Theories of Programming Languages

This textbook is a broad but rigorous survey of the theoretical basis for the design, definition, and implementation of programming languages, and of systems for specifying and proving program behavior. Both imperative and functional programming are covered, as well as the ways of integrating these aspects into more general languages. Recognizing a unity of technique beneath the diversity of research in programming languages, the author presents an integrated treatment of the basic principles of the subject. He identifies the relatively small number of concepts, such as compositional semantics, binding structure, domains, transition systems, and inference rules, that serve as the foundation of the field.

The basic concepts and their properties are described with mathematical rigor, but the mathematical development is balanced by numerous examples of applications, particularly of program specification and proof, concurrent programming, functional programming (including the use of continuations and lazy evaluation), and type systems (including subtyping, polymorphism, and modularization).

Assuming only knowledge of elementary programming and mathematics, this text is perfect for advanced undergraduate and beginning graduate courses in programming language theory, and also will appeal to researchers and professionals in designing or implementing computer languages.

John C. Reynolds is Professor of Computer Science at Carnegie Mellon University.

Theories of Programming Languages

JOHN C. REYNOLDS

CAMBRIDGE UNIVERSITY PRESS
Cambridge, New York, Melbourne, Madrid, Cape Town, Singapore, São Paulo, Delhi

Cambridge University Press
The Edinburgh Building, Cambridge CB2 8RU, UK

Published in the United States of America by Cambridge University Press, New York

www.cambridge.org
Information on this title: www.cambridge.org/9780521106979

First published 1998
This digitally printed version 2009

A catalogue record for this publication is available from the British Library

Library of Congress Cataloguing in Publication data
Reynolds, John C., 1935–
Theories of programming languages / John C. Reynolds.
p.   cm.
Includes bibliographical references and index.
ISBN 0-521-59414-6 (hardbound)
1. Programming languages (Electronic computers)   I. Title.
QA76.7.R495   1998
005.13–dc21   98-20462
                                                        CIP

ISBN 978-0-521-59414-1 hardback
ISBN 978-0-521-10697-9 paperback

Contents

Preface

Peter Landin remarked long ago that the goal of his research was "to tell beautiful stories about computation". Since then many researchers have told many such stories. This book is a collection my favorites in the area of languages for programming and program specification.

In 1992, the Computer Science Department of Carnegie Mellon University replaced the preliminary examinations for its doctoral students by a set of required courses, including CS711, simply titled "Programming Languages", which was intended to be a unified treatment of the basic principles of the subject. Previously, such material had been divided between the programming systems examination and the theory examination, and many important topics had fallen through the cracks between the syllabi. (For example, students were expected to know enough of the theory of program proving to understand Cook completeness, yet they never saw the proof of an actual program beyond a trivial one that computed a square root by iterating over successive natural numbers and squaring them.)

As the most vociferous exponent of such a course, I was put in charge of teaching it, and I soon discovered that there was no suitable textbook. Serious texts in areas such as semantics or verification invariably stressed a particular approach and neglected topics that did not fit well with their point of view. At the opposite extreme, surveys of programming languages usually emphasized superficial differences between languages while slighting more fundamental issues. In effect, what was available were profound novels and journalistic popularizations, but what was needed was a collection of short stories sharing some common characters.

Thus I produced extensive class notes, which in a few years grew into this book. It is intended to be a broad survey of the fundamental principles and issues in programming language research, presented in as consistent a terminology and notation as possible. In writing it, I have come to realize that beneath the diversity of programming language research there is a unity of technique: A relatively small number of concepts, such as compositional semantics, binding structure, domains, transition systems, and inference rules, suffice to describe a diversity of languages and to reveal the principles of their design.

To avoid syntactic distractions, rather than using existing programming languages, I have cast all of the languages discussed in the book into a single uniform syntax. I have also tried, as much as is reasonable, to avoid the theoretical pitfall of treating different aspects of languages in such isolation that their interactions are obscured. The one sad exception is that, for most of the book, imperative and functional programming are treated in isolation. Unfortunately, this is the state of the art: Both of the ways we know for combining these aspects of programming (which I call Iswim-like and Algol-like) destroy much of the simplicity of the individual aspects.

My goal is not to train future theoreticians of programming languages, but to show a broader audience of computer scientists what is known about programming languages and how it can be expressed precisely and rigorously. Thus I have tried to state language properties with mathematical rigor, but with relatively little emphasis on how these properties are proved. I've also avoided advanced mathematical methods (such as category theory) that, although they are powerful tools in the hands of trained theoreticians, tend to obscure the computational insights that are of interest to the broader audience.

I believe there are four reasons why this material, or something much like it, should be taught to all doctoral students in computer science. First, as the fruits of programming-language research become more widely understood, programming is going to become a much more mathematical craft. I believe that in a few years it will become standard professional practice to program in languages with sophisticated type systems, to specify large systems formally, and in safety-critical areas to prove rigorously that programs meet their specifications.

Second, although few software systems are labeled as programming language processors, almost any system that accepts information from human users is such a processor, in the pragmatic sense of being subject to many of the design flaws of programming languages. Current software abounds in operating systems, text processors, symbolic manipulation systems, and other programs that attest dramatically to the need for a wider understanding of language design principles.

Third, even when their immediate research interests are unrelated to programming languages, students may change their specialization radically, either during graduate school or afterwards, and they need a background that is broad enough to support such changes.

Finally, if computer science is to be a unified discipline, then its practitioners must understand the fundamentals of the entire subject, particularly when these fundamentals have a deep intellectual content. Society rightly expects scientists to know the principles of their science, not just their research specialties.

This book is divided roughly into five parts. Chapters 1 to 4 present the simple imperative language (including arrays), along with the classical use of assertions to specify programs and prove their correctness. Nontrivial examples of program proofs are given, and enough theory is developed, especially the rudiments of algebraic semantics and domain theory, to prove the basic properties of binding and substitution, and the soundness of inference rules for program specifications.

In Chapters 5 to 9, the simple imperative language is augmented with a failure mechanism, input-output, nondeterminism (via guarded commands), and concurrency (both via shared-variable programming and communicating sequential processes). To explain these extensions we introduce recursive domain isomorphisms, continuation semantics, structured operational semantics, powerdomains (only of flat domains), and transition-trace semantics.

Chapters 10 to 14 present untyped functional languages: first the pure lambda calculus, then a language using eager evaluation (including extensions with first-class continuations and imperative features using references), and finally a language using normal-order evaluation. Although the discussion of reduction is largely limited to the lambda calculus, all of these languages are defined by both evaluation semantics (i.e. natural operational semantics) and direct denotational semantics. For the eager-evaluation language, we describe implementation by defunctionalizing a continuation semantics to obtain a definition that is essentially a straightforward interpreter. For the normal-order language, we describe lazy evaluation and illustrate the utility of lazy lists.

In Chapters 15 to 18, we present a simple type system for a purely functional language, and then extend this system to encompass subtyping, intersection types, polymorphism, abstract types, and existential types. Inference rules for typing judgements are used to formulate all of the type systems in a uniform manner, and both extrinsic and intrinsic semantics are presented. There are also discussions of coherence conditions for subtyping, of the representation of data by polymorphic functions, and of type systems for specifying modules.

Finally, in Chapter 19, we describe the Algol-like approach to unifying functional and imperative languages. After a discussion of the dual type system that characterizes this approach, we present a semantics that captures the concept of block structure.

Mathematical topics, such as domain theory, that are particular to the subject of this book are presented in the main text as they are needed. On the other hand, the more basic mathematics that is prerequisite to these topics is summarized in the Appendix, along with the particular notations used throughout the book.

To permit flexibility in the choice of topics, I have included more material in this book than is needed for a one-semester course. Any of the following sequences of chapters and sections (or the tails of these sequences) can be omitted without impeding an understanding of the rest of the book:

3, 4, 7.4–7.5	8.6–8.8	14.6
5.7–5.8, 12, 13.3, 13.5, 13.9	10.6, 17.2	15.4, 16.4–16.5, 17.3
7, 8, 9	12.4–12.6, 13.5	15.5–15.6, 16.6, 19.5–19.7
7.2–7.3	13.7–13.8	17, 18

On the other hand, even in a book of this length, limitations of space, time, and knowledge have forced me to exclude more topics than I would have liked. Omissions that are closely related to the topics in the book include methods for solving recursive domain isomorphisms, the Hindley-Milner algorithm, logical relations and parametricity, and propositions as types. Further afield are temporal logic, the π calculus, logic programming, and linear logic. In each case, I have tried to cite suitable references.

My usage of the spelling "premiss" and "premisses" follows Alonzo Church [1956, page 1]. Church attributes this spelling to C. S. Peirce, and argues that it serves to distinguish the logical term from the legal term "premise".

In conclusion, thanks are due to many people: first, to my wife Mary for her constant patience and encouragement; second, to my colleagues at Carnegie Mellon, whose endless discussions of what is worth teaching and how it should be taught have broadened this book substantially; third, to my students, who have endured and often corrected many errors, ranging from serious misconceptions to spelling mistakes; and fourth, to the researchers throughout the world who have not only done the work I describe in this book, but in many cases have patiently explained it to me. In this respect, I must particularly mention two colleagues: Stephen Brookes, who is largely responsible for the virtues (but not the defects) of the material on concurrency (Chapters 8 and 9), as well as a number of exercises, and Bob Harper, whose comments led to substantial improvements in the material on exceptions (Section 13.7) and module specification (Chapter 18).

Finally, thanks are due to my editor, Lauren Cowles, and copy editor, Elise Oranges. They have endured my idiosyncrasies (though remarking that "premisses" looks like a department-store section for young girls) while resisting my barbarisms. (I finally conceded that "data" is plural, and that in English, unlike Algol, one places a comma between "if" and "then".) Most important, they have supported, encouraged, and occasionally demanded my best effort to make this book clear and readable.

I would be delighted to receive comments and corrections, which may be sent to John.Reynolds@cs.cmu.edu. I will try to post errata and other relevant information on my web page at http://www.cs.cmu.edu/~jcr.

John C. Reynolds
Pittsburgh, July 31, 1998

1

Predicate Logic

In this chapter, we introduce four concepts that pervade the study of programming languages: abstract syntax, denotational semantics, inference rules, and binding. These concepts are illustrated by using them to describe a formal language that is not a programming language: predicate logic.

There are three reasons for the oddity of starting a book about programming languages by defining a logic. First, predicate logic is close enough to conventional mathematical notation that the reader's intuitive understanding is likely to be accurate; thus we will be illustrating novel concepts in a familiar setting. Second, since predicate logic has no concept of nontermination, we will be able to define its denotations in terms of ordinary sets, and postpone the more subtle topic of domains until Chapter 2. Finally, as we will see in Chapter 3, predicate logic plays a pivotal role in the formal specification of simple imperative programs.

Although the syntax and semantics of predicate logic are standard topics in logic, we will describe them in the terminology of programming languages: The types of phrases that a logician would call "terms" and "well-formed formulas" we will call "integer expressions" (abbreviated by "intexp") and "assertions" (abbreviated by "assert") respectively. Similarly, "assignments" will be called "states". Moreover, we will usually interpret the operators used to construct terms in a fixed way, as the familiar operations of integer arithmetic.

1.1 Abstract Syntax

It is possible to specify the syntax of a formal language, such as predicate logic or a programming language, by using a context-free grammar (often called BNF or Backus-Naur form) and to define the semantics of the language by a function on the set of strings generated by this grammar. But such a definition would be unnecessarily complicated. The phrases of a formal language are not really character strings, but are abstract entities represented by character strings, in much the same way that natural numbers are abstract entities represented by digit strings. Thus, defining semantics by functions on character strings is as roundabout as defining arithmetic by functions on digit strings.

Instead, one wants to define semantic functions whose domains are sets of *abstract* phrases; the specification of such sets constitutes the *abstract syntax* of a language. Conventional context-free grammars are unsuitable for this purpose since they mix necessary information about the nature of phrases with irrelevant information about how such phrases are represented concretely; for example, what character strings are used to denote constants and variables, which operators are infix, and what are their precedences.

On the other hand, although phrases may be conceptually abstract, one still needs a notation for them. Thus the study of semantics has traditionally used a compromise formalism called an *abstract* grammar, which defines sets of abstract phrases that are independent of any particular representation, but which also provides a simple representation for these phrases without such complications as precedence levels. An abstract grammar for predicate logic, for example, would be

$$\langle \text{intexp} \rangle ::= 0 \mid 1 \mid 2 \mid \cdots$$
$$\mid \langle \text{var} \rangle \mid - \langle \text{intexp} \rangle \mid \langle \text{intexp} \rangle + \langle \text{intexp} \rangle \mid \langle \text{intexp} \rangle - \langle \text{intexp} \rangle$$
$$\mid \langle \text{intexp} \rangle \times \langle \text{intexp} \rangle \mid \langle \text{intexp} \rangle \div \langle \text{intexp} \rangle \mid \langle \text{intexp} \rangle \ \textbf{rem} \ \langle \text{intexp} \rangle$$

$$\langle \text{assert} \rangle ::= \textbf{true} \mid \textbf{false}$$
$$\mid \langle \text{intexp} \rangle = \langle \text{intexp} \rangle \mid \langle \text{intexp} \rangle \neq \langle \text{intexp} \rangle \mid \langle \text{intexp} \rangle < \langle \text{intexp} \rangle$$
$$\mid \langle \text{intexp} \rangle \leq \langle \text{intexp} \rangle \mid \langle \text{intexp} \rangle > \langle \text{intexp} \rangle \mid \langle \text{intexp} \rangle \geq \langle \text{intexp} \rangle$$
$$\mid \neg \langle \text{assert} \rangle \mid \langle \text{assert} \rangle \wedge \langle \text{assert} \rangle \mid \langle \text{assert} \rangle \vee \langle \text{assert} \rangle$$
$$\mid \langle \text{assert} \rangle \Rightarrow \langle \text{assert} \rangle \mid \langle \text{assert} \rangle \Leftrightarrow \langle \text{assert} \rangle$$
$$\mid \forall \langle \text{var} \rangle. \ \langle \text{assert} \rangle \mid \exists \langle \text{var} \rangle. \ \langle \text{assert} \rangle$$

This example illustrates the following general properties of an abstract grammar:

- Just as with context-free grammars, $L ::= \rho_0 \mid \cdots \mid \rho_{k-1}$ abbreviates a set $\{ L ::= \rho_0, \ldots, L ::= \rho_{k-1} \}$ of productions with the same left side. Each unabbreviated production has the form $L ::= s_0 R_0 \ldots R_{n-1} s_n$, where $n \geq 0$, L and the R_i are nonterminals, and the s_i are (possibly empty) strings of terminal symbols.
- Certain *predefined* nonterminals do not occur on the left side of productions. In the above case, $\langle \text{var} \rangle$ is a predefined nonterminal denoting a countably infinite set of variables (with unspecified representations).
- Productions with the same left side always have distinct patterns of terminal symbols. In other words, if $L ::= s_0 R_0 \ldots R_{n-1} s_n$ and $L ::= s'_0 R'_0 \ldots R'_{n'-1} s'_{n'}$ are distinct productions with the same left side, then either $n \neq n'$ or, for some $i \in 0$ to n, $s_i \neq s'_i$.

Although abstract grammars have the same form as ordinary context-free grammars, when interpreted as such they are usually highly ambiguous. Nevertheless, they define an unambiguous concrete representation for phrases — one simply uses the context-free grammar obtained by parenthesizing each nonterminal on the right side of a production. (Strictly speaking, one should use parentheses that do not occur in the original productions or in the representations of members of predefined sets such as $\langle \text{var} \rangle$.) The nonambiguity of this grammar is insured by the parenthesization and the condition on distinct patterns. Precedence plays no role since all of the subphrases are parenthesized.

Of course, when we write complicated phrases we will not put in all of these parentheses, but will use certain conventions about precedence. When these conventions go beyond the common usage of mathematics and most programming languages, we will state them explicitly. A convenient device for this is a *precedence list*, which gives the operators of the language in decreasing order of precedence, with parenthesized groups having the same precedence. Such a list for predicate logic is

$$(\times \div \textbf{rem}) \, (-_{\text{unary}} \, + \, -_{\text{binary}}) \, (= \neq < \leq > \geq) \, \neg \, \wedge \, \vee \, \Rightarrow \, \Leftrightarrow$$

where each of the binary operators is left associative.

Rather than giving them a precedence, we will allow expressions $\forall v. \, a$ that begin with a universal quantifier, or $\exists v. \, a$ that begin with an existential quantifier, to follow any boolean operator, and we will assume that the body a extends to the first *stopping symbol* or the end of the enclosing phrase. For predicate logic, the only stopping symbol is an unmatched closing parenthesis. In the course of this book, however, we will introduce several other stopping symbols (and several other kinds of phrases that are stopped by them). Specifically, the full set of stopping symbols is

- closing delimiters, when unmatched:

$$) \quad] \quad \} \quad : \quad | \quad \textbf{do} \quad \textbf{else} \quad \textbf{fi} \quad \textbf{in} \quad \textbf{od} \quad \textbf{of} \quad \textbf{then}$$

- other stopping symbols, when unparenthesized by any delimiters:

$$; \quad \rightarrow \quad \triangleright \quad \square \quad \| \quad ,$$

The other half of the story about abstract grammars is how they define an abstract syntax that is independent of representation. Basically, while the particular patterns of terminals in productions specify a particular representation for phrases, the rest of the grammar specifies their abstract nature. For example, if we changed the production $\langle \text{intexp} \rangle ::= \langle \text{intexp} \rangle \div \langle \text{intexp} \rangle$ to another, such as $\langle \text{intexp} \rangle ::= \textbf{div} \, \langle \text{intexp} \rangle \, \langle \text{intexp} \rangle$, with the same sequence of nonterminals, we would change the representation of the division operation without changing its abstract character.

Actually, abstractness is lost whenever one defines phrases to be any particular family of sets — of character strings or anything else. What is really abstract about abstract syntax is that one can use any family of sets that satisfies certain conditions.

First, for each nonterminal of the grammar, there must be a set of abstract phrases, called a *carrier*. Thus, in the case of predicate logic, there will be three carriers, named by the nonterminals $\langle$var$\rangle$, $\langle$intexp$\rangle$, and $\langle$assert$\rangle$.

Second, for each production of the abstract grammar, there must be a function among the carriers called a *constructor*. Specifically, a production of the form $L ::= s_0 R_0 \ldots R_{n-1} s_n$ gives rise to a constructor $c \in R_0 \times \cdots \times R_{n-1} \to L$. For example, the production $\langle$intexp$\rangle ::= \langle$intexp$\rangle \div \langle$intexp$\rangle$ gives rise to a constructor in $\langle$intexp$\rangle \times \langle$intexp$\rangle \to \langle$intexp$\rangle$ that we will call $c_\div$. (Note that if we replaced $\langle$intexp$\rangle ::= \langle$intexp$\rangle \div \langle$intexp$\rangle$ by the abstractly equivalent production $\langle$intexp$\rangle ::= \mathbf{div} \langle$intexp$\rangle\langle$intexp$\rangle$, the nature of the constructor $c_\div$ would not change.)

In the case of predicate logic, the constructors (with arbitrary but suggestive names) that correspond to the productions of our abstract grammar are

$$c_0, c_1, c_2, \ldots \in \{\langle\rangle\} \to \langle\text{intexp}\rangle$$

$$c_{\text{var}} \in \langle\text{var}\rangle \to \langle\text{intexp}\rangle$$

$$c_{-\text{unary}} \in \langle\text{intexp}\rangle \to \langle\text{intexp}\rangle$$

$$c_+, c_{-\text{binary}}, c_\times, c_\div, c_{\text{rem}} \in \langle\text{intexp}\rangle \times \langle\text{intexp}\rangle \to \langle\text{intexp}\rangle$$

$$c_{\text{true}}, c_{\text{false}} \in \{\langle\rangle\} \to \langle\text{assert}\rangle \qquad (1.1)$$

$$c_=, c_{\neq}, c_<, c_\leq, c_>, c_\geq \in \langle\text{intexp}\rangle \times \langle\text{intexp}\rangle \to \langle\text{assert}\rangle$$

$$c_\neg \in \langle\text{assert}\rangle \to \langle\text{assert}\rangle$$

$$c_\wedge, c_\vee, c_\Rightarrow, c_\Leftrightarrow \in \langle\text{assert}\rangle \times \langle\text{assert}\rangle \to \langle\text{assert}\rangle$$

$$c_\forall, c_\exists \in \langle\text{var}\rangle \times \langle\text{assert}\rangle \to \langle\text{assert}\rangle.$$

(Here and throughout this book, the operator $\to$ is right associative and has a lower precedence than $\times$.)

Finally, the carriers and constructors must satisfy the following conditions:

- Each constructor must be injective.

- Any two constructors into the same carrier (for example, both in the first part or both in the second part of the list that is displayed above) must have disjoint ranges.

- Every member of each carrier that is not predefined (for example, $\langle$intexp$\rangle$ and $\langle$assert$\rangle$) must be constructible using a finite number of applications of the constructors.

(The reader who is familiar with universal algebra will recognize that these conditions insure that abstract phrases form a many-sorted initial algebra whose operators are the constructors.)

The last condition can be stated more rigorously (though tediously) by first defining sets $\langle \cdots \rangle^j$ of phrases of depth at most j, and then requiring the non-predefined carriers to be the union of these sets over j. For predicate logic, for example, we would define the sets

$$\langle \text{intexp} \rangle^{(0)} = \{\}$$

$$\langle \text{assert} \rangle^{(0)} = \{\}$$

$$\begin{aligned}
\langle \text{intexp} \rangle^{(j+1)} = {}& \{c_0(), c_1(), c_2(), \ldots\} \\
& \cup \{\, c_{\text{var}}(x_0) \mid x_0 \in \langle \text{var} \rangle \,\} \\
& \cup \{\, c_{-\text{unary}}(x_0) \mid x_0 \in \langle \text{intexp} \rangle^{(j)} \,\} \\
& \cup \{\, c_+(x_0, x_1) \mid x_0, x_1 \in \langle \text{intexp} \rangle^{(j)} \,\} \\
& \qquad \vdots
\end{aligned} \tag{1.2}$$

$$\begin{aligned}
\langle \text{assert} \rangle^{(j+1)} = {}& \{c_{\text{true}}(), c_{\text{false}}()\} \\
& \cup \{\, c_=(x_0, x_1) \mid x_0, x_1 \in \langle \text{intexp} \rangle^{(j)} \,\} \\
& \qquad \vdots \\
& \cup \{\, c_\neg(x_0) \mid x_0 \in \langle \text{assert} \rangle^{(j)} \,\} \\
& \cup \{\, c_\wedge(x_0, x_1) \mid x_0, x_1 \in \langle \text{assert} \rangle^{(j)} \,\} \\
& \qquad \vdots \\
& \cup \{\, c_\forall(x_0, x_1) \mid x_0 \in \langle \text{var} \rangle, x_1 \in \langle \text{assert} \rangle^{(j)} \,\} \\
& \qquad \vdots
\end{aligned}$$

Then the finite-construction condition simply requires that every member of each carrier has some finite depth:

$$\langle \text{intexp} \rangle = \bigcup_{j=0}^{\infty} \langle \text{intexp} \rangle^{(j)} \qquad\qquad \langle \text{assert} \rangle = \bigcup_{j=0}^{\infty} \langle \text{assert} \rangle^{(j)}.$$

The above equations provide a standard method for constructing carriers and constructors that satisfy the abstract-syntax conditions. One begins with some "universe" of phrases (which must contain predefined carriers such as $\langle \text{var} \rangle$), and defines the constructors as functions on this universe (with the right arity, i.e. number of arguments) that are injective and have disjoint ranges. Then one takes the above equations as the definition of the carriers.

When we discuss the least fixed-point theorem in Section 2.4, we will see that such a definition gives a family of carriers that is the least solution of the equations that are obtained from Equation (1.2) by dropping the superscripts. These equations insure that the constructors can be restricted to the types displayed in (1.1). Moreover, the restriction preserves the properties of being injective and having disjoint ranges. Thus the carriers and restricted constructors satisfy all of the abstract syntax conditions. For example:

- To obtain the fully parenthesized infix notation described earlier, we can take the universe of phrases to be the set of strings with balanced parentheses, $\langle \text{var} \rangle$ to be some set of alphanumeric strings, and the constructors to be

$$c_0() = 0$$
$$\vdots$$
$$c_{-\text{unary}}(x) = -(x)$$
$$c_+(x, y) = (x) + (y)$$
$$c_{-\text{binary}}(x, y) = (x) - (y)$$
$$\vdots$$

  (Here $(x) + (y)$ denotes concatenation of the strings "(", x, ")+(", y, and ")".) For instance, the phrase $c_+((c_{-\text{binary}}(c_0(), c_1())), c_{-\text{unary}}(c_2()))$ would be the string "$((0) - (1)) + (-(2))$".

- To obtain a parenthesized prefix notation, we can take the universe to be the set of strings with balanced parentheses and no unparenthesized commas, $\langle \text{var} \rangle$ to be some set of alphanumeric strings, and the constructors to be

$$c_0() = 0$$
$$\vdots$$
$$c_{-\text{unary}}(x) = \textbf{negate}(x)$$
$$c_+(x, y) = \textbf{add}(x, y)$$
$$c_{-\text{binary}}(x, y) = \textbf{subtract}(x, y)$$
$$\vdots$$

  For instance, the phrase $c_+((c_{-\text{binary}}(c_0(), c_1())), c_{-\text{unary}}(c_2()))$ would be the string "$\textbf{add}(\textbf{subtract}(0, 1), \textbf{negate}(2))$".

- To obtain a representation by "syntax trees", we can take the universe to be the set of finitary labeled trees, $\langle \text{var} \rangle$ to be a set of terminal nodes labeled with variables, and $c_\ell(x_0, \ldots, x_{n-1})$ to be the tree whose root node is labeled with ℓ and whose n subnodes are the trees $x_0, \ldots, x_{n-1}$. For instance,

$c_+((c_{-\text{binary}}(c_0(), c_1()), c_{-\text{unary}}(c_2())))$ would be the tree

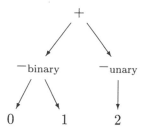

In each case, we obtain a different realization of the same abstract syntax.

Realizations of abstract syntax are also provided by many programming languages. In Standard ML (SML), for example, one can define carriers by *data types*. Then each constructor in $R_0 \times \cdots \times R_{n-1} \to L$ becomes an SML constructor of the data type L that accepts arguments in $R_0 * \cdots * R_{n-1}$. For predicate logic, one might define the data types

```
datatype intexp = c_con of int |
    c_var of string |
    c_unaryminus of intexp |
    c_plus of intexp * intexp |
    c_binaryminus of intexp * intexp |
    c_times of intexp * intexp |
    c_div of intexp * intexp |
    c_rem of intexp * intexp
and assert = c_true | c_false |
    c_equals of intexp * intexp |
    c_unequals of intexp * intexp |
    c_lessthan of intexp * intexp |
    c_lessthanorequals of intexp * intexp |
    c_greaterthan of intexp * intexp |
    c_greaterthanorequals of intexp * intexp |
    c_not of assert |
    c_and of assert * assert |
    c_or of assert * assert |
    c_implies of assert * assert |
    c_iff of assert * assert |
    c_forall of string * assert |
    c_exists of string * assert
```

Here we have used `string` for the predefined carrier ⟨var⟩. We have also coalesced the infinite sequence of constructors $c_0, c_1, c_2, \ldots$ into the application of a single constructor `c_con` to the natural numbers $0, 1, 2, \ldots$. For instance, $c_+((c_{-\text{binary}}(c_0(), c_1()), c_{-\text{unary}}(c_2())))$ would be represented by the SML value `c_plus(c_binaryminus(c_con 0, c_con 1), c_unaryminus(c_con 2))`.

1.2 Denotational Semantics of Predicate Logic

To define the semantics of predicate logic, that is, to define what logicians call a "model" of predicate logic, we must define a pair of *semantic* functions that map integer expressions and assertions into the meanings that these phrases denote. However, we first must answer the prior question of what kinds of meanings are appropriate for such phrases.

Clearly, integer expressions have integer values and assertions have boolean values. But the *meanings* or *denotations* of such phrases are more complex than values, because the value of a phrase depends on the values of its variables. More abstractly, it depends on a *state*, which is a function that maps each variable into its integer value. Let $\mathbf{Z} = \{\ldots, -2, -1, 0, 1, 2, \ldots\}$ and $\mathbf{B} = \{\mathbf{true}, \mathbf{false}\}$. Then, if we write Σ for the set $\langle \mathrm{var} \rangle \to \mathbf{Z}$ of states, the semantic functions that map integer expressions and assertions into their meanings have the following types:

$$\llbracket - \rrbracket_{\mathrm{intexp}} \in \langle \mathrm{intexp} \rangle \to \Sigma \to \mathbf{Z} \qquad \llbracket - \rrbracket_{\mathrm{assert}} \in \langle \mathrm{assert} \rangle \to \Sigma \to \mathbf{B}.$$

These functions can be defined by the following *semantic equations*:

DR SEM EQ: Constants

$$\llbracket 0 \rrbracket_{\mathrm{intexp}} \sigma = 0 \tag{1.3}$$

(and similarly for 1, 2, ...),

DR SEM EQ: Variables

$$\llbracket v \rrbracket_{\mathrm{intexp}} \sigma = \sigma v, \tag{1.4}$$

DR SEM EQ: Unary Operations

$$\llbracket - e \rrbracket_{\mathrm{intexp}} \sigma = - \llbracket e \rrbracket_{\mathrm{intexp}} \sigma, \tag{1.5}$$

DR SEM EQ: Binary Operations

$$\llbracket e_0 + e_1 \rrbracket_{\mathrm{intexp}} \sigma = \llbracket e_0 \rrbracket_{\mathrm{intexp}} \sigma + \llbracket e_1 \rrbracket_{\mathrm{intexp}} \sigma \tag{1.6}$$

(and similarly for $-$, $\times$, $\div$, **rem**),

DR SEM EQ: Boolean Constants

$$\llbracket \mathbf{true} \rrbracket_{\mathrm{assert}} \sigma = \mathbf{true} \qquad \llbracket \mathbf{false} \rrbracket_{\mathrm{assert}} \sigma = \mathbf{false}, \tag{1.7}$$

DR SEM EQ: Relations

$$\llbracket e_0 = e_1 \rrbracket_{\mathrm{assert}} \sigma = (\llbracket e_0 \rrbracket_{\mathrm{intexp}} \sigma = \llbracket e_1 \rrbracket_{\mathrm{intexp}} \sigma) \tag{1.8}$$

(and similarly for $\neq$, $<$, $\leq$, $>$, $\geq$),

DR SEM EQ: Unary Logical Connectives

$$[\![\neg p]\!]_{\text{assert}}\sigma = \neg[\![p]\!]_{\text{assert}}\sigma, \tag{1.9}$$

DR SEM EQ: Binary Logical Connectives

$$[\![p_0 \wedge p_1]\!]_{\text{assert}}\sigma = [\![p_0]\!]_{\text{assert}}\sigma \wedge [\![p_1]\!]_{\text{assert}}\sigma \tag{1.10}$$

(and similarly for $\vee, \Rightarrow, \Leftrightarrow$),

DR SEM EQ: Quantifiers

$$[\![\forall v.\ p]\!]_{\text{assert}}\sigma = \forall n \in \mathbf{Z}.\ [\![p]\!]_{\text{assert}}[\,\sigma \mid v\!:\!n\,]$$
$$[\![\exists v.\ p]\!]_{\text{assert}}\sigma = \exists n \in \mathbf{Z}.\ [\![p]\!]_{\text{assert}}[\,\sigma \mid v\!:\!n\,]. \tag{1.11}$$

Throughout this book, whenever we display a semantic equation (or an inference rule) for a linguistic construction, we will indicate the kind of equation (or rule) as well as the kind of construction. In this case, DR SEM EQ abbreviates *direct semantic equation*, where "direct" distinguishes the kind of semantics from the continuation semantics that will be introduced in Chapter 5. We will also follow the tradition of denoting semantic functions by emphatic brackets.

The notation $[\,\sigma \mid v\!:\!n\,]$ denotes the state that maps v into n and all other variables w into σw. (It is a special case of a notation for varying or extending a function at a single argument that is defined in Section A.3 of the Appendix.)

It is important to distinguish between the language in which semantic equations or other parts of a definition are written, called the *metalanguage*, and the language being defined, called the *object language*. In particular, the variables of the two languages, called *meta*variables and *object* variables, must not be confused. To emphasize this distinction, throughout this book we use italic and Greek letters for metavariables, but we use a sans serif font for object variables. For example, the value of the metavariable v might be the object variable v.

In the metalanguage, we use the common mathematical convention that metavariables, when stripped of subscripts and other decorations, indicate what type of entity they range over. For instance, v and w range over object variables; e over expressions; p, q and r over assertions; σ over states; and m and n over integers. (Occasionally, p will range over phrases of several types.)

On the left side of each equation, the semantic brackets enclose a pattern that is similar to the right side of some production in the abstract grammar, except that metavariables occur in place of nonterminals. Actually, such a pattern stands for an application of the corresponding constructor — for example, $[\![p_0 \wedge p_1]\!]_{\text{assert}}$ stands for $[\![c_{\wedge}(p_0, p_1)]\!]_{\text{assert}}$ — but the patterns are far more readable.

In fact, the semantic equations we have given determine a unique meaning for any phrase of predicate logic. For example, suppose σ is a state that maps the object variable x into 3. Then the semantic equations give

$$\llbracket x + 0 = x \rrbracket_{\text{assert}} \sigma = (\llbracket x + 0 \rrbracket_{\text{intexp}} \sigma = \llbracket x \rrbracket_{\text{intexp}} \sigma)$$
$$= (\llbracket x \rrbracket_{\text{intexp}} \sigma + \llbracket 0 \rrbracket_{\text{intexp}} \sigma = \llbracket x \rrbracket_{\text{intexp}} \sigma) \qquad (1.12)$$
$$= (3 + 0 = 3)$$
$$= \textbf{true}.$$

Moreover, the above argument does not depend on the choice of 3; it holds for any integer n that x might be mapped into by σ. Thus, for any state σ,

$$\llbracket \forall x.\ x + 0 = x \rrbracket_{\text{assert}} \sigma = \forall n \in \mathbf{Z}.\ \llbracket x + 0 = x \rrbracket_{\text{assert}} [\,\sigma \mid x{:}\,n\,] = \textbf{true}.$$

In general, of course, a set of equations can have zero, one, or many solutions. But whenever we call equations "semantic", we imply that they satisfy special conditions that guarantee the existence of a unique solution. Specifically, we will always require semantic equations to satisfy two fundamental conditions:

- There must be one equation for each production of the abstract grammar.
- Each equation must express the meaning of a constructed phrase purely as a function of the meanings of its immediate subphrases (or as a function of the subphrase itself, when the subphrase belongs to a predefined set such as $\langle \text{var} \rangle$.)

(The reader should verify that the above semantic equations actually satisfy these conditions.) A set of equations satisfying these conditions is said to be *syntax-directed* or *homomorphic* (since, if one views abstract phrases as a many-sorted algebra, such equations assert that the function being defined is a homomorphism).

The condition of syntax-directedness, in conjunction with the definition of abstract phrases given in the previous section, insures that the semantic equations possess exactly one solution (which, for predicate logic, will be the pair of functions $\llbracket - \rrbracket_{\text{intexp}}$ and $\llbracket - \rrbracket_{\text{assert}}$). A rigorous proof of this fact is beyond the scope of this book, but the basic idea is that, by induction on the depth j, for each phrase of depth j there is exactly one meaning satisfying the semantic equations. This is trivial for $j = 0$, since there are no phrases of depth 0. If p is a phrase of depth $j + 1$, say an assertion, then, since every phrase is the result of some constructor but the constructors for assertions have disjoint ranges, p is the result of exactly one constructor, say $p = c_\wedge(p_0, p_1)$, which corresponds to exactly one production, $\langle \text{assert} \rangle ::= \langle \text{assert} \rangle \wedge \langle \text{assert} \rangle$, which in turn corresponds to exactly one semantic equation, $\llbracket p_0 \wedge p_1 \rrbracket_{\text{assert}} \sigma = \llbracket p_0 \rrbracket_{\text{assert}} \sigma \wedge \llbracket p_1 \rrbracket_{\text{assert}} \sigma$. Then the injectivity of the constructor $c_\wedge$ insures that there are unique assertions p_0 and p_1 such that $p = c_\wedge(p_0, p_1) = p_0 \wedge p_1$; the induction hypothesis insures that these assertions have unique meanings, say m_0 and m_1; and the semantic equation assigns the function mapping σ into $m_0 \sigma \wedge m_1 \sigma$ as the unique meaning of p.

(The reader who is familiar with universal algebra will again recognize a standard situation: Abstract phrases constitute an initial algebra, the semantic equations assert that the semantic functions are a homomorphism from this algebra to some "target" algebra, and the definition of an initial algebra is that, for any target algebra, there is exactly one homomorphism from the former to the latter. In fact, the argument we have given above is hidden in the proof that abstract phrases really are an initial algebra.)

A further consequence of the syntax-directed nature of semantic equations is that they always define a compositional semantics. A semantics is said to be *compositional* when the meaning of each phrase does not depend on any property of its immediate subphrases except the meanings of these subphrases. This characteristic obviously extends to nonimmediate subphrases. It implies that, in any phrase, one can replace an occurrence of a subphrase by another phrase with the same meaning, without changing the meaning of the enclosing phrase.

It must be admitted that there is an apparent absurdity in the semantic equations we have given, since "0" is defined in terms of "0", "+" in terms of "+", and so forth. Strictly speaking, this does not make our definition circular, since such symbols inside emphatic brackets denote constructors of the object language (predicate logic), while outside emphatic brackets they are part of the metalanguage (conventional mathematical notation). The only oddity is that the object language is a sublanguage of the metalanguage, and features of the object language are explained by the same (or analogous) features of the metalanguage.

This situation is called *metacircularity* (and is frequently a characteristic of definitions of programming languages by interpreters). Its danger is that a misapprehension about the metalanguage, say, that + denotes subtraction, will carry over unchanged to the object language.

In this case, most of the operations are familiar enough that metacircularity is not a real problem. Some of the boolean operations may be less familiar, but here one can give an explicit tabulation:

p_0	p_1	$\neg p_0$	$p_0 \wedge p_1$	$p_0 \vee p_1$	$p_0 \Rightarrow p_1$	$p_0 \Leftrightarrow p_1$
false	false	true	false	false	true	true
false	true	true	false	true	true	false
true	false	false	false	true	false	false
true	true	false	true	true	true	true

However, there is one operation, integer division, that raises a serious issue. As is clear from our definition of predicate logic, every integer expression and assertion must have a value in every state; there is nothing in predicate logic corresponding to nonterminating expressions or error stops. But in conventional mathematics, neither the quotient $m \div n$ nor the remainder m **rem** n has any value when $n = 0$, and in most programming languages such an operation causes an error stop. We will return to this discrepancy in Section 2.7, where we discuss the treatment of arithmetic errors in programming languages, and in Section 3.8, where we discuss the limitations of proving program specifications by methods based on predicate logic.

Notice that our definition of assertions does not include multiple relations such as $e_0 \leq e_1 \leq e_2$ (meaning $e_0 \leq e_1 \wedge e_1 \leq e_2$), despite their ubiquitous usage in mathematics (and occasionally in this book). To keep our presentation simple, we want quantifier-free assertions to be the same as the boolean expressions of the programming language to be introduced in Chapter 2.

1.3 Validity and Inference

A variety of terminology is used to describe the situation where $[\![p]\!]_{\text{assert}}\sigma = \textbf{true}$ for some assertion p and state σ: We say that p is *true* in σ, or that p *holds* for σ, or that p *describes* σ, or that σ *satisfies* p. When $[\![p]\!]_{\text{assert}}\sigma = \textbf{true}$ for all states $\sigma \in \Sigma$, we say that p is *valid*. (Occasionally, when $[\![p]\!]_{\text{assert}}\sigma = \textbf{false}$ for all states $\sigma \in \Sigma$, we say that p is *unsatisfiable*.)

When $p_0 \Rightarrow p_1$ is valid or, equivalently, when every state satisfying p_0 also satisfies p_1, we say that p_0 is *stronger* than p_1 and that p_1 is *weaker* than p_0. (Thus "stronger" and "weaker" are dual preorders, which does not quite jibe with normal English usage. For example, any assertion is both stronger and weaker than itself.) Notice that **true** is weaker than any assertion and **false** is stronger than any assertion.

In general, whenever two phrases of an object language have the same meaning (in the relevant semantics), we say they are *equivalent*. For assertions in particular, p_0 and p_1 will be equivalent when p_0 is both stronger and weaker than p_1.

Predicate logic is the first of many logics we will consider for which one can give a calculus of inference rules. In general, an *inference rule* consists of zero or more *premisses* and a single *conclusion*. (Notationally, we will separate the premisses from the conclusion by a horizontal line.) The premisses and conclusion are each a schema for an assertion, that is, a pattern containing metavariables that each range over some type of phrase, such that one obtains an assertion by replacing each metavariable by any phrase in its range.

An inference rule containing no premisses is called an *axiom schema* or, if it contains no occurrences of metavariables, simply an *axiom*. (In the latter case, we will omit the horizontal line.)

An *instance* of an inference rule is obtained by replacing all occurrences of each metavariable by a phrase in its range. (Sometimes, there will be side conditions on the rule that must be satisfied by the replacement. Also, there may be syntactic operations, such as substitution, that must be carried out after the replacement.)

A *proof* — more precisely, a *formal proof* — is a sequence of assertions, each of which is the conclusion of some instance of an inference rule whose premisses all occur earlier in the sequence. Such a sequence is said to be a proof *of* its final assertion. (Notice the special role of axiom schemas: Their instances are assertions that can appear anywhere in a proof, regardless of what, if anything, precedes them.)

The following are examples of an axiom, an axiom schema, and inference rules with two and one premisses:

$$x + 0 = x \qquad \frac{}{e_1 = e_0 \Rightarrow e_0 = e_1} \qquad \frac{p_0 \qquad p_0 \Rightarrow p_1}{p_1} \qquad \frac{p}{\forall v.\, p}$$

(here x is an object variable, not a metavariable), an instance of each rule:

$$x + 0 = x \qquad \frac{}{x + 0 = x \Rightarrow x = x + 0}$$

$$\frac{x + 0 = x \qquad x + 0 = x \Rightarrow x = x + 0}{x = x + 0} \qquad \frac{x = x + 0}{\forall x.\, x = x + 0}$$

(in the first case, $x + 0 = x$ is the only possible instance, since an axiom contains no metavariables), and a short, dull proof using these instances:

1.	$x + 0 = x$	(First rule)
2.	$x + 0 = x \Rightarrow x = x + 0$	(Second rule)
3.	$x = x + 0$	(Third rule, 1, 2)
4.	$\forall x.\, x = x + 0$	(Fourth rule, 3)

Here we have annotated each step with the name of the rule used to infer it, along with a list of the previous steps that furnished the premisses of the rule.

An alternative form for a formal proof is a tree, where the assertion being proved lies at the root node, and the immediate subtrees are proofs of the premisses of the rule instance used to infer the root assertion. When the root is placed at the bottom, and a horizontal line is placed between each node and its immediate subnodes (which lie above it),

$$\frac{\dfrac{}{x + 0 = x} \qquad \dfrac{}{x + 0 = x \Rightarrow x = x + 0}}{\dfrac{x = x + 0}{\forall x.\, x = x + 0,}}$$

the role of the inference rules is revealed directly: For each line, the assertions immediately above and below the line constitute an instance of the relevant rule.

Proof trees are more perspicuous than sequences, since they show the inferences between assertions directly and do not impose an arbitrary total ordering on the proof steps. In practice, however, all but the smallest proof trees are beyond the limits of typesetting, so one must make do with sequences, usually with annotations to describe the structure.

(When the same assertion is used as a premiss of several proof steps, the proof of this assertion will appear as several subtrees of the proof tree, but need only appear once in the corresponding proof sequence. This distinction will have no effect on our reasoning about proofs.)

Of course, the whole point of the concept of proof is its connection with semantics: If there is a proof of an assertion p, then p should be valid. This will occur provided that each inference rule is *sound*, which means that, for every instance of the rule, if the premisses are all valid, the conclusion is valid.

For example, to see that the penultimate inference rule above is sound, let p_0 and p_1 be any assertions, and suppose that the premisses of the corresponding instance of the rule are valid. Let σ be any state. Then $[\![p_0]\!]_{assert}\sigma = \textbf{true}$ and $[\![p_0 \Rightarrow p_1]\!]_{assert}\sigma = \textbf{true}$. By the semantic equation for $\Rightarrow$, we find $([\![p_0]\!]_{assert}\sigma \Rightarrow [\![p_1]\!]_{assert}\sigma) = \textbf{true}$. Then, since $[\![p_0]\!]_{assert}\sigma = \textbf{true}$, the truth table for $\Rightarrow$ shows that $[\![p_1]\!]_{assert}\sigma = \textbf{true}$ and, since this holds for any σ, p_1 is valid.

As far as predicate logic is concerned, our only interest in inference rules and proofs is to illustrate these concepts in a conventional and familiar setting; the reader who wishes to see adequate sets of inference rules for predicate logic can consult any elementary text on logic. When we come to actual proofs of programs in Chapter 3, we will simply assume that the reader has the mathematical background to decide informally whether elementary assertions about the integers are valid.

The reader who is inexperienced in logic should be cautioned, however, to remember that each step in a proof must be a valid assertion, not just an assertion that is true in particular states. Thus, for example, the assertion x > 0 would never occur as a proof step, since it does not hold for a state that maps x into zero.

A closely related point is that inference, which connects different proof steps, is different than the implication operator $\Rightarrow$, which joins subphrases within a single step. For example, an assertion p may be true in some state without $\forall v.\ p$ being true in the same state. (Suppose v were x and p were x > 0.) Thus

$$p \Rightarrow \forall v.\ p$$

is *not* a sound inference rule. (For instance, it could be used to prove x > 0 $\Rightarrow \forall$x. x > 0, which does not hold in a state where x = 3.) However, if p is valid, then $\forall v.\ p$ is valid. Thus

$$\frac{p}{\forall v.\ p}$$

is a sound inference rule. (The instance obtained by taking p to be x > 0 has a conclusion that is not valid, but neither is its premiss.)

In conclusion, we must mention one aspect of predicate logic about which we will say little in this book. In the theoretical study of logic, considerable attention is paid to the situation where the syntax and semantics of the operations for constructing assertions are fixed, but the semantics of the operations for constructing expressions is varied over arbitrary functions on an arbitrary set (so that one would no longer speak of *integer* expressions). When an assertion holds for all such variations (as well as for all states), it is said to be *logically valid.*

The importance of this concept is its connection with completeness, which is the converse of soundness. A set of inference rules is said to be *complete* if it can be used to prove every valid assertion. If validity is defined as in this chapter, then no finite set of inference rules is complete. (This is Gödel's famous incompleteness theorem.) But if validity is defined to be "logical" validity, then there are finite sets of inference rules that are known to be complete.

However, logical completeness is of little interest in the application of logic to proving that programs meet specifications. In this case, one is usually only interested in giving expressions the same semantics as in a specific programming language. (An exception will be discussed in Section 3.8.)

1.4 Binding and Substitution

In predicate logic, the universal quantifier $\forall v$ and the existential quantifier $\exists v$ are examples of the phenomenon of *binding*, which also occurs in most programming languages and will therefore be a recurrent theme in this book. In this section and Section 2.5, we will examine this phenomenon in considerable detail, since (as we will see when we investigate dynamic binding in Section 11.7) its mistreatment is a surprisingly subtle source of language design errors.

The general idea is that certain occurrences of variables are *binding occurrences* or, more briefly, *binders*, each of which has an associated phrase called its *scope*. In predicate logic, for instance, the binders are the first occurrences of v in $\forall v.\ p$ or $\exists v.\ p$, and their scopes are p. If a nonbinding occurrence of v lies within the scope of a binder of v, it is said to be *bound* by the binder; otherwise, it is a *free* occurrence. (When the nonbinding occurrence of v lies within the scopes of several binders of v, it is bound by the one with the smallest scope.) A phrase with no free occurrences of variables is said to be *closed*.

For example, in

$$\forall\ x\ .\ (\ x\ \neq\ y\ \lor\ \forall\ y\ .\ (\ x\ =\ y\ \lor\ \forall\ x\ .\ x\ +\ y\ \neq\ x\ ))$$
$$\ \ \ 1\ \ \ 1 \qquad\qquad 2\ \ \ 1 \quad 2 \qquad 3\ \ \ 3 \quad 2\ \ \ 3$$

the binding structure is indicated by indices below the variable occurrences: Each binder binds the other variable occurrences with the same index, and the unindexed occurrence of y is free.

Notice that the same variable, such as y in the phrase above, can have both free and bound occurrences in the same phrase. Also, a particular occurrence can be bound in a phrase but free in some subphrase; for example, the final occurrence of y is bound in the phrase above but free in the subphrase beginning with the last quantifier.

The following equations define functions FV_{intexp} and FV_{assert} that map integer expressions and assertions into the sets of variables that occur free in these phrases:

$$FV_{intexp}(0) = \{\}$$

(and similarly for 1, 2, . . .),

$$FV_{intexp}(v) = \{v\}$$

$$FV_{intexp}(-e) = FV_{intexp}(e)$$

$$FV_{intexp}(e_0 + e_1) = FV_{intexp}(e_0) \cup FV_{intexp}(e_1)$$

(and similarly for $-$, $\times$, $\div$, **rem**),

$$FV_{assert}(\textbf{true}) = \{\}$$

$$FV_{assert}(\textbf{false}) = \{\}$$

$$FV_{assert}(e_0 = e_1) = FV_{intexp}(e_0) \cup FV_{intexp}(e_1)$$

(and similarly for $\neq$, $<$, $\leq$, $>$, $\geq$),

$$FV_{assert}(\neg p) = FV_{assert}(p)$$

$$FV_{assert}(p_0 \wedge p_1) = FV_{assert}(p_0) \cup FV_{assert}(p_1)$$

(and similarly for $\vee$, $\Rightarrow$, $\Leftrightarrow$),

$$FV_{assert}(\forall v.\ p) = FV_{assert}(p) - \{v\}$$

$$FV_{assert}(\exists v.\ p) = FV_{assert}(p) - \{v\}.$$

Even though these equations are not "semantic", they are (as the reader may verify) syntax-directed, and thus they define the functions FV_{intexp} and FV_{assert} uniquely.

Semantically, the significance of the variables that occur free in a phrase is that they delineate the only part of the state on which the value of the phrase depends. This is captured by the following proposition:

Proposition 1.1 (Coincidence Theorem) *If p is a phrase of type θ, and σ and σ' are states such that $\sigma w = \sigma' w$ for all $w \in FV_\theta(p)$, then $[\![p]\!]_\theta \sigma = [\![p]\!]_\theta \sigma'$.*

(To avoid reiterating the same property for different types of phrases, we have adopted, here and later, the convention that a proposition containing the symbol θ should hold both when θ is replaced by "integer expression" and by "assertion". In later chapters, θ will range over additional types of phrases.)

The proof of this proposition is a straightforward example of an important method for proving properties of formal languages, called *structural induction*. To use this method to prove that a proposition holds for an arbitrary phrase p, one assumes the hypothesis (called the *induction hypothesis*) that the same proposition holds for the subphrases of p. (Structural induction on a phrase is justified by ordinary natural-number induction on the depth of the phrase, since subphrases always have smaller depth than their parent.)

PROOF   To prove the proposition for an arbitrary p, we assume (in addition to the induction hypothesis that the proposition holds for the subphrases of p) the *hypothesis of the proposition*, that $\sigma w = \sigma' w$ for all $w \in \mathrm{FV}_\theta(p)$, and we prove the *conclusion of the proposition*, that $[\![p]\!]_\theta \sigma = [\![p]\!]_\theta \sigma'$.

As is typical with structural induction, the proof of the conclusion is a case analysis over the constructors that can produce p or, equivalently, over the abstract-grammar productions that can generate the overall form of p:

- If p is an integer constant, such as 0, then the semantic equation for 0 gives

$$[\![0]\!]_{\mathrm{intexp}} \sigma = 0 = [\![0]\!]_{\mathrm{intexp}} \sigma'.$$

- If p is a variable v, then the hypothesis of the proposition gives $\sigma v = \sigma' v$, since v belongs to $\mathrm{FV}_{\mathrm{intexp}}(v) = \{v\}$. Then the semantic equation for v gives

$$[\![v]\!]_{\mathrm{intexp}} \sigma = \sigma v = \sigma' v = [\![v]\!]_{\mathrm{intexp}} \sigma'.$$

- If p is an integer expression of the form $-\,e$, then the hypothesis of the proposition, along with $\mathrm{FV}_{\mathrm{intexp}}(-\,e) = \mathrm{FV}_{\mathrm{intexp}}(e)$, gives $\sigma w = \sigma' w$ for all $w \in \mathrm{FV}_{\mathrm{intexp}}(e)$. Then the induction hypothesis for the subphrase e gives $[\![e]\!]_{\mathrm{intexp}} \sigma = [\![e]\!]_{\mathrm{intexp}} \sigma'$. Finally, the semantic equation for $-\,e$ gives

$$[\![-e]\!]_{\mathrm{intexp}} \sigma = -[\![e]\!]_{\mathrm{intexp}} \sigma = -[\![e]\!]_{\mathrm{intexp}} \sigma' = [\![-e]\!]_{\mathrm{intexp}} \sigma'.$$

- If p is an integer expression of the form $e_0 + e_1$, then the hypothesis of the proposition, along with $\mathrm{FV}_{\mathrm{intexp}}(e_0 + e_1) = \mathrm{FV}_{\mathrm{intexp}}(e_0) \cup \mathrm{FV}_{\mathrm{intexp}}(e_1)$, gives $\sigma w = \sigma' w$ both for all $w \in \mathrm{FV}_{\mathrm{intexp}}(e_0)$ and for all $w \in \mathrm{FV}_{\mathrm{intexp}}(e_1)$. Then the induction hypothesis for the subphrase e_0 gives $[\![e_0]\!]_{\mathrm{intexp}} \sigma = [\![e_0]\!]_{\mathrm{intexp}} \sigma'$, while the induction hypothesis for the subphrase e_1 gives $[\![e_1]\!]_{\mathrm{intexp}} \sigma = [\![e_1]\!]_{\mathrm{intexp}} \sigma'$. Finally, the semantic equation for $e_0 + e_1$ gives

$$\begin{aligned}
[\![e_0 + e_1]\!]_{\mathrm{intexp}} \sigma &= [\![e_0]\!]_{\mathrm{intexp}} \sigma + [\![e_1]\!]_{\mathrm{intexp}} \sigma \\
&= [\![e_0]\!]_{\mathrm{intexp}} \sigma' + [\![e_1]\!]_{\mathrm{intexp}} \sigma' \\
&= [\![e_0 + e_1]\!]_{\mathrm{intexp}} \sigma'.
\end{aligned}$$

The remaining cases for nonbinding constructions are similar. However, the cases for the quantifiers have a novel aspect that is characteristic of binding: In applying the induction hypothesis, which holds for arbitrary states σ and σ', we take σ and σ' to be different states from the σ and σ' for which we are trying to prove the conclusion of the proposition. (In particular, we take σ and σ' to be states that map the variable being bound into a different value.)

- If p is an assertion of the form $\forall v.\ q$, then the hypothesis of the proposition, along with $\mathrm{FV}_{\mathrm{assert}}(\forall v.\ q) = \mathrm{FV}_{\mathrm{assert}}(q) - \{v\}$, gives $\sigma w = \sigma' w$ for all $w \in \mathrm{FV}_{\mathrm{assert}}(q) - \{v\}$. Thus, if n is any integer, $[\sigma \mid v{:}n]w = [\sigma' \mid v{:}n]w$ for all $w \in \mathrm{FV}_{\mathrm{assert}}(q)$. Then the induction hypothesis for the subphrase q gives $[\![q]\!]_{\mathrm{assert}}[\sigma \mid v{:}n] = [\![q]\!]_{\mathrm{assert}}[\sigma' \mid v{:}n]$. Finally, since this equation holds for any integer n, the semantic equation for $\forall v.\ q$ gives

$$
\begin{aligned}
[\![\forall v.\ q]\!]_{\mathrm{assert}}\sigma &= \forall n \in \mathbf{Z}.\ [\![q]\!]_{\mathrm{assert}}[\sigma \mid v{:}n] \\
&= \forall n \in \mathbf{Z}.\ [\![q]\!]_{\mathrm{assert}}[\sigma' \mid v{:}n] \\
&= [\![\forall v.\ q]\!]_{\mathrm{assert}}\sigma'.
\end{aligned}
$$

The case for the existential quantifier is similar.   END OF PROOF

Since the coincidence theorem implies that no command depends on the state for more than a finite number of variables, it suggests that we could develop a semantics using *finite* states, whose domains are finite sets of variables. In fact, we will use finite states in Chapter 13 and finite environments in Section 15.5. We will avoid them for the present, however, since they require cumbersome notation that is unsuitable for an introductory exposition.

Binding has a surprising interaction with substitution. For example, there is a sound axiom schema,

$$
(\forall v.\ p) \Rightarrow (p/v \to e), \tag{1.13}
$$

in which $p/v \to e$ denotes the result of substituting e for v in p (after replacing these metavariables by particular phrases). Now consider replacing p by $\exists y.\ y > x$, v by x, and e by $y + 1$:

$$
(\forall x.\ \exists y.\ y > x) \Rightarrow ((\exists y.\ y > x)/x \to y + 1).
$$

The soundness of the axiom schema implies that this instance of its conclusion must hold for all states. Clearly, the left side of $\Rightarrow$ holds for all states, so the right side must hold for all states. But if we naïvely carry out the substitution by simply replacing the occurrence of x by $y + 1$, we get $\exists y.\ y > y + 1$, which is obviously false.

The problem is that the binder of y in $\exists y.\ y > x$ has nothing to do with the free occurrence of y in $y + 1$, yet the replacement of x by $y + 1$ has caused the occurrence in $y + 1$ to be "captured" by the binder. To avoid this, we must define substitution so that bound variables are renamed before carrying out the replacement whenever such renaming is necessary to avoid capture.

Instead of defining substitution for a single variable, it is simpler to define simultaneous substitution for all variables. Let Δ be the set $\langle\text{var}\rangle \to \langle\text{intexp}\rangle$ of *substitution maps*. When p is an integer expression or assertion and δ is a substitution map, we write p/δ to denote the result of simultaneously substituting δv for each occurrence of each variable v in p. More precisely, $-/-$ denotes a pair of syntactic functions of types $\langle\text{intexp}\rangle \times \Delta \to \langle\text{intexp}\rangle$ and $\langle\text{assert}\rangle \times \Delta \to \langle\text{assert}\rangle$. (To avoid complicated notation, we denote both of these functions the same way.) Their definition is by equations that are syntax-directed in their first argument:

$$0/\delta = 0$$

(and similarly for 1, 2, ..., **true**, **false**),

$$v/\delta = \delta v$$

$$(-e)/\delta = -(e/\delta)$$

(and similarly for ¬),

$$(e_0 + e_1)/\delta = (e_0/\delta) + (e_1/\delta)$$

(and similarly for $-$, $\times$, $\div$, **rem**, $=$, $\neq$, $<$, $\leq$, $>$, $\geq$, $\wedge$, $\vee$, $\Rightarrow$, $\Leftrightarrow$),

$$(\forall v.\ p)/\delta = \forall v_{\text{new}}.\ (p/[\delta \mid v\colon v_{\text{new}}])$$

(and similarly for $\exists$), where

$$v_{\text{new}} \notin \bigcup_{w \in \text{FV}_{\text{assert}}(p) - \{v\}} \text{FV}_{\text{intexp}}(\delta w).$$

Strictly speaking, this definition is ambiguous, since the above condition on v_{new} does not uniquely determine v_{new}. To resolve this ambiguity, we specify that v_{new} will be v when v satisfies the condition; otherwise v_{new} will be the first variable, in some standard ordering of the variables, that satisfies the condition. This is hardly an intuitively obvious definition of substitution, but it has the right properties. In the first place, there are several syntactic properties, each of which is easily proved by structural induction:

Proposition 1.2 *Suppose p is a phrase of type θ. Then:*

(a) *If $\delta w = \delta' w$ for all $w \in \text{FV}_\theta(p)$, then $p/\delta = p/\delta'$.*

(b) $p/c_{\text{var}} = p$.

(c) $\text{FV}_\theta(p/\delta) = \displaystyle\bigcup_{w \in \text{FV}_\theta(p)} \text{FV}_{\text{intexp}}(\delta w).$

(Note that part (b) of this proposition asserts that the constructor c_{var}, which injects variables into the corresponding integer expressions, acts as an identity substitution.) Then the fundamental semantic property of substitution is

Proposition 1.3 (Substitution Theorem) *If p is a phrase of type θ, and $\sigma w = [\![\delta w]\!]_{\text{intexp}}\sigma'$ for all $w \in FV_\theta(p)$, then $[\![p/\delta]\!]_\theta\sigma' = [\![p]\!]_\theta\sigma$.*

PROOF The proof is by structural induction on p, with a case analysis on the constructors of the abstract grammar. As one might expect, the delicate part of the argument deals with the binding constructors. Suppose p is $\forall v.\, q$, and $\sigma w = [\![\delta w]\!]_{\text{intexp}}\sigma'$ holds for all $w \in FV_\theta(p)$. Then the definition of substitution and the semantic equation for the universal quantifier give

$$[\![(\forall v.\, q)/\delta]\!]_{\text{assert}}\sigma' = [\![\forall v_{\text{new}}.\, (q/[\,\delta \mid v\colon v_{\text{new}}\,])]\!]_{\text{assert}}\sigma'$$
$$= \forall n \in \mathbf{Z}.\, [\![q/[\,\delta \mid v\colon v_{\text{new}}\,]]\!]_{\text{assert}}[\,\sigma' \mid v_{\text{new}}\colon n\,]. \qquad (1.14)$$

Now consider the equation

$$[\,\sigma \mid v\colon n\,]w = [\![[\,\delta \mid v\colon v_{\text{new}}\,]w]\!]_{\text{intexp}}[\,\sigma' \mid v_{\text{new}}\colon n\,].$$

This equation holds when $w = v$, and it also holds for all $w \in FV_{\text{assert}}(q) - \{v\}$, since then $v_{\text{new}} \notin FV_{\text{intexp}}(\delta w)$, and therefore $\sigma w = [\![\delta w]\!]_{\text{intexp}}\sigma' = [\![\delta w]\!]_{\text{intexp}}[\,\sigma' \mid v_{\text{new}}\colon n\,]$. Thus the equation holds for all $w \in FV_{\text{assert}}(q)$ and, by the induction hypothesis, the last line of Equation (1.14) equals

$$\forall n \in \mathbf{Z}.\, [\![q]\!]_{\text{assert}}[\,\sigma \mid v\colon n\,] = [\![\forall v.\, q]\!]_{\text{assert}}\sigma.$$

END OF PROOF

Now we can introduce notation denoting substitution for a single variable and simultaneous substitution for a finite set of variables. We write

$$p/v \to e \quad \text{for} \quad p/[\,c_{\text{var}} \mid v\colon e\,]$$

$$p/v_0 \to e_0,\, \ldots,\, v_{n-1} \to e_{n-1} \quad \text{for} \quad p/[\,c_{\text{var}} \mid v_0\colon e_0 \mid \ldots \mid v_{n-1}\colon e_{n-1}\,].$$

Then taking $\sigma = [\,\sigma' \mid v_0\colon [\![e_0]\!]_{\text{intexp}}\sigma' \mid \ldots \mid v_{n-1}\colon [\![e_{n-1}]\!]_{\text{intexp}}\sigma'\,]$ in Proposition 1.3 gives the corollary:

Proposition 1.4 (Finite Substitution Theorem) *If p is a phrase of type θ, then*

$$[\![p/v_0 \to e_0,\, \ldots,\, v_{n-1} \to e_{n-1}]\!]_\theta\sigma'$$
$$= [\![p]\!]_\theta[\,\sigma' \mid v_0\colon [\![e_0]\!]_{\text{intexp}}\sigma' \mid \ldots \mid v_{n-1}\colon [\![e_{n-1}]\!]_{\text{intexp}}\sigma'\,].$$

From this proposition it is easy, for example, to show that the axiom schema (1.13) is valid. The semantics equation for $\Rightarrow$ gives

$$[\![(\forall v.\, p) \Rightarrow (p/v \to e)]\!]_{\text{assert}}\sigma = [\![\forall v.\, p]\!]_{\text{assert}}\sigma \Rightarrow [\![p/v \to e]\!]_{\text{assert}}\sigma.$$

Thus it is enough to show that any σ satisfying $\forall v.\ p$ also satisfies $p/v \to e$. But if $[\![\forall v.\ p]\!]_{\text{assert}}\sigma$ is true, then the semantic equation for the universal quantifier shows that $\forall n \in \mathbf{Z}.\ [\![p]\!]_{\text{assert}}[\,\sigma \mid v\colon n\,]$ is true, so that $[\![p]\!]_{\text{assert}}[\,\sigma \mid v\colon [\![e]\!]_{\text{intexp}}\sigma\,]$ is true and, by Proposition 1.4, $[\![p/v \to e]\!]_{\text{assert}}\sigma$ is true.

A further property of substitution is that the renaming preserves meaning:

Proposition 1.5 (Renaming Theorem) *If* $v_{\text{new}} \notin \text{FV}_{\text{assert}}(q) - \{v\}$, *then*

$$[\![\forall v_{\text{new}}.\ (q/v \to v_{\text{new}})]\!]_{\text{assert}} = [\![\forall v.\ q]\!]_{\text{assert}}.$$

PROOF In proving Proposition 1.3 for binding constructors, we showed that, if $\sigma w = [\![\delta w]\!]_{\text{intexp}}\sigma'$ for all $w \in \text{FV}_{\text{assert}}(\forall v.\ q)$, then

$$[\![\forall v_{\text{new}}.\ (q/[\,\delta \mid v\colon v_{\text{new}}\,])]\!]_{\text{assert}}\sigma' = [\![\forall v.\ q]\!]_{\text{assert}}\sigma.$$

The relationship $\sigma w = [\![\delta w]\!]_{\text{intexp}}\sigma'$ is satisfied by $\delta = c_{\text{var}}$ and $\sigma = \sigma'$. Thus

$$[\![\forall v_{\text{new}}.\ (q/v \to v_{\text{new}})]\!]_{\text{assert}}\sigma = [\![\forall v.\ q]\!]_{\text{assert}}\sigma.$$

The conclusion of the present proposition follows since this holds for all σ.

The only assumption about v_{new} used in the proof is that it does not belong to $\bigcup_{w \in \text{FV}_{\text{assert}}(q) - \{v\}} \text{FV}_{\text{intexp}}(\delta w)$; when $\delta = c_{\text{var}}$ this set reduces to $\text{FV}_{\text{assert}}(q) - \{v\}$.

END OF PROOF

From this proposition and the compositional nature of our semantics, it is clear that, in any context, one can replace an occurrence of a subphrase of the form $\forall v.\ q$ by $\forall v_{\text{new}}.\ (q/v \to v_{\text{new}})$, without changing the meaning of the context. Such a replacement is called a *renaming* of v or an *alpha conversion*. (The latter term comes from the lambda calculus.)

The principle that renaming preserves meaning is a property of all languages with well-behaved binding. (We will see in Section 11.7, however, that this does not include all well-known programming languages.) Indeed, a recent trend in semantics and logic is to regard the names of bound variables as an aspect of concrete, rather than abstract, syntax. From this viewpoint, called *higher-order abstract syntax*, phrases related by renaming, such as $\forall \mathsf{x}.\ \mathsf{x} \times \mathsf{x} \geq 0$ and $\forall \mathsf{y}.\ \mathsf{y} \times \mathsf{y} \geq 0$, would be different representations of the same abstract phrase.

In conclusion, a small warning must be sounded. What we have defined in this section is the substitution of phrases of the object language for object variables. Similarly, we will substitute phrases of the metalanguage for metavariables, and when the binding structure of the metalanguage requires it, we will rename metavariables, though without being formal about the matter. But the replacement of a metavariable by a phrase of the object language, as is done in forming an instance of an inference rule, is something different that we will not call a substitution. It is a replacement of a metavariable by an appropriate value. Such a value will not contain metavariables (though it might contain object variables), so that nothing can be captured and renaming is not necessary.

Bibliographic Notes

A succinct exposition of predicate logic from a theoretical view (and with the traditional vocabulary of logic) is given by Loeckx et al. [1987, Chapter 2]. A more elementary discussion, specifically oriented to the specification of programs, is given by Gries [1981, Part I]. Gries and Schneider have also written an introductory textbook on logic for computer scientists [1993].

Abstract syntax was introduced by McCarthy [1963], and was also pioneered by Landin [1964] (who called abstract grammars "structure definitions"). The connection with algebra was first noticed by Burstall and Landin [1969]; a more mathematically sophisticated treatment was developed by Goguen, Thatcher, Wagner, and Wright [1977].

Although it is not covered in this book, mention should be made of logic programming, where an extension of predicate logic is used as a programming language. Sterling and Shapiro [1986] is an elementary text; O'Keefe [1990] is more advanced.

Higher-order abstract syntax was developed by Pfenning and Elliott [1988].

Exercises

1.1   State the following in predicate logic:

(a) There is at least one integer larger than zero and smaller than two.
(b) There is at most one integer larger than zero and smaller than two.
(c) There are at least two distinct integers larger than zero and smaller than three.
(d) There are at most two distinct integers larger than zero and smaller than three.

1.2   State the following in predicate logic. Assume that variables and expressions only range over natural numbers (that is, nonnegative integers). Do not use the operations $\div$ or **rem**.

(a) **a** is a divisor of **b** (or, equally well, **b** is a multiple of **a**).
(b) **a** is a common divisor of **b** and **c**.
(c) **a** is a greatest common divisor of **b** and **c**.
(d) **p** is prime.

1.3   Define a universe of phrases, and the constructors displayed in (1.1) in Section 1.1, to obtain an unparenthesized prefix notation. For instance, $c_+((c_{-\text{binary}}(c_0(), c_1())), c_{-\text{unary}}(c_2()))$ should be the string "add, subtract, 0, 1, negate, 0". Be sure that the universe of phrases is defined so that the constructors are injective.

1.4   Give the result of substituting (simultaneously)

(a) $x + y + z$ for t in $\forall x.\ \forall z.\ x < t \wedge t \leq z \Rightarrow \exists y.\ x \leq y \wedge y < z$,

(b) n for x and d for y in $\forall d.\ ((\exists n.\ x = n \times d) \Rightarrow (\exists n.\ y = n \times d))$,

(c) y for x, z for y, and x for z in $\forall x.\ \exists y.\ (x < z \Rightarrow x < y \wedge y < z)$.

Do not rename variables unnecessarily.

1.5   Suppose that, when v is a variable and e_0, e_1, and e_2 are integer expressions,

$$\Sigma v : e_0 \textbf{ to } e_1.\ e_2$$

is an integer expression (called a *summation* expression) with the same meaning as the conventional mathematical expression

$$\sum_{v=e_0}^{e_1} e_2.$$

Describe this extension of predicate logic by giving:

(a) an abstract-grammar production;

(b) a semantic equation;

(c) a definition of the set of free variables and the effect of substitution on a summation expression, in such a way that the propositions we have given about binding and substitution remain true;

(d) sound and nontrivial inference rules for the summation expression.

1.6   Suppose the language in the previous exercise is further extended by introducing an integer expression for "indefinite" summation,

$$\Sigma v.\ e,$$

with the same meaning as

$$\sum_{v=0}^{v-1} e.$$

(Notice the similarity to the usual notation $\int dv\ e$ for an indefinite integral.) Discuss the difficulties raised by the binding and substitution properties of this expression.

1.7   Prove the following composition laws about substitution:

(a) If p is a phrase of type θ, and $\delta''w = (\delta w)/\delta'$ for all $w \in \mathrm{FV}_\theta(p)$, then p/δ'' is a renaming of $(p/\delta)/\delta'$.

(b) If p is a phrase of type θ, then $p/v_1 \to e_1, v_0 \to (e_0/v_1 \to e_1)$ is a renaming of $(p/v_0 \to e_0)/v_1 \to e_1$. *Hint* Do not overlook the special case where $v_0 = v_1$.

2

The Simple Imperative Language

Most serious programming languages combine *imperative* aspects, which describe computation in terms of state-transformation operations such as assignment, and *functional* or *applicative* aspects, which describe computation in terms of the definition and application of functions or procedures. To gain a solid understanding, however, it is best to begin by considering each of these aspects in isolation, and to postpone the complications that arise from their interactions.

Thus, beginning in this chapter and continuing through Chapter 7 (nondeterminism) and Chapters 8 and 9 (concurrency), we will limit ourselves to purely imperative languages. Then, beginning in Chapter 10, we will turn to purely functional languages. Languages that combine imperative and functional aspects will be considered in Chapter 13 (Iswim-like languages) and Chapter 19 (Algol-like languages).

In this chapter, we consider a *simple* imperative language that is built out of assignment commands, sequential composition, conditionals (i.e. **if** commands), **while** commands, and (in Section 2.5) variable declarations. We will use this language to illustrate the basic concept of a domain, to demonstrate the properties of binding in imperative languages, and, in the next chapter, to explore formalisms for specifying and proving imperative program behavior. In later chapters we will explore extensions to this language and other approaches to describing its semantics.

At an intuitive level, the simple imperative language is so much a part of every programmer's background that it will hold few surprises for typical readers. As in Chapter 1, we have chosen for clarity's sake to introduce novel concepts such as domains in a familiar context. More surprising languages will come after we have sharpened our tools for specifying them.

2.1 Syntax

Our version of the simple imperative language has three types of phrases: integer expressions, boolean expressions, and commands. Its abstract syntax is described by the following abstract grammar:

$\langle\text{intexp}\rangle ::= 0 \mid 1 \mid 2 \mid \cdots$

$\qquad \mid \langle\text{var}\rangle \mid -\langle\text{intexp}\rangle \mid \langle\text{intexp}\rangle + \langle\text{intexp}\rangle \mid \langle\text{intexp}\rangle - \langle\text{intexp}\rangle$

$\qquad \mid \langle\text{intexp}\rangle \times \langle\text{intexp}\rangle \mid \langle\text{intexp}\rangle \div \langle\text{intexp}\rangle \mid \langle\text{intexp}\rangle \textbf{ rem } \langle\text{intexp}\rangle$

$\langle\text{boolexp}\rangle ::= \textbf{true} \mid \textbf{false}$

$\qquad \mid \langle\text{intexp}\rangle = \langle\text{intexp}\rangle \mid \langle\text{intexp}\rangle \neq \langle\text{intexp}\rangle \mid \langle\text{intexp}\rangle < \langle\text{intexp}\rangle$

$\qquad \mid \langle\text{intexp}\rangle \leq \langle\text{intexp}\rangle \mid \langle\text{intexp}\rangle > \langle\text{intexp}\rangle \mid \langle\text{intexp}\rangle \geq \langle\text{intexp}\rangle$

$\qquad \mid \neg\,\langle\text{boolexp}\rangle \mid \langle\text{boolexp}\rangle \wedge \langle\text{boolexp}\rangle \mid \langle\text{boolexp}\rangle \vee \langle\text{boolexp}\rangle$

$\qquad \mid \langle\text{boolexp}\rangle \Rightarrow \langle\text{boolexp}\rangle \mid \langle\text{boolexp}\rangle \Leftrightarrow \langle\text{boolexp}\rangle$

$\langle\text{comm}\rangle ::= \langle\text{var}\rangle := \langle\text{intexp}\rangle \mid \textbf{skip} \mid \langle\text{comm}\rangle\,;\langle\text{comm}\rangle$

$\qquad \mid \textbf{if } \langle\text{boolexp}\rangle \textbf{ then } \langle\text{comm}\rangle \textbf{ else } \langle\text{comm}\rangle$

$\qquad \mid \textbf{while } \langle\text{boolexp}\rangle \textbf{ do } \langle\text{comm}\rangle$

Anticipating that, in the next chapter, we will use predicate logic to specify programs, we have chosen expressions that are as close as possible to predicate logic: Integer expressions are exactly the same, and boolean expressions are the same as assertions except for the omission of quantifiers (for the obvious reason that they are noncomputable).

We will parenthesize expressions in the same way as in the previous chapter, while giving the assignment and sequencing operators separate levels of precedence that are lower than any of the arithmetic or logical operators. Thus the precedence list is

$$(\times \div \textbf{ rem}) \; (-_{\text{unary}} \; + \; -_{\text{binary}}) \; (= \neq < \leq > \geq) \; \neg \; \wedge \; \vee \; \Rightarrow \; \Leftrightarrow \; := \; ;$$

In the commands $\textbf{if } b \textbf{ then } c_0 \textbf{ else } c_1$ and $\textbf{while } b \textbf{ do } c_1$, the subphrase c_1 will extend to the first stopping symbol or the end of the enclosing phrase. (Note that ";" is a stopping symbol, but ":=" is not.)

Strictly speaking, we should add the assumption that the sequencing operator ";" is left associative. In practice, however, this is unimportant, since we will always give this operator an associative semantics where $(c_0\,;c_1)\,;c_2$ and $c_0\,;(c_1\,;c_2)$ have the same meaning. (Associativity is irrelevant for ":=", since neither $x_0 := (x_1 := x_2)$ nor $(x_0 := x_1) := x_2$ satisfies our abstract syntax.)

Somewhat simplistically, we assume that all variables take on integer values; in particular, there are no boolean variables. We will consider languages with more than one type of variable when we introduce type systems in Chapter 15; for the present, however, multiple types of variables would only complicate our definitions and obscure more important concepts.

2.2 Denotational Semantics

The semantics of integer expressions is the same as in the previous chapter, and, except for the omission of quantifiers, the semantics of boolean expressions is the same as that of assertions in the previous chapter. Thus the semantic functions

$$[\![-]\!]_{\text{intexp}} \in \langle\text{intexp}\rangle \to \Sigma \to \mathbf{Z}$$

$$[\![-]\!]_{\text{boolexp}} \in \langle\text{boolexp}\rangle \to \Sigma \to \mathbf{B}$$

are defined by semantic equations (1.3) to (1.10) in Section 1.2, with the replacement of $[\![-]\!]_{\text{assert}}$ by $[\![-]\!]_{\text{boolexp}}$.

(As in the previous chapter, expressions always terminate without an error stop. In particular, division by zero must produce some integer result. We will discuss this difficulty in Section 2.7.)

The semantics of commands, however, is quite different. Since the behavior of a command is essentially to transform the state of a computation from an initial state to a final state, one would expect the meaning of a command to be a *state-transformation* function from Σ to Σ. However, we must extend the notion of state transformation to deal with the possibility that the execution of a command, for certain initial states, may never terminate. For this purpose, we introduce the symbol $\bot$, usually called "bottom", to denote nontermination, and we take the meanings of commands to be

$$[\![-]\!]_{\text{comm}} \in \langle\text{comm}\rangle \to \Sigma \to \Sigma_\bot,$$

where $\Sigma_\bot$ stands for $\Sigma \cup \{\bot\}$ (assuming that $\bot \notin \Sigma$). Thus the meaning of a command that does not terminate for an initial state σ is a function that maps σ into $\bot$.

(Many writers use an equivalent formalism where the meaning of a command is a partial function from states to states whose result is undefined for initial states that lead to nontermination. We prefer using $\Sigma \to \Sigma_\bot$ since it clarifies the generalization to richer languages.)

The effect of an assignment command $v := e$ is to transform the initial state into a final state that maps v into the value of e (in the initial state) and maps all other variables into the same value as in the initial state. Thus we have the semantic equation

DR SEM EQ: Assignment

$$[\![v := e]\!]_{\text{comm}}\sigma = [\,\sigma \mid v\colon [\![e]\!]_{\text{intexp}}\sigma\,].$$

For instance,

$$[\![\mathsf{x} := \mathsf{x} - 1]\!]_{\text{comm}}\sigma = [\,\sigma \mid \mathsf{x}\colon [\![\mathsf{x} - 1]\!]_{\text{intexp}}\sigma\,] = [\,\sigma \mid \mathsf{x}\colon \sigma\mathsf{x} - 1\,]$$

$$[\![\mathsf{y} := \mathsf{y} + \mathsf{x}]\!]_{\text{comm}}\sigma = [\,\sigma \mid \mathsf{y}\colon [\![\mathsf{y} + \mathsf{x}]\!]_{\text{intexp}}\sigma\,] = [\,\sigma \mid \mathsf{y}\colon \sigma\mathsf{y} + \sigma\mathsf{x}\,].$$

Notice that the meaning of an assignment command never maps a state into $\perp$, since, in this purely imperative language, expressions always terminate (without error stops).

An even more obvious semantic equation is

DR SEM EQ: **skip**

$$[\![\mathbf{skip}]\!]_{\mathrm{comm}}\sigma = \sigma.$$

On the other hand, the sequential composition of commands is complicated by the possibility of nontermination. Naïvely, one would expect to have the equation $[\![c_0\,;c_1]\!]_{\mathrm{comm}}\sigma = [\![c_1]\!]_{\mathrm{comm}}([\![c_0]\!]_{\mathrm{comm}}\sigma)$, but the result of $[\![c_0]\!]_{\mathrm{comm}}\sigma$ can be $\perp$, which is not in the domain of $[\![c_1]\!]_{\mathrm{comm}}$; less formally, the equation fails to capture the fact that, if c_0 never terminates, then $c_0\,;c_1$ never terminates, regardless of c_1.

To solve this problem, we introduce the idea of extending a function to a domain including $\perp$ by mapping $\perp$ into $\perp$. If f is a function from Σ to $\Sigma_\perp$, we write $f_{\perp\perp}$ for the function from $\Sigma_\perp$ to $\Sigma_\perp$ such that

$$f_{\perp\perp}\sigma = \mathbf{if}\ \sigma = \perp\ \mathbf{then}\ \perp\ \mathbf{else}\ f\sigma.$$

(Here we use a conditional construction in the metalanguage to define the function "by cases". Less formally, $f_{\perp\perp}$ maps $\perp$ to $\perp$ and agrees with f on all other arguments.) Then we have the semantic equation

DR SEM EQ: Sequential Composition

$$[\![c_0\,;c_1]\!]_{\mathrm{comm}}\sigma = ([\![c_1]\!]_{\mathrm{comm}})_{\perp\perp}([\![c_0]\!]_{\mathrm{comm}}\sigma).$$

For instance,

$$\begin{aligned}
[\![\mathsf{x} &:= \mathsf{x} - 1\,;\mathsf{y} := \mathsf{y} + \mathsf{x}]\!]_{\mathrm{comm}}\sigma \\
&= ([\![\mathsf{y} := \mathsf{y} + \mathsf{x}]\!]_{\mathrm{comm}})_{\perp\perp}([\![\mathsf{x} := \mathsf{x} - 1]\!]_{\mathrm{comm}}\sigma) \\
&= [\![\mathsf{y} := \mathsf{y} + \mathsf{x}]\!]_{\mathrm{comm}}[\,\sigma\mid\mathsf{x}\colon\sigma\mathsf{x} - 1\,] \\
&= [\,[\,\sigma\mid\mathsf{x}\colon\sigma\mathsf{x} - 1\,]\mid\mathsf{y}\colon[\,\sigma\mid\mathsf{x}\colon\sigma\mathsf{x} - 1\,]\mathsf{y} + [\,\sigma\mid\mathsf{x}\colon\sigma\mathsf{x} - 1\,]\mathsf{x}\,] \\
&= [\,\sigma\mid\mathsf{x}\colon\sigma\mathsf{x} - 1\mid\mathsf{y}\colon\sigma\mathsf{y} + \sigma\mathsf{x} - 1\,].
\end{aligned} \tag{2.1}$$

For conditional commands, we have

DR SEM EQ: Conditional

$$[\![\mathbf{if}\ b\ \mathbf{then}\ c_0\ \mathbf{else}\ c_1]\!]_{\mathrm{comm}}\sigma = \mathbf{if}\ [\![b]\!]_{\mathrm{boolexp}}\sigma\ \mathbf{then}\ [\![c_0]\!]_{\mathrm{comm}}\sigma\ \mathbf{else}\ [\![c_1]\!]_{\mathrm{comm}}\sigma.$$

For instance,

$$\begin{aligned}
[\![\mathbf{if}\ &\mathsf{x} \neq 0\ \mathbf{then}\ \mathsf{x} := \mathsf{x} - 1\ \mathbf{else}\ \mathsf{y} := \mathsf{y} + \mathsf{x}]\!]_{\mathrm{comm}}\sigma \\
&= \mathbf{if}\ [\![\mathsf{x} \neq 0]\!]_{\mathrm{boolexp}}\sigma\ \mathbf{then}\ [\![\mathsf{x} := \mathsf{x} - 1]\!]_{\mathrm{comm}}\sigma\ \mathbf{else}\ [\![\mathsf{y} := \mathsf{y} + \mathsf{x}]\!]_{\mathrm{comm}}\sigma \\
&= \mathbf{if}\ \sigma\mathsf{x} \neq 0\ \mathbf{then}\ [\,\sigma\mid\mathsf{x}\colon\sigma\mathsf{x} - 1\,]\ \mathbf{else}\ [\,\sigma\mid\mathsf{y}\colon\sigma\mathsf{y} + \sigma\mathsf{x}\,].
\end{aligned}$$

Notice how this semantic equation captures the fact that the conditional command executes only one of its subcommands: When $[\![b]\!]_{\text{boolexp}}\sigma$ is true, the equation gives $[\![c_0]\!]_{\text{comm}}\sigma$ even if c_1 fails to terminate for σ (and vice versa when $[\![b]\!]_{\text{boolexp}}\sigma$ is false).

So far, our semantic equations have been a straightforward formalization of the idea of state transformation. With **while** commands, however, we encounter a serious problem whose solution was central to the development of denotational semantics. If one thinks about "unwinding" a **while** command, it is obvious that

$$\textbf{while } b \textbf{ do } c \qquad \text{and} \qquad \textbf{if } b \textbf{ then } (c\,; \textbf{while } b \textbf{ do } c)\textbf{ else skip}$$

have the same meaning. In other words,

$$[\![\textbf{while } b \textbf{ do } c]\!]_{\text{comm}}\sigma = [\![\textbf{if } b \textbf{ then } (c\,; \textbf{while } b \textbf{ do } c)\textbf{ else skip}]\!]_{\text{comm}}\sigma.$$

By applying the semantic equations for conditionals, sequential composition, and **skip** to the right side of this equation, we get

$$
\begin{aligned}
&[\![\textbf{while } b \textbf{ do } c]\!]_{\text{comm}}\sigma \\
&\quad = \textbf{if } [\![b]\!]_{\text{boolexp}}\sigma \textbf{ then } ([\![\textbf{while } b \textbf{ do } c]\!]_{\text{comm}})\bot([\![c]\!]_{\text{comm}}\sigma)\textbf{ else } \sigma.
\end{aligned}
\tag{2.2}
$$

At first sight, this "unwinding equation" seems to be a plausible semantic equation for the **while** command. However, although it is an equation that should be satisfied by the meaning of the **while** command, it is not a *semantic* equation, since it is not syntax-directed: Because of the presence of **while** b **do** c on the right, it does not describe the meaning of the **while** command purely in terms of the meanings of its subphrases b and c. As a consequence, we have no guarantee that the meaning is uniquely determined by this equation.

In general, an equation may have zero, one, or several solutions. In this case, we will find that there is always a solution but, surprisingly, it is not always unique. For example, suppose b is $\mathsf{x} \neq 0$ and c is $\mathsf{x} := \mathsf{x} - 2$. Then $[\![\mathsf{x} \neq 0]\!]_{\text{boolexp}}\sigma = (\sigma\mathsf{x} \neq 0)$ and $[\![\mathsf{x} := \mathsf{x} - 2]\!]_{\text{comm}}\sigma = [\,\sigma \mid \mathsf{x}\!:\sigma\mathsf{x}{-}2\,]$, so that Equation (2.2) reduces to

$$
\begin{aligned}
&[\![\textbf{while } \mathsf{x} \neq 0 \textbf{ do } \mathsf{x} := \mathsf{x} - 2]\!]_{\text{comm}}\sigma \\
&\quad = \textbf{if } \sigma\mathsf{x} \neq 0 \textbf{ then } ([\![\textbf{while } \mathsf{x} \neq 0 \textbf{ do } \mathsf{x} := \mathsf{x} - 2]\!]_{\text{comm}})\bot[\,\sigma \mid \mathsf{x}\!:\sigma\mathsf{x} - 2\,]\textbf{ else } \sigma.
\end{aligned}
$$

As the reader may verify, this equation is satisfied by

$$
[\![\textbf{while } \mathsf{x} \neq 0 \textbf{ do } \mathsf{x} := \mathsf{x} - 2]\!]_{\text{comm}}\sigma = \begin{cases} [\,\sigma \mid \mathsf{x}\!:0\,] & \text{if even}(\sigma\mathsf{x}) \text{ and } \sigma\mathsf{x} \geq 0 \\ \sigma' & \text{if even}(\sigma\mathsf{x}) \text{ and } \sigma\mathsf{x} < 0 \\ \sigma'' & \text{if odd}(\sigma\mathsf{x}), \end{cases}
$$

where σ' and σ'' can be arbitrary states or $\bot$. Since **while** $\mathsf{x} \neq 0$ **do** $\mathsf{x} := \mathsf{x} - 2$ does not terminate when x is either negative or odd, its actual meaning is given by taking $\sigma' = \sigma'' = \bot$, but there is nothing in the unwinding equation that singles out this solution.

As a more extreme example, suppose b is **true** and c is **skip**. Then, since $[\![\textbf{true}]\!]_{\text{assert}}\sigma = \textbf{true}$ and $[\![\textbf{skip}]\!]_{\text{comm}}\sigma$ is σ, the unwinding equation reduces to

$$[\![\textbf{while true do skip}]\!]_{\text{comm}}\sigma = [\![\textbf{while true do skip}]\!]_{\text{comm}}\sigma,$$

which is satisfied by every function in $\Sigma \rightarrow \Sigma_\perp$. In this case, we know that **while true do skip** is a command that never terminates, so that its meaning is the function that maps every state into $\perp$, but again, this is not a consequence of the unwinding equation.

To overcome this problem, we must introduce the rudiments of domain theory. As we will see in the next two sections, the problem can be solved by making the set of meanings into a domain, which is a certain kind of partial ordering, such that the actual meaning of the **while** command is the *least* solution of the unwinding equation.

2.3 Domains and Continuous Functions

A domain is a special kind of partially ordered set (see Section A.6 of the Appendix) where the partial order, written $\sqsubseteq$, is a relationship of "approximation". When $x \sqsubseteq y$, we say that x *approximates* y, or that y *extends* x. The idea (which is quite different from approximation in numerical analysis) is that y provides at least as much information as x.

A *chain* is a countably infinite increasing sequence, $x_0 \sqsubseteq x_1 \sqsubseteq x_2 \sqsubseteq \cdots$. (Strictly speaking, this is a countable chain, but we will not emphasize this qualification, since we will not consider any other kind of chain.) The least upper bound of a chain is called its *limit*. A chain is said to be *interesting* if it does not contain its own limit or, equivalently, if it contains an infinite number of distinct elements.

A partially ordered set P is called a *predomain* if every chain of elements of P has a limit in P. (Note that this requirement is only significant for interesting chains.) A predomain with a least element, which we will denote by $\perp$, is called a *domain*.

When more than one predomain or domain is involved, we will often decorate symbols such as $\sqsubseteq$ and $\perp$ to avoid confusion. For example, the orderings of P and P' might be written as $\sqsubseteq$ and $\sqsubseteq'$, or even as $\sqsubseteq_P$ and $\sqsubseteq_{P'}$.

It should be mentioned that the term "domain" has no universally accepted definition; it has been used with different meanings by different authors, and even by the same author in different publications. Commonly, one requires the existence of limits, not only of chains, but of a more general kind of subset called a "directed set". Often, additional properties such as "algebraicity" and "bounded completeness" are also imposed.

In general, all such definitions impose stronger requirements than are imposed by the definition we have given above, which will be used throughout this book.

These requirements are actually met by the domains we will be using, but they have no consequences that are significant for the semantic issues we will consider.

Unfortunately, following standard mathematical usage, we will also use the word "domain" with a completely different meaning: to refer to the set over which a function or relation is defined. The key to avoiding confusion is the preposition "of": When we say the domain *of* something we will be referring to the standard mathematical concept of the domain of a function or relation, but when we speak of a domain *per se* we will be referring to the above definition. (Thus, oddly, the domain of a function need not be a domain.)

We will often speak of a set "viewed as a predomain". By this we mean that the set is implicitly equipped with the discrete ordering where $x \sqsubseteq y$ if and only if $x = y$. With this ordering, the set is a predomain because its chains cannot contain distinct elements, and so are never interesting.

When P is a predomain, $P_\perp$ is formed from P by adding a least element $\perp$ distinct from any element of P. Except for the extremely uninteresting chain whose every element is $\perp$, the chains of $P_\perp$ are obtained from the chains of P by prefixing zero or more occurrences of $\perp$, and have the same limits. Thus $P_\perp$ is a domain. The operation $(-)_\perp$ is often called *lifting*.

Note that, if the set Σ of states is viewed as a predomain, the set $\Sigma_\perp$ that we defined in the previous section becomes an instance of the lifting construction, and thereby acquires a partial ordering:

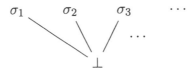

Even in this simple case, the ordering $\sqsubseteq$ is one of increasing information, in the sense that a computation that terminates in some state provides more information than one that never terminates.

More specifically, $\Sigma_\perp$ is an example of a *flat* domain, which is a domain D such that $D - \{\perp\}$ is discretely ordered. Flat domains are suitable for describing the outcomes of computations that either run on forever without producing output or produce output and immediately terminate. They never contain interesting chains.

Richer domains are needed to describe the outcomes of computations that can repeatedly produce output, perhaps ad infinitum. For a class of computations that produce sequences of integers but never terminate, the appropriate domain is the set of finite and infinite sequences of integers, ordered so that $s \sqsubseteq s'$ when s is an initial subsequence of s'. An interesting chain is a sequence of sequences whose lengths grow without limit; each element of such a chain is an initial subsequence of the next, and the limit of the chain is the unique infinite sequence of which every element is an initial subsequence. For example,

$$\langle\rangle \sqsubseteq \langle 3,1\rangle \sqsubseteq \langle 3,1,4\rangle \sqsubseteq \langle 3,1,4,1,5\rangle \sqsubseteq \langle 3,1,4,1,5\rangle \sqsubseteq \langle 3,1,4,1,5,9\rangle \sqsubseteq \cdots$$

is an interesting chain whose limit is the sequence of digits of π. One can think of such a chain as a sequence of snapshots of the output at increasing times, and the limit as the ultimate total result. (We shall investigate a variation of this kind of domain in Sections 5.2 and 5.3.)

For many computations that produce sequences of integers but never terminate, the user is interested only in the set of integers that appear, but not in the order or number of repetitions of these integers. In this situation, the appropriate domain is the powerset of the integers (the set of sets of integers), with $s \sqsubseteq s'$ when $s \subseteq s'$. A chain (interesting or otherwise) is an increasing sequence of sets of integers, and its limit is its union. When the chain elements are all finite sets, one can think of the chain as a sequence of snapshots of the user's interpretation of the output.

In a more extreme case, the user might only be interested in the number of integers that are output. Then the appropriate domain, sometimes called the *vertical* domain of the natural numbers, is the set of natural numbers plus the symbol ∞, ordered by their usual total ordering, $n \sqsubseteq n'$ when $n \leq n'$:

Here the interesting chains are those whose elements increase without limit, and their limits are all ∞. (This is the simplest example of a domain that contains interesting chains.)

A function f from a predomain P to a predomain P' is said to be *continuous from P to P'* if it preserves the limits of chains, that is, if, for every chain $x_0 \sqsubseteq x_1 \sqsubseteq \cdots$ of elements of P, the function f maps the limit of the chain into an element of P' that is the least upper bound of $\{fx_0, fx_1, \ldots\}$.

A continuous function is monotone. To see this, suppose f is continuous and $x \sqsubseteq y$, and consider the chain $x \sqsubseteq y \sqsubseteq y \sqsubseteq \cdots$, whose limit is y. Continuity implies that fy is the least upper bound of $\{fx, fy\}$ and, since a least upper bound is an upper bound, $fx \sqsubseteq' fy$.

On the other hand, a monotone function f will map a chain $x_0 \sqsubseteq x_1 \sqsubseteq \cdots$ into another chain $fx_0 \sqsubseteq fx_1 \sqsubseteq \cdots$, which must possess some limit. In this situation, the condition defining continuity can be written as an equality between two domain elements that are known to exist: If f is a monotone function from a predomain P to a predomain P', then f is continuous if and only if, for all chains $x_0 \sqsubseteq x_1 \sqsubseteq \cdots$ in P,

$$f(\bigsqcup_{i=0}^{\infty} x_i) = \bigsqcup_{i=0}^{\infty}{}' f x_i. \tag{2.3}$$

Nevertheless, there are monotone functions that are not continuous. For example, suppose P is the vertical domain of the natural numbers, and P' is the two-element domain $\{\bot', \top'\}$. Then the monotone function $f x = \mathbf{if}\ x = \infty\ \mathbf{then}\ \top'\ \mathbf{else}\ \bot'$,

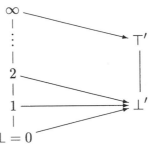

is not continuous, since the limit of $\{0, 1, \ldots\}$ is ∞ and $f\infty$ is $\top'$, but the limit of $\{f0, f1, \ldots\} = \{\bot'\}$ is $\bot'$.

The extra constraint that a monotone function must satisfy in order to be continuous can be characterized as follows:

Proposition 2.1 *Suppose f is a monotone function from a predomain P to a predomain P'. Then f will be continuous if and only if, for all interesting chains $x_0 \sqsubseteq x_1 \sqsubseteq \cdots$ in P,*

$$f(\bigsqcup_{i=0}^{\infty} x_i) \sqsubseteq \bigsqcup_{i=0}^{\infty}{}' f x_i.$$

PROOF We only prove the "if" half of the proposition, since the converse is an immediate consequence of the definition of continuity. Since $\bigsqcup_{i=0}^{\infty} x_i$ is an upper bound of $x_0 \sqsubseteq x_1 \sqsubseteq \cdots$ and f is monotone, $f(\bigsqcup_{i=0}^{\infty} x_i)$ is an upper bound of $f x_0 \sqsubseteq' f x_1 \sqsubseteq' \cdots$, and must therefore extend the least upper bound:

$$\bigsqcup_{i=0}^{\infty}{}' f x_i \sqsubseteq f(\bigsqcup_{i=0}^{\infty} x_i).$$

Thus the opposite inequality is sufficient to imply continuity. Moreover, the opposite inequality holds trivially when the chain $x_0 \sqsubseteq x_1 \sqsubseteq \cdots$ is uninteresting, for then the limit $\bigsqcup_{i=0}^{\infty} x_i$ of the chain belongs to the chain, and it follows that $f(\bigsqcup_{i=0}^{\infty} x_i)$ belongs to $f x_0 \sqsubseteq' f x_1 \sqsubseteq' \cdots$, and thus is bounded by $\bigsqcup_{i=0}^{\infty}{}' f x_i$.

END OF PROOF

When P is finite, or is discretely ordered, or is a flat domain, it contains no interesting chains, so that every monotone function from P to P' is continuous.

Moreover, when P is discretely ordered, all functions from P to P' are monotone, and therefore continuous.

When P and P' are predomains, we write $P \to P'$ for the partially ordered set P'' whose elements are the continuous functions from P to P' and whose ordering is the pointwise extension of the ordering on P':

$$f \sqsubseteq'' g \text{ if and only if, for all } x \in P, \ fx \sqsubseteq' gx.$$

Under this ordering P'' is a predomain and, if P' is a domain, P'' is a domain:

Proposition 2.2 *If P and P' are predomains, $P \to P'$ is a predomain in which the limit of a chain $f_0 \sqsubseteq'' f_1 \sqsubseteq'' \cdots$ of functions is the function such that*

$$\left(\bigsqcup_{i=0}^{\infty}{}'' f_i \right) x = \bigsqcup_{i=0}^{\infty}{}' f_i x$$

for all $x \in P$. Moreover, if P' is a domain, $P \to P'$ is a domain whose least element is the function such that $\perp'' x = \perp'$ for all $x \in P$.

PROOF Let f be the function such that

$$fx = \bigsqcup_{i=0}^{\infty}{}' f_i x$$

for all $x \in P$. (The limit here must exist since the pointwise ordering implies that the $f_i x$ form a chain.) It is easy to see that, under the pointwise ordering, each f_i approximates f and, for any g that is approximated by all of the f_i, f approximates g. Thus f will be the least upper bound of the f_i in $P \to P'$ providing it actually belongs to $P \to P'$, that is, if it is a continuous function.

To see this, let $x_0 \sqsubseteq x_1 \sqsubseteq \cdots$ be a chain in P. Then the definition of f and the continuity of the f_i give

$$f\left(\bigsqcup_{j=0}^{\infty} x_j \right) = \bigsqcup_{i=0}^{\infty}{}' f_i\left(\bigsqcup_{j=0}^{\infty} x_j \right) = \bigsqcup_{i=0}^{\infty}{}' \bigsqcup_{j=0}^{\infty}{}' f_i x_j,$$

while the definition of f also gives

$$\bigsqcup_{j=0}^{\infty}{}' f x_j = \bigsqcup_{j=0}^{\infty}{}' \bigsqcup_{i=0}^{\infty}{}' f_i x_j.$$

By the property of least upper bounds of least upper bounds described in Section A.6 of the Appendix, the right sides of the above equations are both equal to

$$\bigsqcup{}' \{ f_i x_j \mid i \geq 0 \text{ and } j \geq 0 \},$$

and therefore to each other.

When P' is a domain, the pointwise ordering insures that the constant function yielding $\perp'$ is the least element in $P \to P'$. END OF PROOF

When P is discrete, $P \to P'$ contains all of the functions from P to P'; when P' is discrete, $P \to P'$ is discrete. Thus, as long as discrete ordering is the "default" for viewing sets as predomains, our use of $P \to P'$ to denote the predomain of continuous functions from P to P' does not contradict our use of $S \to S'$ to denote the set of all functions from S to S'.

The following proposition establishes that constant and identity functions are continuous, and that composition preserves continuity and is itself a continuous function in each of its arguments:

Proposition 2.3 *Suppose P, P', P'', Q, and Q' are predomains. Then:*

(a) *A constant function from P to P' is a continuous function from P to P'.*

(b) *The identity function on P is a continuous function from P to P.*

(c) *If f is a continuous function from P to P' and g is a continuous function from P' to P'', then $g \cdot f$ is a continuous function from P to P''.*

(d) *If f is a continuous function from P to P', then $- \cdot f$ is a continuous function from $P' \to P''$ to $P \to P''$.*

(e) *If g is a continuous function from P' to P'', then $g \cdot -$ is a continuous function from $P \to P'$ to $P \to P''$.*

Imposing a pointwise ordering makes a domain of the set $\Sigma \to \Sigma_\perp$ of meanings of commands that was introduced in the previous section (since $\Sigma_\perp$ is a domain). In particular, the pointwise ordering is

$$f \sqsubseteq_{\Sigma \to \Sigma_\perp} g \text{ if and only if, for all } \sigma \in \Sigma, \ f\sigma = \perp \text{ or } f\sigma = g\sigma.$$

Again, the ordering is one of increasing information: The computation with meaning g must give the same results as the computation with meaning f, except that it may terminate for more initial states. In the next section, we will find that this ordering is the key to understanding the **while** command.

A function from a domain to a domain is said to be *strict* if it preserves least elements, that is, if it maps $\perp$ into $\perp'$. When $f \in P \to P'$, we write $f_\perp$ (called the *lifting* of f) for the strict function in $P_\perp \to P'_\perp$ such that

$$f_\perp x = \textbf{if } x = \perp \textbf{ then } \perp' \textbf{ else } fx;$$

when $f \in P \to D$ for a domain D, we write $f_{\perp\perp}$ (sometimes called the *source-lifting* of f) for the strict function in $P_\perp \to D$ satisfying the same equation. (Notice that this generalizes the definition in the previous section.) Both of these functions are strict and continuous. On the other hand, the identity injection from P to $P_\perp$, which we denote by $\iota_\uparrow$, is continuous but not strict. Moreover:

Proposition 2.4 *Suppose P, P', and P'' are predomains, D and D' are domains, $e \in P \to P'$, $f \in P' \to P''$, $g \in P'' \to D$, and $h \in D \to D'$,*

$$P \xrightarrow{\ e\ } P' \xrightarrow{\ f\ } P'' \xrightarrow{\ g\ } D \xrightarrow{\ h\ } D'.$$

Then:

(a) $e_\perp$ *is the unique strict extension of e to $P_\perp \to P'_\perp$.*
(b) $g_{\perp\!\perp}$ *is the unique strict extension of g to $P''_\perp \to D$.*
(c) $(f \cdot e)_\perp = f_\perp \cdot e_\perp$.
(d) $(g \cdot f)_{\perp\!\perp} = g_{\perp\!\perp} \cdot f_\perp$.
(e) $(h \cdot g)_{\perp\!\perp} = h \cdot g_{\perp\!\perp}$ *when h is strict.*

Finally, we note that the set of all subsets of a given set can always be regarded as a domain. When S is a set, we write $\mathcal{P}\, S$, called the *powerset domain*, for the domain whose elements are the subsets of S, with inclusion $\subseteq$ as the ordering $\sqsubseteq$. In this case, unions are least upper bounds, so that $\bigsqcup \mathcal{S} = \bigcup \mathcal{S}$ for any $\mathcal{S} \subseteq \mathcal{P}\, S$ (not just chains). The empty set is the least element.

A function f from $\mathcal{P}\, S$ to a predomain P is said to be *finitely generated* if, for all $s \in \mathcal{P}\, S$, $f(s)$ is the least upper bound of $\{\, f(s') \mid s' \stackrel{\text{fin}}{\subseteq} s \,\}$. It can be shown that any finitely generated function is continuous (and, when S is countable, vice versa).

2.4 The Least Fixed-Point Theorem

The following proposition states a fundamental property of domains and continuous functions that underlies the denotational semantics of the **while** command (and also, as we will see in Sections 11.6 and 14.4, of recursion).

Proposition 2.5 (Least Fixed-Point Theorem) *If D is a domain and f is a continuous function from D to D, then*

$$x = \bigsqcup_{n=0}^{\infty} f^n \perp$$

is the least fixed-point of f. In other words, $fx = x$ and, whenever $fy = y$, $x \sqsubseteq y$.

PROOF   Clearly $\perp \sqsubseteq f\perp$ and, if $f^n \perp \sqsubseteq f^{n+1}\perp$, then $f^{n+1}\perp = f(f^n \perp) \sqsubseteq f(f^{n+1}\perp) = f^{n+2}\perp$, since f is monotone. Thus, by induction on n, $\perp \sqsubseteq f\perp \sqsubseteq f^2 \perp \sqsubseteq \cdots$ is a chain, so that x is well defined.

Then, since f is continuous and x is the least upper bound of a chain,

$$fx = f\Big(\bigsqcup_{n=0}^{\infty} f^n \perp\Big) = \bigsqcup_{n=0}^{\infty} f^{n+1}\perp = \bigsqcup_{n=1}^{\infty} f^n \perp = \bigsqcup_{n=0}^{\infty} f^n \perp = x,$$

where the penultimate step is justified since one can always prefix $\perp$ to a chain without changing its least upper bound.

Finally, suppose $fy = y$. Then $\perp \sqsubseteq y$ and, if $f^n\perp \sqsubseteq y$, then $f^{n+1}\perp = f(f^n\perp) \sqsubseteq fy = y$. Thus, by induction on n, y is an upper bound on all of the $f^n\perp$, so that $x = \bigsqcup_{n=0}^{\infty} f^n\perp \sqsubseteq y$.   END OF PROOF

Notice that, in the last paragraph of the above proof, a sufficient hypothesis is $fy \sqsubseteq y$. Thus x is the least solution of $fx \sqsubseteq x$ (and is sometimes called the least *pre-fixed-point* of f) as well as of $fx = x$.

We will write $\mathbf{Y}_D$ for the function from $D \to D$ to D such that

$$\mathbf{Y}_D f = \bigsqcup_{n=0}^{\infty} f^n\perp.$$

Then a more abstract statement of the above proposition is that $\mathbf{Y}_D$ maps continuous functions from D to D into their least fixed-points. It can also be shown that $\mathbf{Y}_D$ itself is a continuous function.

We can now use the mathematical machinery we have developed to explain the **while** command. We know that the meaning of **while** b **do** c should satisfy the "unwinding" equation (2.2) in Section 2.2:

$\llbracket \textbf{while } b \textbf{ do } c \rrbracket_{\text{comm}} \sigma$

$= \textbf{if } \llbracket b \rrbracket_{\text{boolexp}} \sigma \textbf{ then } (\llbracket \textbf{while } b \textbf{ do } c \rrbracket_{\text{comm}})_{\perp\perp}(\llbracket c \rrbracket_{\text{comm}} \sigma) \textbf{ else } \sigma.$

But this equation is simply an assertion that **while** b **do** c is a fixed point of the function $F \in (\Sigma \to \Sigma_\perp) \to (\Sigma \to \Sigma_\perp)$ such that

$$F\, f\, \sigma = \textbf{if } \llbracket b \rrbracket_{\text{boolexp}} \sigma \textbf{ then } f_{\perp\perp}(\llbracket c \rrbracket_{\text{comm}} \sigma) \textbf{ else } \sigma.$$

It can be shown that this function is continuous. Thus, the least fixed-point theorem assures us that the unwinding equation has a solution, and it gives us a criteria — leastness — for picking out a particular solution. If we make the leap of faith that the least solution is the right solution, then we have

DR SEM EQ: **while**

$$\llbracket \textbf{while } b \textbf{ do } c \rrbracket_{\text{comm}} = \mathbf{Y}_{\Sigma \to \Sigma_\perp} F$$

$$\text{where } F\, f\, \sigma = \textbf{if } \llbracket b \rrbracket_{\text{boolexp}} \sigma \textbf{ then } f_{\perp\perp}(\llbracket c \rrbracket_{\text{comm}} \sigma) \textbf{ else } \sigma. \tag{2.4}$$

We cannot *prove* our leap of faith that this semantic equation is correct, because we have no other rigorous definition of the **while** command. But we can give an informal argument that appeals to the reader's intuitive operational understanding. Let $w_0, w_1, \ldots$ be the sequence of commands

$$w_0 \stackrel{\text{def}}{=} \textbf{while true do skip}$$

$$w_i + 1 \stackrel{\text{def}}{=} \textbf{if } b \textbf{ then } (c \,;\, w_n) \textbf{ else skip}.$$

The command w_0 obviously never terminates, so that $[\![w_0]\!]_{\text{comm}} = \bot$, and it is easy to work out that $[\![w_{i+1}]\!]_{\text{comm}} = F[\![w_i]\!]_{\text{comm}}$. Thus

$$[\![w_i]\!]_{\text{comm}} = F^i \bot.$$

Now comes the crucial informal argument: Starting in a particular state σ, the two commands w_i and **while** b **do** c will behave the same way, unless the **while** command executes the test b at least i times, in which case w_i will not terminate. Thus:

- If **while** b **do** c terminates after testing b exactly n times, then

$$[\![w_i]\!]_{\text{comm}}\sigma = \begin{cases} \bot & \text{when } i < n \\ [\![\textbf{while } b \textbf{ do } c]\!]_{\text{comm}}\sigma & \text{when } i \geq n. \end{cases}$$

- If **while** b **do** c does not terminate, then, for all i,

$$[\![w_i]\!]_{\text{comm}}\sigma = \bot = [\![\textbf{while } b \textbf{ do } c]\!]_{\text{comm}}\sigma.$$

In either case, however, $[\![\textbf{while } b \textbf{ do } c]\!]_{\text{comm}}\sigma$ is the limit of the chain $[\![w_0]\!]_{\text{comm}}\sigma$, $[\![w_1]\!]_{\text{comm}}\sigma, \ldots,$

$$[\![\textbf{while } b \textbf{ do } c]\!]_{\text{comm}}\sigma = \bigsqcup_{n=0}^{\infty} [\![w_n]\!]_{\text{comm}}\sigma$$

and, by Proposition 2.2 in the previous section and the least fixed-point theorem,

$$[\![\textbf{while } b \textbf{ do } c]\!]_{\text{comm}} = \bigsqcup_{n=0}^{\infty} [\![w_n]\!]_{\text{comm}} = \bigsqcup_{n=0}^{\infty} F^n \bot = \mathbf{Y}_{\Sigma \to \Sigma_\bot} F.$$

As a trivial example, when b is **true** and c is **skip** the function F is the identity function on $\Sigma \to \Sigma_\bot$, whose least fixed-point is the function mapping every state into $\bot$, which is indeed the meaning of **while true do skip**.

As a nontrivial example, using Equation (2.1) in Section 2.2 we find

$$[\![\textbf{while } \mathsf{x} \neq 0 \textbf{ do } (\mathsf{x} := \mathsf{x} - 1\,;\mathsf{y} := \mathsf{y} + \mathsf{x})]\!]_{\text{comm}} = \mathbf{Y}_{\Sigma \to \Sigma_\bot} F,$$

where

$$F\,f\,\sigma = \textbf{if } \sigma\mathsf{x} \neq 0 \textbf{ then } f_{\bot\bot}[\,\sigma \mid \mathsf{x}{:}\sigma\mathsf{x} - 1 \mid \mathsf{y}{:}\sigma\mathsf{y} + \sigma\mathsf{x} - 1] \textbf{ else } \sigma.$$

There is no universal method for converting such an equation into a more explicit form. In this case, however, our informal expectation is that the "approximate" **while** command w_n, whose meaning is $F^n \bot$, will terminate when $0 \leq \mathsf{x} < n$, and when it terminates it will set x to zero and increase y by each of the integers from $\mathsf{x} - 1$ down to zero. It is known that the sum of these integers is $(\mathsf{x} \times (\mathsf{x} - 1) \div 2)$. Thus we expect

$$F^n \bot \sigma = \textbf{if } 0 \leq \sigma\mathsf{x} < n \textbf{ then } [\,\sigma \mid \mathsf{x}{:}0 \mid \mathsf{y}{:}\sigma\mathsf{y} + \sigma\mathsf{x} \times (\sigma\mathsf{x} - 1) \div 2] \textbf{ else } \bot.$$

In fact, we can prove this equation by induction on n. When $n = 0$, the equation follows from $\bot\sigma = \bot$. The induction step is

$$F^{n+1}\bot\sigma = F(F^n\bot)\sigma$$

$$= \textbf{if } \sigma\mathsf{x} \neq 0 \textbf{ then } (F^n(\bot))_{\bot\bot}[\sigma \mid \mathsf{x}{:}\,\sigma\mathsf{x} - 1 \mid \mathsf{y}{:}\,\sigma\mathsf{y} + \sigma\mathsf{x} - 1] \textbf{ else } \sigma$$

$$= \textbf{if } \sigma\mathsf{x} \neq 0 \textbf{ then}$$

$$\qquad \textbf{if } 0 \leq \sigma\mathsf{x} - 1 < n \textbf{ then}$$

$$\qquad\qquad [\sigma \mid \mathsf{x}{:}\,0 \mid \mathsf{y}{:}\,\sigma\mathsf{y} + \sigma\mathsf{x} - 1 + (\sigma\mathsf{x} - 1) \times (\sigma\mathsf{x} - 2) \div 2]$$

$$\qquad \textbf{else } \bot$$

$$\qquad \textbf{else } \sigma$$

$$= \textbf{if } \sigma\mathsf{x} \neq 0 \textbf{ then}$$

$$\qquad \textbf{if } 1 \leq \sigma\mathsf{x} < n{+}1 \textbf{ then}$$

$$\qquad\qquad [\sigma \mid \mathsf{x}{:}\,0 \mid \mathsf{y}{:}\,\sigma\mathsf{y} + \sigma\mathsf{x} \times (\sigma\mathsf{x} - 1) \div 2]$$

$$\qquad \textbf{else } \bot$$

$$\qquad \textbf{else } \sigma$$

$$= \textbf{if } 0 \leq \sigma\mathsf{x} < n{+}1 \textbf{ then } [\sigma \mid \mathsf{x}{:}\,0 \mid \mathsf{y}{:}\,\sigma\mathsf{y} + \sigma\mathsf{x} \times (\sigma\mathsf{x} - 1) \div 2] \textbf{ else } \bot.$$

Now consider the chain $F^0\bot\sigma$, $F^1\bot\sigma$, ... If $\sigma\mathsf{x} \geq 0$, the chain will consist of some finite number of occurrences of $\bot$, followed by an infinite number of occurrences of $[\sigma \mid \mathsf{x}{:}\,0 \mid \mathsf{y}{:}\,\sigma\mathsf{y} + \sigma\mathsf{x} \times (\sigma\mathsf{x} - 1) \div 2]$, which will be the limit of the chain. On the other hand, if $\sigma\mathsf{x} < 0$, the chain will consist entirely of $\bot$, which will be its limit. Thus

$$[\![\textbf{while } \mathsf{x} \neq 0 \textbf{ do } (\mathsf{x} := \mathsf{x} - 1 \,;\, \mathsf{y} := \mathsf{y} + \mathsf{x})]\!]_{\mathrm{comm}}\sigma$$

$$= \mathbf{Y}_{\Sigma \to \Sigma_\bot}\, F\sigma$$

$$= \bigsqcup_{n=0}^{\infty} F^n\bot\sigma$$

$$= \textbf{if } \sigma\mathsf{x} \geq 0 \textbf{ then } [\sigma \mid \mathsf{x}{:}\,0 \mid \mathsf{y}{:}\,\sigma\mathsf{y} + \sigma\mathsf{x} \times (\sigma\mathsf{x} - 1) \div 2] \textbf{ else } \bot.$$

A very different application of the least fixed-point theorem is to abstract syntax definitions. In Section 1.1, we saw that such a definition can be regarded as a system of equations of the form

$$s_0^{(0)} = \{\} \quad \cdots \quad s_{n-1}^{(0)} = \{\}$$

$$s_0^{(j+1)} = f_0(s_0^{(j)}, \dots, s_{n-1}^{(j)}) \quad \cdots \quad s_{n-1}^{(j+1)} = f_{n-1}(s_0^{(j)}, \dots, s_{n-1}^{(j)})$$

$$s_0 = \bigcup_{j=0}^{\infty} s_0^{(j)} \quad \cdots \quad s_{n-1} = \bigcup_{j=0}^{\infty} s_{n-1}^{(j)},$$

where, for $0 \leq i \leq n - 1$ and $j \geq 0$, the $s_i^{(j)}$ and s_i belong to the powerset $\mathcal{P}\,\mathbf{P}$ of the universe $\mathbf{P}$ of all phrases and the f_i are functions from $(\mathcal{P}\,\mathbf{P})^n$ to $\mathcal{P}\,\mathbf{P}$.

Suppose we define the elements

$$s^{(j)} = \langle s_0^{(j)}, \dots, s_{n-1}^{(j)} \rangle \qquad s = \langle s_0, \dots, s_{n-1} \rangle$$

of the domain $(\mathcal{P}\,\mathbf{P})^n$, and the function $f = f_0 \otimes \cdots \otimes f_{n-1}$ from $(\mathcal{P}\,\mathbf{P})^n$ to $(\mathcal{P}\,\mathbf{P})^n$. Then the above equations can be rewritten more succinctly as

$$s^{(0)} = \langle \{\}, \dots, \{\} \rangle = \bot \qquad s^{(j+1)} = f(s^{(j)}) \qquad s = \bigsqcup_{j=0}^{\infty} s^{(j)},$$

or just

$$s = \bigsqcup_{j=0}^{\infty} f^j \bot.$$

By the least fixed-point theorem, s is the least solution of $s = fs$. In terms of the original equations, $s = \langle s_0, \dots, s_{n-1} \rangle$ is the family of least sets satisfying the original equations with the superscripts (j) omitted.

Of course, this depends on the function f being continuous. In fact, the continuity of f stems from the fact that each f_i is finitely generated in each of its n arguments, which in turn stems from the fact that the constructors of the abstract syntax have a finite number of arguments.

2.5 Variable Declarations and Substitution

In this section, we extend the simple imperative language by adding *variable declarations*. The abstract syntax is given by the production

$$\langle \text{comm} \rangle ::= \textbf{newvar } \langle \text{var} \rangle := \langle \text{intexp} \rangle \textbf{ in } \langle \text{comm} \rangle$$

(We will use the term "declaration" for the subphrase **newvar** $\langle \text{var} \rangle := \langle \text{intexp} \rangle$ and also for the command that begins with this subphrase, which many authors call a "block".) The concrete syntax of this command is similar to the conditional and **while** constructions: It extends to the first stopping symbol or to the end of the enclosing phrase.

Semantically, **newvar** $v := e$ **in** c initializes the variable v to the value of e, executes c, and, if c terminates, resets v to whatever value it had before initialization. This behavior is captured by the semantic equation

$$\llbracket \textbf{newvar } v := e \textbf{ in } c \rrbracket_{\text{comm}} \sigma$$
$$= \textbf{if } \llbracket c \rrbracket_{\text{comm}} [\, \sigma \mid v\colon \llbracket e \rrbracket_{\text{intexp}} \sigma \,] = \bot \textbf{ then } \bot \textbf{ else}$$
$$[\, \llbracket c \rrbracket_{\text{comm}} [\, \sigma \mid v\colon \llbracket e \rrbracket_{\text{intexp}} \sigma \,] \mid v\colon \sigma v \,]$$

or, more abstractly,

DR SEM EQ: Variable Declaration

$$[\![\mathbf{newvar}\ v := e\ \mathbf{in}\ c]\!]_{\text{comm}}\sigma$$
$$= (\lambda\sigma' \in \Sigma.\ [\,\sigma' \mid v\colon\sigma v\,])_{\perp\!\perp}([\![c]\!]_{\text{comm}}[\,\sigma \mid v\colon [\![e]\!]_{\text{intexp}}\sigma\,]).$$

(Here we have used a typed abstraction in the metalanguage. As explained in Section A.3 of the Appendix, $\lambda\sigma' \in \Sigma.\ [\,\sigma' \mid v\colon\sigma v\,]$ stands for the function f such that $f\sigma' = [\,\sigma' \mid v\colon\sigma v\,]$ for all $\sigma' \in \Sigma$.)

Variable declarations are a simple example of a construct that improves the *scalability* of programs. Although they are of little value in small programs, they are essential for the readability of large ones. When a program involves hundreds of variables, it is vital that the programmer be able to indicate the region of the program to which each variable is *local*. (Notice that this notion of locality disconnects the behavior of the variable within the region where it is declared from the behavior of a variable with the same name outside the region. A precise definition of locality will be formalized in Section 3.5.)

We have made a specific design choice in allowing a newly declared variable to be initialized to the value of an arbitrary integer expression. Some languages use a default initialization, typically to zero, but this is unnecessarily restrictive. Many others leave the initialization unspecified, with the pragmatic intention that the initialization may be whatever value happens to lie in the newly allocated word of storage. Such a value, however, will usually be logically unrelated to the variable being declared, and may even be a machine instruction or (in some operating environments) data or code from someone else's computation. This can make debugging extraordinarily difficult, since the behavior of a program that depends on unspecified initial values will be inexplicable in terms of any reasonable semantics, and intelligible only when one understands the details of storage allocation, and perhaps code generation, by the compiler. Indeed, in some environments, the initialization may be determined by factors that make program behavior irreproducible.

In $\mathbf{newvar}\ v := e\ \mathbf{in}\ c$, the occurrence of v is a binder whose scope is c (but not e). In contrast, in the assignment command $v := e$, the occurrence of v is not a binder. Thus the variables occurring free in a command are given by

$$\text{FV}_{\text{comm}}(v := e) = \{v\} \cup \text{FV}_{\text{intexp}}(e)$$

$$\text{FV}_{\text{comm}}(\mathbf{skip}) = \{\}$$

$$\text{FV}_{\text{comm}}(c_0\,;c_1) = \text{FV}_{\text{comm}}(c_0) \cup \text{FV}_{\text{comm}}(c_1)$$

$$\text{FV}_{\text{comm}}(\mathbf{if}\ b\ \mathbf{then}\ c_0\ \mathbf{else}\ c_1) = \text{FV}_{\text{boolexp}}(b) \cup \text{FV}_{\text{comm}}(c_0) \cup \text{FV}_{\text{comm}}(c_1)$$

$$\text{FV}_{\text{comm}}(\mathbf{while}\ b\ \mathbf{do}\ c) = \text{FV}_{\text{boolexp}}(b) \cup \text{FV}_{\text{comm}}(c)$$

$$\text{FV}_{\text{comm}}(\mathbf{newvar}\ v := e\ \mathbf{in}\ c) = (\text{FV}_{\text{comm}}(c) - \{v\}) \cup \text{FV}_{\text{intexp}}(e),$$

where $\text{FV}_{\text{intexp}}$ is the same as in the previous chapter and $\text{FV}_{\text{boolexp}}$ is the same as $\text{FV}_{\text{assert}}$, but restricted to quantifier-free expressions.

One can also define $\text{FA}(c) \subseteq \text{FV}_{\text{comm}}(c)$ to be the set of variables that occur free on the left of an assignment operation in c:

$$\text{FA}(v := e) = \{v\}$$

$$\text{FA}(\textbf{skip}) = \{\}$$

$$\text{FA}(c_0\, ;\, c_1) = \text{FA}(c_0) \cup \text{FA}(c_1)$$

$$\text{FA}(\textbf{if } b \textbf{ then } c_0 \textbf{ else } c_1) = \text{FA}(c_0) \cup \text{FA}(c_1)$$

$$\text{FA}(\textbf{while } b \textbf{ do } c) = \text{FA}(c)$$

$$\text{FA}(\textbf{newvar } v := e \textbf{ in } c) = \text{FA}(c) - \{v\}.$$

Substitution into integer and boolean expressions is defined as in the previous chapter. (Indeed, in the absence of quantifiers it is trivial.) But substitution into commands is much more constrained, since the substitution of an expression that is not a variable for the occurrence of a variable on the left side of an assignment command would produce a syntactically illegal phrase, such as $(\mathsf{x}{:=}\mathsf{x}{+}1)/\mathsf{x} \to 10$, which is $10 := 10 + 1$ or $(\mathsf{x} := \mathsf{x} + 1)/\mathsf{x} \to \mathsf{y} * \mathsf{z}$, which is $\mathsf{y} * \mathsf{z} := \mathsf{y} * \mathsf{z} + 1$.

However, if we limit the substitution map δ to a function that yields variables, so that $\delta \in \langle\text{var}\rangle \to \langle\text{var}\rangle$, then we can define

$$(v := e)/\delta = (\delta v) := (e/\delta)$$

$$\textbf{skip}/\delta = \textbf{skip}$$

$$(c_0\, ;\, c_1)/\delta = (c_0/\delta)\, ;\, (c_1/\delta)$$

$$(\textbf{if } b \textbf{ then } c_0 \textbf{ else } c_1)/\delta = \textbf{if } (b/\delta) \textbf{ then } (c_0/\delta) \textbf{ else } (c_1/\delta)$$

$$(\textbf{while } b \textbf{ do } c)/\delta = \textbf{while } (b/\delta) \textbf{ do } (c/\delta)$$

$$(\textbf{newvar } v := e \textbf{ in } c)/\delta = \textbf{newvar } v_{\text{new}} := (e/\delta) \textbf{ in } (c/[\,\delta \mid v\!: v_{\text{new}}\,]),$$

where

$$v_{\text{new}} \notin \{\, \delta w \mid w \in \text{FV}_{\text{comm}}(c) - \{v\} \,\}.$$

(Actually, we are cheating a little here by assuming that, if δ is a function whose results are variables, it is also a function whose results are integer expressions. Strictly speaking, our abstract grammar does not say that variables are integer expressions, but only that there is an injective constructor c_{var} from variables to integer expressions. However, making this constructor explicit would complicate and obscure the above definition of substitution horribly.)

The properties of free variables and substitution given by Propositions 1.1 to 1.4 in Section 1.4 remain true when θ is "integer expression" or "boolean expression", and the syntactic properties given by Proposition 1.2 also hold when θ is "command". But the semantic properties of free variables and substitution are more complicated for commands.

For instance, in the absence of nontermination, $[\![c]\!]_{\text{comm}}\sigma$ is a state that depends on the entire state σ, not just the part of σ that acts on the free variables of c. However, suppose we consider $[\![c]\!]_{\text{comm}}\sigma w$ for a particular variable w. If w is a free variable of c, then $[\![c]\!]_{\text{comm}}\sigma w$ depends only on the part of σ that acts on the free variables. On the other hand, if w is not a free variable, indeed if w is not assigned by c, then $[\![c]\!]_{\text{comm}}\sigma w$ is the same as σw.

For example, consider $[\![\mathsf{x} := \mathsf{x} + \mathsf{z} \,;\, \mathsf{y} := \mathsf{x} + \mathsf{y}]\!]_{\text{comm}}\sigma$, where $\sigma = [\,\sigma_0 \mid \mathsf{x}{:}\,a \mid \mathsf{y}{:}\,b \mid \mathsf{z}{:}\,c\,]$. If w is x, y, or z, then $[\![\mathsf{x} := \mathsf{x} + \mathsf{z} \,;\, \mathsf{y} := \mathsf{x} + \mathsf{y}]\!]_{\text{comm}}\sigma w$ depends on a, b, and c, but not σ_0; while if w is not x or y, then $[\![\mathsf{x} := \mathsf{x} + \mathsf{z} \,;\, \mathsf{y} := \mathsf{x} + \mathsf{y}]\!]_{\text{comm}}\sigma w = \sigma w$.

In general, one can show

Proposition 2.6 (Coincidence Theorem for Commands)

(a) *If σ and σ' are states such that $\sigma w = \sigma'w$ for all $w \in \text{FV}_{\text{comm}}(c)$, then either $[\![c]\!]_{\text{comm}}\sigma = [\![c]\!]_{\text{comm}}\sigma' = \bot$ or else $[\![c]\!]_{\text{comm}}\sigma$ and $[\![c]\!]_{\text{comm}}\sigma'$ are states such that $([\![c]\!]_{\text{comm}}\sigma)w = ([\![c]\!]_{\text{comm}}\sigma')w$ for all $w \in \text{FV}_{\text{comm}}(c)$.*

(b) *If $[\![c]\!]_{\text{comm}}\sigma \neq \bot$, then $([\![c]\!]_{\text{comm}}\sigma)w = \sigma w$ for all $w \notin \text{FA}(c)$.*

Surprisingly — and disturbingly — the substitution theorem fails for commands. In fact, when a substitution carries distinct variables into the same variable (in which case the distinct variables are said to become *aliases*), it can map commands with the same meaning into commands with different meanings. For example,

$$\mathsf{x} := \mathsf{x} + 1 \,;\, \mathsf{y} := \mathsf{y} * 2 \qquad \text{and} \qquad \mathsf{y} := \mathsf{y} * 2 \,;\, \mathsf{x} := \mathsf{x} + 1$$

have the same meaning, but the aliasing substitution of z for both x and y maps these commands into

$$\mathsf{z} := \mathsf{z} + 1 \,;\, \mathsf{z} := \mathsf{z} * 2 \qquad \text{and} \qquad \mathsf{z} := \mathsf{z} * 2 \,;\, \mathsf{z} := \mathsf{z} + 1,$$

which have different meanings.

Aliasing is an inherent subtlety of imperative programming that is a rich source of programming errors. A less trivial example is

$$\mathsf{y} := 1 \,;\, \textbf{while } \mathsf{x} > 0 \textbf{ do } (\mathsf{y} := \mathsf{y} \times \mathsf{x} \,;\, \mathsf{x} := \mathsf{x} - 1).$$

When $\mathsf{x} \geq 0$, this command sets y to the factorial of the initial value of x. But the command obtained by substituting the same variable z for both x and y,

$$\mathsf{z} := 1 \,;\, \textbf{while } \mathsf{z} > 0 \textbf{ do } (\mathsf{z} := \mathsf{z} \times \mathsf{z} \,;\, \mathsf{z} := \mathsf{z} - 1),$$

does not set z to the factorial of the initial value of z. (We will see in Chapter 13 that aliasing problems are exacerbated when an imperative language is extended with a procedure mechanism that uses call by name or call by reference.)

Even though the substitution theorem fails in general, one can still give a theorem about substitutions that do not create aliases since they map distinct variables into distinct variables:

Proposition 2.7 (Substitution Theorem for Commands) *Suppose c is a command, $\delta \in \langle \text{var} \rangle \to \langle \text{var} \rangle$, and V is a set of variables, such that $\text{FV}_{\text{comm}}(c) \subseteq V$ and $\delta w \neq \delta w'$ whenever w and w' are distinct members of V. If $\sigma w = \sigma'(\delta w)$ for all $w \in V$, then either $[\![c/\delta]\!]_{\text{comm}} \sigma' = [\![c]\!]_{\text{comm}} \sigma = \bot$ or else $[\![c/\delta]\!]_{\text{comm}} \sigma'$ and $[\![c]\!]_{\text{comm}} \sigma$ are states such that $([\![c/\delta]\!]_{\text{comm}} \sigma')(\delta w) = ([\![c]\!]_{\text{comm}} \sigma)w$ for all $w \in V$.*

PROOF As with the substitution theorem for predicate logic (Proposition 1.3 in Section 1.4), the proof is by structural induction (on c) with a case analysis on the constructors of the abstract syntax, and the delicate part of the argument is the case of the binding constructor. We limit our exposition to this case and, to focus on the significant aspects, we only consider initialization to zero.

Suppose c is **newvar** $v := 0$ **in** c', $\text{FV}_{\text{comm}}(c) \subseteq V$, $\delta w \neq \delta w'$ whenever w and w' are distinct members of V, and $\sigma w = \sigma'(\delta w)$ for all $w \in V$. Assume that $v_{\text{new}} \notin \{ \delta w \mid w \in \text{FV}_{\text{comm}}(c') - \{v\} \}$. Consider the equation

$$[\sigma \mid v{:}0]w = [\sigma' \mid v_{\text{new}}{:}0]([\delta \mid v{:}v_{\text{new}}]w).$$

This equation holds when $w = v$, and it also holds for all $w \in \text{FV}_{\text{comm}}(c') - \{v\}$ since then $v_{\text{new}} \neq \delta w$, and thus $\sigma w = \sigma'(\delta w) = [\sigma' \mid v_{\text{new}}{:}0](\delta w)$. Thus the equation holds for all $w \in \text{FV}_{\text{comm}}(c')$.

Moreover, if w and w' are distinct variables in $\text{FV}_{\text{comm}}(c')$, then

$$[\delta \mid v{:}v_{\text{new}}]w \neq [\delta \mid v{:}v_{\text{new}}]w',$$

since either w and w' are both in $\text{FV}_{\text{comm}}(c') - \{v\} = \text{FV}_{\text{comm}}(c) \subseteq V$, in which case $[\delta \mid v{:}v_{\text{new}}]w = \delta w \neq \delta w' = [\delta \mid v{:}v_{\text{new}}]w'$, or one of these variables, say w', is v and the other is in $\text{FV}_{\text{comm}}(c') - \{v\}$, in which case $[\delta \mid v{:}v_{\text{new}}]w = \delta w \neq v_{\text{new}} = [\delta \mid v{:}v_{\text{new}}]w'$.

Thus, we can apply the induction hypothesis, with c replaced by c', V by $\text{FV}_{\text{comm}}(c')$, δ by $[\delta \mid v{:}v_{\text{new}}]$, σ' by $[\sigma' \mid v_{\text{new}}{:}0]$, and σ by $[\sigma \mid v{:}0]$. We find that

$$[\![c'/[\delta \mid v{:}v_{\text{new}}]]\!]_{\text{comm}} [\sigma' \mid v_{\text{new}}{:}0] \qquad \text{and} \qquad [\![c']\!]_{\text{comm}} [\sigma \mid v{:}0]$$

are either both equal to $\bot$ or are states satisfying

$$([\![c'/[\delta \mid v{:}v_{\text{new}}]]\!]_{\text{comm}} [\sigma' \mid v_{\text{new}}{:}0])([\delta \mid v{:}v_{\text{new}}]w) = ([\![c']\!]_{\text{comm}} [\sigma \mid v{:}0])w$$

for all $w \in \text{FV}_{\text{comm}}(c')$.

Now consider the case where termination occurs, and suppose $w \in \mathrm{FV}_{\mathrm{comm}}(c) = \mathrm{FV}_{\mathrm{comm}}(c') - \{v\}$. Then the definition of substitution, the semantic equation for variable declarations, the facts that $v_{\mathrm{new}} \neq \delta w$ and $v \neq w$, the above equation, and again $v \neq w$ and the semantic equation for variable declarations give

$$
\begin{aligned}
(\llbracket c/\delta \rrbracket_{\mathrm{comm}} \sigma')(\delta w) &= (\llbracket (\mathbf{newvar}\ v := 0\ \mathbf{in}\ c')/\delta \rrbracket_{\mathrm{comm}} \sigma')(\delta w) \\
&= (\llbracket \mathbf{newvar}\ v_{\mathrm{new}} := 0\ \mathbf{in}\ (c'/[\,\delta \mid v\!: v_{\mathrm{new}}\,]) \rrbracket_{\mathrm{comm}} \sigma')(\delta w) \\
&= (\llbracket\,\llbracket c'/[\,\delta \mid v\!: v_{\mathrm{new}}\,] \rrbracket_{\mathrm{comm}} [\,\sigma' \mid v_{\mathrm{new}}\!: 0\,] \mid v_{\mathrm{new}}\!: \sigma' v_{\mathrm{new}}\,])(\delta w) \\
&= (\llbracket c'/[\,\delta \mid v\!: v_{\mathrm{new}}\,] \rrbracket_{\mathrm{comm}} [\,\sigma' \mid v_{\mathrm{new}}\!: 0\,])(\delta w) \\
&= (\llbracket c'/[\,\delta \mid v\!: v_{\mathrm{new}}\,] \rrbracket_{\mathrm{comm}} [\,\sigma' \mid v_{\mathrm{new}}\!: 0\,])([\,\delta \mid v\!: v_{\mathrm{new}}\,]w) \\
&= (\llbracket c' \rrbracket_{\mathrm{comm}} [\,\sigma \mid v\!: 0\,])w \\
&= (\llbracket\,\llbracket c' \rrbracket_{\mathrm{comm}} [\,\sigma \mid v\!: 0\,] \mid v\!: \sigma v\,])w \\
&= (\llbracket \mathbf{newvar}\ v := 0\ \mathbf{in}\ c' \rrbracket_{\mathrm{comm}} \sigma)w \\
&= (\llbracket c \rrbracket_{\mathrm{comm}} \sigma)w.
\end{aligned}
$$

On the other hand, in the case of nontermination, the parenthesized expressions immediately following the equality signs in the above display are all equal to $\perp$.

To complete the proof, we must extend the argument for the case of termination to variables in V that do not occur free in c. Suppose $w \in V - \mathrm{FV}_{\mathrm{comm}}(c)$. If δw occurred free in c/δ, then, by Proposition 1.2(c) in Section 1.4, there would be a $w_{\mathrm{free}} \in \mathrm{FV}_{\mathrm{comm}}(c)$ such that $\delta w = \delta w_{\mathrm{free}}$; but then w and w_{free} would be distinct variables in V, so that $\delta w \neq \delta w_{\mathrm{free}}$, which would be contradictory. Thus $\delta w \notin \mathrm{FV}_{\mathrm{comm}}(c/\delta)$. Then, by Proposition 2.6(b),

$$
(\llbracket c/\delta \rrbracket_{\mathrm{comm}} \sigma')(\delta w) = \sigma'(\delta w) = \sigma w = (\llbracket c \rrbracket_{\mathrm{comm}} \sigma)w.
$$

END OF PROOF

The above proposition and its proof illustrate a phenomenon that is typical of subtle induction arguments. Clearly, two important special cases of the proposition arise when V is the set of all variables and, at the opposite extreme, when $V = \mathrm{FV}_{\mathrm{comm}}(c)$. Neither of these cases, however, can be proved directly by structural induction on c. To prove the case where V is the set of all variables, one would have to infer that the injectiveness of δ implies the injectiveness of $[\,\delta \mid v\!: v_{\mathrm{new}}\,]$, which is not true in general. To prove the case where $V = \mathrm{FV}_{\mathrm{comm}}(c)$, in order to use the induction hypothesis when c is $c_0\,;c_1$ (a case that is omitted in the above proof), one would need $\mathrm{FV}_{\mathrm{comm}}(c_0) = \mathrm{FV}_{\mathrm{comm}}(c_1) = \mathrm{FV}_{\mathrm{comm}}(c)$, which is also not true in general. Thus, to prove either of the special cases, one must generalize to the above proposition before employing induction.

Fortunately, the phenomenon of aliasing does not affect the fundamental property of binding that renaming preserves meaning:

Proposition 2.8 (Renaming Theorem for Commands) *If*

$$v_{new} \notin FV_{comm}(c') - \{v\},$$

then

$$[\![\mathbf{newvar}\ v_{new} := e\ \mathbf{in}\ (c'/v \to v_{new})]\!]_{comm}\sigma$$
$$= [\![\mathbf{newvar}\ v := e\ \mathbf{in}\ c']\!]_{comm}\sigma.$$

PROOF We repeat the argument in the previous proof, for the special case where V is the set $\langle var \rangle$ of all variables, δ is the identity function $I_{\langle var \rangle}$, and $\sigma = \sigma'$. (As in the previous proof, for simplicity we only consider the case where $e = 0$.) Then either

$$([\![\mathbf{newvar}\ v_{new} := 0\ \mathbf{in}\ (c'/v \to v_{new})]\!]_{comm}\sigma)w$$
$$= ([\![\mathbf{newvar}\ v := 0\ \mathbf{in}\ c']\!]_{comm}\sigma)w$$

for all $w \in \langle var \rangle$, or the entities in large parentheses are both equal to $\bot$. In either case, the entities in large parentheses are equal. The only assumption made about v_{new} is that it is distinct from δw for all $w \in FV_{comm}(c') - \{v\}$.   END OF PROOF

As we gradually extend the imperative language in later chapters, the above proposition and its analogues for other binding constructs will remain true. Of course, one must extend the definition of the functions FV and FA to encompass the new linguistic constructions. We will give explicit equations for binding constructions and constructions that have variables as immediate subphrases, but we will omit the multitude of equations that merely equate FV or FA of some construction to the union of the same function applied to the immediate subphrases.

2.6 Syntactic Sugar: The for Command

Many imperative languages provide some form of command that iterates a subcommand over an interval of integers. For example, we might introduce a **for** command with the syntax

$$\langle comm \rangle ::= \mathbf{for}\ \langle var \rangle := \langle intexp \rangle\ \mathbf{to}\ \langle intexp \rangle\ \mathbf{do}\ \langle comm \rangle$$

such that **for** $v := e_0$ **to** e_1 **do** c sets v to each integer from e_0 to e_1 inclusive, in increasing order, and after each such assignment executes the subcommand c.

Rather than giving a semantic equation for the **for** command, it is simpler to define its meaning by giving an equivalent command in the language we have already defined:

$$\mathbf{for}\ v := e_0\ \mathbf{to}\ e_1\ \mathbf{do}\ c \stackrel{\mathrm{def}}{=} (v := e_0\ ;\ \mathbf{while}\ v \leq e_1\ \mathbf{do}\ (c\ ;\ v := v + 1)).$$

More precisely, this equation defines the meaning of **for** commands in the following sense: By repeatedly replacing an occurrence of the left side of an instance

of the equation by the right side of the instance, one can translate any phrase
of our language containing **for** commands into one that no longer contains such
commands.

When a language construct can be defined in this way, it is often called *syntactic sugar*, and the translation that eliminates it is called *desugaring*. This
perspicuous terminology was coined by Peter Landin, who used the method to
reduce functional languages to the lambda calculus (as we will describe in Section
11.3).

Obviously, constructions that can be defined as syntactic sugar do not enhance
the expressiveness of a language, that is, the variety of computational processes
that can be described in the language. However, such constructions may allow
certain processes to be described more succinctly or intelligibly.

Despite its seeming simplicity, the **for** command is notorious for the variety of
subtly different designs that are possible, as well as the variety of design mistakes
that can encourage programming errors. In the above definition, we avoided one
common mistake by prescribing that **for** $v := e_0$ **to** e_1 **do** c will not execute c
at all when there are no integers in the interval from e_0 to e_1, which will occur
when $e_0 > e_1$. In contrast, the DO command in early versions of Fortran always
executed its body at least once. In many applications, this forced the programmer
to introduce a special branch to handle the (often rare but essential) case of
iterating over the empty interval.

There are other ways, however, in which the above definition is unsatisfactory.
For instance, the execution of **for** $v := e_0$ **to** e_1 **do** c will have the "side effect" of
resetting the control variable v. But usually the programmer intends v to be a
local variable of the **for** command. Thus a better version of the **for** command is
defined by

$$\textbf{for } v := e_0 \textbf{ to } e_1 \textbf{ do } c \stackrel{\text{def}}{=} \textbf{newvar } v := e_0 \textbf{ in while } v \leq e_1 \textbf{ do } (c \, ; v := v + 1).$$

Both of these versions, however, have the defect that the upper-limit expression
e_1 is reevaluated after every execution of $(c \, ; v := v + 1)$. Thus, if e_1 contains v or
any variable assigned by c, then v will be tested against a changing upper bound.
As an extreme example, **for** $\mathsf{x} := 1$ **to** x **do skip** will never terminate.

It is better to test the control variable against a fixed upper bound that is the
value of e_1 when the **for** command begins execution, as in the definition

$$\textbf{for } v := e_0 \textbf{ to } e_1 \textbf{ do } c$$

$$\stackrel{\text{def}}{=} \textbf{newvar } w := e_1 \textbf{ in newvar } v := e_0 \textbf{ in while } v \leq w \textbf{ do } (c \, ; v := v + 1),$$

where w is distinct from v and does not occur free in either e_0 or c. This version
also has the advantage that e_1, like e_0, is excluded from the scope of the binding
of v.

A final problem is that, if the subcommand c changes the control variable v, then successive executions of c may not occur for consecutive values of v. For example, **for** $x := 1$ **to** 10 **do** $(c' ; x := 2 \times x)$ will execute c' for $x = 1$, 3, and 7. This grotesqueness can be avoided by imposing the restriction $v \notin FA(c)$ on the **for** command.

It is important to understand why our successive redefinitions of the **for** command are improvements. The utility of a properly designed **for** command is that, in comparison with the **while** command, it describes a more restricted form of iteration that is easier to reason about. For instance, if the **for** command is defined by the final equation above, with the restriction $v \notin FA(c)$, and if c always terminates, then **for** $v := e_0$ **to** e_1 **do** c will always execute c the number of times that is the size of the interval e_0 **to** e_1, where e_0 and e_1 are evaluated at the beginning of execution of the **for** command.

2.7 Arithmetic Errors

The language presented in this chapter raises two possibilities for arithmetic error: division by zero and overflow. In this section, we first consider the language design issues raised by these errors, and then the treatment of these issues in terms of the semantics we have presented.

There is a fundamental difference between these kinds of errors: A program that executes an overflow may run without error on a machine with a larger range of representable integers, but a program that divides by zero would not be correct even on a machine with perfect arithmetic. Nevertheless, the ways of treating these errors (and the relative merits of these ways) are similar in both cases.

Basically, the language designer must choose between checking for these errors and reporting them to the user (either by giving an error message or, more flexibly, by the kind of exception mechanism to be discussed in Exercises 5.3 and 5.4, and in Section 13.7), or ignoring the errors and taking whatever results are produced by the underlying hardware. (One can provide both options within a single language, but this merely shifts an essential decision from the language designer to the programmer.)

There are extreme cases where detecting arithmetic errors is not worth the cost in execution time. On the one hand, there are programs for which occasional erroneous behavior is tolerable, for example, programs whose output will be checked by the user or by another program. At the other extreme are programs, particularly in real-time processing, where an error message is just as intolerable as an incorrect answer, so that there is no safe alternative to proving that errors will not occur.

In the vast majority of computer applications, however, a failure to produce a result is far less serious than producing an erroneous result (especially if an error message is given, as opposed to silent nontermination). Indeed, reasoning about overflow is so difficult that it is common programming practice to ignore the issue, write programs that would behave correctly on a machine with perfect arithmetic, and rely on error checking to be sure that the machine does not deviate from such perfection. (Notice that we are *not* considering floating-point arithmetic, where the problem of controlling precision can be far more intractable than that of overflow.) In such applications, it is irresponsible programming to avoid error checking and irresponsible language design to encourage such avoidance.

We now turn to the question of how these contrasting approaches to arithmetic error may be described semantically. The semantics given in this chapter is easy to adopt to languages where arithmetic errors are not detected: One simply takes the arithmetic operations to be the erroneous functions actually computed by the hardware (which must of course be described precisely). The only restriction is that these operations must actually be functional. For example, $x \div 0$ must be some integer function of x, and $x + y$, even when the mathematically correct result would be unrepresentable, must be some integer function of x and y. Thus, for example, the following equivalences would hold, regardless of the particular function denoted by division by zero or addition:

$$\llbracket (x + y) \times 0 \rrbracket_{\text{intexp}} \sigma = 0$$

$$\llbracket x \div 0 = x \div 0 \rrbracket_{\text{boolexp}} \sigma = \textbf{true}$$

$$\llbracket y := x \div 0 \, ; y := e \rrbracket_{\text{comm}} \sigma = \llbracket y := e \rrbracket_{\text{comm}} \sigma \quad \text{when } y \notin \text{FV}_{\text{intexp}}(e)$$

$$\llbracket \textbf{if } x + y = z \textbf{ then } c \textbf{ else } c \rrbracket_{\text{comm}} \sigma = \llbracket c \rrbracket_{\text{comm}} \sigma.$$

On the other hand, to treat the detection of arithmetic errors it is necessary to extend our present semantics in a nontrivial way, such as enlarging the set of results of integer and boolean expressions to include one or more special results denoting errors. We will take this approach to the denotational semantics of expressions when we consider functional languages in Section 11.6.

For the present, however, we will not consider error results for expressions. To do so would distract from our main concerns in studying imperative languages. It would also destroy the close coupling between the simple imperative language and predicate logic that underlies the approach to program specification and proof described in the next chapter.

2.8 Soundness and Full Abstraction

The goal of a denotational semantics is to abstract away from irrelevant details in order to focus on the aspects of a language that are of interest to the user of the semantics. Thus it is natural to ask whether one semantics is more abstract than another, and whether a semantics is excessively or insufficiently abstract for the needs of the user. In fact, these seemingly intuitive questions can be asked precisely, for arbitrary semantic functions on arbitrary languages, as long as the semantics is compositional.

To avoid notational complications, we will limit our discussion to the semantics of a single kind of phrase; the specific example to keep in mind is the semantics of commands in the language of this chapter.

The easy question to formalize is when one semantics is more abstract than another:

- A semantic function $[\![-]\!]_1$ is *at least as abstract* as a semantics function $[\![-]\!]_0$ when, for all phrases p and p', $[\![p]\!]_0 = [\![p']\!]_0$ implies $[\![p]\!]_1 = [\![p']\!]_1$.

To go further, we formalize the "needs of the user" by assuming that there is a set of *observable phrases* and a set $\mathcal{O}$ of *observations*, each of which is a function from the set of observable phrases to some set of *outcomes*.

To deal with compositionality, we define a *context* to be an observable phrase in which some subphrase has been replaced by a "hole" (which we denote by $-$). We write $\mathcal{C}$ for the set of contexts. When C is a context, we write $C[p]$ to denote the result of replacing (not substituting — there is no renaming) the hole in C by the phrase p.

Then we formalize the idea that a semantics is not excessively abstract by

- A semantic function $[\![-]\!]$ is *sound* if and only if, for any commands c and c',

$$[\![c]\!] = [\![c']\!] \text{ implies } \forall O \in \mathcal{O}. \ \forall C \in \mathcal{C}. \ O(C[c]) = O(C[c']).$$

In other words, a semantics is sound if it never equates commands that, in some context, show observably different behavior.

Finally, we formalize the idea that a semantics is sufficiently abstract by

- A semantic function $[\![-]\!]$ is *fully abstract* if and only if, for any commands c and c',

$$[\![c]\!] = [\![c']\!] \text{ if and only if } \forall O \in \mathcal{O}. \ \forall C \in \mathcal{C}. \ O(C[c]) = O(C[c']).$$

In other words, a semantics is fully abstract if it distinguishes commands just when, in some context, they show observably different behavior. It is easy to see that a fully abstract semantics is a sound semantics that is at least as abstract as any sound semantics.

For the specific case of the semantics of the simple imperative language given in Section 2.2, suppose that all commands are observable and that an observation consists of starting the program in some state σ and observing whether it terminates and, if so, what the value of some variable v is. In other words, an observation is a function $O_{\sigma,v} \in \langle \text{comm} \rangle \to \mathbf{Z}_\perp$ such that

$$O_{\sigma,v}(c) = \textbf{if } [\![c]\!]_{\text{comm}}\sigma = \perp \textbf{ then } \perp \textbf{ else } [\![c]\!]_{\text{comm}}\sigma v.$$

Then it is easy to see that $[\![-]\!]_{\text{comm}}$ is fully abstract.

More surprisingly, suppose we limit observable commands to *closed* commands (which contain no occurrences of free variables) and only observe whether such commands terminate (which no longer depends on an initial state, since the commands are closed). Even with such restricted observations, our semantics remains fully abstract. For suppose $[\![c]\!]_{\text{comm}} \neq [\![c']\!]_{\text{comm}}$. Then there is a state σ such that $[\![c]\!]_{\text{comm}}\sigma \neq [\![c']\!]_{\text{comm}}\sigma$. Let $v_0, \ldots, v_{n-1}$ be the variables that occur free in either c or c'; let $\kappa_0, \ldots, \kappa_{n-1}$ be constants whose values are $\sigma v_0, \ldots, \sigma v_{n-1}$ respectively; and let C be the context

$$C \stackrel{\text{def}}{=} \textbf{newvar } v_0 := \kappa_0 \textbf{ in } \cdots \textbf{newvar } v_{n-1} := \kappa_{n-1} \textbf{ in } -.$$

Then, using the coincidence theorem (Proposition 2.6 in Section 2.5),

$$[\![C[c]]\!]_{\text{comm}}\sigma_0 = [\![c]\!]_{\text{comm}}[\,\sigma_0 \mid v_0 \colon \kappa_0 \mid \ldots \mid v_{n-1} \colon \kappa_{n-1}\,] = [\![c]\!]_{\text{comm}}\sigma$$

$$\neq [\![c']\!]_{\text{comm}}\sigma = [\![c']\!]_{\text{comm}}[\,\sigma_0 \mid v_0 \colon \kappa_0 \mid \ldots \mid v_{n-1} \colon \kappa_{n-1}\,] = [\![C[c']]\!]_{\text{comm}}\sigma_0$$

(where σ_0 can be any state, since $C[c]$ and $C[c']$ are closed).

If, starting in σ, one of the commands c or c' does not terminate, then they can be distinguished by observing $C[c]$ and $C[c']$. On the other hand, if both terminate, then there must be a variable v and a constant κ such that $[\![c]\!]_{\text{assert}}\sigma v = \kappa \neq [\![c']\!]_{\text{assert}}\sigma v$. In this case, the command can be distinguished by observing $D[c]$ and $D[c']$, where D is the context

$$D \stackrel{\text{def}}{=} \textbf{newvar } v_0 := \kappa_0 \textbf{ in } \cdots \textbf{newvar } v_{n-1} := \kappa_{n-1} \textbf{ in}$$

$$(- \, ; \textbf{if } v = \kappa \textbf{ then skip else while true do skip}).$$

Although soundness and full abstraction are fundamental properties of semantics, it is vital to realize that they depend on the choice of what is observable, and also on the variety of contexts. For example, because our semantics takes the meaning of a command to be a function from initial states to final states, it abstracts away details of execution that, for some purposes, cannot be ignored. For example, the two commands

$$\mathsf{x} := \mathsf{x} + 1 \, ; \mathsf{x} := \mathsf{x} + 1 \quad \text{and} \quad \mathsf{x} := \mathsf{x} + 2$$

have the same meaning, as do

$$\mathsf{x} := 0 \, ; \textbf{while } \mathsf{x} < 100 \textbf{ do } \mathsf{x} := \mathsf{x} + 1 \quad \text{and} \quad \mathsf{x} := 100$$

or

$$\mathsf{x} := \mathsf{x} + 1 \, ; \mathsf{y} := \mathsf{y} * 2 \quad \text{and} \quad \mathsf{y} := \mathsf{y} * 2 \, ; \mathsf{x} := \mathsf{x} + 1,$$

but there are situations where these pairs should not be considered equivalent. If our concept of observation included execution time or the continuous observation of program variables during execution, then we could distinguish each of the above pairs, so that our present semantics would be unsound.

Semantic definitions that make such distinctions are often called *operational*, in contrast to the *denotational* semantics developed in this chapter. Strictly speaking, however, these terms are relative — one can imagine a wide spectrum of definitions ranging from the extremely denotational to the extremely operational.

(Some authors use "denotational" as a synonym for "compositional". Occasionally it is difficult to tell which is meant, since in practice most denotational definitions are compositional and most operational definitions are not.)

A semantics can also become unsound if the variety of contexts is expanded by extending the language that is being defined. In Chapter 8 we will introduce a construction $c_0 \parallel c_1$ that causes two commands that may share variables to be executed concurrently. In this extended language, it is easy to construct contexts that will distinguish each of the above pairs. In Section 13.1, we will find that the interaction of assignment with a procedure mechanism can cause aliasing, so that assignment to x might change the value of y as well as x. With this kind of language extension, one can define a context that distinguishes the last pair of commands. In both cases, we will need to move to a quite different semantics to avoid unsoundness.

Bibliographic Notes

The basic concept of a domain is due to Scott [1970; 1972], who originally defined a domain to be a complete, continuous, countably based lattice.

The more elementary and less restrictive concept of a domain used in this book is also described by Tennent [1991, Sections 5.2–5.3], Gunter [1992, Chapter 4], and Winskel [1993, Chapter 8]. (Note, however, that what we call predomains are called domains by Tennent and complete partial orders by Gunter and Winskel.)

The simple imperative language is discussed by Loeckx et al. [1987, Section 3.2]; domains and continuous functions are covered in Chapter 4 of the same book, and a denotational semantics for the language is given in Section 5.4.

The more advanced theory of domains, where the conditions of algebraicity and bounded completeness are imposed, is described in Gunter and Scott [1990] and Gunter [1992, Chapter 5]. An explanation of such domains in terms of the more concrete concept of an "information system" was given by Scott [1982], and is also described by Winskel [1993, Chapter 12].

A set of phrases defined by an abstract grammar, such as the set of commands of the simple imperative language, can be enlarged to form a domain by adding partial and infinite phrases appropriately. Moreover, any semantic function from the set of phrases to a domain, such as $[\![-]\!]_{\text{comm}}$, has a unique continuous extension to such a domain of phrases. This fact can be used to give a purely syntactic description of loops and recursion by "unwinding" into infinite phrases. This idea was originally suggested by Scott [1971] and was pursued further by Reynolds [1977], and Goguen, Thatcher, Wagner, and Wright [1977].

Exercises

2.1   A double assignment command has the form $v_0, v_1 := e_0, e_1$. Its effect is
       to evaluate e_0 and e_1 and then assign the resulting values to v_0 and v_1
       respectively. This differs from $v_0 := e_0\,;\, v_1 := e_1$ in that both expressions
       are evaluated before there is any state change.

       Describe the syntax and semantics of this command by giving a produc-
       tion to be added to the abstract grammar in Section 2.1 and a semantic
       equation to be added to those in Section 2.2.

2.2   A **repeat** command has the form **repeat** c **until** b. Its effect is described
       by the following flowchart:

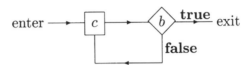

       (a) As in the previous problem, describe the syntax and semantics of
           this command by giving a production to be added to the grammar in
           Section 2.1 and a semantic equation to be added to those in Section
           2.2. The semantic equation should express $[\![\textbf{repeat } c \textbf{ until } b]\!]_{\mathrm{comm}}$ as
           a least fixed-point of a function.
       (b) Define the **repeat** command as syntactic sugar, as in Section 2.6.
       (c) Prove that the definitions in parts (a) and (b) are equivalent.

2.3   Prove that

$$[\![\textbf{while } x \neq 0 \textbf{ do } x := x - 2]\!]_{\mathrm{comm}}\,\sigma = \begin{cases} [\,\sigma \mid x{:}\,0\,] & \text{if } even(\sigma x) \text{ and } \sigma x \geq 0 \\ \bot & \text{if } even(\sigma x) \text{ and } \sigma x < 0 \\ \bot & \text{if } odd(\sigma x). \end{cases}$$

2.4   Prove that the function F in the semantic equation for the **while** com-
       mand (Equation (2.4) in Section 2.4) is continuous.

2.5   Prove that, for all boolean expressions b and all commands c,

$$[\![\textbf{while } b \textbf{ do } c]\!]_{\mathrm{comm}} = [\![\textbf{while } b \textbf{ do } (c; \textbf{if } b \textbf{ then } c \textbf{ else skip})]\!]_{\mathrm{comm}}.$$

2.6   Using the coincidence theorem for commands (Proposition 2.6 in Section
       2.5), prove that, for all commands c_0 and c_1, if

$$\mathrm{FV}_{\mathrm{comm}}(c_0) \cap \mathrm{FA}(c_1) = \mathrm{FA}(c_0) \cap \mathrm{FV}_{\mathrm{comm}}(c_1) = \{\},$$

       then

$$[\![c_0; c_1]\!]_{\mathrm{comm}} = [\![c_1; c_0]\!]_{\mathrm{comm}}.$$

2.7   In Section 2.5, we illustrated aliasing by giving a program for computing the factorial that becomes erroneous when the same variable is substituted for both the input variable x and the output variable y. Rewrite this program so that it still works correctly when the same variable is substituted for x and y.

2.8   Show that the substitution theorem for commands (Proposition 2.7 in Section 2.5) remains true when the condition on δ is weakened from

$$\delta w \neq \delta w' \text{ whenever } w \text{ and } w' \text{ are distinct members of } V$$

to

$$\delta w \neq \delta w' \text{ whenever } w \in \text{FA}(c), w' \in V, \text{ and } w \neq w'.$$

2.9   The final version of the **for** command given in Section 2.6 has the defect that the value of the control value, after the last execution of the subcommand, is set to the next integer beyond the interval of iteration, which can cause unnecessary overflow. Define a **for** command (as syntactic sugar) that will never set the control variable to any integer outside the interval of iteration.

2.10   Consider introducing a **dotwice** construction, defined as syntactic sugar by

$$\mathbf{dotwice}\; c \overset{\text{def}}{=} c\,;c.$$

Explain why this is a valid definition, despite the fact that, when c contains two or more occurrences of **dotwice**, replacing **dotwice** c by $c\,;c$ will increase the number of occurrences of **dotwice**.

3

Program Specifications and Their Proofs

In this chapter, we will explore methods of specifying programs in the simple imperative language and of proving such specifications formally. We will consider both partial correctness, where one specifies that a program will behave properly if it terminates, and total correctness, where one also specifies that a program will terminate. For partial correctness we will use the form of specification invented by C. A. R. Hoare, while for total correctness we will use an analogous form based on the ideas of E. W. Dijkstra.

At the outset, it should be stressed that formal proofs are quite different than the traditional proofs of mathematics. A formal proof is sufficiently detailed that its correctness can be verified mechanically. In contrast, a traditional mathematical proof can be thought of as a blueprint that provides just enough information to allow a well-trained reader to construct a formal proof.

In fact, formal proofs are more prevalent in computer science than in mathematics. The most obvious reason is that only formal methods can be mechanized soundly. A more subtle reason, however, is the different nature of the proof task. Mathematical conjectures often contain no hint of why they might be true, but programs are invariably written by people who have at least a vague idea of why they should work. Thus the task of program proving is not to search over a broad space of arguments, but to refine an already existing argument until all of its flaws have been revealed.

This is not to say that every program merits formal proof. Experience with formal proof methods, however, also increases a programmer's ability to detect flaws in informal arguments. The inference rules introduced in this chapter are fundamental laws about imperative programming, in the same sense that the associative, commutative, and distributive laws are fundamental laws about arithmetic. When mathematically literate people perform or check an elementary algebraic manipulation, they rarely descend to the level of applying such laws explicitly, but their knowledge of these laws, and their experience in applying them, underly their ability to avoid and detect errors. A similar knowledge and experience of program-proof systems can buttress such an ability for programming.

Program-proof systems are also relevant to the task of language design. Such a proof system provides a link between a programming language and a language for the specification of programs. When the system is simple and powerful, it is strong evidence that these languages are uniform and can be reasoned about reliably. For example, a major simplicity of the system described in this chapter is that integer expressions have the same meaning in commands as they do in assertions, and thus in traditional mathematics (with certain exceptions that will be discussed in Section 3.8). The fact that this simplicity would be destroyed if expressions could have side effects is a serious argument against languages that permit such side effects.

Many authors call program-proof systems "axiomatic semantics", but this term is a slight misnomer. Even when proved, the specification of a program is not its meaning, but rather a relationship between its meaning and the meaning of assertions in some logic.

3.1 Syntax and Semantics of Specifications

We begin by introducing a new type of phrase called *specifications*, with two forms called *partial correctness* and *total correctness* specifications:

$$\langle \text{spec} \rangle ::= \{\langle \text{assert} \rangle\}\, \langle \text{comm} \rangle\, \{\langle \text{assert} \rangle\} \qquad \text{(partial correctness)}$$
$$\mid [\, \langle \text{assert} \rangle \,]\, \langle \text{comm} \rangle\, [\, \langle \text{assert} \rangle \,] \qquad \text{(total correctness)}$$

In both forms, the assertion on the left is called the *precedent* (or *precondition*) and the assertion on the right is called the *consequent* (or *postcondition*).

Semantically, the meaning of a specification is simply a truth value:

$$[\![-]\!]_{\text{spec}} \in \langle \text{spec} \rangle \to \mathbf{B}.$$

In particular, $\{p\}\, c\, \{q\}$ is true if and only if, for all states satisfying p, executing c either fails to terminate or terminates in a state satisfying q:

DR SEM EQ: Partial Correctness Specification

$$[\![\{p\}\, c\, \{q\}]\!]_{\text{spec}} = \forall \sigma \in \Sigma.\ [\![p]\!]_{\text{assert}}\sigma \Rightarrow ([\![c]\!]_{\text{comm}}\sigma = \bot \text{ or } [\![q]\!]_{\text{assert}}([\![c]\!]_{\text{comm}}\sigma)).$$

On the other hand, $[p]\, c\, [q]$ is true if and only if, for all states satisfying p, executing c terminates in a state satisfying q:

DR SEM EQ: Total Correctness Specification

$$[\![[p]\, c\, [q]]\!]_{\text{spec}} = \forall \sigma \in \Sigma.\ [\![p]\!]_{\text{assert}}\sigma \Rightarrow ([\![c]\!]_{\text{comm}}\sigma \neq \bot \text{ and } [\![q]\!]_{\text{assert}}([\![c]\!]_{\text{comm}}\sigma)).$$

We will call a specification *valid* when it is true; unlike the case with assertions, we need not add "for all states", since the meaning of specifications is always quantified over all states.

For example, the following are valid partial correctness specifications:

$$\{x - y > 3\}\ x := x - y\ \{x > 3\}$$

$$\{x + y \geq 17\}\ x := x + 10\ \{x + y \geq 27\}$$

$$\{x \leq 10\}\ \textbf{while}\ x \neq 10\ \textbf{do}\ x := x + 1\ \{x = 10\}$$

$$\{\textbf{true}\}\ \textbf{while}\ x \neq 10\ \textbf{do}\ x := x + 1\ \{x = 10\}$$

$$\{x > 10\}\ \textbf{while}\ x \neq 10\ \textbf{do}\ x := x + 1\ \{\textbf{false}\}.$$

On the other hand, for the corresponding total correctness specifications (obtained by replacing braces by square brackets), only the first three cases are valid.

The semantic equations for specifications can be expressed more succinctly by using the two functions p_t and p_f, from the set $\mathbf{B}$ of truth values to the two-element domain $\{\bot, \top\}$, such that

$$p_t\ \textbf{true} = \top \qquad p_t\ \textbf{false} = \bot$$

$$p_f\ \textbf{false} = \top \qquad p_f\ \textbf{true} = \bot.$$

Then, as the reader may verify, specifications are true or false depending on whether certain elements of the domain $\Sigma \to \{\bot, \top\}$ satisfy the ordering on that domain:

DR SEM EQ: Partial Correctness Specification

$$[\![\{p\}\ c\ \{q\}]\!]_{\text{spec}} = ((p_f \cdot [\![q]\!]_{\text{assert}})_{\bot\bot} \cdot [\![c]\!]_{\text{comm}} \sqsubseteq p_f \cdot [\![p]\!]_{\text{assert}}), \qquad (3.1)$$

DR SEM EQ: Total Correctness Specification

$$[\![\,[p]\ c\ [q]\,]\!]_{\text{spec}} = (p_t \cdot [\![p]\!]_{\text{assert}} \sqsubseteq (p_t \cdot [\![q]\!]_{\text{assert}})_{\bot\bot} \cdot [\![c]\!]_{\text{comm}}). \qquad (3.2)$$

Now suppose we regard the meaning of these specifications as a function of the meaning $m = [\![c]\!]_{\text{comm}}$. Then, since functional composition is continuous (Proposition 2.3(e) in Section 2.3),

- If a partial-correctness specification holds for m, it holds for all $m' \sqsubseteq m$. Moreover, if it holds for all members of a chain, it holds for the limit of the chain.
- If a total-correctness specification holds for m, it holds for all $m' \sqsupseteq m$.

In Section 5.2, we will find that these properties characterize partial correctness as a *safety* property and total correctness as a *liveness* property.

It should be emphasized that, although partial correctness is a weaker property than total correctness, it is still practically useful. As we pointed out in Section 2.7, in the vast majority of computer applications a failure to produce a result is far less serious than producing an erroneous result.

3.2 Inference Rules

In the following sections, we will present a collection of inference rules that can be used to prove specifications. As in Section 1.3, an *inference rule* consists of zero or more *premisses* and a single *conclusion*, an *instance* of a rule is formed by replacing all occurrences of each metavariable by a phrase in its range, and a rule is *sound* if and only if, for every instance, if the premisses are all valid, the conclusion is valid. But now the conclusion is a specification instead of an assertion, and the premisses are either specifications or assertions.

A completely formal proof would be a sequence (or tree) of assertions and specifications obtained by using the inference rules for specifications that we are about to give, along with inference rules for assertions that belong to some system of rules for predicate logic (interpreted over the integers). However, we are only interested in formalizing the proof of specifications, not of assertions about the integers. Thus we will define a proof to be a sequence of assertions and specifications such that each specification is the conclusion of an instance of a rule whose premisses occur earlier in the proof, and each assertion is valid (presumably because it has been proved informally).

(Occasionally, we will consider proofs containing assertions or specifications, called *assumptions*, that are not inferred from previous items nor otherwise known to be valid. In this case, what is proved is that the final specification is valid *if* the assumptions are all valid.)

Most of the rules we will present are *compositional*, in the sense that they permit one to conclude a specification about a particular kind of command from specifications of its subcommands. However, there will also be several noncompositional rules that are applicable to arbitrary commands. The compositional rules specifically embody the semantics of commands, while some of the noncompositional rules provide a linkage with the predicate calculus, which embodies the semantics of expressions and assertions.

Each rule exists in two versions, dealing with partial and total correctness. Except, however, for the compositional rule for **while** commands and the noncompositional rule of "constancy", these two versions have exactly the same form. (This reflects the fact that, in the simple imperative language, **while** commands are the only source of nontermination.) In these cases we will display only the partial-correctness version of the rule explicitly; the total-correctness version is obtained simply by replacing braces by square brackets.

3.3 Rules for Assignment and Sequential Composition

We begin our survey of inference rules with a compositional rule for assignment commands. Since an assignment command has no subcommands, the rule has no premisses, and is thus an axiom schema:

SP RULE: Assignment (AS)

$$\frac{}{\{p/v \to e\}\; v := e\; \{p\}.}$$

Here $p/v \to e$ indicates a substitution to be performed after the metavariables p, v, and e have been replaced by an assertion, object variable, and integer expression, respectively. (The label SP RULE abbreviates "inference rule for specifications".)

An example of an instance of this rule is obtained by replacing p by the assertion $x > 3$, v by the variable x, and e by the integer expression $x - y$:

$$\frac{}{\{x - y > 3\}\; x := x - y\; \{x > 3\}.}$$

Another instance is obtained by replacing p by $x - y > 3$, v by x, and e by $2 \times y$:

$$\frac{}{\{(2 \times y) - y > 3\}\; x := 2 \times y\; \{x - y > 3\}.}$$

To see that the assignment rule is sound, suppose σ is a state such that $[\![p/v \to e]\!]_{\text{assert}}\sigma = \textbf{true}$. By the finite substitution theorem (Proposition 1.3 in Section 1.4), $[\![p]\!]_{\text{assert}}[\sigma \mid v: [\![e]\!]_{\text{intexp}}\sigma] = \textbf{true}$. Then, by the semantic equation for assignment commands in Section 2.2, $[\![p]\!]_{\text{assert}}([\![v := e]\!]_{\text{comm}}\sigma) = \textbf{true}$. Since this holds for every σ satisfying $p/v \to e$, the semantic equations for specifications in the previous section show that both $\{p/v \to e\}\; v := e\; \{p\}$ and $[p/v \to e]\; v := e\; [p]$ are valid. Thus both the above rule and the corresponding rule for total correctness are sound.

Next we consider a rule for the sequencing operator:

SP RULE: Sequential Composition (SQ)

$$\frac{\{p\}\; c_1\; \{q\} \qquad \{q\}\; c_2\; \{r\}}{\{p\}\; c_1\; ; c_2\; \{r\}.}$$

Here, and with most of the following rules, we leave the soundness argument to the reader. An example of an instance is

$$\frac{\{(2 \times y) - y > 3\}\; x := 2 \times y\; \{x - y > 3\} \qquad \{x - y > 3\}\; x := x - y\; \{x > 3\}}{\{(2 \times y) - y > 3\}\; x := 2 \times y\; ; x := x - y\; \{x > 3\}.}$$

Next we have two noncompositional rules that provide a linkage with predicate logic by means of premises that are assertions rather than specifications:

SP RULE: Strengthening Precedent (SP)

$$\frac{p \Rightarrow q \qquad \{q\}\ s\ \{r\}}{\{p\}\ s\ \{r\},}$$

SP RULE: Weakening Consequent (WC)

$$\frac{\{p\}\ s\ \{q\} \qquad q \Rightarrow r}{\{p\}\ s\ \{r\}.}$$

Examples of instances are

$$\frac{y > 3 \Rightarrow (2 \times y) - y > 3 \qquad \{(2 \times y) - y > 3\}\ x := 2 \times y \,;\, x := x - y\ \{x > 3\}}{\{y > 3\}\ x := 2 \times y \,;\, x := x - y\ \{x > 3\}}$$

and

$$\frac{\{y > 3\}\ x := 2 \times y \,;\, x := x - y\ \{x > 3\} \qquad x > 3 \Rightarrow x \geq 4}{\{y > 3\}\ x := 2 \times y \,;\, x := x - y\ \{x \geq 4\}.}$$

At this stage, we have gone far enough to give a simple proof of a slightly less than obvious specification. Each step in the proof, except for informally validated assertions, is annotated with the name of the rule used to infer it, plus the numbers of the previous steps that are used as premisses:

1. $\qquad \{(2 \times y) - y > 3\}\ x := 2 \times y\ \{x - y > 3\}$ (AS)
2. $\qquad \{x - y > 3\}\ x := x - y\ \{x > 3\}$ (AS)
3. $\qquad \{(2 \times y) - y > 3\}\ x := 2 \times y \,;\, x := x - y\ \{x > 3\}$ (SQ,1,2)
4. $\qquad y > 3 \Rightarrow (2 \times y) - y > 3$
5. $\qquad \{y > 3\}\ x := 2 \times y \,;\, x := x - y\ \{x > 3\}$ (SP,4,3)
6. $\qquad x > 3 \Rightarrow x \geq 4$
7. $\qquad \{y > 3\}\ x := 2 \times y \,;\, x := x - y\ \{x \geq 4\}$ (WC,5,6)

Notice that the first three steps, which involve only compositional rules, depend on the semantics of commands (specifically of assignment commands and the sequencing operator) but are independent of the interpretation of data types and arithmetic operations; they are "logically valid" specifications in the sense described at the end of Section 1.3. (For example, these specifications would remain valid if the variables x and y ranged over character strings, 3 was a string constant, $\times$ and $-$ were functions on strings, and $>$ was a relation on strings.) On the other hand, the fourth and sixth steps are assertions whose validity is specific to integer arithmetic. It is the rules for strengthening precedents and weakening consequents that are used to bring such data-specific assertions to bear on the proof of specifications, as in the fifth and seventh steps.

Fortunately, the excruciatingly low level of this kind of proof can be alleviated by using *derived* inference rules, which are rules whose soundness is justified by showing that their every instance can be proved using previously justified rules. A family of such rules (indexed by $n > 0$) is given by

SP RULE: Multiple Sequential Composition (MSQ_n)

$$\frac{p_0 \Rightarrow q_0 \quad \{q_0\}\,c_0\,\{p_1\} \quad p_1 \Rightarrow q_1 \quad \cdots \quad \{q_{n-1}\}\,c_{n-1}\,\{p_n\} \quad p_n \Rightarrow q_n}{\{p_0\}\,c_0\,;\,\ldots\,;\,c_{n-1}\,\{q_n\}.}$$

An example of an instance of this rule (where $n = 2$) is

$$\frac{\begin{array}{l} y > 3 \Rightarrow (2 \times y) - y > 3 \\ \quad \{(2 \times y) - y > 3\}\,x := 2 \times y\,\{x - y > 3\} \\ \quad\quad x - y > 3 \Rightarrow x - y > 3 \\ \quad\quad\quad \{x - y > 3\}\,x := x - y\,\{x > 3\} \\ \quad\quad\quad\quad x > 3 \Rightarrow x \geq 4 \end{array}}{\{y > 3\}\,x := 2 \times y\,;\,x := x - y\,\{x \geq 4\}.}$$

To derive the rule MSQ_1,

$$\frac{p_0 \Rightarrow q_0 \quad \{q_0\}\,c_0\,\{p_1\} \quad p_1 \Rightarrow q_1}{\{p_0\}\,c_0\,\{q_1\},}$$

suppose the metavariables stand for assertions and commands that give an instance of the rule with valid premisses. Taking these premisses as assumptions, one can prove

1.	$p_0 \Rightarrow q_0$	assumption
2.	$\{q_0\}\,c_0\,\{p_1\}$	assumption
3.	$\{p_0\}\,c_0\,\{p_1\}$	(SP,1,2)
4.	$p_1 \Rightarrow q_1$	assumption
5.	$\{p_0\}\,c_0\,\{q_1\}$	(WC,3,4)

(Notice that this display is a proof *schema*: Given any replacement of metavariables by object phrases that maps the rule MSQ_1 into an instance with valid premisses, one can obtain a proof of the consequence of the instance by applying the replacement to the proof schema.)

For each $n > 1$, once MSQ_{n-1} has been derived we can use it to derive MSQ_n as follows: Suppose the metavariables stand for assertions and commands giving an instance of the rule MSQ_n with valid premisses. Taking these premisses as assumptions and using MSQ_{n-1} as a derived rule, we have

1.	$p_0 \Rightarrow q_0$	assumption
2.	$\{q_0\}\ c_0\ \{p_1\}$	assumption
3.	$p_1 \Rightarrow q_1$	assumption

$$\vdots$$

$2n-2.$	$\{q_{n-2}\}\ c_{n-2}\ \{p_{n-1}\}$	assumption
$2n-1.$	$p_{n-1} \Rightarrow q_{n-1}$	assumption
$2n.$	$\{p_1\}\ c_0\ ;\ \cdots\ ;\ c_{n-2}\ \{q_{n-1}\}$	$(\text{MSQ}_{n-1}, 1, \ldots, 2n-1)$
$2n+1.$	$\{q_{n-1}\}\ c_{n-1}\ \{p_n\}$	assumption
$2n+2.$	$\{p_0\}\ c_0\ ;\ \cdots\ ;\ c_{n-1}\ \{p_n\}$	$(\text{SQ}, 2n, 2n+1)$
$2n+3.$	$p_n \Rightarrow q_n$	assumption
$2n+4.$	$\{p_0\}\ c_0\ ;\ \cdots\ ;\ c_{n-1}\ \{q_n\}$	$(\text{WC}, 2n+2, 2n+3)$

In using the multiple sequential composition rule in proofs, we will adopt the convention of omitting premiss instances that have the form $p \Rightarrow p$, since they are trivially valid. Thus, for example, the following is a shorter proof with the same conclusion as the previous example:

1.	$y > 3 \Rightarrow (2 \times y) - y > 3$	
2.	$\{(2 \times y) - y > 3\}\ x := -\ 2 \times y\ \{x - y > 3\}$	(AS)
3.	$\{x - y > 3\}\ x := x - y\ \{x > 3\}$	(AS)
4.	$x > 3 \Rightarrow x \geq 4$	
5.	$\{y > 3\}\ x := 2 \times y\ ;\ x := x - y\ \{x \geq 4\}$	(MSQ,1,2,3,4)

(The omitted premiss is $x - y > 3 \Rightarrow x - y > 3$.)

Further brevity is provided by a derived rule that is specific to sequences of assignment commands. For each $n > 0$:

SP RULE: Repeated Assignment (RAS_n)

$$\frac{p \Rightarrow (\cdots (q/v_{n-1} \to e_{n-1}) \cdots /v_0 \to e_0)}{\{p\}\ v_0 := e_0\ ;\ \ldots\ ;\ v_{n-1} := e_{n-1}\ \{q\}.}$$

As an example of an instance of this rule, since $((x \geq 4)/x \to x - y)/x \to 2 \times y$ is $(2 \times y) - y \geq 4$, we have

$$\frac{y > 3 \Rightarrow (2 \times y) - y \geq 4}{\{y > 3\}\ x := 2 \times y\ ;\ x := x - y\ \{x \geq 4\}.}$$

The repeated assignment rule can be derived from MSQ by the proof schema:

1. $\qquad p \Rightarrow (\cdots (q/v_{n-1} \to e_{n-1}) \cdots /v_0 \to e_0) \qquad$ assumption

2. $\qquad \{\cdots (q/v_{n-1} \to e_{n-1}) \cdots /v_0 \to e_0\}\, v_0 := e_0$
   $\qquad\quad \{\cdots (q/v_{n-1} \to e_{n-1}) \cdots /v_1 \to e_1\} \qquad$ (AS)

3. $\qquad \{\cdots (q/v_{n-1} \to e_{n-1}) \cdots /v_1 \to e_1\}\, v_1 := e_1$
   $\qquad\quad \{\cdots (q/v_{n-1} \to e_{n-1}) \cdots /v_2 \to e_2\} \qquad$ (AS)

$$\vdots$$

$n{+}1.\qquad \{q/v_{n-1} \to e_{n-1}\}\, v_{n-1} := e_{n-1}\, \{q\} \qquad$ (AS)

$n{+}2.\qquad \{p\}\, v_0 := e_0\,;\, \ldots\,;\, v_{n-1} := e_{n-1}\, \{q\} \qquad$ (MSQ, 1, ..., $n{+}1$)

Somewhat surprisingly, the repeated assignment rule is not only sound, but also complete. In other words, its conclusion is valid if *and only if* its premiss is valid. (Or, putting the matter the other way round: If the premiss is invalid, the conclusion is invalid.) Thus it can be used to express the validity of any specification of a sequence of assignment commands in terms of the validity of an assertion. For instance, our continuing example is the conclusion of the proof

1. $\qquad y > 3 \Rightarrow (2 \times y) - y \geq 4$

2. $\qquad \{y > 3\}\, x := 2 \times y\,;\, x := x - y\, \{x \geq 4\} \qquad$ (RAS,1)

and thus it is valid if and only if $y > 3 \Rightarrow (2 \times y) - y \geq 4$ is valid (which, happily, it is).

A second, more realistic example is

1. $\qquad (f = \mathrm{fib}(k) \wedge g = \mathrm{fib}(k-1) \wedge k \leq n \wedge k \neq n) \Rightarrow$
   $\qquad\quad (f + g = \mathrm{fib}(k+1) \wedge f = \mathrm{fib}((k+1)-1) \wedge k+1 \leq n)$

2. $\qquad \{f = \mathrm{fib}(k) \wedge g = \mathrm{fib}(k-1) \wedge k \leq n \wedge k \neq n\}$
   $\qquad t := g\,;\, g := f\,;\, f := f + t\,;\, k := k+1$
   $\qquad \{f = \mathrm{fib}(k) \wedge g = \mathrm{fib}(k-1) \wedge k \leq n\} \qquad$ (RAS,1)

Here fib stands for the function mapping i into the ith Fibonacci number, which is the function from integers to integers satisfying

$$\mathrm{fib}(0) = 0 \qquad \mathrm{fib}(1) = 1 \qquad \mathrm{fib}(i) = \mathrm{fib}(i-1) + \mathrm{fib}(i-2). \qquad (3.3)$$

In Section 3.6 we will see that the conclusion of this one-step proof is essentially the specification of the body of a **while** command in a simple program for computing Fibonacci numbers.

3.4 Rules for while Commands

The **while** command is the one program construct that gives rise to different compositional inference rules for partial and total correctness. We will prove the soundness of these rules in detail, since the proofs are good illustrations of how one reasons about least fixed-points.

SP RULE: Partial Correctness of **while** (WHP)

$$\frac{\{i \land b\} \; c \; \{i\}}{\{i\} \; \textbf{while} \; b \; \textbf{do} \; c \; \{i \land \neg b\}.}$$

Here the metavariable i denotes an assertion that is an *invariant* of the **while** command. The basic idea is that, if c preserves the invariant, then, starting in any state satisfying the invariant, the **while** command can only terminate in a state that satisfies the invariant and also falsifies the test b. (Note that c is not required to maintain the truth of i *throughout* its execution, but only to reestablish it by the end of each iteration.) The rule also captures the fact that, since b is true whenever the execution of c begins, c needs to preserve i only when b is true.

To see that this rule is sound, let i, b, and c stand for any assertion, boolean expression, and command such that the premiss $\{i \land b\} \; c \; \{i\}$ is valid, so that by Equation (3.1) in Section 3.1,

$$(\mathsf{p}_f \cdot [\![i]\!]_{\text{assert}})_{\bot\bot} \cdot [\![c]\!]_{\text{comm}} \sqsubseteq \mathsf{p}_f \cdot [\![i \land b]\!]_{\text{assert}},$$

and let $w_n \in \Sigma \to \Sigma_\bot$ be the partial meanings of the **while** command defined in Section 2.4:

$$w_0 \sigma = \bot \qquad w_{n+1} \sigma = \textbf{if} \; [\![b]\!]_{\text{boolexp}} \sigma \; \textbf{then} \; (w_n)_{\bot\bot} ([\![c]\!]_{\text{comm}} \sigma) \; \textbf{else} \; \sigma. \qquad (3.4)$$

According to Equation (3.1), we must show that

$$(\mathsf{p}_f \cdot [\![i \land \neg b]\!]_{\text{assert}})_{\bot\bot} \cdot \left(\bigsqcup_{n=0}^{\infty} w_n \right) \sqsubseteq \mathsf{p}_f \cdot [\![i]\!]_{\text{assert}}.$$

The composition operation here is continuous (by Proposition 2.3(e) in Section 2.3), so that this inequality is equivalent to

$$\bigsqcup_{n=0}^{\infty} \left((\mathsf{p}_f \cdot [\![i \land \neg b]\!]_{\text{assert}})_{\bot\bot} \cdot w_n \right) \sqsubseteq \mathsf{p}_f \cdot [\![i]\!]_{\text{assert}}.$$

The right side will extend the least upper bound of the chain on the left if and only if it is an upper bound of the chain. Thus, we need to show that, for all n,

$$(\mathsf{p}_f \cdot [\![i \land \neg b]\!]_{\text{assert}})_{\bot\bot} \cdot w_n \sqsubseteq \mathsf{p}_f \cdot [\![i]\!]_{\text{assert}}.$$

We will do this by induction on n. For $n = 0$, when σ is any state,

$$(\mathsf{p}_f \cdot [\![i \land \neg b]\!]_{\text{assert}})_{\bot\bot} (w_0 \sigma) = \bot \sqsubseteq (\mathsf{p}_f \cdot [\![i]\!]_{\text{assert}}) \sigma.$$

For the induction step, when σ is any state,

$$(\mathsf{p}_f \cdot [\![i \wedge \neg\, b]\!]_{\text{assert}}) \underline{\perp} (w_{n+1}\sigma)$$
$$= (\mathsf{p}_f \cdot [\![i \wedge \neg\, b]\!]_{\text{assert}}) \underline{\perp} (\textbf{if } [\![b]\!]_{\text{boolexp}}\sigma \textbf{ then } (w_n) \underline{\perp} ([\![c]\!]_{\text{comm}}\sigma) \textbf{ else } \sigma)$$
$$= \textbf{if } [\![b]\!]_{\text{boolexp}}\sigma \textbf{ then } (\mathsf{p}_f \cdot [\![i \wedge \neg\, b]\!]_{\text{assert}}) \underline{\perp} ((w_n) \underline{\perp} ([\![c]\!]_{\text{comm}}\sigma))$$
$$\textbf{else } (\mathsf{p}_f \cdot [\![i \wedge \neg\, b]\!]_{\text{assert}})\sigma.$$

But Proposition 2.4(e) in Section 2.3, the induction hypothesis, and the validity of the premiss give

$$(\mathsf{p}_f \cdot [\![i \wedge \neg\, b]\!]_{\text{assert}}) \underline{\perp} ((w_n) \underline{\perp} ([\![c]\!]_{\text{comm}}\sigma))$$
$$= ((\mathsf{p}_f \cdot [\![i \wedge \neg\, b]\!]_{\text{assert}}) \underline{\perp} \cdot w_n) \underline{\perp} ([\![c]\!]_{\text{comm}}\sigma)$$
$$\sqsubseteq (\mathsf{p}_f \cdot [\![i]\!]_{\text{assert}}) \underline{\perp} ([\![c]\!]_{\text{comm}}\sigma)$$
$$\sqsubseteq (\mathsf{p}_f \cdot [\![i \wedge b]\!]_{\text{assert}})\sigma.$$

Thus

$$(\mathsf{p}_f \cdot [\![i \wedge \neg\, b]\!]_{\text{assert}}) \underline{\perp} (w_{n+1}\sigma)$$
$$\sqsubseteq \textbf{if } [\![b]\!]_{\text{boolexp}}\sigma \textbf{ then } (\mathsf{p}_f \cdot [\![i \wedge b]\!]_{\text{assert}})\sigma \textbf{ else } (\mathsf{p}_f \cdot [\![i \wedge \neg\, b]\!]_{\text{assert}})\sigma$$
$$= \textbf{if } [\![b]\!]_{\text{boolexp}}\sigma \textbf{ then } (\mathsf{p}_f \cdot [\![i]\!]_{\text{assert}})\sigma \textbf{ else } (\mathsf{p}_f \cdot [\![i]\!]_{\text{assert}})\sigma$$
$$= (\mathsf{p}_f \cdot [\![i]\!]_{\text{assert}})\sigma,$$

where the penultimate step follows because $[\![i \wedge b]\!]_{\text{assert}}\sigma = [\![i]\!]_{\text{assert}}\sigma$ holds when $[\![b]\!]_{\text{assert}}\sigma$ is true, and $[\![i \wedge \neg\, b]\!]_{\text{assert}}\sigma = [\![i]\!]_{\text{assert}}\sigma$ holds when $[\![b]\!]_{\text{assert}}\sigma$ is false.

Next we consider how to modify the above inference rule to deal with total-correctness specifications. The essential idea is that **while** b **do** c must terminate if there is some integer expression e, called the *variant* of the **while** command, that is always decreased by execution of c but will never be negative when c begins execution. To impose the second requirement, we will introduce the assertion $i \wedge b \Rightarrow e \geq 0$ as an additional premiss; this suffices since $i \wedge b$ will hold whenever c begins execution. To impose the first requirement, we must augment the premiss describing the behavior of c so that it insures that c decreases e. But here we encounter a problem: Assertions describe a single state of the computation, so that they cannot directly describe a relationship between values of e in different states.

The way around this problem is to use a *ghost variable*, which is a variable that occurs in a specification without occurring in the command being specified:

SP RULE: Total Correctness of **while** (WHT)

$$\frac{[\,i \wedge b \wedge e = v_0\,]\, c\, [\,i \wedge e < v_0\,] \qquad i \wedge b \Rightarrow e \geq 0}{[\,i\,]\ \textbf{while } b \textbf{ do } c\ [\,i \wedge \neg\, b\,]}$$

when v_0 does not occur free in i, b, c, or e.

In this rule, we specify that if the variant equals the ghost variable v_0 before executing c, then the variant is less than the ghost variable afterward. Thus, since c does not change the ghost variable, it must decrease the variant.

To see the soundness of this rule, suppose v_0, i, b, c, and e stand for a variable, assertion, boolean expression, command, and integer expression such that v_0 does not occur free in the other phrases and the premises of the rule are valid. Then, from Equation (3.2) in Section 3.1,

$$\mathsf{p}_t \cdot [\![i \wedge b \wedge e = v_0]\!]_{\text{assert}} \sqsubseteq (\mathsf{p}_t \cdot [\![i \wedge e < v_0]\!]_{\text{assert}})_{\bot\!\bot} \cdot [\![c]\!]_{\text{comm}}, \tag{3.5}$$

and from the semantics of assertions,

$$\forall \sigma \in \Sigma. \ [\![i]\!]_{\text{assert}} \sigma \text{ and } [\![b]\!]_{\text{assert}} \sigma \text{ implies } [\![e]\!]_{\text{intexp}} \sigma \geq 0. \tag{3.6}$$

According to Equation (3.2), we need to show

$$\mathsf{p}_t \cdot [\![i]\!]_{\text{assert}} \sqsubseteq (\mathsf{p}_t \cdot [\![i \wedge \neg \, b]\!]_{\text{assert}})_{\bot\!\bot} \cdot \left(\bigsqcup_{n=0}^{\infty} w_n \right)$$

or, equivalently, for all states σ,

$$\mathsf{p}_t([\![i]\!]_{\text{assert}} \sigma) \sqsubseteq \bigsqcup_{n=0}^{\infty} (\mathsf{p}_t \cdot [\![i \wedge \neg \, b]\!]_{\text{assert}})_{\bot\!\bot}(w_n \sigma),$$

since $(\bigsqcup_{n=0}^{\infty} w_n)\sigma = \bigsqcup_{n=0}^{\infty} w_n \sigma$ and $(\mathsf{p}_t \cdot [\![i \wedge \neg \, b]\!]_{\text{assert}})_{\bot\!\bot}$ is easily seen to be continuous. Here the left side is $\bot$ unless $[\![i]\!]_{\text{assert}} \sigma$ is true, and the right side is the limit of an increasing chain in the two-element domain $\{\bot, \top\}$. Thus we must show that, whenever $[\![i]\!]_{\text{assert}} \sigma$ is true, there is a sufficiently large n such that the chain rises to $\top$.

In fact, the variant e provides a bound on this n. We will show, by induction on n, that for all $n \geq 0$ and $\sigma \in \Sigma$,

$$[\![i]\!]_{\text{assert}} \sigma \text{ and } [\![e]\!]_{\text{intexp}} \sigma < n \text{ implies } (\mathsf{p}_t \cdot [\![i \wedge \neg \, b]\!]_{\text{assert}})_{\bot\!\bot}(w_{n+1} \sigma) = \top,$$

which is sufficient to insure soundness.

In the base case, $[\![i]\!]_{\text{assert}} \sigma$ and $[\![e]\!]_{\text{intexp}} \sigma < 0$ and (3.6) imply that $[\![b]\!]_{\text{assert}} \sigma$ is false. Then $w_{n+1} \sigma = \sigma$, and $[\![i]\!]_{\text{assert}} \sigma$ gives $(\mathsf{p}_t \cdot [\![i \wedge \neg \, b]\!]_{\text{assert}})_{\bot\!\bot}(w_{n+1} \sigma) = \top$.

For the induction step, if $[\![b]\!]_{\text{assert}} \sigma$ is false, then the same argument holds as for $n = 0$. Otherwise, assume $[\![i]\!]_{\text{assert}} \sigma$ and $[\![e]\!]_{\text{intexp}} \sigma < n + 1$ and $[\![b]\!]_{\text{assert}} \sigma$, and let $\sigma' = [\sigma \mid v_0 \colon [\![e]\!]_{\text{intexp}} \sigma]$. Since v_0 does not occur free in i, b, or e, the coincidence theorem (Proposition 1.1 in Section 1.4) implies that

$$[\![i \wedge b \wedge e = v_0]\!]_{\text{assert}} \sigma' = [\![i]\!]_{\text{assert}} \sigma \wedge [\![b]\!]_{\text{assert}} \sigma \wedge ([\![e]\!]_{\text{intexp}} \sigma = [\![e]\!]_{\text{intexp}} \sigma) = \textbf{true}.$$

Then Condition (3.5) gives

$$(\mathsf{p}_t \cdot [\![i \wedge e < v_0]\!]_{\text{assert}})_{\bot\!\bot}([\![c]\!]_{\text{comm}} \sigma') = \top,$$

so that $[\![c]\!]_{\text{comm}}\sigma'$ is a state, $[\![i]\!]_{\text{assert}}([\![c]\!]_{\text{comm}}\sigma')$ is true, and $[\![e]\!]_{\text{intexp}}([\![c]\!]_{\text{comm}}\sigma') < [\![v_0]\!]_{\text{intexp}}([\![c]\!]_{\text{comm}}\sigma')$.

Since v_0 does not occur free in c, the coincidence theorem for commands (Proposition 2.6 in Section 2.5) shows that $[\![c]\!]_{\text{comm}}\sigma$ is a state and

$$[\![c]\!]_{\text{comm}}\sigma' = [\,[\![c]\!]_{\text{comm}}\sigma \mid v_0 \colon \sigma'v_0\,] = [\,[\![c]\!]_{\text{comm}}\sigma \mid v_0 \colon [\![e]\!]_{\text{intexp}}\sigma\,].$$

Then, since v_0 does not occur in i or e, we find that

$$[\![i]\!]_{\text{assert}}([\![c]\!]_{\text{comm}}\sigma) = [\![i]\!]_{\text{assert}}([\![c]\!]_{\text{comm}}\sigma') = \textbf{true}$$

and

$$[\![e]\!]_{\text{intexp}}([\![c]\!]_{\text{comm}}\sigma) = [\![e]\!]_{\text{intexp}}([\![c]\!]_{\text{comm}}\sigma') < [\![v_0]\!]_{\text{intexp}}([\![c]\!]_{\text{comm}}\sigma') = [\![e]\!]_{\text{intexp}}\sigma,$$

and since $[\![e]\!]_{\text{intexp}}\sigma < n+1$, we have $[\![e]\!]_{\text{intexp}}([\![c]\!]_{\text{comm}}\sigma) < n$.

Since $[\![i]\!]_{\text{assert}}([\![c]\!]_{\text{comm}}\sigma)$ is true and $[\![e]\!]_{\text{intexp}}([\![c]\!]_{\text{comm}}\sigma) < n$, we may apply the induction hypothesis, with σ replaced by $[\![c]\!]_{\text{comm}}\sigma$, to obtain

$$(\mathsf{p}_t \cdot [\![i \wedge \neg\, b]\!]_{\text{assert}}) \!\perp\!\! (w_{n+1}([\![c]\!]_{\text{comm}}\sigma)) = \top.$$

Then, by using the second equation in (3.4) to expand w_{n-2}, and using the facts that $[\![b]\!]_{\text{assert}}\sigma$ is true and $[\![c]\!]_{\text{comm}}$ is a state, we have

$$w_{n+2}\sigma = (w_{n+1}) \!\perp\!\! ([\![c]\!]_{\text{comm}}\sigma) = w_{n+1}([\![c]\!]_{\text{comm}}\sigma),$$

so that $(\mathsf{p}_t \cdot [\![i \wedge \neg\, b]\!]_{\text{assert}}) \!\perp\!\! (w_{n+2}\sigma) = \top$.

It should be noted that a more general total-correctness rule can be formulated by using a logic for assertions that accommodates a variety of data types, since then variants can range over any set with a well-founded ordering, rather than just the nonnegative integers.

3.5 Further Rules

In this section, we give the remaining inference rules needed to reason about the simple imperative language. With one exception, each rule has the same form for partial and total correctness. Their soundness is left to the reader.

There are more rules about specific kinds of commands. The first is obvious:

SP RULE: **skip** (SK)

$$\overline{\{p\}\ \textbf{skip}\ \{p\}.}$$

From SK and SP one can derive a slightly more convenient rule for **skip**:

SP RULE: Implication and **skip** (ISK)

$$\frac{p \Rightarrow q}{\{p\}\ \textbf{skip}\ \{q\}.}$$

The rule for conditional commands captures the idea that the specification for such a command must be met by each subcommand, except that one can assume the truth or falsity of the test when the subcommand begins execution:

SP RULE: Conditional (CD)

$$\frac{\{p \wedge b\}\, c_0\, \{q\} \qquad \{p \wedge \neg\, b\}\, c_1\, \{q\}}{\{p\}\ \textbf{if}\ b\ \textbf{then}\ c_0\ \textbf{else}\ c_1\ \{q\}}.$$

The rule for variable declarations has an unusual noncompositional form. It allows one to infer a specification of a command sequence containing a declaration from a similar specification in which the declaration is replaced by an initializing assignment command — provided that the variable being declared does not occur free in the consequent of the specification:

SP RULE: Variable Declaration (DC)

$$\frac{\{p\}\ s\,;v := e\,;c\,\{q\}}{\{p\}\ s\,;\textbf{newvar}\ v := e\ \textbf{in}\ c\,\{q\}}$$

when v does not occur free in q.

(Here the metavariable s ranges over sequential compositions of zero or more commands. When s is empty, the following semicolon is omitted.)

In this rule, the requirement on v formalizes the concept of locality: that the value of the declared variable plays no further role after execution of the scope of the declaration.

It is important to realize that locality is a property of the specification of a command rather than just the command itself, since it depends on the use to which the command may be put. For example, the same command satisfies both of the specifications

$$\{\textbf{true}\}\ t := x + y\,;z := t \times t\ \{z = (x + y)^2\}$$

$$\{\textbf{true}\}\ t := x + y\,;z := t \times t\ \{z = (x + y)^2 \wedge t = x + y\}.$$

But the variable t is local only in the first case, so that **newvar** t:=x+y **in** z:=t×t meets only the first specification.

At first sight, it might appear that the declaration rule is inadequate to deal with declarations that mask a more global usage of the variable being declared. The effect of a command beginning with such a declaration is to preserve the value of the variable, so that, for example,

$$\{x = 0\}\ \textbf{newvar}\ x := 1\ \textbf{in}\ x := x + 1\ \{x = 0\}$$

is valid. But one cannot prove this by a direct application of DC since the variable being declared occurs in the consequent.

However, one can use the fact that renaming, in either assertions or commands, preserves meaning. One can prove

1. $\{x = 0\}\ y := 1\ ;\ y := y + 1\ \{x = 0\}$ (AS)

2. $\{x = 0\}\ \textbf{newvar}\ y := 1\ \textbf{in}\ y := y + 1\ \{x = 0\}$ (DC,1)

and then rename the bound variable y by x.

The use of renaming can be formalized by a noncompositional rule:

SP RULE: Renaming (RN)

$$\frac{\{p\}\ c\ \{q\}}{\{p'\}\ c'\ \{q'\},}$$

where p', c', and q' are obtained from p, c, and q by zero or more renamings of bound variables (see Propositions 1.5 in Section 1.4 and 2.8 in Section 2.5).

Finally, we come to several noncompositional rules that, although they are not logically necessary, are often useful for shortening large proofs. The first two describe ways of combining different specifications of the same command:

SP RULE: Conjunction of Assertions (CA)

$$\frac{\{p_0\}\ c\ \{q_0\} \qquad \{p_1\}\ c\ \{q_1\}}{\{p_0 \wedge p_1\}\ c\ \{q_0 \wedge q_1\},}$$

SP RULE: Disjunction of Assertions (DA)

$$\frac{\{p_0\}\ c\ \{q_0\} \qquad \{p_1\}\ c\ \{q_1\}}{\{p_0 \vee p_1\}\ c\ \{q_0 \vee q_1\}.}$$

Then there are rules that capture the fact that a command only affects the variables that it assigns to. For partial correctness, this is stated quite simply:

SP RULE: Constancy for Partial Correctness (CSP)

$$\frac{}{\{p\}\ c\ \{p\}}$$

when no variable occurs both free in p and free on the left of an assignment command in c.

For total correctness, however, the precedent of the conclusion must guarantee termination. A convenient form of such a rule is

SP RULE: Constancy for Total Correctness (CST)

$$\frac{[\,p\,]\ c\ [\,q\,]}{[\,p \wedge r\,]\ c\ [\,q \wedge r\,]}$$

when no variable occurs both free in r and free on the left of an assignment command in c.

(Note that the partial-correctness rule analogous to CST can be derived from CSP and CA.)

3.6 Computing Fibonacci Numbers

To illustrate the use of the inference rules described in this chapter, we give proofs of the partial and total correctness of a simple program that computes Fibonacci numbers:

$$\textbf{if } n = 0 \textbf{ then } f := 0 \textbf{ else}$$

$$\textbf{newvar } k := 1 \textbf{ in newvar } g := 0 \textbf{ in } (f := 1;$$

$$\textbf{while } k \neq n \textbf{ do}$$

$$\textbf{newvar } t := g \textbf{ in } (g := f \, ; f := f + t \, ; k := k + 1)).$$

Specifically, we will prove that, beginning in any state in which $n \geq 0$, this program produces a state in which $f = \mathrm{fib}(n)$, where fib is defined by Equations (3.3) in Section 3.3.

Within the program, a conditional command is used to treat the case of $n = 0$ separately; the remaining cases are treated by a **while** loop whose invariant is

$$f = \mathrm{fib}(k) \wedge g = \mathrm{fib}(k - 1) \wedge k \leq n.$$

The following is the proof of partial correctness:

1. $(f = \mathrm{fib}(k) \wedge g = \mathrm{fib}(k - 1) \wedge k \leq n \wedge k \neq n) \Rightarrow$

    $(f + g = \mathrm{fib}(k + 1) \wedge f = \mathrm{fib}((k + 1) - 1) \wedge k + 1 \leq n)$

2. $\{f = \mathrm{fib}(k) \wedge g = \mathrm{fib}(k - 1) \wedge k \leq n \wedge k \neq n\}$

    $t := g \, ; g := f \, ; f := f + t \, ; k := k + 1$

    $\{f = \mathrm{fib}(k) \wedge g = \mathrm{fib}(k - 1) \wedge k \leq n\}$ (RAS,1)

3. $\{f = \mathrm{fib}(k) \wedge g = \mathrm{fib}(k - 1) \wedge k \leq n \wedge k \neq n\}$

    $\textbf{newvar } t := g \textbf{ in } (g := f \, ; f := f + t \, ; k := k + 1)$

    $\{f = \mathrm{fib}(k) \wedge g = \mathrm{fib}(k - 1) \wedge k \leq n\}$ (DC,2)

4. $\{f = \mathrm{fib}(k) \wedge g = \mathrm{fib}(k - 1) \wedge k \leq n\}$

    $\textbf{while } k \neq n \textbf{ do}$

    $\quad \textbf{newvar } t := g \textbf{ in } (g := f \, ; f := f + t \, ; k := k + 1)$

    $\{f = \mathrm{fib}(k) \wedge g = \mathrm{fib}(k - 1) \wedge k \leq n \wedge \neg \, k \neq n\}$ (WHP,3)

5. $(n \geq 0 \wedge \neg \, n = 0) \Rightarrow (1 = \mathrm{fib}(1) \wedge 0 = \mathrm{fib}(1 - 1) \wedge 1 \leq n)$

6. $\{n \geq 0 \wedge \neg\, n = 0\}$
   $k := 1 \,;\, g := 0 \,;\, f := 1$
   $\{f = \text{fib}(k) \wedge g = \text{fib}(k-1) \wedge k \leq n\}$ (RAS,5)

7. $(f = \text{fib}(k) \wedge g = \text{fib}(k-1) \wedge k \leq n \wedge \neg\, k \neq n) \Rightarrow f = \text{fib}(n)$

8. $\{n \geq 0 \wedge \neg\, n = 0\}$
   $k := 1 \,;\, g := 0 \,;\, f := 1;$
   while $k \neq n$ **do**
       newvar $t := g$ **in** $(g := f \,;\, f := f + t \,;\, k := k + 1)$
   $\{f = \text{fib}(n)\}$ (MSQ,6,4,7)

9. $\{n \geq 0 \wedge \neg\, n = 0\}$
   $k := 1 \,;\,$ **newvar** $g := 0$ **in** $(f := 1;$
       while $k \neq n$ **do**
           newvar $t := g$ **in** $(g := f \,;\, f := f + t \,;\, k := k + 1))$
   $\{f = \text{fib}(n)\}$ (DC,8)

10. $\{n \geq 0 \wedge \neg\, n = 0\}$
    newvar $k := 1$ **in newvar** $g := 0$ **in** $(f := 1;$
        while $k \neq n$ **do**
            newvar $t := g$ **in** $(g := f \,;\, f := f + t \,;\, k := k + 1))$
    $\{f = \text{fib}(n)\}$ (DC,9)

11. $(n \geq 0 \wedge n = 0) \Rightarrow 0 = \text{fib}(n)$

12. $\{n \geq 0 \wedge n = 0\}\ f := 0\ \{f = \text{fib}(n)\}$ (RAS,11)

13. $\{n \geq 0\}$
    if $n = 0$ **then** $f := 0$ **else**
        newvar $k := 1$ **in newvar** $g := 0$ **in** $(f := 1;$
            while $k \neq n$ **do**
                newvar $t := g$ **in** $(g := f \,;\, f := f + t \,;\, k := k + 1))$
    $\{f = \text{fib}(n)\}$ (CD,12,10)

To obtain a proof of total correctness, we note that the body of the **while** command increases k and leaves n unchanged, and the invariant guarantees that k never exceeds n. Thus we can use $n - k$ as a variant. The first five steps of the total-correctness proof are

1. $(f = \mathrm{fib}(k) \wedge g = \mathrm{fib}(k-1) \wedge k \leq n \wedge k \neq n \wedge n - k = v_0) \Rightarrow$
    $(f + g = \mathrm{fib}(k+1) \wedge f = \mathrm{fib}((k+1) - 1) \wedge k + 1 \leq n \wedge n - (k+1) < v_0)$

2. $[f = \mathrm{fib}(k) \wedge g = \mathrm{fib}(k-1) \wedge k \leq n \wedge k \neq n \wedge n - k = v_0]$
    $t := g \,;\, g := f \,;\, f := f + t \,;\, k := k + 1$
    $[f = \mathrm{fib}(k) \wedge g = \mathrm{fib}(k-1) \wedge k \leq n \wedge n - k < v_0]$ (RAS,1)

3. $[f = \mathrm{fib}(k) \wedge g = \mathrm{fib}(k-1) \wedge k \leq n \wedge k \neq n \wedge n - k = v_0]$
    newvar $t := g$ **in** $(g := f \,;\, f := f + t \,;\, k := k + 1)$
    $[f = \mathrm{fib}(k) \wedge g = \mathrm{fib}(k-1) \wedge k \leq n \wedge n - k < v_0]$ (DC,2)

3a. $(f = \mathrm{fib}(k) \wedge g = \mathrm{fib}(k-1) \wedge k \leq n \wedge k \neq n) \Rightarrow n - k \geq 0$

4. $[f = \mathrm{fib}(k) \wedge g = \mathrm{fib}(k-1) \wedge k \leq n]$
    while $k \neq n$ **do**
        newvar $t := g$ **in** $(g := f \,;\, f := f + t \,;\, k := k + 1)$
    $[f = \mathrm{fib}(k) \wedge g = \mathrm{fib}(k-1) \wedge k \leq n \wedge \neg\, k \neq n]$ (WHT,3a)

The remaining steps are the same as in the previous proof (except for the use of total- rather than partial-correctness specifications).

3.7 Fast Exponentiation

As a second example, we will prove the total correctness of a program that computes x^n in $\log n$ time. In this case, we want to demonstrate that one does not have to prove programs after the fact, but that program proof can go hand in hand with program construction.

Suppose we wish to construct a program that, starting in a state where $n \geq 0$, will set y to x^n. An obvious choice for a simple **while**-loop program is the invariant $y \times x^k = x^n \wedge k \geq 0$, where k is a decreasing variable that, roughly speaking, measures the amount of computation remaining to be done. One can achieve this invariant by setting k to n and y to one, and one can terminate the computation when k is zero, since then x^k is one.

However, to write a fast program, one needs a more general invariant that will permit more freedom in the body of the **while** command, while retaining the easy initialization and termination. One possibility is to introduce an additional variable z to generalize the invariant to

$$y \times z^k = x^n \wedge k \geq 0.$$

This is almost as easy to achieve — all that is needed is the additional assignment $z := x$ — and $k = 0$ still allows one to terminate. But now the **while** body will have the extra freedom to change z.

At this point, we have an informal account of the first step in a top-down program construction: We know how to write the program if we can write a **while** body B with certain properties. Before proceeding further, however, we can formalize these properties by a specification of B, and use this specification as an assumption in a proof that is actually a schema in the metavariable B:

7a. $[y \times z^k = x^n \wedge k \geq 0 \wedge k \neq 0 \wedge k = k_0]$

       B

       $[y \times z^k = x^n \wedge k \geq 0 \wedge k < k_0]$ assumption

8. $(y \times z^k = x^n \wedge k \geq 0 \wedge k \neq 0) \Rightarrow k \geq 0$

9. $[y \times z^k = x^n \wedge k \geq 0]$

       while $k \neq 0$ **do** B

       $[y \times z^k = x^n \wedge k \geq 0 \wedge \neg\, k \neq 0]$ (WHT,7,8)

10. $(n \geq 0) \Rightarrow (1 \times x^n = x^n \wedge n \geq 0)$

11. $[n \geq 0]$

       $k := n\,;\, z := x\,;\, y := 1$

       $[y \times z^k = x^n \wedge k \geq 0]$ (RAS,10)

12. $(y \times z^k = x^n \wedge k \geq 0 \wedge \neg\, k \neq 0) \Rightarrow y = x^n$

13. $[n \geq 0]$

       $k := n\,;\, z := x\,;\, y := 1\,;\,$ **while** $k \neq 0$ **do** B

       $[y = x^n]$ (MSQ,11,9,12)

14. $[n \geq 0]$

       $k := n\,;\,$ **newvar** $z := x$ **in**

           $idy := 1\,;\,$ **while** $k \neq 0$ **do** $B)$

       $[y = x^n]$ (DC,13)

15. $[n \geq 0]$

       newvar $k := n$ **in newvar** $z := x$ **in**

           $(y := 1\,;\,$ **while** $k \neq 0$ **do** $B)$

       $[y = x^n]$ (DC,14)

An obvious choice for B is $k := k - 1 \, ; \, y := y \times z$. In this case, the correctness is based on the exponential law that $z^k = z \times z^{k-1}$ when k is positive:

1. $(y \times z^k = x^n \wedge k \geq 0 \wedge k \neq 0 \wedge k = k_0) \Rightarrow$

   $((y \times z) \times z^{k-1} = x^n \wedge k - 1 \geq 0 \wedge k - 1 < k_0)$

2. $[y \times z^k = x^n \wedge k \geq 0 \wedge k \neq 0 \wedge k = k_0]$

   $k := k - 1 \, ; \, y := y \times z$

   $[y \times z^k = x^n \wedge k \geq 0 \wedge k < k_0]$ (RAS,1)

However, this choice of B gives a slow program that takes time proportional to n. The key to speed lies in another exponential law, that $z^k = (z \times z)^{k \div 2}$ when k is even and nonnegative. This allows us to halve k in a single execution of the **while** body, but unfortunately it only works when k is even:

3. $(y \times z^k = x^n \wedge k \geq 0 \wedge k \neq 0 \wedge k = k_0 \wedge \textbf{even } k) \Rightarrow$

   $(y \times (z \times z)^{k \div 2} = x^n \wedge k \div 2 \geq 0 \wedge k \div 2 < k_0)$

4. $[y \times z^k = x^n \wedge k \geq 0 \wedge k \neq 0 \wedge k = k_0 \wedge \textbf{even } k]$

   $k := k \div 2 \, ; \, z := z \times z$

   $[y \times z^k = x^n \wedge k \geq 0 \wedge k < k_0]$ (RAS,3)

The obvious solution is to branch on whether k is even or not, halving k when it is correct to do so, and decreasing it by one otherwise. (We assume that the predicate "**even**" is available in our programming language.)

5. $(y \times z^k = x^n \wedge k \geq 0 \wedge k \neq 0 \wedge k = k_0 \wedge \neg \textbf{ even } k) \Rightarrow$

   $(y \times z^k = x^n \wedge k \geq 0 \wedge k \neq 0 \wedge k = k_0)$

6. $[y \times z^k = x^n \wedge k \geq 0 \wedge k \neq 0 \wedge k = k_0 \wedge \neg \textbf{ even } k]$

   $k := k - 1 \, ; \, y := y \times z$

   $[y \times z^k = x^n \wedge k \geq 0 \wedge k < k_0]$ (SP,5,2)

7. $[y \times z^k = x^n \wedge k \geq 0 \wedge k \neq 0 \wedge k = k_0]$

   if even k **then** $(k := k \div 2 \, ; \, z := z \times z)$

       else $(k := k - 1 \, ; \, y := y \times z)$

   $[y \times z^k = x^n \wedge k \geq 0 \wedge k < k_0]$ (CD,4,6)

This exactly matches the assumption needed to prove the overall program: If we take the proof schema we began with and replace the occurrences of B by the command in Step 7, then Steps 7 and 7a become identical and our proof fragments dovetail into a complete proof.

3.8 Complications and Limitations

There are several limitations to the method for specifying and proving programs described in this chapter. The first has already been mentioned in the discussion of the total-correctness rule for **while** commands: Since assertions are descriptions of single states of the computation, they cannot directly describe relationships between different states. However, as in Section 3.4, it is easy to overcome this limitation by using ghost variables.

This problem arises with "in-place" programs that alter their input. For example, suppose P is the fast exponentiation program of the previous section and P' is obtained from P by deleting the declaration and initialization of k:

> **newvar** $z := x$ **in** $(y := 1$; **while** $k \neq 0$ **do**
>
> **if even** k **then** $(k := k \div 2 ; z := z \times z)$ **else** $(k := k - 1 ; y := y \times z))$.

Since the only usage of n in P was to provide the initialization of k, it is clear that P' will do unto the initial value of k as P did unto n. In other words, if the initial value of k is nonnegative, the program will terminate with y equal to x raised to the initial value of k.

This cannot be expressed directly by an assertion about the final state since k will no longer have its initial value. But one can prove the specification

$$[\,k \geq 0 \wedge k = k_0\,]\ P'\ [\,y = x^{k_0}\,].$$

Here k_0 is a variable, called a *ghost variable*, that does not occur free in P'. Thus its value does not affect, and is not affected by, the behavior of P'. In conjunction with the above specification, this fact (which is not itself part of the meaning of the specification) implies that P' has the desired behavior.

Another complication arises when a program may be executed in language implementations with varied arithmetic. In this situation, one needs to use a predicate logic that is weak enough to be sound for more than one semantics. A simple example is the division of negative integers. Integer arithmetic on computers normally satisfies the axioms

$$y \neq 0 \Rightarrow x = (x \div y) \times y + x \ \mathbf{rem}\ y$$
$$x \geq 0 \wedge y > 0 \Rightarrow 0 \leq x \ \mathbf{rem}\ y < y, \tag{3.7}$$

where x **rem** y denotes the remainder of dividing x by y. (We are ignoring overflow for the moment.) However, although most machines provide division that is "odd" in x and y:

$$y \neq 0 \Rightarrow (-x) \div y = -(x \div y)$$
$$y \neq 0 \Rightarrow x \div (-y) = -(x \div y), \tag{3.8}$$

a few machines provide a "number-theoretic" division satisfying

$$y > 0 \Rightarrow 0 \leq x \textbf{ rem } y < y, \tag{3.9}$$

so that, for example, $-3 \div 2 = -2$ and $-3 \textbf{ rem } 2 = 1$. In this situation, one can easily obtain a logic that is sound for both kinds of division by limiting the axioms about division to (3.7). One can even add a monotonicity law, since it holds in both situations:

$$y > 0 \wedge x \leq x' \Rightarrow x \div y \leq x' \div y. \tag{3.10}$$

Weak logics with a multiplicity of models are also needed to deal with arithmetic errors in programming languages where such errors are not checked. With overflow, for instance, one typically wants to prove that a program will execute correctly on all machines where the arithmetic operations coincide with true arithmetic whenever their results lie within an interval of representable numbers (delimited, say, by symbolic constants **minint** and **maxint**). For this purpose, one can use a logic that is weak enough to be sound for all such semantics. Similarly, for division by zero, one would want a logic that is weak enough to be sound for all functional definitions of division by zero.

The details of such logics are beyond the scope of this book. However, it should be noted that they are still instances of predicate logic and thus incorporate the assumption that operations are total functions. For example, one can use the rules in Section 3.3 to prove

$$[\textbf{true}] \, y := x \div 0 \, ; y := 7 \, [y = 7],$$

which is sound since the second assignment will overwrite whatever value is possessed by $x \div 0$, and

$$[x = 7] \textbf{ if } x + y = z \textbf{ then } x := x + 1 \textbf{ else } x := x - 1 \, [x = 8 \vee x = 6],$$

which is sound since $x + y = z$ must yield true or false even when $x + y$ overflows. Moreover, as long as equality is axiomatized in the standard way, since the logic incorporates the assumption that the same operation applied to the same operands yields the same result, one can prove $x \div 0 = x \div 0$. Similarly, as long as multiplication by zero is standard, one can prove $(x + y) \times 0 = 0$.

For languages where arithmetic errors are checked, the kind of logic described in this chapter still works for partial correctness, provided that error stops are regarded as nontermination. For total correctness, however, one must move from predicate logic to some richer logic that can deal with erroneous or nonterminating results. (A similar situation holds when one introduces recursive function definitions that can define nonterminating functions.) Such partial-function logics are an important topic of current research.

In summary, the logic of standard arithmetic suffices for the partial correctness of programs when all errors are checked at runtime; weaker logics are needed for partial correctness when unchecked errors may occur, and suffice for total correctness when there is no error checking; and partial-function logics are needed for total correctness in the presence of error checking or nonterminating functions.

Finally, something needs to be said about scaling: whether the formal specification and proof of programs remain a viable endeavor when one moves from trivial programs such as the examples in this chapter to programs that are so complex that the avoidance of errors is a serious challenge. Sheer size does not appear to be a severe problem; in the author's experience, formal proofs of well-structured programs tend to have sizes of order $n \log n$ in the size of the program, which is probably a more modest growth rate than that of the cost of debugging.

The real difficulty arises from the complexity and variety of real-world problem domains. When one moves from a mathematically well-understood area such as integer arithmetic to a domain such as text formatting or income-tax preparation, specifications quickly become unwieldly and can be as subject to error as the programs that they specify, so that the heart of the problem moves from meeting the specification to formulating it. Even here, however, formal methods provide powerful tools for avoiding ambiguity and contradiction.

Bibliographic Notes

The inference rules discussed in this chapter are given a more theoretical treatment by Loeckx et al. [1987, Chapter 8], who deal with completeness issues as well as soundness (and who include a stronger total-correctness **while** rule using well-founded orderings); other books are better for examples of real proofs. A number of partial-correctness proofs, in a formalism similar to that of this chapter, are given in Reynolds [1981a, Chapter 1]. Various total-correctness proofs are given by Gries [1981], but in a formalism using guarded commands and weakest preconditions, which we will discuss in Chapter 7.

The original papers in this area are unusually clear and well worth reading. The use of assertions to specify and prove correctness of flowchart programs was developed independently by Naur [1966] and Floyd [1967], although the essential idea goes back to the origins of computer programming, in unpublished reports by Goldstine and von Neumann [1947] and Turing [1950]. Then Hoare [1969] developed the partial-correctness system described in this chapter. (Arithmetic with unchecked overflow was also formalized in this paper.) Later, Hoare [1971] gave an exemplary proof of a median-finding program which made it clear that program-proving could be integrated with top-down program construction. The soundness of Hoare's system was first proved by Lauer [1971] (as summarized in Hoare and Lauer [1974]). A short history of the development of the subject, with an extensive bibliography, has been given by Jones [1992].

Program-specification logics that accommodate partial functions were devised by Barringer, Cheng, and Jones [1984] and Jones and Middelburg [1994]. Surveys of this area include Cheng and Jones [1991] and Owe [1993].

A logic for reasoning about assembly-language programs has been devised by Necula [1997].

Exercises

3.1   Fill in the missing precedents indicated by question marks to make the following specifications true. The assertions that you provide should be as weak as possible, but they should not be unnecessarily complicated.

$$[\,?\,]\; x := x + 1\,;\, y := y + 2 \times x - 1\; [\, y = x^2\,]$$

$$[\,?\,]\; x := x + y\,;\, y := x - y\,;\, x := x - y\; [\, x = z \wedge y = w\,]$$

$$[\,?\,]\; \textbf{while}\; a < b\; \textbf{do}\; (a := a + 1\,;\, y := x + y)\; [\, y = x \times b\,]$$

$$\{?\}\; \textbf{while true do skip}\; \{\textbf{false}\}$$

$$[\,?\,]\; \textbf{while true do skip}\; [\,\textbf{false}\,].$$

3.2   Write a program P that satisfies the following total-correctness specification:

$$[\, a \geq 0 \wedge b \geq 0\,]\; P\; [\, c = \gcd(a, b)\,]$$

(and does not assign to the input variables a or b), where $\gcd(x, y)$ denotes the greatest common divisor of the integers x and y. (By convention, $\gcd(0, 0) = 0$.)

Then give a formal proof of the specification using the inference rules given in this chapter. (You need not include formal proofs of the assertions that occur as steps in the proof, but they all should be valid. To save writing, you may define metavariables to stand for assertions that occur repeatedly.)

The following mathematical facts are relevant:

$$\gcd(y, x \,\textbf{rem}\, y) = \gcd(x, y) \qquad\qquad \gcd(x, 0) = x \text{ when } x \geq 0$$

$$0 \leq x \,\textbf{rem}\, y < y \text{ when } x \geq 0 \text{ and } y > 0.$$

3.3   For each of the following total-correctness specifications, complete the program "skeletons" in such a way that the programs meet their specifications, use the indicated invariants, and do not assign to the input variables x or y. (Although it is not indicated by the skeletons, your programs should begin with declarations of all local variables. In the first two cases, you may use multiplication or division by two as a primitive operation but not multiplication or division by an arbitrary number.)

Then give a formal proof of the specifications that uses the inference rules given in this chapter. (You need not include formal proofs of the assertions that occur as steps in the proof, but they all should be valid. To save writing, you may define metavariables to stand for assertions that occur repeatedly.)

(a) Logarithmic-Time Multiplication

$$[y \geq 0]$$

"Achieve invariant I" ;

while $k \neq 0$ **do** "Preserve invariant I while decreasing k"

$$[z = x \times y]$$

where

$$I \stackrel{\text{def}}{=} z + w \times k = x \times y \wedge k \geq 0.$$

(b) Logarithmic-Time Division

$$[x \geq 0 \wedge y > 0]$$

"Achieve invariant I_0" ;

while $z \leq x$ **do** "Preserve invariant I_0 while increasing z" ;

"Achieve invariant I_1" ;

while $n \neq 0$ **do** "Preserve invariant I_1 while decreasing n"

$$[x = q \times y + r \wedge 0 \leq r < y]$$

where

$$I_0 \stackrel{\text{def}}{=} z = y \times 2^n \wedge n \geq 0 \wedge x \geq 0 \wedge y > 0$$

$$I_1 \stackrel{\text{def}}{=} x = q \times z + r \wedge 0 \leq r < z \wedge z = y \times 2^n \wedge n \geq 0.$$

(c) Logarithmic-Time Square Root

$$[x \geq 0]$$

"Achieve invariant I_0" ;

while $w \times w \leq x$ **do** "Preserve invariant I_0 while increasing w" ;

"Achieve invariant I_1" ;

while $n \neq 0$ **do** "Preserve invariant I_1 while decreasing n"

$$[z^2 \leq x < (z+1)^2]$$

where

$$I_0 \stackrel{\text{def}}{=} w = 2^n \wedge n \geq 0 \wedge x \geq 0$$

$$I_1 \stackrel{\text{def}}{=} z^2 \leq x < (z+w)^2 \wedge w = 2^n \wedge n \geq 0.$$

3.4   Give a formal proof, using the inference rules of this chapter, of the total-correctness specification

$$[x \geq 0 \land x = x_0 \land y = y_0]$$
$$\textbf{while } x \neq 0 \textbf{ do } (x := x - 1 \,; y := y + x)$$
$$[y = y_0 + x_0 \times (x_0 - 1) \div 2].$$

3.5   Derive the total-correctness specification $[\,\textbf{false}\,] \; c \; [\,\textbf{false}\,]$ by structural induction on the command c.

3.6   Give inference rules for proving partial- and total-correctness specifications of the **repeat** command described in Exercise 2.2. These rules should be compositional, so that the premisses that are specifications should be specifications of the subcommand of the **repeat** command.

   The answer to this question will be more complex than one might expect. This reflects an inherent complexity in the **repeat** command, which is closely related to the fact that this command (like the DO command in early Fortran) always executes its body at least once.

   Derive your partial-correctness rule from the definition of the **repeat** command as syntactic sugar, obtained in Exercise 2.2(b).

3.7   The following definition of the **for** command as syntactic sugar was given at the end of Section 2.6:

$$\textbf{for } v := e_0 \textbf{ to } e_1 \textbf{ do } c$$
$$\overset{\text{def}}{=} \textbf{newvar } w := e_1 \textbf{ in newvar } v := e_0 \textbf{ in}$$
$$\textbf{while } v \leq w \textbf{ do } (c \,; v := v + 1)$$

when w is distinct from v and does not occur free in either e_0 or c, and v is not assigned by c. An appropriate total-correctness inference rule for this kind of **for** command is

$$\frac{[\, i \land v \leq u \,] \; c \; [\, i/v \to v + 1 \,]}{[\, i/v \to e_0 \land e_1 = u \land e_0 \leq e_1 + 1 \,] \; \textbf{for } v := e_0 \textbf{ to } e_1 \textbf{ do } c \; [\, i/v \to u + 1 \,],}$$

where the variable u is distinct from v and is not assigned by c. Derive this rule from the above definition. In other words, give a proof schema that begins with the premise of the rule as an assumption and ends with the conclusion, except that the **for** command in the conclusion is replaced by its definition.

Hint Use $i \land w = u \land v \leq w + 1$ as the invariant of the **while** command. Without loss of generality, you may assume w is distinct from u and does not occur free in i (since these conditions can be obtained by renaming w). Do not overlook the rule of constancy at the end of Section 3.5.

3.8   The following is an alternative inference rule for conditional commands
       where the precedents of the premisses can be arbitrary assertions:

$$\frac{\{p_0\}\ c_0\ \{q\} \qquad \{p_1\}\ c_1\ \{q\}}{\{(b \Rightarrow p_0) \wedge (\neg b \Rightarrow p_1)\}\ \textbf{if } b \textbf{ then } c_0 \textbf{ else } c_1\ \{q\}.}$$

       Derive this rule from the rule CD in Section 3.5, and vice versa.

3.9   Prove the soundness of inference rule DC for variable declarations in Sec-
       tion 3.5, for both partial and total correctness.

3.10   The following is a compositional rule for declarations:

$$\frac{\{p\}\ c\ \{q\}}{\{p/v \to e\}\ \textbf{newvar } v := e \textbf{ in } c\ \{q\}}$$

       when v does not occur free in q. Derive this rule from the assignment rule
       AS in Section 3.3 and the noncompositional rule DC for declarations in
       Section 3.5.

       Explain why the noncompositional rule can be more convenient to use.
       Hint Try to do the Fibonacci example with the compositional rule.

3.11   Suppose $[\,p\,]\ c\ [\,q\,]$ is a valid specification and $\delta \in \langle \text{var} \rangle \to \langle \text{var} \rangle$ maps
       distinct variables in $\text{FV}_{\text{assert}}(p) \cup \text{FV}_{\text{comm}}(c) \cup \text{FV}_{\text{assert}}(q)$ into distinct
       variables. Show that $[\,p/\delta\,]\ (c/\delta)\ [\,q/\delta\,]$ is a valid specification.

       Give a counterexample showing that this proposition can fail when δ
       maps distinct variables into the same variable.

4

Arrays

In this chapter, we extend the simple imperative language and the methods for reasoning about its programs to include one-dimensional arrays with integer subscripts. Although more elaborate and varied forms of arrays are provided by many programming languages, such simple arrays are enough to demonstrate the basic semantical and logical properties of arrays.

There are two complementary ways to think about arrays. In the older view, which was first made explicit in early work on semantics by Christopher Strachey, an array variable is something that one can apply to an integer (called a subscript) to obtain an "array element" (in Strachey's terminology, an "L-value"), which in turn can be either evaluated, to obtain a value, or assigned, to alter the state of the computation. In the newer view, which is largely due to Hoare but has roots in the work of McCarthy, an array variable, like an ordinary variable, has a value — but this value is a function mapping subscripts into ordinary values. Strachey's view is essential for languages that are rich enough that arrays can share elements. But for the simple imperative language, and especially for the kind of reasoning about programs developed in the previous chapter, Hoare's view is much more straightforward.

4.1 Abstract Syntax

Clearly, array variables are a different *type* of variable than the integer variables used in previous chapters. In general, there are three ways in which variables of different types may be distinguished:

(a) The type of a variable occurrence may be determined by the declaration (or other phrase) that binds it. In this approach, which is used in most modern programming languages, different occurrences of the same variable may have different types if they are bound by binders with different scopes.

(b) The type of a variable may be determined by the variable itself. In early versions of Fortran, for example, variables beginning with i, j, k, l, m, or n were integer variables. Although this approach is rare for programming languages, it is common in mathematical notation, where different types of variables often have different fonts.

(c) If the type of every variable occurrence can be determined from its context, then different occurrences of the same variable can have different types, even within the same nest of scopes; one simply modifies the definition of binding so that an occurrence of v is bound by the innermost binder of v that has the same type. In Standard ML, for example, this approach is applied to the distinction between ordinary variables and type variables. (The latter are actually variables that range over types. For purposes of this discussion, however, they are simply variables of a different type than ordinary variables.)

In Chapter 15 and later, when we study type systems, we will use the first approach, but at present it would be a distracting complication. Instead, to keep things as simple as possible, we will follow the second approach. Specifically, we will assume that, in addition to the predefined set ⟨var⟩ of variables, there is a disjoint predefined set ⟨arrayvar⟩ of array variables. In examples, we will use lower case to represent members of ⟨var⟩ and upper case to represent members of ⟨arrayvar⟩.

To emphasize the view that array variables have functions as values, in the same sense that integer variables have integers as values, we will distinguish between variables and expressions just as we did for integers. An occurrence of an array variable that indicates evaluation, for example within the right side of an assignment command, will be classified as an array expression; but an occurrence that indicates a change in value, for example at the left of an assignment command, will not be classified as an expression. This is a rather precious distinction to make in the syntax of our programming language, since array variables will be the only form of array expression in the language, but later we will introduce other forms into the logic for reasoning about programs. (Of course, one could introduce complex array expressions into the programming language, as in APL.)

These considerations lead to the following additions to the abstract grammar given in Section 2.1:

⟨arrayexp⟩ ::= ⟨arrayvar⟩

⟨intexp⟩ ::= ⟨arrayexp⟩(⟨intexp⟩)

⟨comm⟩ ::= ⟨arrayvar⟩(⟨intexp⟩) := ⟨intexp⟩

    | **newarray** ⟨arrayvar⟩ (⟨intexp⟩ **to** ⟨intexp⟩) := ⟨intexp⟩ **in** ⟨comm⟩

The last production describes array declarations: **newarray** w (e_0 **to** e_1):=e **in** c declares w to be an array whose subscript ranges over the interval e_0 **to** e_1, and initializes this array to (the constant function whose result is) e. The occurrence of w is a binder whose scope is c, but not e_0, e_1, or e. More generally, the sets of variables that occur free and that are assigned are given by

$$FV_{\text{arrayexp}}(w) = \{w\}$$

$$FV_{\text{comm}}(w(e_0) := e_1) = \{w\} \cup FV_{\text{intexp}}(e_0) \cup FV_{\text{intexp}}(e_1)$$

$FV_{\text{comm}}(\textbf{newarray}\ w\ (e_0\ \textbf{to}\ e_1) := e\ \textbf{in}\ c)$
$$= (FV_{\text{comm}}(c) - \{w\}) \cup FV_{\text{intexp}}(e_0) \cup FV_{\text{intexp}}(e_1) \cup FV_{\text{intexp}}(e)$$

$$FA(w(e_0) := e_1) = \{w\}$$

$$FA(\textbf{newarray}\ w\ (e_0\ \textbf{to}\ e_1) := e\ \textbf{in}\ c) = FA(c) - \{w\}.$$

To make the above syntax concrete, we assume that the application of an array variable to a subscript is left-associative and has higher precedence than any previously introduced operation.

4.2 Denotational Semantics

To formalize Hoare's view that array values are functions, we define the set of array values to be

$$\mathbf{A} = \bigcup_{l,u \in \mathbf{Z}} (l\ \textbf{to}\ u) \to \mathbf{Z}.$$

As discussed in Section A.1 of the Appendix, we will call the set $l\ \textbf{to}\ u = \{\, i \mid l \leq i \leq u \,\}$ the *interval from l to u*. Note that this set has size

$$\textbf{if}\ u - l + 1 \geq 0\ \textbf{then}\ u - l + 1\ \textbf{else}\ 0$$

and contains l and u whenever it is nonempty. When $u - l + 1 \geq 0$, so that size is given by the "**then**" branch of the above conditional, we will call the interval from l to u *regular* (even though, strictly speaking, it is the representation of the interval by l and u that is regular, not the interval itself).

Clearly, the concept of a state must be generalized to map ordinary variables into integers and array variables into array values. The obvious definition would be $\Sigma = Z^{\langle\text{var}\rangle} \times A^{\langle\text{arrayvar}\rangle}$, but this would force us to write $\sigma_1 v$ or $\sigma_2 w$ when applying states to ordinary or array variables. To avoid the subscripts, we define

$$\Sigma = \prod_{v \in \langle\text{var}\rangle \cup \langle\text{arrayvar}\rangle} \textbf{if}\ v \in \langle\text{var}\rangle\ \textbf{then}\ \mathbf{Z}\ \textbf{else}\ \mathbf{A}.$$

(The product notation used here is defined in Section A.3 of the Appendix.) Then the semantics in Section 2.2 is extended with a new semantic function:

$$[\![-]\!]_{\text{arrayexp}} \in \langle\text{arrayexp}\rangle \to (\Sigma \to \mathbf{A})$$

and the following semantic equations:

DR SEM EQ: Array Variables

$$\llbracket w \rrbracket_{\text{arrayexp}} \sigma = \sigma w,$$

DR SEM EQ: Array Application

$$\llbracket a(e) \rrbracket_{\text{intexp}} \sigma = \textbf{if } \llbracket e \rrbracket_{\text{intexp}} \sigma \in \text{dom}(\llbracket a \rrbracket_{\text{arrayexp}} \sigma)$$
$$\textbf{then } (\llbracket a \rrbracket_{\text{arrayexp}} \sigma)(\llbracket e \rrbracket_{\text{intexp}} \sigma)$$
$$\textbf{else } 0,$$

DR SEM EQ: Array Assignment

$$\llbracket w(e_0) := e_1 \rrbracket_{\text{comm}} \sigma = \textbf{if } \llbracket e_0 \rrbracket_{\text{intexp}} \sigma \in \text{dom}(\sigma w)$$
$$\textbf{then } [\, \sigma \mid w \colon [\, \sigma w \mid \llbracket e_0 \rrbracket_{\text{intexp}} \sigma \colon \llbracket e_1 \rrbracket_{\text{intexp}} \sigma \,]\,]$$
$$\textbf{else } \bot,$$

DR SEM EQ: Array Declaration

$$\llbracket \textbf{newarray } w \ (e_0 \textbf{ to } e_1) := e \textbf{ in } c \rrbracket_{\text{comm}} \sigma$$
$$= (\lambda \sigma' \in \Sigma. \ [\, \sigma' \mid w \colon \sigma w \,])_{\bot\!\bot}$$
$$(\llbracket c \rrbracket_{\text{comm}} [\, \sigma \mid w \colon \lambda k \in \llbracket e_0 \rrbracket_{\text{intexp}} \sigma \textbf{ to } \llbracket e_1 \rrbracket_{\text{intexp}} \sigma. \ \llbracket e \rrbracket_{\text{intexp}} \sigma \,]).$$

Our intent here is to describe a language where out-of-range subscripts are always checked. However, as discussed briefly in Section 2.7, this would force us to introduce an "error result" for expressions. To avoid such a diversion, we have treated subscript errors in expressions unrealistically: Application of an array value to a subscript outside its domain gives a default value of zero. With array assignments, however, we have been more realistic: Assignment with an out-of-range subscript gives an error stop that is formalized as a failure to terminate. (This fails to distinguish between programs that give error messages and those that run on forever. We will discuss the pros and cons of overlooking this distinction when we consider functional programming languages in Chapter 11.)

Something cautionary needs to be said about languages where out-of-range subscripts are not checked. In contrast to the situation with unchecked arithmetic errors, when arrays are applied to out-of-range subscripts in expressions, they may not behave as single-valued functions. For example, if 100 does not belong to the domain of X, then

$$t := X(100) \,; y := 7 \,; \textbf{if } t = X(100) \textbf{ then } c \textbf{ else } c'$$

may execute c', since the location of the hundredth element of X may actually be the location of the variable y. Even worse, an assignment to an array at an out-of-range subscript can alter a seemingly unrelated variable, so that

$$t := y \,; X(100) := 7 \,; \textbf{if } t = y \textbf{ then } c \textbf{ else } c'$$

may execute c'.

Since they can cause logically unrelated variables (or even storage containing machine instructions) to be assigned to as well as evaluated, unchecked subscript errors are even more problematic than uninitialized variables. Thus the omission of subscript checking should be tolerated only in extreme situations, either where unpredictable and undebuggable behavior is acceptable, or where care has been taken to prove that out-of-range subscripts cannot occur. (Sadly, however, it is common practice to omit subscript checking in many cases where the gain in efficiency is not justified by the loss of reliability.)

Semantically, a program that can execute an unchecked subscript error can only be regarded as meaningless. This raises the difficult technical problem of restricting the domain of semantic functions to sets of phrases that are themselves determined by a semantic criteria. (This problem is addressed by certain advanced type systems that are beyond the scope of this book.)

4.3 Binary Search

As we will see in the next section, proofs of programs containing array assignments require a new inference rule. However, the rules developed in the previous chapter suffice for programs that only evaluate arrays, such as a program for binary search. As with fast exponentiation in Section 3.7, we will prove the total correctness of such a program in parallel with its construction.

The program P will search the ordered array X over the subscripts in the regular interval from a to b to find an element that is equal to the test value y. If such an element exists, the variable c will be set to its subscript; otherwise, c will be set to $\mathsf{b}+1$. More precisely, P should satisfy the specification

$$[\mathsf{a}-1 \le \mathsf{b} \wedge R]$$

$$P$$

$$[\mathsf{a} \le \mathsf{c} \le \mathsf{b} \wedge \mathsf{X}(\mathsf{c}) = \mathsf{y} \vee \mathsf{c} = \mathsf{b}+1 \wedge \forall \mathsf{i}.\ \mathsf{a} \le \mathsf{i} \le \mathsf{b} \Rightarrow \mathsf{X}(\mathsf{i}) \ne \mathsf{y}]$$

where the metavariable R abbreviates the assertion that X is in nonstrict increasing order from a to b:

$$R \stackrel{\mathrm{def}}{=} \forall \mathsf{i}.\ \forall \mathsf{j}.\ \mathsf{a} \le \mathsf{i} \le \mathsf{j} \le \mathsf{b} \Rightarrow \mathsf{X}(\mathsf{i}) \le \mathsf{X}(\mathsf{j}).$$

(Here and in the proof to follow, we use the common mathematical notation for multiple inequalities; for example, we write $\mathsf{a} \le \mathsf{i} \le \mathsf{j} \le \mathsf{b}$ to abbreviate $\mathsf{a} \le \mathsf{i} \wedge \mathsf{i} \le \mathsf{j} \wedge \mathsf{j} \le \mathsf{b}$.) Note that $\mathsf{a} - 1 \le \mathsf{b}$ in the precedent of the specification of P asserts that a **to** b is regular.

The heart of the program will be a **while** command whose invariant

$$I \stackrel{\text{def}}{=} a - 1 \le c \le d - 1 \le b \wedge R \wedge$$
$$(\forall i.\, a \le i \le c \Rightarrow X(i) \le y) \wedge (\forall i.\, d \le i \le b \Rightarrow X(i) > y)$$

asserts that the interval to be searched is partitioned into three regular subintervals: from a to c, from c + 1 to d − 1, and from d to b; and that the values of X over the first subinterval are all less than or equal to the test value, while those over the third subinterval are all greater.

It is easy to achieve this invariant initially by making the first and third intervals empty. Now suppose we can write a **while** command that preserves the invariant while emptying the middle interval. Then, at its completion, the invariant will assure that the test value occurs only in the segment of X over the first subinterval, and the ordering of X will assure that any such occurrences must be at the upper end of this subinterval.

This leads to the following proof, which starts with the assumption that the body B of the **while** command preserves the invariant and decreases the size d − 1 − c of the middle subinterval:

9a. $[I \wedge d - 1 - c > 0 \wedge d - 1 - c = k_0]$

    B

    $[I \wedge d - 1 - c < k_0]$ assumption

10. $(I \wedge d - 1 - c > 0) \Rightarrow d - 1 - c \ge 0$

11. $[I]$

    while d − 1 − c > 0 **do** B

    $[I \wedge \neg\, d - 1 - c > 0]$ (WHT,9,10)

12. $(a - 1 \le b \wedge R) \Rightarrow$

    $(a - 1 \le a - 1 \le b + 1 - 1 \le b \wedge R \wedge$

    $(\forall i.\, a \le i \le a - 1 \Rightarrow X(i) \le y) \wedge$

    $(\forall i.\, b + 1 \le i \le b \Rightarrow X(i) > y))$

13. $[a - 1 \le b \wedge R]$

    c := a − 1 ; d := b + 1

    $[I]$ (RAS,12)

14. $(I \wedge \neg\, d - 1 - c > 0 \wedge a \le c \wedge X(c) = y) \Rightarrow$

    $(a \le c \le b \wedge X(c) = y \;\vee$

    $c = b + 1 \wedge \forall i.\, a \le i \le b \Rightarrow X(i) \ne y)$

15. $[I \wedge \neg\ d - 1 - c > 0 \wedge a \le c \wedge X(c) = y]$

    skip

    $[a \le c \le b \wedge X(c) = y \vee$
    $\qquad c = b + 1 \wedge \forall i.\ a \le i \le b \Rightarrow X(i) \ne y]$ $\qquad\qquad$ (ISK,14)

16. $(I \wedge \neg\ d - 1 - c > 0 \wedge \neg(a \le c \wedge X(c) = y)) \Rightarrow$
    $\qquad (a \le b + 1 \le b \wedge X(b + 1) = y \vee$
    $\qquad\qquad b + 1 = b + 1 \wedge \forall i.\ a \le i \le b \Rightarrow X(i) \ne y)$

17. $[I \wedge \neg\ d - 1 - c > 0 \wedge \neg(a \le c \wedge X(c) = y)]$

    $c := b + 1$

    $[a \le c \le b \wedge X(c) = y \vee$
    $\qquad c = b + 1 \wedge \forall i.\ a \le i \le b \Rightarrow X(i) \ne y]$ $\qquad\qquad$ (RAS,16)

18. $[I \wedge \neg\ d - 1 - c > 0]$

    if $a \le c \wedge X(c) = y$ **then skip else** $c := b + 1$

    $[a \le c \le b \wedge X(c) = y \vee$
    $\qquad c = b + 1 \wedge \forall i.\ a \le i \le b \Rightarrow X(i) \ne y]$ $\qquad\qquad$ (CD,15,17)

19. $[a - 1 \le b \wedge R]$

    $c := a - 1\,;\, d := b + 1;$

    $\qquad$ **while** $d - 1 - c > 0$ **do** $B;$

    $\qquad$ **if** $a \le c \wedge X(c) = y$ **then skip else** $c := b + 1$

    $[a \le c \le b \wedge X(c) = y \vee$
    $\qquad c = b + 1 \wedge \forall i.\ a \le i \le b \Rightarrow X(i) \ne y]$ $\qquad\qquad$ (MSQ,13,11,18)

20. $[a - 1 \le b \wedge R]$

    $c := a - 1\,;\,$ **newvar** $d := b + 1$ **in**

    $\qquad (\textbf{while}\ d - 1 - c > 0\ \textbf{do}\ B;$

    $\qquad$ **if** $a \le c \wedge X(c) = y$ **then skip else** $c := b + 1)$

    $[a \le c \le b \wedge X(c) = y \vee$
    $\qquad c = b + 1 \wedge \forall i.\ a \le i \le b \Rightarrow X(i) \ne y]$ $\qquad\qquad$ (DC,19)

When the **while** body B begins execution, the middle subinterval will be nonempty, so that a local variable j can be set to some member of this interval, which we assume will be given by an expression E. Next, $X(j)$ can be compared with the test value y. If it is less than or equal to y, then, because of the ordering, every previous element is also less than or equal to y, so that the invariant will be preserved if the first subinterval is extended upward to include j. By a symmetric argument, if $X(j)$ is greater than y, then the third subinterval can be extended downward to include j. In either case, at least j will be removed from the middle interval, whose size will decrease.

This argument is formalized by the following proof:

2a. $[I \wedge d - 1 - c > 0 \wedge d - 1 - c = k_0]$

    $j := E$

    $[I \wedge c + 1 \leq j \leq d - 1 \wedge d - 1 - c = k_0]$ assumption

3. $(I \wedge c + 1 \leq j \leq d - 1 \wedge d - 1 - c = k_0 \wedge X(j) \leq y) \Rightarrow$

      $(a - 1 \leq j \leq d - 1 \leq b \wedge R \wedge$

          $(\forall i.\ a \leq i \leq j \Rightarrow X(i) \leq y) \wedge (\forall i.\ d \leq i \leq b \Rightarrow X(i) > y) \wedge$

         $d - 1 - j < k_0)$

4. $[I \wedge c + 1 \leq j \leq d - 1 \wedge d - 1 - c = k_0 \wedge X(j) \leq y]$

    $c := j$

    $[I \wedge d - 1 - c < k_0]$ (RAS,3)

5. $(I \wedge c + 1 \leq j \leq d - 1 \wedge d - 1 - c = k_0 \wedge \neg\, X(j) \leq y) \Rightarrow$

      $(a - 1 \leq c \leq j - 1 \leq b \wedge R \wedge$

         $(\forall i.\ a \leq i \leq c \Rightarrow X(i) \leq y) \wedge (\forall i.\ j \leq i \leq b \Rightarrow X(i) > y) \wedge$

         $j - 1 - c < k_0)$

6. $[I \wedge c + 1 \leq j \leq d - 1 \wedge d - 1 - c = k_0 \wedge \neg\, X(j) \leq y]$

    $d := j$

    $[I \wedge d - 1 - c < k_0]$ (RAS,5)

7. $[I \wedge c + 1 \leq j \leq d - 1 \wedge d - 1 - c = k_0]$

    if $X(j) \leq y$ **then** $c := j$ **else** $d := j$

    $[I \wedge d - 1 - c < k_0]$ (CD,4,6)

8. $[I \wedge d - 1 - c > 0 \wedge d - 1 - c = k_0]$

    $j := E$; **if** $X(j) \leq y$ **then** $c := j$ **else** $d := j$

    $[I \wedge d - 1 - c < k_0]$ (MSQ,2,7)

9. $[I \wedge d - 1 - c > 0 \wedge d - 1 - c = k_0]$

    newvar $j := E$ **in** (**if** $X(j) \leq y$ **then** $c := j$ **else** $d := j$)

    $[I \wedge d - 1 - c < k_0]$ (DC,8)

Finally, we must write the expression E. Here the problem is not just to meet the specification, but also to make the program efficient. For example, taking E to be $c + 1$ or $d - 1$ would be correct, but it would lead to a program taking time proportional to the size of the interval from a to b. However, if we choose E to be $(c + d) \div 2$, which is as close as possible to the midpoint of the middle interval, the program will take time proportional to the logarithm of the size of the interval to be searched. The completion of the proof is

1. $(I \wedge d - 1 - c > 0 \wedge d - 1 - c = k_0) \Rightarrow$

    $(I \wedge c + 1 \le (c + d) \div 2 \le d - 1 \wedge d - 1 - c = k_0)$

2. $[I \wedge d - 1 - c > 0 \wedge d - 1 - c = k_0]$

    $j := (c + d) \div 2$

    $[I \wedge c + 1 \le j \le d - 1 \wedge d - 1 - c = k_0]$ (RAS,1)

At first sight, it would seem that the implication in Step 1 might be difficult to prove, since the dividend $(c + d)$ might be negative. But in fact it holds as long as division by two inverts multiplication by two and satisfies the monotonicity law (3.10) in Section 3.8. To see this, note that $d - 1 - c > 0$ implies

$$2 \times (c + 1) \le c + d \le 2 \times (d - 1),$$

from which monotonicity gives

$$(2 \times (c + 1)) \div 2 \le (c + d) \div 2 \le (2 \times (d - 1)) \div 2$$

and, since the first and last divisions are exact,

$$c + 1 \le (c + d) \div 2 \le d - 1.$$

The conclusion of this proof (Step 20) is valid for the semantics of array expressions given in the previous section. However, only the corresponding partial correctness specification is valid for an implementation where evaluating array expressions gives an error stop, rather than zero, when a subscript is out of range.

To obtain total correctness when out-of-range subscripts cause error stops, one must obviously add an assertion such as

$$\forall i. \; a \le i \wedge i \le b \Rightarrow i \in \mathbf{dom}\, X$$

(using an obvious notation that will be formalized in the next section) to the precedent of the program specification (Step 20). However, there is also a more subtle problem. To avoid unnecessary subscript errors that would falsify the total correctness specification, the test $a \le c \wedge X(c) = y$ in the final conditional command must be implemented with "short circuit" evaluation. In other words, $X(c) = y$ should not be evaluated if $a \le c$ is false.

It should also be noted that the program meets the stronger specification obtained from Step 20 by deleting the regularity condition $a - 1 \le b$ from the precedent. Somewhat surprisingly, the easiest way to show this (in a proof using inequalities) is to prove the irregular case $a - 1 > b$ separately, and then use the rule DA to combine the cases.

4.4 Inference Rules for Arrays

The inference rule AS in Section 3.3 for assignment to ordinary variables,

$$\overline{\{p/v \to e\}\ v := e\ \{p\}},$$

is inadequate to deal with assignments to array elements. If we try to apply this rule to, say, $X(i) := y$, we obtain

$$\{p/X(i) \to y\}\ X(i) := y\ \{p\}.$$

However, it is unclear what it means to substitute something for the array application $X(i)$. We might reasonably infer

$$\{y = z\}\ X(i) := y\ \{X(i) = z\} \qquad \text{or} \qquad \{w = z\}\ X(i) := y\ \{w = z\},$$

but it is far from obvious what happens when, say, p is $X(j) = z$. In fact,

$$\{j = i \land y = z \lor j \ne i \land X(j) = z\}\ X(i) := y\ \{X(j) = z\}$$

is a valid specification, but it would require a substantial extension of the concept of substitution to regard the precedent of this specification as the result of the substitution $(X(j) = z)/X(i) \to y$.

A way around this difficulty was first suggested by Hoare. The basic idea is to regard an assignment such as $X(i) := y$ as an assignment to the entire array X of the function that is similar to the prior value of X, except that it maps i into y:

$$X := [X \mid i : y].$$

To formalize this idea, we first extend the syntax of array expressions to include a form that describes the single-point variation of an array value. (Strictly speaking, this should be an extension of array expressions occurring within assertions, but not within commands.) We also extend assertions to include a form which asserts that an integer belongs to the domain of an array value:

$$\langle \text{arrayexp} \rangle ::= [\, \langle \text{arrayexp} \rangle \mid \langle \text{intexp} \rangle : \langle \text{intexp} \rangle \,]$$

$$\langle \text{assert} \rangle ::= \langle \text{intexp} \rangle \in \textbf{dom}\ \langle \text{arrayexp} \rangle$$

(In the first line, the occurrence of "|" denotes a symbol of the object language, not the metasymbol that separates parts of a compound production.)

Next we give semantic equations for these constructs:

DR SEM EQ: Single-Point Array Variation

$$[\![\,a \mid e_0\colon e_1\,]\!]_{\mathrm{arrayexp}}\sigma = [\,[\![a]\!]_{\mathrm{arrayexp}}\sigma \mid [\![e_0]\!]_{\mathrm{intexp}}\sigma\colon [\![e_1]\!]_{\mathrm{intexp}}\sigma\,],$$

DR SEM EQ: Array Domain Membership

$$[\![e \in \mathbf{dom}\ a]\!]_{\mathrm{assert}}\sigma = ([\![e]\!]_{\mathrm{intexp}}\sigma \in \mathrm{dom}([\![a]\!]_{\mathrm{arrayexp}}\sigma)).$$

(Notice that the notation for single-point variation will extend the domain of the array value a if $[\![e_0]\!]_{\mathrm{intexp}}\sigma \notin \mathrm{dom}([\![a]\!]_{\mathrm{arrayexp}}\sigma)$, so that the notation can be used to denote functions whose domains are not intervals. The utility of such "lacy array values" will be illustrated in the next section.)

With these extensions of syntax and semantics, we can formulate inference rules for array assignments and declarations. Except for a total-correctness requirement prohibiting out-of-range subscripts, the assignment rules can be derived from the rule AS in Section 3.3 by regarding $w(e_0) := e_1$ as an abbreviation for $w := [\,w \mid e_0\colon e_1\,]$:

SP RULE: Partial Correctness for Array Assignment (AAP)

$$\overline{\{p/w \to [\,w \mid e_0\colon e_1\,]\}\ w(e_0) := e_1\ \{p\}},$$

SP RULE: Total Correctness for Array Assignment (AAT)

$$\overline{[\,p/w \to ([\,w \mid e_0\colon e_1\,]) \wedge e_0 \in \mathbf{dom}\ w\,]\ w(e_0) := e_1\ [\,p\,]},$$

SP RULE: Array Declaration (AD)

$$\frac{\{p \wedge \forall k.\ e_0 \le k \wedge k \le e_1 \Rightarrow k \in \mathbf{dom}\ w \wedge w(k) = e\}\ c\ \{q\}}{\{p\}\ \mathbf{newarray}\ w\ (e_0\ \mathbf{to}\ e_1) := e\ \mathbf{in}\ c\ \{q\}}$$

when w does not occur free in e_0, e_1, e, p, or q, and k is distinct from w and does not occur free in e_0, e_1, or e.

The total-correctness rule for array declarations has the same form as the partial-correctness rule. Notice that, unlike the case for simple variables, we cannot give a rule for array declarations that expresses the initialization in terms of an assignment command, since we do not have an assignment command that assigns a new value to an entire array.

These rules correctly handle the subtleties of aliasing between array variables. For example, consider the following partial-correctness proof of a program that simply copies two adjacent elements from one array to another:

1. $(X(i) = a \wedge X(i+1) = b) \Rightarrow ([Y \mid j: X(i)](j) = a \wedge X(i+1) = b)$

2. $\{[Y \mid j: X(i)](j) = a \wedge X(i+1) = b\}$
    $Y(j) := X(i)$
    $\{Y(j) = a \wedge X(i+1) = b\}$ (AAP)

3. $(Y(j) = a \wedge X(i+1) = b) \Rightarrow$
        $([Y \mid j+1: X(i+1)](j) = a \wedge [Y \mid j+1: X(i+1)](j+1) = b)$

4. $\{[Y \mid j+1: X(i+1)](j) = a \wedge [Y \mid j+1: X(i+1)](j+1) = b\}$
    $Y(j+1) := X(i+1)$
    $\{Y(j) = a \wedge Y(j+1) = b\}$ (AAP)

5. $\{X(i) = a \wedge X(i+1) = b\}$
    $Y(j) := X(i) \, ; \, Y(j+1) := X(i+1)$
    $\{Y(j) = a \wedge Y(j+1) = b\}$ (MSQ,1,2,3,4)

In the specification proved here, if we alias X and Y by substituting the same array variable, say Z, for both of them, then the resulting specification is neither valid nor provable, because the assignments $Z(j) := Z(i) \, ; \, Z(j+1) := Z(i+1)$ will set both $Z(j)$ and $Z(j+1)$ to $Z(i) = a$ when $j = i+1$. However, the aliased specification can be proved if we add the condition $j \neq i+1$ to its precedent:

1. $(Z(i) = a \wedge Z(i+1) = b \wedge j \neq i+1) \Rightarrow$
        $([Z \mid j: Z(i)](j) = a \wedge [Z \mid j: Z(i)](i+1) = b)$

2. $\{[Z \mid j: Z(i)](j) = a \wedge [Z \mid j: Z(i)](i+1) = b\}$
    $Z(j) := Z(i)$
    $\{Z(j) = a \wedge Z(i+1) = b\}$ (AAP)

3. $(Z(j) = a \wedge Z(i+1) = b) \Rightarrow$
        $([Z \mid j+1: Z(i+1)](j) = a \wedge [Z \mid j+1: Z(i+1)](j+1) = b)$

4. $\{[Z \mid j+1: Z(i+1)](j) = a \wedge [Z \mid j+1: Z(i+1)](j+1) = b\}$
    $Z(j+1) := Z(i+1)$
    $\{Z(j) = a \wedge Z(j+1) = b\}$ (AAP)

5. $\{Z(i) = a \wedge Z(i+1) = b \wedge j \neq i+1\}$
    $Z(j) := Z(i) \, ; \, Z(j+1) := Z(i+1)$
    $\{Z(j) = a \wedge Z(j+1) = b\}$ (MSQ,1,2,3,4)

Even more startling behavior can arise when an array variable reoccurs in its own subscript, as in $X(X(0))$ in the following instance of rule AAP:

$$\{[\,X\mid X(0)\!:1\,]([\,X\mid X(0)\!:1\,](0)) = 7\}\ X(X(0)) := 1\ \{X(X(0)) = 7\}.$$

Suppose $X(0) = 0$ and $X(1) = 7$. This implies

$$[\,X\mid X(0)\!:1\,]([\,X\mid X(0)\!:1\,](0)) = [\,X\mid X(0)\!:1\,](1) = X(1) = 7.$$

Thus, if we apply rule SP for strengthening precedents to this implication and the instance of AAP, we obtain the valid specification

$$\{X(0) = 0 \wedge X(1) = 7\}\ X(X(0)) := 1\ \{X(X(0)) = 7\}.$$

In other words, $X(X(0))$ is an entity that takes on the value 7 when (in certain states) it is assigned the value 1. This illustrates the danger of regarding the left side of an array assignment command as a variable.

4.5 Higher-Order Assertions About Arrays

To give concise specifications of programs that assign to arrays, it is necessary to use a much richer logic than that described in Chapter 1. Specifically, one needs a *higher-order* logic, which is a logic where variables bound by quantifiers can range over sets of integers, and over array values and other functions on sets of integers. One also needs to be able to define *predicates*, which are functions whose results are truth values.

It is beyond the scope of this book to formalize such a logic or to give proofs that use it, but we will give a few examples of predicate definitions and program specifications that illustrate its expressiveness. For the assertions in these examples, we employ a notation that is similar to the mathematical metalanguage used throughout this book.

Some useful predicates are

- The function F is monotone (i.e. in non-strict increasing order):

$$\mathrm{monotone}(F) \overset{\mathrm{def}}{=} \forall x \in \mathrm{dom}\, F.\ \forall y \in \mathrm{dom}\, F.\ x \le y \Rightarrow F(x) \le F(y).$$

- The function F is an isomorphism from the set S to the set T (or, equivalently, a bijection or a permutation):

$$\mathrm{isomorphism}(F, S, T) \overset{\mathrm{def}}{=} F \in S \to T \wedge \exists G \in T \to S.\ G \cdot F = I_S \wedge F \cdot G = I_T.$$

- The function X is a *rearrangement* of the function Y:

$$\mathrm{rearrangement}(X, Y)$$
$$\overset{\mathrm{def}}{=} \exists F \in \mathrm{dom}\, X \to \mathrm{dom}\, Y.$$
$$\mathrm{isomorphism}(F, \mathrm{dom}\, X, \mathrm{dom}\, Y) \wedge X = Y \cdot F.$$

- The function X is a *realignment* of the function Y, which is a rearrangement where the order of occurrence of values is preserved:

  realignment(X, Y)

  $\stackrel{\text{def}}{=} \exists F \in \text{dom}\, X \to \text{dom}\, Y.$

  isomorphism$(F, \text{dom}\, X, \text{dom}\, Y) \wedge$ monotone$(F) \wedge X = Y \cdot F.$

Using these predicates, we can give specifications such as the following:

- An in-place sorting program that rearranges an array with subscripts from a to b so that the array is in nonstrict increasing order:

  $[a \text{ to } b = \text{dom}\, X \wedge X = X_0]$

  $\ldots$

  $[\text{monotone}(X) \wedge \text{rearrangement}(X, X_0)].$

Note the use of a ghost array variable to relate array values in the initial and final states.

- An in-place program that accepts an array with subscripts from a to b, filters out elements with negative values, and leaves the final array value in a left subsegment of the original array, with c set to the new upper limit of the subscripts:

  $[a \text{ to } b = \text{dom}\, X \wedge X = X_0]$

  $\ldots$

  $[\text{realignment}(X{\rceil}(a \text{ to } c), X_0{\rceil}\{\, i \mid i \in \text{dom}\, X_0 \wedge X_0(i) \geq 0 \,\})].$

Here the restricted function $X_0{\rceil}\{\, i \mid i \in \text{dom}\, X_0 \wedge X_0(i) \geq 0 \,\}$ is a "lacy array value", which is a function whose domain is a finite set of integers but not necessarily an interval.

- An in-place program for sorting on keys that gives a "stable" rearrangement, which is one where items with the same key retain the same order of occurrence. Here the elements of the array X range over some set of "items", rather than integers, and K is the function mapping items into their keys, which are integers:

  $[a \text{ to } b = \text{dom}\, X \wedge X = X_0]$

  $\ldots$

  $[\text{monotone}(K \cdot X) \wedge$

  $\quad \forall k \in \mathbf{Z}. \text{realignment}(X{\rceil}\{\, i \mid K(X(i)) = k \,\}, X_0{\rceil}\{\, i \mid K(X_0(i)) = k \,\})].$

Bibliographic Notes

The inference rule for array assignment was originally introduced by Hoare and Wirth [1973] in their axiomatic definition of Pascal. An alternative rule, based on substitution for array applications, was devised by Gries and Levin [1980] and is also described in Gries [1981, Chapter 9]. Examples of specifications and (mostly semiformal) proofs concerning arrays, including the concepts described in Section 4.5, are given in Reynolds [1981a, Chapter 2].

Exercises

4.1   Fill in the missing precedents indicated by question marks to make the following total-correctness specifications true. The assertions you provide should be as weak as possible, but they should not be unnecessarily complicated. In particular, notation such as $[\mathsf{X} \mid \mathsf{i}\colon \mathsf{a}]$ for the variation of a function at an argument should be avoided.

$$[\,?\,]\,\mathsf{X}(\mathsf{i}) := \mathsf{a}\,;\mathsf{X}(\mathsf{j}) := \mathsf{b}\,[\,\mathsf{X}(\mathsf{i}) = \mathsf{a} \wedge \mathsf{X}(\mathsf{j}) = \mathsf{b}\,]$$
$$[\,?\,]\,\mathsf{X}(\mathsf{X}(\mathsf{i}) + \mathsf{X}(\mathsf{j})) := 7\,[\,\mathsf{X}(\mathsf{X}(\mathsf{i}) + \mathsf{X}(\mathsf{j})) = 7\,].$$

4.2   Give an alternative semantics for array operations where evaluating the application of an array to an out-of-range subscript gives the value to which the array was initialized by its declaration.

4.3   For each of the following total-correctness specifications, complete the program "skeletons" in such a way that the programs meet their specifications and use the indicated invariants.

Then give a formal proof of the specifications that uses the inference rules given in this and the preceding chapter. (You need not include formal proofs of the assertions that occur as steps in the proof, but all of them should be valid. To save writing, you may define metavariables to stand for assertions that occur repeatedly.)

(a) Finding the Minimum of an Array

$$[\mathsf{b} \leq \mathsf{c}]$$
newvar $\mathsf{k} :=$ "initial value of k" **in**
  ("Achieve invariant I_0" ;
   while $\mathsf{k} < \mathsf{c}$ **do** "Preserve invariant I_0 while increasing k")
$$[\mathsf{b} \leq \mathsf{i} \leq \mathsf{c} \wedge \forall \mathsf{j}.\ \mathsf{b} \leq \mathsf{j} \leq \mathsf{c} \Rightarrow \mathsf{X}(\mathsf{i}) \leq \mathsf{X}(\mathsf{j})],$$

  where

$$I_0 \overset{\mathrm{def}}{=} \mathsf{b} \leq \mathsf{i} \leq \mathsf{k} \leq \mathsf{c} \wedge \forall \mathsf{j}.\ \mathsf{b} \leq \mathsf{j} \leq \mathsf{k} \Rightarrow \mathsf{X}(\mathsf{i}) \leq \mathsf{X}(\mathsf{j}).$$

This program should not assign to b, c, or the array X.

(b) Exchanging Array Elements

$$[b \in \text{dom}\,X \wedge i \in \text{dom}\,X \wedge p/X \rightarrow [\,X \mid b{:}X(i) \mid i{:}X(b)\,]\,]$$

"Exchange $X(b)$ and $X(i)$"

$$[p].$$

This program should not assign to b or i. The metavariable p denotes an arbitrary assertion.

Hint You may assume that any local variables declared in your program do not occur in the assertion p, since otherwise, without changing its meaning, your program could be renamed so that its local variables do not occur in p.

(c) Sorting by Finding Minima

$$[\forall j.\ a \leq j \leq c \Rightarrow j \in \text{dom}\,X]$$

newvar b := a **in while** b $\leq$ c **do**

$\quad$ (**newvar** i := 0 **in**

$\qquad$ ("Set i to minimum element of X over b **to** c" ;

$\qquad$ "Exchange $X(b)$ and $X(i)$") ;

$\qquad$ "Preserve invariant I_1 while increasing b")

$$[\forall j.\ \forall k.\ a \leq j \leq k \leq c \Rightarrow X(j) \leq X(k)],$$

where

$$I_1 \overset{\text{def}}{=} \forall j.\ \forall k.\ a \leq j \leq b - 1 \wedge j \leq k \leq c \Rightarrow X(j) \leq X(k).$$

This program should not assign to a or c.

(d) Sorting by Finding Minima (continued)

$$[\forall j.\ a \leq j \leq c \Rightarrow j \in \text{dom}\,X \wedge X = X_0]$$

newvar b := a **in while** b $\leq$ c **do**

$\quad$ (**newvar** i := 0 **in**

$\qquad$ ("Set i to minimum element of X over b **to** c" ;

$\qquad$ "Exchange $X(b)$ and $X(i)$") ;

$\qquad$ "Preserve invariant I_1 while increasing b")

$$[\text{rearrangement}(X, X_0)].$$

Here the program should be the same as in the previous part. The predicate "rearrangement" is defined in Section 4.5. It is an equivalence relation that satisfies

$$i \in \text{dom}\,X \wedge j \in \text{dom}\,X \Rightarrow \text{rearrangement}([\,X \mid i{:}X(j) \mid j{:}X(i)\,], X).$$

5

Failure, Input-Output, and Continuations

In this chapter, we will go beyond the simple imperative language to consider a **fail** command and operations for output and input. These extensions will require significant changes to the semantic framework developed in previous chapters. First we will develop a generalization of the "direct" denotational semantics used in Chapter 2; then we will introduce an alternative approach called continuation semantics.

In investigating these topics, we will encounter a richer variety of domains than in previous chapters. In particular, to describe computations whose input and output can go on forever, we will use recursively defined domains.

5.1 The fail Command

Suppose we wish to augment the simple imperative language with a command **fail** that causes a program to cease execution. The abstract syntax is obvious:

$$\langle\text{comm}\rangle ::= \textbf{fail}$$

but the semantics raises a serious problem: How do we insure that, regardless of the context in which it is embedded, if the **fail** command is executed, it determines the final result of the program?

Consider, for example, the composition $c_0 ; c_1$, and ignore for the moment the possibility of nontermination, so that the semantic equation is simply

$$[\![c_0 ; c_1]\!]_{\text{comm}}\sigma = [\![c_1]\!]_{\text{comm}}([\![c_0]\!]_{\text{comm}}\sigma).$$

If the command c_0 fails, then the composition $c_0 ; c_1$ also fails, regardless of c_1. However, if $[\![c_1]\!]_{\text{comm}}$ can be any function from Σ to Σ, there is no value we can give to $[\![c_0]\!]_{\text{comm}}\sigma$ that is guaranteed to be the value of $[\![c_1]\!]_{\text{comm}}([\![c_0]\!]_{\text{comm}}\sigma)$, because, if $[\![c_1]\!]_{\text{comm}}$ is a constant function, its result will be unaffected by $[\![c_0]\!]_{\text{comm}}\sigma$.

Actually, even nontermination raises this problem, since, if c_0 runs forever, then so must $c_0 ; c_1$, regardless of c_1. In Chapter 2 we solved this problem by taking the domain of command meanings to be $\Sigma \to \Sigma_\perp$ and using the semantic equation

$$[\![c_0 \,;\, c_1]\!]_{\text{comm}} \sigma = ([\![c_1]\!]_{\text{comm}})_{\perp\!\perp}([\![c_0]\!]_{\text{comm}} \sigma),$$

where the subscript $\perp\!\perp$ indicates the extension of a function $f \in \Sigma \to \Sigma_\perp$ to $f_{\perp\!\perp} \in \Sigma_\perp \to \Sigma_\perp$ such that

$$f_{\perp\!\perp} \perp = \perp$$

$$f_{\perp\!\perp} \sigma = f\sigma,$$

which guarantees that $([\![c_1]\!]_{\text{comm}})_{\perp\!\perp}$ will preserve $\perp$, regardless of c_1.

A similar approach can be used for failure. We take $[\![c]\!]_{\text{comm}} \sigma$ to be $\perp$ if c does not terminate, the state σ' if c terminates normally (without failure) in the state σ', and the pair $\langle \mathbf{abort}, \sigma' \rangle$ if c terminates by executing $\mathbf{fail}$ in the state σ'. Thus the meaning of commands satisfies

$$[\![-]\!]_{\text{comm}} \in \langle \text{comm} \rangle \to \Sigma \to \hat{\Sigma}_\perp,$$

where $\hat{\Sigma}_\perp = (\hat{\Sigma})_\perp$ and

$$\hat{\Sigma} = \Sigma \cup \{\, \langle \mathbf{abort}, \sigma \rangle \mid \sigma \in \Sigma \,\} = \Sigma \cup \{\mathbf{abort}\} \times \Sigma.$$

(More abstractly, $\hat{\Sigma}$ must be the union of two disjoint sets that are each isomorphic to Σ. A more canonical choice might be $\hat{\Sigma} = \{\mathbf{finish}, \mathbf{abort}\} \times \Sigma$ or $\hat{\Sigma} = \Sigma + \Sigma$, where $+$ is the disjoint union operator described in Sections A.3 and A.5 of the Appendix. But by making Σ a subset of $\hat{\Sigma}$, we avoid having to change the semantic equations we have already given for assignment commands and $\mathbf{skip}$.)

Then the semantics of $\mathbf{fail}$ is given by

DR SEM EQ: **fail**

$$[\![\mathbf{fail}]\!]_{\text{comm}} \sigma = \langle \mathbf{abort}, \sigma \rangle,$$

while the semantic equation for composition becomes

DR SEM EQ: Sequential Composition

$$[\![c_0 \,;\, c_1]\!]_{\text{comm}} \sigma = ([\![c_1]\!]_{\text{comm}})_*([\![c_0]\!]_{\text{comm}} \sigma),$$

where $*$ indicates the extension of a function $f \in \Sigma \to \hat{\Sigma}_\perp$ to $f_* \in \hat{\Sigma}_\perp \to \hat{\Sigma}_\perp$ such that

$$f_* \perp = \perp$$

$$f_* \sigma = f\sigma$$

$$f_* \langle \mathbf{abort}, \sigma \rangle = \langle \mathbf{abort}, \sigma \rangle.$$

This definition guarantees that $(\llbracket c_1 \rrbracket_{\text{comm}})_*$ preserves both $\bot$ and the results $\langle \textbf{abort}, \sigma \rangle$ of **fail** commands.

A similar generalization from $\bot\!\bot$ to $*$ occurs in the semantic equations for **while** commands:

DR SEM EQ: **while**

$$\llbracket \textbf{while } b \textbf{ do } c \rrbracket_{\text{comm}} = \mathbf{Y}_{\Sigma \to \hat{\Sigma}_\bot} F$$
$$\text{where } F(f)\sigma = \textbf{if } \llbracket b \rrbracket_{\text{boolexp}}\sigma \textbf{ then } f_*(\llbracket c \rrbracket_{\text{comm}}\sigma) \textbf{ else } \sigma.$$

The remaining semantic equations in Section 2.2 are unchanged, except for the equation for variable declarations, where one might expect

$$\llbracket \textbf{newvar } v := e \textbf{ in } c \rrbracket_{\text{comm}}\sigma$$
$$= (\lambda \sigma' \in \Sigma. \, [\, \sigma' \mid v \colon \sigma v \,])_*(\llbracket c \rrbracket_{\text{comm}}[\, \sigma \mid v \colon \llbracket e \rrbracket_{\text{intexp}}\sigma \,]). \tag{5.1}$$

Here, however, there is a serious problem. For example, we would have

$$\llbracket \mathsf{x} := 0 \, ; \textbf{newvar } \mathsf{x} := 1 \textbf{ in fail} \rrbracket_{\text{comm}}\sigma = \langle \textbf{abort}, [\, \sigma \mid \mathsf{x} \colon 1 \,] \rangle$$

and

$$\llbracket \mathsf{x} := 0 \, ; \textbf{newvar } \mathsf{y} := 1 \textbf{ in fail} \rrbracket_{\text{comm}}\sigma = \langle \textbf{abort}, [\, \sigma \mid \mathsf{x} \colon 0 \mid \mathsf{y} \colon 1 \,] \rangle,$$

but the commands in these equations can be obtained from one another by re-naming, so that they should have the same meaning.

To avoid this problem, the result of executing a command that fails must be a state that records the values of the free variables of that command, rather than of the local variables that are active when a **fail** instruction is executed. For this reason, when a **fail** command is executed, each variable in the local state that is bound by a declaration whose scope encloses the **fail** must revert to the value it had before the declaration took effect.

Thus variable declarations must reset final states that arise from failure as well as from normal termination. To indicate this, we change the kind of function extension used in the semantic equation for variable declarations:

DR SEM EQ: Variable Declaration

$$\llbracket \textbf{newvar } v := e \textbf{ in } c \rrbracket_{\text{comm}}\sigma$$
$$= (\lambda \sigma' \in \Sigma. \, [\, \sigma' \mid v \colon \sigma v \,])_\dagger(\llbracket c \rrbracket_{\text{comm}}[\, \sigma \mid v \colon \llbracket e \rrbracket_{\text{intexp}}\sigma \,]). \tag{5.2}$$

Here, if $f \in \Sigma \to \Sigma$, then $f_\dagger \in \hat{\Sigma}_\bot \to \hat{\Sigma}_\bot$ is the extension such that

$$f_\dagger \bot = \bot$$
$$f_\dagger \sigma = f\sigma$$
$$f_\dagger \langle \textbf{abort}, \sigma \rangle = \langle \textbf{abort}, f\sigma \rangle.$$

We must also extend the meaning of specifications to accommodate the introduction of **fail**. The simplest approach is to treat failure in the same way as nontermination, so that it is permitted by partial correctness but prohibited by total correctness. More precisely, the semantic equations at the beginning of Section 3.1 become

DR SEM EQ: Partial Correctness Specification

$$[\![\{p\}\ c\ \{q\}]\!]_{\text{spec}} = \forall \sigma \in \Sigma.\ [\![p]\!]_{\text{assert}}\sigma \Rightarrow$$
$$([\![c]\!]_{\text{comm}}\sigma = \bot \text{ or } [\![c]\!]_{\text{comm}}\sigma \in \{\textbf{abort}\} \times \Sigma \text{ or } [\![q]\!]_{\text{assert}}([\![c]\!]_{\text{comm}}\sigma)),$$

DR SEM EQ: Total Correctness Specification

$$[\![\,[p]\ c\ [q]\,]\!]_{\text{spec}} = \forall \sigma \in \Sigma.\ [\![p]\!]_{\text{assert}}\sigma \Rightarrow$$
$$([\![c]\!]_{\text{comm}}\sigma \neq \bot \text{ and } [\![c]\!]_{\text{comm}}\sigma \notin \{\textbf{abort}\} \times \Sigma \text{ and } [\![q]\!]_{\text{assert}}([\![c]\!]_{\text{comm}}\sigma)).$$

From these equations, it is easy to see the soundness of the following inference rules for specifications:

SP RULE: Partial Correctness of **fail** (FLP)

$$\{\textbf{true}\}\ \textbf{fail}\ \{\textbf{false}\},$$

SP RULE: Total Correctness of **fail** (FLT)

$$[\,\textbf{false}\,]\ \textbf{fail}\ [\,\textbf{false}\,].$$

In conclusion, we note that the addition of the **fail** command, although it might naïvely seem to be a minor language extension, is in fact a serious change in the imperative language. A symptom of its seriousness is that it cannot be described by merely adding another semantic equation; instead, we had to change the underlying domain containing the range of the semantic function, from $\Sigma \to \Sigma_\bot$ to $\Sigma \to \hat{\Sigma}_\bot$. (Analogously, when we consider the operational semantics of **fail** in Section 6.3, we will have to change the set of terminal configurations.)

When a language extension requires such a global change to the underlying semantic framework, one should suspect that it may have surprising interactions with the rest of the language, changing properties that might naïvely seem to be unrelated to the extension. In fact, this is the case at present: The language described in previous chapters satisfies, for example, the law that

$$c\,;\textbf{while true do skip} \quad \text{and} \quad \textbf{while true do skip}$$

have the same meaning for any command c. But when **fail** is added to the language, this seemingly unrelated equivalence law ceases to be valid.

In the following sections, we will consider extensions to intermediate output and input that also require changes to the underlying semantic framework.

5.2 Intermediate Output and a Domain of Sequences

We next consider extending the simple imperative language with a command

$$\langle comm \rangle ::= \ ! \ \langle intexp \rangle$$

that causes output of the value of its operand without terminating program execution. (We will give ! the same precedence as the operator := for assignment.) At the outset, it should be emphasized that this is a major change in our view of how programs can behave. Until now, we have assumed that all programs that fail to terminate (for some particular initial state) have indistinguishable behavior (for that initial state). But now such programs can produce output, which in the most interesting case can be endless. Thus we are moving closer to a situation that characterizes a large part of real-world computer applications, where the most interesting and useful programs never terminate. (We assume that output cannot be revoked, that is, it becomes available to a user who can be confident that it will not be rescinded by anything like a "rewind" operation.)

Specifically, once intermediate output is introduced, there are three possibilities for program execution:

(a) The program may output a finite sequence of integers and then run on forever without further output.
(b) The program may output a finite sequence of integers and then terminate (normally or abortively) in a final state.
(c) The program may output an endless sequence of integers.

In each of these cases, the total output of the computation can be described by a sequence:

(a) a finite sequence of integers,
(b) a finite sequence where the last element is a state (or other member of $\hat{\Sigma}$) and the preceding elements are integers,
(c) an infinite sequence of integers.

Thus we define the *output* domain Ω to consist of these three kinds of sequences. But now we encounter a surprise: Not only can the members of Ω be used to describe the total output of a computation at "infinite" time, but they also can be used to describe the accumulated output at some finite time (perhaps before the computation terminates). This suggests how Ω should be ordered: $\omega \sqsubseteq \omega'$ should hold just when ω and ω' could be outputs of the same computation at earlier and later (or equal) times. In other words, $\omega \sqsubseteq \omega'$ if and only if ω is an initial subsequence of ω' (which includes the possibility that $\omega = \omega'$).

Now consider a sequence of domain members that give "snapshots" of the accumulated output of a computation at increasing (but finite) times. For the cases listed above, we would have:

(a) An uninteresting chain whose elements are finite sequences of integers. For example:

$$\langle\rangle \sqsubseteq \langle 3, 1\rangle \sqsubseteq \langle 3, 1, 4\rangle \sqsubseteq \langle 3, 1, 4\rangle \sqsubseteq \langle 3, 1, 4\rangle \sqsubseteq \cdots .$$

(b) An uninteresting chain whose elements are finite sequences of integers, except for the final element, which is a finite sequence where the last distinct element is a state (or other member of $\hat{\Sigma}$) and the preceding elements are integers. For example:

$$\langle\rangle \sqsubseteq \langle 3, 1\rangle \sqsubseteq \langle 3, 1, 4\rangle \sqsubseteq \langle 3, 1, 4, \sigma\rangle \sqsubseteq \langle 3, 1, 4, \sigma\rangle \sqsubseteq \cdots .$$

(c) An interesting chain whose elements are finite sequences of integers. For example:

$$\langle\rangle \sqsubseteq \langle 3, 1\rangle \sqsubseteq \langle 3, 1, 4\rangle \sqsubseteq \langle 3, 1, 4, 1, 5\rangle \sqsubseteq \langle 3, 1, 4, 1, 5\rangle \sqsubseteq \langle 3, 1, 4, 1, 5, 9\rangle \sqsubseteq \cdots .$$

In the first two cases, the limit of the chain is its last distinct element. In the third case, the limit is the infinite sequence of integers whose ith component is the ith component of every element of the infinite sequence that has at least i components:

$$\langle 3, 1, 4, 1, 5, 9, \ldots \rangle.$$

In all cases, however, the limit of the chain of snapshots is the domain element that describes the total output of the computation. (Of course, one can delete or replicate elements in any of these chains to obtain a differently paced "movie" of the same computation.)

It is worthwhile to spell out in more detail the argument about the limit in the third case. If ω and ω' are distinct members of Ω such that $\omega \sqsubseteq \omega'$, then ω is a finite sequence of integers, ω' is a longer sequence, and, whenever ω has an ith component, ω' has the same ith component. Thus the distinct members of the interesting chain must have ever-increasing length and any upper bound of the entire chain must be infinite. Moreover, the ith component of an upper bound must be the ith component of the infinitely many chain elements that have ith components. Thus the upper bound of an interesting chain of finite sequences of integers is uniquely determined, and therefore must be the least upper bound.

Finally, we note that, whenever a chain element is not a finite sequence of integers, there is no distinct member of Ω that extends it, so that the chain must be uninteresting. Thus every interesting chain is an instance of our third case and has a least upper bound, so that Ω is indeed a domain. (The least element $\bot$ is the empty sequence, which represents the result of a computation that runs on forever without any output.)

We can now give a denotational semantics for our extended language where the meaning of a command maps an initial state into a sequence in Ω that describes the output behavior and possible final termination of the resulting execution:

$$\llbracket - \rrbracket_{\text{comm}} \in \langle \text{comm} \rangle \to \Sigma \to \Omega.$$

The semantic equations for assignment commands, **skip**, and **fail** are the same as before, except that the final state (or **abort**-state pair) must be injected into a single-element sequence:

DR SEM EQ: Assignment

$$\llbracket v := e \rrbracket_{\text{comm}} \sigma = \langle [\, \sigma \mid v : \llbracket e \rrbracket_{\text{intexp}} \sigma \,] \rangle,$$

DR SEM EQ: **skip**

$$\llbracket \text{skip} \rrbracket_{\text{comm}} \sigma = \langle \sigma \rangle,$$

DR SEM EQ: **fail**

$$\llbracket \text{fail} \rrbracket_{\text{comm}} \sigma = \langle \langle \text{abort}, \sigma \rangle \rangle.$$

On the other hand, an output command gives an integer followed by the initial state (since this state is not altered by the command):

DR SEM EQ: Output

$$\llbracket !\, e \rrbracket_{\text{comm}} \sigma = \langle \llbracket e \rrbracket_{\text{intexp}} \sigma, \sigma \rangle.$$

When we come to the sequential composition $c_0 ; c_1$ of commands, the situation is more complicated. If the execution of c_0, starting in some initial state, runs on forever (with either finite or infinite output) or results in an abortion, then the execution of $c_0 ; c_1$ will behave similarly. But if the execution of c_0 outputs the integers $n_0, \ldots, n_{k-1}$ and terminates normally in state σ', then the result of executing $c_0 ; c_1$ is obtained by prefixing $n_0, \ldots, n_{k-1}$ to the result of executing c_1 in the state σ'. This can still be described by the semantic equation

DR SEM EQ: Sequential Composition

$$\llbracket c_0 ; c_1 \rrbracket_{\text{comm}} \sigma = (\llbracket c_1 \rrbracket_{\text{comm}})_* (\llbracket c_0 \rrbracket_{\text{comm}} \sigma).$$

But now the asterisk describes the extension from $f \in \Sigma \to \Omega$ to $f_* \in \Omega \to \Omega$ such that

$$f_* \langle n_0, \ldots, n_{k-1} \rangle = \langle n_0, \ldots, n_{k-1} \rangle$$

$$f_* \langle n_0, \ldots, n_{k-1}, \sigma \rangle = \langle n_0, \ldots, n_{k-1} \rangle \circ (f\sigma)$$

$$f_* \langle n_0, \ldots, n_{k-1}, \langle \text{abort}, \sigma \rangle \rangle = \langle n_0, \ldots, n_{k-1}, \langle \text{abort}, \sigma \rangle \rangle$$

$$f_* \langle n_0, n_1, \ldots \rangle = \langle n_0, n_1, \ldots \rangle,$$

(5.3)

where $\circ$ denotes the concatenation of sequences.

The semantic equation

DR SEM EQ: Variable Declaration

$$[\![\textbf{newvar } v := e \textbf{ in } c]\!]_{\text{comm}}\sigma$$
$$= (\lambda\sigma' \in \Sigma. \, [\sigma' \mid v{:}\,\sigma v])_\dagger([\![c]\!]_{\text{comm}}[\sigma \mid v{:}\, [\![e]\!]_{\text{intexp}}\sigma])$$

requires a similar treatment. Here $\dagger$ describes the extension of $f \in \Sigma \to \Sigma$ to $f_\dagger \in \Omega \to \Omega$ such that

$$f_\dagger\langle n_0, \ldots, n_{k-1}\rangle = \langle n_0, \ldots, n_{k-1}\rangle$$
$$f_\dagger\langle n_0, \ldots, n_{k-1}, \sigma\rangle = \langle n_0, \ldots, n_{k-1}, f\sigma\rangle$$
$$f_\dagger\langle n_0, \ldots, n_{k-1}, \langle\textbf{abort}, \sigma\rangle\rangle = \langle n_0, \ldots, n_{k-1}, \langle\textbf{abort}, f\sigma\rangle\rangle \tag{5.4}$$
$$f_\dagger\langle n_0, n_1, \ldots\rangle = \langle n_0, n_1, \ldots\rangle.$$

The remaining semantic equations are straightforward: The equation for conditionals remains unchanged from the previous section, but the equation for **while** commands is changed slightly to inject the final state into a single-element sequence:

DR SEM EQ: **while**

$$[\![\textbf{while } b \textbf{ do } c]\!]_{\text{comm}} = \mathbf{Y}_{\Sigma \to \Omega}\, F$$
$$\text{where } F(f)\sigma = \textbf{if } [\![b]\!]_{\text{boolexp}}\sigma \textbf{ then } f_*([\![c]\!]_{\text{comm}}\sigma) \textbf{ else } \langle\sigma\rangle.$$

In devising the denotational semantics in this section, our task has been eased by the concrete nature of the domain Ω as a partially ordered set of sequences. Unfortunately, when we consider input in Section 5.6, the domain Ω will become a much more abstract object that is defined by a recursive isomorphism. To prepare for this development, it is useful to rewrite our semantic equations and the relevant function extensions in terms of certain injections into Ω.

From Equations (5.3), it is easy to show that f_* is continuous and satisfies the following equations:

$$f_*\langle\rangle = \langle\rangle$$
$$f_*\langle\sigma\rangle = f\sigma$$
$$f_*\langle\langle\textbf{abort}, \sigma\rangle\rangle = \langle\langle\textbf{abort}, \sigma\rangle\rangle \tag{5.5}$$
$$f_*(\langle n\rangle \circ \omega) = \langle n\rangle \circ f_*\omega.$$

If we introduce the following functions into Ω, which have disjoint ranges and are each injective:

$$\iota_\perp \in \{\langle\rangle\} \to \Omega \quad \text{such that} \quad \iota_\perp() = \langle\rangle = \perp_\Omega$$

$$\iota_{\text{term}} \in \Sigma \to \Omega \quad \text{such that} \quad \iota_{\text{term}}(\sigma) = \langle\sigma\rangle$$

$$\iota_{\text{abort}} \in \Sigma \to \Omega \quad \text{such that} \quad \iota_{\text{abort}}(\sigma) = \langle\langle\textbf{abort}, \sigma\rangle\rangle \tag{5.6}$$

$$\iota_{\text{out}} \in \mathbf{Z} \times \Omega \to \Omega \quad \text{such that} \quad \iota_{\text{out}}(n, \omega) = \langle n\rangle \circ \omega,$$

then we can rewrite Equations (5.5) as

$$f_*\perp = \perp$$

$$f_*(\iota_{\text{term}}\sigma) = f\sigma$$

$$f_*(\iota_{\text{abort}}\sigma) = \iota_{\text{abort}}\sigma \tag{5.7}$$

$$f_*(\iota_{\text{out}}(n, \omega)) = \iota_{\text{out}}(n, f_*\omega).$$

In fact, f_* is the unique continuous solution of these equations. Despite the fact that Ω is not a very syntactic entity, this can be shown by an extension of the arguments about abstract syntax and semantic equations in Sections 1.1 and 1.2. Since the functions defined by Equations (5.6) are injective and have disjoint ranges, and the sequences that can be obtained by applying these functions a finite number of times are exactly the finite sequences in Ω, we can regard these functions as the constructors of an abstract syntax whose phrases are the finite sequences in Ω (where Σ and $\mathbf{Z}$ are predefined sets). With respect to these constructors, Equations (5.7) are syntax-directed, so that they have a unique solution over the finite sequences in Ω. (In (5.7) we have simplified the first equation by writing $\perp$ instead of the equivalent $\iota_\perp()$.)

By itself, this argument does not extend to the infinite sequences in Ω, which cannot be obtained by applying the constructors any finite number of times. However, since every infinite sequence in Ω is a limit of finite sequences, requiring the solution to be continuous extends its uniqueness to the entirety of Ω. (The domain Ω is an example of an initial *continuous* algebra, for which the above constructors are the operations and f_* is a homomorphism.)

In a similar manner, the function $f_\dagger$ defined by Equations (5.4) satisfies

$$f_\dagger\langle\rangle = \langle\rangle$$

$$f_\dagger\langle\sigma\rangle = \langle f\sigma\rangle$$

$$f_\dagger\langle\langle\textbf{abort}, \sigma\rangle\rangle = \langle\langle\textbf{abort}, f\sigma\rangle\rangle \tag{5.8}$$

$$f_\dagger(\langle n\rangle \circ \omega) = \langle n\rangle \circ f_\dagger\omega$$

or, in terms of the injections in Equations (5.6),

$$f_\dagger \bot = \bot$$
$$f_\dagger(\iota_{\text{term}}\sigma) = \iota_{\text{term}}(f\sigma)$$
$$f_\dagger(\iota_{\text{abort}}\sigma) = \iota_{\text{abort}}(f\sigma) \tag{5.9}$$
$$f_\dagger(\iota_{\text{out}}(n,\omega)) = \iota_{\text{out}}(n, f_\dagger\omega).$$

By a similar argument, $f_\dagger$ can be shown to be the unique continuous solution of these equations.

Finally, we rewrite the semantic equations themselves in terms of the injections into Ω, rather than operations on sequences:

DR SEM EQ: Assignment

$$[\![v := e]\!]_{\text{comm}}\sigma = \iota_{\text{term}}[\,\sigma \mid v{:}\, [\![e]\!]_{\text{intexp}}\sigma\,],$$

DR SEM EQ: **skip**

$$[\![\mathbf{skip}]\!]_{\text{comm}}\sigma = \iota_{\text{term}}\sigma,$$

DR SEM EQ: **fail**

$$[\![\mathbf{fail}]\!]_{\text{comm}}\sigma = \iota_{\text{abort}}\sigma,$$

DR SEM EQ: Output

$$[\![!\, e]\!]_{\text{comm}}\sigma = \iota_{\text{out}}([\![e]\!]_{\text{intexp}}\sigma, \iota_{\text{term}}\sigma),$$

DR SEM EQ: Sequential Composition

$$[\![c_0\,;\,c_1]\!]_{\text{comm}}\sigma = ([\![c_1]\!]_{\text{comm}})_*([\![c_0]\!]_{\text{comm}}\sigma),$$

DR SEM EQ: Variable Declaration

$$[\![\mathbf{newvar}\ v := e\ \mathbf{in}\ c]\!]_{\text{comm}}\sigma$$
$$= (\lambda\sigma' \in \Sigma.\ [\,\sigma' \mid v{:}\,\sigma v\,])_\dagger([\![c]\!]_{\text{comm}}[\,\sigma \mid v{:}\,[\![e]\!]_{\text{intexp}}\sigma\,]),$$

DR SEM EQ: Conditional

$$[\![\mathbf{if}\ b\ \mathbf{then}\ c_0\ \mathbf{else}\ c_1]\!]_{\text{comm}}\sigma = \mathbf{if}\ [\![b]\!]_{\text{boolexp}}\sigma\ \mathbf{then}\ [\![c_0]\!]_{\text{comm}}\sigma\ \mathbf{else}\ [\![c_1]\!]_{\text{comm}}\sigma,$$

DR SEM EQ: **while**

$$[\![\mathbf{while}\ b\ \mathbf{do}\ c]\!]_{\text{comm}} = \mathbf{Y}_{\Sigma\to\Omega}\ F$$
$$\text{where } F(f)\sigma = \mathbf{if}\ [\![b]\!]_{\text{boolexp}}\sigma\ \mathbf{then}\ f_*([\![c]\!]_{\text{comm}}\sigma)\ \mathbf{else}\ \iota_{\text{term}}\sigma.$$

Here f_* and $f_\dagger$ are the unique solutions of Equations (5.7) and (5.9).

In conclusion, some general remarks about output domains are appropriate. Although domains such as Ω are needed to describe the output of physical processes, others are needed to describe the meanings of such output from the viewpoint of a user. For example, a common use of computations that can generate endless sequences of integers is the enumeration of sets of integers. Here the user is not interested in the order or the number of times each integer occurs in the physical output sequence s, but only in the set μs, where μ maps each $s \in \Omega$ into the set of integers that occur in s. The sense of increasing information is given by the inclusion relation, so that the relevant domain is $\mathcal{P}\,\mathbf{Z}$. It is easily seen that μ is a continuous function from Ω to $\mathcal{P}\,\mathbf{Z}$.

These domains also provide illustrations of the notions of safety and liveness properties. A property defined over the elements of a domain is called a

- *safety property* if, whenever it holds for x, it holds for all $x' \sqsubseteq x$, and, whenever it holds for a chain, it holds for the limit of the chain,
- *liveness property* if, whenever it holds for x, it holds for all $x' \sqsupseteq x$.

Intuitively, a safety property insures that certain events will not occur, while a liveness property insures that certain events will occur.

For example, consider a computation in our language with intermediate output (starting from some fixed initial state). A typical safety property over Ω is that only primes are output, that is, every integer occurring in the output s is prime. A typical liveness property is that every prime is output, that is, every prime occurs in s. Equally well, one can define analogous properties over $\mathcal{P}\,\mathbf{Z}$ and apply them to μs: the safety property of a set that every member is prime, or the liveness property that every prime is a member.

As remarked in Section 3.1, the partial and total correctness specifications defined by Equations (3.1) and (3.2) are safety and liveness properties, respectively, of the meaning of the commands being specified.

5.3 The Physical Argument for Continuity

The domain Ω of sequences introduced in the previous section is rich enough to illustrate clearly what we mean by an ordering of "increasing information": $s \sqsubseteq s'$ holds when observing the output s at some time during the computation is compatible with observing the output s' later (or with s' being the total output of the computation). Chains are "movies" of possible computations, that is, time-ordered sequences of snapshots of the output. When such a chain is interesting, it depicts a computation with endless output and provides enough information to determine the output completely.

This domain can be used to illustrate the basic argument as to why only continuous functions are physically realizable. Imagine an observer (either human or mechanical) whose input is the output of a computation of the kind we have just described, and whose own output is of a similar kind. This observer might be given tasks such as the following:

- Output one if you receive an infinite sequence of integers, or zero otherwise.
- Output one if you never receive the integer 37, or zero otherwise.
- Output one if you receive the digit expansion of a rational number, or zero otherwise.

In each case, as long as the input consists of, say, single-digit integers, there is never anything that the observer can safely output. Thus the above tasks, each of which describes the computation of a noncontinuous function, are impossible.

The general argument (for a domain like Ω) is the following: Suppose that the task is to evaluate some function f and, for a particular execution, $x_0 \sqsubseteq x_1 \sqsubseteq \cdots$ is a sequence of snapshots of the input at increasing times and $y_0 \sqsubseteq y_1 \sqsubseteq \cdots$ is a sequence of snapshots of the output at the same times. Then the ultimate input and output are

$$x = \bigsqcup_{n=0}^{\infty} x_n \qquad \text{and} \qquad y = \bigsqcup_{n=0}^{\infty} y_n,$$

and the function f must satisfy $f(x) = y$.

To see that f is monotonic, suppose $x \sqsubseteq x'$, and consider an execution where x is the limit of the input chain. At time n, all the observer knows about the input is that it is approximated by x_n, which holds for x' as well as x. Thus the output y_n must approximate $f(x')$ as well as $f(x)$. Since this situation holds for all n, $f(x')$ must be an upper bound on all of the y_n, and thus must extend the least upper bound $f(x)$.

To see that f is also continuous, let $x_0 \sqsubseteq x_1 \sqsubseteq \cdots$ be any interesting chain, and suppose that this chain describes the input to a computation of f. At time n, all the observer knows about the input is that it is approximated by x_n, which holds for x_n as well as x. Thus the output y_n must approximate $f(x_n)$ and, since this situation holds for all n,

$$\bigsqcup_{n=0}^{\infty} y_n \sqsubseteq \bigsqcup_{n=0}^{\infty} f(x_n).$$

But the left side here is $y = f(x) = f(\bigsqcup_{n=0}^{\infty} x_n)$.

Notice that this argument has nothing to do with the Turing concept of computability, which is based on the observer being controlled by a finite program. Instead, it is based on the physical limitations of communication: one cannot predict the future of input, nor receive an infinite amount of information in a finite amount of time, nor produce output except at finite times.

5.4 Products and Disjoint Unions of Predomains

To understand how domains such as Ω can be described by recursive domain isomorphisms, we must first extend the concepts of product and disjoint union (defined in Sections A.3 and A.5 of the Appendix) from sets to predomains. Although this generalization actually applies to products and disjoint unions over arbitrary sets, we limit our discussion to n-ary products and disjoint unions.

When $P_0, \ldots, P_{n-1}$ are predomains, we write $P_0 \times \cdots \times P_{n-1}$ for the partially ordered set obtained by equipping the Cartesian product of sets,

$$P_0 \times \cdots \times P_{n-1} = \{\, \langle x_0, \ldots, x_{n-1} \rangle \mid x_0 \in P_0 \text{ and } \cdots \text{ and } x_{n-1} \in P_{n-1} \,\},$$

with the componentwise ordering

$$\langle x_0, \ldots, x_{n-1} \rangle \sqsubseteq \langle y_0, \ldots, y_{n-1} \rangle$$

if and only if $x_0 \sqsubseteq_0 y_0$ and $\cdots$ and $x_{n-1} \sqsubseteq_{n-1} y_{n-1}$.

This ordering gives a predomain for which the limit of a chain of n-tuples is computed componentwise:

$$\bigsqcup_{k=0}^{\infty} \langle x_0^{(k)}, \ldots, x_{n-1}^{(k)} \rangle = \langle \bigsqcup_{k=0}^{\infty}{}^{0} x_0^{(k)}, \ldots, \bigsqcup_{k=0}^{\infty}{}^{n-1} x_{n-1}^{(k)} \rangle. \tag{5.10}$$

Moreover, if the P_i are all domains, then $P_0 \times \cdots \times P_{n-1}$ is a domain whose least element is the n-tuple $\bot = \langle \bot_0, \ldots, \bot_{n-1} \rangle$.

If the P_i are all discrete, then so is $P_0 \times \cdots \times P_{n-1}$; thus the componentwise ordering of products is compatible with the convention that sets are discretely ordered.

As with sets, we write P^n for the product of P with itself n times.

The projection functions associated with the product are continuous, and the function constructors preserve continuity. In particular:

Proposition 5.1 *Suppose P, Q, and, for $0 \le i \le n - 1$, P_i and Q_i are predomains. Then*

(a) *The projection functions π_i satisfying $\pi_i \langle x_0, \ldots, x_{n-1} \rangle = x_i$ are continuous functions from $P_0 \times \cdots \times P_{n-1}$ to P_i.*

(b) *If the n functions $f_i \in P \to P_i$ are continuous, then the "target-tupling" function $f_0 \otimes \cdots \otimes f_{n-1}$ satisfying*

$$(f_0 \otimes \cdots \otimes f_{n-1}) x = \langle f_0\, x, \ldots, f_{n-1}\, x \rangle$$

is a continuous function from P to $P_0 \times \cdots \times P_{n-1}$.

(c) *If the n functions $f_i \in P_i \to Q_i$ are continuous, then the function $f_0 \times \cdots \times f_{n-1}$ satisfying*

$$(f_0 \times \cdots \times f_{n-1}) \langle x_0, \ldots, x_{n-1} \rangle = \langle f_0\, x_0, \ldots, f_{n-1}\, x_{n-1} \rangle$$

is a continuous function from $P_0 \times \cdots \times P_{n-1}$ to $Q_0 \times \cdots \times Q_{n-1}$.

In a similar spirit, when $P_0, \ldots, P_{n-1}$ are predomains, we want to equip the disjoint union,

$$P_0 + \cdots + P_{n-1} = \{\, \langle 0, x \rangle \mid x \in P_0 \,\} \cup \cdots \cup \{\, \langle n-1, x \rangle \mid x \in P_{n-1} \,\},$$

with an appropriate ordering that will make it a predomain. We want each component $\{\, \langle i, x \rangle \mid x \in P_i \,\}$ to have the same ordering as P_i, and members of distinct components to be incomparable. Thus we use the ordering

$$\langle i, x \rangle \sqsubseteq \langle j, y \rangle \text{ if and only if } i = j \text{ and } x \sqsubseteq_i y.$$

Any chain in the disjoint union must be a sequence of pairs with the same first component; the limit of such a chain is

$$\bigsqcup_{k=0}^{\infty} \langle i, x_k \rangle = \langle i, \bigsqcup_{k=0}^{\infty}{}^i x_k \rangle.$$

Even when all of the P_i are domains, their disjoint union is only a predomain, since (except when $n = 1$) there is no least element.

As with the product construction, if the P_i are all discrete, then so is $P_0 + \cdots + P_{n-1}$; thus the ordering of the disjoint union is compatible with the convention that sets are discretely ordered.

The injection functions associated with the disjoint union are continuous, and the function constructors preserve continuity. In particular:

Proposition 5.2 *Suppose P, Q, and, for $0 \le i \le n - 1$, P_i and Q_i are predomains. Then*

(a) *The injection functions ι_i satisfying*

$$\iota_i(x) = \langle i, x \rangle$$

are continuous functions from P_i to $P_0 + \cdots + P_{n-1}$.

(b) *If the n functions $f_i \in P_i \to P$ are continuous, then the "source-tupling" function $f_0 \oplus \cdots \oplus f_{n-1}$ satisfying*

$$(f_0 \oplus \cdots \oplus f_{n-1})\langle i, x \rangle = f_i x$$

is a continuous function from $P_0 + \cdots + P_{n-1}$ to P.

(c) *If the n functions $f_i \in P_i \to Q_i$ are continuous, then the function $f_0 + \cdots + f_{n-1}$ satisfying*

$$(f_0 + \cdots + f_{n-1})\langle i, x \rangle = \langle i, f_i x \rangle$$

is a continuous function from $P_0 + \cdots + P_{n-1}$ to $Q_0 + \cdots + Q_{n-1}$.

5.5 Recursive Domain Isomorphisms

Pictorially, the domain Ω looks like this:

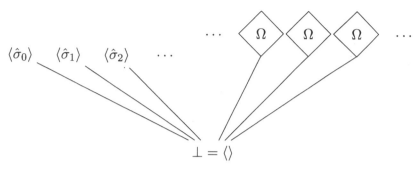

The least element is the empty sequence, the $\langle \hat{\sigma}_i \rangle$ on the left are single-element sequences containing states or **abort**-state pairs, and each diamond on the right contains all sequences that begin with a particular integer. But then, since the sequences in Ω that begin with, say 17, are the sequences that are obtained by prefixing 17 to arbitrary sequences in Ω, each diamond is isomorphic to Ω itself.

Now consider the product $\mathbf{Z} \times \Omega$, where $\mathbf{Z}$ is discretely ordered. This predomain consists of a copy of Ω for each $n \in Z$, formed by pairing n with the members of Ω. Moreover, the componentwise ordering is

$$\langle n, \omega \rangle \sqsubseteq \langle n', \omega' \rangle \text{ if and only if } n = n' \text{ and } \omega \sqsubseteq_\Omega \omega',$$

so that each copy is ordered in the same way as Ω itself, and members of different copies are incomparable. Thus the collection of diamonds in the above diagram is isomorphic to $\mathbf{Z} \times \Omega$, and Ω itself is isomorphic to

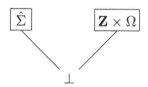

To within an isomorphism, nothing in this diagram changes if we pair each member of $\hat{\Sigma}$ with zero and each member of $\mathbf{Z} \times \Omega$ with one, as long as we maintain the ordering within these components and keep members of distinct components incomparable. Thus Ω is isomorphic to $(\hat{\Sigma} + \mathbf{Z} \times \Omega)_\perp$, which we indicate by writing

$$\Omega \approx (\hat{\Sigma} + \mathbf{Z} \times \Omega)_\perp.$$

This means that there are continuous functions

$$\Omega \xrightleftharpoons[\psi]{\phi} (\hat{\Sigma} + \mathbf{Z} \times \Omega)_\perp$$

such that the compositions $\psi \cdot \phi$ and $\phi \cdot \psi$ are both identity functions.

The injections defined in Equations (5.6) in Section 5.2 can be redefined in terms of this isomorphism. We begin with the following diagram of functions, all of which are injections:

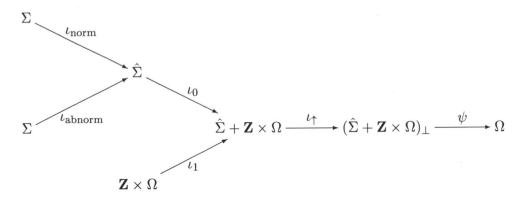

Here, $\iota_{\text{norm}}\sigma = \sigma$, $\iota_{\text{abnorm}}\sigma = \langle \mathbf{abort}, \sigma \rangle$, ι_0 and ι_1 are the injections associated with the disjoint union, $\iota_\uparrow$ is the injection associated with lifting (defined in Section 2.3), and ψ is part of the isomorphism (and therefore a bijection). Then we define the compositions:

$$\iota_{\text{term}} = \psi \cdot \iota_\uparrow \cdot \iota_0 \cdot \iota_{\text{norm}} \in \Sigma \to \Omega$$

$$\iota_{\text{abort}} = \psi \cdot \iota_\uparrow \cdot \iota_0 \cdot \iota_{\text{abnorm}} \in \Sigma \to \Omega$$

$$\iota_{\text{out}} = \psi \cdot \iota_\uparrow \cdot \iota_1 \in \mathbf{Z} \times \Omega \to \Omega.$$

By using these definitions instead of Equations (5.6), we free our semantic equations from a dependency on the specific construction of Ω as a domain of sequences of integers and states. (The fact that these functions, along with $\iota_\perp \in \{\langle \rangle\} \to \Omega$ such that $\iota_\perp() = \perp$, are continuous injections with disjoint ranges is enough to insure that they have the properties we need.)

The isomorphism $\Omega \approx (\hat{\Sigma} + \mathbf{Z} \times \Omega)_\perp$ is our first encounter with an instance of a large class of domain isomorphisms that possess solutions. Specifically, if T is any function mapping domains into domains that is constructed from constant predomains and operations such as $+$, $\times$, $\to$, and $(-)_\perp$ (and others that will be introduced later), then there is a domain D satisfying the isomorphism $D \approx T(D)$. Although we will repeated rely on this fact, the "inverse limit" construction that proves it is beyond the scope of this book.

This kind of domain isomorphism is similar to a fixed-point equation for an element of a domain, in that it always has at least one solution but often has more than one. One can even define a sense of "least" that singles out the solution given by the construction and insures that such equations as (5.7) and (5.9) in Section 5.2 have unique solutions. But even this definition of "least" (initiality in an appropriate category) is beyond the scope of this book.

5.6 Intermediate Input and a Domain of Resumptions

Next we consider extending the language of Section 5.2 with a command

$$\langle \text{comm} \rangle ::= \, ? \, \langle \text{var} \rangle$$

that causes an integer to be read from the input medium and to become the value of the operand. (We will give the operator ? the same precedence as the assignment operator :=.)

To see how this extension affects our semantics, suppose that applying the meaning of a program to an initial state produces some $\omega \in \Omega$. Instead of thinking of ω as an "output", we can think of it as describing the behavior of the *process* of executing the command. In the absence of input commands, when $\Omega \approx (\hat{\Sigma} + \mathbf{Z} \times \Omega)_{\perp}$ as in Section 5.5, there are four possibilities:

(a) If $\omega = \perp$, the process executes forever without performing input or output.

(b) If $\omega = \iota_{\text{term}} \sigma$, the process terminates normally in the state σ.

(c) If $\omega = \iota_{\text{abort}} \sigma$, the process aborts in the state σ.

(d) If $\omega = \iota_{\text{out}}(n, \omega')$, the process outputs the integer n and thereafter behaves as described by ω'.

To describe an input operation, we must introduce a fifth possibility, where behavior depending on the input is described by a function g that maps the input into a member of Ω:

(e) If $\omega = \iota_{\text{in}} g$, where $g \in \mathbf{Z} \to \Omega$, the process inputs an integer k and thereafter behaves as described by $g \, k$.

To accommodate this extra alternative, we take Ω to be a solution of

$$\Omega \approx (\hat{\Sigma} + (\mathbf{Z} \times \Omega) + (\mathbf{Z} \to \Omega))_{\perp}.$$

A domain satisfying such an isomorphism is often called a domain of *resumptions*, since the occurrences of Ω on the right refer to behavior when the process resumes execution after input or output. The new injection is the composition

$$\iota_{\text{in}} = \psi \cdot \iota_{\uparrow} \cdot \iota_2 \in (\mathbf{Z} \to \Omega) \to \Omega.$$

When executed in the state σ, the input command ? v yields a function (injected into Ω) that maps an input k into the altered state $[\sigma \mid v\!:\!k]$. Thus the new semantic equation is

DR SEM EQ: Input

$$[\![?\,v]\!]_{\text{comm}}\sigma = \iota_{\text{in}}(\lambda k \in \mathbf{Z}.\ \iota_{\text{term}}[\sigma \mid v\!:\!k]).$$

The previous semantic equations in Section 5.2 remain unchanged, except that the definitions of f_* by Equations (5.7) and $f_\dagger$ by Equations (5.9) must be augmented to deal with the new injection. In both cases, when the extended function is applied to $\iota_{\text{in}}g$, it is recursively applied pointwise, that is, to the results of g:

$$f_* \bot = \bot$$
$$f_*(\iota_{\text{term}}\sigma) = f\sigma$$
$$f_*(\iota_{\text{abort}}\sigma) = \iota_{\text{abort}}\sigma \qquad\qquad (5.11)$$
$$f_*(\iota_{\text{out}}(n,\omega)) = \iota_{\text{out}}(n, f_*\omega)$$
$$f_*(\iota_{\text{in}}g) = \iota_{\text{in}}(\lambda k \in \mathbf{Z}.\ f_*(g\,k)),$$

$$f_\dagger \bot = \bot$$
$$f_\dagger(\iota_{\text{term}}\sigma) = \iota_{\text{term}}(f\sigma)$$
$$f_\dagger(\iota_{\text{abort}}\sigma) = \iota_{\text{abort}}(f\sigma) \qquad\qquad (5.12)$$
$$f_\dagger(\iota_{\text{out}}(n,\omega)) = \iota_{\text{out}}(n, f_\dagger\omega)$$
$$f_\dagger(\iota_{\text{in}}g) = \iota_{\text{in}}(\lambda k \in \mathbf{Z}.\ f_\dagger(g\,k)).$$

As an example, consider the command

$$\mathsf{x} := 0\,;\,\textbf{while true do } (?\,\mathsf{y}\,;\,\mathsf{x} := \mathsf{x} + \mathsf{y}\,;\,!\,\mathsf{x}).$$

By repeated application of the semantic equations and the above equations for f_*, one obtains

$$
\begin{aligned}
&[\![\mathsf{x} := 0\,;\,\textbf{while true do }(?\,\mathsf{y}\,;\,\mathsf{x} := \mathsf{x}+\mathsf{y}\,;\,!\,\mathsf{x})]\!]_{\text{comm}}\sigma \\
&= ([\![\textbf{while true do }(?\,\mathsf{y}\,;\,\mathsf{x} := \mathsf{x}+\mathsf{y}\,;\,!\,\mathsf{x})]\!]_{\text{comm}})_*([\![\mathsf{x} := 0]\!]_{\text{comm}}\sigma) \\
&= ([\![\textbf{while true do }(?\,\mathsf{y}\,;\,\mathsf{x} := \mathsf{x}+\mathsf{y}\,;\,!\,\mathsf{x})]\!]_{\text{comm}})_*(\iota_{\text{term}}[\sigma \mid \mathsf{x}\!:\!0]) \\
&= [\![\textbf{while true do }(?\,\mathsf{y}\,;\,\mathsf{x} := \mathsf{x}+\mathsf{y}\,;\,!\,\mathsf{x})]\!]_{\text{comm}}[\sigma \mid \mathsf{x}\!:\!0] \\
&= (\mathbf{Y}_{\Sigma \to \Omega}\,F)[\sigma \mid \mathsf{x}\!:\!0] \\
&= \left(\bigsqcup_{n=0}^{\infty}{}^{\Sigma \to \Omega} F^n(\bot)\right)[\sigma \mid \mathsf{x}\!:\!0] \\
&= \bigsqcup_{n=0}^{\infty}{}^{\Omega} F^n(\bot)[\sigma \mid \mathsf{x}\!:\!0],
\end{aligned}
$$

where

$$F(f)\sigma = \textbf{if } [\![\textbf{true}]\!]_{\text{boolexp}}\sigma \textbf{ then } f_*([\![?\,\text{y}\,;\,\text{x}:=\text{x}+\text{y}\,;\,!\,\text{x}]\!]_{\text{comm}}\sigma) \textbf{ else } \iota_{\text{term}}\sigma$$

$$= f_*([\![?\,\text{y}\,;\,\text{x}:=\text{x}+\text{y}\,;\,!\,\text{x}]\!]_{\text{comm}}\sigma)$$

$$= f_*(([\![\text{x}:=\text{x}+\text{y}\,;\,!\,\text{x}]\!]_{\text{comm}})_*([\![?\,\text{y}]\!]_{\text{comm}}\sigma))$$

$$= f_*(([\![\text{x}:=\text{x}+\text{y}\,;\,!\,\text{x}]\!]_{\text{comm}})_*(\iota_{\text{in}}(\lambda k \in \mathbf{Z}.\ \iota_{\text{term}}[\,\sigma \mid \text{y}:k\,])))$$

$$= f_*(\iota_{\text{in}}(\lambda k \in \mathbf{Z}.\ ([\![\text{x}:=\text{x}+\text{y}\,;\,!\,\text{x}]\!]_{\text{comm}})_*(\iota_{\text{term}}[\,\sigma \mid \text{y}:k\,])))$$

$$= f_*(\iota_{\text{in}}(\lambda k \in \mathbf{Z}.\ [\![\text{x}:=\text{x}+\text{y}\,;\,!\,\text{x}]\!]_{\text{comm}}[\,\sigma \mid \text{y}:k\,]))$$

$$= f_*(\iota_{\text{in}}(\lambda k \in \mathbf{Z}.\ ([\![!\,\text{x}]\!]_{\text{comm}})_*([\![\text{x}:=\text{x}+\text{y}]\!]_{\text{comm}}[\,\sigma \mid \text{y}:k\,])))$$

$$= f_*(\iota_{\text{in}}(\lambda k \in \mathbf{Z}.\ ([\![!\,\text{x}]\!]_{\text{comm}})_*(\iota_{\text{term}}[\,\sigma \mid \text{y}:k \mid \text{x}:\sigma\text{x}+k\,])))$$

$$= f_*(\iota_{\text{in}}(\lambda k \in \mathbf{Z}.\ [\![!\,\text{x}]\!]_{\text{comm}}[\,\sigma \mid \text{y}:k \mid \text{x}:\sigma\text{x}+k\,]))$$

$$= f_*(\iota_{\text{in}}(\lambda k \in \mathbf{Z}.\ \iota_{\text{out}}(\sigma\text{x}+k, \iota_{\text{term}}[\,\sigma \mid \text{y}:k \mid \text{x}:\sigma\text{x}+k\,])))$$

$$= \iota_{\text{in}}(\lambda k \in \mathbf{Z}.\ f_*(\iota_{\text{out}}(\sigma\text{x}+k, \iota_{\text{term}}[\,\sigma \mid \text{y}:k \mid \text{x}:\sigma\text{x}+k\,])))$$

$$= \iota_{\text{in}}(\lambda k \in \mathbf{Z}.\ \iota_{\text{out}}(\sigma\text{x}+k, f_*(\iota_{\text{term}}[\,\sigma \mid \text{y}:k \mid \text{x}:\sigma\text{x}+k\,])))$$

$$= \iota_{\text{in}}(\lambda k \in \mathbf{Z}.\ \iota_{\text{out}}(\sigma\text{x}+k, f[\,\sigma \mid \text{y}:k \mid \text{x}:\sigma\text{x}+k\,])).$$

From this result, it is straightforward to show by induction on n that

$$F^n(\bot)[\,\sigma \mid \text{x}:0\,] = \iota_{\text{in}}(\lambda k_0 \in \mathbf{Z}.\ \iota_{\text{out}}(k_0, \iota_{\text{in}}(\lambda k_1 \in \mathbf{Z}.\ \iota_{\text{out}}(k_0 + k_1, \ldots$$

$$\iota_{\text{in}}(\lambda k_{n-1} \in \mathbf{Z}.\ \iota_{\text{out}}(k_0 + \cdots + k_{n-1}, \bot))\ldots)))),$$

which has the limit

$$[\![\text{x}:=0\,;\,\textbf{while true do } (?\,\text{y}\,;\,\text{x}:=\text{x}+\text{y}\,;\,!\,\text{x})]\!]_{\text{comm}}\sigma$$

$$= \bigsqcup_{n=0}^{\infty}{}^{\Omega} F^n(\bot)[\,\sigma \mid \text{x}:0\,]$$

$$= \iota_{\text{in}}(\lambda k_0 \in \mathbf{Z}.\ \iota_{\text{out}}(k_0, \iota_{\text{in}}(\lambda k_1 \in \mathbf{Z}.\ \iota_{\text{out}}(k_0 + k_1,$$

$$\iota_{\text{in}}(\lambda k_2 \in \mathbf{Z}.\ \iota_{\text{out}}(k_0 + k_1 + k_2, \ldots)))))).$$

5.7 Continuation Semantics

One can argue that the denotational semantics given in this chapter is unnatural. A particularly disturbing symptom is that, when introducing language features that seem unrelated to the sequencing of commands, we have repeatedly had to complicate the definition of command sequencing by changing the definition of the extension f_*. By the last section, f_* has become an elaborate function that is a far cry from the way any implementor would think about command sequencing.

Fundamentally, the composition $([\![c_1]\!]_{\text{comm}})_* \cdot [\![c_0]\!]_{\text{comm}}$, where $[\![c_1]\!]_{\text{comm}}$ determines the result of the computation except as it is constrained by the operation $(-)_*$, does not reflect the way in which $c_0\,;\,c_1$ is actually implemented on a computer, where c_0 has complete control over the computation until if and when it passes control to c_1. The latter situation would be more closely mirrored by the opposite composition $[\![c_0]\!]_{\mathrm{comm}} \cdot [\![c_1]\!]_{\mathrm{comm}}$, where $[\![c_0]\!]_{\mathrm{comm}}$ would be a constant function if c_0 never relinquished control.

The key to achieving such a semantics is to make the meaning of every command a function whose result is the final result of the entire program, and to provide an extra argument to the command meaning, called a *continuation*, that is a function from states to final results describing the behavior of the "rest of the program" that will occur if the command relinquishes control. Thus the semantic function for commands has the type

$$[\![-]\!]_{\mathrm{comm}} \in \langle \mathrm{comm} \rangle \to (\Sigma \to \Omega) \to \Sigma \to \Omega,$$

where Ω is the domain of final results (which we leave unspecified for the moment) and $\Sigma \to \Omega$ is the domain of continuations. If the command c, when executed in the state σ, never relinquishes control, then the final result $[\![c]\!]_{\mathrm{comm}}\kappa\sigma$ is independent of the continuation κ; if it produces a state σ' and relinquishes control, then $[\![c]\!]_{\mathrm{comm}}\kappa\sigma$ is $\kappa\sigma'$.

A denotational semantics of this kind is called a *continuation* semantics, as opposed to the kind of semantics discussed heretofore, which is often called *direct* semantics. We will begin by giving a continuation semantics for the simple imperative language of Chapter 2, and then we will consider the various extensions discussed in this chapter.

Assignment and **skip** commands always relinquish control, so the final result is obtained by applying the continuation argument to the appropriate state. (We write CN SEM EQ to abbreviate "continuation semantic equation".)

CN SEM EQ: Assignment

$$[\![v := e]\!]_{\mathrm{comm}}\kappa\sigma = \kappa[\,\sigma \mid v: [\![e]\!]_{\mathrm{intexp}}\sigma\,],$$

CN SEM EQ: **skip**

$$[\![\mathbf{skip}]\!]_{\mathrm{comm}}\kappa\sigma = \kappa\sigma.$$

(Note that, although we are changing from a direct to a continuation semantics of commands, the semantics of expressions remains the same. A continuation semantics for expressions will be introduced, in the context of functional languages, in Section 12.1.)

The composition $c_0\,;\,c_1$ is more subtle. Since c_0 gains control first, the final result given by $[\![c_0\,;\,c_1]\!]_{\mathrm{comm}}$ when applied to a continuation κ and a state σ should be the final result given by $[\![c_0]\!]_{\mathrm{comm}}$ when applied to some continuation κ' and the initial state σ. If c_0 relinquishes control in a state σ', the final result will be $\kappa'\sigma'$, which should be given by $[\![c_1]\!]_{\mathrm{comm}}$ applied to some continuation κ'' and the intermediate state σ'. Then, if c_1 relinquishes control in a state σ'', the final result will be $\kappa''\sigma''$. But when c_1 relinquishes control the entire composition will have finished execution, so that the continuation κ'' should be the continuation κ to which $[\![c_0\,;c_1]\!]_{\text{comm}}$ was applied. Thus

$$[\![c_0\,;c_1]\!]_{\text{comm}}\kappa\sigma = [\![c_0]\!]_{\text{comm}}(\lambda\sigma' \in \Sigma.\,[\![c_1]\!]_{\text{comm}}\kappa\sigma')\sigma.$$

The apparent complexity of this equation vanishes from a more abstract viewpoint. If $f\sigma = g\sigma$ holds for all $\sigma \in \Sigma$, then $f = g$. Applying this fact to both σ and σ' in the above equation gives

CN SEM EQ: Sequential Composition

$$[\![c_0\,;c_1]\!]_{\text{comm}}\kappa = [\![c_0]\!]_{\text{comm}}([\![c_1]\!]_{\text{comm}}\kappa)$$

or, as suggested earlier,

$$[\![c_0\,;c_1]\!]_{\text{comm}} = [\![c_0]\!]_{\text{comm}} \cdot [\![c_1]\!]_{\text{comm}}.$$

Conditionals are more straightforward. Depending on whether the initial state satisfies b, one or the other of the subcommands is executed in the initial state; if it relinquishes control, the rest of the computation is the same as the rest of the computation after the entire conditional. Thus

CN SEM EQ: Conditional

$$[\![\textbf{if } b \textbf{ then } c_0 \textbf{ else } c_1]\!]_{\text{comm}}\kappa\sigma$$
$$= \textbf{if } [\![b]\!]_{\text{boolexp}}\sigma \textbf{ then } [\![c_0]\!]_{\text{comm}}\kappa\sigma \textbf{ else } [\![c_1]\!]_{\text{comm}}\kappa\sigma.$$

Just as with direct semantics, a semantic equation for the **while** command can be obtained by applying the fixed-point theorem to an "unwinding" equation:

$$[\![\textbf{while } b \textbf{ do } c]\!]_{\text{comm}}\kappa\sigma$$
$$= [\![\textbf{if } b \textbf{ then } (c\,;\textbf{while } b \textbf{ do } c) \textbf{ else skip}]\!]_{\text{comm}}\kappa\sigma$$
$$= \textbf{if } [\![b]\!]_{\text{boolexp}}\sigma \textbf{ then } [\![c]\!]_{\text{comm}}([\![\textbf{while } b \textbf{ do } c]\!]_{\text{comm}}\kappa)\sigma \textbf{ else } \kappa\sigma.$$

This equation expresses $[\![\textbf{while } b \textbf{ do } c]\!]_{\text{comm}}$ as a function of itself, specifically as a fixed point of type $(\Sigma \to \Omega) \to \Sigma \to \Omega$. However, the equation has the special property that every occurrence of $[\![\textbf{while } b \textbf{ do } c]\!]_{\text{comm}}$ is applied to the same continuation κ, so that the equation also expresses $[\![\textbf{while } b \textbf{ do } c]\!]_{\text{comm}}\kappa$ as a function of itself. This fixed-point characterization is simpler because it has the simpler type $\Sigma \to \Omega$:

CN SEM EQ: **while**

$$[\![\textbf{while } b \textbf{ do } c]\!]_{\text{comm}}\kappa = \mathbf{Y}_{\Sigma\to\Omega}\, F,$$

where, for all $w \in \Sigma \to \Omega$ and $\sigma \in \Sigma$,

$$Fw\sigma = \textbf{if } [\![b]\!]_{\text{boolexp}}\sigma \textbf{ then } [\![c]\!]_{\text{comm}}w\sigma \textbf{ else } \kappa\sigma.$$

(We can take the fixed point at the lower type because, operationally, the "rest of the program" is the same after each execution of the **while** body. This is what distinguishes a loop from an arbitrary recursion.)

Finally, we have the semantic equation for variable declarations, where the continuation restores the declared variable to its initial value:

CN SEM EQ: Variable Declaration

$$[\![\textbf{newvar } v := e \textbf{ in } c]\!]_{\text{comm}}\kappa\sigma$$
$$= [\![c]\!]_{\text{comm}}(\lambda\sigma' \in \Sigma.\ \kappa[\sigma' \mid v{:}\sigma v])[\sigma \mid v{:}[\![e]\!]_{\text{intexp}}\sigma].$$

It can be shown that this continuation semantics bears the following relationship to the direct semantics given in Chapter 2: For all commands c of the (unextended) simple imperative language, continuations κ, and states σ,

$$[\![c]\!]_{\text{comm}}^{\text{continuation}}\kappa\sigma = \kappa_{\perp\!\perp}([\![c]\!]_{\text{comm}}^{\text{direct}}\sigma).$$

In particular, one can take the domain Ω of final results to be $\Sigma_\perp$, and κ to be the "final continuation" that injects Σ into $\Sigma_\perp$; then $\kappa_{\perp\!\perp}$ is the identity function on $\Sigma_\perp$, so that the continuation semantics applied to the final continuation and an initial state coincides with the direct semantics applied to the same initial state.

In fact, the equation displayed above holds for any choice of the domain Ω. (In other words, it is "polymorphic" in Ω.) The nature of Ω will become specific, however, when we consider extensions to the simple imperative language.

5.8 Continuation Semantics of Extensions

The various language features introduced in this chapter can be described by continuation semantics much more simply than by direct semantics. In particular, there is no need to introduce the function extensions f_* and $f_\dagger$.

However, we must specify the domain Ω of "final results". In particular, we take Ω to be the domain of resumptions defined in Section 5.6 (so that "total behavior" might be a more accurate term than "final result"). We also take

$$\iota_{\text{term}} \in \Sigma \to \Omega \qquad \iota_{\text{abort}} \in \Sigma \to \Omega \qquad \iota_{\text{out}} \in \mathbf{Z} \times \Omega \to \Omega \qquad \iota_{\text{in}} \in (\mathbf{Z} \to \Omega) \to \Omega$$

to be the injections defined in Sections 5.6 and 5.5.

Now consider the **fail** command. Essentially, its final result is the state in which it is executed — which is clearly expressed by the semantic equation

$$[\![\textbf{fail}]\!]_{\text{comm}}\kappa\sigma = \iota_{\text{abort}}\sigma.$$

Here, the fact that $[\![\textbf{fail}]\!]_{\text{comm}}\kappa\sigma$ is independent of the behavior κ of the rest of the program makes it obvious that **fail** does not execute the rest of the program.

Unfortunately, however, by taking the final result to be the current state, we raise the problem with variable declarations that was discussed at the end of

Section 5.1. When an occurrence of **fail** within the scope of a variable declaration is executed, if the current state is taken to be the final result without resetting the declared variable to its more global value, then variable renaming will not preserve meaning.

We will describe the solution to this problem at the end of this section, but first we consider the simpler problem of treating intermediate output and input.

The final result of a program that executes the output command $!\,e$ consists of the value of e followed by the final result of the rest of the program. This is captured by the semantic equation

CN SEM EQ: Output

$$[\![!\,e]\!]_{\text{comm}} \kappa \sigma = \iota_{\text{out}}([\![e]\!]_{\text{intexp}}\sigma, \kappa\sigma).$$

On the other hand, the final result of a program that executes the input command $?\,v$ is a function mapping the input integer into the final result for an appropriately altered state. Thus

CN SEM EQ: Input

$$[\![?\,v]\!]_{\text{comm}} \kappa \sigma = \iota_{\text{in}}(\lambda k \in \mathbf{Z}.\ \kappa[\,\sigma \mid v{:}\,k\,]).$$

It can be shown that this continuation semantics bears the following relationship to the direct semantics described earlier in this chapter (provided that the direct semantics of variable declarations is defined by Equation (5.1) in Section 5.1, even though the preservation of meaning under renaming is violated):

$$[\![c]\!]_{\text{comm}}^{\text{continuation}} \kappa\sigma = \kappa_*([\![c]\!]_{\text{comm}}^{\text{direct}}\sigma),$$

where $(-)_*$ is defined by Equations (5.11) in Section 5.6. As a special case, where κ is taken to be the "final" continuation ι_{term}, we have

$$[\![c]\!]_{\text{comm}}^{\text{continuation}} \iota_{\text{term}}\sigma = [\![c]\!]_{\text{comm}}^{\text{direct}}\sigma,$$

since $(\iota_{\text{term}})_*$ can be shown to be the identity function on Ω.

Finally, we return to the problem of resetting local variables in failure states to preserve meaning under the renaming of variables. The solution here is a global, though straightforward, change in the semantics: The meanings of commands become functions accepting two continuations: κ_t, which is used to map a state into a final result if the command terminates normally in that state, and κ_f, which is used to map a state into a final result if the command fails in that state. Then the new continuation κ_f is used to reset a local variable when a **fail** occurring within the scope of a variable declaration is executed.

Thus the continuation semantics of commands satisfies

$$[\![-]\!]_{\text{comm}} \in \langle\text{comm}\rangle \to (\Sigma \to \Omega) \to (\Sigma \to \Omega) \to \Sigma \to \Omega,$$

and the relevant semantic equations are

CN SEM EQ: Assignment

$$[\![v := e]\!]_{\text{comm}} \kappa_t \kappa_f \sigma = \kappa_t [\sigma \mid v{:}\, [\![e]\!]_{\text{intexp}} \sigma],$$

CN SEM EQ: **skip**

$$[\![\textbf{skip}]\!]_{\text{comm}} \kappa_t \kappa_f \sigma = \kappa_t \sigma,$$

CN SEM EQ: Sequential Composition

$$[\![c_0 \,;\, c_1]\!]_{\text{comm}} \kappa_t \kappa_f = [\![c_0]\!]_{\text{comm}} ([\![c_1]\!]_{\text{comm}} \kappa_t \kappa_f) \kappa_f,$$

CN SEM EQ: Conditional

$$[\![\textbf{if } b \textbf{ then } c_0 \textbf{ else } c_1]\!]_{\text{comm}} \kappa_t \kappa_f \sigma$$
$$= \textbf{if } [\![b]\!]_{\text{boolexp}} \sigma \textbf{ then } [\![c_0]\!]_{\text{comm}} \kappa_t \kappa_f \sigma \textbf{ else } [\![c_1]\!]_{\text{comm}} \kappa_t \kappa_f \sigma,$$

CN SEM EQ: **while**

$$[\![\textbf{while } b \textbf{ do } c]\!]_{\text{comm}} \kappa_t \kappa_f = \mathbf{Y}_{\Sigma \to \Omega}\, F$$
$$\text{where } Fw\sigma = \textbf{if } [\![b]\!]_{\text{boolexp}} \sigma \textbf{ then } [\![c]\!]_{\text{comm}} w\kappa_f \sigma \textbf{ else } \kappa_t \sigma,$$

CN SEM EQ: Variable Declaration

$$[\![\textbf{newvar } v := e \textbf{ in } c]\!]_{\text{comm}} \kappa_t \kappa_f \sigma$$
$$= [\![c]\!]_{\text{comm}} (\lambda \sigma' \in \Sigma.\ \kappa_t [\sigma' \mid v{:}\, \sigma v])$$
$$(\lambda \sigma' \in \Sigma.\ \kappa_f [\sigma' \mid v{:}\, \sigma v]) [\sigma \mid v{:}\, [\![e]\!]_{\text{intexp}} \sigma],$$

CN SEM EQ: **fail**

$$[\![\textbf{fail}]\!]_{\text{comm}} \kappa_t \kappa_f \sigma = \kappa_f \sigma,$$

CN SEM EQ: Output

$$[\![!\, e]\!]_{\text{comm}} \kappa_t \kappa_f \sigma = \iota_{\text{out}} ([\![e]\!]_{\text{intexp}} \sigma, \kappa_t \sigma),$$

CN SEM EQ: Input

$$[\![?\, v]\!]_{\text{comm}} \kappa_t \kappa_f \sigma = \iota_{\text{in}} (\lambda k \in \mathbf{Z}.\ \kappa_t [\sigma \mid v{:}\, k]).$$

It can be shown that this continuation semantics bears the following relationship to the direct semantics described earlier (provided that variable declarations are defined by Equation (5.2) in Section 5.1, so that renaming preserves meaning):

$$[\![c]\!]_{\text{comm}}^{\text{continuation}} \kappa_t \kappa_f \sigma = (\kappa_t, \kappa_f)_* ([\![c]\!]_{\text{comm}}^{\text{direct}} \sigma),$$

where $(\kappa_t, \kappa_f)_*$ satisfies

$$(\kappa_t, \kappa_f)_* \perp = \perp$$

$$(\kappa_t, \kappa_f)_*(\iota_{\text{term}}\sigma) = \kappa_t \sigma$$

$$(\kappa_t, \kappa_f)_*(\iota_{\text{abort}}\sigma) = \kappa_f \sigma$$

$$(\kappa_t, \kappa_f)_*(\iota_{\text{out}}(n, \omega)) = \iota_{\text{out}}(n, (\kappa_t, \kappa_f)_*\omega)$$

$$(\kappa_t, \kappa_f)_*(\iota_{\text{in}}g) = \iota_{\text{in}}(\lambda k \in \mathbf{Z}. \ (\kappa_t, \kappa_f)_*(g\,k)).$$

It can also be shown that $(\iota_{\text{term}}, \iota_{\text{abort}})_*$ is the identity function on Ω. Thus, as a special case,

$$[\![c]\!]_{\text{comm}}^{\text{continuation}} \iota_{\text{term}}\iota_{\text{abort}}\sigma = [\![c]\!]_{\text{comm}}^{\text{direct}}\sigma,$$

where ι_{term} and ι_{abort} can be thought of as the final continuations for normal and abortive termination.

Bibliographic Notes

The concept of continuous algebras was developed by Goguen, Thatcher, Wagner, and Wright [1977].

There are a variety of approaches to solving domain isomorphisms. The earliest was the inverse limit construction, which was originally devised by Scott [1971; 1972], generalized by Reynolds [1972b], and eventually generalized and abstracted much further by Wand [1975; 1979] and by Smyth and Plotkin [1982]. More elementary accounts are given in Tennent [1991, Chapter 10], Schmidt [1986, Chapter 11], and Gunter [1992, Section 10.1].

A later method, also due to Scott [1976], expressed the solution of a domain isomorphism as the set of fixed points of an idempotent function (i.e. satisfying $f = f \cdot f$) on a "universal" domain. This method comes in three flavors, depending on whether one uses arbitrary idempotent functions (called retractions) or restricts such functions to be approximations of the identity function (called projections) or extensions of the identity function (called closures). It is described in Gunter and Scott [1990, Section 6] and Gunter [1992, Section 8.2].

Still more recently, Larsen and Winskel [1991] developed a method using Scott's [1982] information systems. This approach is also described in Winskel [1993, Chapter 12].

Resumptions were introduced (in the more complex setting of concurrent computation) by Plotkin [1976] and Hennessy and Plotkin [1979].

Most of the literature on continuations discusses the concept in the setting of functional languages (where we will return to continuations in Section 12.1). However, the properties of continuation semantics for imperative languages are described, perhaps to excess, by Reynolds [1977].

Both the various extension operations, such as $(-)_\perp$ and $(-)_*$, and the use of continuations are special cases of a general treatment of computational effects as monads that was devised by Moggi [1991] in the setting of functional languages. More intuitive descriptions, also in the functional setting, have been given by Wadler [1992; 1993].

Exercises

5.1   Let c be the command

$$\textbf{while } x \neq 0 \textbf{ do if } x = 1 \textbf{ then fail else } x := x - 2.$$

For simplicity, assume that the set $\langle\text{var}\rangle$ contains only x, so that $[x{:}\,m]$ is a typical state.

(a) What is $[\![c]\!]_{\text{comm}}[x{:}\,m]$, where $[\![-]\!]_{\text{comm}}$ is the direct semantic function defined in Chapter 2 and extended in Section 5.1?

(b) What is $[\![c]\!]_{\text{comm}}\kappa_t\kappa_f[x{:}\,m]$, where $[\![-]\!]_{\text{comm}}$ is the two-continuation semantic function defined in Section 5.8?

(c) Derive the answer to part (a) from the relevant semantic equations.

(d) Give preconditions such that

$$\{?\} \ c \ \{x = 0\} \qquad \{?\} \ c \ \{x = 5\} \qquad [\,?\,] \ c \ [\,x = 0\,].$$

Your preconditions should be as weak as possible.

(e) Prove the last specification in part (d).

5.2   Extend the continuation semantics of Section 5.7, and also the more elaborate continuation semantics of Section 5.8, by giving semantic equations for the **repeat** command described in Exercise 2.2.

5.3   Consider extending the simple imperative language (including **fail**) by adding a new command,

$$\langle\text{comm}\rangle ::= \textbf{catchin } \langle\text{comm}\rangle \textbf{ with } \langle\text{comm}\rangle$$

that resumes computation after failure. Specifically, **catchin** c_0 **with** c_1 causes c_0 to be executed, and, if c_0 terminates normally (that is, without any failure that is not caught by a lower-level occurrence of **catchin**), then **catchin** c_0 **with** c_1 terminates normally without executing c_1. But if c_0 terminates with an uncaught failure, then c_1 is executed (beginning in the state that resulted from the execution of c_0) and **catchin** c_0 **with** c_1 terminates normally or fails, depending on whether c_1 terminates normally or fails.

(a) Extend the direct semantics of Section 5.1 to describe this extension. The type of meaning of commands should remain the same.

(b) Extend the continuation semantics of Section 5.8 (using two continuations κ_t and κ_f) to describe this extension. Again, the type of meaning of commands should remain the same.

5.4   Consider a further extension of the simple imperative language where failures have labels:

$$\langle comm \rangle ::= \textbf{fail } \langle label \rangle \mid \textbf{catch } \langle label \rangle \textbf{ in } \langle comm \rangle \textbf{ with } \langle comm \rangle$$

(where $\langle label \rangle$ denotes a countably infinite predefined set of *labels*). Now **fail** ℓ causes a failure *named* ℓ. The command **catch** ℓ **in** c_0 **with** c_1 causes c_0 to be executed, and, if c_0 terminates normally or with a uncaught failure with a name different than ℓ, then **catch** ℓ **in** c_0 **with** c_1 terminates normally or with a similarly named failure, without executing c_1. But if c_0 terminates with an uncaught failure named ℓ, then c_1 is executed (beginning in the state that resulted from the execution of c_0) and **catch** ℓ **in** c_0 **with** c_1 terminates normally or fails, depending on whether c_1 terminates normally or fails. For example,

> **catch** cold **in catch** cold **in** $(x := 0 \,;\textbf{fail}\text{ cold})$ **with** $y := 0$ **with** $z := 0$

is equivalent to $x := 0 \,; y := 0$, but

> **catch** cold **in catch** flu **in** $(x := 0 \,;\textbf{fail}\text{ cold})$ **with** $y := 0$ **with** $z := 0$

is equivalent to $x := 0 \,; z := 0$.

(a) Extend the direct semantics of Section 5.1 to describe this language extension. The type of command meanings should still be $[\![-]\!]_{comm} \in \langle comm \rangle \to \Sigma \to \hat{\Sigma}_\perp$, but now

$$\hat{\Sigma} = \Sigma \cup (\langle label \rangle \times \Sigma),$$

where $\langle \ell, \sigma \rangle$ is the result of a command that fails with label ℓ.

(b) Extend the continuation semantics of Section 5.8 to describe this language extension. The type of command meanings should now be

$$[\![-]\!]_{comm} \in \langle comm \rangle \to (\Sigma \to \Omega) \to (\langle label \rangle \to \Sigma \to \Omega) \to \Sigma \to \Omega.$$

Here the meaning of a command c is applied to a continuation κ_t that describes the "rest of the computation" to be done in case c completes execution normally, and to a function κ_f such that $\kappa_f \ell$ describes the rest of the computation to be done in case c completes execution with a failure named ℓ. The domain Ω of final results is still the domain of resumptions used in Sections 5.6 to 5.8, except that now $\hat{\Sigma} = \Sigma \cup (\langle label \rangle \times \Sigma)$, where a final result $\langle \ell, \sigma \rangle$ arises when the program terminates with an uncaught failure named ℓ.

5.5   Use either the direct or continuation semantics that you defined in Exercise 5.4 to prove that, for all commands c and labels ℓ,

$$[\![\mathbf{catch}\ \ell\ \mathbf{in}\ c\ \mathbf{with}\ \mathbf{fail}\ \ell]\!]_{\mathrm{comm}} = [\![c]\!]_{\mathrm{comm}}.$$

5.6   In Section 5.1, we redefined program specifications to treat failure in the same way as nontermination. This makes it impossible to assert anything about the state in which a failure occurs; as a consequence, these forms of specification are inadequate for reasoning about the **catchin** commands introduced in Exercise 5.3.

To avoid these limitations, one can work with a more elaborate kind of specification containing two consequents. These new specifications have the form $[p]c[q][r]$, where q describes the final states in which normal termination occurs, while r describes the final states in which failure occurs. More precisely (for determinate commands with no input or output),

$$[p]c[q][r] = \forall \sigma \in \Sigma.\ [\![p]\!]_{\mathrm{assert}}\sigma \Rightarrow ([\![c]\!]_{\mathrm{comm}}\sigma \neq \bot\ \text{and}$$
$$((\exists \sigma' \in \Sigma.\ [\![c]\!]_{\mathrm{comm}}\sigma = \sigma'\ \text{and}\ [\![q]\!]_{\mathrm{assert}}\sigma')$$
$$\text{or}\ (\exists \sigma' \in \Sigma.\ [\![c]\!]_{\mathrm{comm}}\sigma = \langle\mathbf{abort}, \sigma'\rangle\ \text{and}\ [\![r]\!]_{\mathrm{assert}}\sigma'))).$$

Give inference rules for inferring specifications of this new kind for assignment commands, **skip**, **fail**, sequential composition, **catchin**, and conditional commands.

5.7   Suppose $f \in \Sigma \to \Omega$ and let $f_* \in \Omega \to \Omega$ be the function defined by Equations 5.3 in Section 5.2. Prove that f_* is continuous.

5.8   Let S be the domain of finite and infinite sequences of integers with $x \sqsubseteq y$ if and only if x is a prefix of y, that is, if there is a sequence z such that y is the concatenation of x and z. Let $\mathcal{P}\mathbf{Z}$ be the powerset of the integers, ordered under inclusion. Prove that the function that maps a sequence of integers into the set of its elements is a continuous function from S to $\mathcal{P}\mathbf{Z}$. (Note that this function is essentially a simplification of the function μ described in Section 5.2.)

5.9   Prove that the composition function cmp such that

$$\mathrm{cmp}\langle f, g\rangle = g \cdot f$$

is a continuous function from $(P \to P') \times (P' \to P'')$ to $P \to P''$.

5.10   Suppose we have domains D and D' and a pair of monotone functions $\phi \in D \to D'$ and $\psi \in D' \to D$ that satisfy the equations for an isomorphism:

$$\psi \cdot \phi = I_D \qquad \text{and} \qquad \phi \cdot \psi = I_{D'}.$$

Show that ϕ and ψ are strict and continuous.

5.11   In Section A.3 of the Appendix, it is stated that

$$\underbrace{S + \cdots + S}_{n \text{ times}} = n \times S,$$

where n is interpreted as the set 0 **to** $n - 1$. Show that this equality remains true when S is an arbitrary predomain, provided that 0 **to** $n - 1$ is discretely ordered.

6

Transition Semantics

In this chapter, we consider the operational semantics of the simple imperative language, including various extensions. Although this is an interesting topic in its own right, our main purpose is to lay a groundwork for the study of nondeterminate and concurrent programs, whose operational semantics is much more tractable than their domain-theoretic semantics.

We use an approach, devised by Gordon Plotkin, that is called "transition semantics", "structural operational semantics", or sometimes "small-step semantics". The basic idea is that the execution of a program can be formalized as a sequence $\gamma_0 \rightarrow \gamma_1 \rightarrow \cdots$ of configurations, each of which (for the simple imperative language of Chapter 2) is either a state, in the case of a terminal configuration, or a state paired with a command determining the rest of the computation, in the case of a nonterminal configuration.

For example, the execution of $x := x + 1 \,; y := y + x \,; x := x + 1$ in an initial state mapping x into 3 and y into 7 would be formalized by the sequence

$$\langle x := x + 1 \,; y := y + x \,; x := x + 1, [\, x \colon 3 \mid y \colon 7 \,] \rangle$$
$$\rightarrow \langle y := y + x \,; x := x + 1, [\, x \colon 4 \mid y \colon 7 \,] \rangle$$
$$\rightarrow \langle x := x + 1, [\, x \colon 4 \mid y \colon 11 \,] \rangle$$
$$\rightarrow [\, x \colon 5 \mid y \colon 11 \,].$$

(To keep the examples given in this chapter brief, we will limit the domain $\langle \mathrm{var} \rangle$ of states to the set of variables that are actually relevant to each example.)

6.1 Configurations and the Transition Relation

In general, a transition semantics is given by specifying a set Γ of *configurations*, partitioned into disjoint sets Γ_N of *nonterminal* configurations and Γ_T of *terminal* configurations, and a *transition* relation from Γ_N to Γ. The transition relation is denoted by $\rightarrow$ and can be thought of as "moves in one step to".

An execution is a finite or infinite sequence of configurations, each of which is related to the next by the transition relation. Clearly, all configurations in an execution, except perhaps the final configuration of a finite execution, must be nonterminal. For configurations γ and γ', we write $\gamma \to^* \gamma'$ if there is a finite execution beginning with γ and ending with γ'; we write $\gamma \uparrow$, and say that γ diverges, if there is an infinite execution beginning with γ. (Note that $\to^*$ is the transitive and reflexive closure of the relation $\to$, as discussed in Section A.6 of the Appendix.)

For both the simple imperative language of Chapter 2 and the extensions discussed in Chapter 5, the transition relation (which we will define in the following sections) can be shown to be a function. This means that:

- No nonterminal configuration can move in one step to more than one configuration. In other words, the semantics is *determinate*.
- No nonterminal configuration can move in one step to less than one configuration. In other words, executions never get *stuck*.

It follows that, for every configuration γ, there is a unique *maximal* execution (that is, an execution that is not an initial subsequence of any longer execution) beginning with γ, and that this maximal execution is either infinite or ends with a terminal configuration. In the first case γ diverges, while in the second case there is exactly one terminal configuration γ' such that $\gamma \to^* \gamma'$.

6.2 Inference Rules for the Simple Language

In this section, we give a transition semantics for the simple imperative language described in Chapter 2. In this simple case, the set of nonterminal configurations is $\Gamma_N = \langle \text{comm} \rangle \times \Sigma$ and the set of terminal configurations is $\Gamma_T = \Sigma$.

The main novelty in Plotkin's approach to operational semantics is the use of inference rules to define the transition relation: An instance of $\gamma \to \gamma'$ is true if and only if it can be proved from a set of inference rules whose premises and conclusions have the form $\gamma \to \gamma'$. There are one or more rules for each construct of the programming language. (We use the label TR RULE to abbreviate "transition rule".)

The rules for assignment and **skip** commands are obvious axiom schemas:

TR RULE: Assignment

$$\langle v := e, \sigma \rangle \to [\,\sigma \mid v \colon \llbracket e \rrbracket_{\text{intexp}} \sigma\,],$$

TR RULE: **skip**

$$\langle \mathbf{skip}, \sigma \rangle \to \sigma.$$

(Notice that, although we are giving an operational semantics for commands, we are still using the same denotational semantics for expressions as in Chapter 2.)

For sequential composition there are two rules, one for when c_0 terminates in one step and one for when it does not:

TR RULE: Sequential Composition

$$\frac{\langle c_0, \sigma \rangle \rightarrow \sigma'}{\langle c_0 \, ; c_1, \sigma \rangle \rightarrow \langle c_1, \sigma' \rangle}$$

$$\frac{\langle c_0, \sigma \rangle \rightarrow \langle c_0', \sigma' \rangle}{\langle c_0 \, ; c_1, \sigma \rangle \rightarrow \langle c_0' \, ; c_1, \sigma' \rangle.}$$

An example of the use of the rules for assignment and sequencing is the following proof (of the first step of the execution given at the beginning of this chapter). We assume that the sequencing operator ; is left associative.

1. $\langle x := x + 1, [x\colon 3 \mid y\colon 7] \rangle \rightarrow [x\colon 4 \mid y\colon 7]$ (Assignment)

2. $\langle x := x + 1 \, ; y := y + x, [x\colon 3 \mid y\colon 7] \rangle$
    $\rightarrow \langle y := y + x, [x\colon 4 \mid y\colon 7] \rangle$ (Sequential Composition (a), 1)

3. $\langle (x := x + 1 \, ; y := y + x) \, ; x := x + 1, [x\colon 3 \mid y\colon 7] \rangle$
    $\rightarrow \langle y := y + x \, ; x := x + 1, [x\colon 4 \mid y\colon 7] \rangle$ (Sequential Composition (b), 2)

For conditional commands, two rules are needed to describe the two branches of control:

TR RULE: Conditional

$$\frac{}{\langle \textbf{if } b \textbf{ then } c_0 \textbf{ else } c_1, \sigma \rangle \rightarrow \langle c_0, \sigma \rangle} \qquad \text{when } [\![b]\!]_{\text{boolexp}} \sigma = \textbf{true}$$

$$\frac{}{\langle \textbf{if } b \textbf{ then } c_0 \textbf{ else } c_1, \sigma \rangle \rightarrow \langle c_1, \sigma \rangle} \qquad \text{when } [\![b]\!]_{\text{boolexp}} \sigma = \textbf{false}.$$

Similarly, two rules are needed for the **while** command:

TR RULE: **while**

$$\frac{}{\langle \textbf{while } b \textbf{ do } c, \sigma \rangle \rightarrow \langle c \, ; \textbf{while } b \textbf{ do } c, \sigma \rangle} \qquad \text{when } [\![b]\!]_{\text{boolexp}} \sigma = \textbf{true}$$

$$\frac{}{\langle \textbf{while } b \textbf{ do } c, \sigma \rangle \rightarrow \sigma} \qquad \text{when } [\![b]\!]_{\text{boolexp}} \sigma = \textbf{false}.$$

Finally, we consider variable declarations, which raise a subtle complication. A naïve approach — that we will not follow — employs a single rule, where an assignment command is added to the "rest of the computation" to restore the declared variable to its earlier value when the scope of the declaration has completed execution:

$$\langle \textbf{newvar } v := e \textbf{ in } c, \sigma \rangle \rightarrow \langle c \,;\, v := n, [\,\sigma \mid v\colon [\![e]\!]_{\text{intexp}} \sigma \,] \rangle \qquad \text{where } n = \sigma v.$$

With this rule, one would have, for example:

$$\langle \textbf{newvar } \mathsf{x} := 0 \textbf{ in } (\mathsf{y} := \mathsf{y} \times \mathsf{x} \,;\, \mathsf{x} := \mathsf{x} + 1 \,;\, \mathsf{y} := \mathsf{y} + \mathsf{x}), [\,\mathsf{x}\colon 100 \mid \mathsf{y}\colon 200\,] \rangle$$
$$\rightarrow \langle \mathsf{y} := \mathsf{y} \times \mathsf{x} \,;\, \mathsf{x} := \mathsf{x} + 1 \,;\, \mathsf{y} := \mathsf{y} + \mathsf{x} \,;\, \mathsf{x} := 100, [\,\mathsf{x}\colon 0 \mid \mathsf{y}\colon 200\,] \rangle$$
$$\rightarrow \langle \mathsf{x} := \mathsf{x} + 1 \,;\, \mathsf{y} := \mathsf{y} + \mathsf{x} \,;\, \mathsf{x} := 100, [\,\mathsf{x}\colon 0 \mid \mathsf{y}\colon 0\,] \rangle$$
$$\rightarrow \langle \mathsf{y} := \mathsf{y} + \mathsf{x} \,;\, \mathsf{x} := 100, [\,\mathsf{x}\colon 1 \mid \mathsf{y}\colon 0\,] \rangle$$
$$\rightarrow \langle \mathsf{x} := 100, [\,\mathsf{x}\colon 1 \mid \mathsf{y}\colon 1\,] \rangle$$
$$\rightarrow [\,\mathsf{x}\colon 100 \mid \mathsf{y}\colon 1\,].$$

To understand why this is unsatisfactory, we must anticipate the extension of this semantics to concurrency, which will be considered in Chapters 8 and 9. Then it will become possible for a command beginning with a variable declaration, such as that above, to be executed concurrently with some other command, which will cause the executions of the two commands to be interleaved. For example, any execution of

$$\mathsf{x} := 82 \parallel \textbf{newvar } \mathsf{x} := 0 \textbf{ in } (\mathsf{y} := \mathsf{y} \times \mathsf{x} \,;\, \mathsf{x} := \mathsf{x} + 1 \,;\, \mathsf{y} := \mathsf{y} + \mathsf{x})$$

will contain an interleaved transition of the form $\langle \ldots, \sigma \rangle \rightarrow \langle \ldots, [\,\sigma \mid \mathsf{x}\colon 82\,] \rangle$ (or $\langle \ldots, \sigma \rangle \rightarrow [\,\sigma \mid \mathsf{x}\colon 82\,]$). But the assignment $\mathsf{x} := 82$ lies outside the scope of the variable declaration, so that it refers to a different, more global variable than the bound occurrences of x within the scope. Thus, for the interleaving to work properly, the states in the execution of the command beginning with the declaration must refer to the more global variable.

In other words, while the scope of the declaration has the execution

$$\langle \mathsf{y} := \mathsf{y} \times \mathsf{x} \,;\, \mathsf{x} := \mathsf{x} + 1 \,;\, \mathsf{y} := \mathsf{y} + \mathsf{x}, [\,\mathsf{x}\colon 0 \mid \mathsf{y}\colon 200\,] \rangle$$
$$\rightarrow \langle \mathsf{x} := \mathsf{x} + 1 \,;\, \mathsf{y} := \mathsf{y} + \mathsf{x}, [\,\mathsf{x}\colon 0 \mid \mathsf{y}\colon 0\,] \rangle$$
$$\rightarrow \langle \mathsf{y} := \mathsf{y} + \mathsf{x}, [\,\mathsf{x}\colon 1 \mid \mathsf{y}\colon 0\,] \rangle$$
$$\rightarrow [\,\mathsf{x}\colon 1 \mid \mathsf{y}\colon 1\,],$$

the enclosing command beginning with the declaration should have an execution with the same form but with states that give x its global values:

$$\langle \textbf{newvar } \mathsf{x} := 0 \textbf{ in } (\mathsf{y} := \mathsf{y} \times \mathsf{x} \,;\, \mathsf{x} := \mathsf{x} + 1 \,;\, \mathsf{y} := \mathsf{y} + \mathsf{x}), [\,\mathsf{x}\colon 100 \mid \mathsf{y}\colon 200\,] \rangle$$
$$\rightarrow \langle \ldots, [\,\mathsf{x}\colon 100 \mid \mathsf{y}\colon 0\,] \rangle$$
$$\rightarrow \langle \ldots, [\,\mathsf{x}\colon 100 \mid \mathsf{y}\colon 0\,] \rangle$$
$$\rightarrow [\,\mathsf{x}\colon 100 \mid \mathsf{y}\colon 1\,].$$

However, the values of the local x must still be embedded somewhere in the intermediate configurations. This can be accomplished by using an ingenious idea suggested by Eugene Fink: We prefix the commands in the intermediate configurations with variable declarations whose initializations store the local values. This leads to the following inference rules:

TR RULE: Variable Declaration

$$\frac{\langle c, [\,\sigma \mid v{:}\, [\![e]\!]_{\mathrm{intexp}}\sigma\,]\rangle \to \sigma'}{\langle \mathbf{newvar}\; v := e \;\mathbf{in}\; c, \sigma \rangle \to [\,\sigma' \mid v{:}\, \sigma v\,]}$$

$$\frac{\langle c, [\,\sigma \mid v{:}\, [\![e]\!]_{\mathrm{intexp}}\sigma\,]\rangle \to \langle c', \sigma' \rangle}{\langle \mathbf{newvar}\; v := e \;\mathbf{in}\; c, \sigma \rangle \to \langle \mathbf{newvar}\; v := \sigma'v \;\mathbf{in}\; c', [\,\sigma' \mid v{:}\, \sigma v\,]\rangle.}$$

Then, for example, we have

$$\langle \mathbf{newvar}\; \mathsf{x} := 0 \;\mathbf{in}\; (\mathsf{y} := \mathsf{y} \times \mathsf{x}\,;\mathsf{x} := \mathsf{x}+1\,;\mathsf{y} := \mathsf{y}+\mathsf{x}), [\,\mathsf{x}{:}\,100 \mid \mathsf{y}{:}\,200\,]\rangle$$
$$\to \langle \mathbf{newvar}\; \mathsf{x} := 0 \;\mathbf{in}\; (\mathsf{x} := \mathsf{x}+1\,;\mathsf{y} := \mathsf{y}+\mathsf{x}), [\,\mathsf{x}{:}\,100 \mid \mathsf{y}{:}\,0\,]\rangle$$
$$\to \langle \mathbf{newvar}\; \mathsf{x} := 1 \;\mathbf{in}\; \mathsf{y} := \mathsf{y}+\mathsf{x}, [\,\mathsf{x}{:}\,100 \mid \mathsf{y}{:}\,0\,]\rangle$$
$$\to [\,\mathsf{x}{:}\,100 \mid \mathsf{y}{:}\,1\,],$$

where the following is a proof of the second step:

1. $\langle \mathsf{x} := \mathsf{x}+1, [\,\mathsf{x}{:}\,0 \mid \mathsf{y}{:}\,0\,]\rangle \to [\,\mathsf{x}{:}\,1 \mid \mathsf{y}{:}\,0\,]$ (Assignment)

2. $\langle \mathsf{x} := \mathsf{x}+1\,;\mathsf{y} := \mathsf{y}+\mathsf{x}, [\,\mathsf{x}{:}\,0 \mid \mathsf{y}{:}\,0\,]\rangle$
    $\to \langle \mathsf{y} := \mathsf{y}+\mathsf{x}, [\,\mathsf{x}{:}\,1 \mid \mathsf{y}{:}\,0\,]\rangle$ (Sequential Composition (a), 1)

3. $\langle \mathbf{newvar}\; \mathsf{x} := 0 \;\mathbf{in}\; (\mathsf{x} := \mathsf{x}+1\,;\mathsf{y} := \mathsf{y}+\mathsf{x}), [\,\mathsf{x}{:}\,100 \mid \mathsf{y}{:}\,0\,]\rangle$
    $\to \langle \mathbf{newvar}\; \mathsf{x} := 1 \;\mathbf{in}\; \mathsf{y} := \mathsf{y}+\mathsf{x}, [\,\mathsf{x}{:}\,100 \mid \mathsf{y}{:}\,0\,]\rangle$ (Variable Decl. (b), 2)

It can be shown that the transition relation defined by the rules we have given is a function. As remarked in the previous section, this implies that, for any configuration, there is a unique longest execution starting with that configuration, which is either infinite or ends in a terminal configuration. Thus the following defines a function $[\![-]\!]_{\mathrm{comm}} \in \langle \mathrm{comm}\rangle \to \Sigma \to \Sigma_\bot$:

$$[\![c]\!]_{\mathrm{comm}}\sigma = \begin{cases} \bot & \text{when } \langle c, \sigma \rangle \uparrow \\ \sigma' & \text{when } \langle c, \sigma \rangle \to^* \sigma'. \end{cases}$$

It can be shown that this coincides with the direct semantic function defined in Chapter 2.

Finally, we note that the relation $\to^*$ can be defined in terms of $\to$ by inference rules:

TR RULE: Transitive and Reflexive Closure

$$\frac{\gamma \to \gamma'}{\gamma \to^* \gamma'} \qquad \frac{\gamma \to^* \gamma' \qquad \gamma' \to^* \gamma''}{\gamma \to^* \gamma''} \qquad \frac{}{\gamma \to^* \gamma.}$$

(The metavariable γ ranges over all configurations, both nonterminal and terminal.) On the other hand, the property $\gamma \uparrow$ of divergence cannot be defined in terms of $\to$ by inference rules.

6.3 Transition Semantics of fail

We next consider augmenting the simple language of the previous section with the **fail** command described in Section 5.1. To accommodate this generalization, we introduce **abort**-state pairs as additional terminal configurations. Thus the set of terminal configurations becomes

$$\Gamma_T = \hat{\Sigma} = \Sigma \cup \{\mathbf{abort}\} \times \Sigma.$$

Then a single axiom schema suffices to define the semantics of **fail**:

TR RULE: **fail**

$$\frac{}{\langle \mathbf{fail}, \sigma \rangle \to \langle \mathbf{abort}, \sigma \rangle.}$$

However, we must also introduce additional rules for certain other commands. Specifically, when the rules we have already given have premises that describe the first step of some subcommand, an additional rule is needed to describe the case where the first step gives **abort**.

Thus we must add another rule for sequencing, to deal with the case where the first step gives **abort**. In essence, this rule captures the fact that **fail** will stop the execution of a larger program in which it is embedded:

TR RULE: Sequential Composition (for **abort**)

$$\frac{\langle c_0, \sigma \rangle \to \langle \mathbf{abort}, \sigma' \rangle}{\langle c_0 \,;\, c_1, \sigma \rangle \to \langle \mathbf{abort}, \sigma' \rangle.}$$

We must also add another rule for variable declaration:

TR RULE: Variable Declaration (for **abort**)

$$\frac{\langle c, [\,\sigma \mid v\colon [\![e]\!]_{\mathrm{intexp}}\sigma\,] \rangle \to \langle \mathbf{abort}, \sigma' \rangle}{\langle \mathbf{newvar}\ v := e\ \mathbf{in}\ c, \sigma \rangle \to \langle \mathbf{abort}, [\,\sigma' \mid v\colon \sigma v\,] \rangle.}$$

The extension we have made to accommodate the **fail** command does not alter the fact that the transition relation is a function, so that, for any configuration, there is a unique longest execution starting with that configuration, which is either infinite or ends in a terminal configuration. Thus the following defines a function $[\![-]\!]_{\mathrm{comm}} \in \langle\mathrm{comm}\rangle \to \Sigma \to \hat{\Sigma}_\perp$:

$$[\![c]\!]_{\mathrm{comm}}\sigma = \begin{cases} \perp & \text{when } \langle c, \sigma \rangle \uparrow \\ \sigma' & \text{when } \langle c, \sigma \rangle \to^* \sigma' \\ \langle \mathbf{abort}, \sigma' \rangle & \text{when } \langle c, \sigma \rangle \to^* \langle \mathbf{abort}, \sigma' \rangle. \end{cases}$$

It can be shown that this coincides with the direct semantic function defined in Section 5.1.

6.4 Input and Output

To deal with input and output, we place labels on the transitions between configurations, writing $?\,n$ when the integer n is input and $!\,n$ when the integer n is output. For example, the following is an execution of the program in Section 5.6:

$\langle x := 0 \,;\, \textbf{while true do } (?\,y \,;\, x := x + y \,;\, !\,x), [\,x\!: 100 \mid y\!: 100\,]\rangle$

$\quad \to \langle \textbf{while true do } (?\,y \,;\, x := x + y \,;\, !\,x), [\,x\!: 0 \mid y\!: 100\,]\rangle$

$\quad \to \langle ?\,y \,;\, x := x + y \,;\, !\,x \,;\, \textbf{while true do } (?\,y \,;\, x := x + y \,;\, !\,x), [\,x\!: 0 \mid y\!: 100\,]\rangle$

$\quad \xrightarrow{?\,7} \langle x := x + y \,;\, !\,x \,;\, \textbf{while true do } (?\,y \,;\, x := x + y \,;\, !\,x), [\,x\!: 0 \mid y\!: 7\,]\rangle$

$\quad \to \langle !\,x \,;\, \textbf{while true do } (?\,y \,;\, x := x + y \,;\, !\,x), [\,x\!: 7 \mid y\!: 7\,]\rangle$

$\quad \xrightarrow{!\,7} \langle \textbf{while true do } (?\,y \,;\, x := x + y \,;\, !\,x), [\,x\!: 7 \mid y\!: 7\,]\rangle$

$\quad \to \langle ?\,y \,;\, x := x + y \,;\, !\,x \,;\, \textbf{while true do } (?\,y \,;\, x := x + y \,;\, !\,x), [\,x\!: 7 \mid y\!: 7\,]\rangle$

$\quad \xrightarrow{?\,5} \langle x := x + y \,;\, !\,x \,;\, \textbf{while true do } (?\,y \,;\, x := x + y \,;\, !\,x), [\,x\!: 7 \mid y\!: 5\,]\rangle$

$\quad \to \langle !\,x \,;\, \textbf{while true do } (?\,y \,;\, x := x + y \,;\, !\,x), [\,x\!: 12 \mid y\!: 5\,]\rangle$

$\quad \xrightarrow{!\,12} \cdots .$

To formalize this, we make the transition relation a trinary relation that is a subset of $\Gamma_N \times \Lambda \times \Gamma$, where Λ is the set of *labels*:

$$\Lambda = \{\epsilon\} \cup \{\, ?\,n \mid n \in \mathbf{Z} \,\} \cup \{\, !\,n \mid n \in \mathbf{Z} \,\},$$

and we write $\langle c, \sigma \rangle \xrightarrow{\lambda} \gamma$ to indicate that $\langle\langle c, \sigma \rangle, \lambda, \gamma\rangle$ belongs to the transition relation. However, when λ is the *null* label ϵ, it is omitted over the arrow, and the corresponding transition is called a *silent* transition. Thus the rules in previous sections become rules about silent transitions.

Two more rules are needed to deal with input and output:

TR RULE: Input

$$\langle ?\, v, \sigma \rangle \xrightarrow{?\,n} [\,\sigma \mid v\!:\!n\,],$$

TR RULE: Output

$$\langle !\, e, \sigma \rangle \xrightarrow{!\,n} \sigma \qquad \text{when } n = [\![e]\!]_{\text{intexp}}\sigma.$$

However, we must also generalize the rules of Section 6.2 that have a premiss, to allow the transition in the premiss to have an arbitrary label (denoted by the metavariable λ) that is carried over to the conclusion: In particular:

TR RULE: Sequential Composition

$$\frac{\langle c_0, \sigma \rangle \xrightarrow{\lambda} \sigma'}{\langle c_0\,;\,c_1, \sigma \rangle \xrightarrow{\lambda} \langle c_1, \sigma' \rangle}$$

$$\frac{\langle c_0, \sigma \rangle \xrightarrow{\lambda} \langle c_0', \sigma' \rangle}{\langle c_0\,;\,c_1, \sigma \rangle \xrightarrow{\lambda} \langle c_0'\,;\,c_1, \sigma' \rangle}$$

$$\frac{\langle c_0, \sigma \rangle \xrightarrow{\lambda} \langle \mathbf{abort}, \sigma \rangle}{\langle c_0\,;\,c_1, \sigma \rangle \xrightarrow{\lambda} \langle \mathbf{abort}, \sigma \rangle},$$

TR RULE: Variable Declaration

$$\frac{\langle c, [\,\sigma \mid v\!:\![\![e]\!]_{\text{intexp}}\sigma\,] \rangle \xrightarrow{\lambda} \sigma'}{\langle \mathbf{newvar}\ v := e\ \mathbf{in}\ c, \sigma \rangle \xrightarrow{\lambda} [\,\sigma' \mid v\!:\!\sigma v\,]}$$

$$\frac{\langle c, [\,\sigma \mid v\!:\![\![e]\!]_{\text{intexp}}\sigma\,] \rangle \xrightarrow{\lambda} \langle c', \sigma' \rangle}{\langle \mathbf{newvar}\ v := e\ \mathbf{in}\ c, \sigma \rangle \xrightarrow{\lambda} \langle \mathbf{newvar}\ v := \sigma'v\ \mathbf{in}\ c', [\,\sigma' \mid v\!:\!\sigma v\,] \rangle}$$

$$\frac{\langle c, [\,\sigma \mid v\!:\![\![e]\!]_{\text{intexp}}\sigma\,] \rangle \xrightarrow{\lambda} \langle \mathbf{abort}, \sigma' \rangle}{\langle \mathbf{newvar}\ v := e\ \mathbf{in}\ c, \sigma \rangle \xrightarrow{\lambda} \langle \mathbf{abort}, [\,\sigma' \mid v\!:\!\sigma v\,] \rangle.}$$

Although our transition relation is no longer a function, or even a binary relation, the semantics is still determinate and executions never get stuck. Let $\langle c, \sigma \rangle$ be an arbitrary nonterminal configuration. Then it can be shown that exactly one of the following cases holds:

- There is exactly one transition from $\langle c, \sigma \rangle$. It is a silent transition of the form $\langle c, \sigma \rangle \to \gamma$.
- There is exactly one transition from $\langle c, \sigma \rangle$. It is an output transition of the form $\langle c, \sigma \rangle \xrightarrow{!n} \gamma$.
- Every transition from $\langle c, \sigma \rangle$ is an input transition of the form $\langle c, \sigma \rangle \xrightarrow{?n} \gamma_n$. There is one such transition for each $n \in \mathbf{Z}$.

It follows that, from any configuration, there is a unique longest sequence of silent transitions, which is either

- infinite,
- or ends with a terminal configuration,
- or ends with a nonterminal configuration from which a unique output transition is possible,
- or ends with a nonterminal configuration from which exactly one input transition is possible for every integer.

Let $\Omega \approx (\hat{\Sigma} + (\mathbf{Z} \times \Omega) + (\mathbf{Z} \to \Omega))_\perp$ be the domain of resumptions used in Section 5.6 and $F \in \Gamma \to \Omega$ be the least function satisfying

$$
F\gamma = \begin{cases}
\perp & \text{when } \gamma \uparrow \\
\iota_{\text{term}} \sigma' & \text{when } \gamma \to^* \sigma' \\
\iota_{\text{abort}} \sigma' & \text{when } \gamma \to^* \langle \mathbf{abort}, \sigma' \rangle \\
\iota_{\text{out}}(n, F\gamma'') & \text{when } \exists \gamma' \in \Gamma. \ \gamma \to^* \gamma' \text{ and } \gamma' \xrightarrow{!n} \gamma'' \\
\iota_{\text{in}}(\lambda n \in \mathbf{Z}. \ F\gamma_n) & \text{when } \exists \gamma' \in \Gamma. \ \forall n \in \mathbf{Z}. \ \gamma \to^* \gamma' \text{ and } \gamma' \xrightarrow{?n} \gamma_n.
\end{cases}
$$

(Note that $\gamma \to^* \gamma'$ means that there is an execution from γ to γ' consisting of zero or more *silent* transitions.) Then it can be shown that the direct semantic function defined in Section 5.6 satisfies $[\![c]\!]_{\text{comm}} \sigma = F\langle c, \sigma \rangle$.

Bibliographic Notes

Transition semantics was originally developed to describe programming languages for concurrent processing. It was introduced by Hennessy and Plotkin [1979] and applied to a variety of languages by Plotkin [1981; 1983].

Exercises

6.1   Let c be the command considered in Exercise 5.1:

while $x \neq 0$ **do if** $x = 1$ **then fail else** $x := x - 2$.

(a) Give an execution that begins with the configuration $\langle c, [x : 3] \rangle$.

(b) Prove the second transition of this execution.

6.2   Extend the transition semantics given in Sections 6.2 and 6.3 (including **fail** but not input-output) by giving inference rules for the following constructs:

(a) The **repeat** command described in Exercise 2.2.
(b) The **catchin** command described in Exercise 5.3.
(c) The **catch**-label command described in Exercise 5.4. Assume that the set of terminal configurations is $\hat{\Sigma} = \Sigma \cup (\langle\text{label}\rangle \times \Sigma)$, where $\langle \ell, \sigma \rangle$ is produced by a command that fails with label ℓ.

6.3   Extend the transition semantics of Section 6.4 by giving inference rules for a command describing input to a subscripted array variable with the syntax

$$\langle\text{comm}\rangle ::= ?\,\langle\text{arrayvar}\rangle(\langle\text{intexp}\rangle)$$

When $?\,w(e)$ is executed in state σ, an integer value should be input and assigned to the array element denoted by $w(e)$ in the state σ, unless a subscript error occurs, in which case execution should fail without performing input. (Assume that a state maps ordinary variables into integers and array variables into functions, as in Section 4.2.)

6.4   In contrast to the transition semantics presented in this chapter, there is another kind of operational semantics called *evaluation semantics*, or sometimes "natural semantics" or "big-step semantics", that is based on a relation $\Rightarrow$ between nonterminal configurations and terminal configurations, such that $\gamma \Rightarrow \gamma'$ holds in evaluation semantics if and only if $\gamma \rightarrow^* \gamma'$ holds in transition semantics. (The relations $\Rightarrow$ and $\rightarrow^*$ are not exactly the same, however, since they are defined over different sets.) Nonterminal and terminal configurations and the relation $\rightarrow^*$ are the same as in Section 6.1.

    Beginning in Section 10.3, we will use evaluation semantics to describe the behavior of functional languages, but it can also be used for the simple imperative language.

    Define the evaluation semantics of the simple imperative language, plus **fail** but without input or output, by giving inference rules for formulas of the form $\langle c, \sigma \rangle \Rightarrow \gamma$, where σ is a state, γ is a state or **abort**-state pair, and c is an assignment command, **skip**, **fail**, sequential composition, conditional command, **while** command, or variable declaration. The premisses and conclusions of the rules all must be formulas whose main operator is $\Rightarrow$, though there may be side conditions that depend on the value of boolean expressions. The rules should not contain occurrences of $\rightarrow$ or $\rightarrow^*$.

Hint Remember that inference rules can have more than one premiss.

7

Nondeterminism and Guarded Commands

A *nondeterministic* program is one that does not completely determine the behavior of a computer, so that different executions of the same program with the same initial state and input can give different results. Although concurrent programs are usually nondeterministic, the topics of nondeterminism and concurrency are distinct, and it is pedagogically sensible to consider nondeterminism by itself before plunging on to concurrency.

Moreover, even with purely sequential computation, nondeterministic programs are often desirable because they avoid unnecessary commitments. Such commitments can make programs harder to read and to reason about. Even more seriously, in programs that use abstract types, they can place unnecessary constraints on the choice of data representations.

(Just as one can have nondeterministic sequential programs, one can also have deterministic concurrent ones — often called parallel programs — as will be evident when we consider functional programming languages.)

In this chapter we will explore Dijkstra's guarded commands, which are the most widely accepted and studied mechanism for extending the simple imperative language to nondeterministic programming.

In contrast to the previous chapters, we will begin with operational semantics, extending the development of the previous chapter. Then, after introducing powerdomains, we will give a direct denotational semantics for our nondeterministic language (excluding intermediate input and output). Finally, we will extend the specification methods of Chapter 3 to nondeterminism (again excluding input and output) and also deal briefly with weakest preconditions.

Before proceeding further, however, we must clear up a potential confusion. In automata theory, the result of a *nondeterministic automaton* is defined to be the the union of the results of *all* possible executions. In this book, however, we will only consider a very different view of nondeterminacy, where any *single* execution is an acceptable implementation of a nondeterministic program. (Thus, for example, a program that either terminates with x = 6 or runs on forever is very different from a program that always terminates with x = 6.)

7.1 Syntax and Transition Semantics

Despite their name, guarded commands are a new syntactic category rather than a new kind of command. Thus we augment the syntax of the simple imperative language by introducing a new nonterminal ⟨gdcomm⟩ denoting the set of guarded commands:

$$\langle \text{gdcomm} \rangle ::= \langle \text{boolexp} \rangle \rightarrow \langle \text{comm} \rangle \mid \langle \text{gdcomm} \rangle \; \square \; \langle \text{gdcomm} \rangle$$

(The operator $\rightarrow$ will be given the same precedence as :=, while $\square$ will given a lower precedence.) In a simple guarded command of the form $b \rightarrow c$ the command c is said to be *guarded* by the boolean expression b, indicating that c will be executed only when b is true. More generally, guarded commands can be combined with the operator $\square$. (Dijkstra calls these combinations "guarded command sets", but we will regard them as belonging to the same syntactic category as simple guarded commands since they have the same kind of meaning.)

Two new kinds of commands, the *alternative* and *repetitive* commands, are then defined in terms of guarded commands:

$$\langle \text{comm} \rangle ::= \textbf{if } \langle \text{gdcomm} \rangle \textbf{ fi} \mid \textbf{do } \langle \text{gdcomm} \rangle \textbf{ od}$$

The repetitive command is equivalent to a **while** command whose body is an alternative command, and the alternative command is *roughly* similar to a nest of conditional commands:

$$\textbf{do } b_0 \rightarrow c_0 \; \square \; \cdots \; \square \; b_{n-1} \rightarrow c_{n-1} \textbf{ od}$$
$$= \textbf{while } b_0 \vee \cdots \vee b_{n-1} \textbf{ do if } b_0 \rightarrow c_0 \; \square \; \cdots \; \square \; b_{n-1} \rightarrow c_{n-1} \textbf{ fi}$$

$$\textbf{if } b_0 \rightarrow c_0 \; \square \; \cdots \; \square \; b_{n-1} \rightarrow c_{n-1} \textbf{ fi}$$
$$\overset{?}{=} \textbf{if } b_0 \textbf{ then } c_0 \textbf{ else } \cdots \textbf{ if } b_{n-1} \textbf{ then } c_{n-1} \textbf{ else fail}.$$

(Note that the test $b_0 \vee \cdots \vee b_{n-1}$ insures that the repetitive command cannot execute the final **fail** within the alternative command.) But there is one profound difference: If more than one of the guards b_i are true, then the implementation of **if** $\cdots$ **fi** (and therefore of **do** $\cdots$ **od**) is free to execute any one of the corresponding commands c_i.

As a consequence, when we extend the transition semantics of Chapter 6, we will lose the guarantee that the transition relation is a function (though it will still be a total relation, since executions never get "stuck"). Thus, for a given initial configuration there may be more than one execution that is maximal (in the sense of not being an initial subsequence of a longer execution, and thus either being infinite or ending in a terminal configuration).

A further complication is that guarded commands have a more complex meaning than ordinary commands since, in addition to diverging or terminating normally or abortively, a guarded command may report that all of its guards are false. We will model this new possibility by a transition from a configuration containing the guarded command to a new terminal configuration **false**. Thus the set of nonterminal configurations will be $(\langle \text{comm} \rangle \times \Sigma) \cup (\langle \text{gdcomm} \rangle \times \Sigma)$ and the set of terminal configurations will be $\hat{\Sigma} \cup \{\textbf{false}\}$, where $\hat{\Sigma} = \Sigma \cup (\{\textbf{abort}\} \times \Sigma)$. However, the transition relation will never hold between a configuration in $\langle \text{comm} \rangle \times \Sigma$ and either **false** or a configuration in $\langle \text{gdcomm} \rangle \times \Sigma$, so that no execution beginning with an ordinary command will end with **false**.

More precisely, the possible transitions are limited to those shown in the following diagram:

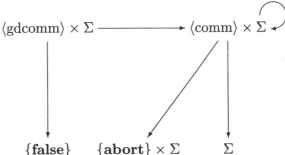

Once the configurations are understood, the inference rules for transition semantics are straightforward. The rules for guarded commands are

TR RULE: Simple Guarded Command

$$\frac{}{\langle b \rightarrow c, \sigma \rangle \rightarrow \langle c, \sigma \rangle} \qquad \text{when } \llbracket b \rrbracket_{\text{boolexp}} \sigma = \textbf{true}$$

$$\frac{}{\langle b \rightarrow c, \sigma \rangle \rightarrow \textbf{false}} \qquad \text{when } \llbracket b \rrbracket_{\text{boolexp}} \sigma = \textbf{false},$$

TR RULE: Compound Guarded Command

$$\frac{\langle g_0, \sigma \rangle \rightarrow \langle c, \sigma \rangle}{\langle g_0 \ \Box \ g_1, \sigma \rangle \rightarrow \langle c, \sigma \rangle} \qquad\qquad \frac{\langle g_1, \sigma \rangle \rightarrow \langle c, \sigma \rangle}{\langle g_0 \ \Box \ g_1, \sigma \rangle \rightarrow \langle c, \sigma \rangle}$$

$$\frac{\langle g_0, \sigma \rangle \rightarrow \textbf{false} \qquad \langle g_1, \sigma \rangle \rightarrow \textbf{false}}{\langle g_0 \ \Box \ g_1, \sigma \rangle \rightarrow \textbf{false},}$$

and the rules for the new ordinary commands (in addition to those of Chapter 6) are

TR RULE: Alternative Command

$$\frac{\langle g, \sigma \rangle \rightarrow \langle c, \sigma \rangle}{\langle \textbf{if } g \textbf{ fi}, \sigma \rangle \rightarrow \langle c, \sigma \rangle} \qquad\qquad \frac{\langle g, \sigma \rangle \rightarrow \textbf{false}}{\langle \textbf{if } g \textbf{ fi}, \sigma \rangle \rightarrow \langle \textbf{abort}, \sigma \rangle,}$$

TR RULE: Repetitive Command

$$\frac{\langle g, \sigma \rangle \to \langle c, \sigma \rangle}{\langle \textbf{do } g \textbf{ od}, \sigma \rangle \to \langle c \text{ ; } \textbf{do } g \textbf{ od}, \sigma \rangle} \qquad\qquad \frac{\langle g, \sigma \rangle \to \textbf{false}}{\langle \textbf{do } g \textbf{ od}, \sigma \rangle \to \sigma.}$$

7.2 Bounded Nondeterminism and Powerdomains

In the previous section, we described the addition of guarded commands and related facilities to the language discussed in Chapters 5 and 6, which included **fail** commands and intermediate input-output. (Although the new inference rules mention only silent transitions, nonsilent transitions still occur in the rules inherited from Chapter 6.) For the rest of this chapter, however, we consider this language without any facilities for input or output.

As in Chapter 6, we write $\gamma \to^* \gamma'$ when there is a finite execution beginning with γ and ending with γ', and $\gamma \uparrow$ when there is an infinite execution beginning with γ.

In Sections 6.2 and 6.3, we expressed direct denotational semantics in terms of transition semantics by taking the denotational meaning of a command c in a state σ to be either the unique terminal configuration γ such that $\langle c, \sigma \rangle \to^* \gamma$, or $\bot$ if $\langle c, \sigma \rangle \uparrow$. Once nondeterminism has appeared, however, we must take the meaning of a command (or guarded command) in a state to be a set of such results:

$$[\![g]\!]_{\text{gdcomm}} \sigma = \{ \gamma \mid \langle g, \sigma \rangle \to^* \gamma \wedge \gamma \text{ terminal} \} \cup (\textbf{if } \langle g, \sigma \rangle \uparrow \textbf{ then } \{\bot\} \textbf{ else } \{\})$$

$$[\![c]\!]_{\text{comm}} \sigma = \{ \gamma \mid \langle c, \sigma \rangle \to^* \gamma \wedge \gamma \text{ terminal} \} \cup (\textbf{if } \langle c, \sigma \rangle \uparrow \textbf{ then } \{\bot\} \textbf{ else } \{\}).$$

It is evident that

$$[\![-]\!]_{\text{gdcomm}} \in \langle \text{gdcomm} \rangle \to \Sigma \to \mathcal{P}((\hat{\Sigma} \cup \{\textbf{false}\})_\bot)$$

and, since no execution goes from a configuration in $\langle \text{comm} \rangle \times \Sigma$ to the configuration **false**,

$$[\![-]\!]_{\text{comm}} \in \langle \text{comm} \rangle \to \Sigma \to \mathcal{P}(\hat{\Sigma}_\bot).$$

However, one can say more about the nature of the sets $[\![g]\!]_{\text{gdcomm}} \sigma$ and $[\![c]\!]_{\text{comm}} \sigma$. Since executions never get stuck, from any starting configuration there is always either an infinite path or a path to some terminal configuration; thus these sets are never empty. A more subtle property, which is called *bounded nondeterminism* and has profound consequences for the denotational semantics and proof theory of guarded commands, is that whenever these sets are infinite they contain $\bot$.

To see that bounded nondeterminism holds, we first note that, for any configuration γ, the set $\{\,\gamma' \mid \gamma \to \gamma'\,\}$ of configurations to which the computation can move in one step is finite. (This can be proved from the inference rules in the previous section, by structural induction on the command or guarded command that is the first component of γ.)

Now let γ_0 be $\langle g, \sigma \rangle$ (or $\langle c, \sigma \rangle$), and suppose that $[\![g]\!]_{\text{gdcomm}}\sigma$ (or $[\![c]\!]_{\text{comm}}\sigma$) is infinite. Then the set $\{\,\gamma \mid \gamma_0 \to^* \gamma\,\}$ of all configurations reachable from γ_0 is infinite, since it includes every member of $[\![g]\!]_{\text{gdcomm}}\sigma$ (or $[\![c]\!]_{\text{comm}}\sigma$) except perhaps $\bot$. To show that γ_0 diverges one can construct, by induction on n, an infinite execution $\gamma_0 \to \gamma_1 \to \cdots$ such that, for each γ_n, the set $\{\,\gamma \mid \gamma_n \to^* \gamma\,\}$ is infinite.

For suppose this set is infinite for γ_n. It consists of γ_n itself plus the union of the sets of configurations reachable from each γ' that can be reached in one step from γ_n:

$$\{\,\gamma \mid \gamma_n \to^* \gamma\,\} = \{\gamma_n\} \cup \bigcup \{\,\{\,\gamma \mid \gamma' \to^* \gamma\,\} \mid \gamma_n \to \gamma'\,\}.$$

Since $\{\,\gamma' \mid \gamma_n \to \gamma'\,\}$ is finite, the union on the right expresses an infinite set as the union of a finite set of sets. It follows that at least one member $\{\,\gamma \mid \gamma' \to^* \gamma\,\}$ of this set of sets must be infinite, so that the corresponding γ' can be chosen as γ_{n+1}.

(This argument is an instance of "König's Lemma". A more usual statement is that there is an infinite path in any infinite tree with finite branching.)

It is instructive to consider the kind of language constructs that would violate bounded nondeterminism. For example, the command

$$\langle \text{comm} \rangle ::= \textbf{anynum}\ \langle \text{var} \rangle$$

with the transition semantics

$$\overline{\langle \textbf{anynum}\ v, \sigma \rangle \to [\,\sigma \mid v{:}n\,]} \qquad \text{whenever } n \geq 0,$$

moves in one step to an infinite set of terminal configurations, so that the set

$$[\![\textbf{anynum}\ v]\!]_{\text{comm}}\sigma = \{\,[\,\sigma \mid v{:}n\,] \mid n \geq 0\,\}$$

is infinite but does not contain $\bot$.

More subtly, bounded nondeterminism would fail if one were to impose a "fairness" constraint on guarded commands that guarantees that, in a repetition, any guard that was true an infinite number of times would eventually cause the corresponding command to be selected. For example, such a constraint would insure the termination of

$$\textbf{newvar}\ \mathsf{y} := 0\ \textbf{in}\ (\mathsf{x} := 0\,;\, \textbf{do}\ \mathsf{y} = 0 \to \mathsf{x} := \mathsf{x} + 1 \,\square\, \mathsf{y} = 0 \to \mathsf{y} := 1\ \textbf{od}),$$

which then would have the same behavior as **anynum** x.

As long as nondeterminism is bounded, however, the semantic functions satisfy

$$[\![-]\!]_{\text{gdcomm}} \in \langle\text{gdcomm}\rangle \to \Sigma \to \mathcal{P}_{\text{DOM}}((\hat{\Sigma} \cup \{\textbf{false}\})_\bot)$$

$$[\![-]\!]_{\text{comm}} \in \langle\text{comm}\rangle \to \Sigma \to \mathcal{P}_{\text{DOM}}(\hat{\Sigma}_\bot),$$

where

$$\mathcal{P}_{\text{DOM}}(S_\bot) = \{\, X \mid X \subseteq S_\bot \wedge X \neq \{\} \wedge (X \text{ infinite} \Rightarrow \bot \in X)\,\}$$

is called the *powerdomain* of $S_\bot$.

The obvious intent is that $\mathcal{P}_{\text{DOM}}(S_\bot)$ should be a domain. In general, the appropriate notion of approximation is

$$X \sqsubseteq Y \text{ if and only if } (\forall x \in X. \exists y \in Y. x \sqsubseteq y) \wedge (\forall y \in Y. \exists x \in X. x \sqsubseteq y),$$

which is called the *Egli-Milner ordering*. It is easy to see that $\{\bot\}$ is the least element in this ordering.

To see how the Egli-Milner ordering captures the concept of increasing information, consider a collection of computers, all simultaneously executing transition sequences for the same nondeterministic program with the same initial state. Let the "output" of a particular computer at a particular time be γ if the computer has reached the terminal configuration γ, or $\bot$ if the computer is in a nonterminal configuration. Let the "output" of a particular computer at infinite time be γ if the computer ever reaches the terminal state γ or $\bot$ if the computer runs on forever. If X and Y are the sets of outputs of all members of the collection when observed at an earlier and a later (or infinite) time, then every member of X should have an extension in Y and every member of Y should have an approximation in X — which is precisely the Egli-Milner ordering $X \sqsubseteq Y$.

In fact, this argument extends to languages with input-output and other enrichments. The outputs of the individual computers can range over a wide class of domains, as long as $x \sqsubseteq y$ holds whenever x and y are outputs of the same computer at earlier and later times. In these more general cases, however, the mathematics needed to construct the powerdomain is difficult. One basic problem is that, for subsets of nontrivial nonflat domains, the Egli-Milner ordering ceases to be an antisymmetric relation. For example, for subsets of the domain $\{1, 2, 3\}$ with the ordering $1 \sqsubseteq 2 \sqsubseteq 3$, the Egli-Milner ordering gives $\{1, 3\} \sqsubseteq \{1, 2, 3\} \sqsubseteq \{1, 3\}$. Because of such difficulties, in this book we will consider powerdomains of only flat domains (which is why we exclude input-output operations).

In the particular case of the powerdomain of a flat domain, the Egli-Milner ordering is a partial order that simplifies to

$$X \sqsubseteq Y \quad \text{if and only if} \quad \textbf{if } \bot \in X \textbf{ then } X \subseteq Y \cup \{\bot\} \textbf{ else } X = Y$$

or, equivalently, $X \sqsubseteq Y$ if and only if $X \cup \{\bot\} \subseteq Y \cup \{\bot\}$ and either $\bot \in X$ or $X = Y$. In this case, the following proposition establishes that every chain has a least upper bound, so that $\mathcal{P}_{\mathrm{DOM}}(S_\bot)$ is indeed a domain:

Proposition 7.1 *Let X_0, X_1, ... be a sequence of members of the power-domain $\mathcal{P}_{\mathrm{DOM}}(S_\bot)$ of a flat domain.*

(a) *Suppose every X_i contains $\bot$. Then the sequence is a chain $X_0 \sqsubseteq X_1 \sqsubseteq \cdots$ if and only if it is an inclusion sequence:*

$$X_0 \subseteq X_1 \subseteq \cdots \, ;$$

and, if so, its union is its limit:

$$\bigsqcup_{k=0}^{\infty} X_k = \bigcup_{k=0}^{\infty} X_k.$$

(b) *Suppose there is a least $n \geq 0$, which we will call the "completion point" of the sequence, such that X_n does not contain $\bot$. Then the sequence is a chain if and only if the X_n are finite sets satisfying*

$$X_0 \subseteq \cdots \subseteq X_{n-1} \hat{\subseteq} X_n = X_{n+1} = \cdots \, ,$$

where $X_{n-1} \hat{\subseteq} X_n$ stands for

$$X_{n-1} \subseteq X_n \cup \{\bot\} \quad \text{and} \quad \bot \in X_{n-1} \quad \text{and} \quad \bot \notin X_n;$$

and, if so, the members of the sequence are all finite and their limit is

$$\bigsqcup_{k=0}^{\infty} X_k = X_n = \left(\bigcup_{k=0}^{\infty} X_k \right) - \{\bot\}.$$

The proof is left to the reader.

Finally, we consider the question of whether the pointwise union of a set of chains preserves limits:

Proposition 7.2 *Let $S_\bot$ be a flat domain and suppose, for each i in some nonempty set I, that $X_0^{(i)} \sqsubseteq X_1^{(i)} \sqsubseteq \cdots$ is a chain of elements of $\mathcal{P}_{\mathrm{DOM}}(S_\bot)$. If either I is finite or, for some $i_0 \in I$, all $X_k^{(i_0)}$ contain $\bot$, then*

$$\bigcup_{i \in I} X_0^{(i)} \sqsubseteq \bigcup_{i \in I} X_1^{(i)} \sqsubseteq \cdots$$

is a chain whose limit is

$$\bigsqcup_{k=0}^{\infty} \bigcup_{i \in I} X_k^{(i)} = \bigcup_{i \in I} \bigsqcup_{k=0}^{\infty} X_k^{(i)}.$$

PROOF We first consider the case where there is some i_0 such that $\perp \in X_k^{(i_0)}$ for all k. On the one hand, for every $i \in I$, since $X_0^{(i)} \sqsubseteq X_1^{(i)} \sqsubseteq \cdots$ is a chain, we have

$$X_0^{(i)} \cup \{\perp\} \subseteq X_1^{(i)} \cup \{\perp\} \subseteq \cdots .$$

Thus

$$\bigcup_{i \in I}(X_0^{(i)} \cup \{\perp\}) \subseteq \bigcup_{i \in I}(X_1^{(i)} \cup \{\perp\}) \subseteq \cdots .$$

But the unions here include $i = i_0$, so that each $\bigcup_{i \in I} X_k^{(i)}$ itself contains $\perp$. Thus

$$\bigcup_{i \in I} X_0^{(i)} \subseteq \bigcup_{i \in I} X_1^{(i)} \subseteq \cdots ,$$

and since every set in this inclusion sequence contains $\perp$, it is a chain

$$\bigcup_{i \in I} X_0^{(i)} \sqsubseteq \bigcup_{i \in I} X_1^{(i)} \sqsubseteq \cdots ,$$

whose limit is

$$\bigsqcup_{k=0}^{\infty} \bigcup_{i \in I} X_k^{(i)} = \bigcup_{k=0}^{\infty} \bigcup_{i \in I} X_k^{(i)} = \bigcup_{i \in I} \bigcup_{k=0}^{\infty} X_k^{(i)}.$$

On the other hand, for each $i \in I$, $\bigsqcup_{k=0}^{\infty} X_k^{(i)}$ is either $\bigcup_{k=0}^{\infty} X_k^{(i)}$ or $\bigcup_{k=0}^{\infty} X_k^{(i)} - \{\perp\}$, and the first of these cases holds when $i = i_0$. Thus

$$\bigcup_{i \in I} \bigsqcup_{k=0}^{\infty} X_k^{(i)} = \bigcup_{i \in I} \bigcup_{k=0}^{\infty} X_k^{(i)}.$$

Next consider the case where I is finite and every chain $X_0^{(i)} \sqsubseteq X_1^{(i)} \sqsubseteq \cdots$ has a completion point n_i, so that, by the second part of Proposition 7.1,

$$X_0^{(i)} \subseteq \cdots \subseteq X_{n_i-1}^{(i)} \hat{\subseteq} X_{n_i}^{(i)} = X_{n_i+1}^{(i)} = \cdots ,$$

and the $X_n^{(i)}$ are all finite. Let n be the maximum of the completion points n_i over $i \in I$. It is easy to see that, by adding $\perp$ to the $X_k^{(i)}$ for $n_i \le k < n$ (or equally well for $0 \le k < n$, since $\perp$ already occurs in the earlier $X_k^{(i)}$), we can raise the completion point of the ith chain:

$$X_0^{(i)} \cup \{\perp\} \subseteq \cdots \subseteq X_{n-1}^{(i)} \cup \{\perp\} \hat{\subseteq} X_n^{(i)} = X_{n+1}^{(i)} = \cdots .$$

Thus the unions of the elements over $i \in I$ satisfy

$$\bigcup_{i \in I}(X_0^{(i)} \cup \{\perp\}) \subseteq \cdots \subseteq \bigcup_{i \in I}(X_{n-1}^{(i)} \cup \{\perp\}) \hat{\subseteq} \bigcup_{i \in I} X_n^{(i)} = \bigcup_{i \in I} X_{n+1}^{(i)} = \cdots ,$$

and since each union is finite (being the union of finite sets over a finite set), this sequence is also a chain in $\mathcal{P}_{\text{DOM}}(S_\perp)$.

For $k < n$, however, the union $\bigcup_{i \in I} X_k^{(i)}$ already contains $\perp$, since $X_k^{(i)}$ contains $\perp$ when i is a member of I for which the completion point n_i takes on the maximum value n. Thus the above chain is

$$\bigcup_{i \in I} X_0^{(i)} \subseteq \cdots \subseteq \bigcup_{i \in I} X_{n-1}^{(i)} \,\hat{\subseteq}\, \bigcup_{i \in I} X_n^{(i)} = \bigcup_{i \in I} X_{n+1}^{(i)} = \cdots,$$

whose limit is

$$\overset{\infty}{\underset{k=0}{\bigsqcup}} \bigcup_{i \in I} X_k^{(i)} = \Big(\overset{\infty}{\underset{k=0}{\bigcup}} \bigcup_{i \in I} X_k^{(i)}\Big) - \{\perp\}$$

$$= \Big(\bigcup_{i \in I} \overset{\infty}{\underset{k=0}{\bigcup}} X_k^{(i)}\Big) - \{\perp\}$$

$$= \bigcup_{i \in I} \Big(\overset{\infty}{\underset{k=0}{\bigcup}} X_k^{(i)} - \{\perp\}\Big)$$

$$= \bigcup_{i \in I} \overset{\infty}{\underset{k=0}{\bigsqcup}} X_k^{(i)}.$$

END OF PROOF

Notice that the hypotheses of this proposition are necessary. To see this, suppose $I = \mathbf{N}$ and, for $i \in I$ and $0 \leq k < \infty$,

$$X_k^{(i)} = \textbf{if } k < i \textbf{ then } F^{(i)} \cup \{\perp\} \textbf{ else } F^{(i)},$$

where each $F^{(i)}$ is some finite subset of S. Then

$$\overset{\infty}{\underset{k=0}{\bigsqcup}} \bigcup_{i \in I} X_k^{(i)} = \Big(\bigcup_{i \in I} F^{(i)}\Big) \cup \{\perp\}$$

but

$$\bigcup_{i \in I} \overset{\infty}{\underset{k=0}{\bigsqcup}} X_k^{(i)} = \bigcup_{i \in I} F^{(i)}.$$

Indeed, the latter set may even be an infinite subset of S, which would not belong to $\mathcal{P}_{\mathrm{DOM}}(S_\perp)$.

7.3 Semantic Equations

The direct semantic functions that were defined in the previous section in terms of transition semantics can also be defined by semantic equations. For assignment, **skip**, and **fail**, the equations are straightforward:

DR SEM EQ: Assignment

$$\llbracket v := e \rrbracket_{\mathrm{comm}} \sigma = \{[\, \sigma \mid v{:}\, \llbracket e \rrbracket_{\mathrm{intexp}} \sigma \,]\},$$

DR SEM EQ: **skip**

$$\llbracket \textbf{skip} \rrbracket_{\text{comm}} \sigma = \{\sigma\},$$

DR SEM EQ: **fail**

$$\llbracket \textbf{fail} \rrbracket_{\text{comm}} \sigma = \{\langle \textbf{abort}, \sigma \rangle\}.$$

However, sequential composition requires an extension operator $(-)_*$ that raises a function from $\Sigma \to \mathcal{P}_{\text{DOM}}(\hat{\Sigma}_\perp)$ to $\mathcal{P}_{\text{DOM}}(\hat{\Sigma}_\perp) \to \mathcal{P}_{\text{DOM}}(\hat{\Sigma}_\perp)$:

DR SEM EQ: Sequential Composition

$$\llbracket c_0 \,;\, c_1 \rrbracket_{\text{comm}} \sigma = (\llbracket c_1 \rrbracket_{\text{comm}})_* (\llbracket c_0 \rrbracket_{\text{comm}} \sigma),$$

where

$$f_* X = \bigcup_{\sigma \in X} \textbf{if } \sigma = \perp \text{ or } \sigma \in \{\textbf{abort}\} \times \Sigma \textbf{ then } \{\sigma\} \textbf{ else } f\sigma. \qquad (7.1)$$

For guarded commands, we have

DR SEM EQ: Simple Guarded Command

$$\llbracket b \to c \rrbracket_{\text{gdcomm}} \sigma = \textbf{if } \llbracket b \rrbracket_{\text{boolexp}} \sigma \textbf{ then } \llbracket c \rrbracket_{\text{comm}} \sigma \textbf{ else } \{\textbf{false}\},$$

DR SEM EQ: Compound Guarded Command

$$\llbracket g_0 \mathbin{\square} g_1 \rrbracket_{\text{gdcomm}} \sigma = (\llbracket g_0 \rrbracket_{\text{gdcomm}} \sigma \quad \{\textbf{false}\}) \cup (\llbracket g_1 \rrbracket_{\text{gdcomm}} \sigma - \{\textbf{false}\}) \cup$$
$$(\textbf{if false} \in \llbracket g_0 \rrbracket_{\text{gdcomm}} \sigma \textbf{ and false} \in \llbracket g_1 \rrbracket_{\text{gdcomm}} \sigma \textbf{ then } \{\textbf{false}\} \textbf{ else } \{\}).$$

(The reader may verify that, for any guarded command g, the set $\llbracket g \rrbracket_{\text{gdcomm}} \sigma$ is either $\{\textbf{false}\}$ or a set that does not contain **false**.)

Then for the alternative and repetitive constructs we have

DR SEM EQ: Alternative Command

$$\llbracket \textbf{if } g \textbf{ fi} \rrbracket_{\text{comm}} \sigma$$
$$= (\lambda \sigma' \in \Sigma. \textbf{ if } \sigma' = \textbf{false then } \{\langle \textbf{abort}, \sigma \rangle\} \textbf{ else } \{\sigma'\})_* (\llbracket g \rrbracket_{\text{gdcomm}} \sigma),$$

DR SEM EQ: Repetitive Command

$$\llbracket \textbf{do } g \textbf{ od} \rrbracket_{\text{comm}} = \textbf{Y}_{\Sigma \to \mathcal{P}_{\text{DOM}}(\hat{\Sigma}_\perp)} F = \bigsqcup_{n=0}^{\infty} F^n \perp,$$

where

$$Fw\sigma = (\lambda \sigma' \in \Sigma. \textbf{ if } \sigma' = \textbf{false then } \{\sigma\} \textbf{ else } w\sigma')_* (\llbracket g \rrbracket_{\text{gdcomm}} \sigma).$$

(Although the operator $(-)_*$ here still satisfies Equation (7.1), it has a different type than the similar operator used earlier in this section, since it raises a function from $(\Sigma \cup \{\mathbf{false}\}) \to \mathcal{P}_{\mathrm{DOM}}(\hat{\Sigma}_\perp)$ to $\mathcal{P}_{\mathrm{DOM}}((\hat{\Sigma} \cup \{\mathbf{false}\})_\perp) \to \mathcal{P}_{\mathrm{DOM}}(\hat{\Sigma}_\perp)$.)

Finally, for variable declarations we have

DR SEM EQ: Variable Declaration

$$[\![\mathbf{newvar}\ v := e\ \mathbf{in}\ c]\!]_{\mathrm{comm}}\sigma$$
$$= (\lambda\sigma' \in \Sigma.\ [\sigma'\ |\ v{:}\sigma v])_\dagger([\![c]\!]_{\mathrm{comm}}[\sigma\ |\ v{:}[\![e]\!]_{\mathrm{intexp}}\sigma]),$$

where $(-)_\dagger$ raises a function from $\Sigma \to \Sigma$ to $\mathcal{P}_{\mathrm{DOM}}(\hat{\Sigma}_\perp) \to \mathcal{P}_{\mathrm{DOM}}(\hat{\Sigma}_\perp)$ as follows:

$$f_\dagger X = \{\,f\sigma\ |\ \sigma \in X\ \text{and}\ \sigma \in \Sigma\,\} \cup \{\,\langle\mathbf{abort}, f\sigma\rangle\ |\ \langle\mathbf{abort}, \sigma\rangle \in X\ \text{and}\ \sigma \in \Sigma\,\}$$
$$\cup\,(\mathbf{if}\ \perp\ \in X\ \mathbf{then}\ \{\perp\}\ \mathbf{else}\ \{\}).$$

We will not attempt to derive these semantic equations from the connection between denotational and transition semantics described in the previous section. But we will show that the function F in the equation for the repetitive construct is continuous. Let $w_0 \sqsubseteq w_1 \sqsubseteq \cdots$ be a chain in $\Sigma \to \mathcal{P}_{\mathrm{DOM}}(\hat{\Sigma}_\perp)$ and $\sigma \in \Sigma$. Then, using the definitions of F and $(-)_*$, Proposition 2.2 in Section 2.3 and the fact that the limit of a constant chain is its only member, obvious properties of conditionals, and the definition of F again, one obtains

$$F(\bigsqcup_{n=0}^{\infty} w_n)\sigma = \bigcup_{\sigma' \in [\![g]\!]_{\mathrm{gdcomm}}\sigma} \mathbf{if}\ \sigma' = \perp\ \text{or}\ \sigma' \in \{\mathbf{abort}\} \times \Sigma\ \mathbf{then}\ \{\sigma'\}\ \mathbf{else}$$
$$\mathbf{if}\ \sigma' = \mathbf{false}\ \mathbf{then}\ \{\sigma\}\ \mathbf{else}\ (\bigsqcup_{n=0}^{\infty} w_n)\sigma'$$

$$= \bigcup_{\sigma' \in [\![g]\!]_{\mathrm{gdcomm}}\sigma} \mathbf{if}\ \sigma' = \perp\ \text{or}\ \sigma' \in \{\mathbf{abort}\} \times \Sigma\ \mathbf{then}\ \bigsqcup_{n=0}^{\infty}\{\sigma'\}\ \mathbf{else}$$
$$\mathbf{if}\ \sigma' = \mathbf{false}\ \mathbf{then}\ \bigsqcup_{n=0}^{\infty}\{\sigma\}\ \mathbf{else}\ \bigsqcup_{n=0}^{\infty} w_n\sigma'$$

$$= \bigcup_{\sigma' \in [\![g]\!]_{\mathrm{gdcomm}}\sigma} \bigsqcup_{n=0}^{\infty} \mathbf{if}\ \sigma' = \perp\ \text{or}\ \sigma' \in \{\mathbf{abort}\} \times \Sigma\ \mathbf{then}\ \{\sigma'\}\ \mathbf{else}$$
$$\mathbf{if}\ \sigma' = \mathbf{false}\ \mathbf{then}\ \{\sigma\}\ \mathbf{else}\ w_n\sigma'$$

$$\overset{?}{=} \bigsqcup_{n=0}^{\infty} \bigcup_{\sigma' \in [\![g]\!]_{\mathrm{gdcomm}}\sigma} \mathbf{if}\ \sigma' = \perp\ \text{or}\ \sigma' \in \{\mathbf{abort}\} \times \Sigma\ \mathbf{then}\ \{\sigma'\}\ \mathbf{else}$$
$$\mathbf{if}\ \sigma' = \mathbf{false}\ \mathbf{then}\ \{\sigma\}\ \mathbf{else}\ w_n\sigma'$$

$$= \bigsqcup_{n=0}^{\infty} Fw_n\sigma,$$

provided that the equality marked with "?" holds. But this equality has the form

$$\bigcup_{\sigma' \in S} \bigsqcup_{n=0}^{\infty} w'_n \sigma' \stackrel{?}{=} \bigsqcup_{n=0}^{\infty} \bigcup_{\sigma' \in S} w'_n \sigma',$$

where $S = [\![g]\!]_{\text{gdcomm}} \sigma$, each w'_n is a strict function, and each $w'_0 \sigma' \sqsubseteq w'_1 \sigma' \sqsubseteq \cdots$ is a chain.

If S is infinite, then, by bounded nondeterminism, it must contain $\bot$. But then, since the w'_n are strict, every element of the chain $w'_0 \bot \sqsubseteq w'_1 \bot \sqsubseteq \cdots$ is $\{\bot\}$. Thus, Proposition 7.2 in the previous section implies that the above equality holds, and that the $\bigcup_{\sigma' \in S} w'_n \sigma' = Fw_n \sigma$ are chains over n.

Finally, the pointwise order on $\Sigma \to \mathcal{P}_{\text{DOM}}(\hat{\Sigma}_\bot)$ implies that the Fw_n are a chain over n, so that Proposition 2.2 in Section 2.3 gives

$$\bigsqcup_{n=0}^{\infty} Fw_n \sigma = (\bigsqcup_{n=0}^{\infty} Fw_n)\sigma,$$

which completes the proof that F is continuous.

It is important to realize that this argument — and continuity — fails if nondeterminism is unbounded. For example, suppose g is the guarded command in

do x $< 0 \to$ **anynum** x $\square$ x $> 0 \to$ x $:=$ x $- 1$ **od**

and σ is a state in which x has the value -3. For any integer n, it is possible for this repetitive command to run on for more than n iterations, so that $F^n \bot \sigma$, which describes the behavior of a repetitive command limited to n iterations, must contain $\bot$. Since this holds for all n, the limit of these terms, which is **Y** F, must also contain $\bot$. But in fact, the above repetitive command always terminates. (The counterexample does not even require guarded commands; one could use **while** x $\neq 0$ **do if** x < 0 **then anynum** x **else** x $:=$ x $- 1$.)

This failure of continuity is a symptom of the fact that our powerdomain semantics is limited to bounded nondeterminacy. (It is possible, however, to generalize powerdomains to treat unbounded nondeterminacy, by using a weaker notion of continuity based on transfinite limits.)

7.4 Program Specification and Proof

We can continue to reason about programs (excluding input-output) by using the same kinds of specifications as were introduced in Chapter 3 (and extended to treat **fail** in Section 5.1), but the definition of these specifications must be generalized to encompass nondeterminism: Essentially, the specification of a command must be true regardless of which of the possible executions of the command is selected nondeterministically. More precisely, the definitions in Sections 3.1 and 5.1 must be replaced by

DR SEM EQ: Partial Correctness Specification

$$[\![\{p\}\, c\, \{q\}]\!]_{\text{spec}} = \forall \sigma \in \Sigma.\ [\![p]\!]_{\text{assert}}\sigma \Rightarrow \forall \sigma' \in [\![c]\!]_{\text{comm}}\sigma.$$
$$(\sigma' = \bot \text{ or } \sigma' \in \{\mathbf{abort}\} \times \Sigma \text{ or } [\![q]\!]_{\text{assert}}\sigma'),$$

DR SEM EQ: Total Correctness Specification

$$[\![[\,p\,]\, c\, [\,q\,]]\!]_{\text{spec}} = \forall \sigma \in \Sigma.\ [\![p]\!]_{\text{assert}}\sigma \Rightarrow \forall \sigma' \in [\![c]\!]_{\text{comm}}\sigma.$$
$$(\sigma' \neq \bot \text{ and } \sigma' \notin \{\mathbf{abort}\} \times \Sigma \text{ and } [\![q]\!]_{\text{assert}}\sigma').$$

In addition, we must introduce specifications of guarded commands:

$$\langle\text{spec}\rangle ::= \{\langle\text{assert}\rangle\}\, \langle\text{gdcomm}\rangle\, \{\langle\text{assert}\rangle\} \qquad\qquad \text{(partial correctness)}$$
$$\mid\, [\,\langle\text{assert}\rangle\,]\, \langle\text{gdcomm}\rangle\, [\,\langle\text{assert}\rangle\,] \qquad\qquad \text{(total correctness)}$$

These specifications have a slightly different meaning than those for ordinary commands, since they permit execution of the guarded command to give **false**:

DR SEM EQ: Partial Correctness Specification for Guarded Commands

$$[\![\{p\}\, g\, \{q\}]\!]_{\text{spec}} = \forall \sigma \in \Sigma.\ [\![p]\!]_{\text{assert}}\sigma \Rightarrow \forall \sigma' \in [\![g]\!]_{\text{gdcomm}}\sigma.$$
$$(\sigma' = \bot \text{ or } \sigma' \in \{\mathbf{abort}\} \times \Sigma \text{ or } \sigma' = \mathbf{false} \text{ or } [\![q]\!]_{\text{assert}}\sigma'),$$

DR SEM EQ: Total Correctness Specification for Guarded Commands

$$[\![[\,p\,]\, g\, [\,q\,]]\!]_{\text{spec}} = \forall \sigma \in \Sigma.\ [\![p]\!]_{\text{assert}}\sigma \Rightarrow \forall \sigma' \in [\![g]\!]_{\text{gdcomm}}\sigma.$$
$$(\sigma' \neq \bot \text{ and } \sigma' \notin \{\mathbf{abort}\} \times \Sigma \text{ and } (\sigma' = \mathbf{false} \text{ or } [\![q]\!]_{\text{assert}}\sigma')).$$

Finally, we introduce a syntactic function $\mathcal{D}$ from $\langle\text{gdcomm}\rangle$ to $\langle\text{boolexp}\rangle$ that maps guarded commands into the disjunction of their guards:

$$\mathcal{D}(b \to c) = b$$
$$\mathcal{D}(g_0 \,\square\, g_1) = \mathcal{D}\,g_0 \vee \mathcal{D}\,g_1.$$

It is easily seen that $\mathcal{D}$ satisfies

$$[\![\mathcal{D}\,g]\!]_{\text{assert}}\sigma \text{ if and only if } \mathbf{false} \notin [\![g]\!]_{\text{gdcomm}}\sigma.$$

Happily, the inference rules given in Chapter 3 remain sound in the generalized setting of nondeterminism (as long as the nondeterminism is bounded). However, additional rules are needed to reason about the new constructs that we have introduced. For guarded commands, these rules are the same for partial and total correctness (except for the use of braces in one case and square brackets in the other), but for the alternative and repetitive constructs they are different.

SP RULE: Simple Guarded Command (SGC)

$$\frac{\{p \wedge b\}\, c\, \{q\}}{\{p\}\, b \rightarrow c\, \{q\}},$$

SP RULE: Compound Guarded Command (CGC)

$$\frac{\{p\}\, g_0\, \{q\} \qquad \{p\}\, g_1\, \{q\}}{\{p\}\, g_0 \,\square\, g_1\, \{q\}},$$

SP RULE: Partial Correctness of Alternative Command (ACP)

$$\frac{\{p\}\, g\, \{q\}}{\{p\}\, \mathbf{if}\ g\ \mathbf{fi}\, \{q\}},$$

SP RULE: Total Correctness of Alternative Command (ACT)

$$\frac{[\,p\,]\, g\, [\,q\,]}{[\,p \wedge \mathcal{D}\,g\,]\, \mathbf{if}\ g\ \mathbf{fi}\, [\,q\,]},$$

SP RULE: Partial Correctness of Repetitive Command (RCP)

$$\frac{\{i\}\, g\, \{i\}}{\{i\}\, \mathbf{do}\ g\ \mathbf{od}\, \{i \wedge \neg\, \mathcal{D}\,g\}},$$

SP RULE: Total Correctness of Repetitive Command (RCT)

$$\frac{[\,i \wedge e = v_0\,]\, g\, [\,i \wedge e < v_0\,] \qquad i \wedge \mathcal{D}\,g \Rightarrow e \geq 0}{[\,i\,]\, \mathbf{do}\ g\ \mathbf{od}\, [\,i \wedge \neg\, \mathcal{D}\,g\,]}$$

when v_0 does not occur free in i, g, or e.

7.5 Weakest Preconditions

Instead of using the inference rules in the previous section or in Chapter 3, Dijkstra and several other writers prefer to reason about programs by using *weakest preconditions*. (Historically, weakest preconditions are associated with nondeterminism and guarded commands, but there is no logically necessary connection. One can reason about guarded commands by using the inference rules in the previous section, or about the determinate language of Chapter 2 by using weakest preconditions.)

To introduce weakest preconditions, we extend the syntax of assertions by introducing a new constructor, **wp**, that builds an assertion out of a command and an assertion:

$$\langle \text{assert} \rangle ::= \mathbf{wp}(\langle \text{comm} \rangle, \langle \text{assert} \rangle)$$

A state σ satisfies the assertion $\mathbf{wp}(c,q)$ when every execution of the command c starting in state σ terminates normally in a state that satisfies the assertion q:

DR SEM EQ: Weakest Precondition

$$[\![\mathbf{wp}(c,q)]\!]_{\text{assert}}\sigma$$
$$= \forall\sigma' \in [\![c]\!]_{\text{comm}}\sigma. \ (\sigma' \neq \perp \text{ and } \sigma' \notin \{\mathbf{abort}\} \times \Sigma \text{ and } [\![q]\!]_{\text{assert}}\sigma').$$

It is easy to see that $[\, \mathbf{wp}(c,q) \,] \, c \, [\, q\,]$, and that $\mathbf{wp}(c,q)$ is weaker than p whenever $[\,p\,]\,c\,[\,q\,]$. This justifies the terminology that $\mathbf{wp}(c,q)$ is the *weakest precondition of c and q*.

(In Dijkstra's original formulation, $\mathbf{wp}$ was regarded as a function, called a *predicate transformer*, that maps commands and assertions into assertions, rather than as a novel constructor for assertions. Unfortunately, this approach cannot be made rigorous, since there are c and q for which there is no assertion in predicate logic that meets the requirements placed on $\mathbf{wp}(c,q)$.)

From this definition, one can show the soundness of several noncompositional inference rules that hold for arbitrary commands. (We abbreviate "weakest precondition rule" by WP RULE.)

WP RULE: Law of the Excluded Miracle

$$\mathbf{wp}(c,\mathbf{false}) \Leftrightarrow \mathbf{false},$$

WP RULE: Monotonicity

$$\frac{p \Rightarrow q}{\mathbf{wp}(c,p) \Rightarrow \mathbf{wp}(c,q),}$$

WP RULE: Conjunction

$$(\mathbf{wp}(c,p) \wedge \mathbf{wp}(c,q)) \Leftrightarrow \mathbf{wp}(c,p \wedge q),$$

WP RULE: Disjunction

$$(\mathbf{wp}(c,p) \vee \mathbf{wp}(c,q)) \Rightarrow \mathbf{wp}(c,p \vee q),$$

WP RULE: Continuity

$$\frac{\forall v. \ v \geq 0 \Rightarrow (q \Rightarrow (q/v \to v + 1))}{\mathbf{wp}(c, \exists v. \ v \geq 0 \wedge q) \Leftrightarrow \exists v. \ v \geq 0 \wedge \mathbf{wp}(c,q)}$$

when v does not occur free in c.

For most commands, one can give an axiom schema that expresses the weakest precondition in terms of the weakest preconditions of subcommands:

WP RULE: Assignment

$$\mathbf{wp}(v := e, q) \Leftrightarrow (q/v \to e),$$

WP RULE: **skip**

$$\mathbf{wp}(\mathbf{skip}, q) \Leftrightarrow q,$$

WP RULE: Sequential Composition

$$\mathbf{wp}(c_0 \,;\, c_1, q) \Leftrightarrow \mathbf{wp}(c_0, \mathbf{wp}(c_1, q)),$$

WP RULE: Conditional

$$\mathbf{wp}(\mathbf{if}\ b\ \mathbf{then}\ c_0\ \mathbf{else}\ c_1, q) \Leftrightarrow (b \Rightarrow \mathbf{wp}(c_0, q)) \land (\neg\, b \Rightarrow \mathbf{wp}(c_1, q)),$$

WP RULE: Variable Declaration

$$\mathbf{wp}(\mathbf{newvar}\ v := e\ \mathbf{in}\ c, q) \Leftrightarrow (\mathbf{wp}(c, q)/v \to e)$$

when v is not free in q,

WP RULE: **fail**

$$\mathbf{wp}(\mathbf{fail}, q) \Leftrightarrow \mathbf{false},$$

WP RULE: Alternative Command

$$\mathbf{wp}(\mathbf{if}\ b_0 \to c_0 \;\square\; \cdots \;\square\; b_{n-1} \to c_{n-1}\ \mathbf{fi}, q)$$
$$\Leftrightarrow (b_0 \lor \cdots \lor b_{n-1}) \land (b_0 \Rightarrow \mathbf{wp}(c_0, q)) \land \cdots \land (b_{n-1} \Rightarrow \mathbf{wp}(c_{n-1}, q)).$$

For repetitive commands (or **while** commands), however, the situation is more complex. Sometimes, one can find an assertion p containing a variable v that is true exactly when the weakest precondition of a repetitive command is true *and* the repetitive command will always terminate in less than v iterations. Then one can use the inference rule:

WP RULE: Repetitive Command (Equivalence)

$$(p/v \to 0) \Leftrightarrow \mathbf{false}$$
$$\forall v.\ v \geq 0 \Rightarrow ((p/v \to v+1) \Leftrightarrow (q \land \neg\, \mathcal{D}g) \lor \mathbf{wp}(\mathbf{if}\ g\ \mathbf{fi}, p))$$
$$\overline{(\exists v.\ v \geq 0 \land p) \Leftrightarrow \mathbf{wp}(\mathbf{do}\ g\ \mathbf{od}, q)}$$

when v is not free in g or q.

(Here g denotes a guarded command and $\mathcal{D}g$ the disjunction of its guards.) In other situations, it is necessary or convenient to use a p that implies the weakest precondition and termination in less than v iterations. Then the appropriate rule is

WP RULE: Repetitive Command (Implication)

$(p/v \to 0) \Rightarrow \textbf{false}$

$$\frac{\forall v.\ v \geq 0 \Rightarrow ((p/v \to v+1) \Rightarrow (q \wedge \neg\ \mathcal{D}\,g) \vee \textbf{wp}(\textbf{if}\ g\ \textbf{fi}, p))}{(\exists v.\ v \geq 0 \wedge p) \Rightarrow \textbf{wp}(\textbf{do}\ g\ \textbf{od}, q)}$$

when v is not free in g or q.

In conclusion, we note that the concept of weakest precondition developed in this section describes only total correctness. Although we will not pursue the matter, it is also possible to reason with weakest *liberal* preconditions, which describe partial correctness:

DR SEM EQ: Weakest Liberal Precondition

$$[\![\textbf{wlp}(c, q)]\!]_{\text{assert}}\sigma = \forall\sigma' \in [\![c]\!]_{\text{comm}}\sigma.\ (\sigma' = \bot \text{ or } \sigma' \in \{\textbf{abort}\} \times \Sigma \text{ or } [\![q]\!]_{\text{assert}}\sigma').$$

Bibliographic Notes

Guarded commands and weakest preconditions were invented by Dijkstra [1975] and explored in more detail, with many examples, in Dijkstra [1976]. They are also used extensively in Gries [1981]. Refinement logics, which are a generalization of the weakest-precondition approach, have become an active research area in recent years; the standard text is Morgan [1994].

Several examples of programs that use abstract types, where nondeterminism is needed to avoid constraining the choice of data representations, are given in Reynolds [1981a, Chapter 5].

Powerdomains were discovered by Plotkin [1976] and developed further by Smyth [1978]. The conflict between powerdomains and unbounded nondeterminacy was analyzed by Apt and Plotkin [1986], and a generalization of powerdomains that resolves this conflict by weakening the notion of continuity was devised by Plotkin [1982]. An interesting generalization of powerdomains to categories has been given by Lehmann [1976].

Exercises

7.1   For each of the following programs, give a precise description of the set of possible final states. Are there any infinite executions?

(a) $x := 0$;

   $\textbf{do}\ x \leq 3 \to x := x + 1\ \square\ odd(x) \to x := x - 1\ \textbf{od}.$

(b) $x := 0\,;\, y := 0$;

   $\textbf{do}\ x \leq 16 \to x := x + 1\ \square\ x \geq 13 \wedge y = 0 \to y := x\ \textbf{od}.$

7.2 Fill in the missing precedent to make the following total-correctness specification true. The assertion you provide should be as weak as possible, but it should not be unnecessarily complicated.

$$[\,?\,] \textbf{ if } x \geq 0 \rightarrow y := y - 1 \,\square\, \textbf{even } x \rightarrow y := y + 1 \textbf{ fi } [\,y = 0\,].$$

7.3 Using the inference rules of Chapter 3 and Section 7.4, prove the following total-correctness specification (of a program that computes the greatest common divisor of three positive integers):

$$[\gcd(x, y, z) = g_0 \wedge x \geq 1 \wedge y \geq 1 \wedge z \geq 1]$$
$$\textbf{do } x > y \rightarrow x := x - y$$
$$\square\, y > z \rightarrow y := y - z$$
$$\square\, z > x \rightarrow z := z - x$$
$$\textbf{od}$$
$$[x = g_0].$$

You may use the following mathematical facts:

$$\gcd(x - y, y, z) = \gcd(x, y - z, z) = \gcd(x, y, z - x) = \gcd(x, y, z)$$

$$x \geq 1 \text{ implies } \gcd(x, x, x) = x.$$

7.4 Extend the language described in this chapter with a nondeterministic guarded command of the form

$$\langle gdcomm \rangle ::= \langle boolexp \rangle \xrightarrow{?} \langle comm \rangle$$

When b is false, $b \xrightarrow{?} c$ will make a transition to **false**, just as an ordinary (interruptible) guarded command would. But when b is true, $b \xrightarrow{?} c$ may either execute c or make a transition to **false** (while an ordinary guarded command could only execute c).

For this new guarded command:

(a) Give inference rules in the style of Section 7.1 for its transition semantics.

(b) Give a semantic equation in the style of Section 7.3 for its denotational semantics.

(c) Give an inference rule in the style of Section 7.4 for proving its specifications. Also extend the definition of $\mathcal{D}$ to apply to the new command, in such a way that

$$[\![\mathcal{D}\,g]\!]_{\text{assert}}\sigma \text{ if and only if } \textbf{false} \notin [\![g]\!]_{\text{gdcomm}}\sigma$$

remains true. (It will no longer be true that $\mathcal{D}$ maps all guarded commands into the disjunction of their guards.)

(d) Using your new rule, prove the partial correctness specification

$$\{z = y \times 2^n \wedge n \geq 0 \wedge y > 0\}$$

do $z \leq x \rightarrow n := n+1\,;z := z \times 2$ □ **true** $\xrightarrow{?}$ $n := n+1\,;z := z \times 2$ **od**

$$\{z = y \times 2^n \wedge n \geq 0 \wedge y > 0 \wedge \neg\, z \leq x\}$$

(of a novel version of part of Exercise 3.3(b)). You may assume

$$\{z = y \times 2^n \wedge n \geq 0 \wedge y > 0\}$$
$$n := n+1\,;z := z \times 2$$
$$\{z = y \times 2^n \wedge n \geq 0 \wedge y > 0\}.$$

(e) Consider the total correctness specification that is analogous to the specification in the previous part of this exercise. Discuss briefly whether this specification is valid, and how this question relates to the topics discussed in Section 7.2.

7.5   Extend the evaluation semantics of Exercise 6.4 to encompass guarded commands, by giving inference rules for formulas of the form $\langle c, \sigma \rangle \Rightarrow \gamma$, where σ is a state; γ is a state, **abort**-state pair, or (when c is a guarded command) **false**; and c is an assignment command, **skip**, **fail**, sequential composition, conditional command, **while** command, variable declaration, simple or compound guarded command, or alternative or repetitive construct (built from a guarded command). As before, the premises and conclusions of the rules all must be formulas whose main operator is $\Rightarrow$, though there may be side conditions that depend on the value of boolean expressions. The rules should not contain occurrences of $\rightarrow$ or $\rightarrow^*$.

Hint You will reduce the number of rules by using a metavariable ranging over terminal configurations other than **false**.

7.6   Show that the inference rule for disjunction given in Section 7.5 can be strengthened to

$$\overline{(\mathbf{wp}(c, p) \vee \mathbf{wp}(c, q)) \Leftrightarrow \mathbf{wp}(c, p \vee q)}$$

when c is a determinate command. Give an example of a nondeterminate command for which this strengthened rule is unsound.

7.7   Show that the inference rule for continuity given in Section 7.5 becomes unsound when c is a command, such as **anynum** x, that exhibits unbounded nondeterminism.

7.8   Prove the soundness of the inference rule for continuity in Section 7.5.

8

Shared-Variable Concurrency

In recent years, the dramatic drop in the cost of computing hardware has made it practical, in an ever-increasing variety of contexts, to execute different parts of a program simultaneously. Many authors use the terms "concurrent" or "parallel" indifferently to describe such computations. Following increasingly common usage, however, we will use *concurrent* to describe computations where the simultaneously executing processes can interact with one another, and we will reserve *parallel* to describe computations where the behavior of each process is unaffected by the behavior of the others.

Our present concern is concurrency. In this chapter, we consider an approach where processes communicate through shared variables. This approach mirrors the situation where a common memory, typically containing a shared database, is accessed by several physical processors — or perhaps by a single processor that is time-shared among several logical processes. (An alternative approach to concurrency, where processes communicate by passing messages, will be described in Chapter 9.)

Except in trivial cases, the interaction between concurrent processes will depend on the relative speed of the physical processors or on the decisions by a scheduler of when to switch a physical processor from one logical process to another. Thus concurrent programs are usually nondeterminate. This nondeterminacy makes concurrent programs especially difficult to reason about, since one must consider all possible orders of execution. Moreover, the efficacy of debugging is undermined by the irreproducibility of executions and by the fact that the actual occurrences of obscure and possibly erroneous orders of execution may be very infrequent.

8.1 Concurrent Composition

As a first step, we introduce the concurrent composition of commands:

$$\langle \text{comm} \rangle ::= \langle \text{comm} \rangle \parallel \langle \text{comm} \rangle$$

For concrete notation, we assume that $\parallel$ has a lower precedence than $\square$ or any of the other operators introduced in previous chapters. We will also assume that $\parallel$ is left associative, although it will usually behave associatively.

Informally, executing $c_0 \parallel c_1$ means executing c_0 and c_1 at the same time, for example on separate physical processors. But the closest we can come to this in the transition semantics of Chapter 6 is to say that an execution of $c_0 \parallel c_1$ consists of the steps of c_0 interleaved with the steps of c_1 in arbitrary order.

This is captured by the following inference rules for transition semantics:

TR RULE: Concurrent Composition

$$\frac{\langle c_0, \sigma \rangle \overset{\lambda}{\to} \langle c_0', \sigma' \rangle}{\langle c_0 \parallel c_1, \sigma \rangle \overset{\lambda}{\to} \langle c_0' \parallel c_1, \sigma' \rangle} \qquad \frac{\langle c_1, \sigma \rangle \overset{\lambda}{\to} \langle c_1', \sigma' \rangle}{\langle c_0 \parallel c_1, \sigma \rangle \overset{\lambda}{\to} \langle c_0 \parallel c_1', \sigma' \rangle}$$

$$\frac{\langle c_0, \sigma \rangle \overset{\lambda}{\to} \sigma'}{\langle c_0 \parallel c_1, \sigma \rangle \overset{\lambda}{\to} \langle c_1, \sigma' \rangle} \qquad \frac{\langle c_1, \sigma \rangle \overset{\lambda}{\to} \sigma'}{\langle c_0 \parallel c_1, \sigma \rangle \overset{\lambda}{\to} \langle c_0, \sigma' \rangle}$$

$$\frac{\langle c_0, \sigma \rangle \to \langle \textbf{abort}, \sigma' \rangle}{\langle c_0 \parallel c_1, \sigma \rangle \to \langle \textbf{abort}, \sigma' \rangle} \qquad \frac{\langle c_1, \sigma \rangle \to \langle \textbf{abort}, \sigma' \rangle}{\langle c_0 \parallel c_1, \sigma \rangle \to \langle \textbf{abort}, \sigma' \rangle}.$$

Here the rules on the left describe the case where c_0 is selected to provide the first step of execution, while the symmetric rules on the right describe the case where c_1 is selected. Notice that, if both c_0 and c_1 terminate normally, then $c_0 \parallel c_1$ terminates normally; if either terminates by failure, then $c_0 \parallel c_1$ terminates by failure; otherwise, it runs on forever.

Two commands c_0 and c_1 are said to *interfere* if either can assign to any variable that is assigned or evaluated by the other, that is, if the set

$$(\text{FA}(c_0) \cap \text{FV}_{\text{comm}}(c_1)) \cup (\text{FA}(c_1) \cap \text{FV}_{\text{comm}}(c_0)) \tag{8.1}$$

is nonempty. When c_0 and c_1 do not interfere, nor terminate by failure, the concurrent composition $c_0 \parallel c_1$ is determinate. More precisely, from a given starting state, although the composition may give rise to a variety of executions, all of these executions lead to the same final state, or all run on forever. For example, the command

$$\mathsf{t} := \mathsf{g} \,;\, \mathsf{g} := \mathsf{f} \,;\, \mathsf{f} := \mathsf{f} + \mathsf{t} \,;\, \mathsf{k} := \mathsf{k} + 1$$

(which is the body of the **while** command in the Fibonacci-number program of Section 3.6, except for the declaration of t) can be replaced by the determinate concurrent command

$$((\mathsf{t} := \mathsf{g} \parallel \mathsf{u} := \mathsf{f}) \,;\, (\mathsf{g} := \mathsf{u} \parallel \mathsf{f} := \mathsf{u} + \mathsf{t})) \parallel \mathsf{k} := \mathsf{k} + 1$$

(where u is a new variable).

On the other hand, the concurrent execution of interfering commands can be nondeterminate. For example,

$$x := 0 \;;\; (x := x + 1 \;;\; x := x + 1 \;\|\; y := x)$$

might set y to 0, 1, or 2. A more useful example is the following program, which searches for a nonnegative result of a function f. Specifically, it sets k to a value such that $0 \leq k \leq n$ and $f(k) \geq 0$, or to -1 if there is no such value. Two processes are used to test even and odd integers concurrently:

> $k := -1$;
>
> $(\mathbf{newvar}\ i := 0\ \mathbf{in\ while}\ i \leq n \wedge k = -1\ \mathbf{do}$
>
> $\quad \mathbf{if}\ f(i) \geq 0\ \mathbf{then}\ k := i\ \mathbf{else}\ i := i + 2$
>
> $\|\ \mathbf{newvar}\ i := 1\ \mathbf{in\ while}\ i \leq n \wedge k = -1\ \mathbf{do}$
>
> $\quad \mathbf{if}\ f(i) \geq 0\ \mathbf{then}\ k := i\ \mathbf{else}\ i := i + 2).$

If there are both even and odd values of k such that $f(k) \geq 0$, then, depending on the relative speeds of the two processes, k may be set to either the least even value or least odd value such that $f(k) \geq 0$.

8.2 Critical Regions

Suppose we try to modify the previous program so that, in addition to setting k, it also sets r to the value of $f(k)$:

> $k := -1$;
>
> $(\mathbf{newvar}\ i := 0\ \mathbf{in\ while}\ i \leq n \wedge k = -1\ \mathbf{do}$
>
> $\quad \mathbf{if}\ f(i) \geq 0\ \mathbf{then}\ k := i \;;\; r := f(i)\ \mathbf{else}\ i := i + 2$
>
> $\|\ \mathbf{newvar}\ i := 1\ \mathbf{in\ while}\ i \leq n \wedge k = -1\ \mathbf{do}$
>
> $\quad \mathbf{if}\ f(i) \geq 0\ \mathbf{then}\ k := i \;;\; r := f(i)\ \mathbf{else}\ i := i + 2).$

Here there is a problem: If, at about the same time, the two processes find values i_0 and i_1 that meet the search criteria, it is possible for the assignments to k and r to be interleaved as follows:

$$k := i_0 \;;\; k := i_1 \;;\; r := f(i_1) \;;\; r := f(i_0),$$

so that r would not be $f(k)$. This example illustrates the need for *critical regions*, which are regions within concurrent processes where a sequence of several operations can be performed exclusive of any interleaving with other processes.

In this section, we write **crit** c for such a critical region, where c is a command, called a $\langle\text{critcomm}\rangle$, that is restricted to avoid nontermination, input-output, or concurrency. More specifically,

$$\langle\text{comm}\rangle ::= \textbf{crit } \langle\text{critcomm}\rangle$$

$$\langle\text{critcomm}\rangle ::= \langle\text{var}\rangle := \langle\text{intexp}\rangle \mid \textbf{skip} \mid \langle\text{critcomm}\rangle \text{ ; } \langle\text{critcomm}\rangle$$
$$\mid \textbf{if } \langle\text{boolexp}\rangle \textbf{ then } \langle\text{critcomm}\rangle \textbf{ else } \langle\text{critcomm}\rangle \mid \textbf{fail}$$
$$\mid \textbf{newvar } \langle\text{var}\rangle := \langle\text{intexp}\rangle \textbf{ in } \langle\text{critcomm}\rangle$$

(In the phrase **crit** c, the command c extends to the first stopping symbol or the end of the enclosing phrase.) The semantics is that **crit** c performs the entire execution of c as a single transition or "atomic action":

TR RULE: Critical Region

$$\frac{\langle c, \sigma\rangle \to^* \gamma}{\langle\textbf{crit } c, \sigma\rangle \to \gamma} \qquad \text{when } \gamma \text{ is terminal.}$$

Using this construction, it is straightforward to avoid the problems in the previous program:

$$k := -1;$$
$$(\textbf{newvar } i := 0 \textbf{ in while } i \le n \wedge k = -1 \textbf{ do}$$
$$\quad \textbf{if } f(i) \ge 0 \textbf{ then crit } (k := i \text{ ; } r := f(i)) \textbf{ else } i := i + 2$$
$$\| \textbf{ newvar } i := 1 \textbf{ in while } i \le n \wedge k = -1 \textbf{ do}$$
$$\quad \textbf{if } f(i) \ge 0 \textbf{ then crit } (k := i \text{ ; } r := f(i)) \textbf{ else } i := i + 2).$$

In effect, critical regions give the programmer control over the size of atomic actions, as opposed to imposing the "default" that each assignment or conditional test is an atomic action. In fact, this default is unrealistic. In a real implementation, the default atomic actions would normally be the individual accesses to shared memory. Thus

$$x := x + 1 \parallel x := 2 \times x$$

might be implemented as though it were

$$(t := x + 1 \text{ ; } x := t) \parallel (u := 2 \times x \text{ ; } x := u),$$

which could set x to $2 \times (x + 1)$, $(2 \times x) + 1$, $x + 1$, or $2 \times x$.

(Indeed, even stranger things can happen when the shared variable occupies more than one physical word, as is often the case for floating-point numbers. For example, x might have half of its contents set to $x + 1$ and the other half to $2 \times x$.)

This suggests that one should require the use of critical regions whenever the extent of atomic actions is semantically significant. For the simple imperative language, this requirement could be imposed by restricting the variables in the set (8.1) (in Section 8.1) to occurrences within critical regions. Unfortunately, for more general languages with procedures (using either call by address or call by name) the problem of aliasing prohibits such a simple solution.

8.3 Mutual Exclusion and Conditional Critical Regions

It is usually undesirable to enclose a time-consuming command in a critical region, since while one process is executing the critical region no other process can execute at all. A less draconian approach is to use mutual exclusion. A collection of regions is said to be *mutually exclusive* if it is never possible for more than one process to execute commands within any of the regions at the same time. (However, while one process executes within a mutually exclusive region, other processes can still execute outside of the mutually exclusive regions.)

For instance, suppose we wish to alter our running example so that it prints out, for every i such that $0 \leq i \leq n$ and $f(i) \geq 0$, the integers i and $f(i)$. In the following program, to insure a sensible order of output, it is sufficient that the two underlined pairs of output commands should be mutually exclusive:

$$\textbf{newvar } i := 0 \textbf{ in while } i \leq n \textbf{ do}$$
$$(\textbf{if } f(i) \geq 0 \textbf{ then } !\,i\,;\,!\,f(i) \textbf{ else skip }; i := i + 2)$$
$$\|\ \textbf{newvar } i := 1 \textbf{ in while } i \leq n \textbf{ do}$$
$$(\textbf{if } f(i) \geq 0 \textbf{ then } !\,i\,;\,!\,f(i) \textbf{ else skip }; i := i + 2).$$

To impose this mutual exclusion, we will use a binary semaphore, which we will implement with a generalization of the critical region called a *conditional* critical region.

For conditional critical regions, we use the syntax

$$\langle\text{comm}\rangle ::= \textbf{await } \langle\text{boolexp}\rangle \textbf{ then } \langle\text{critcomm}\rangle$$

(In **await** b **then** c, the command c extends to the first stopping symbol or the end of the enclosing phrase.)

The effect of **await** b **then** c is the same as

$$\textbf{while } \neg b \textbf{ do skip }; c,$$

except that the final evaluation of b, along with the following execution of c, are performed as a single atomic action. Thus the transition semantics is given by

TR RULE: Conditional Critical Region

$$\frac{\langle c,\sigma\rangle \to^* \gamma}{\langle \textbf{await } b \textbf{ then } c,\sigma\rangle \to \gamma} \qquad \text{when } \gamma \text{ is terminal and } [\![b]\!]_{\text{boolexp}}\sigma \text{ is true,}$$

$$\overline{\langle \textbf{await } b \textbf{ then } c,\sigma\rangle \to \langle \textbf{skip ; await } b \textbf{ then } c,\sigma\rangle} \qquad \text{when } [\![b]\!]_{\text{boolexp}}\sigma \text{ is false.}$$

$$(8.2)$$

Here the second rule describes a kind of semantics called *busy waiting*, where the **await** command cycles without affecting the state as long as b is false.

Notice that the unconditional critical region, written **crit** c in the previous section, can now be written as **await true then** c.

Into the previous program, we will introduce a global variable busy, called a *semaphore*, that will be one if some process is currently producing output and zero otherwise. Then, just before each process is about to produce output, it waits until busy is zero and then sets it to one before producing its own output, and back to zero afterwards:

newvar busy := 0 **in**

(**newvar** i := 0 **in while** i ≤ n **do**

   (**if** f(i) ≥ 0 **then** (**await** busy = 0 **then** busy := 1) ; ! i ; ! f(i) ; busy := 0

      else skip ; i := i + 2)

   ∥ **newvar** i := 1 **in while** i ≤ n **do**

   (**if** f(i) ≥ 0 **then** (**await** busy = 0 **then** busy := 1) ; ! i ; ! f(i) ; busy := 0

      else skip ; i := i + 2)).

We can prove that there is no execution of the above program where both processes are simultaneously in the program regions that perform output. First, we divide the commands that can occur in any configuration in any execution of either process into the "exclusive" commands

$$! i ; ! f(i) ; busy := 0 ; i := i + 2 ; w$$

$$! f(i) ; busy := 0 ; i := i + 2 ; w$$

$$busy := 0 ; i := i + 2 ; w$$

(where w is the **while** command occurring in each process of the above program), and all of the other commands, which we call "nonexclusive". (To clarify our argument, we are ignoring the fact that the above commands will be prefixed by **newvar** i := ... **in** .)

Next, we note that all transitions taken by a single process, other than a transition to a terminal state, have one of the following forms:

- from a configuration containing a nonexclusive command to another containing a nonexclusive command, without changing the value of busy,
- from a configuration containing the nonexclusive command

$$(\textbf{await busy} = 0 \textbf{ then busy} := 1) \,;\, !\,i \,;\, !\,f(i) \,;\, \text{busy} := 0 \,;\, i := i + 2 \,;\, w,$$

paired with a state in which busy $= 0$, to an exclusive command paired with a state in which busy $= 1$,
- from a configuration containing an exclusive command to another containing an exclusive command, without changing the value of busy,
- from a configuration containing the exclusive command

$$\text{busy} := 0 \,;\, i := i + 2 \,;\, w$$

to a nonexclusive command paired with a state in which busy $= 0$.

Finally, by induction on the length of executions, making use of the fact that every transition of a concurrent command is formed from a transition of one of its components, one can show that every configuration of the form $\langle c_0 \parallel c_1, \sigma \rangle$ in any execution of the entire program satisfies one of the following conditions:

- c_0 and c_1 are both nonexclusive and $\sigma(\text{busy}) = 0$.
- c_0 is exclusive and c_1 is nonexclusive, or vice versa, and $\sigma(\text{busy}) = 1$.

In particular, c_0 and c_1 are never both exclusive.

Note that it is crucial to this argument that **await** busy $= 0$ **then** busy $:= 1$ is an atomic operation when busy $= 0$. If another process could interrupt between the test busy $= 0$ and the command busy $:= 1$ — and execute its own **await** command — then both processes could enter their exclusive regions together.

8.4 Deadlock

The introduction of conditional critical regions raises the possibility of *deadlock*, which occurs when all processes are executing conditional critical regions with false conditions.

In the simplest case, if one executes **await** b **then** c by itself, rather than as part of a concurrent composition, and if b is false in the starting state σ, then deadlock occurs immediately. More generally, if b is false in σ and the execution of c' never makes b true, never causes a failure, and always terminates, then **await** b **then** $c \parallel c'$ deadlocks eventually, since every execution beginning with $\langle \textbf{await } b \textbf{ then } c \parallel c', \sigma \rangle$ leads to a configuration $\langle \textbf{await } b \textbf{ then } c, \sigma' \rangle$ where b is still false in σ'.

In more complex cases, deadlock is a possible but not certain outcome. For example, from a starting state where $x = 0$, the command

$$\textbf{await } x = 1 \textbf{ then } x := 10 \parallel x := x + 1 \,;\, x := x + 1$$

can either terminate with $x = 11$ or deadlock with $x = 2$.

A more realistic example occurs when nested exclusive regions, based on two distinct semaphores, are entered in opposite order by different processes:

...**await** $b = 0$ **then** $b := 1$; ... ; **await** $b' = 0$ **then** $b' := 1$; ... ; $b' := 0$; $b := 0$

|| ...**await** $b' = 0$ **then** $b' := 1$; ... ; **await** $b = 0$ **then** $b := 1$; ... ; $b := 0$; $b' := 0$.

Here, if the two processes both execute their first **await** before either executes its second **await**, deadlock will occur in a configuration

$$\langle \textbf{await } b' = 0 \textbf{ then } \ldots \parallel \textbf{await } b = 0 \textbf{ then } \ldots, \sigma \rangle,$$

where σ is a state where b and b' are both one.

8.5 Fairness

Consider the following generalization of the program at the end of Section 8.1, which searches through *all* nonnegative integers for a k such that $f(k) \geq 0$:

$$k := -1;$$
$$(\textbf{newvar } i := 0 \textbf{ in while } k = -1 \textbf{ do}$$
$$\qquad \textbf{if } f(i) \geq 0 \textbf{ then } k := i \textbf{ else } i := i + 2$$
$$\parallel \textbf{newvar } i := 1 \textbf{ in while } k = -1 \textbf{ do}$$
$$\qquad \textbf{if } f(i) \geq 0 \textbf{ then } k := i \textbf{ else } i := i + 2).$$

If $f(k) \geq 0$ never holds for even k, then, according to our transition semantics, there is an infinite execution that, after the initialization step, has the form

$$\langle c_0 \parallel c', \sigma_0 \rangle \to \langle c_1 \parallel c', \sigma_1 \rangle \to \langle c_2 \parallel c', \sigma_2 \rangle \to \cdots,$$

where every transition of the concurrent composition arises from a transition of the first process, so that the second process never executes at all and the function f is never tested for odd arguments. Such an execution is said to be *unfair*.

More generally, an execution of concurrent processes is *unfair* if it does not terminate but, after some finite number of steps, there is an unterminated process that never makes a transition.

Unfortunately, our transition semantics (unlike the denotational semantics that we will present in Sections 8.7 and 8.8) does not permit a straightforward definition of unfairness in the general case where concurrent compositions may be embedded within larger constructs (which may themselves be concurrent compositions). Therefore, we limit this discussion to the case where the overall program is an n-ary concurrent composition of sequential subprograms.

In this case, an execution is said to be *unfair* if it is an infinite sequence that, after some finite number of transitions, has the form

$$\langle c_0^{(0)} \| \cdots \| c_0^{(n-1)}, \sigma_0 \rangle \xrightarrow{\lambda_0} \langle c_1^{(0)} \| \cdots \| c_1^{(n-1)}, \sigma_1 \rangle \xrightarrow{\lambda_1} \langle c_2^{(0)} \| \cdots \| c_2^{(n-1)}, \sigma_2 \rangle \xrightarrow{\lambda_2} \cdots ,$$

where, for some i, the $c_k^{(i)}$ are identical.

(For this definition to formalize the notion that the ith process is never selected for execution, it is vital that our semantics never specifies a transition $\langle c, \sigma \rangle \to \langle c, \sigma' \rangle$ where the command does not change. This is the reason for using rule (8.2) for conditional critical regions in Section 8.3, instead of the simpler rule that omits **skip** on the right side.)

It is clear that some, though not all, concurrent programs require a *fair* implementation that excludes unfair executions. Such an implementation is straightforward when one has enough physical processors that a processor can be dedicated to each process in the program (assuming that the hardware resolves conflicts between accesses to shared memory fairly). Otherwise, some form of scheduler that switches from one process to another, such as a round-robin scheduler, is required to guarantee fairness. (Indeed, fairness can be regarded as a way of describing the essence of such a scheduler while abstracting away the details of its behavior.)

In the extreme case where only a single processor is available, the simplest implementation of $c \| c'$ would be $c \, ; c'$. But this would be unfair if c runs on forever.

It should be noticed that, just as in Section 7.2, the imposition of fairness raises the possibility of unbounded nondeterminism. For example, a fair execution of

$$\textbf{newvar } y := 0 \textbf{ in } (x := 0 \, ; (\textbf{while } y = 0 \textbf{ do } x := x + 1 \| y := 1))$$

will always terminate, but it can set x to any natural number. For the kind of sequential nondeterminism considered in Chapter 7, this possibility suggested that fairness is an unnatural requirement to impose on repetitive constructs. For concurrency, however, fairness is a vital concept that cannot be evaded, despite its mathematical complexities.

Stronger concepts of fairness are sometimes considered in the theoretical literature on shared-variable concurrency. For example, such concepts would rule out the infinite execution of

$$\textbf{newvar } y := 0 \textbf{ in } (x := 0 \, ; (\textbf{while } y = 0 \textbf{ do } x := 1 - x \| \textbf{await } x = 1 \textbf{ then } y := 1)),$$

since the **await** command is "enabled" infinitely often, though not at every execution step. Since general implementations of these strong forms of fairness are highly inefficient, however, we will not consider them here.

8.6 Resumption Semantics

We now consider several approaches to the denotational semantics of shared-variable concurrency. Since we already have a transition semantics in hand, we begin by defining these denotational semantics in terms of the transition semantics and postpone for a moment the details of defining the denotational semantics compositionally by semantic equations. (To avoid complications that would distract us from the fundamental problems of concurrency, we will ignore failure, input-output, and guarded commands for the rest of this chapter.)

As in Section 7.2, one can define the function

$$\llbracket - \rrbracket_{\mathrm{comm}} \in \langle \mathrm{comm} \rangle \to \Sigma \to \mathcal{P}_{\mathrm{DOM}}(\hat{\Sigma}_\perp)$$

such that

$$\llbracket c \rrbracket_{\mathrm{comm}} \sigma = \{ \gamma \mid \langle c, \sigma \rangle \to^* \gamma \wedge \gamma \text{ terminal} \} \cup (\textbf{if } \langle c, \sigma \rangle \uparrow \textbf{ then } \{\perp\} \textbf{ else } \{\}).$$

(Strictly speaking, because of the problem of unbounded nondeterminacy, unfair computations must be permitted to insure that the results of this function always belong to $\mathcal{P}_{\mathrm{DOM}}(\hat{\Sigma}_\perp)$.) In the presence of concurrency, however, this function no longer provides a compositional semantics, since $\llbracket c_0 \parallel c_1 \rrbracket_{\mathrm{comm}}$ is not a function of $\llbracket c_0 \rrbracket_{\mathrm{comm}}$ and $\llbracket c_1 \rrbracket_{\mathrm{comm}}$.

To see this, note that

$$\llbracket \mathsf{x} := \mathsf{x} + 2 \rrbracket_{\mathrm{comm}} = \llbracket \mathsf{x} := \mathsf{x} + 1 \, ; \mathsf{x} := \mathsf{x} + 1 \rrbracket_{\mathrm{comm}},$$

but

$$\llbracket \mathsf{x} := \mathsf{x} + 2 \parallel \mathsf{x} := 2 \times \mathsf{x} \rrbracket_{\mathrm{comm}} \neq \llbracket (\mathsf{x} := \mathsf{x} + 1 \, ; \mathsf{x} := \mathsf{x} + 1) \parallel \mathsf{x} := 2 \times \mathsf{x} \rrbracket_{\mathrm{comm}},$$

since there is a possible execution of the command on the right of the last equation where $\mathsf{x} := 2 \times \mathsf{x}$ is executed between the two executions of $\mathsf{x} := \mathsf{x} + 1$. Thus, $\llbracket c_0 \parallel c_1 \rrbracket_{\mathrm{comm}}$ must depend on some property of c_0 other than $\llbracket c_0 \rrbracket_{\mathrm{comm}}$. It follows then that the function $\llbracket - \rrbracket_{\mathrm{comm}}$ cannot be defined by semantic equations.

The problem is that $\llbracket - \rrbracket_{\mathrm{comm}}$ describes "overall" state transformations, while an adequate denotational semantics must also deal with intermediate states. Specifically, it must provide enough information about a command to determine the effects of interrupting execution of the command with a change of state induced by some other process.

The earliest such semantics, devised by Hennessy and Plotkin, used resumptions (in the sense of Section 5.6) and powerdomains. It was based on a function $\mathcal{R} \in \langle \mathrm{comm} \rangle \to R$, where R is a domain of resumptions satisfying the isomorphism

$$R \approx \Sigma \to \mathcal{P}_{\mathrm{DOM}}(\Sigma + (\Sigma \times R))_\perp.$$

Essentially, $\mathcal{R}[\![c]\!]$ maps an initial state into a set containing all of the terminal states that can be reached in one step, plus all of the nonterminal states that can be reached in one step, each paired with the meaning of the command describing the remainder of the computation. In other words,

$$\mathcal{R}[\![c]\!]\sigma = \{\,\sigma' \mid \langle c, \sigma \rangle \to \sigma'\,\} + \{\,\langle \sigma', \mathcal{R}[\![c']\!]\rangle \mid \langle c, \sigma \rangle \to \langle c', \sigma' \rangle\,\}.$$

Although this kind of resumption semantics can be defined compositionally, there are several problems:

- Complex mathematical constructions are needed to construct powerdomains of nonflat domains and, even more so, to solve recursive domain isomorphisms containing the operator $\mathcal{P}_{\text{DOM}}$.

- Since ordinary powerdomains impose bounded nondeterminacy, fairness cannot be imposed (without using a weaker notion of continuity based on transfinite limits).

- Resumption semantics makes unnecessary distinctions among commands, so that it is far from fully abstract. For example, the three commands

$$c \qquad \mathbf{skip}\,;c \qquad c\,;\mathbf{skip}$$

have different meanings.

For these reasons, we will not consider resumption semantics further in this book.

8.7 Transition Traces

Some of the shortcomings of resumption semantics can be avoided by using a denotational semantics, originally suggested by David Park, that is based on the idea of transition traces.

When the execution of a command c_0 can be interrupted by other processes, the sequence of transitions induced by such an execution will have the form

$$\langle c_0, \sigma_0 \rangle \to \langle c_1, \sigma_0' \rangle, \ \langle c_1, \sigma_1 \rangle \to \langle c_2, \sigma_1' \rangle, \ \ldots, \ \langle c_{n-1}, \sigma_{n-1} \rangle \to \sigma_{n-1}'$$

if the execution terminates, or

$$\langle c_0, \sigma_0 \rangle \to \langle c_1, \sigma_0' \rangle, \ \langle c_1, \sigma_1 \rangle \to \langle c_2, \sigma_1' \rangle, \ \ldots$$

if it runs on forever. Notice that, for $0 < i < n$, each σ_i may differ from σ_{i-1}', since the state may be changed by the intervention of other processes between successive transitions.

As far as the rest of the program is concerned, the commands $c_0, c_1, \ldots$ are invisible, and all that matters is the sequence of before-and-after state pairs: either the finite sequence

$$\langle \sigma_0, \sigma_0' \rangle, \langle \sigma_1, \sigma_1' \rangle, \ldots, \langle \sigma_{n-1}, \sigma_{n-1}' \rangle$$

or the infinite sequence

$$\langle \sigma_0, \sigma_0' \rangle, \langle \sigma_1, \sigma_1' \rangle, \ldots.$$

Such a sequence, which is called a *transition trace*, reflects a computation that alternates between two steps:

(a) A single step of the computation of c changes the state from σ_i to σ_i'.
(b) Intervention by zero or more other processes changes the state from σ_i' to σ_{i+1}.

In the special case where each $\sigma_i' = \sigma_{i+1}$, reflecting the situation where no other process intervenes, the transition trace is said to be *interference-free*.

The set of transition traces induced by the command c_0 is

$$\mathcal{T}[\![c_0]\!] = \{ \langle \langle \sigma_0, \sigma_0' \rangle, \langle \sigma_1, \sigma_1' \rangle, \ldots, \langle \sigma_{n-1}, \sigma_{n-1}' \rangle \rangle \mid n > 0 \text{ and } \exists c_1, c_2, \ldots, c_{n-1}.$$
$$(\forall i \in 0 \textbf{ to } n - 2. \langle c_i, \sigma_i \rangle \rightarrow \langle c_{i+1}, \sigma_i' \rangle) \text{ and } \langle c_{n-1}, \sigma_{n-1} \rangle \rightarrow \sigma_{n-1}' \}$$
$$\cup \{ \langle \langle \sigma_0, \sigma_0' \rangle, \langle \sigma_1, \sigma_1' \rangle, \ldots \rangle \mid \exists c_1, c_2, \ldots . \forall i \geq 0. \langle c_i, \sigma_i \rangle \rightarrow \langle c_{i+1}, \sigma_i' \rangle \}.$$

This set is called the *transition-trace semantics* (not to be confused with the transition semantics) of c_0. There are actually two semantic functions, $\mathcal{T}_{\text{unfair}}$ and $\mathcal{T}_{\text{fair}}$, depending on whether one includes or excludes infinite transition traces that describe unfair execution sequences. (We will postpone making this distinction rigorous until we formulate the semantic equation for concurrent composition.)

Clearly, $\mathcal{T} \in \langle \text{comm} \rangle \rightarrow \mathcal{P}((\Sigma \times \Sigma)^\infty)$, where $(\Sigma \times \Sigma)^\infty$ (as defined in Section A.3 of the Appendix) is the set of finite and infinite sequences of state pairs.

Since the semantics given by $\mathcal{T}$ is compositional, this function can be defined by semantic equations. Moreover, given $\mathcal{T}[\![c]\!]$ for a complete program c (or at least for a command that is not a subphrase of a concurrent composition), one can describe the overall state transformation caused by c in terms of its interference-free traces. First we define the *contraction* of an interference-free transition trace to be

$$\text{contract}\langle \langle \sigma_0, \sigma_1 \rangle, \langle \sigma_1, \sigma_2 \rangle, \ldots, \langle \sigma_{n-1}, \sigma_n \rangle \rangle \stackrel{\text{def}}{=} \langle \sigma_0, \sigma_n \rangle$$

$$\text{contract}\langle \langle \sigma_0, \sigma_1 \rangle, \langle \sigma_1, \sigma_2 \rangle, \ldots \rangle \stackrel{\text{def}}{=} \langle \sigma_0, \bot \rangle.$$

Then

$$[\![c]\!]_{\text{comm}} \sigma = \{ \sigma' \mid \exists \alpha \in \mathcal{T}[\![c]\!]. \alpha \text{ is interference-free and } \langle \sigma, \sigma' \rangle = \text{contract } \alpha \}.$$
$$(8.3)$$

To give the semantic equations for transition-trace semantics, we first extend the notion of concatenating sequences such as transition traces to include infinite sequences: When α_0 and α_1 are finite or infinite sequences, we write $\alpha_0 \circ \alpha_1$ for the sequence whose length is the sum of the lengths of α_0 and α_1 (assuming that a sum is infinity when either of its arguments is infinity), such that

$$(\alpha_0 \circ \alpha_1)_i = \begin{cases} (\alpha_0)_i & \text{when } i < n \\ (\alpha_1)_{i-n} & \text{otherwise,} \end{cases}$$

where $n = \# \operatorname{dom} \alpha_0$ is the length of α_0. Notice that $\alpha_0 \circ \alpha_1 = \alpha_0$ when α_0 is an infinite sequence.

Concatenation is associative, even when infinite sequences are involved. Indeed, one can directly define the concatenation of a sequence of sequences in a way that extends to an infinite sequence of sequences:

$$\operatorname{dom}(\alpha_0 \circ \cdots \circ \alpha_{n-1}) = 0 \text{ to } \sum_{i=0}^{n-1} \# \operatorname{dom} \alpha_i$$

$$\operatorname{dom}(\alpha_0 \circ \alpha_1 \circ \cdots) = 0 \text{ to } \sum_{i=0}^{\infty} \# \operatorname{dom} \alpha_i$$

$$(\alpha_0 \circ \cdots \circ \alpha_{n-1})_i = (\alpha_k)_{i'}$$

$$(\alpha_0 \circ \alpha_1 \circ \cdots)_i = (\alpha_k)_{i'},$$

where

$$i' = i - \sum_{i=0}^{k-1} \# \operatorname{dom} \alpha_i$$

and k is the greatest integer such that i' is nonnegative. Here, when any of the sequences being concatenated is infinite, the first such infinite sequence completes the concatenation. Thus, when α_i is infinite, both the finite concatenation $\alpha_0 \circ \cdots \circ \alpha_i \circ \cdots \circ \alpha_n$ and the infinite concatenation $\alpha_0 \circ \cdots \circ \alpha_i \circ \cdots$ are equal to $\alpha_0 \circ \cdots \circ \alpha_i$.

We also introduce some notation for sets of sequences:

$$S \, ; S' \stackrel{\text{def}}{=} \{ \alpha \circ \beta \mid \alpha \in S \text{ and } \beta \in S' \}$$

$$S^0 \stackrel{\text{def}}{=} \{ \langle \rangle \}$$

$$S^{n+1} \stackrel{\text{def}}{=} S \, ; S^n$$

$$S^* \stackrel{\text{def}}{=} \bigcup_{n=0}^{\infty} S^n$$

$$S^\omega \stackrel{\text{def}}{=} \{ \alpha_0 \circ \alpha_1 \circ \cdots \mid \forall i \geq 0. \, \alpha_i \in S \}.$$

(For the rest of this chapter, this notation supersedes the more general notation for the exponentiation of arbitrary sets given in Section A.3 of the Appendix.)

Then the following semantic equations are straightforward:

DR SEM EQ: Assignment

$$\mathcal{T}[\![v := e]\!] = \{\, \langle\langle \sigma, [\,\sigma \mid v\!: [\![e]\!]_{\mathrm{intexp}}\sigma\,]\rangle\rangle \mid \sigma \in \Sigma \,\},$$

DR SEM EQ: **skip**

$$\mathcal{T}[\![\mathbf{skip}]\!] = \{\, \langle\langle \sigma, \sigma \rangle\rangle \mid \sigma \in \Sigma \,\},$$

DR SEM EQ: Sequential Composition

$$\mathcal{T}[\![c_0 \,;\, c_1]\!] = \mathcal{T}[\![c_0]\!] \,;\, \mathcal{T}[\![c_1]\!].$$

A transition trace of the conditional command **if** b **then** c_0 **else** c_1 will consist of either a pair $\langle \sigma, \sigma \rangle$ for some σ such that $[\![b]\!]_{\mathrm{boolexp}}\sigma$ is true (corresponding to the transition $\langle \mathbf{if}\ b\ \mathbf{then}\ c_0\ \mathbf{else}\ c_1, \sigma \rangle \to \langle c_0, \sigma \rangle$), followed by a transition trace of c_0, or a pair $\langle \sigma, \sigma \rangle$ for some σ such that $[\![b]\!]_{\mathrm{boolexp}}\sigma$ is false (corresponding to the transition $\langle \mathbf{if}\ b\ \mathbf{then}\ c_0\ \mathbf{else}\ c_1, \sigma \rangle \to \langle c_1, \sigma \rangle$), followed by a transition trace of c_1. Thus,

DR SEM EQ: Conditional

$$\mathcal{T}[\![\mathbf{if}\ b\ \mathbf{then}\ c_0\ \mathbf{else}\ c_1]\!] = \mathcal{B}[\![b]\!] \,;\, \mathcal{T}[\![c_0]\!] \cup \mathcal{B}[\![\neg b]\!] \,;\, \mathcal{T}[\![c_1]\!],$$

where

$$\mathcal{B}[\![b]\!] = \{\, \langle\langle \sigma, \sigma \rangle\rangle \mid [\![b]\!]_{\mathrm{boolexp}}\sigma = \mathbf{true} \,\}.$$

The command **while** b **do** c will have two kinds of transition traces corresponding to executions that loop a finite or infinite number of times. The first kind will alternate some finite number of times between pairs $\langle \sigma, \sigma \rangle$ where $[\![b]\!]_{\mathrm{boolexp}}\sigma$ is true (corresponding to the transition $\langle \mathbf{while}\ b\ \mathbf{do}\ c, \sigma \rangle \to \langle c\,;\mathbf{while}\ b\ \mathbf{do}\ c, \sigma \rangle$) and traces of c, and then will end with a pair $\langle \sigma, \sigma \rangle$ where $[\![b]\!]_{\mathrm{boolexp}}\sigma$ is false (corresponding to the final transition $\langle \mathbf{while}\ b\ \mathbf{do}\ c, \sigma \rangle \to \sigma$). The second kind will alternate ad infinitum between pairs $\langle \sigma, \sigma \rangle$ where $[\![b]\!]_{\mathrm{boolexp}}\sigma$ is true and traces of c. Thus

DR SEM EQ: **while**

$$\mathcal{T}[\![\mathbf{while}\ b\ \mathbf{do}\ c]\!] = (\mathcal{B}[\![b]\!] \,;\, \mathcal{T}[\![c]\!])^* \,;\, \mathcal{B}[\![\neg b]\!] \cup (\mathcal{B}[\![b]\!] \,;\, \mathcal{T}[\![c]\!])^\omega.$$

Let the powerset T of the set of transition traces be ordered under the dual of inclusion, so that $\sqsubseteq$ is $\supseteq$. Then T is a *complete lattice*, which is a domain in which all subsets have least upper bounds. Moreover, it can be shown that $\mathcal{T}[\![\mathbf{while}\ b\ \mathbf{do}\ c]\!]$ is the least fixed-point of the function F from T to T such that

$$F\,S = (\mathcal{B}[\![b]\!] \,;\, \mathcal{T}[\![c]\!] \,;\, S) \cup \mathcal{B}[\![\neg b]\!].$$

Nevertheless, transition-trace semantics is not a conventional domain-theoretic semantics, because the dual of inclusion between sets of traces is not a notion of approximation in the usual sense. In particular, the function defined by Equation (8.3), which maps the set $\mathcal{T}[\![c]\!]$ of transition traces into the overall behavior $[\![c]\!]_{\text{comm}}$, is not a continuous function from T to $\Sigma \to \mathcal{P}_{\text{DOM}}(\hat{\Sigma}_\perp)$.

To understand variable declarations, notice that the command **newvar** $v :=$ e **in** c will have a finite or infinite trace

$$\hat{\alpha} = \langle \langle \hat{\sigma}_0, \hat{\sigma}_0' \rangle, \langle \hat{\sigma}_1, \hat{\sigma}_1' \rangle, \ldots \rangle$$

when the command c has a trace

$$\alpha = \langle \langle \sigma_0, \sigma_0' \rangle, \langle \sigma_1, \sigma_1' \rangle, \ldots \rangle$$

such that

- $\hat{\alpha}$ has the same length as α.
- Corresponding states give the same value to all variables except v:

$$\hat{\sigma}_i w = \sigma_i w \text{ and } \hat{\sigma}_i' w = \sigma_i' w \text{ when } w \neq v.$$

- The value of v in the states of α is never changed externally:

$$\sigma_{i+1} v = \sigma_i' v.$$

- The value of v in the states of $\hat{\alpha}$ is never changed internally:

$$\hat{\sigma}_i' v - \hat{\sigma}_i v.$$

- The initial value of v in α is the value of e in the initial state of $\hat{\alpha}$:

$$\sigma_0 v = [\![e]\!]_{\text{intexp}} \hat{\sigma}_0.$$

Let local-global$(v, e, \alpha, \hat{\alpha})$ be the predicate that is true when the above conditions are satisfied. Then

DR SEM EQ: Variable Declaration

$$\mathcal{T}[\![\textbf{newvar } v := e \textbf{ in } c]\!] = \{\, \hat{\alpha} \mid \exists \alpha \in \mathcal{T}[\![c]\!].\, \text{local-global}(v, e, \alpha, \hat{\alpha}) \,\}.$$

In the semantic equation for concurrent composition, we must distinguish between including and excluding unfair executions. First consider the case where unfair executions are excluded. Then $c_0 \parallel c_1$ will have a trace γ when c_0 has a trace α and c_1 has a trace β such that γ is a *fair merge* of α and β, which means that every element of α and of β occurs in γ, in the same order as in α or in β, and no other elements occur in γ. To make this notion precise, we consider the functions f and g that map positions in α and β respectively into positions in γ. Specifically, let fair-merge(α, β, γ) be the predicate on transition traces that is true when there are functions $f \in \text{dom}\,\alpha \to \text{dom}\,\gamma$ and $g \in \text{dom}\,\beta \to \text{dom}\,\gamma$ such that:

- f and g are monotone injections:

$$fi < fj \text{ and } gi < gj \text{ when } i < j.$$

- The ranges of f and g partition the domain of γ:

$$\operatorname{ran} f \cap \operatorname{ran} g = \{\} \text{ and } \operatorname{ran} f \cup \operatorname{ran} g = \operatorname{dom} \gamma.$$

- f (or g) maps each position of a state-pair in α (or in β) to a position of the same state-pair in γ:

$$\gamma_{fi} = \alpha_i \text{ and } \gamma_{gi} = \beta_i.$$

Then

DR SEM EQ: Fair Concurrent Composition

$$\mathcal{T}_{\text{fair}}[\![c_0 \parallel c_1]\!] = \{\, \gamma \mid \exists \alpha \in \mathcal{T}_{\text{fair}}[\![c_0]\!].\ \exists \beta \in \mathcal{T}_{\text{fair}}[\![c_1]\!].\ \text{fair-merge}(\alpha, \beta, \gamma) \,\}.$$

When unfair executions are included, the set of merges of α and β must be enlarged to include traces that only include a finite prefix of β when α is infinite, and vice versa. Thus we define the predicate

unfair-merge(α, β, γ)

$$\stackrel{\text{def}}{=} \text{fair-merge}(\alpha, \beta, \gamma)$$

$$\text{or } \# \operatorname{dom} \alpha = \infty \text{ and } \exists \beta_0, \beta_1.\ \beta = \beta_0 \circ \beta_1 \text{ and fair-merge}(\alpha, \beta_0, \gamma)$$

$$\text{or } \# \operatorname{dom} \beta = \infty \text{ and } \exists \alpha_0, \alpha_1.\ \alpha = \alpha_0 \circ \alpha_1 \text{ and fair-merge}(\alpha_0, \beta, \gamma).$$

Then

DR SEM EQ: Unfair Concurrent Composition

$$\mathcal{T}_{\text{unfair}}[\![c_0 \parallel c_1]\!] = \{\, \gamma \mid \exists \alpha \in \mathcal{T}_{\text{unfair}}[\![c_0]\!].\ \exists \beta \in \mathcal{T}_{\text{unfair}}[\![c_1]\!].\ \text{unfair-merge}(\alpha, \beta, \gamma) \,\}.$$

Finally, we come to the semantic equation for conditional critical regions. The command **await** b **then** c has two kinds of transition traces: First there are finite traces where pairs $\langle \sigma, \sigma \rangle$ for which $[\![b]\!]_{\text{boolexp}}\sigma$ is false (corresponding to the transition $\langle$**await** b **then** $c, \sigma\rangle \to \langle$**skip**; **await** b **then** $c, \sigma\rangle)$ alternate some finite number of times with pairs $\langle \sigma, \sigma \rangle$ for arbitrary σ (corresponding to the transition $\langle$**skip** ; **await** b **then** $c, \sigma\rangle \to \langle$**await** b **then** $c, \sigma\rangle)$, and then there is a single final transition $\langle \sigma_0, \sigma' \rangle$ for which $[\![b]\!]_{\text{boolexp}}\sigma_0$ is true and the entire execution of c changes σ_0 to σ'. Second, there are infinite traces where the alternating pairs go on forever. Thus

DR SEM EQ: Conditional Critical Region

$\mathcal{T}[\![\textbf{await } b \textbf{ then } c]\!]$

$= (\mathcal{B}[\![\neg b]\!] \,;\, \mathcal{T}[\![\textbf{skip}]\!])^* \,;$

$\quad \{\, \langle\langle \sigma_0, \sigma' \rangle\rangle \mid [\![b]\!]_{\text{boolexp}} \sigma_0 = \textbf{true} \text{ and}$

$\qquad \exists \sigma_1, \ldots, \sigma_n.\ \langle\langle \sigma_0, \sigma_1 \rangle, \langle \sigma_1, \sigma_2 \rangle, \ldots, \langle \sigma_n, \sigma' \rangle\rangle \in \mathcal{T}[\![c]\!] \,\}$

$\cup\ (\mathcal{B}[\![\neg b]\!] \,;\, \mathcal{T}[\![\textbf{skip}]\!])^{\omega}.$

8.8 Stuttering and Mumbling

The transition-trace semantics given in the previous section is not as abstract as one might hope; it gives different meanings to commands that one would expect to be equivalent, since their behaviors are indistinguishable. For example,

$$\mathcal{T}[\![\text{x} := \text{x} + 1]\!] = \{\, \langle\langle \sigma, [\,\sigma \mid \text{x}: \sigma\text{x} + 1\,] \rangle\rangle \mid \sigma \in \Sigma \,\}$$

$$\mathcal{T}[\![\textbf{skip} \,;\, \text{x} := \text{x} + 1]\!] = \{\, \langle\langle \sigma', \sigma' \rangle, \langle \sigma, [\,\sigma \mid \text{x}: \sigma\text{x} + 1\,] \rangle\rangle \mid \sigma, \sigma' \in \Sigma \,\}$$

$$\mathcal{T}[\![\text{x} := \text{x} + 1 \,;\, \textbf{skip}]\!] = \{\, \langle\langle \sigma, [\,\sigma \mid \text{x}: \sigma\text{x} + 1\,] \rangle, \langle \sigma', \sigma' \rangle\rangle \mid \sigma, \sigma' \in \Sigma \,\}.$$

A second example is most easily seen if we momentarily add a **choice** operation to our language, such that the command c_0 **choice** c_1 nondeterministically executes either c_0 or c_1:

$$\mathcal{T}[\![c_0 \textbf{ choice } c_1]\!] = \mathcal{T}[\![c_0]\!] \cup \mathcal{T}[\![c_1]\!].$$

Then

$\mathcal{T}[\![\text{x} := \text{x} + 1 \,;\, \text{x} := \text{x} + 1]\!]$

$\quad = \{\, \langle\langle \sigma, [\,\sigma \mid \text{x}: \sigma\text{x} + 1\,] \rangle, \langle \sigma', [\,\sigma' \mid \text{x}: \sigma'\text{x} + 1\,] \rangle\rangle \mid \sigma, \sigma' \in \Sigma \,\}$

$\mathcal{T}[\![(\text{x} := \text{x} + 1 \,;\, \text{x} := \text{x} + 1) \textbf{ choice } \text{x} := \text{x} + 2]\!]$

$\quad = \{\, \langle\langle \sigma, [\,\sigma \mid \text{x}: \sigma\text{x} + 1\,] \rangle, \langle \sigma', [\,\sigma' \mid \text{x}: \sigma'\text{x} + 1\,] \rangle\rangle \mid \sigma, \sigma' \in \Sigma \,\}$

$\quad \cup \{\, \langle\langle \sigma, [\,\sigma \mid \text{x}: \sigma\text{x} + 2\,] \rangle\rangle \mid \sigma \in \Sigma \,\}$

are distinct, despite the fact that adding the choice of x:=x+2 only adds behaviors that are already possible for $\text{x} := \text{x} + 1 \,;\, \text{x} := \text{x} + 1$ (i.e. the behaviors where no other process interrupts between the two assignment operations).

Recently, Stephen Brookes devised a transition-trace semantics that avoids these difficulties. His basic innovation was to use transition traces where the individual state-pairs describe an arbitrary finite number of computational steps, rather than a single step. Such a trace reflects a computation that alternates between the two actions:

(a) Zero or more steps of the computation of c change the state from σ_i to σ_i'.

(b) Intervention by zero or more other processes changes the state from σ_i' to σ_{i+1}.

This leads to the semantic function

$$
\begin{aligned}
&\mathcal{T}^*[\![c_0]\!] \\
&= \{\, \langle \langle \sigma_0, \sigma_0' \rangle, \langle \sigma_1, \sigma_1' \rangle, \ldots, \langle \sigma_{n-1}, \sigma_{n-1}' \rangle \rangle \mid n \geq m > 0 \text{ and } \exists c_1, c_2, \ldots, c_{m-1}. \\
&\qquad (\forall i \in 0 \text{ to } m-2.\ \langle c_i, \sigma_i \rangle \to^* \langle c_{i+1}, \sigma_i' \rangle) \text{ and } \langle c_{m-1}, \sigma_{m-1} \rangle \to^* \sigma_{m-1}' \\
&\qquad\quad \text{and } (\forall i \in m \text{ to } n-1.\ \sigma_i = \sigma_i') \,\} \\
&\cup \{\, \langle \langle \sigma_0, \sigma_0' \rangle, \langle \sigma_1, \sigma_1' \rangle, \ldots \rangle \mid \exists c_1, c_2, \ldots. \\
&\qquad (\forall i \geq 0.\ \langle c_i, \sigma_i \rangle \to^* \langle c_{i+1}, \sigma_i' \rangle) \\
&\qquad\quad \text{and for infinitely many } i \geq 0,\ \langle c_i, \sigma_i \rangle \to^+ \langle c_{i+1}, \sigma_i' \rangle \,\}.
\end{aligned}
$$

Notice that the conditions on finite traces in this equation permit $n - m \geq 0$ state-pairs, in which the state does not change, to occur after c has terminated. The final condition on infinite traces insures that every trace describes a complete computation of c, by prohibiting the situation where c is endlessly interrupted without taking any steps. (Again we will distinguish between $\mathcal{T}^*_{\text{unfair}}$ and $\mathcal{T}^*_{\text{fair}}$, where the latter excludes infinite transition traces that describe unfair executions.)

To ascertain the relationship between $\mathcal{T}^*$ and the semantic function $\mathcal{T}$ defined in the previous section, notice that a state-pair $\langle \sigma_i, \sigma_i' \rangle$ will occur in a trace in $\mathcal{T}^*[\![c_0]\!]$ under either of two circumstances:

(a) corresponding to the condition $\langle c_i, \sigma_i \rangle \to^k \langle c_{i+1}, \sigma_i' \rangle$ or $\langle c_i, \sigma_i \rangle \to^k \sigma_i'$ for some $k > 0$ — in this case, there will be an execution sequence

$$\langle c_i, \sigma_i \rangle \to \langle c_{i,1}, \sigma_{i,1} \rangle \to \cdots \to \langle c_{i,k-1}, \sigma_{i,k-1} \rangle \to \langle c_{i+1}, \sigma_i' \rangle$$

or

$$\langle c_i, \sigma_i \rangle \to \langle c_{i,1}, \sigma_{i,1} \rangle \to \cdots \to \langle c_{i,k-1}, \sigma_{i,k-1} \rangle \to \sigma_i',$$

so that the finite nonempty interference-free sequence

$$\langle \sigma_i, \sigma_{i,1} \rangle, \langle \sigma_{i,1}, \sigma_{i,2} \rangle, \ldots, \langle \sigma_{i,k-1}, \sigma_i' \rangle$$

will occur as a portion of some trace in $\mathcal{T}[\![c_0]\!]$;

(b) corresponding to the condition $\langle c_i, \sigma_i \rangle \to^0 \langle c_{i+1}, \sigma_i' \rangle$ or $\sigma_i = \sigma_i'$ — in this case, the state-pair will be $\langle \sigma, \sigma \rangle$, where σ can be any state.

Now suppose a finite trace $\alpha \in \mathcal{T}[\![c_0]\!]$ can be written as a finite concatenation $\alpha_0 \circ \cdots \circ \alpha_{n-1}$, or an infinite trace $\alpha \in \mathcal{T}[\![c_0]\!]$ can be written as an infinite concatenation $\alpha_0 \circ \alpha_1 \circ \cdots$, where each α_i is either a finite nonempty interference-free trace or the empty sequence.

(a) When α_i is nonempty, let $\hat{\alpha}_i = \text{contract}\,\alpha_i$, called a *mumbling contraction*.

(b) When α_i is empty, let $\hat{\alpha}_i = \langle \sigma, \sigma \rangle$ (where σ is any state), called a *stuttering expansion*.

Then the finite sequence $\hat{\alpha} = \langle \hat{\alpha}_0, \ldots, \hat{\alpha}_{n-1} \rangle$ or the infinite sequence $\hat{\alpha} = \langle \hat{\alpha}_0, \hat{\alpha}_1, \ldots \rangle$ is called a *stuttering-mumbling variant* of α. (Notice that we do not permit a finite α to be written as an infinite concatenation — which could happen only if an infinite number of the α_i were empty — since the infinite variant would describe a nonterminating computation while α describes a terminating computation.)

Next let

$$S^\dagger \stackrel{\text{def}}{=} \{ \hat{\alpha} \mid \exists \alpha \in S.\ \hat{\alpha} \text{ is a stuttering-mumbling variant of } \alpha \}.$$

Then it can be shown that

$$\mathcal{T}^*[\![c]\!] = (\mathcal{T}[\![c]\!])^\dagger.$$

It can also be shown that $S \subseteq S^\dagger$ and that, whenever $\alpha \in S^\dagger$, every stuttering-mumbling variant of α also belongs to $S^\dagger$. Thus $S^\dagger$ is called the *closure of S under stuttering and mumbling*.

From the above equation it is easy to work out, for the examples given earlier, that

$$\mathcal{T}^*[\![\mathsf{x} := \mathsf{x} + 1]\!] = \mathcal{T}^*[\![\mathbf{skip}\,;\mathsf{x} := \mathsf{x} + 1]\!] = \mathcal{T}^*[\![\mathsf{x} := \mathsf{x} + 1\,;\mathbf{skip}]\!]$$

and

$$\mathcal{T}^*[\![\mathsf{x} := \mathsf{x} + 1\,;\mathsf{x} := \mathsf{x} + 1]\!] = \mathcal{T}^*[\![(\mathsf{x} := \mathsf{x} + 1\,;\mathsf{x} := \mathsf{x} + 1)\ \mathbf{choice}\ \mathsf{x} := \mathsf{x} + 2]\!].$$

One can also derive semantic equations for $\mathcal{T}^*$ from the semantic equations for $\mathcal{T}$. Each semantic equation for $\mathcal{T}$ can be written in the syntax-directed form

$$\mathcal{T}[\![c(z_0, \ldots, z_{m-1}, c_0, \ldots, c_{n-1})]\!] = F_c(z_0, \ldots, z_{m-1}, \mathcal{T}[\![c_0]\!], \ldots, \mathcal{T}[\![c_{n-1}]\!]),$$

where c is a constructor of the abstract syntax; $c_0, \ldots, c_{n-1}$ are commands; $z_0, \ldots, z_{m-1}$ are variables or expressions; and F_c is a function from variables, expressions, and sets of transition traces into sets of transition traces. Moreover, it is possible to show that each F_c satisfies

$$F_c(z_0, \ldots, z_{m-1}, S_0, \ldots, S_{n-1}) \subseteq F_c(z_0, \ldots, z_{m-1}, S_0^\dagger, \ldots, S_{n-1}^\dagger)$$

$$\subseteq (F_c(z_0, \ldots, z_{m-1}, S_0, \ldots, S_{n-1}))^\dagger.$$

By applying $(-)^\dagger$ (which is monotone) to each term of this inclusion, and using the fact that $(S^\dagger)^\dagger = S^\dagger$ (which is a general property of closure operators), one finds that

$$(F_c(z_0, \ldots, z_{m-1}, S_0, \ldots, S_{n-1}))^\dagger = (F_c(z_0, \ldots, z_{m-1}, S_0^\dagger, \ldots, S_{n-1}^\dagger))^\dagger,$$

so that

$$\mathcal{T}^*[\![c(z_0, \ldots, z_{m-1}, c_0, \ldots, c_{n-1})]\!] = (F_c(z_0, \ldots, z_{m-1}, \mathcal{T}^*[\![c_0]\!], \ldots, \mathcal{T}^*[\![c_{n-1}]\!]))^\dagger.$$

Thus each semantic equation for $\mathcal{T}^*$ can be obtained from the corresponding equation for $\mathcal{T}$ by applying the closure operation $(-)^\dagger$ to the right side:

DR SEM EQ: Assignment

$$\mathcal{T}^*[\![v := e]\!] = (\{\, \langle\langle \sigma, [\,\sigma \mid v\colon [\![e]\!]_{\text{intexp}} \sigma\,]\rangle\rangle \mid \sigma \in \Sigma \,\})^\dagger,$$

DR SEM EQ: **skip**

$$\mathcal{T}^*[\![\mathbf{skip}]\!] = (\{\, \langle\langle \sigma, \sigma \rangle\rangle \mid \sigma \in \Sigma \,\})^\dagger,$$

DR SEM EQ: Sequential Composition

$$\mathcal{T}^*[\![c_0 \,;\, c_1]\!] = (\mathcal{T}^*[\![c_0]\!] \,;\, \mathcal{T}^*[\![c_1]\!])^\dagger,$$

DR SEM EQ: Conditional

$$\mathcal{T}^*[\![\mathbf{if}\ b\ \mathbf{then}\ c_0\ \mathbf{else}\ c_1]\!] = (\mathcal{B}[\![b]\!] \,;\, \mathcal{T}^*[\![c_0]\!] \cup \mathcal{B}[\![\neg b]\!] \,;\, \mathcal{T}^*[\![c_1]\!])^\dagger,$$

DR SEM EQ: **while**

$$\mathcal{T}^*[\![\mathbf{while}\ b\ \mathbf{do}\ c]\!] = ((\mathcal{B}[\![b]\!] \,;\, \mathcal{T}^*[\![c]\!])^* \,;\, \mathcal{B}[\![\neg b]\!] \cup (\mathcal{B}[\![b]\!] \,;\, \mathcal{T}^*[\![c]\!])^\omega)^\dagger,$$

DR SEM EQ: Variable Declaration

$$\mathcal{T}^*[\![\mathbf{newvar}\ v := e\ \mathbf{in}\ c]\!] = (\{\, \hat{\alpha} \mid \exists \alpha \in \mathcal{T}^*[\![c]\!].\ \text{local-global}(v, e, \alpha, \hat{\alpha}) \,\})^\dagger,$$

DR SEM EQ: Fair Concurrent Composition

$$\mathcal{T}^*_{\text{fair}}[\![c_0 \parallel c_1]\!] = (\{\, \gamma \mid \exists \alpha \in \mathcal{T}^*_{\text{fair}}[\![c_0]\!].\ \exists \beta \in \mathcal{T}^*_{\text{fair}}[\![c_1]\!].\ \text{fair-merge}(\alpha, \beta, \gamma) \,\})^\dagger,$$

DR SEM EQ: Unfair Concurrent Composition

$$\mathcal{T}^*_{\text{unfair}}[\![c_0 \parallel c_1]\!]$$
$$= (\{\, \gamma \mid \exists \alpha \in \mathcal{T}^*_{\text{unfair}}[\![c_0]\!].\ \exists \beta \in \mathcal{T}^*_{\text{unfair}}[\![c_1]\!].\ \text{unfair-merge}(\alpha, \beta, \gamma) \,\})^\dagger,$$

DR SEM EQ: Conditional Critical Region

$$\mathcal{T}^*[\![\mathbf{await}\ b\ \mathbf{then}\ c]\!]$$
$$= ((\mathcal{B}[\![\neg b]\!] \,;\, \mathcal{T}^*[\![\mathbf{skip}]\!])^* \,;$$
$$\{\, \langle\langle \sigma_0, \sigma' \rangle\rangle \mid [\![b]\!]_{\text{boolexp}} \sigma_0 = \mathbf{true}\ \text{and}$$
$$\exists \sigma_1, \ldots, \sigma_n.\ \langle\langle \sigma_0, \sigma_1 \rangle, \langle \sigma_1, \sigma_2 \rangle, \ldots, \langle \sigma_n, \sigma' \rangle\rangle \in \mathcal{T}^*[\![c]\!] \,\}$$
$$\cup (\mathcal{B}[\![\neg b]\!] \,;\, \mathcal{T}^*[\![\mathbf{skip}]\!])^\omega)^\dagger.$$

We have seen that $\mathcal{T}^*$ is a more abstract semantic function than $\mathcal{T}$. In fact, $\mathcal{T}^*_{\text{fair}}$ is fully abstract, in the sense defined in Section 2.8, if all commands are observable and one is permitted to observe intermediate states.

One might hope that $\mathcal{T}^*_{\text{fair}}$ would be fully abstract if one only observed the state-transformation function of a command, that is, if the function $[\![-]\!]_{\text{comm}}$ were the only member of the set $\mathcal{O}$ of observations. In the absence of failure or output operations, however, this hope is unrealistic, since there is no context that will produce an observable difference between two commands that never terminate.

On the other hand, it has been shown that $\mathcal{T}^*_{\text{fair}}$ is fully abstract when the set $\mathcal{O}$ of observations contains the function

$$\mathcal{M}[\![c]\!] = \{\, \alpha \mid \alpha \in \mathcal{T}^*_{\text{fair}}[\![c]\!] \text{ and } \alpha \text{ is interference-free} \,\},$$

which describes the interference-free behavior of a command.

Bibliographic Notes

The basic concepts of shared-variable concurrent processing were clearly delineated by Hoare [1972].

Both transition semantics and resumption semantics for shared-variable concurrency were devised by Hennessy and Plotkin [1979]. Transition-trace semantics was developed by Park [1980], and the use of stuttering and mumbling was introduced and shown to give full abstraction by Brookes [1993; 1996b]. An entire book devoted to fairness is Francez [1986].

An early but influential technique for concurrent program verification is due to Owicki and Gries [1976]. Such verification methods have been surveyed by Barringer [1985] and described extensively by Apt and Olderog [1991, Chapter 6]. A more recent approach has been developed by Brookes [1992].

A very different approach to reasoning about concurrent programming, using temporal logic, was first proposed by Pnueli [1977; 1981]. In this form of logic, one can make statements such as "Eventually it will be true that x will always be zero", which are particularly useful for reasoning about programs that interact with their environment without ever terminating. An extensive exposition appears in Manna and Pnueli [1992, Part II].

A good general text on concurrent programming is Andrews [1991].

Exercises

8.1   For each of the following concurrent programs, give a precise description of the set of possible final states. (In the last case, also describe the set of possible output sequences.) Also describe any infinite computations and state whether they are fair or unfair.

(a) $x := 0 ; t := 0 ;$

$\quad$ ($\textbf{while } t = 0 \textbf{ do } x := x + 1$

$\quad$ $\| \textbf{ await } x \geq 13 \textbf{ then } (y := x ; t := 1)).$

(b) $x := 0 ; t := 0 ;$

$\quad$ ($\textbf{while } t = 0 \textbf{ do } x := x + 1$

$\quad$ $\| (\textbf{await } x \geq 13 \textbf{ then } y := x) ; t := 1).$

(c) $x := 0 ; t := 0 ;$

$\quad$ ($\textbf{while } t = 0 \textbf{ do } x := x + 1$

$\quad$ $\| \textbf{ while } x < 13 \textbf{ do skip} ; y := x ; t := 1).$

(d) $x := 0 ; t := 0 ;$

$\quad$ ($\textbf{while } t = 0 \textbf{ do } x := x + 1$

$\quad$ $\| \textbf{ await } odd(x) \textbf{ then } (y := x ; t := 1)).$

(e) $x := 0 ; t := 0 ;$

$\quad$ ($\textbf{while } t = 0 \textbf{ do } (x := x + 1 ; x := x + 1)$

$\quad$ $\| \textbf{ await } odd(x) \textbf{ then } (y := x ; t := 1)).$

(f) $i := 0 ; j := 0 ; x := 0 ;$

$\quad$ ($\textbf{while } i < 100 \textbf{ do } x := x + 1 ; !x ; i := i + 1$

$\quad$ $\| \textbf{ while } j < 100 \textbf{ do } x := x + 1 ; j := j + 1).$

8.2   The following shared-variable concurrent program, called Peterson's algorithm, provides a method for achieving mutual exclusion without critical regions, conditional or otherwise:

$$c_0 := 1 ; c_1 := 1 ; turn := 0 ; (P_0 \| P_1),$$

where P_0 is the process

$\quad$ $\textbf{while true do}$

$\quad\quad$ ($c_0 := 0 ; turn := 1 ; \textbf{while } c_1 = 0 \wedge turn = 1 \textbf{ do skip} ;$

$\quad\quad$ *excluded region*$_0$; $c_0 := 1$; *nonexcluded region*$_0$)

and P_1 is the process

$\quad$ $\textbf{while true do}$

$\quad\quad$ ($c_1 := 0 ; turn := 0 ; \textbf{while } c_0 = 0 \wedge turn = 0 \textbf{ do skip} ;$

$\quad\quad$ *excluded region*$_1$; $c_1 := 1$; *nonexcluded region*$_1$).

It is assumed that the variables c_0, c_1, and **turn** do not occur in the excluded regions or nonexcluded regions.

(a) Give an *informal* argument as to why both processes cannot be in their excluded regions at the same time.

Hint First establish a relationship among the variables c_0, c_1, and **turn** that holds whenever P_0 finishes executing its inner **while** command. Then establish that this relationship must continue to hold as long as P_0 is executing its excluded region, except when P_1 is at a specific point in its program that is outside its excluded region. Finally, assume that both processes are in their excluded regions, so that both the relationship and a symmetric one for P_1 hold, and show that this leads to a contradiction.

(b) Give an *informal* argument, assuming fairness and that P_0 does not stay within its excluded region forever, that P_1 does not execute its inner **while** command forever.

(c) Suppose the assignments $c_0:=0$ and **turn**$:=1$ in P_0 were interchanged. Show that then there would be an execution where both processes are in their excluded regions at the same time.

8.3   Using the shared-variable concurrency language of this chapter, write a program to solve the "unisex bathroom" problem. Specifically, write protocols (i.e. commands) M_{entry}, M_{exit}, W_{entry}, and W_{exit} so that in all executions of the program

$$M_0 \parallel \cdots \parallel M_{m-1} \parallel W_0 \parallel \cdots \parallel W_{w-1},$$

where

$$M_i \equiv \textbf{while true do } (M_{\text{entry}} ; m_i ; M_{\text{exit}})$$
$$W_j \equiv \textbf{while true do } (W_{\text{entry}} ; w_j ; W_{\text{exit}}),$$

no m_i is ever executing at the same time as a w_j. Your solution should allow as much concurrency as is permitted by this specification. (For example, several m_i can execute concurrently if no w_j is executing at the same time, and vice versa.) Note that all M_i use the same M_{entry} and M_{exit}, and all W_j use the same W_{entry} and W_{exit}. These protocols may use global variables whose declarations enclose the entire concurrent program.

Give an informal argument justifying the correctness of your program.

8.4   Suppose U is a user process that requires an endless sequence of values
       $f(0), f(1), f(2), \ldots$ of a function f whose computation time is significant
       and varies widely for different arguments. Then it is reasonable to have
       many concurrent processes $P_0, \ldots, P_{m-1}$ precomputing different values of
       f before they are needed by U, and to buffer up to n of the results of
       these computations. (You may assume that m and n are constants that
       will both be at least one.)

       Using the shared-variable concurrency language of this chapter, write
       a program to control the interaction of these processes. The overall form
       of your program should be

$$\textbf{newvar } k := 0 \textbf{ in newvar } l := 0 \textbf{ in}$$
$$\textbf{newarray } R \ (0 \textbf{ to } n - 1) := 0 \textbf{ in}$$
$$\textbf{newarray } V \ (0 \textbf{ to } n - 1) := 0 \textbf{ in}$$
$$(P_0 \parallel \cdots \parallel P_{m-1} \parallel U).$$

(In the actual program, n would be replaced by an integer constant specifying the buffer size.)

       What you should write is

(a) The commands $P_0, \ldots, P_{m-1}$ (which will all be the same).

(b) A command U_{fetch}, which will occur within U, that will obtain the
    successive values $f(0), f(1), f(2), \ldots$. Each time U_{fetch} is executed, it
    should set a local variable v of U to the next value occurring in this
    sequence.

Your program should satisfy the following conditions:

(a) k should be the number of times U_{fetch} has been executed, so that the
    next value to be fetched is $f(k)$.

(b) $f(0), \ldots, f(l - 1)$, where $l \geq k$, are the values that either have been
    computed or are being computed by the P_i.

(c) Each element of the array R indicates whether a yet-to-be-fetched
    result of f is stored in the corresponding element of the array V.
    Specifically, for all i such that $k \leq i < k + n$:

$$R(i \textbf{ rem } n) \neq 0 \text{ implies } V(i \textbf{ rem } n) = f(i).$$

(d) As long as there is enough space in the buffer, all of the P_i should be
    kept busy.

8.5 Suppose that, in a program in the language of this chapter, several processes need to compute values of an integer-to-integer function f for arguments between 0 and 999 inclusive. Write a program that will "memoize"
the function. More precisely, your program should save the values of the
function in an array S with domain 0 **to** 999, so that the function is never
computed more than once for the same argument.

Specifically, you should write a command, identical copies of which will
occur in each process that needs to evaluate f, that will set the variable y
to the value of f applied to an argument given by the variable x (where x
and y are local variables of the process). Assume that there is a command
c_f that evaluates f x and stores the result in y. (Since c_f may be a time-
consuming command, it should not occur within a critical region.)

You will also need to write the declarations of S and any other necessary
variables or arrays. (These declarations will enclose the entire program.)
You may assume fair execution.

Hint Use a second array T to keep track of the status of the computation
of f for each argument:

$$T(i) = \begin{cases} 0 & \text{if the ith value of f has never been requested,} \\ 1 & \text{if the ith value of f is currently being computed,} \\ 2 & \text{if the ith value of f is stored in } S(i). \end{cases}$$

8.6 Which of the following pairs of commands are equivalent (i.e. have the
same meaning) in the $\mathcal{T}^*_{\text{fair}}$ semantics of Section 8.8?

$$\textbf{while } b \textbf{ do } c \overset{?}{\equiv} \textbf{ if } b \textbf{ then while } b \textbf{ do } c \textbf{ else skip}$$

$$\textbf{await } b \textbf{ then } c \overset{?}{\equiv} \textbf{ while } \neg b \textbf{ do skip} \,;\, c$$

$$x := 0 \,;\, x := 1 \overset{?}{\equiv} x := 0 \,;\, (\textbf{await } x = 1 \textbf{ then skip} \parallel x := 1)$$

8.7 In Section 8.8, we mentioned a **choice** operation such that the command
c_0 **choice** c_1 nondeterministically executes either c_0 or c_1:

$$\mathcal{T}[\![c_0 \textbf{ choice } c_1]\!] = \mathcal{T}[\![c_0]\!] \cup \mathcal{T}[\![c_1]\!].$$

(a) Define this operation as syntactic sugar in terms of the guarded-
command constructions of Chapter 7.
(b) Define this operation as syntactic sugar in terms of concurrent composition, that is, in terms of the language used in this chapter (but
without guarded commands).

In both cases, although you need not prove it, your definition should have
the same denotational semantics (in the sense of $\mathcal{T}^*$ rather than $\mathcal{T}$) as
the **choice** operation, but its execution sequences may be longer.

8.8   Consider altering the language described in this chapter so that expression evaluation is still atomic but assignment commands (outside of conditional critical regions) are no longer atomic. In other words, an assignment $v := e$ can be interrupted after the value of e has been determined, but when completed will update v with that value (even if the state has changed meanwhile). For example,

$$x := x + 1 \parallel x := x - 1$$

can either leave the value of x unchanged, increase it by one, or decrease it by one.

(a) Give inference rules for the transition semantics of this interruptible assignment command. (If necessary, you may augment the variety of configurations by introducing additional kinds of commands.)

(b) Change the equations for $\mathcal{T}[\![v := e]\!]$ in Section 8.7 and $\mathcal{T}^*[\![v := e]\!]$ in Section 8.8 to describe the denotational semantics of this interruptible assignment command.

8.9   Show that the semantic equation for conditional critical regions in Section 8.8 is equivalent to the following simpler equation:

$$\mathcal{T}^*[\![\textbf{await } b \textbf{ then } c]\!]$$
$$= (\{ \langle\langle \sigma, \sigma' \rangle\rangle \mid \langle\langle \sigma, \sigma' \rangle\rangle \in \mathcal{T}^*[\![c]\!] \text{ and } [\![b]\!]_{\text{boolexp}} \sigma = \textbf{true} \})^{\dagger}$$
$$\cup ((\mathcal{B}[\![\neg b]\!])^{\omega})^{\dagger}.$$

8.10   Explain why the evaluation semantics of Exercises 6.4 and 7.5 is unsuited for describing shared-variable concurrency.

8.11   Data are said to be *packed* when several variables are implemented by separate fields in the same physical word. Assume that an assignment to such a variable causes the contents of the entire word to be read from memory to a central processor, and then the altered contents of the entire word to be written back into memory. Discuss the problems this raises for shared-variable concurrent processing.

9

Communicating Sequential Processes

In this chapter, we use operational semantics to explore an approach to concurrency where processes communicate by passing messages. This approach is based on Hoare's communicating sequential processes (often abbreviated CSP), but differs in two details: communication is by named "channels" instead of between named processes, and the nondeterminate selection of input-output operations is performed by an "input-output guarded command" in which all of the guards are input-output commands, instead of Hoare's generalization of Dijkstra's guarded command, where guards can contain both boolean expressions and input-output commands. (Specifically, our input-output command is similar to a guarded command of Hoare's where the boolean part of each guard is **true**.)

9.1 Syntax

To define abstract syntax, we assume that $\langle chname \rangle$ is a countably infinite predefined set of *channel names*, which will name channels for internal communication between concurrent processes. (Formally, $\langle chname \rangle$ is a set of variables disjoint from either $\langle var \rangle$ or $\langle arrayvar \rangle$. In examples, however, we will use a, b, c, and d as channel names.) Then we introduce two *internal input-output commands*, denoted by the new nonterminal $\langle iocomm \rangle$:

$$\langle comm \rangle ::= \langle iocomm \rangle$$

$$\langle iocomm \rangle ::= \langle chname \rangle \, ? \, \langle var \rangle \mid \langle chname \rangle \, ! \, \langle intexp \rangle$$

These forms (including their precedence) are similar to the input and output commands in Sections 5.2 and 5.6, except that they include the name of the channel to be used: The *input* command $h \, ? \, v$ inputs an integer from channel h and assigns it to the variable v, while the *output* command $h \, ! \, e$ outputs the value of the expression e to channel h.

Channels are not buffers; they are mechanisms for synchronizing concurrent processes. Thus output from a process to a channel will not occur until some other process performs input from the same channel, and vice versa. If this never happens, then the process trying to execute the unmated input-output command is stuck — and if all of the processes are stuck, the computation is deadlocked.

An additional construction is needed so that a process may simultaneously attempt several input-output operations and then proceed if any of the operations is successful. For this purpose, we introduce (internal) *input-output guarded commands*, denoted by the new nonterminal $\langle \text{iogdcomm} \rangle$:

$$\langle \text{comm} \rangle ::= \langle \text{iogdcomm} \rangle$$

$$\langle \text{iogdcomm} \rangle ::= \langle \text{iocomm} \rangle \rhd \langle \text{comm} \rangle \mid \langle \text{iogdcomm} \rangle \,\Box\, \langle \text{iogdcomm} \rangle$$

Here, $c_{io} \rhd c$ causes the input-output operation c_{io} to be attempted; if this operation is successful, then the command c is executed. (We use $\rhd$ here rather than $\rightarrow$ to emphasize the distinction between these forms and the guarded commands of Chapter 7. However, the two operators have the same precedence.) The compound form $c_0 \,\Box\, c_1$ may execute either c_0 or c_1, but it will always execute one or the other if either is possible.

Despite their superficial resemblance to the guarded commands of Chapter 7, input-output guarded commands are subtly different. In particular, there is nothing like the alternative or repetitive constructs that might be used to branch when no guard can proceed. In our transition semantics, this will be mirrored by the fact that input-output guarded commands that cannot proceed will have no transitions, rather than a transition to the special symbol **false**, and thus will have the same kind of meaning as other commands. The nonterminals $\langle \text{iocomm} \rangle$ and $\langle \text{iogdcomm} \rangle$ (but not the $\langle \text{gdcomm} \rangle$ of Chapter 7) denote subsets of $\langle \text{comm} \rangle$ that are distinguished only to impose the syntactic restriction that only an internal input-output command can occur on the left of the operator $\rhd$.

To complete the abstract syntax, we introduce a form for declaring channels:

$$\langle \text{comm} \rangle ::= \textbf{channel} \ \langle \text{chname} \rangle \ \textbf{in} \ \langle \text{comm} \rangle$$

Here the command **channel** h **in** c declares h to be a local channel name with scope c. Syntactically, the command c extends to the first stopping symbol or the end of the enclosing phrase.

The new equations for free variables and free assigned variables are

$$\text{FV}_{\text{comm}}(h \, ? \, v) = \{h, v\}$$

$$\text{FV}_{\text{comm}}(h \, ! \, e) = \{h\} \cup \text{FV}_{\text{intexp}}(e)$$

$$\text{FV}_{\text{comm}}(\textbf{channel} \ h \ \textbf{in} \ c) = \text{FV}_{\text{comm}}(c) - \{h\}$$

$$\text{FA}(h \, ? \, v) = \{v\}$$

$$\text{FA}(h \, ! \, e) = \{\}$$

$$\text{FA}(\textbf{channel} \ h \ \textbf{in} \ c) = \text{FA}(c) - \{h\}.$$

(The last equation is written this way to emphasize the similarity to other kinds of declarations. One could just as well write $FA(\textbf{channel } h \textbf{ in } c) = FA(c)$, since $FA(c)$ will never contain a channel name.)

Unless the variable occurrences in a concurrent composition $c_0 \parallel c_1$ are restricted, the processes c_0 and c_1 will be able to interact via shared variables, as in the previous chapter, as well as through internal input-output. Although such a combination of approaches is semantically consistent, most research on CSP assumes the absence of shared variables, except perhaps variables that are not assigned by any process.

To prohibit shared-variable interactions between c_0 and c_1 (i.e. to prohibit c_0 and c_1 from interfering, in the sense of the previous chapter), it is sufficient to require the set (8.1) in Section 8.1,

$$(FA(c_0) \cap FV_{comm}(c_1)) \cup (FA(c_1) \cap FV_{comm}(c_0)),$$

to be empty.

9.2 Transition Semantics

To give meaning to the language extensions in the previous section, we extend the transition semantics of previous chapters by introducing labelled internal input-output transitions, which will be similar to the transitions of Section 6.4, except that their labels will include channel names. Thus the sets of nonterminal and terminal configurations are still as in Chapter 7:

$$\Gamma_N = (\langle \text{gdcomm} \rangle \cup \langle \text{comm} \rangle) \times \Sigma$$

$$\Gamma_T = \hat{\Sigma} \cup \{\textbf{false}\}$$
$$= \Sigma \cup (\{\textbf{abort}\} \times \Sigma) \cup \{\textbf{false}\},$$

but the set of labels is expanded to include internal as well as external communications:

$$\Lambda = \{\epsilon\} \cup \{ h\,?\,n \mid h \in \langle \text{chname} \rangle \wedge n \in \textbf{Z} \} \cup \{ h\,!\,n \mid h \in \langle \text{chname} \rangle \wedge n \in \textbf{Z} \}$$
$$\cup \{ ?\,n \mid n \in \textbf{Z} \} \cup \{ !\,n \mid n \in \textbf{Z} \}.$$

As in Section 6.4, we write $\langle c, \sigma \rangle \xrightarrow{\lambda} \gamma$ (with λ omitted when it is the silent transition ϵ) to indicate that $\langle \langle c, \sigma \rangle, \lambda, \gamma \rangle$ belongs to the trinary transition relation, which is a subset of $\Gamma_N \times \Lambda \times \Gamma$.

The inference rules for internal input-output and guarded input-output are straightforward:

TR RULE: Internal Input

$$\langle h \, ? \, v, \sigma \rangle \xrightarrow{h?n} [\sigma \mid v{:}\, n],$$

TR RULE: Internal Output

$$\langle h \, ! \, e, \sigma \rangle \xrightarrow{h!n} \sigma \qquad \text{when } n = [\![e]\!]_{\text{intexp}} \sigma,$$

TR RULE: Simple Input-Output Guarded Command

$$\frac{\langle c_{io}, \sigma \rangle \xrightarrow{\lambda} \sigma'}{\langle c_{io} \vartriangleright c, \sigma \rangle \xrightarrow{\lambda} \langle c, \sigma' \rangle,}$$

TR RULE: Compound Input-Output Guarded Command

$$\frac{\langle c_0, \sigma \rangle \xrightarrow{\lambda} \langle c, \sigma' \rangle}{\langle c_0 \, \square \, c_1, \sigma \rangle \xrightarrow{\lambda} \langle c, \sigma' \rangle} \qquad \frac{\langle c_1, \sigma \rangle \xrightarrow{\lambda} \langle c, \sigma' \rangle}{\langle c_0 \, \square \, c_1, \sigma \rangle \xrightarrow{\lambda} \langle c, \sigma' \rangle.}$$

Notice that every transition from a configuration that starts with an input-output command or a input-output guarded command is labeled with either $h?n$ or $h!n$, reflecting the fact that these commands cannot proceed without communicating.

The heart of the semantics lies in the following rules for the concurrent execution of commands (which augment the rules given in Section 8.1):

TR RULE: Concurrent Composition with Internal Input-Output

$$\frac{\langle c_0, \sigma \rangle \xrightarrow{h!n} \langle c_0', \sigma \rangle \qquad \langle c_1, \sigma \rangle \xrightarrow{h?n} \langle c_1', \sigma' \rangle}{\langle c_0 \parallel c_1, \sigma \rangle \to \langle c_0' \parallel c_1', \sigma' \rangle}$$

$$\frac{\langle c_0, \sigma \rangle \xrightarrow{h?n} \langle c_0', \sigma' \rangle \qquad \langle c_1, \sigma \rangle \xrightarrow{h!n} \langle c_1', \sigma \rangle}{\langle c_0 \parallel c_1, \sigma \rangle \to \langle c_0' \parallel c_1', \sigma' \rangle}$$

$$\frac{\langle c_0, \sigma \rangle \xrightarrow{h!n} \langle c_0', \sigma \rangle \qquad \langle c_1, \sigma \rangle \xrightarrow{h?n} \sigma'}{\langle c_0 \parallel c_1, \sigma \rangle \to \langle c_0', \sigma' \rangle}$$

$$\frac{\langle c_0, \sigma \rangle \xrightarrow{h?n} \sigma' \qquad \langle c_1, \sigma \rangle \xrightarrow{h!n} \langle c_1', \sigma \rangle}{\langle c_0 \parallel c_1, \sigma \rangle \to \langle c_1', \sigma' \rangle}$$

$$\frac{\langle c_0, \sigma \rangle \xrightarrow{h!n} \sigma \qquad \langle c_1, \sigma \rangle \xrightarrow{h?n} \langle c_1', \sigma' \rangle}{\langle c_0 \parallel c_1, \sigma \rangle \to \langle c_1', \sigma' \rangle}$$

$$\frac{\langle c_0, \sigma \rangle \xrightarrow{h?n} \langle c_0', \sigma' \rangle \qquad \langle c_1, \sigma \rangle \xrightarrow{h!n} \sigma}{\langle c_0 \parallel c_1, \sigma \rangle \to \langle c_0', \sigma' \rangle}$$

$$\frac{\langle c_0, \sigma \rangle \xrightarrow{h!n} \sigma \qquad \langle c_1, \sigma \rangle \xrightarrow{h?n} \sigma'}{\langle c_0 \parallel c_1, \sigma \rangle \to \sigma'}$$

$$\frac{\langle c_0, \sigma \rangle \xrightarrow{h?n} \sigma' \qquad \langle c_1, \sigma \rangle \xrightarrow{h!n} \sigma}{\langle c_0 \parallel c_1, \sigma \rangle \to \sigma'.}$$

These rules capture the possibility that, if two processes executing concurrently perform matching input and output transitions, then they can communicate with one another, so that the combined process executes a single silent transition. (Note that the resulting state is always the changed state of the input transition, not the unchanged state of the output transition.)

On the other hand, the rules for concurrent execution in Section 8.1 permit the combined process to make a single transition of either subprocess, even when this is an input or output transition. This allows the subprocesses to communicate with other processes occurring at a higher textual level.

Such communication is cut off by a channel declaration: The transitions from a configuration containing **channel** h **in** c are those for the corresponding subcommand c, except for unmated inputs or outputs on the channel h (since any reference to h at a higher textual level refers to a different channel):

TR RULE: Channel Declaration

$$\frac{\langle c, \sigma \rangle \xrightarrow{\lambda} \langle c', \sigma' \rangle}{\langle \textbf{channel } h \textbf{ in } c, \sigma \rangle \xrightarrow{\lambda} \langle \textbf{channel } h \textbf{ in } c', \sigma' \rangle}$$

unless λ is either $h\,?\,n$ or $h\,!\,n$ (for any integer n),

$$\frac{\langle c, \sigma \rangle \xrightarrow{\lambda} \sigma'}{\langle \textbf{channel } h \textbf{ in } c, \sigma \rangle \xrightarrow{\lambda} \sigma'}$$

unless λ is either $h\,?\,n$ or $h\,!\,n$ (for any integer n),

$$\frac{\langle c, \sigma \rangle \to \langle \textbf{abort}, \sigma' \rangle}{\langle \textbf{channel } h \textbf{ in } c, \sigma \rangle \to \langle \textbf{abort}, \sigma' \rangle.}$$

As a simple example, consider

channel c in channel d in $(c\,?\,x \rhd d\,?\,y \;\square\; d\,?\,x \rhd c\,?\,y \parallel c\,!\,3 \parallel d\,!\,4).$

Here the guarded command in the first process permits the outputs of the second and third processes to be read in either order, while the channel declarations prevent all three processes from communicating (via channel c or d) with any other process. Thus there are two possible executions:

$$\langle \textbf{channel c in channel d in } (\mathsf{c\,?\,x} \rhd \mathsf{d\,?\,y} \;\square\; \mathsf{d\,?\,x} \rhd \mathsf{c\,?\,y} \parallel \mathsf{c\,!\,3} \parallel \mathsf{d\,!\,4}), \sigma\rangle$$
$$\rightarrow \langle \textbf{channel c in channel d in } (\mathsf{d\,?\,y} \parallel \mathsf{d\,!\,4}), [\sigma \mid \mathsf{x:3}]\rangle$$
$$\rightarrow [\sigma \mid \mathsf{x:3} \mid \mathsf{y:4}]$$

$$\langle \textbf{channel c in channel d in } (\mathsf{c\,?\,x} \rhd \mathsf{d\,?\,y} \;\square\; \mathsf{d\,?\,x} \rhd \mathsf{c\,?\,y} \parallel \mathsf{c\,!\,3} \parallel \mathsf{d\,!\,4}), \sigma\rangle$$
$$\rightarrow \langle \textbf{channel c in channel d in } (\mathsf{c\,?\,y} \parallel \mathsf{c\,!\,3}), [\sigma \mid \mathsf{x:4}]\rangle$$
$$\rightarrow [\sigma \mid \mathsf{x:4} \mid \mathsf{y:3}].$$

The following is a proof of the first transition in the first of these executions, using the inference rules of the previous section, plus the Concurrent Composition rule in Section 8.1:

1. $\langle \mathsf{c\,?\,x}, \sigma\rangle \xrightarrow{\mathsf{c?3}} [\sigma \mid \mathsf{x:3}]$ (Internal Input)

2. $\langle \mathsf{c\,?\,x} \rhd \mathsf{d\,?\,y}, \sigma\rangle \xrightarrow{\mathsf{c?3}} \langle \mathsf{d\,?\,y}, [\sigma \mid \mathsf{x:3}]\rangle$

    (Simple I-O Guarded Command, 1)

3. $\langle \mathsf{c\,?\,x} \rhd \mathsf{d\,?\,y} \;\square\; \mathsf{d\,?\,x} \rhd \mathsf{c\,?\,y}, \sigma\rangle \xrightarrow{\mathsf{c?3}} \langle \mathsf{d\,?\,y}, [\sigma \mid \mathsf{x:3}]\rangle$

    (Compound I-O Guarded Command (a), 2)

4. $\langle \mathsf{c\,!\,3}, \sigma\rangle \xrightarrow{\mathsf{c!3}} \sigma$ (Internal Output)

5. $\langle \mathsf{c\,?\,x} \rhd \mathsf{d\,?\,y} \;\square\; \mathsf{d\,?\,x} \rhd \mathsf{c\,?\,y} \parallel \mathsf{c\,!\,3}, \sigma\rangle \rightarrow \langle \mathsf{d\,?\,y}, [\sigma \mid \mathsf{x:3}]\rangle$

    (Concurrent Composition with Internal I-O (e), 3, 4)

6. $\langle \mathsf{c\,?\,x} \rhd \mathsf{d\,?\,y} \;\square\; \mathsf{d\,?\,x} \rhd \mathsf{c\,?\,y} \parallel \mathsf{c\,!\,3} \parallel \mathsf{d\,!\,4}, \sigma\rangle \rightarrow \langle \mathsf{d\,?\,y} \parallel \mathsf{d\,!\,4}, [\sigma \mid \mathsf{x:3}]\rangle$

    (Concurrent Composition (a), 5)

7. $\langle \textbf{channel d in } (\mathsf{c\,?\,x} \rhd \mathsf{d\,?\,y} \;\square\; \mathsf{d\,?\,x} \rhd \mathsf{c\,?\,y} \parallel \mathsf{c\,!\,3} \parallel \mathsf{d\,!\,4}), \sigma\rangle$
    $\rightarrow \langle \textbf{channel d in } (\mathsf{d\,?\,y} \parallel \mathsf{d\,!\,4}), [\sigma \mid \mathsf{x:3}]\rangle$

    (Channel Declaration (a), 6)

8. $\langle \textbf{channel c in channel d in } (\mathsf{c\,?\,x} \rhd \mathsf{d\,?\,y} \;\square\; \mathsf{d\,?\,x} \rhd \mathsf{c\,?\,y} \parallel \mathsf{c\,!\,3} \parallel \mathsf{d\,!\,4}), \sigma\rangle$
    $\rightarrow \langle \textbf{channel c in channel d in } (\mathsf{d\,?\,y} \parallel \mathsf{d\,!\,4}), [\sigma \mid \mathsf{x:3}]\rangle$

    (Channel Declaration (a), 7)

9.3 Possible Restrictions

As illustrated in the example at the end of the previous section, the usual cause of nondeterminacy in CSP is the interaction of an input-output guarded command with concurrent processes. Nondeterminacy can also arise, however, when several processes output to the same channel (or input from the same channel). For example,

$$\langle \textbf{channel } c \textbf{ in } (c\,?\,x\,;c\,?\,y\,\|\,c\,!\,3\,\|\,c\,!\,4), \sigma \rangle$$
$$\rightarrow \langle \textbf{channel } c \textbf{ in } (c\,?\,y\,\|\,c\,!\,4), [\,\sigma\,|\,x\colon 3\,] \rangle$$
$$\rightarrow [\,\sigma\,|\,x\colon 3\,|\,y\colon 4\,]$$

and

$$\langle \textbf{channel } c \textbf{ in } (c\,?\,x\,;c\,?\,y\,\|\,c\,!\,3\,\|\,c\,!\,4), \sigma \rangle$$
$$\rightarrow \langle \textbf{channel } c \textbf{ in } (c\,?\,y\,\|\,c\,!\,3), [\,\sigma\,|\,x\colon 4\,] \rangle$$
$$\rightarrow [\,\sigma\,|\,x\colon 4\,|\,y\colon 3\,].$$

In many versions of CSP, the latter kind of nondeterminacy is prohibited by restricting each channel to communicating between two specified processes. In one approach to doing this, the syntax of the channel declaration is changed so that more than one channel can be declared, and so that the body must be a binary concurrent composition:

$$\langle \text{comm} \rangle ::= \textbf{channel } \langle \text{chname} \rangle, \ldots, \langle \text{chname} \rangle \textbf{ in } (\langle \text{comm} \rangle \| \langle \text{comm} \rangle)$$

Then, in **channel** $h_1, \ldots, h_n$ **in** $(c_0 \| c_1)$, the declared channels are used to communicate between c_0 and c_1, while any other channel is used to communicate between c_0 and higher-level processes, or c_1 and higher-level processes, but not both. Syntactically, in **channel** $h_1, \ldots, h_n$ **in** $(c_0 \| c_1)$, the declared channels $h_1, \ldots, h_n$ are permitted to appear in both c_0 and c_1, but any other channel names must occur in at most one of c_0 and c_1. Similarly, when $c_0 \| c_1$ is not an immediate subphrase of a channel declaration, each channel name must occur in at most one of c_0 and c_1.

A further possible restriction is to make each channel one-way. An obvious notation is to suffix each channel name in a declaration with $\rightarrow$ if c_0 is to send information to c_1, or with $\leftarrow$ in the opposite case:

$$\langle \text{comm} \rangle ::= \textbf{channel } \langle \text{chname} \rangle \langle \text{arrow} \rangle, \ldots, \langle \text{chname} \rangle \langle \text{arrow} \rangle \textbf{ in }$$
$$(\langle \text{comm} \rangle \| \langle \text{comm} \rangle)$$

$$\langle \text{arrow} \rangle ::= \rightarrow \mid \leftarrow$$

9.4 Examples

The following illustrates the use of a simple one-element buffer:

channel c **in channel** d **in**

$$(c_0 \; ; c \,! \, x \; ; c_1 \; ; c \,! \, x \; ; c_2 \; ; \dots \; \|$$

$$\textbf{while true do } (c \,? \, y \; ; d \,! \, y) \; \|$$

$$c_0' \; ; d \,? \, z \; ; c_1' \; ; d \,? \, z \; ; c_2' \; ; \dots \;).$$

One can chain such buffers together:

channel c **in channel** d **in channel** e **in**

$$(c_0 \; ; c \,! \, x \; ; c_1 \; ; c \,! \, x \; ; c_2 \; ; \dots \; \|$$

$$\textbf{while true do } (c \,? \, y \; ; d \,! \, y) \; \|$$

$$\textbf{while true do } (d \,? \, z \; ; e \,! \, z) \; \|$$

$$c_0' \; ; e \,? \, w \; ; c_1' \; ; e \,? \, w \; ; c_2' \; ; \dots \;)$$

or, more practically, one can use an array to construct a multielement buffer:

newarray X $(0 \textbf{ to } 9) := 0$ **in**

   newvar inp $:= 0$ **in newvar** out $:= 0$ **in**

      do out $<$ inp $<$ out $+ 10 \rightarrow$

         $(c \,?\, X(\text{inp } \textbf{rem } 10) \rhd$ inp $:=$ inp $+ 1$

            $\Box \; d \,!\, X(\text{out } \textbf{rem } 10) \rhd$ out $:=$ out $+ 1)$

        $\Box$ out $=$ inp $\rightarrow (c \,?\, X(\text{inp } \textbf{rem } 10) \rhd$ inp $:=$ inp $+ 1)$

        $\Box$ inp $=$ out $+ 10 \rightarrow (d \,!\, X(\text{out } \textbf{rem } 10) \rhd$ out $:=$ out $+ 1)$

      od.

Here the variables inp and out count the number of items that have entered and left the buffer respectively, so that the number of items currently in the buffer is inp $-$ out. The invariant of the repetitive construct is $0 \leq$ out $\leq$ inp $\leq$ out $+ 10$. (The initialization of the array is arbitrary.)

Finally, we give an alternative version of the program in Section 8.3, which uses CSP rather than shared variables and conditional critical regions. Again, the goal is to print out k and f(k) for all k such that $0 \leq k \leq n$ and f(k) ≥ 0, and again two processes are used to examine even and odd arguments. But now these processes send their results, via distinct channels, to a third process, which sends them on to the external world, but whose internal input operations are arranged to avoid mixing up pairs of numbers from different processors:

channel c **in channel** d **in**

    ((**newvar** i := 0 **in while** i ≤ n **do**

          (**if** $f(i) \geq 0$ **then** c ! i ; c ! f(i) **else skip** ; i := i + 2)

        || **newvar** i := 1 **in while** i ≤ n **do**

          (**if** $f(i) \geq 0$ **then** d ! i ; d ! f(i) **else skip** ; i := i + 2));

    fail

    || **newvar** i := 0 **in while true do** (c ? i ▷ ! i ; c ? i ; ! i □ d ? i ▷ ! i ; d ? i ; ! i)).

When the first two processes are completed, a failure is used to force termination of the third process, so that the entire program terminates with a failure. (The initialization of i in the third process is arbitrary.)

9.5 Deadlock

As in shared-variable concurrency, deadlock occurs when all processes become stuck. But now processes are stuck by unrequited input-output operations rather than by conditional critical regions, and the condition of being stuck is formalized by a nonterminal configuration with no transitions, rather than by busy waiting.

    The question of whether some execution of a program can end in deadlock is surprisingly subtle. For example, consider

channel a **in channel** b **in channel** c **in** (a ! 0 ; b ? y || P),

where P is one of the following processes:

a ? x ; (b ! x ▷ **skip** □ c ! x ▷ **skip**)

a ? x ▷ b ! x □ a ? x ▷ c ! x

a ? x ; **if true** → b ! x □ **true** → c ! x **fi**.

The first case will never deadlock, but the second and third cases may deadlock.

9.6 Fairness

The concept of fairness is more complex for communicating sequential processes than for shared-variable concurrency. As in Section 8.5, we limit our discussion to the case of an n-ary concurrent composition of sequential subprograms. Moreover, we assume that this composition is enclosed in an implicit declaration of all channel names, so that its transitions cannot be unmated internal input-output operations, and we ignore external input-output. We also assume that the concurrent subprocesses do not share variables, so that internal input-output is the only way in which they interfere.

As in Section 8.5, unfair executions are infinite sequences that, after some finite number of transitions, have the form

$$\langle c_0^{(0)} \| \cdots \| c_0^{(n-1)}, \sigma_0 \rangle \to \langle c_1^{(0)} \| \cdots \| c_1^{(n-1)}, \sigma_1 \rangle \to \langle c_2^{(0)} \| \cdots \| c_2^{(n-1)}, \sigma_2 \rangle \to \cdots , \quad (9.1)$$

where, for some i,

(a) The $c_k^{(i)}$ are identical (i.e. $c_k^{(i)} = c^{(i)}$ for all k), reflecting the fact that the ith process is never selected for execution.

By itself, however, this property is not sufficient to define unfairness, since it does not distinguish an unfair execution from one where the ith process is attempting unrequited internal communication. For this purpose, we say that $c^{(i)}$ is *enabled* for k, if either there is a silent transition $\langle c^{(i)}, \sigma_k \rangle \to \gamma$ or there is a pair of transitions $\langle c^{(i)}, \sigma_k \rangle \xrightarrow{\lambda} \gamma$ and $\langle c_k^{(j)}, \sigma_k \rangle \xrightarrow{\lambda'} \gamma'$, where λ and λ' are matching internal input-output operations.

We now can define two kinds of unfairness: An execution is said to be *strongly unfair* if, after some finite number of transitions, it has the form (9.1), where condition (a) holds, and

(b) $c^{(i)}$ is enabled for all k.

An execution is said to be *weakly unfair* if, after some finite number of transitions, it has the form (9.1), where condition (a) holds, and

(b') $c^{(i)}$ is enabled for infinitely many k.

Conversely, any execution that is not *strongly unfair* is *weakly fair*, and any execution that is not *weakly unfair* is *strongly fair*.

strongly unfair	weakly fair	
(a) and (b) hold	(a) and (b') hold, but not (b)	other infinite executions
	weakly unfair	strongly fair

For example, there is an infinite execution of

$$\textbf{while true do } x := x + 1 \ \| \ y := y + 1$$

where the second process never terminates; it is strongly unfair because $y := y+1$ (which does not attempt input or output) is enabled at all times. Similarly,

$$\textbf{while true do } x := x + 1 \ \| \ c \ ! \ 3 \ \| \ c \ ? \ y$$

has an infinite execution where the second and third processes never execute; it is strongly unfair because each of these processes is enabled (to communicate with the other) at every transition.

On the other hand, there is an infinite execution of

$$\textbf{while true do } \mathsf{c\,!\,3} \parallel \textbf{while true do } \mathsf{c\,?\,x} \parallel \mathsf{c\,?\,y}$$

where the third process never executes; this execution is weakly but not strongly unfair. To see why this is so, note that the first process oscillates between configurations of the form $\langle\textbf{while true do } \mathsf{c!3}, \ldots\rangle$, which are not ready to communicate, and configurations of the form $\langle \mathsf{c\,!\,3}\,;\,\textbf{while true do } \mathsf{c\,!\,3}, \ldots\rangle$, which are ready to communicate. Thus, $\mathsf{c\,?\,y}$ is enabled (to communicate with the first process) infinitely often, but it is also not-enabled infinitely often.

Finally, consider

$$\textbf{while true do } \mathsf{x} := \mathsf{x} + 1 \parallel \textbf{if } \mathsf{x} \leq 13 \textbf{ then } \mathsf{c\,!\,3} \textbf{ else skip} \parallel \mathsf{c\,?\,y}.$$

Here there is an infinite execution where the second process executes when $\mathsf{x} > 13$ and the third process never executes. Since the third process is only enabled a finite number of times, this execution is strongly fair.

In practice, when a program requires the imposition of fairness, it is usually strong fairness that is required.

Bibliographic Notes

Communicating sequential processes were introduced in Hoare [1978], which is a model of clear exposition. More details will be found in Hoare [1985]. Our transition semantics is loosely based on the work of Plotkin [1983].

Methods for reasoning about CSP have been developed by Brookes, Hoare, and Roscoe [1984] and Brookes [1994], and have been surveyed by Apt and Olderog [1991, Chapter 8]. A denotational semantics using "communication" traces has been given by Brookes and Older [1995] and Older [1996]. Since then, Brookes [1997] has explored the integration of CSP with Algol-like languages, using a variant of CSP where channels can buffer information, so that a process can write data to a channel and then continue execution before the data are read. (The deterministic case of processes with buffered communication was originally formalized by Kahn [1974] and Kahn and MacQueen [1977].)

A different and more algebraic approach to processes that interact by message passing, called the Calculus of Communicating Systems, has been developed by Milner [1980; 1989]. Since then, he and his colleagues have developed the π-*calculus* [Milner, Parrow, and Walker, 1992; Milner, 1991], in which processes interact by passing names. Still more recently, Milner has explored further generalizations called *action calculi* [1993; 1994; 1996].

Exercises

9.1   For the following program, give a precise description of the set of possible final configurations (which may include deadlocked configurations as well as normal or failed terminal configurations). Also describe any infinite computations and state whether they are strongly unfair, weakly but not strongly unfair, or strongly fair.

channel c in channel d in

$$(c!0 ; (c!1 \triangleright \textbf{skip} \;\square\; d!2 \triangleright \textbf{skip})$$
$$\| \, d!3 ; (c!4 \triangleright \textbf{skip} \;\square\; d!5 \triangleright \textbf{skip})$$
$$\| \, c?x ; d?y ; c?z ; d?w).$$

9.2   Give all of the possible executions of the following program, starting in an arbitrary state σ:

channel c in

$$(c!3 \triangleright c?x \;\square\; c?x \triangleright c!3 \;\|\; c!4 \triangleright c?y \;\square\; c?y \triangleright c!4).$$

Then give a formal proof of the first transition in one of these sequences.

9.3   Consider the following program, which is similar to the one at the end of Section 9.4, except that the search is unlimited:

channel c in channel d in

$\quad$ (**newvar** $i := 0$ **in while true do**

$\qquad$ (**if** $f(i) \geq 0$ **then** $c!i ; c!f(i)$ **else skip** ; $i := i+2$)

$\quad$ $\|$ **newvar** $i := 1$ **in while true do**

$\qquad$ (**if** $f(i) \geq 0$ **then** $d!i ; d!f(i)$ **else skip** ; $i := i+2$)

$\quad$ $\|$ **newvar** $i := 0$ **in while true do**

$\qquad$ ($c?i \triangleright !i ; c?i ; !i \;\square\; d?i \triangleright !i ; d?i ; !i$)).

In each of the following cases, indicate which of the execution sequences are strongly unfair, weakly but not strongly unfair, or strongly fair.

(a) when $f(n) \geq 0$ holds if and only if $n \geq 1000$,

(b) when $f(n) \geq 0$ holds for infinitely many even numbers and no odd numbers,

(c) when $f(n) \geq 0$ holds for infinitely many even numbers and all odd numbers greater than 1000,

(d) when $f(n) \geq 0$ holds only for $n = 42$.

(You can assume that, for all values of n, evaluating $f(n)$ terminates.)

9.4   Show that, for all commands c_0, c_1, c_0', c_1', all labels λ, and all channels h such that $h \notin \text{FV}_{\text{comm}}(c_1)$,

$$\langle \textbf{channel } h \textbf{ in } (c_0 \parallel c_1), \sigma \rangle \xrightarrow{\lambda} \langle \textbf{channel } h \textbf{ in } (c_0' \parallel c_1'), \sigma' \rangle$$

if and only if

$$\langle (\textbf{channel } h \textbf{ in } c_0) \parallel c_1, \sigma \rangle \xrightarrow{\lambda} \langle (\textbf{channel } h \textbf{ in } c_0') \parallel c_1', \sigma' \rangle.$$

9.5   Using the language of this chapter (without shared variables), write a process that implements a two-element stack. Specifically, your process should read numbers from a channel named in and write them to a channel named out, subject to two constraints:

- At all times #out $\leq$ #in $\leq$ #(out + 2), where #in is the number of input operations performed so far and #out is the number of output operations performed so far.
- When a number is output, it is the most recently read item that has not yet been output.

9.6   Suppose f is a function whose computation time is significant and varies widely for different arguments. Then a useful device is an "f-engine" that computes several values of f concurrently, but may return results in a different order than it is supplied with arguments. So that results can be matched up with arguments, each argument is paired with an index, and the corresponding result is paired with the same index.

Use the language of this chapter (without shared variables) to write:

(a) An n-ary f-engine. Specifically, your f-engine should read an endless sequence of alternating indices and arguments, $i_0, x_0, i_1, x_1, \ldots,$ from channel a, and write an endless sequence of alternating indices and results, $i_{k_0}, f(x_{k_0}), i_{k_1}, f(x_{k_1}), \ldots,$ to channel b. Assume f always terminates; then whenever i, x appears in the input, $i, f(x)$ should eventually appear in the output. Your program should evaluate up to n values of f concurrently, and will thus contain at least n processes.

(b) A process that, when run concurrently with an f-engine, reads an endless sequence of arguments, $x_0, x_1, \ldots,$ from channel c, and writes the sequence of corresponding results, in the same order, $f(x_0), f(x_1), \ldots,$ to channel d.

Hint Use an array to buffer arguments, as in the example in Section 9.4, and a second array to store the corresponding results. In the second array, you will need a special value to indicate that a result is not yet known. For this purpose, you may assume that $f(x)$ is never -1.

10

The Lambda Calculus

Now we turn to *functional* programming languages (sometimes called *applicative* languages), where computation is based on the evaluation of expressions and the application of functions rather than on assignment and state change. We begin our study with the lambda calculus, which underlies all functional languages as well as the procedural facilities of many more general languages. Originally developed and investigated in the 1930's by logicians such as Church, Curry, and Rosser, this calculus has influenced the design of programming languages ever since Lisp and Algol 60.

Although one can program in the lambda calculus itself, its real importance to computer science is that many problems of language design and implementation, especially those concerning procedure mechanisms or type structure, can be posed and investigated more easily in the calculus than in more complex languages.

To see how the lambda calculus hides behind most procedure facilities, consider a functional procedure definition, as in

$$\textbf{let } f(x) \equiv x \times x + 1 \textbf{ in } B.$$

This definition specifies the meaning of f, but not of x, which is merely a bound variable within the description of the function being defined. Conceptually, this can be made clear by placing the binder of x in a subexpression that denotes the function being defined:

$$\textbf{let } f \equiv \lambda x.\, x \times x + 1 \textbf{ in } B.$$

Here the subexpression $\lambda x.\, x \times x + 1$, called an *abstraction* or *lambda expression*, denotes the function that "when applied to an argument x yields $x \times x + 1$". By itself, this abstraction does not specify that any variable is a name of this function; the association of this function with the variable f is made by the enclosing definition of f.

The ability to denote functions without giving them names makes abstractions particularly useful for describing functions that are arguments to other "higher order" functions. For example, suppose $\textsf{integrate}(a, b, f)$ integrates the function

f from a to b. In many programming languages, a call of integrate requires using a definition to name its third argument, so that to compute, say $\int_0^1 dx\, x^2 + 1$, one would write

$$\textbf{let } f(x) \equiv x \times x + 1 \textbf{ in } \text{integrate}(0, 1, f).$$

If the language provides abstractions, however, then one can simply write

$$\text{integrate}(0, 1, \lambda x.\ x \times x + 1).$$

Multiple integration provides an even more dramatic example: To compute $\int_0^1 dx \int_0^x dy\ (x + y)^2$ without abstractions, one must write the impenetrable expression

$$\textbf{let } f(x) \equiv (\textbf{let } g(y) \equiv (x + y) \times (x + y) \textbf{ in } \text{integrate}(0, x, g)) \textbf{ in } \text{integrate}(0, 1, f),$$

as opposed to

$$\text{integrate}(0, 1, \lambda x.\ \text{integrate}(0, x, \lambda y.\ (x + y) \times (x + y))).$$

At the outset, one point must be emphasized to avoid confusion: An abstraction is not a function. It is an expression that *denotes* a function in much the same way that an integer expression denotes an integer. In particular, if it contains occurrences of free variables, it may denote different functions for different values of those free variables. For example, $\lambda y.\ x + y$ denotes an identity function when x is zero but the successor function when x is one. Similarly, in the expression displayed above, the function denoted by $\lambda y.\ (x + y) \times (x + y)$ depends on the variable x.

It should also be understood that there are no type distinctions in the lambda calculus; variables and expressions range over a single universe of values that includes functions and possibly other entities. To emphasize this characteristic and to distinguish the language from various typed languages based on the lambda calculus (which will be studied in Chapter 15 and later), one often speaks of the *untyped* lambda calculus. Historically, however, the untyped version of the language is the oldest, and thus is properly named "the lambda calculus" without qualification.

From a computational viewpoint, untyped languages are simpler to describe than typed languages, which is why we will study them first. But from the view of mathematics and logic, the opposite situation holds: The typed lambda calculus can be understood in terms of conventional mathematical functions — indeed, we have already used typed lambda expressions in our metalanguage, in Sections 2.5 and 5.6 for example — but, as we will see in Section 10.5, the untyped language raises serious foundational problems.

10.1 Syntax

Expressions of the lambda calculus (often called *terms*) have the following abstract syntax:

$$\langle \text{exp} \rangle ::= \langle \text{var} \rangle \mid \langle \text{exp} \rangle \langle \text{exp} \rangle \mid \lambda \langle \text{var} \rangle.\ \langle \text{exp} \rangle$$

Here, $\langle \text{var} \rangle$ (as before) is a predefined countably infinite set of *variables*. Expressions of the form $\langle \text{exp} \rangle \langle \text{exp} \rangle$ are called *applications*, and expressions of the form $\lambda \langle \text{var} \rangle.\ \langle \text{exp} \rangle$ are called *abstractions* or *lambda expressions*. Within an application $e_0 e_1$, e_0 is called the *operator* and e_1 is called the *operand*.

As we will see in the next few chapters, the lambda calculus can be extended in a variety of interesting ways, from the addition of constants to much more elaborate constructions. Thus the above language is sometimes called the *pure* lambda calculus.

We assume that application is left associative and that, in $\lambda v.\ e$, the subexpression e extends to the first stopping symbol or to the end of the enclosing phrase. (In many texts on the lambda calculus, $\lambda x_1.\ \cdots \lambda x_n.\ e$ is abbreviated by $\lambda x_1 \cdots x_n.\ e$, but we will not use such abbreviations in this book.) Thus, for example,

$$\lambda \text{x}.\ (\lambda \text{y}.\ \text{xyx})\text{x} \quad \text{stands for} \quad \lambda \text{x}.\ ((\lambda \text{y}.\ ((\text{xy})\text{x}))\text{x}).$$

In $\lambda v.\ e$, the occurrence of v is a binder whose scope is e. Indeed, we can define free and bound variable occurrences and substitution just as with the predicate calculus in Section 1.4: The set $\text{FV}(e)$ of variables occurring free in e is defined by

$$\text{FV}(v) = \{v\}$$

$$\text{FV}(e_0 e_1) = \text{FV}(e_0) \cup \text{FV}(e_1)$$

$$\text{FV}(\lambda v.\ e) = \text{FV}(e) - \{v\},$$

and the result e/δ of simultaneously substituting δv for each occurrence of each variable v in e is defined by

$$v/\delta = \delta v$$

$$(e_0 e_1)/\delta = (e_0/\delta)(e_1/\delta)$$

$$(\lambda v.\ e)/\delta = \lambda v_{\text{new}}.\ (e/[\,\delta \mid v\!:\! v_{\text{new}}\,]),$$

where

$$v_{\text{new}} \notin \bigcup_{w \in \text{FV}(e) - \{v\}} \text{FV}(\delta w).$$

(As in Section 1.4, we resolve the ambiguity here by specifying that v_{new} will be v when v satisfies the above condition, while otherwise v_{new} will be the first variable, in some standard ordering of the variables, that satisfies the condition.) These entities can be shown to satisfy the analogue of Proposition 1.2 in Section 1.4:

Proposition 10.1 *Suppose e is an expression of the lambda calculus. Then:*

(a) *If $\delta w = \delta' w$ for all $w \in \mathrm{FV}(e)$, then $e/\delta = e/\delta'$.*

(b) *$e/I_{\langle \mathrm{var} \rangle} = e$.*

(c) *$\mathrm{FV}(e/\delta) = \bigcup\limits_{w \in \mathrm{FV}(e)} \mathrm{FV}(\delta w)$.*

As in Section 1.4, we also introduce notations describing substitution for a single variable:

$$e/v \to e' \qquad \text{for} \qquad e/[\, I_{\langle \mathrm{var} \rangle} \mid v\colon e'\,],$$

and for a finite set of variables:

$$e/v_0 \to e_0, \ldots, v_{n-1} \to e_{n-1} \qquad \text{for} \qquad e/[\, I_{\langle \mathrm{var} \rangle} \mid v_0\colon e_0 \mid \ldots \mid v_{n-1}\colon e_{n-1}\,].$$

The operation of replacing an occurrence of a lambda expression $\lambda v.\ e$ by $\lambda v_{\mathrm{new}}.\ (e/v \to v_{\mathrm{new}})$, where v_{new} is any variable not in the set $\mathrm{FV}(e) - \{v\}$, is called a *renaming* or *change of bound variable*. If e' is obtained from e by performing zero or more renamings of occurrences of subphrases, we say that e' is obtained from e *by renaming* or, in the jargon of the lambda calculus, that e *α-converts to e'*; since it can be shown that this is an equivalence relation, we also say that e and e' are *renaming-equivalent* or *α-equivalent*, and write $e \equiv e'$.

The intent is that renaming should preserve meaning in any semantics of the lambda calculus or its extensions. In fact, this property holds for most modern programming languages (functional or otherwise) but fails for a few early languages such as Lisp, Snobol, and APL. (As we will see in Section 11.7, its failure in such languages is a rich source of programming errors.)

10.2 Reduction

Historically, an operational semantics of the lambda calculus was understood long before its denotational semantics. This operational semantics, called *reduction semantics*, is similar to the transition semantics discussed in Chapter 6, except that the configurations (both terminal and nonterminal) are simply expressions. But it is traditional to use different terminology: transitions are called *contractions*, multiple transitions are called *reductions*, and executions are called *reduction sequences*.

The underlying idea is that the process of reduction should simplify an expression or make its meaning more explicit, without changing that meaning. Since there can be many reduction sequences that begin with the same expression, reduction semantics is nondeterministic. In contrast to the situation with nondeterministic imperative languages, however, different reduction sequences cannot lead to arbitrarily different results, but only to results that are "similar" — in a rather subtle sense described by a central proposition called the Church-Rosser Theorem.

An expression of the form $(\lambda v.\ e)e'$ is called a *redex*. Intuitively, it represents the application of the function $(\lambda v.\ e)$ to the argument e', which should yield the value that is denoted by e when v denotes the value of e'. But this should also be the value of the "simpler" expression obtained by substituting e' for v in e.

To formalize this intuition, suppose an expression e_0 contains an occurrence of a redex $(\lambda v.\ e)e'$. Let e_1 be obtained from e_0 by replacing the occurrence of the redex by $e/v \to e'$ and then possibly renaming e_1 or its subexpressions. Then we write $e_0 \to e_1$, and say that e_0 *contracts* to e_1 (despite the possibility that, when e contains more than one occurrence of v, e_1 may be a longer expression than e_0).

As in Chapter 6, this transition relation can be defined by inference rules:

TR RULE: β-reduction

$$(\lambda v.\ e)e' \to (e/v \to e'),$$

TR RULE: Renaming

$$\frac{e_0 \to e_1 \qquad e_1 \equiv e_1'}{e_0 \to e_1',}$$

TR RULE: Contextual Closure

$$\frac{e_0 \to e_1}{e_0' \to e_1',}$$

where e_1' is obtained from e_0' by replacing one occurrence of e_0 in e_0' by e_1.

If e' is obtained from e by zero or more contractions (or just by renaming), then we say that e *reduces* to e', and we write $e \to^* e'$. In terms of inference rules (much as in Section 6.2):

TR RULE: Transitive and Reflexive Closure

$$\frac{e_0 \to e_1}{e_0 \to^* e_1}$$

$$\frac{e_0 \to^* e_1 \qquad e_1 \to^* e_2}{e_0 \to^* e_2}$$

$$\frac{e_0 \equiv e_1}{e_0 \to^* e_1.}$$

If reduction sequences are a kind of execution, with expressions as configurations, then the obvious notion of terminal configuration is an expression that contain no redices. Such expressions are called *normal forms*. Moreover, if e reduces to a normal form e', then e' is called a normal form *of* the expression e.

The Greek letter β is meant to distinguish the particular reduction rule given above. Sometimes, in the presence of several reduction rules, one speaks of β-*contraction* (written $\xrightarrow{\beta}$), β-*reduction* (written $\xrightarrow{\beta}*$), and β-*normal forms* to refer to the versions of these notions induced by using only the β-reduction rule. Similarly, the left side of the β-reduction rule is called a β-*redex*. (In general, a redex is simply the left side of a reduction rule.)

The following are examples of reduction sequences, each terminating in a normal form:

$$(\lambda x.\ y)(\lambda z.\ z) \to y$$

$$(\lambda x.\ x)(\lambda z.\ z) \to (\lambda z.\ z)$$

$$(\lambda x.\ x\,x)(\lambda z.\ z) \to (\lambda z.\ z)(\lambda z.\ z) \to (\lambda z.\ z)$$

$$(\lambda x.\ (\lambda y.\ y\,x)z)(z\,w) \to (\lambda x.\ z\,x)(z\,w) \to z(z\,w)$$

$$(\lambda x.\ (\lambda y.\ y\,x)z)(z\,w) \to (\lambda y.\ y(z\,w))z \to z(z\,w).$$

The last two lines here are reduction sequences that start with the same expression and move off in different directions (by reducing different redices), but eventually return to the same expression. The following proposition, whose proof is beyond the scope of this book, shows that this is a general phenomenon:

Proposition 10.2 (Church-Rosser Theorem) *If $e \to^* e_0$ and $e \to^* e_1$, then there is an expression e' such that $e_0 \to^* e'$ and $e_1 \to^* e'$.*

As a special case, since normal forms only reduce by renaming, if e_0 and e_1 are normal forms, then they both must be renaming-equivalent to e', and therefore to each other. Thus

Proposition 10.3 *To within renaming equivalence, every expression has at most one normal form.*

However, contraction does not always simplify expressions, and there are reduction sequences that never terminate:

$$(\lambda x.\ x\,x)(\lambda x.\ x\,x) \to (\lambda x.\ x\,x)(\lambda x.\ x\,x) \to \cdots$$

$$(\lambda x.\ x\,x\,y)(\lambda x.\ x\,x\,y) \to (\lambda x.\ x\,x\,y)(\lambda x.\ x\,x\,y)y \to \cdots$$

$$(\lambda x.\ f(x\,x))(\lambda x.\ f(x\,x)) \to f((\lambda x.\ f(x\,x))(\lambda x.\ f(x\,x))) \to \cdots.$$

In each of these cases, there are no other reduction sequences with the same initial expression, so that these initial expressions have no normal form. However, there are also cases where both terminating and nonterminating sequences begin with the same expression:

$$(\lambda u.\ \lambda v.\ v)((\lambda x.\ xx)(\lambda x.\ xx)) \rightarrow \lambda v.\ v$$

$$(\lambda u.\ \lambda v.\ v)((\lambda x.\ xx)(\lambda x.\ xx)) \rightarrow (\lambda u.\ \lambda v.\ v)((\lambda x.\ xx)(\lambda x.\ xx)) \rightarrow \cdots.$$

This raises the question of whether, given an initial expression, there is some way of choosing a reduction sequence that will terminate if any such sequence does. To state the answer, we first define an *outermost* redex of an expression to be a redex that is not contained within any other redex of the expression. Next, a *normal-order* reduction sequence is one in which, at each step, an expression is contracted on the leftmost of its outermost redices. Then it can be shown that

Proposition 10.4 (Standardization Theorem) *If any reduction sequence beginning with e terminates, then the normal-order reduction sequence beginning with e terminates.*

For example, in the pair of reduction sequences displayed above, the terminating one is the normal-order sequence.

(Notice that the above definition of normal-order reduction can be applied to either the concrete representation of an expression or to a representation by an abstract syntax tree, provided that the operator subnode of each application lies to the left of of the operand subnode. In fact, when the conventional concrete representation is used, the textually leftmost redex must be outermost, so that a normal-order reduction sequence is simply one where each expression is contracted on its textually leftmost redex.)

Finally, we note that, in addition to β-reduction, there is another kind of reduction, called η-reduction, that is also studied for the pure lambda calculus.

An *η-redex* is an expression of the form $\lambda v.\ ev$, where the variable v does not occur free in the subexpression e. Clearly, for any e', the application $(\lambda v.\ ev)e'$ β-contracts to ee'. Thus, if one accepts the intuition that every expression denotes an *extensional* function, which is a function whose value is completely determined by the results it gives when applied to all possible arguments, then one would expect $\lambda v.\ ev$ to contract to e. This motivates the reduction rule

TR RULE: η-reduction

$$\frac{}{\lambda v.\ ev \rightarrow e} \qquad \text{where } v \text{ does not occur free in } e.$$

We will be much less concerned with η-reduction than β-reduction since our long-range interest is in functional languages that, although they extend the lambda calculus, permit expressions that do not always denote functions (extensional or otherwise), so that η-reduction does not always preserve meaning.

10.3 Normal-Order Evaluation

Although reduction to normal form might be considered a kind of "evaluation", we will always use the latter term to describe the evaluation process used for functional programming languages, which is a less general process than the reduction to normal form described in the previous section. In the first place, one only evaluates expressions that are *closed*, which are expressions that contain no free occurrences of variables (since the evaluation of an expression with variables — in the absence of values for these variables — is more a kind of formula manipulation than of evaluation).

In the second place, rather than continuing to reduce an expression all the way to a normal form, evaluation terminates as soon as a *canonical form* is obtained. In general, the concept of a canonical form may vary between different functional languages, but it always includes abstractions, which are the only canonical forms in the pure lambda calculus. Thus, for the remainder of this chapter, we define a *canonical form* to be an abstraction. (The underlying idea is that once one knows that the result of a reduction is an abstraction, one knows that this result denotes a function, and one should not explicate the result by reducing it further, but only by applying it to various arguments.)

Consider, for example, the normal-order reduction sequence

$$(\lambda x.\ x(\lambda y.\ x\, y\, y)x)(\lambda z.\ \lambda w.\ z) \to (\lambda z.\ \lambda w.\ z)(\lambda y.\ (\lambda z.\ \lambda w.\ z)y\, y)(\lambda z.\ \lambda w.\ z)$$

$$\to (\lambda w.\ \lambda y.\ (\lambda z.\ \lambda w.\ z)y\, y)(\lambda z.\ \lambda w.\ z)$$

$$\to \lambda y.\ (\lambda z.\ \lambda w.\ z)y\, y$$

$$\to \lambda y.\ (\lambda w.\ y)y$$

$$\to \lambda y.\ y.$$

For the closed expression beginning this sequence, evaluation terminates after three steps with $\lambda y.\ (\lambda z.\ \lambda w.\ z)y\, y$, which is the first canonical form in the reduction sequence.

In general, for a closed expression e, we say that e *evaluates* to z and write $e \Rightarrow z$ when z is the first canonical form in the normal-order reduction sequence beginning with e. If there is no such canonical form z, we say that e *diverges* and write $e \uparrow$.

Before going further, we mention some general facts about closed expressions. It is easy to see that reduction never introduces free variable occurrences, so that a closed expression only contracts or reduces to a closed expression. Moreover, a closed expression cannot be a variable, so it must be either a canonical form or an application. Also:

Proposition 10.5 *A closed application cannot be a normal form.*

PROOF Beginning with the closed application, repeatedly take its operator part (i.e. its left subexpression) until this operator is no longer an application. The resulting operator cannot be a variable, since it is part of a closed expression but is not within the scope of any binder. It is therefore an abstraction that is the operator of an application, which is therefore a redex. Thus the original closed application is not a normal form.   END OF PROOF

It follows that a closed normal form, since it cannot be a variable or an application, must be an abstraction, and therefore a canonical form. On the other hand, not every closed canonical form is a normal form. Thus, for a closed expression e, there are three possibilities:

- The normal-order reduction sequence terminates in a normal form. Since this normal form is a canonical form, the reduction sequence must contain a first canonical form z, so that $e \Rightarrow z$. For example, in

$$(\lambda x.\ \lambda y.\ x\, y)(\lambda x.\ x) \rightarrow \lambda y.\ (\lambda x.\ x)\, y \rightarrow \lambda y.\ y,$$

  the first canonical form is $z = \lambda y.\ (\lambda x.\ x)\, y$.

- The normal-order reduction sequence does not terminate, but it contains a canonical form, and therefore a first canonical form z. Again $e \Rightarrow z$. For example, in

$$(\lambda x.\ \lambda y.\ x\, x)(\lambda x.\ x\, x) \rightarrow \lambda y.\ (\lambda x.\ x\, x)(\lambda x.\ x\, x) \rightarrow \lambda y.\ (\lambda x.\ x\, x)(\lambda x.\ x\, x) \rightarrow \cdots,$$

  the first canonical form is $z = \lambda y.\ (\lambda x.\ x\, x)(\lambda x.\ x\, x)$.

- The normal-order reduction sequence does not terminate, and it contains no canonical forms. Then e diverges, (i.e. $e \uparrow$). For example, in

$$(\lambda x.\ x\, x)(\lambda x.\ x\, x) \rightarrow (\lambda x.\ x\, x)(\lambda x.\ x\, x) \rightarrow \cdots,$$

  there is no canonical form.

Evaluation can also be defined by a natural or "big-step" semantics that is similar to the one discussed in Exercise 6.4. Here, we give inference rules (called *evaluation rules* and abbreviated EV RULE) for the relation $\Rightarrow$ rather than $\rightarrow$:

EV RULE: Canonical Forms

$$\overline{\lambda v.\ e \Rightarrow \lambda v.\ e},$$

EV RULE: Application (β-evaluation)

$$\frac{e \Rightarrow \lambda v.\ \hat{e} \qquad (\hat{e}/v \rightarrow e') \Rightarrow z}{e\, e' \Rightarrow z.}$$

For example, these rules are used in the following proof, which corresponds to the example of evaluation given earlier:

1. $(\lambda x.\, x(\lambda y.\, x\,y\,y)x) \Rightarrow (\lambda x.\, x(\lambda y.\, x\,y\,y)x)$ (termination)

2. $(\lambda z.\, \lambda w.\, z) \Rightarrow (\lambda z.\, \lambda w.\, z)$ (termination)

3. $(\lambda w.\, \lambda y.\, (\lambda z.\, \lambda w.\, z)y\,y) \Rightarrow (\lambda w.\, \lambda y.\, (\lambda z.\, \lambda w.\, z)y\,y)$ (termination)

4. $(\lambda z.\, \lambda w.\, z)(\lambda y.\, (\lambda z.\, \lambda w.\, z)y\,y) \Rightarrow (\lambda w.\, \lambda y.\, (\lambda z.\, \lambda w.\, z)y\,y)$ (β-eval,2,3)

5. $\lambda y.\, (\lambda z.\, \lambda w.\, z)y\,y \Rightarrow \lambda y.\, (\lambda z.\, \lambda w.\, z)y\,y$ (termination)

6. $(\lambda z.\, \lambda w.\, z)(\lambda y.\, (\lambda z.\, \lambda w.\, z)y\,y)(\lambda z.\, \lambda w.\, z) \Rightarrow \lambda y.\, (\lambda z.\, \lambda w.\, z)y\,y$

           (β-eval,4,5)

7. $(\lambda x.\, x(\lambda y.\, x y\,y)x)(\lambda z.\, \lambda w.\, z) \Rightarrow \lambda y.\, (\lambda z.\, \lambda w.\, z)y\,y$ (β-eval,1,6)

The following proposition establishes that the inference rules are actually equivalent to the definition of evaluation in terms of reduction:

Proposition 10.6 *For any closed expression e and canonical form z, $e \Rightarrow z$ holds if and only if there is a proof of $e \Rightarrow z$ from the above rules.*

PROOF We first prove the "if" half of the proposition, which is that the above rules are *sound*, by induction on the length of a proof. If the last line of the proof is obtained by the rule for termination (in which case it will be the only line of the proof), it has the form $\lambda v.\, e \Rightarrow \lambda v.\, e$, which holds because $\lambda v.\, e$ is a canonical form.

On the other hand, suppose the last line of the proof is obtained by the rule for β-evaluation. Then it has the form $ee' \Rightarrow z$, and there are shorter proofs of the premisses $e \Rightarrow \lambda v.\, \hat{e}$ and $(\hat{e}/v \to e') \Rightarrow z$, which by the induction hypothesis must be true. From the first premiss, there is a normal-order reduction sequence

$$e \to \cdots \to \lambda v.\, \hat{e},$$

where the last term is the first canonical form; in other words, each term is contracted on the leftmost of its outermost redices, and only the last term is an abstraction. This implies that

$$ee' \to \cdots \to (\lambda v.\, \hat{e})e'$$

is a reduction sequence where each term is contracted on the leftmost of its outermost redices and no term is an abstraction. But now we can complete this sequence with a β-contraction and the sequence whose existence is asserted by the second premiss:

$$ee' \to \cdots \to (\lambda v.\, \hat{e})e' \to (\hat{e}/v \to e') \to \cdots \to z.$$

This is a normal-order reduction sequence in which z is the first canonical form; thus $ee' \Rightarrow z$.

Next, we prove the "only if" half of the proposition, which is that the above rules are *complete*. Here we assume that we have a normal-order reduction sequence $e \to \cdots \to z$ in which only the last term is a canonical form, and we show, by induction on the length of the reduction sequence, the existence of the corresponding proof of $e \Rightarrow z$. If the reduction sequence begins with an abstraction, it must consist of the single term $\lambda v.\ e$, without any contractions, and the corresponding proof is a single use of the rule for termination.

On the other hand, if the reduction sequence begins with an application, let $n \geq 0$ be the index of the first term in this reduction sequence that is not an application whose left subterm is also an application. (Such a term must exist since z does not have this form.) Then the reduction sequence has the form

$$e_0 e_0' \to \cdots \to e_{n-1} e_{n-1}' \to \cdots,$$

where $e_0, \ldots, e_{n-1}$ are all applications, and therefore, by Proposition 10.5, contain redices. Moreover, the fact that this reduction sequence is normal-order implies that it has the form

$$e_0 e_0' \to \cdots \to e_{n-1} e_0' \to e_n e_0' \to \cdots,$$

where

$$e_0 \to \cdots \to e_{n-1} \to e_n$$

is also a normal-order reduction sequence. Also, the definition of n insures that e_n is not an application, and is therefore (since it is closed) an abstraction, say $\lambda v.\ \hat{e}$. Then the induction hypothesis implies that there is a proof of $e_0 \Rightarrow \lambda v.\ \hat{e}$.

Since $e_n = \lambda v.\ \hat{e}$, the term $e_n e_0' = (\lambda v.\ \hat{e}) e_0'$ is a redex, and the rest of the original reduction sequence must have the form

$$(\lambda v.\ \hat{e}) e_0' \to (\hat{e}/v \to e_0') \to \cdots \to z,$$

where only the last term is a canonical form. Then the induction hypothesis implies that there is a proof of $(\hat{e}/v \to e_0') \Rightarrow z$.

Finally, from the proofs of $e_0 \Rightarrow \lambda v.\ \hat{e}$ and $(\hat{e}/v \to e_0') \Rightarrow z$, one can use the rule for β-evaluation to construct a proof of $e_0 e_0' \Rightarrow z$.   END OF PROOF

The inference rules for evaluation lead to a recursive method for evaluating closed expressions that is more direct than the process of reduction. To see this, consider a proof of $e_c \Rightarrow z$, where e_c is closed:

(a) If e_c is an abstraction, then the final (and only) step of the proof must use the termination rule, and z must be e_c.

(b) If e_c is an application ee', then the final step of the proof must use the β-evaluation rule, and must be preceded by proofs that e evaluates to some $\lambda v.\ \hat{e}$ and that $\hat{e}/v \to e'$ evaluates to z.

It follows that e_c can be evaluated by the following recursive procedure:

(a) If e_c is an abstraction, it evaluates to itself.
(b) If e_c is an application ee', evaluate e to obtain an abstraction $\lambda v.\ \hat{e}$. Then evaluate $\hat{e}/v \to e'$ to obtain the value of e_c.

The connection between proofs of evaluation and this recursive procedure is clarified by an indented form for displaying the proofs. The basic idea is that a proof whose final step is an application of the rule for β-evaluation,

$$\frac{e \Rightarrow \lambda v.\ \hat{e} \qquad (\hat{e}/v \to e') \Rightarrow z}{ee' \Rightarrow z,}$$

is displayed as

ee'

　　display of proof of $e \Rightarrow \lambda v.\ \hat{e}$

　　display of proof of $(\hat{e}/v \to e') \Rightarrow z$

$\Rightarrow z.$

(A proof whose only step is an application of the premiss-free rule for termination is displayed as a single line containing its conclusion.) For example, the indented form of the proof given earlier in this section is

$(\lambda\mathsf{x}.\ \mathsf{x}(\lambda\mathsf{y}.\ \mathsf{x\,y\,y})\mathsf{x})(\lambda\mathsf{z}.\ \lambda\mathsf{w}.\ \mathsf{z})$

　　$\lambda\mathsf{x}.\ \mathsf{x}(\lambda\mathsf{y}.\ \mathsf{x\,y\,y})\mathsf{x} \Rightarrow \lambda\mathsf{x}.\ \mathsf{x}(\lambda\mathsf{y}.\ \mathsf{x\,y\,y})\mathsf{x}$

　　$(\lambda\mathsf{z}.\ \lambda\mathsf{w}.\ \mathsf{z})(\lambda\mathsf{y}.\ (\lambda\mathsf{z}.\ \lambda\mathsf{w}.\ \mathsf{z})\mathsf{y\,y})(\lambda\mathsf{z}.\ \lambda\mathsf{w}.\ \mathsf{z})$

　　　　$(\lambda\mathsf{z}.\ \lambda\mathsf{w}.\ \mathsf{z})(\lambda\mathsf{y}.\ (\lambda\mathsf{z}.\ \lambda\mathsf{w}.\ \mathsf{z})\mathsf{y\,y})$

　　　　　　$\lambda\mathsf{z}.\ \lambda\mathsf{w}.\ \mathsf{z} \Rightarrow \lambda\mathsf{z}.\ \lambda\mathsf{w}.\ \mathsf{z}$

　　　　　　$\lambda\mathsf{w}.\ \lambda\mathsf{y}.\ (\lambda\mathsf{z}.\ \lambda\mathsf{w}.\ \mathsf{z})\mathsf{y\,y} \Rightarrow \lambda\mathsf{w}.\ \lambda\mathsf{y}.\ (\lambda\mathsf{z}.\ \lambda\mathsf{w}.\ \mathsf{z})\mathsf{y\,y}$

　　　　$\Rightarrow \lambda\mathsf{w}.\ \lambda\mathsf{y}.\ (\lambda\mathsf{z}.\ \lambda\mathsf{w}.\ \mathsf{z})\mathsf{y\,y}$

　　　　　　$\lambda\mathsf{y}.\ (\lambda\mathsf{z}.\ \lambda\mathsf{w}.\ \mathsf{z})\mathsf{y\,y} \Rightarrow \lambda\mathsf{y}.\ (\lambda\mathsf{z}.\ \lambda\mathsf{w}.\ \mathsf{z})\mathsf{y\,y}$

　　　　$\Rightarrow \lambda\mathsf{y}.\ (\lambda\mathsf{z}.\ \lambda\mathsf{w}.\ \mathsf{z})\mathsf{y\,y}$

　　$\Rightarrow \lambda\mathsf{y}.\ (\lambda\mathsf{z}.\ \lambda\mathsf{w}.\ \mathsf{z})\mathsf{y\,y}.$

Such a display can be viewed as a trace of a recursive evaluation, where each recursive call is described by an indented section that begins with an expression to be evaluated (the argument to the call) and ends with its value (the result of the call).

Henceforth, we will call the kind of evaluation described in this section *normal-order* evaluation, to distinguish it from the *eager* evaluation described in the next section.

10.4 Eager Evaluation

The normal-order evaluation of $(\lambda x.\, xx)((\lambda y.\, y)(\lambda z.\, z))$ takes four contractions:

$$(\lambda x.\, xx)((\lambda y.\, y)(\lambda z.\, z)) \to ((\lambda y.\, y)(\lambda z.\, z))((\lambda y.\, y)(\lambda z.\, z))$$
$$\to (\lambda z.\, z)((\lambda y.\, y)(\lambda z.\, z))$$
$$\to (\lambda y.\, y)(\lambda z.\, z)$$
$$\to \lambda z.\, z,$$

but the same expression can be reduced to a canonical form in three contractions if one deviates from normal order:

$$(\lambda x.\, xx)((\lambda y.\, y)(\lambda z.\, z)) \to (\lambda x.\, xx)(\lambda z.\, z)$$
$$\to (\lambda z.\, z)(\lambda z.\, z)$$
$$\to (\lambda z.\, z).$$

The strategy here, which is called *eager* evaluation, is to postpone a contraction $(\lambda v.\, e)e' \to (e/v \to e')$ until e' is a canonical form, rather than to carry out the substitution and then reduce each of perhaps many copies of e' separately.

To make this precise, we define a β_E-redex to be a β-redex whose operand is a canonical form or a variable, and β_E-reduction to be the restriction of β-reduction to β_E-redices:

TR RULE: β_E-reduction

$$\overline{(\lambda v.\, e)z \to (e/v \to z)} \qquad \text{where } z \text{ is a canonical form or a variable.}$$

Then a closed expression e is said to evaluate *eagerly* to a canonical form z, written $e \Rightarrow_E z$, if there is a reduction sequence from e to z in which each contraction acts on the leftmost β_E-redex that is not a subexpression of a canonical form.

(The reader may wonder why we permit the operand of a β_E-redex to be a variable when the process of eager evaluation only contracts redices that are closed expressions. When we discuss the denotational semantics of eager evaluation, however, in Section 10.5, we will find that the more general form of β_E-reduction preserves meaning.)

Eager evaluation can also be defined directly by evaluation rules:

EV RULE: Canonical Forms

$$\overline{\lambda v.\, e \Rightarrow_E \lambda v.\, e,}$$

EV RULE: β_E-evaluation

$$\frac{e \Rightarrow_E \lambda v.\, \hat{e} \qquad e' \Rightarrow_E z' \qquad (\hat{e}/v \to z') \Rightarrow_E z}{ee' \Rightarrow_E z.}$$

As with normal-order, proofs of eager evaluation can be displayed perspicuously in an indented form, where an application of the β_E-reduction rule has the form

$$ee'$$

display of proof of $e \Rightarrow_E \lambda v.\,\hat{e}$

display of proof of $e' \Rightarrow_E z'$

display of proof of $(\hat{e}/v \to z') \Rightarrow_E z$

$\Rightarrow_E z.$

For example, the following is a proof of the eager evaluation shown earlier:

$$(\lambda x.\, xx)((\lambda y.\, y)(\lambda z.\, z))$$

$\lambda x.\, xx \Rightarrow_E \lambda x.\, xx$

$(\lambda y.\, y)(\lambda z.\, z)$

$\lambda y.\, y \Rightarrow_E \lambda y.\, y$

$\lambda z.\, z \Rightarrow_E \lambda z.\, z$

$\lambda z.\, z \Rightarrow_E \lambda z.\, z$

$\Rightarrow_E \lambda z.\, z$

$(\lambda z.\, z)(\lambda z.\, z)$

$\lambda z.\, z \Rightarrow_E \lambda z.\, z$

$\lambda z.\, z \Rightarrow_E \lambda z.\, z$

$\lambda z.\, z \Rightarrow_E \lambda z.\, z$

$\Rightarrow_E \lambda z.\, z$

$\Rightarrow_E \lambda z.\, z.$

Although eager evaluation can be faster than normal-order evaluation when it postpones a contraction that would make multiple copies of its operand, it can be slower when the postponed contraction would make zero copies. Indeed, in this case eager evaluation can be infinitely slower, as is illustrated by an example from Section 10.2. The normal order evaluation

$$(\lambda u.\, \lambda v.\, v)((\lambda x.\, xx)(\lambda x.\, xx)) \to \lambda v.\, v$$

terminates, but the eager evaluation

$$(\lambda u.\, \lambda v.\, v)((\lambda x.\, xx)(\lambda x.\, xx)) \to (\lambda u.\, \lambda v.\, v)((\lambda x.\, xx)(\lambda x.\, xx)) \to \cdots$$

diverges.

Finally, some warnings must be sounded about terminology. What we have called normal-order and eager evaluation are often called "call by name" and "call by value", but we prefer to limit the latter terms to their original meanings, which refer to parameter-passing mechanisms in Algol-like languages. What we have called normal-order evaluation is also sometimes called "lazy evaluation". Again, however, we prefer to use the latter term with its original meaning, which is a particular method for implementing normal-order evaluation (to be described in Section 14.6) that avoids *both* repeated and unnecessary evaluation of subexpressions.

10.5 Denotational Semantics

To capture the intuition behind the lambda calculus, a denotational semantics should interpret applications as the applications of functions to arguments. Moreover, since reduction represents the "working out" of such applications, it should preserve meaning. Surprisingly, more than three decades elapsed from the invention of the lambda calculus to the discovery of such a semantics. The difficulty was that, since the lambda calculus is untyped, it permits functions to be applied to themselves, and thus can be used to formalize paradoxes that are similar to those discovered by Bertrand Russell around the turn of the century.

To see this, we first note that, if there is a set S of "values" such that functions from values to values are themselves values, that is, such that $S \to S \subseteq S$, then every function in $S \to S$ has a fixed point. For suppose $f \in S \to S$, and let $p \in S \to S$ be some function such that $p\,x = f(x\,x)$ for all $x \in S \to S$. (If x is in S but not $S \to S$, it does not matter what $p\,x$ is.) Then $p\,p = f(p\,p)$, so that $p\,p$ is a fixed point of the function f.

This argument can be formalized in the lambda calculus directly. Suppose that the function f is denoted by some expression e in the lambda calculus and that x is a variable not occurring free in e. Then $\lambda x.\ e(xx)$ denotes p, and $(\lambda x.\ e(xx))(\lambda x.\ e(xx))$ denotes $p\,p$. But

$$(\lambda x.\ e(xx))(\lambda x.\ e(xx)) \to e((\lambda x.\ e(xx))(\lambda x.\ e(xx))).$$

Thus, if applications denote function applications, and if β-reduction preserves meaning, then $(\lambda x.\ e(xx))(\lambda x.\ e(xx))$ denotes a fixed point of f.

Indeed, let Y stand for the expression $\lambda f.\ (\lambda x.\ f(xx))(\lambda x.\ f(xx))$. Then

$$Y e \to (\lambda x.\ e(xx))(\lambda x.\ e(xx)),$$

so that Y denotes a function mapping every function into its fixed point.

The trouble with all this is that, if S contains more than one member, then there are functions in $S \to S$ that have no fixed point. For example, if 0 and 1 are distinct members of S, then the function $f \in S \to S$ such that $f\,x = $ **if** $x = 0$ **then** 1 **else** 0 has no fixed point.

Even before the invention of the lambda calculus, a contradiction like this led Russell to formulate a theory of types that excluded self-applicative functions (and was a precursor of the simple type system that we will study in Chapter 15).

But half a century later, Dana Scott found another way around the contradiction: One can limit the functions denoted by the lambda calculus to continuous functions from a domain to itself, which all possess fixed points.

After discovering how to solve the kind of domain isomorphisms that we discussed at the end of Section 5.2, Scott constructed a domain D_∞ that was a nontrivial solution to the isomorphism

$$D_\infty \xrightleftharpoons[\psi]{\phi} D_\infty \to D_\infty.$$

(By "nontrivial" we mean that D_∞ contains more than one element.)

It is beyond the scope of this book to describe the construction of D_∞, but it is straightforward to use it to give a denotational semantics for the lambda calculus. Since the value of an expression depends on the values of its free variables, the meaning of an expression will be a continuous function from $D_\infty^{\langle \mathrm{var} \rangle}$ to D_∞:

$$\llbracket - \rrbracket \in \langle \exp \rangle \to (D_\infty^{\langle \mathrm{var} \rangle} \to D_\infty). \tag{10.1}$$

This is much like the meaning of integer expressions given in Section 1.2, except that the set of integers has been replaced by the domain D_∞ and meanings are now required to be continuous functions. Also, in deference to the common usage for functional languages, we will call the members of $D_\infty^{\langle \mathrm{var} \rangle}$ *environments* rather than states. (The metavariable η will range over environments.)

The semantic equations are straightforward: One simply uses the function ϕ or ψ whenever it is necessary to convert a value into a function, or vice versa.

DR SEM EQ: Variables

$$\llbracket v \rrbracket \eta = \eta v, \tag{10.2}$$

DR SEM EQ: Application

$$\llbracket e_0 e_1 \rrbracket \eta = \phi(\llbracket e_0 \rrbracket \eta)(\llbracket e_1 \rrbracket \eta), \tag{10.3}$$

DR SEM EQ: Abstraction

$$\llbracket \lambda v.\, e \rrbracket \eta = \psi(\lambda x \in D_\infty.\, \llbracket e \rrbracket [\eta \mid v{:}x]). \tag{10.4}$$

(Note that the lambda notation in the metalanguage on the right of the last equation is properly typed, and thus does not raise the semantic difficulties of the untyped lambda calculus. It simply denotes the function f from D_∞ to D_∞ such that $fx = \llbracket e \rrbracket [\eta \mid v{:}x]$ for all $x \in D_\infty$.)

To be rigorous, we must show that the above semantic equations are correctly typed, so as to satisfy condition (10.1). This is nontrivial, because asserting that a function belongs to $D \to D'$ implies that the function is continuous. For example, each meaning $\llbracket e \rrbracket$ must be a continuous function from $D_\infty^{\langle \mathrm{var} \rangle}$ to D_∞, and the argument $\lambda x \in D_\infty.\, \llbracket e \rrbracket [\eta \mid v{:}x]$ of ψ in Equation (10.4) must be a continuous function from D_∞ to D_∞. To modularize our proof, and to simplify later arguments about continuity, we will first develop the properties of certain basic operations on functions and environments, and then reexpress the semantic equations in terms of these operations.

Proposition 10.7 *Suppose P, P', and P'' are predomains and $v \in \langle \text{var} \rangle$. Then*

(a) *The function* get_{Pv} *satisfying*

$$\text{get}_{Pv}\, \eta = \eta\, v$$

is a continuous function from $P^{\langle \text{var} \rangle}$ to P.

(b) *The function* ext_{Pv} *satisfying*

$$\text{ext}_{Pv}\langle \eta, x \rangle = [\, \eta \mid v{:}x\,]$$

is a continuous function from $P^{\langle \text{var} \rangle} \times P$ to $P^{\langle \text{var} \rangle}$.

(c) *The "application" function* $\text{ap}_{PP'}$ *satisfying*

$$\text{ap}_{PP'}\langle f, x \rangle = f x$$

is a continuous function from $(P \to P') \times P$ to P'.

(d) *If f is a continuous function from $P \times P'$ to P'' and* $\text{ab}\, f$ *(sometimes called the "Currying" of f) satisfies*

$$((\text{ab}\, f)\, x)\, y = f\langle x, y \rangle,$$

then $\text{ab}\, f$ *is a continuous function from P to $P' \to P''$.*

(Notice that, since $P' \to P''$ denotes a set of continuous functions, part (d) implies that, for all $x \in P$, $(\text{ab}\, f)\, x$ is a continuous function.)

PROOF We omit most of the proof, but give the argument for part (c), since it illustrates why a continuous function is required to preserve only the least upper bounds of chains, rather than those of arbitrary sets. Let $\langle f_0, x_0 \rangle \sqsubseteq \langle f_1, x_1 \rangle \sqsubseteq \cdots$ be a chain in $(P \to P') \times P$. From Equation (5.10) in Section 5.4, the definition of $\text{ap}_{PP'}$, and Proposition 2.2 and Equation (2.3) in Section 2.3, we have

$$\text{ap}_{PP'}\Big(\bigsqcup_{i=0}^{\infty}{}^{(P\to P')\times P}\langle f_i, x_i \rangle\Big) = \text{ap}_{PP'}\Big\langle \bigsqcup_{i=0}^{\infty}{}^{P\to P'} f_i,\ \bigsqcup_{i=0}^{\infty}{}^{P} x_i \Big\rangle$$

$$= \Big(\bigsqcup_{i=0}^{\infty}{}^{P\to P'} f_i\Big)\Big(\bigsqcup_{i=0}^{\infty}{}^{P} x_i\Big)$$

$$= \bigsqcup_{i=0}^{\infty}{}^{P'} f_i\Big(\bigsqcup_{i=0}^{\infty}{}^{P} x_i\Big)$$

$$= \bigsqcup_{i=0}^{\infty}{}^{P'}\ \bigsqcup_{j=0}^{\infty}{}^{P'} f_i x_j.$$

(Notice that the last step here is an example of renaming in the metalanguage. In detail it is justified by the equation obtained by substituting f_i for f in Equation (2.3). But i is free in f_i and has a binding occurrence on the right of Equation (2.3) whose scope contains a free occurrence of f. Thus the right-side occurrences of i are renamed to avoid capturing the free occurrence of i in f_i.)

As discussed in Section A.6 of the Appendix, the last term of the above equation is the least upper bound of the set

$$\{\, f_i x_j \mid i \geq 0 \text{ and } j \geq 0 \,\}.$$

Compare this set with

$$\{\, f_k x_k \mid k \geq 0 \,\}.$$

Obviously, every member of the second set belongs to the first. On the other hand, suppose $f_i x_j$ belongs to the first set, and let k be the maximum of i and j. Then, since the f_i are a chain, the pointwise ordering of $P \to P'$ implies $f_i x_j \sqsubseteq f_k x_j$, and, since the x_j are a chain, the monotonicity of f_k gives $f_k x_j \sqsubseteq f_k x_k$. Thus $f_k x_k$ is a member of the second set that extends $f_i x_j$.

Thus every member of either of the above sets is extended by some member of the other. It then follows that any upper bound of either is an upper bound of the other. Therefore, the sets must have the same least upper bound, and we can continue our sequence of equalities with

$$\bigsqcup_{i=0}^{\infty}{}^{P'} \bigsqcup_{j=0}^{\infty}{}^{P'} f_i x_j = \bigsqcup_{k=0}^{\infty}{}^{P'} f_k x_k = \bigsqcup_{k=0}^{\infty}{}^{P'} \mathsf{ap}_{PP'} \langle f_k, x_k \rangle.$$

END OF PROOF

Proposition 10.8 *The function defined by the semantic equations (10.2) to (10.4) is well-typed and satisfies condition (10.1).*

PROOF The proof is by structural induction on the argument e of the semantic function $[\![-]\!]$, with a case analysis on the three ways of constructing expressions:

(a) Suppose e is a variable v. Equation (10.2) can be rewritten as

$$[\![v]\!] = \mathsf{get}_{D_\infty v}\,.$$

Proposition 10.7(a) implies that $[\![v]\!]$ is a continuous function from $D_\infty^{\langle \mathrm{var} \rangle}$ to D_∞ or, more succinctly,

$$[\![v]\!] \in D_\infty^{\langle \mathrm{var} \rangle} \to D_\infty.$$

(b) Suppose e is an application $e_0 e_1$. Equation (10.3) can be rewritten as

$$[\![e_0 e_1]\!] = \mathsf{ap}_{D_\infty D_\infty} \cdot ((\phi \cdot [\![e_0]\!]) \otimes [\![e_1]\!]).$$

Then:

- By the induction hypothesis,

$$[\![e_0]\!], [\![e_1]\!] \in D_\infty^{\langle \text{var} \rangle} \to D_\infty.$$

- Since $\phi \in D_\infty \to (D_\infty \to D_\infty)$ and functional composition preserves continuity (Proposition 2.3(ii) in Section 2.3)),

$$\phi \cdot [\![e_0]\!] \in D_\infty^{\langle \text{var} \rangle} \to (D_\infty \to D_\infty).$$

- Proposition 5.1(ii) in Section 5.4 implies

$$(\phi \cdot [\![e_0]\!]) \otimes [\![e_1]\!] \in D_\infty^{\langle \text{var} \rangle} \to (D_\infty \to D_\infty) \times D_\infty.$$

- Proposition 10.7(c) implies

$$\text{ap}_{D_\infty D_\infty} \in (D_\infty \to D_\infty) \times D_\infty \to D_\infty.$$

- Since composition preserves continuity,

$$\text{ap}_{D_\infty D_\infty} \cdot ((\phi \cdot [\![e_0]\!]) \otimes [\![e_1]\!]) \in D_\infty^{\langle \text{var} \rangle} \to D_\infty.$$

(c) Suppose e is an abstraction $\lambda v.\, e'$. Equation (10.4) can be rewritten as

$$[\![\lambda v.\, e']\!] = \psi \cdot \text{ab}([\![e']\!] \cdot \text{ext}_{D_\infty} v).$$

Then:

- By the induction hypothesis,

$$[\![e']\!] \in D_\infty^{\langle \text{var} \rangle} \to D_\infty.$$

- Proposition 10.7(b) implies that

$$\text{ext}_{D_\infty} v \in D_\infty^{\langle \text{var} \rangle} \times D_\infty \to D_\infty^{\langle \text{var} \rangle}.$$

- Since composition preserves continuity,

$$[\![e']\!] \cdot \text{ext}_{D_\infty} v \in D_\infty^{\langle \text{var} \rangle} \times D_\infty \to D_\infty.$$

- Proposition 10.7(d) implies that

$$\text{ab}([\![e']\!] \cdot \text{ext}_{D_\infty} v) \in D_\infty^{\langle \text{var} \rangle} \to (D_\infty \to D_\infty).$$

- Since $\psi \in (D_\infty \to D_\infty) \to D_\infty$ and composition preserves continuity,

$$\psi \cdot \text{ab}([\![e']\!] \cdot \text{ext}_{D_\infty} v) \in D_\infty^{\langle \text{var} \rangle} \to D_\infty.$$

END OF PROOF

Despite the fact that we have moved from sets to domains, many of the basic properties of the predicate calculus also hold for the lambda calculus. In the same way as in Section 1.4 (and without using the fact that ϕ and ψ form an isomorphism), one can show

Proposition 10.9 (Coincidence Theorem) *If $\eta w = \eta' w$ for all $w \in$ FV(e), then $[\![e]\!]\eta = [\![e]\!]\eta'$.*

Proposition 10.10 (Substitution Theorem) *If $[\![\delta w]\!]\eta' = \eta w$ for all $w \in$ FV(e), then $[\![e/\delta]\!]\eta' = [\![e]\!]\eta$.*

Proposition 10.11 (Finite Substitution Theorem)

$$[\![e/v_0 \to e_0, \ldots, v_{n-1} \to e_{n-1}]\!]\eta' = [\![e]\!][\,\eta' \mid v_0\colon [\![e_0]\!]\eta' \mid \ldots \mid v_{n-1}\colon [\![e_{n-1}]\!]\eta'\,].$$

Proposition 10.12 (Soundness of Renaming) *If*

$$v_{\text{new}} \notin \text{FV}(e) - \{v\},$$

then

$$[\![\lambda v_{\text{new}}.\ (e/v \to v_{\text{new}})]\!] = [\![\lambda v.\ e]\!].$$

From these results it is easy to show that the two equations that characterize the isomorphism between D_∞ and $D_\infty \to D_\infty$,

$$\phi \cdot \psi = I_{D_\infty \to D_\infty} \qquad \text{and} \qquad \psi \cdot \phi = I_{D_\infty}, \qquad (10.5)$$

respectively imply that β-contraction and η-contraction are *sound*, that is, that these operations preserve meaning:

Proposition 10.13 (Soundness of β-Contraction)

$$[\![(\lambda v.\ e)e']\!] = [\![e/v \to e']\!].$$

PROOF Let η be any environment. Then, by the semantic equations for applications and abstractions, the isomorphism equation $\phi \cdot \psi = I_{D_\infty \to D_\infty}$, β-contraction in the metalanguage, and the finite substitution theorem (for $n = 1$):

$$\begin{aligned}
[\![(\lambda v.\ e)e']\!]\eta &= \phi([\![\lambda v.\ e]\!]\eta)([\![e']\!]\eta) \\
&= \phi(\psi(\lambda x \in D_\infty.\ [\![e]\!][\,\eta \mid v\colon x\,]))([\![e']\!]\eta) \\
&= (\lambda x \in D_\infty.\ [\![e]\!][\,\eta \mid v\colon x\,])([\![e']\!]\eta) \\
&= [\![e]\!][\,\eta \mid v\colon [\![e']\!]\eta\,] \\
&= [\![e/v \to e']\!]\eta.
\end{aligned}$$

END OF PROOF

Proposition 10.14 (Soundness of η-Contraction) *If v does not occur free in e, then*

$$[\![\lambda v.\ ev]\!] = [\![e]\!].$$

PROOF Let η be any environment. Then, by the semantic equations for abstractions, applications, and variables, the coincidence theorem, η-contraction in the metalanguage, and the isomorphism equation $\psi \cdot \phi = I_{D_\infty}$:

$$
\begin{aligned}
[\![\lambda v.\ ev]\!]\eta &= \psi(\lambda x \in D_\infty.\ [\![ev]\!][\,\eta \mid v\!:x\,]) \\
&= \psi(\lambda x \in D_\infty.\ \phi([\![e]\!][\,\eta \mid v\!:x\,])([\![v]\!][\,\eta \mid v\!:x\,])) \\
&= \psi(\lambda x \in D_\infty.\ \phi([\![e]\!][\,\eta \mid v\!:x\,])x) \\
&= \psi(\lambda x \in D_\infty.\ \phi([\![e]\!]\eta)x) \\
&= \psi(\phi([\![e]\!]\eta)) \\
&= [\![e]\!]\eta.
\end{aligned}
$$

END OF PROOF

Since β-reduction is sound, the expression $Y = \lambda f.\ (\lambda x.\ f(xx))(\lambda x.\ f(xx))$ denotes a function that maps functions into their fixed points. In fact, Y always yields *least* fixed-points; more precisely, $[\![Y]\!]\eta = \psi(\mathbf{Y}_D \cdot \phi)$, where $\mathbf{Y}_D$ is the least fixed-point operator defined in Section 2.4. (This fact depends on the specific construction of D_∞, not just the isomorphism between D_∞ and $D_\infty \to D_\infty$.)

In Sections 11.6 and 14.4, we will use the fixed-point operator $\mathbf{Y}_D$ to describe the semantics of recursion.

The denotational semantics given by D_∞ incorporates the assumption that (to within an isomorphism) all members of D_∞ are extensional functions, which is reasonable for interpreting reduction to normal form in the pure lambda calculus. However, it is not appropriate to normal-order *evaluation* in the sense of Section 10.3. For example, $(\lambda x.\ xx)(\lambda x.\ xx)$, which diverges, and the canonical form $\lambda y.\ (\lambda x.\ xx)(\lambda x.\ xx)y$, which evaluates to itself, are both given the meaning $\bot \in D_\infty$ (for any environment).

To obtain a denotational model for normal-order evaluation, we must distinguish the least element of D, which corresponds to a diverging computation in the evaluation semantics, from the functions in $D \to D$, which correspond to canonical forms in the evaluation semantics — even from the least element in $D \to D$, which corresponds to an abstraction whose applications always diverge but which does not diverge itself. Thus we want

$$D = V_\bot \quad \text{where } V \simeq D \to D.$$

Here the elements of V are the denotations of canonical forms, while the extra element $\bot \in V_\bot$ is the denotation of divergent expressions. To emphasize this distinction, we will henceforth use the term *value* for the elements of V, but not for $\bot$. (We will occasionally use the term *result* to encompass all of D.)

Let the isomorphism connecting V and $D \to D$ be

$$V \underset{\psi}{\overset{\phi}{\rightleftarrows}} D \to D.$$

Then

$$D = V_\perp \xrightarrow[\iota_\uparrow \cdot \psi]{\phi_{\perp\!\perp}} D \to D,$$

where $\iota_\uparrow$ is the injection associated with the lifting operator $(-)_\perp$, and $\phi_{\perp\!\perp}$ is the function from $V_\perp$ to $D \to D$ that is the strict extension of ϕ. (The continuity of $\phi_{\perp\!\perp}$ is a consequence of Proposition 2.4(b) in Section 2.3, while the continuity of $\iota_\uparrow \cdot \psi$ follows from the continuity of $\iota_\uparrow$ and the preservation of continuity by composition.)

With the replacement of D_∞ by the new D, ϕ by $\phi_{\perp\!\perp}$, and ψ by $\iota_\uparrow \cdot \psi$, Equations (10.2) to (10.4) become semantic equations for normal-order evaluation:

DR SEM EQ: Variables

$$[\![v]\!]\eta = \eta v,$$

DR SEM EQ: Application

$$[\![e_0 e_1]\!]\eta = \phi_{\perp\!\perp}([\![e_0]\!]\eta)([\![e_1]\!]\eta),$$

DR SEM EQ: Abstraction

$$[\![\lambda v.\ e]\!]\eta = (\iota_\uparrow \cdot \psi)(\lambda x \in D_\infty.\ [\![e]\!][\,\eta \mid v{:}x\,]).$$

(The type-correctness of the semantic equations is still established as in the proof of Proposition 10.8.) These equations imply, for example, that

$$[\![(\lambda \mathsf{x}.\ \mathsf{x}\mathsf{x})(\lambda \mathsf{x}.\ \mathsf{x}\mathsf{x})]\!]\eta = \perp$$

and

$$[\![\lambda \mathsf{y}.\ (\lambda \mathsf{x}.\ \mathsf{x}\mathsf{x})(\lambda \mathsf{x}.\ \mathsf{x}\mathsf{x})]\!]\eta = (\iota_\uparrow \cdot \psi)(\lambda x \in D.\ \perp) \neq \perp$$

are distinct. More generally, the pair $\phi_{\perp\!\perp}$ and $\iota_\uparrow \cdot \psi$ is not an isomorphism — the first of the isomorphism equations (10.5) still holds:

$$\phi_{\perp\!\perp} \cdot (\iota_\uparrow \cdot \psi) = I_{D \to D},$$

but the other does not. Indeed, this semantics satisfies Propositions 10.9 to 10.13, but not Proposition 10.14, so that β-contraction is sound but η-contraction is not. (The expression $Y = \lambda \mathsf{f}.\ (\lambda \mathsf{x}.\ \mathsf{f}(\mathsf{x}\mathsf{x}))(\lambda \mathsf{x}.\ \mathsf{f}(\mathsf{x}\mathsf{x}))$ still maps functions into their least fixed-points.)

Finally, we consider the denotational semantics of eager evaluation. Operationally, the essential change from normal-order evaluation is that operands are preevaluated, so that only canonical forms are passed to functions or substituted for variables. Denotationally, this is mirrored by limiting the arguments of functions and the elements of environments to values (which are the denotations of canonical forms) but excluding the least element $\perp$ of D (which is the denotation of divergent expressions). Thus D must satisfy

$$D = V_\perp \quad \text{where } V \simeq V \to D,$$

and the semantic equation must satisfy

$$[\![-]\!] \in \langle \exp \rangle \to (V^{\langle \mathrm{var} \rangle} \to D).$$

Let the isomorphism connecting V and $V \to D$ be

$$V \underset{\psi}{\overset{\phi}{\rightleftarrows}} V \to D.$$

Then the semantic equations are

DR SEM EQ: Variables

$$[\![v]\!]\eta = \iota_\uparrow(\eta v),$$

DR SEM EQ: Application

$$[\![e_0 e_1]\!]\eta = (\phi_{\perp\!\perp}([\![e_0]\!]\eta))_{\perp\!\perp}([\![e_1]\!]\eta),$$

DR SEM EQ: Abstraction

$$[\![\lambda v.\ e]\!]\eta = (\iota_\uparrow \cdot \psi)(\lambda x \in V.\ [\![e]\!][\,\eta \mid v{:}x\,]).$$

In the semantic equation for application, the outer occurrence of the extension operator $(-)_{\perp\!\perp}$ expresses the fact that an application will diverge whenever its operand diverges.

For the semantics of eager evaluation, all of the propositions in this section fail, except the coincidence theorem (10.9) and the soundness of renaming (10.12). However, it still can be shown that β_E-contraction (i.e. the contraction of a β-redex whose operand is a canonical form or a variable) preserves meaning.

The expression $Y = \lambda f.\ (\lambda x.\ f(xx))(\lambda x.\ f(xx))$ is no longer a fixed-point operator in eager evaluation; one can show that $[\![Y\ e]\!]\eta = \perp_D$ for any expression e. The recursion definition of functions in eager-evaluation languages will be introduced in Section 11.3, and its semantics will be defined in terms of least fixed-points in Section 11.6.

10.6 Programming in the Lambda Calculus

Our main interest in the lambda calculus lies in the functional languages that can be obtained by extending it, but in passing it should be noted that one can actually program in the pure calculus, provided that "computation" is interpreted as normal-order reduction to normal form. The basic trick is to encode truth values, natural numbers, and other types of primitive data by appropriate closed expressions in normal form. (Of course, these encodings actually denote functions, but the behavior of these functions mimics the primitive data.)

For example, it is conventional to encode the truth values by

$$TRUE \stackrel{\text{def}}{=} \lambda x.\ \lambda y.\ x \qquad FALSE \stackrel{\text{def}}{=} \lambda x.\ \lambda y.\ y.$$

(Throughout this section, we will use metavariables such as $TRUE$ and $FALSE$ to abbreviate various closed expressions.) With this encoding, the conditional expression **if** b **then** e_0 **else** e_1 can be written simply as be_0e_1, since

$$TRUE\ e_0e_1 \rightarrow^* e_0 \qquad FALSE\ e_0e_1 \rightarrow^* e_1.$$

Similarly, one can define

$$NOT \stackrel{\text{def}}{=} \lambda b.\ \lambda x.\ \lambda y.\ b\, y\, x$$

$$AND \stackrel{\text{def}}{=} \lambda b.\ \lambda c.\ \lambda x.\ \lambda y.\ b(c\, x\, y)y,$$

since

$$NOT\ TRUE \rightarrow^* FALSE \qquad\qquad NOT\ FALSE \rightarrow^* TRUE$$

$$AND\ TRUE\ TRUE \rightarrow^* TRUE \qquad AND\ TRUE\ FALSE \rightarrow^* FALSE$$

$$AND\ FALSE\ TRUE \rightarrow^* FALSE \qquad AND\ FALSE\ FALSE \rightarrow^* FALSE.$$

(Notice that AND gives short-circuit evaluation: $AND\ FALSE\ e \rightarrow^* FALSE$ even when e has no normal form.)

To encode natural numbers, one can use the "Church numerals":

$$NUM_0 \stackrel{\text{def}}{=} \lambda f.\ \lambda x.\ x \qquad NUM_1 \stackrel{\text{def}}{=} \lambda f.\ \lambda x.\ f\, x \qquad NUM_2 \stackrel{\text{def}}{=} \lambda f.\ \lambda x.\ f(f\, x) \quad \cdots ,$$

or in general

$$NUM_n \stackrel{\text{def}}{=} \lambda f.\ \lambda x.\ f^n x,$$

where $f^n x$ abbreviates n applications of f to x. Then one can take the successor function and the predicate that tests for zero to be

$$SUCC \stackrel{\text{def}}{=} \lambda n.\ \lambda f.\ \lambda x.\ f(n\, f\, x) \qquad ISZERO \stackrel{\text{def}}{=} \lambda n.\ \lambda x.\ \lambda y.\ n(\lambda z.\ y)x,$$

since then

$$SUCC\ NUM_n \rightarrow^* NUM_{n+1}$$

and

$$ISZERO\ NUM_0 \rightarrow^* TRUE \qquad ISZERO\ NUM_{n+1} \rightarrow^* FALSE.$$

By using these encodings plus the fixed-point operator Y, one can actually (though rather tediously) program any computable function on the natural numbers. More interestingly, the particular encodings provide some intriguing short cuts, such as

$$ADD \overset{\text{def}}{=} \lambda m.\ \lambda n.\ \lambda f.\ \lambda x.\ m\, f(n\, f\, x) \qquad MULT \overset{\text{def}}{=} \lambda m.\ \lambda n.\ \lambda f.\ m(n\, f).$$

Aside from practical inefficiency, the major shortcoming of this approach is that the encodings have accidental properties that do not make sense for the entities being encoded. In this case, for example, $NUM_0 \equiv FALSE$. Also, there is an alternative, equally valid encoding of the successor function,

$$SUCC' \overset{\text{def}}{=} \lambda n.\ \lambda f.\ \lambda x.\ n\, f(f\, x),$$

that differs from $SUCC$ when applied to certain expressions that do not encode natural numbers. (These problems are avoided when similar encodings are used in the polymorphic typed lambda calculus. In Section 17.2, after we have introduced polymorphic typing, we will explore this kind of programming much further.)

It should be emphasized that this kind of programming in the lambda calculus requires normal-order reduction. For example, to mimic conditional expressions correctly, $TRUE\, e_0 e_1$ must reduce to e_0 even when e_1 diverges. Moreover, an expression must be reduced to its normal form (not just to a canonical form) to determine what number or truth value it represents. For example, one must reduce

$$
\begin{aligned}
MULT\ NUM_2\ NUM_3 &\to (\lambda n.\ \lambda f.\ NUM_2(n\, f))\ NUM_3 \\
&\to \lambda f.\ NUM_2(NUM_3\, f) \\
&\to \lambda f.\ \lambda x.\ (NUM_3\, f)((NUM_3\, f)\, x) \\
&\to \lambda f.\ \lambda x.\ (\lambda x.\ f(f(f\, x)))((NUM_3\, f)\, x) \\
&\to \lambda f.\ \lambda x.\ f(f(f((NUM_3\, f)\, x))) \\
&\to \lambda f.\ \lambda x.\ f(f(f((\lambda x.\ f(f(f\, x)))\, x))) \\
&\to \lambda f.\ \lambda x.\ f(f(f(f(f(f\, x)))))
\end{aligned}
$$

all the way to the normal form NUM_6.

A further complication is that NUM_1 actually has two forms, $\lambda f.\ \lambda x.\ f\, x$ and $\lambda f.\ f$, which are related by η-reduction but not β-reduction. Thus, strictly speaking, computations with Church numerals should be based on reduction to $\beta\eta$-normal form, that is, to an expression that contains neither β- nor η-redices. (In fact, it is sufficient to first perform a normal-order reduction to β-normal form and then eliminate any η-redices by η-reduction.)

Bibliographic Notes

It is still fascinating to read the brief monograph by Church [1941] that summarizes research on the lambda calculus during the 1930's, such as the proof of the

Church-Rosser theorem [Church and Rosser, 1936]. For example, in Section 18, Church mentions what we now call the distinction between eager and normal-order evaluation, and credits the idea to Bernays [1936], in a review of Church and Rosser [1936]. This is a powerful antidote to the belief that only recent ideas are significant in computer science.

Seventeen years later, Curry and Feys [1958] wrote an exhaustively thorough treatise that also covers the closely related topic of combinatory logic. The definitive modern text is Barendregt [1984], while a more introductory exposition is Hindley and Seldin [1986].

The domain-theoretic models such as D_∞ were originally introduced by Scott [1970] and have been thoroughly explored by Wadsworth [1976; 1978]. The basic construction of such models is explained in Hindley and Seldin [1986, Chapter 12] and Barendregt [1984, Chapter 18].

The connection between reduction and evaluation is based on work by Plotkin [1975]. The domain used to provide denotational semantics for normal-order evaluation was introduced and related to evaluation by Abramsky and Ong [1993]. More recently, Abramsky and McCusker [1995] and McCusker [1998] have developed a fully abstract game-theoretic semantics.

The indented format for proofs of evaluation was devised by Launchbury [1993].

Exercises

10.1   Consider the following expressions of the lambda calculus:

$$(\lambda f.\ \lambda x.\ f\,(f\,x))\,(\lambda b.\ \lambda x.\ \lambda y.\ b\,y\,x)(\lambda z.\ \lambda w.\ z)$$

$$(\lambda d.\ d\,d)(\lambda f.\ \lambda x.\ f(f\,x))$$

$$(\lambda x.\ x\,(\lambda w.\ w)\,(\lambda t.\ (\lambda s.\ s)\,t))(\lambda y.\ (\lambda z.\ z\,z\,z)(y\,(\lambda x.\ \lambda y.\ x)))\,(\lambda t.\ t).$$

For each of these expressions:

(a) Give the normal-order reduction sequence from this expression to its normal form.

(b) Indicate where this reduction sequence would end if it stopped at the first canonical form.

(c) Give a proof of the normal-order evaluation of this expression using the inference rules in Section 10.3.

(d) Give the eager reduction sequence from this expression to the first canonical form.

(e) Give a proof of the eager evaluation of this expression using the inference rules in Section 10.4.

Be careful to rename bound variables when necessary.

10.2   Prove that, for any closed expression e and canonical form z, the expression e evaluates eagerly to z if and only if there is a proof of $e \Rightarrow_E z$ from the inference rules in Section 10.4.

10.3   For any predomain P and domain D, the operation $(-)_{\perp\!\perp}$ is a function from $P \to D$ to $P_\perp \to D$. Show that this function is continuous.

10.4   Prove the type correctness (in the sense of Proposition 10.8 in Section 10.5) of the semantic equations for eager evaluation. (You will need the result of the previous exercise.)

10.5   Prove Proposition 10.7(d) in Section 10.5. In other words, suppose P, P', and P'' are predomains, f is a continuous function from $P \times P'$ to P'', and $\mathsf{ab}\, f$ is such that $((\mathsf{ab}\, f)\, x)\, y = f\langle x, y \rangle$. Then prove that

   (a) For any $x \in P$, $(\mathsf{ab}\, f)\, x$ is a continuous function from P' to P''.
   (b) $\mathsf{ab}\, f$ is a continuous function from P to $P' \to P''$.

   Also give examples showing that neither $(\mathsf{ab}\, f)\, x$ nor $\mathsf{ab}\, f$ need be strict when f is strict (and P, P', and P'' are domains).

10.6   Let D be a domain and F be the function from $D \to D$ to $D \to D$ such that $F f x = f(fx)$. Show that F is continuous. (Notice that, since the argument of F belongs to $D \to D$, you may assume that the argument is a continuous function.)

10.7   Let f be the function from $\mathcal{P}\,\mathbf{Z}$ (the powerset of the integers) to $\mathcal{P}\,\mathbf{Z}$ such that

$$f(s) = \{\, x + y \mid x \in s \text{ and } y \in s \,\}.$$

   Assuming that $\mathcal{P}\,\mathbf{Z}$ is ordered by inclusion, show that f is continuous.
   Describe the least fixed-point, the greatest fixed-point, and at least one other fixed point of this function.

10.8   Let D be a domain and $\mathbf{Y}_D$ be the least-fixed-point function from $D \to D$ to D such that

$$\mathbf{Y}_D f = \bigsqcup_{n=0}^{\infty} f^n \perp.$$

   Show that $\mathbf{Y}_D$ is continuous.

10.9   Let f and g be functions from $\mathcal{P}\,\mathbf{N}$ to $\mathcal{P}(\mathbf{N}^\infty)$ (where $\mathcal{P}$ is the powerset operator), such that f (or g) maps a set S of nonnegative integers into the set of finite sequences (or infinite sequences) of members of S:

$$fS = \{\, \langle i_0, \ldots, i_{n-1} \rangle \mid n \geq 0 \wedge \forall k \in 0 \text{ to } n - 1.\ i_k \in S \,\}$$

$$gS = \{\, \langle i_0, i_1, \ldots \rangle \mid \forall k \geq 0.\ i_k \in S \,\}.$$

Assume that the powersets are ordered by set-inclusion. Show that f is continuous. Show that g is not continuous.

10.10 Prove that

$$(\lambda v_0. \; \cdots \lambda v_{n-1}.\; e)e_0 \cdots e_{n-1} \to^* e/v_0 \to e_0, \; \ldots, \; v_{n-1} \to e_{n-1}$$

(even when some of the variables v_i are the same).
Hint Use the definition of $e/v_0 \to e_0, \; \ldots, \; v_{n-1} \to e_{n-1}$ in Section 1.4 and the result of Part (a) of Exercise 1.7.

10.11 Prove that the following variant of the substitution theorem (Proposition 10.10 in Section 10.5) holds for the denotational semantics of eager evaluation: If $[\![\delta w]\!]\eta' = \iota_\uparrow(\eta w)$ for all $w \in FV(e)$, then $[\![e/\delta]\!]\eta' = [\![e]\!]\eta$.

10.12 Use the variant of the substitution theorem stated in Exercise 10.11 to prove the soundness of β_E-contraction for the denotational semantics of eager evaluation, that is, that $(\lambda v.\; e)z$ and $e/v \to z$ have the same meaning when z is a canonical form or a variable.

10.13 Give a definition of OR analogous to the definition of AND in Section 10.6. Then, for each of the followings pairs of expressions, show that the two expressions have the same $\beta\eta$-normal form:

$$AND\,(AND\,b\,c)\,d \qquad AND\,b\,(AND\,c\,d)$$

$$NOT\,(NOT\,b) \qquad b$$

$$AND\,(NOT\,b)\,(NOT\,c) \qquad NOT\,(OR\,b\,c).$$

10.14 Prove that, with the encodings of natural numbers in Section 10.6, the expression

$$EXP \stackrel{\text{def}}{=} \lambda m.\; \lambda n.\; nm$$

behaves as an exponentiation function, this is, that

$$EXP\,NUM_m\,NUM_n \to^* NUM_{(m^n)},$$

where $m^0 = 1$ and $m^{n+1} = m \times m^n$ when $n \geq 0$. (Remember that NUM_1 has the two forms $\lambda f.\; \lambda x.\; f\,x$ and $\lambda f.\; f.$)

11

An Eager Functional Language

Now we extend the lambda calculus to a more general functional language that uses eager evaluation. This language will combine the arithmetic and logical operations of Chapter 1 with the functional constructions of Chapter 10, and will also provide conditional and definitional expressions, and constructions for synthesizing and analyzing tuples, alternatives, and lists.

In this chapter, we present the syntax, operational semantics, and direct denotational semantics of this language, along with examples of its use. In later chapters, we will explore language extensions that provide continuations as values and imperative constructs such as assignment, a variation of the language that uses normal-order evaluation, and the imposition of various type disciplines.

11.1 Concrete Syntax

Since our language is rather complex, we will introduce its abstract syntax as we go along. At the beginning, however, it is useful to summarize briefly the concrete syntax of the entire language, including the various extensions and variations that will be introduced in the rest of this book. The precedence list is

$$. \ (\text{FA} \ @ \ \textbf{callcc} \ \textbf{throw} \ \textbf{mkref} \ \textbf{val}) \ (\times \div \ \textbf{rem}) \ (-_{\text{unary}} \ + \ -_{\text{binary}})$$

$$(= \neq \ < \leq \ > \geq \ =_{\text{ref}}) \ \neg \ \wedge \ \vee \ \Rightarrow \ \Leftrightarrow \ :: \ (:= \ !) \ ; \ \equiv \ ,$$

Here "FA" stands for the function-application operator, which is an empty string (so that e_0 applied to e_1 is written $e_0 \ e_1$), but still has a precedence and associativity. The binary operators :: and := are right-associative. As in earlier chapters, unparenthesized multiple combinations of the relational operators $=$, $\neq$, $<$, $\leq$, $>$, and $\geq$ are not permitted. The remaining binary operators are left-associative.

Our reason for prohibiting relational combinations such as $e_0 \leq e_1 \leq e_2$ is that the usual mathematical meaning of such combinations (e.g. $e_0 \leq e_1 \wedge e_1 \leq e_2$) is rarely provided in programming languages and, more seriously, is difficult to generalize cleanly to encompass side effects. (In the above expression, for example, is e_1 evaluated once or twice?)

In each of the expressions

if $\cdots$ **then** $\cdots$ **else** e

$\lambda \cdots . e$

let $\cdots$ **in** e

letrec $\cdots$ **in** e

newvar $\cdots$ **in** e

while $\cdots$ **do** e

rec e

$\Lambda \cdots . e$

letrectype $\cdots$ **in** e

lettranstype $\cdots$ **in** e

letabstype $\cdots$ **in** e

pack $\cdots$ **as** e

open $\cdots$ **in** e

the subexpression e extends to the first stopping symbol (as defined in Section 1.1) or the end of the enclosing phrase.

11.2 Evaluation Semantics

Our first approach to defining our functional language is to give inference rules for the evaluation relation $\Rightarrow_E$. (Since only eager evaluation is considered in this chapter, we will henceforth omit the subscript E.)

As with the pure lambda calculus, the evaluation relation relates closed expressions to canonical forms; indeed, since the language is determinate, this relation is actually a partial function. But in the present language there are values of several different run-time types. Thus we divide the set $\langle \text{cfm} \rangle$ of canonical forms according to the types of values denoted by these forms:

$$\langle \text{cfm} \rangle ::= \langle \text{intcfm} \rangle \mid \langle \text{boolcfm} \rangle \mid \langle \text{funccfm} \rangle \mid \langle \text{tuplecfm} \rangle \mid \langle \text{altcfm} \rangle$$

(Occasionally, we will say that an expression evaluates to an integer, boolean, function, tuple, or alternative when we mean that it evaluates to a canonical form of the corresponding kind.)

In the above paragraph, we have used the phrase "run-time type" to describe certain sets of values (in a yet-to-be-specified denotational semantics). This unfortunate phrase is computer jargon that was coined without regard for the historical usage of "type" in logic. In logic, where the term was originally used, a "type" is a syntactic property of (closed) expressions, sometimes called a "compile-time type" in computer science. In Chapter 15 and later, we will use the term with this standard meaning. Roughly speaking, however, it will turn out that all closed expressions with a given type in the logical sense will denote semantic values of the same run-time type. Thus the run-time types considered here will eventually reappear as the meanings of logical types.

A further difference between the present language and the pure lambda calculus is that evaluation can produce errors, either because an operation is applied to an argument of inappropriate type or because an operation (such as division) is undefined for a particular argument (such as zero). Evaluation semantics can be used to describe the detection of such errors by introducing a special canonical form **error** (or even several forms denoting different kinds of errors) and giving inference rules that show when errors are detected and how they are propagated. Such a semantics would answer such questions as "If e fails to terminate, does **true** $+ e$ give an error stop or fail to terminate?"

The difficulty is that such a semantics is extremely complicated: Dealing with errors roughly triples the number of inference rules. Moreover, it invalidates laws such as $e + e' = e' + e$ that fail to hold only if one distinguishes between errors and nontermination, or between different kinds of errors. For these reasons, we limit our presentation in this section to a simpler evaluation semantics where error stops are not distinguished from nontermination, and we postpone a more precise treatment of errors until we consider denotational semantics in Section 11.6. In the present treatment, when the evaluation of e either fails to terminate or gives an error stop, there will be no canonical form z such that $e \Rightarrow z$; in either of these cases we will write $e \uparrow$ and say that e *diverges*.

In the inference rules for evaluation semantics, the following metavariables, sometimes with primes or subscripts, will be used with the following ranges:

$$
\begin{array}{llll}
e & \langle \exp \rangle_{\text{closed}} & i & \mathbf{Z} \\
\hat{e} & \langle \exp \rangle & k, n & \mathbf{N} \\
z & \langle \text{cfm} \rangle & b & \mathbf{B} \\
v, u & \langle \text{var} \rangle & p & \langle \text{pat} \rangle \quad (\text{patterns}).
\end{array}
$$

Most of the inference rules for evaluation are particular to a single aspect of the language, but one is pervasive: Canonical forms always evaluate to themselves.

EV RULE: Canonical Forms

$$z \Rightarrow z.$$

Turning to the more specific aspects of the language, we begin with the constants and primitive operations for computing with integers and boolean values:

$\langle \text{natconst} \rangle ::= 0 \mid 1 \mid 2 \mid \cdots$

$\langle \text{boolconst} \rangle ::= \textbf{true} \mid \textbf{false}$

$\langle \exp \rangle ::= \langle \text{natconst} \rangle \mid \langle \text{boolconst} \rangle$
$\quad \mid -\langle \exp \rangle \mid \langle \exp \rangle + \langle \exp \rangle \mid \langle \exp \rangle - \langle \exp \rangle$
$\quad \mid \langle \exp \rangle \times \langle \exp \rangle \mid \langle \exp \rangle \div \langle \exp \rangle \mid \langle \exp \rangle \textbf{ rem } \langle \exp \rangle$
$\quad \mid \langle \exp \rangle = \langle \exp \rangle \mid \langle \exp \rangle \neq \langle \exp \rangle \mid \langle \exp \rangle < \langle \exp \rangle$
$\quad \mid \langle \exp \rangle \leq \langle \exp \rangle \mid \langle \exp \rangle > \langle \exp \rangle \mid \langle \exp \rangle \geq \langle \exp \rangle$
$\quad \mid \neg \langle \exp \rangle \mid \langle \exp \rangle \wedge \langle \exp \rangle \mid \langle \exp \rangle \vee \langle \exp \rangle \mid \langle \exp \rangle \Rightarrow \langle \exp \rangle \mid \langle \exp \rangle \Leftrightarrow \langle \exp \rangle$

$$\langle\text{intcfm}\rangle ::= \cdots \mid -2 \mid -1 \mid 0 \mid 1 \mid 2 \mid \cdots$$

$$\langle\text{boolcfm}\rangle ::= \langle\text{boolconst}\rangle$$

Notice that the two sets of canonical forms are isomorphic to the sets **Z** of integers and **B** of boolean values respectively. To deal with these isomorphisms, we use the following notational trick: If "$-$" is a metaexpression denoting a member of **Z** or **B**, we write $\lfloor - \rfloor$ for the corresponding member of $\langle\text{intcfm}\rangle$ or $\langle\text{boolcfm}\rangle$. For example, if i denotes the integer 2 and i' denotes the integer -3, then $\lfloor i + i' \rfloor$ denotes the member of $\langle\text{intcfm}\rangle$ written -1 (which, strictly speaking, is an abstract phrase rather than an integer).

Then the inference rules for arithmetic, relational, and boolean operations are

EV RULE: Unary Operations

$$\frac{e \Rightarrow \lfloor i \rfloor}{- e \Rightarrow \lfloor -i \rfloor} \qquad \frac{e \Rightarrow \lfloor b \rfloor}{\neg e \Rightarrow \lfloor \neg b \rfloor},$$

EV RULE: Binary Operations

$$\frac{e \Rightarrow \lfloor i \rfloor \quad e' \Rightarrow \lfloor i' \rfloor}{e \text{ op } e' \Rightarrow \lfloor i \text{ op } i' \rfloor} \qquad \begin{array}{l} \text{when op} \in \{+, -, \times, =, \neq, <, \leq, >, \geq\} \\ \text{or } i' \neq 0 \text{ and op} \in \{\div, \mathbf{rem}\} \end{array}$$

$$\frac{e \Rightarrow \lfloor b \rfloor \quad e' \Rightarrow \lfloor b' \rfloor}{e \text{ op } e' \Rightarrow \lfloor b \text{ op } b' \rfloor} \qquad \text{when op} \in \{\wedge, \vee, \rightarrow, \leftrightarrow\}.$$

Each form of expression we have described so far always evaluates all of its subexpressions (in the absence of nontermination or errors during these evaluations). Even in a language using eager evaluation, however, there must be some mechanism for choosing, on the basis of a computed value, between the evaluation of different subexpressions. The simplest of such mechanisms is the conditional expression (a close relative of the conditional command of Chapter 2),

$$\langle\text{exp}\rangle ::= \mathbf{if}\ \langle\text{exp}\rangle\ \mathbf{then}\ \langle\text{exp}\rangle\ \mathbf{else}\ \langle\text{exp}\rangle$$

which evaluates its first subexpression to obtain a boolean value and then, depending on this value, evaluates one of the two remaining subexpressions:

EV RULE: Conditional Expressions

$$\frac{e \Rightarrow \mathbf{true} \quad e' \Rightarrow z}{\mathbf{if}\ e\ \mathbf{then}\ e'\ \mathbf{else}\ e'' \Rightarrow z} \qquad \frac{e \Rightarrow \mathbf{false} \quad e'' \Rightarrow z}{\mathbf{if}\ e\ \mathbf{then}\ e'\ \mathbf{else}\ e'' \Rightarrow z.}$$

It should be noted that some of the binary boolean operations described earlier, specifically $\wedge$, $\vee$, and $\Rightarrow$, give results that, for some values of their first operand, are independent of the value of their second operand. We could have defined these operations so that, like the conditional, they do not always evaluate all of their operands. For example, we might have defined $e \wedge e'$ to have the same behavior as **if** e **then** e' **else false**, so that e' is not evaluated when e is false. However, although there are strong pragmatic reasons for preferring such "short circuit" evaluation, we will postpone the topic until we consider normal-order evaluation.

The syntax of variables, applications, and abstractions is the same as for the lambda calculus:

$$\langle \text{exp} \rangle ::= \langle \text{var} \rangle \mid \langle \text{exp} \rangle \langle \text{exp} \rangle \mid \lambda \langle \text{var} \rangle. \langle \text{exp} \rangle$$

$$\langle \text{funcfm} \rangle ::= \lambda \langle \text{var} \rangle. \langle \text{exp} \rangle$$

as is the inference rule for eager evaluation:

EV RULE: Application (β_E-evaluation)

$$\frac{e \Rightarrow \lambda v.\, \hat{e} \qquad e' \Rightarrow z' \qquad (\hat{e}/v \to z') \Rightarrow z}{ee' \Rightarrow z.}$$

(In the next section, we will generalize the syntax and semantics of abstractions to permit binding by patterns.)

Now we introduce two language constructs that go beyond the arithmetic, logical, and functional facilities of previous chapters. The first of these is the *tuple*, which is a mathematical construct that is appropriate to a purely functional language, yet mirrors records in languages such as Algol W or Pascal and objects in object-oriented languages.

Here there are two possible approaches, depending on whether the *tag* used to select a field of a tuple is a number indicating position, or an explicitly attached name. At present, we will limit ourselves to numbered tuples, but the alternative of named tuples will be explored in Chapter 16.

For tuples with numbered fields, we use the syntax

$$\langle \text{exp} \rangle ::= \langle\!\langle \text{exp} \rangle, \ldots, \langle \text{exp} \rangle\!\rangle \mid \langle \text{exp} \rangle.\langle \text{tag} \rangle$$

$$\langle \text{tag} \rangle ::= \langle \text{natconst} \rangle$$

$$\langle \text{tuplecfm} \rangle ::= \langle\!\langle \text{cfm} \rangle, \ldots, \langle \text{cfm} \rangle\!\rangle$$

(In this and later grammars, we enlarge the object-language angle brackets enclosing tuples to distinguish them from the metalanguage angle brackets enclosing nonterminals.) For example, $\langle 10, 20 \rangle$ denotes a two-field tuple where the field numbered zero is 10 and the field numbered one is 20; if x denotes such a tuple, then x.0 and x.1 denote its fields (which we will occasionally call the first field and the second field, even though the tags are zero and one).

Notice that the numerical tags in the selection operation are required to be constants. This restriction anticipates the type systems that we will later impose on this language, where the type of $e.k$ will depend on k, so that the value of k must be known at compile time to do type checking.

The rules for evaluation are

EV RULE: Tuples

$$\frac{e_0 \Rightarrow z_0 \quad \cdots \quad e_{n-1} \Rightarrow z_{n-1}}{\langle e_0, \ldots, e_{n-1} \rangle \Rightarrow \langle z_0, \ldots, z_{n-1} \rangle}$$

$$\frac{e \Rightarrow \langle z_0, \ldots, z_{n-1} \rangle}{e.k \Rightarrow z_k} \qquad \text{when } k < n.$$

Finally, we introduce an *alternative* construct (often called a sum, or disjoint union, and closely related to the variant-record construct in Pascal), where a value can be paired with a *tag* that must be branched upon in order to process the value. As with tuples, we limit ourselves to numeric tags (postponing named tags until Chapter 16):

$\langle \text{exp} \rangle ::= @ \langle \text{tag} \rangle \langle \text{exp} \rangle \mid \textbf{sumcase } \langle \text{exp} \rangle \textbf{ of } (\langle \text{exp} \rangle, \ldots, \langle \text{exp} \rangle)$

$\langle \text{tag} \rangle ::= \langle \text{natconst} \rangle$

$\langle \text{altcfm} \rangle ::= @ \langle \text{tag} \rangle \langle \text{cfm} \rangle$

The value of $@ \, k \, e$ is the value of e paired with the tag k. If e' has the value x paired with the tag k, and $f_0, \ldots, f_{n-1}$ are functions, then the value of $\textbf{sumcase } e' \textbf{ of } (f_0, \ldots, f_{n-1})$ is the result of applying the function f_k to x. The evaluation rules are

EV RULE: Alternatives

$$\frac{e \Rightarrow z}{@ \, k \, e \Rightarrow @ \, k \, z}$$

$$\frac{e \Rightarrow @ \, k \, z \qquad e_k \, z \Rightarrow z'}{\textbf{sumcase } e \textbf{ of } (e_0, \ldots, e_{n-1}) \Rightarrow z'} \qquad \text{when } k < n.$$

Strictly speaking, $@ \, k \, e$ is a pair like $\langle k, e \rangle$. But we consider them to be different kinds of pairs since they will be treated differently by most type systems. (The type of e in $@ \, k \, e$, but not in $\langle k, e \rangle$, may depend on k, so that compile-time type checking will require k to be a constant.)

Finally, we introduce expressions that explicitly force either an ordinary error stop or a type-error stop:

$$\langle \text{exp} \rangle ::= \textbf{error} \mid \textbf{typeerror}$$

We will give meaning to these expressions, and explain the distinction between them, when we consider denotational semantics in Section 11.6. In our simple evaluation semantics, however, they are merely expressions that always diverge — a fact that is captured trivially by giving no inference rules at all.

11.3 Definitions, Patterns, and Recursion

It is useful to extend our language to provide a definitional expression of the form

$$\textbf{let } v_0 \equiv e_0, \ \ldots, \ v_{n-1} \equiv e_{n-1} \textbf{ in } e,$$

which evaluates e while taking each variable v_i to stand for the value of e_i.

A second useful extension is to generalize the binding occurrences of variables in both definitions and abstractions to permit patterns of variables that can match against tuples. For example, if e_0 evaluates to $\langle 3, 4 \rangle$, then $\textbf{let } \langle x, y \rangle \equiv e_0 \textbf{ in } x + y$ matches the pattern $\langle x, y \rangle$ against $\langle 3, 4 \rangle$, takes x to stand for 3 and y to stand for 4, and evaluates $x + y$ to 7. Similarly, when $\lambda \langle x, y \rangle . \ x + y$ is applied to the tuple $\langle 3, 4 \rangle$, the pattern $\langle x, y \rangle$ is matched against $\langle 3, 4 \rangle$, so that the result of the application is 7.

These generalizations are described by the following grammar, which introduces patterns for matching tuples and allows such patterns to be nested:

$$\langle \text{pat} \rangle ::= \langle \text{var} \rangle \mid \langle \langle \text{pat} \rangle, \ldots, \langle \text{pat} \rangle \rangle$$

$$\langle \text{exp} \rangle ::= \lambda \langle \text{pat} \rangle . \ \langle \text{exp} \rangle \mid \textbf{let } \langle \text{pat} \rangle \equiv \langle \text{exp} \rangle, \ \ldots, \langle \text{pat} \rangle \equiv \langle \text{exp} \rangle \textbf{ in } \langle \text{exp} \rangle$$

Note that an abstraction of the form $\lambda \langle \text{pat} \rangle . \ \langle \text{exp} \rangle$ is not a canonical form when the pattern $\langle \text{pat} \rangle$ is not a variable.

In the abstraction $\lambda p. \ e$, each variable occurrence in the pattern p is a binder whose scope is e. Similarly, in $\textbf{let } p_0 \equiv e_0, \ \ldots, \ p_{n-1} \equiv e_{n-1} \textbf{ in } e$, each variable occurrence in each p_i is a binder whose scope is e. Thus

$$\text{FV}(\lambda p. \ e)$$
$$= \text{FV}(e) - \text{FV}_{\text{pat}}(p)$$

$$\text{FV}(\textbf{let } p_0 \equiv e_0, \ \ldots, \ p_{n-1} \equiv e_{n-1} \textbf{ in } e)$$
$$= FV(e_0) \cup \cdots \cup \text{FV}(e_{n-1}) \cup (\text{FV}(e) - \text{FV}_{\text{pat}}(p_0) - \cdots - \text{FV}_{\text{pat}}(p_{n-1})),$$

where

$$\text{FV}_{\text{pat}}(v) = \{v\}$$

$$\text{FV}_{\text{pat}}(\langle p_0, \ \ldots, \ p_{n-1} \rangle) = \text{FV}_{\text{pat}}(p_0) \cup \cdots \cup \text{FV}_{\text{pat}}(p_{n-1}).$$

Notice that two binding occurrences of variables in the same pattern, or in patterns in the same **let** definition, have the same scope. Thus, if the variables are the same, as in $\textbf{let } x \equiv 0, x \equiv 1 \textbf{ in } x + 1$, it is not clear from the definition of binding in Section 1.4 which of the binding occurrences binds the occurrences of the same variable in their common scope. Actually, the definition we are about to give will resolve this question unambiguously. But pragmatically, such repeated bindings of the same variable would almost certainly be a programming error. In most languages, one prohibits the situation by requiring that no two binding occurrences of the same variable may have the same scope.

Although definitions and patterns can be defined by evaluation rules, it is more straightforward to regard them as syntactic sugar, in the sense of Section 2.6:

$$\textbf{let } p_0 \equiv e_0, \ldots, p_{n-1} \equiv e_{n-1} \textbf{ in } e$$
$$\stackrel{\text{def}}{=} (\lambda p_0.\ \ldots \lambda p_{n-1}.\ e)\, e_0 \cdots e_{n-1}$$

$$\lambda\langle p_0, \ldots, p_{n-1}\rangle.\ e \stackrel{\text{def}}{=} \lambda v.\ \textbf{let } p_0 \equiv v.0, \ldots, p_{n-1} \equiv v.\lfloor n-1 \rfloor \textbf{ in } e,$$

where v is a variable that does not occur free in e. Thus, for example,

$$\textbf{let } \langle \mathsf{x}, \mathsf{y} \rangle \equiv \mathsf{w},\ \mathsf{z} \equiv 2 \times \mathsf{n} \textbf{ in } \mathsf{x} + \mathsf{y} + \mathsf{z}$$
$$\stackrel{\text{def}}{=} (\lambda \langle \mathsf{x}, \mathsf{y} \rangle.\ \lambda \mathsf{z}.\ \mathsf{x} + \mathsf{y} + \mathsf{z})\, \mathsf{w}\, (2 \times \mathsf{n})$$
$$\stackrel{\text{def}}{=} (\lambda \mathsf{v}.\ \textbf{let } \mathsf{x} \equiv \mathsf{v}.0,\ \mathsf{y} \equiv \mathsf{v}.1 \textbf{ in } \lambda \mathsf{z}.\ \mathsf{x} + \mathsf{y} + \mathsf{z})\, \mathsf{w}\, (2 \times \mathsf{n})$$
$$\stackrel{\text{def}}{=} (\lambda \mathsf{v}.\ (\lambda \mathsf{x}.\ \lambda \mathsf{y}.\ \lambda \mathsf{z}.\ \mathsf{x} + \mathsf{y} + \mathsf{z})(\mathsf{v}.0)(\mathsf{v}.1))\, \mathsf{w}\, (2 \times \mathsf{n}).$$

Indeed, definitional expressions are the primal case of syntactic sugar, since this phrase was coined by Peter Landin to describe the above definition of **let** (in the absence of patterns).

In a definition such as **let** $v_0 \equiv e_0$ **in** e the scope of the binder of v_0 does not include the expression e_0, so that occurrences of v_0 in e_0 are either free or bound "further out" in the program, and thus cannot represent recursive calls of functions. To remedy this shortcoming, we introduce a second form of definition specifically designed to provide recursion:

$$\langle \text{exp} \rangle ::= \textbf{letrec } \langle \text{var} \rangle \equiv \lambda \langle \text{pat} \rangle.\ \langle \text{exp} \rangle, \ldots, \langle \text{var} \rangle \equiv \lambda \langle \text{pat} \rangle.\ \langle \text{exp} \rangle \textbf{ in } \langle \text{exp} \rangle$$

(The restrictions on this form of recursive definition, that compound patterns are not permitted on the left of $\equiv$, and that the expressions on the right of $\equiv$ must be abstractions, so that only functions can be defined recursively, are a peculiarity of eager evaluation. As we will see in Section 14.2, in a language with normal-order evaluation, **letrec** definitions can have the same general form as **let** definitions.)

In **letrec** $v_0 \equiv \lambda p_0.\ e_0, \ldots, v_{n-1} \equiv \lambda p_{n-1}.\ e_{n-1}$ **in** e the variable occurrences $v_0, \ldots, v_{n-1}$ are binders whose common scope consists of both e and the abstractions $\lambda p_0.\ e_0, \ldots, \lambda p_{n-1}.\ e_{n-1}$. Thus

$$\text{FV}(\textbf{letrec } v_0 \equiv \lambda p_0.\ e_0, \ldots, v_{n-1} \equiv \lambda p_{n-1}.\ e_{n-1} \textbf{ in } e)$$
$$= (\text{FV}(\lambda p_0.\ e_0) \cup \cdots \cup \text{FV}(\lambda p_{n-1}.\ e_{n-1}) \cup \text{FV}(e)) - \{v_0, \ldots, v_{n-1}\}$$
$$= ((\text{FV}(e_0) - \text{FV}_{\text{pat}}(p_0)) \cup \cdots \cup (\text{FV}(e_{n-1}) - \text{FV}_{\text{pat}}(p_{n-1})) \cup \text{FV}(e))$$
$$\qquad - \{v_0, \ldots, v_{n-1}\}.$$

In giving meaning to recursive definitions, we can limit our attention to the case where the abstractions bind variables rather than arbitrary patterns, since abstractions using compound patterns have already been defined as abbreviations.

Since the difference between **letrec** $v_0 \equiv \lambda u_0.\, e_0,\, \ldots,\, v_{n-1} \equiv \lambda u_{n-1}.\, e_{n-1}$ **in** e and **let** $v_0 \equiv \lambda u_0.\, e_0,\, \ldots,\, v_{n-1} \equiv \lambda u_{n-1}.\, e_{n-1}$ **in** e is that the $e_0,\, \ldots,\, e_{n-1}$ feel the new bindings of $v_0,\, \ldots,\, v_{n-1}$ in the former but not the latter, it is plausible to consider the **letrec** definition as an abbreviation for a **let** definition in which the e_i are enclosed within copies of the **letrec**:

$$\textbf{letrec } v_0 \equiv \lambda u_0.\, e_0,\, \ldots,\, v_{n-1} \equiv \lambda u_{n-1}.\, e_{n-1} \textbf{ in } e$$
$$\stackrel{\text{def}}{=} \textbf{let } v_0 \equiv \lambda u_0.\, e_0^*,\, \ldots,\, v_{n-1} \equiv \lambda u_{n-1}.\, e_{n-1}^* \textbf{ in } e,$$

where each e_i^* is

$$\textbf{letrec } v_0 \equiv \lambda u_0.\, e_0,\, \ldots,\, v_{n-1} \equiv \lambda u_{n-1}.\, e_{n-1} \textbf{ in } e_i$$

and $v_0,\, \ldots v_{n-1} \notin \{u_0, \ldots, u_{n-1}\}$. (The restriction on the v_i, which must be imposed since the **letrec**'s are moved into the scopes of the u_i, can always be met by renaming.)

However, although the two sides of this purported equational definition of **letrec** have the same meaning, it is not really a definition, because its repeated application will never eliminate all occurrences of **letrec**.

Nevertheless, the equation suggests how to obtain an inference rule for the evaluation of **letrec** definitions. As a preliminary step, we replace the **let** definition on the right of the equation by its desugaring:

$$\textbf{letrec } v_0 \equiv \lambda u_0.\, e_0,\, \ldots,\, v_{n-1} \equiv \lambda u_{n-1}.\, e_{n-1} \textbf{ in } e$$
$$\stackrel{\text{def}}{=} (\lambda v_0.\, \ldots \lambda v_{n-1}.\, e)(\lambda u_0.\, e_0^*) \cdots (\lambda u_{n-1}.\, e_{n-1}^*).$$

Then we formulate a rule that lets us infer a value for the left side of this equation when the same value can be inferred for the right side:

EV RULE: Recursion

$$\frac{(\lambda v_0.\, \ldots \lambda v_{n-1}.\, e)(\lambda u_0.\, e_0^*) \cdots (\lambda u_{n-1}.\, e_{n-1}^*) \Rightarrow z}{\textbf{letrec } v_0 \equiv \lambda u_0.\, e_0,\, \ldots,\, v_{n-1} \equiv \lambda u_{n-1}.\, e_{n-1} \textbf{ in } e \Rightarrow z,}$$

where each e_i^* is

$$\textbf{letrec } v_0 \equiv \lambda u_0.\, e_0,\, \ldots,\, v_{n-1} \equiv \lambda u_{n-1}.\, e_{n-1} \textbf{ in } e_i$$

and

$$v_0,\, \ldots v_{n-1} \notin \{u_0, \ldots, u_{n-1}\}.$$

The reason this rule works is that the $\lambda u_i.\ e_i^*$ are canonical forms. Thus the **letrec**'s within them will not be evaluated unless the application of some $\lambda u_i.\ e_i^*$ to an argument is evaluated, that is, unless a recursive call is evaluated.

11.4 Lists

Ever since the development of Lisp in the early 1960's, functional programming and list processing have been closely associated. For the construction of lists in our language, we use the Lisp primitives **nil** for the empty list and **cons** for prefixing an element to a list, except that we denote **cons** by the infix operator ::, as in Standard ML. For the analysis of lists, however, we use a case construction. An abstract grammar for these operations is

$$\langle\text{exp}\rangle ::= \textbf{nil} \mid \langle\text{exp}\rangle :: \langle\text{exp}\rangle \mid \textbf{listcase}\ \langle\text{exp}\rangle\ \textbf{of}\ (\langle\text{exp}\rangle, \langle\text{exp}\rangle)$$

$$\langle\text{cfm}\rangle ::= \textbf{nil} \mid \langle\text{cfm}\rangle :: \langle\text{cfm}\rangle$$

When e is an empty list, **listcase** e **of** $(e_\text{e}, e_\text{ne})$ gives the value of e_e while, when e is a list with initial element i and remainder r, **listcase** e **of** $(e_\text{e}, e_\text{ne})$ gives the value of the application $e_\text{ne}\ i\ r$.

More formally, the behavior of lists can be described by the following inference rules:

EV RULE: Lists

$$\overline{\textbf{nil} \Rightarrow \textbf{nil}}$$

$$\frac{e \Rightarrow z \qquad e' \Rightarrow z'}{e :: e' \Rightarrow z :: z'}$$

$$\frac{e \Rightarrow \textbf{nil} \qquad e_\text{e} \Rightarrow z}{\textbf{listcase}\ e\ \textbf{of}\ (e_\text{e}, e_\text{ne}) \Rightarrow z}$$

$$\frac{e \Rightarrow z :: z' \qquad e_\text{ne}\ z\ z' \Rightarrow z''}{\textbf{listcase}\ e\ \textbf{of}\ (e_\text{e}, e_\text{ne}) \Rightarrow z''.}$$

In fact, rather than treating lists as a new kind of value, we will regard them as complex data structures built out of alternatives and tuples. Specifically, we take a list to be an alternative value that is either the tag zero followed by an empty tuple, or the tag one followed by a pair giving the initial element and remainder of the list. Then all of the list operations can be defined as syntactic sugar in terms of the operations for alternatives and tuples:

$$\mathbf{nil} \overset{\mathrm{def}}{=} @ \, 0 \, \langle \rangle$$

$$e :: e' \overset{\mathrm{def}}{=} @ \, 1 \, \langle e, e' \rangle$$

$$\mathbf{listcase} \; e \; \mathbf{of} \; (e_{\mathrm{e}}, e_{\mathrm{ne}}) \overset{\mathrm{def}}{=} \mathbf{sumcase} \; e \; \mathbf{of} \; (\lambda \langle \rangle. \; e_{\mathrm{e}}, \lambda \langle x, y \rangle. \; e_{\mathrm{ne}} \, x \, y),$$

where x and y do not occur free in e_{ne}. These definitions imply that **nil** is a canonical form and that the **cons** of two canonical forms is a canonical form. They can also be used to derive the inference rules displayed above.

The **listcase** construction provides the same expressive power as the usual Lisp primitives null, car, and cdr for analyzing lists. (Our reason for preferring the former is that it has better typing properties; see Exercise 15.5.) In fact, one can use definitional expressions to define the latter in terms of the former:

$$\mathbf{let} \; \mathsf{null} \equiv \lambda \mathsf{x}. \; \mathbf{listcase} \; \mathsf{x} \; \mathbf{of} \; (\mathbf{true}, \lambda \mathsf{i}. \; \lambda \mathsf{r}. \; \mathbf{false}) \; \cdots$$

$$\mathbf{let} \; \mathsf{car} \equiv \lambda \mathsf{x}. \; \mathbf{listcase} \; \mathsf{x} \; \mathbf{of} \; (\mathbf{error}, \lambda \mathsf{i}. \; \lambda \mathsf{r}. \; \mathsf{i}) \; \cdots$$

$$\mathbf{let} \; \mathsf{cdr} \equiv \lambda \mathsf{x}. \; \mathbf{listcase} \; \mathsf{x} \; \mathbf{of} \; (\mathbf{error}, \lambda \mathsf{i}. \; \lambda \mathsf{r}. \; \mathsf{r}) \; \cdots.$$

Equally well (at the metalevel), one could use the Lisp primitives to define **listcase**:

$$\mathbf{listcase} \; e \; \mathbf{of} \; (e_{\mathrm{e}}, e_{\mathrm{ne}}) \overset{\mathrm{def}}{=} \mathbf{if} \; \mathsf{null} \, e \; \mathbf{then} \; e_{\mathrm{e}} \; \mathbf{else} \; e_{\mathrm{ne}}(\mathsf{car} \, e)(\mathsf{cdr} \, e).$$

Readers who are familiar with Lisp will have noticed that we have said nothing about the primitive equality test **eq**. When both x and y are represented by pointers, $\mathbf{eq}(x, y)$ will give **true** only when these pointers are the same. Unfortunately, the implementation-dependence of this operation makes it impossible to describe in any semantics that abstracts away from the use of pointers. Nevertheless, even in a purely functional language **eq** can be useful, since it is an efficient test such that $\mathbf{eq}(x, y)$ implies $x = y$.

11.5 Examples

Our language permits the recursive definition of conventional numeric functions, such as

$$\mathbf{letrec} \; \mathsf{fact} \equiv \lambda \mathsf{n}. \; \mathbf{if} \; \mathsf{n} = 0 \; \mathbf{then} \; 1 \; \mathbf{else} \; \mathsf{n} \times \mathsf{fact}(\mathsf{n} - 1) \; \cdots,$$

as well as higher-order numeric functions, such as

$$\mathbf{letrec} \; \mathsf{iterate} \equiv \lambda \mathsf{n}. \; \lambda \mathsf{f}. \; \lambda \mathsf{x}. \; \mathbf{if} \; \mathsf{n} = 0 \; \mathbf{then} \; \mathsf{x} \; \mathbf{else} \; \mathsf{f}(\mathsf{iterate}(\mathsf{n} - 1) \, \mathsf{f} \, \mathsf{x}) \; \cdots,$$

which, when applied to n, f, and x, gives $f^n \, x$ (which is $f \, (\cdots (f \, x) \cdots)$ with n occurrences of f).

For list processing, the **listcase** operation leads to more compact recursive definitions than in Lisp. For example,

> **letrec** append $\equiv$ λx. λy. **listcase** x **of** (y, λi. λr. i :: append r y) $\cdots$
>
> **letrec** mapcar $\equiv$ λf. λx. **listcase** x **of** (**nil**, λi. λr. f i :: mapcar f r) $\cdots$
>
> **letrec** filter $\equiv$ λx. λp.
>
>   **listcase** x **of** (**nil**, λi. λr. **if** p i **then** i :: filter r p **else** filter r p) $\cdots$.

Somewhat more complex are functions that recur on more than one list, such as a function for testing two lists of integers for equality:

> **letrec** eqlist $\equiv$ λx. λx'. **listcase** x **of** (
>
>   **listcase** x' **of** (**true**, λi'. λr'. **false**),
>
> λi. λr. **listcase** x' **of** (**false**, λi'. λr'.
>
>   **if** i = i' **then** eqlist r r' **else** **false**)) $\cdots$,

or a function for merging two ordered lists of integers:

> **letrec** merge $\equiv$ λx. λx'. **listcase** x **of** (x', λi. λr.
>
>   **listcase** x' **of** (x, λi'. λr'.
>
>   **if** i = i' **then** i :: merge r r' **else**
>
>   **if** i < i' **then** i :: merge r x' **else**
>
>   i' :: merge x r')) $\cdots$.

Specifically, merge accepts two ordered lists and returns an ordered list of the elements that occur in either argument, eliminating duplicates between lists but not within lists.

A particularly general function for iterating over lists is

> **letrec** reduce $\equiv$ λx. λf. λa. **listcase** x **of** (a, λi. λr. f i (reduce r f a)) $\cdots$,

which, when applied to a list x_0 :: $\cdots$ :: x_{n-1} :: **nil**, a function f, and a "starting value" a, gives $f\, x_0\, (\cdots (f\, x_{n-1}\, a) \cdots)$. For example, once one has defined reduce recursively, one can use this function to give nonrecursive definitions such as

> **let** append $\equiv$ λx. λy. reduce x (λi. λz. i :: z) y $\cdots$
>
> **let** mapcar $\equiv$ λf. λx. reduce x (λi. λz. f i :: z) **nil** $\cdots$
>
> **let** filter $\equiv$ λx. λp. reduce x (λi. λz. **if** p i **then** i :: z **else** z) **nil** $\cdots$.

(The name reduce comes from the language APL and has no connection with the concept of reduction in the lambda calculus.)

On the other hand, consider

    letrec search $\equiv \lambda$x. λp. λf. λg.

        listcase x **of** (g$\langle\rangle$, λi. λr. **if** p i **then** f i **else** search r p f g) $\cdots$.

Here the function **search** accepts a list, a predicate, and two functions f and g. If some element of the list satisfies the predicate, then f of the first such element is returned; otherwise, the result of g$\langle\rangle$ is returned. Because a successful search may be completed without examining the entire list, **search** cannot be defined nonrecursively in terms of **reduce** in an eager-evaluation language. (In Section 14.3, we will see that the situation is quite different in a normal-order evaluation language, where the functional argument to **reduce** need not evaluate all of its arguments.)

Notice that the parameter **g** is a function that is applied to the "dummy" argument $\langle\rangle$. This application does not provide useful information to **g** (since **g** is never applied to any other argument), but it is needed to avoid performing the computation of g$\langle\rangle$ unless the search fails. This is a common technique in eager-evaluation languages (which, as we will see in Section 14.3, is unnecessary in languages that use normal-order evaluation).

Lists are only the simplest example (albeit the only one for which we have defined a special notation) of the complex data structures that can be built up using alternatives and tuples. A slightly more elaborate example is binary trees with integer-labeled terminal nodes. Such a binary tree is either

$$@\, 0\, n,$$

called a *terminal node labeled by the integer n*, or

$$@\, 1\, \langle l, r \rangle,$$

called a *nonterminal node with left subtree l and right subtree r*.

The *fringe* of such a binary tree is a list of the integers labeling its terminal nodes, from left to right. It is computed by the function

    letrec fringelist $\equiv \lambda$t. **sumcase** t

        of (λn. n :: **nil**, $\lambda\langle l, r \rangle$. append (fringelist l)(fringelist r)) $\cdots$

or, much more efficiently, by

        let fringelist $\equiv \lambda$t.

            letrec frl $\equiv \lambda$t. λx. **sumcase** t

                of (λn. n :: x, $\lambda\langle l, r \rangle$. frl l (frl r x)) **in**

            frl t **nil** $\cdots$.

Here the subsidiary function frl appends the fringe of its first argument to the list that is its second argument.

11.6 Direct Denotational Semantics

In this section, we will extend the denotational semantics of eager evaluation, presented in Section 10.5, to define the language of this chapter. As with the simple imperative language, we will call this semantics *direct* to distinguish it from continuation semantics, which will be considered in the next chapter.

The extension from the lambda calculus to a full-blown functional language complicates denotational semantics for two reasons. The first reason is the possibility of error stops, which we will now distinguish from nontermination. For this purpose, we extend the domain of *results* (called D in Section 10.5) to contain, in addition to the predomain V of *values* and the undefined result $\bot$, two elements, **typeerror** and **error**, which denote the results of computations that are terminated by error stops. We write

$$V_* = (V + \{\textbf{error}, \textbf{typeerror}\})_\bot$$

for this domain of results, and we define the injection

$$\iota_{\text{norm}} = \iota_\uparrow \cdot \iota_0 \in V \to V_*$$

and two constants

$$\text{err} = \iota_\uparrow(\iota_1 \, \textbf{error})$$

$$\text{tyerr} = \iota_\uparrow(\iota_1 \, \textbf{typeerror}).$$

We also define an appropriate notion of function extension: If $f \in V \to V_*$, then $f_* \in V_* \to V_*$ is the extension of f that preserves error stops and $\bot$:

$$f_*(\iota_{\text{norm}} \, z) = f \, z$$

$$f_*(\text{err}) = \text{err}$$

$$f_*(\text{tyerr}) = \text{tyerr}$$

$$f_*(\bot) = \bot.$$

The distinction here between two kinds of error stops anticipates the introduction of type systems. At present we will use **typeerror** for errors that can be detected by type checking, such as using **true** as an operand of addition, but **error** for errors that cannot be detected during compilation, such as division by zero. Eventually, when we consider the semantics of type systems in Section 15.4, we will show that no well-typed expression gives the result **typeerror**.

(Of course, it would also be possible to give a simpler denotational semantics that, like the evaluation semantics of Section 11.2, equates error stops with nontermination. In fact, such a semantics can be obtained from what follows by reinterpreting V_* as $V_\bot$, ι_{norm} as $\iota_\uparrow$, err and tyerr as $\bot$, and f_* as $f_{\bot\bot}$.)

The second complication in our language is that the set of values now forms a predomain (rather than a domain) that is isomorphic to a disjoint union over five different kinds (or run-time types) of values. Specifically, the predomain V of values for the eager language satisfies the isomorphism

$$V \xrightarrow[\psi]{\phi} V_{\text{int}} + V_{\text{bool}} + V_{\text{fun}} + V_{\text{tuple}} + V_{\text{alt}},$$

where

$$V_{\text{int}} = \mathbf{Z}$$

$$V_{\text{bool}} = \mathbf{B}$$

$$V_{\text{fun}} = V \to V_*$$

$$V_{\text{tuple}} = V^* = \bigcup_{n=0}^{\infty} V^n$$

$$V_{\text{alt}} = \mathbf{N} \times V.$$

(Here, V_{tuple} is ordered like a disjoint union of n-ary products, so that tuples of different lengths never approximate one another.) To deal with this disjoint union $V_{\text{int}} + \cdots + V_{\text{alt}}$ succinctly, we define the injections

$$\iota_{\text{int}} = \psi \cdot \iota_0 \in V_{\text{int}} \to V$$

$$\iota_{\text{bool}} = \psi \cdot \iota_1 \in V_{\text{bool}} \to V$$

$$\iota_{\text{fun}} = \psi \cdot \iota_2 \in V_{\text{fun}} \to V$$

$$\iota_{\text{tuple}} = \psi \cdot \iota_3 \in V_{\text{tuple}} \to V$$

$$\iota_{\text{alt}} = \psi \cdot \iota_4 \in V_{\text{alt}} \to V.$$

We also need to define a general notation for extending functions on particular types of values to functions on arbitrary values. For this purpose, we use the variable θ, often with subscripts, to range over the set

$$\{\text{int}, \text{bool}, \text{fun}, \text{tuple}, \text{alt}\}.$$

Then, when $f \in V_\theta \to V_*$, we write f_θ for the function in $V \to V_*$ such that

$$f_\theta(\iota_\theta x) = f\, x \tag{11.1}$$

for $x \in V_\theta$, and

$$f_\theta\, z = \text{tyerr}$$

when z is not in the range of ι_θ. (It is the functions defined by this extension that will perform most of the run-time type checking in our definition.)

Frequently we will need to extend a function from $V_\theta \to V_*$ to $V_* \to V_*$ by applying first $(-)_\theta$ and then $(-)_*$. For this purpose, it is useful to introduce the abbreviation

$$f_{\theta*} = (f_\theta)_*.$$

Now we can define the semantic function. Let

$$E = \langle \text{var} \rangle \to V$$

be the predomain of *environments*. Then

$$[\![-]\!] \in \langle \text{exp} \rangle \to (E \to V_*).$$

Within the semantic equations for this function, the following variables, with occasional primes and subscripts, will have the following ranges:

e	$\langle \text{exp} \rangle$		i	$V_{\text{int}} = \mathbf{Z}$
v	$\langle \text{var} \rangle$		b	$V_{\text{bool}} = \mathbf{B}$
η	E		f	$V_{\text{fun}} = V \to V_*$
z	V		t	$V_{\text{tuple}} = V^*.$
k, n	$\mathbf{N}$			

We begin our tour of the semantic equations with the equations for explicitly indicated errors:

DR SEM EQ: Errors

$$[\![\mathbf{error}]\!] \eta = \text{err}$$

$$[\![\mathbf{typeerror}]\!] \eta = \text{tyerr}.$$

Then, for arithmetic constants and operations we have

DR SEM EQ: Constants

$$[\![\lfloor k \rfloor]\!] \eta = \iota_{\text{norm}}(\iota_{\text{int}} \, k),$$

DR SEM EQ: Unary Operations

$$[\![-e]\!] \eta = (\lambda i. \, \iota_{\text{norm}}(\iota_{\text{int}}(-i)))_{\text{int}*}([\![e]\!] \eta),$$

DR SEM EQ: Binary Operations

$$[\![e + e']\!] \eta = (\lambda i. \, (\lambda i'. \, \iota_{\text{norm}}(\iota_{\text{int}}(i + i')))_{\text{int}*}([\![e']\!] \eta))_{\text{int}*}([\![e]\!] \eta).$$

Notice that, in the last equation, the extensions make it clear that nontermination and (run-time) type checking of the first operand take precedence over nontermination and type checking of the second operand. For example, if $[\![e]\!] \eta = \bot$, then $[\![e + \mathbf{true}]\!] \eta = \bot$ but $[\![\mathbf{true} + e]\!] \eta = \text{tyerr}$.

The remaining arithmetic and logical operations are treated similarly, except for the complication of division (and remainder) by zero:

DR SEM EQ: Division

$$[\![e \div e']\!]\eta$$
$$= (\lambda i.\ (\lambda i'.\ \textbf{if}\ i' = 0\ \textbf{then}\ \mathrm{err}\ \textbf{else}\ \iota_{\mathrm{norm}}(\iota_{\mathrm{int}}(i \div i')))_{\mathrm{int}*}([\![e']\!]\eta))_{\mathrm{int}*}([\![e]\!]\eta).$$

Conditional expressions are described by

DR SEM EQ: Conditional Expressions

$$[\![\textbf{if}\ e\ \textbf{then}\ e'\ \textbf{else}\ e'']\!]\eta = (\lambda b.\ \textbf{if}\ b\ \textbf{then}\ [\![e']\!]\eta\ \textbf{else}\ [\![e'']\!]\eta)_{\mathrm{bool}*}([\![e]\!]\eta).$$

For the lambda-calculus part of the language, we have

DR SEM EQ: Variables

$$[\![v]\!]\eta = \iota_{\mathrm{norm}}(\eta v),$$

DR SEM EQ: Application

$$[\![ee']\!]\eta = (\lambda f.\ (\lambda z.\ f\ z)_*([\![e']\!]\eta))_{\mathrm{fun}*}([\![e]\!]\eta),$$

DR SEM EQ: Abstraction

$$[\![\lambda v.\ e]\!]\eta = \iota_{\mathrm{norm}}(\iota_{\mathrm{fun}}(\lambda z.\ [\![e]\!][\,\eta\mid v{:}\,z\,])).$$

Notice that, in the second equation, errors and nontermination are treated the same way as with arithmetic operations, except that z can be any type of value.

The value of a tuple is a sequence in V^*. Thus the construction and analysis of tuples are described by

DR SEM EQ: Tuples

$$[\![\langle e_0,\ \ldots,\ e_{n-1}\rangle]\!]\eta$$
$$= (\lambda z_0.\ \cdots (\lambda z_{n-1}.\ \iota_{\mathrm{norm}}(\iota_{\mathrm{tuple}}\langle z_0,\ \ldots,\ z_{n-1}\rangle))_*([\![e_{n-1}]\!]\eta)\ \cdots)_*([\![e_0]\!]\eta)$$

$$[\![e.\lfloor k\rfloor]\!]\eta$$
$$= (\lambda t.\ \textbf{if}\ k \in \mathrm{dom}\ t\ \textbf{then}\ \iota_{\mathrm{norm}}(t_k)\ \textbf{else}\ \mathrm{tyerr})_{\mathrm{tuple}*}([\![e]\!]\eta).$$

On the other hand, the value of an alternative construction @ $k\ e$ is simply the tag k paired with the value of e, so that

DR SEM EQ: Alternatives

$$[\![@\ \lfloor k\rfloor\ e]\!]\eta = (\lambda z.\ \iota_{\mathrm{norm}}(\iota_{\mathrm{alt}}\langle k,\ z\rangle))_*([\![e]\!]\eta)$$

$$[\![\textbf{sumcase}\ e\ \textbf{of}\ (e_0,\ \ldots,\ e_{n-1})]\!]\eta$$
$$= (\lambda\langle k, z\rangle.\ \textbf{if}\ k < n\ \textbf{then}\ (\lambda f.\ f\ z)_{\mathrm{fun}*}([\![e_k]\!]\eta)\ \textbf{else}\ \mathrm{tyerr})_{\mathrm{alt}*}([\![e]\!]\eta).$$

Earlier in this chapter, we defined nonrecursive definitions, patterns, and list-processing operations as abbreviations, so that any expression containing these constructions could be desugared into an equivalent expression where they are absent. Since this process is indifferent to the semantics given to desugared expressions, it is just as applicable to denotational as operational semantics, so that we need not give semantic equations for these constructions.

What remains are recursive definitions, whose semantics depends on the least fixed-point theorem of Section 2.4, but in a somewhat complicated way that is characteristic of eager evaluation. To understand the details, we first consider a **letrec** expression defining a single recursive function. We expect that the meaning of this expression in an environment η will be the meaning of its body in an extended environment η':

$$[\![\textbf{letrec } v_0 \equiv \lambda u_0.\ e_0 \textbf{ in } e]\!]\eta = [\![e]\!]\eta',$$

where η' should be similar to η, except that it maps the variable v_0 into the meaning of $\lambda u_0.\ e_0$ in η':

$$\eta' = [\,\eta \mid v_0 \colon [\![\lambda u_0.\ e_0]\!]\eta'\,].$$

Notice that, by using η' rather than η on the right side of this equation, we express the basic concept of recursion, which is that the free occurrences of v_0 in $\lambda u_0.\ e_0$ stand for the meaning of the function being defined.

Unfortunately, the above equation does not make sense, since η' must map v_0 into a value in V, but $[\![\lambda u_0.\ e_0]\!]\eta'$ is a result in V_*. From the semantic equation for abstractions, however,

$$[\![\lambda u_0.\ e_0]\!]\eta' = \iota_{\mathrm{norm}}(\iota_{\mathrm{fun}}(\lambda z.\ [\![e_0]\!][\,\eta' \mid u_0 \colon z\,])),$$

we find that the right side is obtained by applying the injection ι_{norm} to a value. By mapping v_0 into this value, we obtain the sensible equation

$$\eta' = [\,\eta \mid v_0 \colon \iota_{\mathrm{fun}}(\lambda z.\ [\![e_0]\!][\,\eta' \mid u_0 \colon z\,])\,]. \tag{11.2}$$

(Notice that the above argument depends critically on the fact that $\lambda u_0.\ e_0$ is an abstraction, which is an expression that always evaluates to a function without giving nontermination or an error. This is the real reason why recursive definitions in an eager-evaluation language are limited to the definition of functions.)

In essence, we have defined recursion in our object language by means of a recursive equation for the environment η' in the metalanguage. One can show that the right side of this equation is a continuous function of η'. Unfortunately, however, one cannot use the least fixed-point theorem directly to describe η'. The difficulty is that the set E of environments is a predomain, but not a domain. In particular, there is no least environment $\perp_E$, so that $\mathbf{Y}_E F = \bigsqcup_{n=0}^{\infty} F^n \perp_E$ makes no sense.

To see the way around this complication, let $f_0 \in V_{\text{fun}} = V \to V_*$ be the function

$$f_0 = \lambda z.\ [\![e_0]\!][\eta' \mid u_0\colon z],$$

so that

$$\eta' = [\eta \mid v_0\colon \iota_{\text{fun}} f_0]. \tag{11.3}$$

By substituting the last equation into the previous one we obtain

$$f_0 = \lambda z.\ [\![e_0]\!][\eta \mid v_0\colon \iota_{\text{fun}} f_0 \mid u_0\colon z], \tag{11.4}$$

which describes f_0 as the fixed point of a continuous function from V_{fun} to V_{fun}. But V_{fun} is a domain, so that now we can use the least fixed-point theorem to obtain

$$f_0 = \mathbf{Y}_{V_{\text{fun}}}(\lambda f.\ \lambda z.\ [\![e_0]\!][\eta \mid v_0\colon \iota_{\text{fun}} f \mid u_0\colon z]). \tag{11.5}$$

One can give an operational argument based on depth of recursion, which is similar to the argument in Section 2.4 based on the number of iterations, that justifies choosing f_0 to be the least of the solutions of Equation (11.4).

(It can be shown that the environment η' defined by Equations (11.3) and (11.5) is the least solution of Equation (11.2). But it is f_0 rather than η that can be obtained by applying the operator $\mathbf{Y}\,F = \bigsqcup_{n=0}^{\infty} F^n \bot$.)

The generalization to multiple recursion is straightforward:

DR SEM EQ: Recursion

$$[\![\textbf{letrec}\ v_0 \equiv \lambda u_0.\ e_0,\ \ldots,\ v_{n-1} \equiv \lambda u_{n-1}.\ e_{n-1}\ \textbf{in}\ e]\!]\eta = [\![e]\!]\eta',$$

where η' is the least solution of

$$\eta' = [\eta \mid v_0\colon \iota_{\text{fun}} f_0 \mid \ldots \mid v_{n-1}\colon \iota_{\text{fun}} f_{n-1}]$$
$$f_0 = \lambda z.\ [\![e_0]\!][\eta' \mid u_0\colon z]$$
$$\vdots$$
$$f_{n-1} = \lambda z.\ [\![e_{n-1}]\!][\eta' \mid u_{n-1}\colon z].$$

(To use the least fixed-point theorem, one must convert the above equations into a straightforward but lengthy equation for the n-tuple $\langle f_0, \ldots, f_{n-1} \rangle$, which belongs to the domain V_{fun}^n.)

The definition of a functional language that we have given in this section is typical of the earliest applications of denotational semantics to programming languages, which occurred in the early 1970's and constituted a major breakthrough in the art of defining languages. Prior to this work, functional languages were defined operationally, by definitions along the lines of the first-order semantics we will describe in Section 12.4. It was immediately apparent that, in contrast to operational definitions, denotational semantics directly captured the information-hiding properties of functional values that are the essence of functional programming.

Consider, for example,

$$\lambda x.\, x + 2$$

$$\lambda y.\, y + 2$$

$$\lambda x.\, x + 1 + 1$$

$$\lambda x.\ \textbf{if}\ x = 0\ \textbf{then}\ 2\ \textbf{else}\ x + 1 + 1,$$

or even

> **letrec** f $\equiv \lambda$x.
>
> > **if** x = 0 **then** 2 **else if** x > 0 **then** f(x − 1) + 1 **else** f(x + 1) − 1
>
> **in** f.

Since these expressions denote the same "mathematical" function, one expects that their differences will be hidden, so that (except for considerations of execution time and storage requirements) they can be used interchangeably. (In the terminology of logic, one expects functions to behave extensionally.)

In the semantics of this section (or in the continuation semantics to be presented in Section 12.1), these expressions have the same meaning. Thus, since the semantics is compositional, one can interchange these expressions whenever they occur as subphrases of a larger context, without changing the meaning of the larger context. Notice that this fact depends on the semantic equations for the subphrases of the expressions, and on the general property of compositionality, but not on any semantic equations for language constructs that do not occur in the expressions, but may occur in the larger context.

In contrast, in the evaluation semantics of Section 11.2 (or the first-order semantics to be given in Section 12.4), the above expressions do not have the same meaning, nor are these semantics compositional. Thus, to show that one can interchange the expressions in a larger context, one must take into account the semantics of every language construct that might occur in the context.

In fact, some early languages based on interpreters, such as Lisp, permitted contexts that distinguish between the "functions" defined by the expressions displayed above. Such a design flaw is hard to see from the interpreter, which is really a kind of operational semantics, but it becomes obvious when one tries to define the language denotationally (or when one tries to construct a compiler for the language).

11.7 Dynamic Binding

In the previous section, we gave the following semantic equations for application and abstraction:

$$\llbracket ee' \rrbracket \eta = (\lambda f. \, (\lambda z. \, f \, z)_* (\llbracket e' \rrbracket \eta))_{\text{fun}*}(\llbracket e \rrbracket \eta)$$

$$\llbracket \lambda v. \, e \rrbracket \eta = \iota_{\text{norm}}(\iota_{\text{fun}}(\lambda z. \, \llbracket e \rrbracket [\, \eta \mid v\!: z \,])).$$

According to these equations, when the operator in an application evaluates to the value of an abstraction (even when the abstraction occurs in a different part of the program), the body of the abstraction is evaluated in an environment that extends the environment used to evaluate the abstraction. In an alternative approach called *dynamic binding*, this environment is an extension of the environment used to evaluate the application. To describe this alternative in direct semantics, we must alter both the above equations and the domain V_{fun}:

$$V_{\text{fun}} = V \to E \to V_*$$

$$\llbracket ee' \rrbracket \eta = (\lambda f. \, (\lambda z. \, f \, z \, \eta)_* (\llbracket e' \rrbracket \eta))_{\text{fun}*}(\llbracket e \rrbracket \eta)$$

$$\llbracket \lambda v. \, e \rrbracket \eta = \iota_{\text{norm}}(\iota_{\text{fun}}(\lambda z. \, \lambda \eta'. \, \llbracket e \rrbracket [\, \eta' \mid v\!: z \,])).$$

Dynamic binding was used in several early languages, including Snobol and APL, both of which required dynamic binding, and Lisp, which permitted either dynamic or ordinary binding (which is sometimes called *static* binding). It is even employed in a few more recent systems such as the macro facility of TEX. Nowadays, however, it is widely and unequivocally regarded as a design error.

To see why, consider

$$\llbracket (\lambda x'. \, x' \, 3)(\lambda y. \, y + x) \rrbracket [\, \eta \mid x\!: \iota_{\text{int}} \, 1 \,],$$

where y is an identifier that is distinct from x or x'. From the semantic equations for dynamic binding, one finds that the above expression equals

$$\llbracket y + x \rrbracket [\, \eta \mid x\!: \iota_{\text{int}} \, 1 \mid x'\!: \iota_{\text{fun}}(\lambda z. \, \lambda \eta'. \, \llbracket y + x \rrbracket [\, \eta' \mid y\!: z \,]) \mid y\!: \iota_{\text{int}} \, 3 \,],$$

which gives the integer 4 (as would ordinary binding) when x and x' are distinct identifiers, but gives a type error when these identifiers are the same.

This demonstrates that dynamic binding violates the principle that renaming (of $\lambda x'. \, x' \, 3$ in the example) should preserve meaning. The practical consequence in languages such as Lisp is that, in certain contexts, the programmer is forced to invent obscure bound variables that (one hopes) will not be used accidentally elsewhere in the program. The author vividly remembers that, in the original Lisp I system, the lambda expression for the function maplist (actually, the expression on the property list of the atom maplist) began (in our notation)

$$\lambda\langle\text{verylongatomunlikelytobeusedbyprogrammer1},$$

$$\text{verylongatomunlikelytobeusedbyprogrammer2}\rangle.\ \cdots.$$

Similar difficulties motivated the provision of underscored variables in APL and private control symbols (e.g. containing the character @) in T_EX.

Bibliographic Notes

Untyped functional languages using eager evaluation (and extended to include imperative operations, as discussed in Chapter 13, and sometimes continuations as values, as discussed in Section 12.2) have a long history. The earliest such language (despite its mistreatment of variable binding) was LISP (for LISt Processor) [McCarthy, 1960; McCarthy et al., 1962]. Then, the late 1960's saw the design of several more theoretical languages: ISWIM (for "If you See What I Mean") [Landin, 1966c], PAL (for "Pedagogic Algorithmic Language") [Evans, 1968], and Gedanken [Reynolds, 1970]. But the first such language to achieve both theoretical cleanliness and a reasonably efficient implementation was Scheme [Sussman and Steele Jr., 1975].

There are also typed languages whose functional sublanguages use eager evaluation. The best known examples are Algol 68 [van Wijngaarden et al., 1969; 1975] and, more recently, Standard ML [Milner, Tofte, and Harper, 1990; Milner and Tofte, 1991; Ullman, 1994; Paulson, 1996].

Shortly after Scott [1970] formulated the concept of a domain, he and Strachey [1971] showed how the concept could be used to provide denotational semantics. The next few years saw elaborate denotational definitions of such languages as Algol 60 by Mosses [1974], Algol 68 by Milne [1974], and PL/I by a group of researchers at the IBM Vienna Laboratory [Bekić et al., 1974]. A more modest and readable example was the definition of Gedanken by Tennent [1976].

Patterns were introduced in the language Hope [Burstall, MacQueen, and Sannella, 1980] and play a major role in Standard ML. They have been extended to deal with alternatives as well as tuples by Kesner, Puel, and Tannen [1996].

Textbooks on functional programming include Henderson [1980], Field and Harrison [1988], Bird and Wadler [1988], and Reade [1989]. A variety of papers on implementation issues may be found in Lee [1991].

Exercises

11.1   Extend the evaluation semantics of Section 11.2 to describe the treatment of errors. This can be done by allowing expressions to evaluate to **error** and **typeerror** as well as to canonical forms. For binary arithmetic and logical operations, for example, one would introduce the following additional rules to describe the error-checking of operands:

$$\frac{e \Rightarrow \lfloor i \rfloor \qquad e' \Rightarrow \lfloor 0 \rfloor}{e \text{ op } e' \Rightarrow \textbf{error}} \qquad \text{when op} \in \{\div, \textbf{rem}\}$$

$$\frac{e \Rightarrow z}{e \text{ op } e' \Rightarrow \textbf{typeerror}} \qquad \begin{array}{l} \text{when } z \notin \langle\text{intcfm}\rangle \text{ and} \\ \text{op} \in \{+, -, \times, \div, \textbf{rem}, =, \neq, <, \leq, >, \geq\} \end{array}$$

$$\frac{e \Rightarrow \lfloor i \rfloor \qquad e' \Rightarrow z'}{e \text{ op } e' \Rightarrow \textbf{typeerror}} \qquad \begin{array}{l} \text{when } z' \notin \langle\text{intcfm}\rangle \text{ and} \\ \text{op} \in \{+, -, \times, \div, \textbf{rem}, =, \neq, <, \leq, >, \geq\} \end{array}$$

$$\frac{e \Rightarrow z}{e \text{ op } e' \Rightarrow \textbf{typeerror}} \qquad \begin{array}{l} \text{when } z \notin \langle\text{boolcfm}\rangle \text{ and} \\ \text{op} \in \{\wedge, \vee, \Rightarrow, \Leftrightarrow\} \end{array}$$

$$\frac{e \Rightarrow \lfloor b \rfloor \qquad e' \Rightarrow z'}{e \text{ op } e' \Rightarrow \textbf{typeerror}} \qquad \begin{array}{l} \text{when } z' \notin \langle\text{boolcfm}\rangle \text{ and} \\ \text{op} \in \{\wedge, \vee, \Rightarrow, \Leftrightarrow\}, \end{array}$$

plus the following rules to describe the propagation of errors:

$$\frac{e \Rightarrow \varepsilon}{e \text{ op } e' \Rightarrow \varepsilon} \qquad \begin{array}{l} \text{when } \varepsilon \in \{\textbf{error}, \textbf{typeerror}\} \text{ and} \\ \text{op} \in \{+, -, \times, \div, \textbf{rem}, \\ \qquad\quad =, \neq, <, \leq, >, \geq, \wedge, \vee, \Rightarrow, \Leftrightarrow\} \end{array}$$

$$\frac{e \Rightarrow \lfloor i \rfloor \qquad e' \Rightarrow \varepsilon}{e \text{ op } e' \Rightarrow \varepsilon} \qquad \begin{array}{l} \text{when } \varepsilon \in \{\textbf{error}, \textbf{typeerror}\} \text{ and} \\ \text{op} \in \{+, -, \times, \div, \textbf{rem}, =, \neq, <, \leq, >, \geq\} \end{array}$$

$$\frac{e \Rightarrow \lfloor b \rfloor \qquad e' \Rightarrow \varepsilon}{e \text{ op } e' \Rightarrow \varepsilon} \qquad \begin{array}{l} \text{when } \varepsilon \in \{\textbf{error}, \textbf{typeerror}\} \text{ and} \\ \text{op} \in \{\wedge, \vee, \Rightarrow, \Leftrightarrow\}. \end{array}$$

(Notice that the range of the metavariable z includes canonical forms but not **error** or **typeerror**.) To coincide with the denotational semantics in Section 11.6, your rules should describe a regime where each subexpression is completely checked before the next subexpression is evaluated. Thus, for example,

$$\textbf{true} \div e \Rightarrow \textbf{typeerror},$$

even when the subexpression e fails to terminate, evaluates to **error**, or evaluates to zero.

11.2   As in Exercise 11.1, extend evaluation semantics to describe the treatment of errors, but now describe a regime where, except in conditional expressions, all subexpressions are evaluated (from left to right) before the run-time type of any subexpression is checked. Thus, for example, **true** $\div e$ should evaluate to **error** or fail to terminate if e does so, and should only evaluate to **typeerror** otherwise.

11.3   Revise the denotational semantics in Section 11.6 to reflect the evaluation regime described in Exercise 11.2.

This is a surprisingly tricky problem. To keep it tractable, it is useful to define extensions of curried functions of several arguments. When

$$f \in \underbrace{V \to \cdots \to V}_{n \text{ times}} \to V_*,$$

let f_{*n} be the function

$$f_{*n} \in \underbrace{V_* \to \cdots \to V_*}_{n \text{ times}} \to V_*$$

such that

$$f_{*n}(\iota_{\text{norm}} z_0) \cdots (\iota_{\text{norm}} z_{n-1}) = f z_0 \cdots z_{n-1}$$

and, for $k < n$,

$$f_{*n}(\iota_{\text{norm}} z_0) \cdots (\iota_{\text{norm}} z_{k-1})(\text{err}) \, x_{k+1} \cdots x_{n-1} = \text{err}$$

$$f_{*n}(\iota_{\text{norm}} z_0) \cdots (\iota_{\text{norm}} z_{k-1})(\text{tyerr}) \, x_{k+1} \cdots x_{n-1} = \text{tyerr}$$

$$f_{*n}(\iota_{\text{norm}} z_0) \cdots (\iota_{\text{norm}} z_{k-1}) \perp x_{k+1} \cdots x_{n-1} = \perp.$$

In essence, the result of f_{*n} is the same as the result of f, unless some argument is an error or $\perp$, in which case the result is the first such argument.

A similar notation is useful for extending functions on particular types of values to functions on arbitrary values. When

$$f \in V_{\theta_0} \to \cdots \to V_{\theta_{n-1}} \to V_*,$$

let $f_{\theta_0,\ldots,\theta_{n-1}}$ be the function

$$f_{\theta_0,\ldots,\theta_{n-1}} \in V \to \cdots \to V \to V_*$$

such that

$$f_{\theta_0,\ldots,\theta_{n-1}}(\iota_{\theta_0} x_0) \cdots (\iota_{\theta_{n-1}} x_{n-1}) = f x_0 \cdots x_{n-1}$$

and

$$f_{\theta_0,\ldots,\theta_{n-1}} z_0 \cdots z_{n-1} = \text{tyerr}$$

whenever some z_k is not in the range of ι_{θ_k}. (It is also useful to generalize this extension by allowing the θ_k to take the value "all", with V_{all} defined to be V and ι_{all} defined to be the identity function on V.)

11.4   In place of numbered tuples many programming languages use named tuples, often called *records* or (roughly speaking) *objects*. (In Section 16.2, we will find that named tuples, and also named sums, lead to a richer subtyping discipline than numbered tuples.)

An appropriate abstract syntax for named tuples is

$$\langle \text{exp} \rangle ::= \langle \langle \text{id} \rangle \equiv \langle \text{exp} \rangle, \dots, \langle \text{id} \rangle \equiv \langle \text{exp} \rangle \rangle \mid \langle \text{exp} \rangle.\langle \text{tag} \rangle$$

$$\langle \text{tag} \rangle ::= \langle \text{id} \rangle$$

$$\langle \text{tuplecfm} \rangle ::= \langle \langle \text{id} \rangle \equiv \langle \text{cfm} \rangle, \dots, \langle \text{id} \rangle \equiv \langle \text{cfm} \rangle \rangle$$

where $\langle \text{id} \rangle$ denotes a predefined set of *identifiers*, and the identifiers ι_0, $\dots, \iota_{n-1}$ in $\iota_0 \equiv e_0, \dots, \iota_{n-1} \equiv e_{n-1}$ must be distinct. For example, $\langle \text{real} \equiv 10, \text{imag} \equiv 20 \rangle$ denotes a two-field tuple where the field named real is 10 and the field named imag is 20; if x is such a tuple, then x.real and x.imag denote its fields. The inference rules for evaluation are

EV RULE: Named Tuples

$$\frac{e_0 \Rightarrow z_0 \quad \cdots \quad e_{n-1} \Rightarrow z_{n-1}}{\langle \iota_0 \equiv e_0, \dots, \iota_{n-1} \equiv e_{n-1} \rangle \Rightarrow \langle \iota_0 \equiv z_0, \dots, \iota_{n-1} \equiv z_{n-1} \rangle}$$

$$\frac{e \Rightarrow \langle \iota_0 \equiv z_0, \dots, \iota_{n-1} \equiv z_{n-1} \rangle}{e.\iota_k \Rightarrow z_k} \qquad \text{when } k < n.$$

In the direct denotational semantics, the predomain V_{tuple} of tuple values is the union, over all finite sets F of identifiers, of the sets of functions from F to V:

$$V_{\text{tuple}} = \bigcup \{ V^F \mid F \overset{\text{fin}}{\subseteq} \langle \text{id} \rangle \},$$

and the relevant semantic equations are

DR SEM EQ: Named Tuples

$$[\![\langle \iota_0 \equiv e_0, \dots, \iota_{n-1} \equiv e_{n-1} \rangle]\!] \eta$$
$$= (\lambda z_0. \ \cdots$$
$$\qquad (\lambda z_{n-1}. \ \iota_{\text{norm}}(\iota_{\text{tuple}}[\iota_0{:}\, z_0 \mid \dots \mid \iota_{n-1}{:}\, z_{n-1}]))_* ([\![e_{n-1}]\!] \eta)$$
$$\cdots)_* ([\![e_0]\!] \eta)$$

$$[\![e.\iota]\!] \eta = (\lambda t. \ \textbf{if } \iota \in \text{dom}\, t \ \textbf{then } \iota_{\text{norm}}(t\, \iota) \ \textbf{else } \text{tyerr})_{\text{tuple}*} ([\![e]\!] \eta).$$

Notice that, if all of its subexpressions terminate without errors, the meaning of a named tuple will be independent of the order of its fields, since no selection operation will distinguish between, for example, $\langle \text{real} \equiv 10, \text{imag} \equiv 20 \rangle$ and $\langle \text{imag} \equiv 20, \text{real} \equiv 10 \rangle$.

Now assume that identifiers and variables are the same thing, so that $\langle \text{id} \rangle$ and $\langle \text{var} \rangle$ are the same predefined set. Describe an extension of the language with named tuples to include an expression **open** e **in** e'. If, in an environment η, the expression e has the value $\langle \iota_0 \equiv z_0, \dots, \iota_{n-1} \equiv z_{n-1} \rangle$, then the value of **open** e **in** e' in η should be the value of e' in the environment that is like η, except that it maps ι_i into z_i for each i from zero to $n-1$. (If the value of e is not a tuple, the **open** expression should give a type error.)

For example, the value of

let r $\equiv \langle$ y $\equiv 1,$ z $\equiv 10 \rangle$, x $\equiv 100$, y $\equiv 1000$ **in open** r **in** x $+$ y $+$ z

should be 111.

Specifically, you should give the following for the **open** construct:

(a) an abstract grammar production,

(b) an inference rule for eager evaluation, as in Section 11.2,

(c) a semantic equation for the direct denotational semantics, as in Section 11.6.

11.5 Using the inference rules for evaluation in Section 11.2, derive the rules for evaluating list operations in Section 11.4 from the definition of these lists as syntactic sugar. (Note that you will first have to desugar the patterns in the definition of **listcase**, by using the definitions in Section 11.3.)

11.6 The evaluation rule for a binary arithmetic operation e op e',

$$\frac{e \Rightarrow \lfloor i \rfloor \qquad e' \Rightarrow \lfloor i' \rfloor}{e \text{ op } e' \Rightarrow \lfloor i \text{ op } i' \rfloor,}$$

makes it clear that the subexpressions e and e' can be evaluated in parallel, without introducing nondeterminacy (provided that error stops are equated with nontermination) and without the "speculative" evaluation of expressions whose values may be unnecessary.

(a) Describe all of the opportunities for such determinate, nonspeculative parallelism that are evident from the evaluation semantics of Section 11.2.

(b) Describe informally several ways of handling errors during such parallel evaluation.

11.7   Let binary trees be defined as in Section 11.5. Let the *reduction* of a
        binary tree with respect to a function f and a function g be

   • If the tree is a terminal node labeled with the integer n, then $f\,n$.
   • If the main node of the tree is a nonterminal node with two subtrees,
     then $g\,r_l\,r_r$, where r_l and r_r are the reductions of the left and right
     subtrees with respect to the same functions.

   Then

   (a) Recursively define a function redtree such that redtree $t\,f\,g$ gives the
       reduction of the tree t with respect to the functions f and g.
   (b) Use redtree to give a nonrecursive definition of the function fringelist in
       Section 11.5. Your program should perform n cons operations (i.e. n
       of the operations ":") when applied to a tree with n terminal nodes,
       as does the second definition of fringelist in Section 11.5.

11.8   Consider the following variant of the function reduce (which was defined
        in Section 11.5):

   letrec lazyreduce $\equiv$

   λx. λf. λa. $\lambda\langle\rangle$. **listcase** x **of** $\left(\mathsf{a}\langle\rangle, \lambda\mathsf{i}.\ \lambda\mathsf{r}.\ \mathsf{f}\ \mathsf{i}\,(\mathsf{lazyreduce}\ \mathsf{r}\ \mathsf{f}\ \mathsf{a})\right)\ \cdots$.

   The result of lazyreduce x f a is a function (of the dummy argument $\langle\rangle$)
   that will not analyze the list x or make a recursive call of lazyreduce unless
   it is applied to an argument. Moreover, lazyreduce expects its argument **a**
   to be a function of a dummy argument, which will be evaluated only when
   x is an empty list. The advantage of lazyreduce is that it can be used to
   define functions on lists that sometimes give a result without inspecting
   the entire list.

   Let member be the function such that member m x gives **true** if the integer m occurs in the list x of integers, and **false** otherwise. Define member
   nonrecursively in terms of lazyreduce, in such a way that member m x does
   not search the entire list x when m occurs near the beginning of x.

11.9   Define the function eqlist of Section 11.5 that compares two lists of in-
        tegers for equality, in terms of the function reduce, which is also defined
        in Section 11.5. Your definition should express eqlist in terms of reduce
        nonrecursively (i.e. using **let** rather than **letrec**).
        Hint Take advantage of the fact that eqlist is curried, so that eqlist x is
        the function, mapping a list of integers into true or false, that compares
        its argument to the list x. Define eqlist to be λx. reduce x $(\cdots)\,(\cdots)$, where
        reduce x $(\cdots)\,(\cdots)$ gives the desired comparison function.

        Suppose the function you have defined is applied to two lists whose first
        elements are different. State how its execution time will depend on the
        lengths of these lists.

11.10 Show that the following expression behaves like the factorial function on nonnegative integers:

$$\textbf{let } f \equiv \lambda h.\ \lambda n.\ \textbf{if } n = 0 \textbf{ then } 1 \textbf{ else } n \times (h\ h\ (n-1)) \textbf{ in } f\ f.$$

This is an example of a nonrecursive definition achieving the effect of recursion through self-application.

11.11 A recursively defined function on the integers is said to *loop* if, during an application to an integer at some recursive level, there is a lower-level application to the same integer. Looping is one way (but not the only way) for a recursively defined function to run on forever.

Write a function loopcheck that checks for looping. Specifically, the function loopcheck should accept a function F from integer-accepting functions to integer-accepting functions, and should produce a function that computes the same result as does the least fixed-point f of F (i.e. the function that would be defined by **letrec** $f \equiv \lambda n.\ F\ f\ n$ **in** f), except that an application of loopcheck F will give an error stop when the application of f to the same argument would loop.

11.12 The direct denotational semantics of Section 11.6 is based on an isomorphism of predomains:

$$V \simeq \mathbf{Z} + \mathbf{B} + (V \to V_*) + \left(\sum_{n=0}^{\infty} V^n\right) + (N \times V),$$

where

$$V_* = (V + \{\textbf{error}, \textbf{typeerror}\})_\perp.$$

(Here we have used $\sum$ instead of $\bigcup$ to make the disjointness of the V^n more explicit.) But the standard construction for solving such isomorphisms works for domains rather than predomains.

This difficulty can be overcome by eliminating V and expressing the domain V_* as an isomorphism in terms of itself. To do so, one must use the *smash product* and *smash sum* (or *coalesced sum*) of domains:

$$D_0 \times_{\text{smash}} \cdots \times_{\text{smash}} D_{n-1} \stackrel{\text{def}}{=} ((D_0 - \perp_{D_0}) \times \cdots \times (D_{n-1} - \perp_{D_{n-1}}))_\perp$$

$$D_0 +_{\text{smash}} \cdots +_{\text{smash}} D_{n-1} \stackrel{\text{def}}{=} ((D_0 - \perp_{D_0}) + \cdots + (D_{n-1} - \perp_{D_{n-1}}))_\perp,$$

along with the domain of strict functions:

$$D \xrightarrow{\text{strict}} D' = \{\,f \mid f \in D \to D' \text{ and } f \perp = \perp\,\}$$

(with the same ordering as $D \to D'$). Fortunately, these operations are sufficiently well-behaved that the construction of the isomorphism goes through. (This would not be the case if we needed to use a "smash $\to$"

operation, which would happen if V_{fun} were $V \to V$ rather than $V \to V_*$. In this case, the isomorphism would have no solution.)

(a) Show the isomorphisms

$$(P_0 \times \cdots \times P_{n-1})_\perp \simeq (P_0)_\perp \times_{\text{smash}} \cdots \times_{\text{smash}} (P_{n-1})_\perp$$

$$(P_0 + \cdots + P_{n-1})_\perp \simeq (P_0)_\perp +_{\text{smash}} \cdots +_{\text{smash}} (P_{n-1})_\perp$$

$$P \to D \simeq P_\perp \xrightarrow{\text{strict}} D,$$

where the P_i are predomains and D is a domain.

(b) Use the above isomorphisms, along with the obvious analogues for "smash" versions of V^n and $\sum$, to obtain an isomorphism expressing V_* in terms of itself.

11.13 Describe failures of renaming, due to dynamic binding or other causes, in programming languages (or other formal languages that are used as input to computer systems) you are familiar with.

Continuations in a Functional Language

In this chapter, we introduce continuations into the setting of a functional language using eager evaluation. We begin by defining a continuation semantics for the language of the previous chapter. Next, we extend this language by introducing continuations as values. Finally, we derive a first-order semantics that reveals how one might implement the extended language interpretively.

12.1 Continuation Semantics

When the evaluation of an expression gives an error or fails to terminate, this "computational effect" is the final result of the entire program. In the direct denotational semantics of Section 11.6, this behavior is expressed by passing err, tyerr, or $\perp$ through a chain of *-extended functions that preserve these results.

An alternative approach is to use a continuation semantics, similar to the one discussed in Section 5.7, in which the semantic function, when applied to an expression e, an environment η, and a new argument κ called a *continuation*, produces the final result of the entire program in which e is embedded. If the evaluation of e gives a value, then the final result is obtained by applying κ to this value; but if the evaluation gives an error stop or fails to terminate (or executes a **throw** operation, which we will discuss in the next section), this result is produced directly without using the continuation. This makes it immediately evident that the "rest of the computation", which is represented by the continuation, has no effect on the final result. (We will use the metavariable κ, with occasional primes and subscripts, for continuations.)

Since continuations are functions from values to final results, the domain of continuations is

$$V_{\text{cont}} = V \to V_*.$$

(Our choice of the name V_{cont} anticipates the use of continuations as values, which will be explored in the next section.) Thus the new semantic function satisfies

$$[\![-]\!] \in \langle \text{exp} \rangle \to (E \to V_{\text{cont}} \to V_*).$$

There is one further change in the semantic domains. Since the values in V_{fun} are functions that may give an error stop or fail to terminate when applied to an argument, these functional values also accept a new argument that is a continuation, and their result is the final result of the program. Thus the domain V_{fun} of functional values is redefined to be

$$V_{\text{fun}} = V \to V_{\text{cont}} \to V_*.$$

The remaining semantic domains and predomains are defined in the same way as in the direct semantics of Section 11.6. The domain of results is

$$V_* = (V + \{\textbf{error}, \textbf{typeerror}\})_\perp,$$

with associated injections and constants

$$\iota_{\text{norm}} = \iota_\uparrow \cdot \iota_0 \in V \to V_*$$

$$\text{err} = \iota_\uparrow(\iota_1\,\textbf{error})$$

$$\text{tyerr} = \iota_\uparrow(\iota_1\,\textbf{typeerror}).$$

Also as in Section 11.6, the predomain of values satisfies the isomorphism

$$V \underset{\psi}{\overset{\phi}{\rightleftarrows}} V_{\text{int}} + V_{\text{bool}} + V_{\text{fun}} + V_{\text{tuple}} + V_{\text{alt}},$$

where all but the domain of functional values remain unchanged:

$$V_{\text{int}} = \mathbf{Z}$$

$$V_{\text{bool}} = \mathbf{B}$$

$$V_{\text{fun}} = V \to V_{\text{cont}} \to V_*$$

$$V_{\text{tuple}} = V^* = \bigcup_{n=0}^{\infty} V^n$$

$$V_{\text{alt}} = \mathbf{N} \times V.$$

As before, for $\theta \in \{\text{int}, \text{bool}, \text{fun}, \text{tuple}, \text{alt}\}$, we define ι_θ to be the obvious injection from V_θ to V, and when $f \in V_\theta \to V_*$ we define $f_\theta \in V \to V_*$ to be the extension such that

$$f_\theta(\iota_\theta x) = f\,x$$

for $x \in V_\theta$, and

$$f_\theta\,z = \text{tyerr}$$

when z is not in the range of ι_θ.

Having summarized the relevant domains and related entities, we turn to the semantic equations. Since the evaluation of **error** or **typeerror** always produces an error stop, regardless of the rest of the program, we have

CN SEM EQ: Errors

$$[\![\mathbf{error}]\!]\eta\kappa = \mathrm{err}$$

$$[\![\mathbf{typeerror}]\!]\eta\kappa = \mathrm{tyerr}.$$

At the opposite extreme, constants always give a value, which is passed to their continuation:

CN SEM EQ: Constants

$$[\![\lfloor k \rfloor]\!]\eta\kappa = \kappa(\iota_{\mathrm{int}} k).$$

The meaning of a unary operation such as negation is obtained by giving the meaning of the subexpression a new continuation that negates the value it receives, before passing it on to the original continuation:

CN SEM EQ: Unary Operations

$$[\![-e]\!]\eta\kappa = [\![e]\!]\eta\left(\lambda i.\ \kappa(\iota_{\mathrm{int}}(-i))\right)_{\mathrm{int}}.$$

Here, as is typical of continuation semantics, the check that the value of e is an integer is expressed by using $(\cdots)_{\mathrm{int}}$ to extend a function that accepts only integers into the continuation that accepts the value of the subexpression.

With binary operations, the left subexpression is evaluated with a continuation that evaluates the right subexpression, with a second continuation that carries out the binary operation and passes the result to the original continuation:

CN SEM EQ: Binary Operations

$$[\![e + e']\!]\eta\kappa = [\![e]\!]\eta\left(\lambda i.\ [\![e']\!]\eta\left(\lambda i'.\ \kappa(\iota_{\mathrm{int}}(i + i'))\right)_{\mathrm{int}}\right)_{\mathrm{int}},$$

CN SEM EQ: Division

$$[\![e \div e']\!]\eta\kappa = [\![e]\!]\eta\left(\lambda i.\ [\![e']\!]\eta\left(\lambda i'.\ \mathbf{if}\ i' = 0\ \mathbf{then}\ \mathrm{err}\ \mathbf{else}\ \kappa(\iota_{\mathrm{int}}(i \div i'))\right)_{\mathrm{int}}\right)_{\mathrm{int}}.$$

Notice that the fact that the subexpressions are evaluated from left to right is made far more obvious here than in direct denotational semantics or evaluation semantics.

For conditional expressions, the value of the first subexpression is passed to a continuation that evaluates one of the remaining subexpressions with the original continuation:

CN SEM EQ: Conditional Expressions

$$[\![\textbf{if } e \textbf{ then } e' \textbf{ else } e'']\!]\eta\kappa = [\![e]\!]\eta\,(\lambda b.\ \textbf{if } b \textbf{ then } [\![e']\!]\eta\kappa \textbf{ else } [\![e'']\!]\eta\kappa)_{\text{bool}}.$$

Variables, like constants, always produce values, which are passed to their continuation:

CN SEM EQ: Variables

$$[\![v]\!]\eta\kappa = \kappa(\eta v).$$

Function application uses continuations to express the order of evaluation in the same way as with binary arithmetic operations:

CN SEM EQ: Application

$$[\![ee']\!]\eta\kappa = [\![e]\!]\eta\,(\lambda f.\ [\![e']\!]\eta\,(\lambda z.\ f\,z\,\kappa))_{\text{fun}}.$$

Abstractions, also like constants, always produce values, which are passed to their continuation. But now, the value is a function that, when applied to an argument, accepts a second continuation κ', which receives the result of the function application and carries out the rest of the computation:

CN SEM EQ: Abstraction

$$[\![\lambda v.\ e]\!]\eta\kappa = \kappa(\iota_{\text{fun}}(\lambda z.\ \lambda\kappa'.\ [\![e]\!][\,\eta\mid v{:}z\,]\kappa')).$$

For an n-ary tuple constructor, n continuations are used to show that the subexpressions are evaluated from left to right:

CN SEM EQ: Tuples

$$[\![\langle e_0,\ \ldots,\ e_{n-1}\rangle]\!]\eta\kappa = [\![e_0]\!]\eta\,(\lambda z_0.\ \cdots$$
$$[\![e_{n-1}]\!]\eta\,(\lambda z_{n-1}.\ \kappa(\iota_{\text{tuple}}\langle z_0,\ \ldots,\ z_{n-1}\rangle))\cdots)$$

$$[\![e.\lfloor k\rfloor]\!]\eta\kappa = [\![e]\!]\eta\,(\lambda t.\ \textbf{if } k \in \text{dom}\,t \textbf{ then } \kappa(t_k) \textbf{ else } \text{tyerr})_{\text{tuple}}.$$

The continuation semantics for the remaining constructions of our language follows the same basic approach. For alternatives, we have

CN SEM EQ: Alternatives

$$[\![@\,\lfloor k\rfloor\,e]\!]\eta\kappa = [\![e]\!]\eta\,(\lambda z.\ \kappa(\iota_{\text{alt}}\langle k,z\rangle))$$

$$[\![\textbf{sumcase } e \textbf{ of } (e_0,\ \ldots,\ e_{n-1})]\!]\eta\kappa = [\![e]\!]\eta\,(\lambda\langle k,z\rangle.\ \textbf{if } k < n \textbf{ then}$$
$$[\![e_k]\!]\eta\,(\lambda f.\ f\,z\,\kappa)_{\text{fun}} \textbf{ else } \text{tyerr})_{\text{alt}}.$$

And, finally, for recursive function definitions we have

CN SEM EQ: Recursion

$$[\![\mathbf{letrec}\ v_0 \equiv \lambda u_0.\ e_0,\ \ldots\ ,v_{n-1} \equiv \lambda u_{n-1}.\ e_{n-1}\ \mathbf{in}\ e]\!]\eta\kappa = [\![e]\!]\eta'\kappa,$$

where the environment η' is the least solution of

$$\eta' = [\,\eta \mid v_0\colon \iota_{\mathrm{fun}} f_0 \mid \ldots \mid v_{n-1}\colon \iota_{\mathrm{fun}} f_{n-1}\,]$$
$$f_0 = \lambda z.\ \lambda\kappa'.\ [\![e_0]\!][\,\eta' \mid u_0\colon z\,]\kappa'$$
$$\vdots$$
$$f_{n_1} = \lambda z.\ \lambda\kappa'.\ [\![e_{n-1}]\!][\,\eta' \mid u_{n-1}\colon z\,]\kappa'.$$

To obtain the result of a complete program, the meaning of the program must be applied to an initial environment η_0 and an initial continuation κ_0. Since the latter will be used to map the value of the complete program into the final result, it should be the appropriate injection

$$\kappa_0 = \iota_{\mathrm{norm}}.$$

On the other hand, since a complete program will be a closed expression, its result will be independent of η_0, which can be any environment.

12.2 Continuations as Values

Many eager-evaluation functional languages, such as Scheme and some versions of ML, permit continuations to occur as values. It is easy to extend the continuation semantics of the previous section to encompass this feature.

The first step is to add the set of continuation values $V_{\mathrm{cont}} = V \to V_*$ as another alternative in the isomorphism for V:

$$V \underset{\psi}{\overset{\phi}{\rightleftarrows}} V_{\mathrm{int}} + V_{\mathrm{bool}} + V_{\mathrm{fun}} + V_{\mathrm{tuple}} + V_{\mathrm{alt}} + V_{\mathrm{cont}},$$

to define the injection

$$\iota_{\mathrm{cont}} = \psi \cdot \iota_5 \in V_{\mathrm{cont}} \to V,$$

and to add "cont" to the range of the metavariable θ, so that the extension $(-)_{\mathrm{cont}}$ from $V_{\mathrm{cont}} \to V_*$ to $V \to V_*$ is defined.

Then we introduce two new forms of expressions:

$$\langle\exp\rangle ::= \mathbf{callcc}\ \langle\exp\rangle \mid \mathbf{throw}\ \langle\exp\rangle\ \langle\exp\rangle$$

and define their continuation semantics by semantic equations. The expression **callcc** e (pronounced "call e with current continuation") evaluates e to obtain a function, and then applies this function to the current continuation (as well as giving the current continuation to the function as its continuation):

CN SEM EQ: **callcc**

$$[\![\textbf{callcc } e]\!]\eta\kappa = [\![e]\!]\eta\,(\lambda f.\ f\,(\iota_{\text{cont}}\,\kappa)\,\kappa)_{\text{fun}}.$$

The expression **throw** $e\ e'$ evaluates e to obtain a continuation and then evaluates e', giving it the continuation that is the value of e, rather than the continuation that is given to the **throw** expression itself:

CN SEM EQ: **throw**

$$[\![\textbf{throw } e\ e']\!]\eta\kappa = [\![e]\!]\eta\,(\lambda\kappa'.\ [\![e']\!]\eta\kappa')_{\text{cont}}.$$

Basically, the effect of evaluating **throw** $e\ e'$ is to make the value of e' the result of the **callcc** expression which introduced the continuation that is the value of e. As a simple example, the value of

$$\textbf{callcc }(\lambda\text{k}.\ 2 + \textbf{throw } \text{k}\,(3 \times 4))$$

is 12, which is obtained without executing the addition operation, as can be seen from the continuation semantic equations and Equation (11.1) in Section 11.6:

$$
\begin{aligned}
&[\![\textbf{callcc }(\lambda\text{k}.\ 2 + \textbf{throw } \text{k}\,(3\times 4))]\!]\eta\kappa\\
&= [\![\lambda\text{k}.\ 2 + \textbf{throw } \text{k}\,(3\times 4)]\!]\eta\,(\lambda f.\ f\,(\iota_{\text{cont}}\,\kappa)\,\kappa)_{\text{fun}}\\
&= (\lambda f.\ f\,(\iota_{\text{cont}}\,\kappa)\,\kappa)_{\text{fun}}(\iota_{\text{fun}}(\lambda z.\ \lambda\kappa'.\ [\![2 + \textbf{throw } \text{k}\,(3\times 4)]\!][\,\eta\mid \text{k}\!:\!z\,]\kappa'))\\
&= (\lambda z.\ \lambda\kappa'.\ [\![2 + \textbf{throw } \text{k}\,(3\times 4)]\!][\,\eta\mid \text{k}\!:\!z\,]\kappa')\,(\iota_{\text{cont}}\,\kappa)\,\kappa\\
&= [\![2 + \textbf{throw } \text{k}\,(3\times 4)]\!][\,\eta\mid \text{k}\!:\!\iota_{\text{cont}}\,\kappa\,]\kappa\\
&= [\![2]\!][\,\eta\mid \text{k}\!:\!\iota_{\text{cont}}\,\kappa\,]\,(\lambda i.\ [\![\textbf{throw } \text{k}\,(3\times 4)]\!][\,\eta\mid \text{k}\!:\!\iota_{\text{cont}}\,\kappa\,]\,(\lambda i'.\ \cdots)_{\text{int}})_{\text{int}}\\
&= (\lambda i.\ [\![\textbf{throw } \text{k}\,(3\times 4)]\!][\,\eta\mid \text{k}\!:\!\iota_{\text{cont}}\,\kappa\,]\,(\lambda i'.\ \cdots)_{\text{int}})_{\text{int}}(\iota_{\text{int}}\,2)\\
&= [\![\textbf{throw } \text{k}\,(3\times 4)]\!][\,\eta\mid \text{k}\!:\!\iota_{\text{cont}}\,\kappa\,]\,(\lambda i'.\ \cdots)_{\text{int}}\\
&= [\![\text{k}]\!][\,\eta\mid \text{k}\!:\!\iota_{\text{cont}}\,\kappa\,]\,(\lambda\kappa'.\ [\![3\times 4]\!][\,\eta\mid \text{k}\!:\!\iota_{\text{cont}}\,\kappa\,]\kappa')_{\text{cont}}\\
&= (\lambda\kappa'.\ [\![3\times 4]\!][\,\eta\mid \text{k}\!:\!\iota_{\text{cont}}\,\kappa\,]\kappa')_{\text{cont}}(\iota_{\text{cont}}\,\kappa)\\
&= [\![3\times 4]\!][\,\eta\mid \text{k}\!:\!\iota_{\text{cont}}\,\kappa\,]\kappa\\
&\ \ \vdots\\
&= \kappa\,(12).
\end{aligned}
$$

Less trivially, the following function computes the product of a list of integers, without performing any multiplications if the list contains zero:

$$
\begin{aligned}
&\textbf{let } \text{multlist} \equiv \lambda\text{x}.\ \textbf{callcc }(\lambda\text{k}.\\
&\quad\textbf{letrec } \text{mt} \equiv \lambda\text{x}.\ \textbf{listcase } \text{x } \textbf{of } (1,\\
&\quad\quad \lambda i.\ \lambda\text{r}.\ \textbf{if } i = 0 \textbf{ then throw } \text{k}\,0 \textbf{ else } i \times \text{mt r})\\
&\quad\textbf{in } \text{mt x})\ \cdots.
\end{aligned}
$$

This example shows the similarity between continuations and exceptions. As we will see in Section 13.7, however, there are significant differences between continuations and the kind of *dynamic* exception mechanism that is provided in many languages.

The use of continuations to skip part of the evaluation process is relatively straightforward. In more exotic usage, they can cause part of the evaluation to be repeated. In the following example, the continuation $(\lambda f.\ f(\iota_{\text{int}}6)\kappa)_{\text{fun}}$, which accepts the result of the **callcc** expression, is applied twice, to different functions:

$$
\begin{aligned}
&[\![\textbf{let } f \equiv \textbf{callcc } \lambda k.\ \lambda x.\ \textbf{throw } k\ (\lambda y.\ x+y) \textbf{ in } f\ 6]\!]\eta\kappa \\
&= [\![(\lambda f.\ f\ 6)(\textbf{callcc } \lambda k.\ \lambda x.\ \textbf{throw } k\ (\lambda y.\ x+y))]\!]\eta\kappa \\
&= [\![\textbf{callcc } \lambda k.\ \lambda x.\ \textbf{throw } k\ (\lambda y.\ x+y)]\!]\eta(\lambda f.\ f(\iota_{\text{int}}6)\kappa)_{\text{fun}} \\
&= [\![\lambda x.\ \textbf{throw } k\ (\lambda y.\ x+y)]\!][\,\eta \mid k\colon \iota_{\text{cont}}(\lambda f.\ f(\iota_{\text{int}}6)\kappa)_{\text{fun}}\,](\lambda f.\ f(\iota_{\text{int}}6)\kappa)_{\text{fun}} \\
&= [\![\textbf{throw } k\ (\lambda y.\ x+y)]\!][\,\eta \mid k\colon \iota_{\text{cont}}(\lambda f.\ f(\iota_{\text{int}}6)\kappa)_{\text{fun}} \mid x\colon \iota_{\text{int}}6\,]\kappa \\
&= [\![\lambda y.\ x+y]\!][\,\eta \mid k\colon \iota_{\text{cont}}(\lambda f.\ f(\iota_{\text{int}}6)\kappa)_{\text{fun}} \mid x\colon \iota_{\text{int}}6\,](\lambda f.\ f(\iota_{\text{int}}6)\kappa)_{\text{fun}} \\
&= [\![x+y]\!][\,\eta \mid k\colon \iota_{\text{cont}}(\lambda f.\ f(\iota_{\text{int}}6)\kappa)_{\text{fun}} \mid x\colon \iota_{\text{int}}6 \mid y\colon \iota_{\text{int}}6\,]\kappa \\
&= \kappa(\iota_{\text{int}}12).
\end{aligned}
$$

In Section 13.8, we will use this kind of repeated execution to backtrack the evaluation of nondeterministic functions.

12.3 Continuations as a Programming Technique

When a functional language does not provide continuations as values, a similar kind of capability can be obtained by subjecting functions in the object language to the same kind of transformation (called the *continuation-passing transformation*) that converts direct semantics into continuation semantics.

Consider the problem posed in the previous section, of multiplying a list of integers without performing any multiplications if the list contains zero. In the absence of **catch** and **throw**, we begin with a program that does not avoid the unnecessary multiplications:

$$
\begin{aligned}
&\textbf{let } \text{multlist} \equiv \lambda x. \\
&\qquad \textbf{letrec } \text{mt} \equiv \lambda x.\ \textbf{listcase } x \textbf{ of } (1, \\
&\qquad\qquad \lambda i.\ \lambda r.\ i \times \text{mt } r) \\
&\qquad \textbf{in } \text{mt } x \cdots.
\end{aligned}
$$

Now we subject the subsidiary function **mt** to the continuation-passing transformation. Specifically, we rewrite the function **mt** so that

(a) It accepts an additional argument k, called a continuation, that maps the result of the untransformed mt (which was the product of the list x) into the final result to be produced by multlist.

(b) Every call mt x k produces the final result of multlist, by applying k to the product of x.

(c) The function mt is *tail recursive*, which means that, whenever it calls itself, the result returned by the called function becomes the result of the calling function.

This leads to

$$\textbf{let } \text{multlist} \equiv \lambda x.$$
$$\textbf{letrec } \text{mt} \equiv \lambda x. \; \lambda k. \; \textbf{listcase } x \textbf{ of } (k\,1,$$
$$\lambda i. \; \lambda r. \; \text{mt } r\,(\lambda z. \; k(i \times z)))$$
$$\textbf{in } \text{mt } x\,(\lambda z. \; z) \; \cdots .$$

Here, instead of multiplying the result of its recursive call by i (which would violate tail recursion), the function mt achieves the same effect by embedding the multiplication in the continuation that is an argument to the recursive call. Specifically, this continuation first multiplies its argument by i and then applies the continuation that was an argument to the calling function.

Now we can add the special treatment of zero: When its first argument is zero, mt ignores its continuation argument (including the multiplications embedded within it) and returns zero, which, because of the tail recursion, becomes the result of multlist:

$$\textbf{let } \text{multlist} \equiv \lambda x.$$
$$\textbf{letrec } \text{mt} \equiv \lambda x. \; \lambda k. \; \textbf{listcase } x \textbf{ of } (k\,1,$$
$$\lambda i. \; \lambda r. \; \textbf{if } i = 0 \textbf{ then } 0 \textbf{ else } \text{mt } r\,(\lambda z. \; k(i \times z)))$$
$$\textbf{in } \text{mt } x\,(\lambda z. \; z) \; \cdots .$$

12.4 Deriving a First-Order Semantics

None of the definitions presented so far in this chapter make it obvious how one might reasonably implement an eager-evaluation functional language. Although it would be straightforward to program evaluation semantics, its use of explicit substitution would create major inefficiencies. On the other hand, although both direct and continuation denotational semantics look much like programs for interpreters, they use functions so heavily that the corresponding interpreters would have to be written in a language that is just as functional — and just as difficult to implement — as the language being interpreted.

It is possible, however, to transform the denotational definitions so that their semantic functions become *first-order* rather than *higher-order* functions, that is, so that these functions no longer accept or produce functional data. When continuation semantics is transformed in this way, it becomes a state-transformation interpreter that is easily programmed in any language that supports list processing.

To motivate the development, we will derive our first-order semantics in a very informal and intuitive manner. Then in the next section we will give a precise description of the relation between continuation semantics and the transformed definition. To avoid distracting complications, we will limit tuple constructors to zero or two components, and recursive definitions to a single function.

The key to the "defunctionalizing" transformation is to replace a function by a record giving the information necessary to compute the function. Thus the three sets of functional data occurring in the continuation semantics,

$$V_{\text{cont}} = V \to V_*$$

$$V_{\text{fun}} = V \to V_{\text{cont}} \to V_*$$

$$E = \langle \text{var} \rangle \to V,$$

will each become a set of records (whose exact nature we will specify later). For each of these sets, there will be an *interpretive function* that maps the records into the functions that they represent:

$$\text{cont} \in V_{\text{cont}} \to V \to V_*$$

$$\text{apply} \in V_{\text{fun}} \to V \to V_{\text{cont}} \to V_*$$

$$\text{get} \in E \to \langle \text{var} \rangle \to V.$$

In each application (in the metalanguage) of a function in one of the above sets, we will replace the function being applied (which we will indicate by overlining) by an application of the appropriate interpretive function. For example, in the semantic equation for constants,

$$[\![\lfloor k \rfloor]\!]\eta\kappa = \overline{\kappa}(\iota_{\text{int}}k),$$

the application of the overlined occurrence of the continuation κ is replaced by an application of the interpretive function "cont" to κ and its operands:

$$[\![\lfloor k \rfloor]\!]\eta\kappa = \text{cont } \kappa \, (\iota_{\text{int}}k).$$

Whenever an expression in the metalanguage defines a function in one of the above sets, the expression (which we will indicate by underlining) will be *defunctionalized*, that is, it will be replaced by an operation that creates a record of the values of its free variables. This record will actually be a tuple in the metalanguage, beginning with a name that identifies the defining expression. (Such names will be written in boldface.) For example, in the semantic equation for negation,

$$\llbracket -e \rrbracket \eta \kappa = \llbracket e \rrbracket \eta \, \underline{(\lambda i. \, \overline{\kappa}(\iota_{\text{int}}(-i)))_{\text{int}}},$$

the continuation-defining expression $(\lambda i. \, \kappa(\iota_{\text{int}}(-i)))_{\text{int}}$ is replaced by an operation that creates a record containing the arbitrarily chosen name **negate** and the value of κ, which is the only variable occurring free in the defining expression:

$$\llbracket -e \rrbracket \eta \kappa = \llbracket e \rrbracket \eta \langle \textbf{negate}, \kappa \rangle.$$

Then the definition of the appropriate interpretive function will contain a case that interprets such records as the function that they represent. For example, we would have

$$\text{cont} \, \langle \textbf{negate}, \kappa \rangle \, z = \left(\lambda i. \, \overline{\kappa}(\iota_{\text{int}}(-i)) \right)_{\text{int}} z,$$

except that $\overline{\kappa}$ must be replaced by an application of **cont**:

$$\text{cont} \, \langle \textbf{negate}, \kappa \rangle \, z = \left(\lambda i. \, \text{cont} \, \kappa(\iota_{\text{int}}(-i)) \right)_{\text{int}} z.$$

Such an equation may appear to be higher order, but this is only because of the use of the $(\cdots)_{\text{int}}$ notation to express a case analysis concisely. It could be written more cumbersomely as

$$\text{cont} \, \langle \textbf{negate}, \kappa \rangle \, (\iota_{\text{int}} i) = \text{cont} \, \kappa \, (\iota_{\text{int}}(-i))$$

$$\text{cont} \, \langle \textbf{negate}, \kappa \rangle \, z = \text{tyerr} \quad \text{when } z \notin \text{ran} \, \iota_{\text{int}}.$$

The treatment of the semantic equations for binary operations is somewhat more complex. In

$$\llbracket e + e' \rrbracket \eta \kappa = \llbracket e \rrbracket \eta \, \underline{(\lambda i. \, \llbracket e' \rrbracket \eta \, (\lambda i'. \, \overline{\kappa}(\iota_{\text{int}}(i + i'))))_{\text{int}})_{\text{int}}},$$

both underlined expressions define continuations. We defunctionalize the outer expression first:

$$\llbracket e + e' \rrbracket \eta \kappa = \llbracket e \rrbracket \eta \langle \textbf{add}_1, e', \eta, \kappa \rangle,$$

where

$$\text{cont} \, \langle \textbf{add}_1, e', \eta, \kappa \rangle \, z = \left(\lambda i. \, \llbracket e' \rrbracket \eta \, \underline{(\lambda i'. \, \overline{\kappa}(\iota_{\text{int}}(i + i')))_{\text{int}}} \right)_{\text{int}} z.$$

But this equation still contains the inner defining expression, whose defunctionalization gives

$$\text{cont} \, \langle \textbf{add}_1, e', \eta, \kappa \rangle \, z = \left(\lambda i. \, \llbracket e' \rrbracket \eta \, \langle \textbf{add}_2, i, \kappa \rangle \right)_{\text{int}} z,$$

where

$$\text{cont} \, \langle \textbf{add}_2, i, \kappa \rangle \, z = \left(\lambda i'. \, \text{cont} \, \kappa(\iota_{\text{int}}(i + i')) \right)_{\text{int}} z$$

(where again we have replaced the application of $\overline{\kappa}$ with an application of cont to κ).

The treatment of division is similar: From

$$[\![e \div e']\!]\eta\kappa = [\![e]\!]\eta\,(\lambda i.\,[\![e']\!]\eta\,(\lambda i'.\,\textbf{if}\ i' = 0\ \textbf{then}\ \text{err}\ \textbf{else}\ \overline{\kappa}(\iota_{\text{int}}(i \div i')))_{\text{int}})_{\text{int}},$$

one obtains

$$[\![e \div e']\!]\eta\kappa = [\![e]\!]\eta\langle\textbf{div}_1, e', \eta, \kappa\rangle$$

$$\text{cont}\,\langle\textbf{div}_1, e', \eta, \kappa\rangle\,z = (\lambda i.\,[\![e']\!]\eta\,\langle\textbf{div}_2, i, \kappa\rangle)_{\text{int}}z$$

$$\text{cont}\,\langle\textbf{div}_2, i, \kappa\rangle\,z = (\lambda i'.\,\textbf{if}\ i' = 0\ \textbf{then}\ \text{err}\ \textbf{else}\ \text{cont}\,\kappa(\iota_{\text{int}}(i + i')))_{\text{int}}z.$$

Conditional expressions, on the other hand, introduce only a single defunctionalized continuation, which branches between the evaluation of two subexpressions. From

$$[\![\textbf{if}\ e\ \textbf{then}\ e'\ \textbf{else}\ e'']\!]\eta\kappa = [\![e]\!]\eta\,(\lambda b.\,\textbf{if}\ b\ \textbf{then}\ [\![e']\!]\eta\kappa\ \textbf{else}\ [\![e'']\!]\eta\kappa)_{\text{bool}},$$

we have

$$[\![\textbf{if}\ e\ \textbf{then}\ e'\ \textbf{else}\ e'']\!]\eta\kappa = [\![e]\!]\eta\langle\textbf{cond}, e', e'', \eta, \kappa\rangle$$

$$\text{cont}\,\langle\textbf{cond}, e', e'', \eta, \kappa\rangle\,z = (\lambda b.\,\textbf{if}\ b\ \textbf{then}\ [\![e']\!]\eta\kappa\ \textbf{else}\ [\![e'']\!]\eta\kappa)_{\text{bool}}\,z.$$

When we come to variables and applications, we encounter additional interpretive functions. In the semantic equation for variables,

$$[\![v]\!]\eta\kappa = \overline{\kappa}(\overline{\eta}v),$$

the application of the environment η to a variable becomes an application of the function "get" to the environment and variable:

$$[\![v]\!]\eta\kappa = \text{cont}\,\kappa\,(\text{get}\,\eta\,v).$$

In the equation for applications,

$$[\![ee']\!]\eta\kappa = [\![e]\!]\eta\,(\lambda f.\,[\![e']\!]\eta\,(\lambda z.\,\overline{f}\,z\,\kappa))_{\text{fun}},$$

the defunctionalization of the underlined expressions is the same as with binary arithmetic operations, but then the application of the function value $\overline{f}$ to the value z and the continuation κ becomes an application of the interpretive function "apply":

$$[\![ee']\!]\eta\kappa = [\![e]\!]\eta\langle\textbf{app}_1, e', \eta, \kappa\rangle$$

$$\text{cont}\,\langle\textbf{app}_1, e', \eta, \kappa\rangle\,z = (\lambda f.\,[\![e']\!]\eta\langle\textbf{app}_2, f, \kappa\rangle)_{\text{fun}}z$$

$$\text{cont}\,\langle\textbf{app}_2, f, \kappa\rangle\,z = \text{apply}\,f\,z\,\kappa.$$

In the equation for abstractions,

$$[\![\lambda v.\,e]\!]\eta\kappa = \overline{\kappa}(\iota_{\text{fun}}(\lambda z.\,\lambda\kappa'.\,[\![e]\!][\,\eta \mid v{:}z\,]\kappa')), \tag{12.1}$$

the functional value that is an argument to ι_{fun} is defunctionalized into a record in V_{fun}, while the extended environment $[\,\eta \mid v\!:\!z\,]$ is defunctionalized into a record in E:

$$[\![\lambda v.\ e]\!]\eta\kappa = \text{cont}\ \kappa\ (\iota_{\text{fun}}\langle\mathbf{abstract}, v, e, \eta\rangle)$$

$$\text{apply}\ \langle\mathbf{abstract}, v, e, \eta\rangle\ z\ \kappa' = [\![e]\!]\langle\mathbf{extend}, v, z, \eta\rangle\kappa'$$

$$\text{get}\ \langle\mathbf{extend}, v, z, \eta\rangle\ w = [\,\text{get}\ \eta \mid v\!:\!z\,]\ w$$
$$= \textbf{if}\ w = v\ \textbf{then}\ z\ \textbf{else}\ \text{get}\ \eta\ w.$$

The transformation of the semantic equations for constructing tuples with zero and two components is similar to that of the equations for constants and binary operations, respectively. We leave it to the reader to check the resulting equations:

$$[\![\langle\rangle]\!]\eta\kappa = \text{cont}\ \kappa(\iota_{\text{tuple}}\langle\rangle)$$

$$[\![\langle e, e'\rangle]\!]\eta\kappa = [\![e]\!]\eta\langle\mathbf{tuple}_1, e', \eta, \kappa\rangle$$

$$\text{cont}\ \langle\mathbf{tuple}_1, e', \eta, \kappa\rangle\ z = [\![e']\!]\eta\ \langle\mathbf{tuple}_2, z, \kappa\rangle$$

$$\text{cont}\ \langle\mathbf{tuple}_2, z, \kappa\rangle\ z' = \text{cont}\ \kappa(\iota_{\text{tuple}}\langle z, z'\rangle),$$

as well as the transformed equations for tuple selection:

$$[\![e.\lfloor k\rfloor]\!]\eta\kappa = [\![e]\!]\eta\langle\mathbf{sel}, k, \kappa\rangle$$

$$\text{cont}\ \langle\mathbf{sel}, k, \kappa\rangle\ z = (\lambda t.\ \textbf{if}\ k \in \text{dom}\ t\ \textbf{then}\ \text{cont}\ \kappa(t_k)\ \textbf{else}\ \text{tyerr})_{\text{tuple}}\ z,$$

alternative constructions:

$$[\![@\ \lfloor k\rfloor\ e]\!]\eta\kappa = [\![e]\!]\eta\langle\mathbf{alt}, k, \kappa\rangle$$

$$\text{cont}\ \langle\mathbf{alt}, k, \kappa\rangle\ z = \text{cont}\ \kappa\ (\iota_{\text{alt}}\langle k, z\rangle),$$

and the **sumcase** expression:

$$[\![\textbf{sumcase}\ e\ \textbf{of}\ (e_0, \ldots, e_{n-1})]\!]\eta\kappa = [\![e]\!]\eta\langle\mathbf{scase}_1, \langle e_0,\ \ldots\ , e_{n-1}\rangle, \eta, \kappa\rangle$$

$$\text{cont}\ \langle\mathbf{scase}_1, \langle e_0,\ \ldots\ , e_{n-1}\rangle, \eta, \kappa\rangle\ z = (\lambda\langle k, z\rangle.\ \textbf{if}\ k < n\ \textbf{then}$$
$$[\![e_k]\!]\eta\langle\mathbf{scase}_2, z, \kappa\rangle\ \textbf{else}\ \text{tyerr})_{\text{alt}}\ z$$

$$\text{cont}\ \langle\mathbf{scase}_2, z, \kappa\rangle\ z' = (\lambda f.\ \text{apply}\ f\ z\ \kappa)_{\text{fun}}\ z'.$$

Recursive definitions, however, are more difficult. Using the least fixed-point operator $\mathbf{Y}_{V_{\text{fun}}}$, one can write the semantic equation as

$$[\![\textbf{letrec}\ v_0 \equiv \lambda u_0.\ e_0\ \textbf{in}\ e]\!]\eta\kappa = [\![e]\!][\,\eta \mid v_0\!:\!\iota_{\text{fun}}(\mathbf{Y}_{V_{\text{fun}}}(\cdots))\,]\kappa,$$

where $\mathbf{Y}_{V_{\mathrm{fun}}}(\cdots)$ abbreviates

$$\mathbf{Y}_{V_{\mathrm{fun}}}(\lambda f.\ \lambda z.\ \lambda \kappa'.\ [\![e_0]\!][[\eta \mid v_0 \colon \iota_{\mathrm{fun}} f] \mid u_0 \colon z]\kappa').$$

When we defunctionalize $[\eta \mid v_0 \colon \iota_{\mathrm{fun}}(\mathbf{Y}_{V_{\mathrm{fun}}}(\cdots))]$, we obtain

$$[\![\mathbf{letrec}\ v_0 \equiv \lambda u_0.\ e_0\ \mathbf{in}\ e]\!]\eta\kappa = [\![e]\!]\langle \mathbf{recenv}, \eta, v_0, u_0, e_0\rangle \kappa,$$

where

$$\begin{aligned}
\mathrm{get}\ \langle \mathbf{recenv}, \eta, v_0, u_0, e_0\rangle w &= [\,\mathrm{get}\ \eta \mid v_0 \colon \iota_{\mathrm{fun}}(\mathbf{Y}_{V_{\mathrm{fun}}}(\cdots))\,]w \\
&= \mathbf{if}\ w = v_0\ \mathbf{then}\ \iota_{\mathrm{fun}}(\mathbf{Y}_{V_{\mathrm{fun}}}(\cdots))\ \mathbf{else}\ \mathrm{get}\ \eta\,w.
\end{aligned}$$

To defunctionalize $\mathbf{Y}_{V_{\mathrm{fun}}}(\cdots)$, however, we must first replace this expression by its fixed-point expansion:

$$\begin{aligned}
\mathbf{Y}_{V_{\mathrm{fun}}}(\cdots) &= (\lambda f.\ \lambda z.\ \lambda \kappa'.\ [\![e_0]\!][[\eta \mid v_0 \colon \iota_{\mathrm{fun}} f] \mid u_0 \colon z]\kappa')(\mathbf{Y}_{V_{\mathrm{fun}}}(\cdots)) \\
&= \lambda z.\ \lambda \kappa'.\ [\![e_0]\!][[\eta \mid v_0 \colon \iota_{\mathrm{fun}}(\mathbf{Y}_{V_{\mathrm{fun}}}(\cdots))] \mid u_0 \colon z]\kappa',
\end{aligned}$$

to obtain

$$\begin{aligned}
&\mathrm{get}\ \langle \mathbf{recenv}, \eta, v_0, u_0, e_0\rangle w \\
&\quad = \mathbf{if}\ w = v_0\ \mathbf{then}\ \iota_{\mathrm{fun}}(\lambda z.\ \lambda \kappa'.\ [\![e_0]\!][[\eta \mid v_0 \colon \iota_{\mathrm{fun}}(\mathbf{Y}_{V_{\mathrm{fun}}}(\cdots))] \mid u_0 \colon z]\kappa') \\
&\quad \ \mathbf{else}\ \mathrm{get}\ \eta\,w.
\end{aligned}$$

At this point, we may exploit the similarity with the semantic equation (12.1) for abstractions. In transforming that equation, we defined the action of "apply" on records labeled with **abstract** so that $\lambda z.\ \lambda \kappa'.\ [\![e]\!][\eta \mid v \colon z]\kappa'$ could be defunctionalized into $\langle \mathbf{abstract}, v, e, \eta\rangle$. Thus we can defunctionalize

$$\lambda z.\ \lambda \kappa'.\ [\![e_0]\!][[\eta \mid v_0 \colon \iota_{\mathrm{fun}}(\mathbf{Y}_{V_{\mathrm{fun}}}(\cdots))] \mid u_0 \colon z]\kappa'$$

into

$$\langle \mathbf{abstract}, u_0, e_0, [\eta \mid v_0 \colon \iota_{\mathrm{fun}}(\mathbf{Y}_{V_{\mathrm{fun}}}(\cdots))]\rangle.$$

All that remains is to defunctionalize $[\eta \mid v_0 \colon \iota_{\mathrm{fun}}(\mathbf{Y}_{V_{\mathrm{fun}}}(\cdots))]$. But here we have finally closed the recursive circle: We have already defunctionalized this expression into $\langle \mathbf{recenv}, \eta, v_0, u_0, e_0\rangle$. Thus, the completely defunctionalized action of "get" on **recenv** records is

$$\begin{aligned}
&\mathrm{get}\ \langle \mathbf{recenv}, \eta, v_0, u_0, e_0\rangle w \\
&\quad = \mathbf{if}\ w = v_0\ \mathbf{then}\ \iota_{\mathrm{fun}}(\langle \mathbf{abstract}, u_0, e_0, \langle \mathbf{recenv}, \eta, v_0, u_0, e_0\rangle\rangle) \\
&\quad \ \mathbf{else}\ \mathrm{get}\ \eta\,w.
\end{aligned}$$

In essence, when one looks up a recursively defined function in an environment, one obtains an **abstract** record containing the same environment.

The **callcc** and **throw** constructs introduced in Section 12.2 can also be defunctionalized:

$$[\![\mathbf{callcc}\ e]\!]\eta\kappa = [\![e]\!]\eta\langle\mathbf{ccc}, \kappa\rangle$$

$$\mathrm{cont}\ \langle\mathbf{ccc}, \kappa\rangle\ z = (\lambda f.\ \mathrm{apply}\ f\ (\iota_{\mathrm{cont}}\ \kappa)\ \kappa)_{\mathrm{fun}}\ z$$

$$[\![\mathbf{throw}\ e\ e']\!]\eta\kappa = [\![e]\!]\eta\langle\mathbf{thw}, e', \eta\rangle$$

$$\mathrm{cont}\ \langle\mathbf{thw}, e', \eta\rangle\ z = (\lambda\kappa'.\ [\![e']\!]\eta\kappa')_{\mathrm{cont}}\ z.$$

The details of the derivations are left to the reader.

Finally, there are the semantic equations for explicit error stops, which are unchanged by defunctionalization:

$$[\![\mathbf{error}]\!]\eta\kappa = \mathrm{err}$$

$$[\![\mathbf{typeerror}]\!]\eta\kappa = \mathrm{tyerr}.$$

Also, we must defunctionalize the initial continuation κ_0 and initial environment e_0 that are used to evaluate a complete program. From $\kappa_0 = \iota_{\mathrm{norm}}$ we have

$$\kappa_0 = \langle\mathbf{initcont}\rangle \quad \text{where} \quad \mathrm{cont}\ \langle\mathbf{initcont}\rangle\ z = \iota_{\mathrm{norm}}\ z.$$

On the other hand, e_0 can be any environment. If we choose, for example, the environment that maps all variables into the integer value zero, then we have

$$\eta_0 = \langle\mathbf{initenv}\rangle \quad \text{where} \quad \mathrm{get}\ \langle\mathbf{initenv}\rangle\ v = \iota_{\mathrm{int}}\ 0.$$

12.5 First-Order Semantics Summarized

Having derived our first-order semantics piecemeal, we need to give it a more compact and rigorous presentation, freed of the scaffolding of its construction.

First, we must carefully specify the underlying domains and predomains of our definition, since it is not just V_{cont}, V_{fun}, and E that are changed by the transformation to first order. Because these entities are defined by mutual recursion, they all change, except for the sets V_{int} and V_{bool} of primitive values.

We will indicate the changed domains and predomains by adding hats to their names. (To be completely precise, we should also decorate the names of the associated injections and function extensions, but this would be excessively cumbersome.) Thus the domain of results is

$$\hat{V}_* = (\hat{V} + \{\mathbf{error}, \mathbf{typeerror}\})_\perp,$$

where the predomain $\hat{V}$ of values satisfies the isomorphism

$$\hat{V} \xrightarrow[\psi]{\phi} V_{\mathrm{int}} + V_{\mathrm{bool}} + \hat{V}_{\mathrm{fun}} + \hat{V}_{\mathrm{tuple}} + \hat{V}_{\mathrm{alt}} + \hat{V}_{\mathrm{cont}},$$

where

$$V_{\text{int}} = \mathbf{Z}$$

$$V_{\text{bool}} = \mathbf{B}$$

$$\hat{V}_{\text{tuple}} = \hat{V}^* = \bigcup_{n=0}^{\infty} \hat{V}^n$$

$$\hat{V}_{\text{alt}} = \mathbf{N} \times \hat{V}.$$

To complete the circle, we must describe $\hat{V}_{\text{cont}}$, $\hat{V}_{\text{fun}}$, and $\hat{E}$, which are predomains of records. To do this, we simply take these predomains to be a union of the various forms of records that were accumulated in the course of our derivation:

$$
\begin{aligned}
\hat{V}_{\text{cont}} = {} & \{\mathbf{negate}\} \times \hat{V}_{\text{cont}} \\
& \cup \{\mathbf{add_1}\} \times \langle \exp \rangle \times \hat{E} \times \hat{V}_{\text{cont}} \cup \{\mathbf{add_2}\} \times V_{\text{int}} \times \hat{V}_{\text{cont}} \\
& \cup \{\mathbf{div_1}\} \times \langle \exp \rangle \times \hat{E} \times \hat{V}_{\text{cont}} \cup \{\mathbf{div_2}\} \times V_{\text{int}} \times \hat{V}_{\text{cont}} \\
& \cup \{\mathbf{cond}\} \times \langle \exp \rangle \times \langle \mathrm{cxp} \rangle \times \hat{E} \times \hat{V}_{\text{cont}} \\
& \cup \{\mathbf{app_1}\} \times \langle \exp \rangle \times \hat{E} \times \hat{V}_{\text{cont}} \cup \{\mathbf{app_2}\} \times \hat{V}_{\text{fun}} \times \hat{V}_{\text{cont}} \\
& \cup \{\mathbf{tuple_1}\} \times \langle \exp \rangle \times \hat{E} \times \hat{V}_{\text{cont}} \cup \{\mathbf{tuple_2}\} \times \hat{V} \times \hat{V}_{\text{cont}} \\
& \cup \{\mathbf{sel}\} \times \mathbf{N} \times \hat{V}_{\text{cont}} \cup \{\mathbf{alt}\} \times \mathbf{N} \times \hat{V}_{\text{cont}} \\
& \cup \{\mathbf{scase_1}\} \times \langle \exp \rangle^* \times \hat{E} \times \hat{V}_{\text{cont}} \cup \{\mathbf{scase_2}\} \times \hat{V} \times \hat{V}_{\text{cont}} \\
& \cup \{\mathbf{ccc}\} \times \hat{V}_{\text{cont}} \cup \{\mathbf{thw}\} \times \langle \exp \rangle \times \hat{E} \cup \{\mathbf{initcont}\} \\[6pt]
\hat{V}_{\text{fun}} = {} & \{\mathbf{abstract}\} \times \langle \mathrm{var} \rangle \times \langle \exp \rangle \times \hat{E} \\[6pt]
\hat{E} = {} & \{\mathbf{extend}\} \times \langle \mathrm{var} \rangle \times \hat{V} \times \hat{E} \\
& \cup \{\mathbf{recenv}\} \times \hat{E} \times \langle \mathrm{var} \rangle \times \langle \mathrm{var} \rangle \times \langle \exp \rangle \cup \{\mathbf{initenv}\}.
\end{aligned}
$$

(Of course, there would be additional terms in the equation for $\hat{V}_{\text{cont}}$ because of additional arithmetic and boolean operations.) The distinct names in these equations insure that the components of the unions are disjoint. Indeed, we could have used a disjoint union in our definitions of the record sets:

$$
\begin{aligned}
\hat{V}_{\text{cont}} = {} & \hat{V}_{\text{cont}} \\
& + \langle \exp \rangle \times \hat{E} \times \hat{V}_{\text{cont}} + V_{\text{int}} \times \hat{V}_{\text{cont}} \\
& + \langle \exp \rangle \times \hat{E} \times \hat{V}_{\text{cont}} + V_{\text{int}} \times \hat{V}_{\text{cont}} \\
& \vdots
\end{aligned}
$$

For readability, however, we have used named rather than numbered alternatives in the metalanguage. Nevertheless, the above predomains are ordered in the same way as for a disjoint union: Records with distinct names never approximate one another, while records with the same name are ordered componentwise.

Notice that the predomains $\hat{V}$, $\hat{E}$, and the various $\hat{V}_\theta$ are defined by a mutual recursion that does not contain $\hat{V}_*$, lifting, or $\rightarrow$, but only involves sets, finite products, explicit disjoint unions, and ordinary unions that are in fact disjoint. These are all operations that preserve discrete ordering, that is, they map sets into sets. Moreover, they are finitely generated. Under these conditions, we can take $\hat{V}$, $\hat{E}$, and the various $\hat{V}_\theta$ to be the least sets satisfying the above equations (as in the construction given at the end of Section 2.4). Thus, all of the predomains in our first-order definition, except $\hat{V}_*$, are discretely ordered sets, while $\hat{V}_*$ is obviously a flat domain.

Once we have established these predomains, the rest of our first-order semantics can be obtained by collating the results of the previous section. We have a semantic function (henceforth distinguished by the subscript "fo") and three interpretive functions:

$$[\![-]\!]_{\mathrm{fo}} \in \langle \exp \rangle \rightarrow (\hat{E} \rightarrow \hat{V}_{\mathrm{cont}} \rightarrow \hat{V}_*)$$

$$\mathrm{cont} \in \hat{V}_{\mathrm{cont}} \rightarrow \hat{V} \rightarrow \hat{V}_*$$

$$\mathrm{apply} \in \hat{V}_{\mathrm{fun}} \rightarrow \hat{V} \rightarrow \hat{V}_{\mathrm{cont}} \rightarrow \hat{V}_*$$

$$\mathrm{get} \in \hat{E} \rightarrow \langle \mathrm{var} \rangle \rightarrow \hat{V},$$

where the semantic function satisfies:

$$[\![\lfloor k \rfloor]\!]_{\mathrm{fo}}\eta\kappa = \mathrm{cont}\ \kappa\ (\iota_{\mathrm{int}}k)$$

$$[\![-e]\!]_{\mathrm{fo}}\eta\kappa = [\![e]\!]_{\mathrm{fo}}\eta\langle \mathbf{negate}, \kappa \rangle$$

$$[\![e + e']\!]_{\mathrm{fo}}\eta\kappa = [\![e]\!]_{\mathrm{fo}}\eta\langle \mathbf{add}_1, e', \eta, \kappa \rangle$$

$$[\![e \div e']\!]_{\mathrm{fo}}\eta\kappa = [\![e]\!]_{\mathrm{fo}}\eta\langle \mathbf{div}_1, e', \eta, \kappa \rangle$$

$$[\![\mathbf{if}\ e\ \mathbf{then}\ e'\ \mathbf{else}\ e'']\!]_{\mathrm{fo}}\eta\kappa = [\![e]\!]_{\mathrm{fo}}\eta\langle \mathbf{cond}, e', e'', \eta, \kappa \rangle$$

$$[\![v]\!]_{\mathrm{fo}}\eta\kappa = \mathrm{cont}\ \kappa\ (\mathrm{get}\ \eta\ v)$$

$$[\![ee']\!]_{\mathrm{fo}}\eta\kappa = [\![e]\!]_{\mathrm{fo}}\eta\langle \mathbf{app}_1, e', \eta, \kappa \rangle$$

$$[\![\lambda v.\ e]\!]_{\mathrm{fo}}\eta\kappa = \mathrm{cont}\ \kappa\ (\iota_{\mathrm{fun}}\langle \mathbf{abstract}, v, e, \eta \rangle)$$

$$[\![\langle \rangle]\!]_{\mathrm{fo}}\eta\kappa = \mathrm{cont}\ \kappa(\iota_{\mathrm{tuple}}\langle \rangle)$$

$$[\![\langle e, e' \rangle]\!]_{\mathrm{fo}}\eta\kappa = [\![e]\!]_{\mathrm{fo}}\eta\langle \mathbf{tuple}_1, e', \eta, \kappa \rangle$$

$$[\![e.\lfloor k \rfloor]\!]_{\mathrm{fo}}\eta\kappa = [\![e]\!]_{\mathrm{fo}}\eta\langle \mathbf{sel}, k, \kappa \rangle$$

$$[\![@\ \lfloor k \rfloor\ e]\!]_{\mathrm{fo}}\eta\kappa = [\![e]\!]_{\mathrm{fo}}\eta\langle \mathbf{alt}, k, \kappa \rangle$$

$$[\![\textbf{sumcase } e \textbf{ of } (e_0, \ldots, e_{n-1})]\!]_{\text{fo}} \eta \kappa = [\![e]\!]_{\text{fo}} \eta \langle \textbf{scase}_1, \langle e_0, \ldots, e_{n-1} \rangle, \eta, \kappa \rangle$$

$$[\![\textbf{letrec } v_0 \equiv \lambda u_0.\ e_0 \textbf{ in } e]\!]_{\text{fo}} \eta \kappa = [\![e]\!]_{\text{fo}} \langle \textbf{recenv}, \eta, v_0, u_0, e_0 \rangle \kappa$$

$$[\![\textbf{callcc } e]\!]_{\text{fo}} \eta \kappa = [\![e]\!]_{\text{fo}} \eta \langle \textbf{ccc}, \kappa \rangle$$

$$[\![\textbf{throw } e\ e']\!]_{\text{fo}} \eta \kappa = [\![e]\!]_{\text{fo}} \eta \langle \textbf{thw}, e', \eta \rangle$$

$$[\![\textbf{error}]\!]_{\text{fo}} \eta \kappa = \text{err}$$

$$[\![\textbf{typeerror}]\!]_{\text{fo}} \eta \kappa = \text{tyerr},$$

while "cont" satisfies:

$$\text{cont } \langle \textbf{negate}, \kappa \rangle\, z = (\lambda i.\ \text{cont } \kappa(\iota_{\text{int}}(-i)))_{\text{int}} z$$

$$\text{cont } \langle \textbf{add}_1, e', \eta, \kappa \rangle\, z = (\lambda i.\ [\![e']\!]_{\text{fo}} \eta\, \langle \textbf{add}_2, i, \kappa \rangle)_{\text{int}} z$$

$$\text{cont } \langle \textbf{add}_2, i, \kappa \rangle\, z = (\lambda i'.\ \text{cont } \kappa(\iota_{\text{int}}(i + i')))_{\text{int}} z$$

$$\text{cont } \langle \textbf{div}_1, e', \eta, \kappa \rangle\, z = (\lambda i.\ [\![e']\!]_{\text{fo}} \eta\, \langle \textbf{div}_2, i, \kappa \rangle)_{\text{int}} z$$

$$\text{cont } \langle \textbf{div}_2, i, \kappa \rangle\, z = (\lambda i'.\ \textbf{if } i' = 0 \textbf{ then } \text{err} \textbf{ else } \text{cont } \kappa(\iota_{\text{int}}(i + i')))_{\text{int}} z$$

$$\text{cont } \langle \textbf{cond}, e', e'', \eta, \kappa \rangle\, z = (\lambda b.\ \textbf{if } b \textbf{ then } [\![e']\!]_{\text{fo}} \eta \kappa \textbf{ else } [\![e'']\!]_{\text{fo}} \eta \kappa)_{\text{bool}} z$$

$$\text{cont } \langle \textbf{app}_1, e', \eta, \kappa \rangle\, z = (\lambda f.\ [\![e']\!]_{\text{fo}} \eta \langle \textbf{app}_2, f, \kappa \rangle)_{\text{fun}} z$$

$$\text{cont } \langle \textbf{app}_2, f, \kappa \rangle\, z = \text{apply } f\, z\, \kappa$$

$$\text{cont } \langle \textbf{tuple}_1, e', \eta, \kappa \rangle\, z = [\![e']\!]_{\text{fo}} \eta\, \langle \textbf{tuple}_2, z, \kappa \rangle$$

$$\text{cont } \langle \textbf{tuple}_2, z, \kappa \rangle\, z' = \text{cont } \kappa(\iota_{\text{tuple}} \langle z, z' \rangle)$$

$$\text{cont } \langle \textbf{sel}, k, \kappa \rangle\, z = (\lambda t.\ \textbf{if } k \in \text{dom } t \textbf{ then } \text{cont } \kappa(t_k) \textbf{ else } \text{tyerr})_{\text{tuple}} z$$

$$\text{cont } \langle \textbf{alt}, k, \kappa \rangle\, z = \text{cont } \kappa\, (\iota_{\text{alt}} \langle k, z \rangle)$$

$$\text{cont } \langle \textbf{scase}_1, \langle e_0, \ldots, e_{n-1} \rangle, \eta, \kappa \rangle\, z$$
$$= (\lambda \langle k, z \rangle.\ \textbf{if } k < n \textbf{ then } [\![e_k]\!]_{\text{fo}} \eta \langle \textbf{scase}_2, z, \kappa \rangle \textbf{ else } \text{tyerr})_{\text{alt}} z$$

$$\text{cont } \langle \textbf{scase}_2, z, \kappa \rangle\, z' = (\lambda f.\ \text{apply } f\, z\, \kappa)_{\text{fun}} z'$$

$$\text{cont } \langle \textbf{ccc}, \kappa \rangle\, z = (\lambda f.\ \text{apply } f\, (\iota_{\text{cont}} \kappa)\, \kappa)_{\text{fun}} z$$

$$\text{cont } \langle \textbf{thw}, e', \eta \rangle\, z = (\lambda \kappa'.\ [\![e']\!]_{\text{fo}} \eta \kappa')_{\text{cont}} z$$

$$\text{cont } \langle \textbf{initcont} \rangle\, z = \iota_{\text{norm}}\, z,$$

"apply" satisfies:

$$\text{apply } \langle \textbf{abstract}, v, e, \eta \rangle\, z\, \kappa' = [\![e]\!]_{\text{fo}} \langle \textbf{extend}, v, z, \eta \rangle \kappa',$$

and "get" satisfies:

$$\text{get } \langle \textbf{extend}, v, z, \eta \rangle \, w = \textbf{if } w = v \textbf{ then } z \textbf{ else get } \eta \, w$$

$$\text{get } \langle \textbf{recenv}, \eta, v_0, u_0, e_0 \rangle w = \textbf{if } w = v_0 \textbf{ then}$$

$$\iota_{\text{fun}}(\langle \textbf{abstract}, u_0, e_0, \langle \textbf{recenv}, \eta, v_0, u_0, e_0 \rangle \rangle)$$

$$\textbf{else get } \eta \, w$$

$$\text{get } \langle \textbf{initenv} \rangle \, v = \iota_{\text{int}} \, 0.$$

To complete the first-order definition, we need only add the initial continuation and environment:

$$\kappa_0 = \langle \textbf{initcont} \rangle \qquad\qquad \eta_0 = \langle \textbf{initenv} \rangle.$$

Once the first-order definition is displayed explicitly, its operational character becomes evident. The environments in E are lists of variable-value associations (except for the **recenv** environments used to implement recursion), and "get" is their lookup function. The members of V_{fun}, which are called *closures*, consist of function-denoting phrases paired with environments that specify the values of their free variables. Finally, the continuations in V_{cont} are lists of instructions to be executed after the current expression has been evaluated, and "cont" is the interpreter for these instructions.

The semantic function $[\![-]\!]_{\text{fo}}$ and the functions "cont" and "apply" are tail recursive: Whenever one of these functions calls itself or another, the result of the called function becomes the result of the calling function. By induction on the number of calls, it follows that the result of every call of any of these functions is the result of the initial call $[\![e_0]\!]_{\text{fo}} \eta_0 \kappa_0$ (where the expression e_0 is the complete program to be evaluated).

Such a collection of first-order tail-recursive functions can be viewed as a transition semantics in which a configuration is reached each time a function is called. Specifically, each nonterminal configuration consists of a function name appended to a list of arguments to the function, the terminal configurations are the results in V_*, and each line in each function definition gives rise to one or more premiss-free transition rules. For example,

$$\text{cont } \langle \textbf{add}_1, e', \eta, \kappa \rangle \, z = (\lambda i. \, [\![e']\!]_{\text{fo}} \eta \, \langle \textbf{add}_2, i, \kappa \rangle)_{\text{int}} z$$

gives rise to the rules

$$\frac{}{\text{cont } \langle \textbf{add}_1, e', \eta, \kappa \rangle \, z \to \text{fo } \eta \, \langle \textbf{add}_2, i, \kappa \rangle} \qquad \text{when } z = \iota_{\text{int}}(i)$$

and

$$\frac{}{\text{cont } \langle \textbf{add}_1, e', \eta, \kappa \rangle \, z \to \text{tyerr}} \qquad \text{when } z \notin \text{ran } \iota_{\text{int}},$$

where "fo" is used to name the semantic function $[\![-]\!]_{\text{fo}}$.

12.6 Relating First-Order and Continuation Semantics

Our final task is to specify the relationship between our first-order semantics and the continuation semantics from which it was derived.

Although the informal description of our derivation might suggest that there is a one-to-one correspondence between the closure records in $\hat{V}_{\text{fun}}$ and the functions in V_{fun} that they represent, this correspondence is actually just a relation (which we will call R_{fun}), since the same function may be represented by many closures (describing different methods of computation) or even by no closure (if the function is not computable).

In fact, we must specify a representation relation between each of the predomains in the first-order definition and the corresponding predomain in the continuation semantics:

(a) $\langle \hat{i}, i \rangle \in R_{\text{int}} \subseteq V_{\text{int}} \times V_{\text{int}}$ if and only if

$$\hat{i} = i.$$

(b) $\langle \hat{b}, b \rangle \in R_{\text{bool}} \subseteq V_{\text{bool}} \times V_{\text{bool}}$ if and only if

$$\hat{b} = b.$$

(c) $\langle \hat{f}, f \rangle \in R_{\text{fun}} \subseteq \hat{V}_{\text{fun}} \times V_{\text{fun}}$ if and only if, when $\langle \hat{z}, z \rangle \in R$ and $\langle \hat{\kappa}, \kappa \rangle \in R_{\text{cont}}$,

$$\langle \text{apply } \hat{f} \, \hat{z} \, \hat{\kappa}, f \, z \, \kappa \rangle \in R_*.$$

(d) $\langle \hat{t}, t \rangle \in R_{\text{tuple}} \subseteq \hat{V}_{\text{tuple}} \times V_{\text{tuple}}$ if and only if $\operatorname{dom} \hat{t} = \operatorname{dom} t$ and, for all $k \in \operatorname{dom} t$,

$$\langle \hat{t}_k, t_k \rangle \in R.$$

(e) $\langle \langle \hat{k}, \hat{z} \rangle, \langle k, z \rangle \rangle \in R_{\text{alt}} \subseteq \hat{V}_{\text{alt}} \times V_{\text{alt}}$ if and only if

$$\hat{k} = k \text{ and } \langle \hat{z}, z \rangle \in R.$$

(f) $\langle \hat{\kappa}, \kappa \rangle \in R_{\text{cont}} \subseteq \hat{V}_{\text{cont}} \times V_{\text{cont}}$ if and only if, whenever $\langle \hat{z}, z \rangle \in R$,

$$\langle \text{cont } \hat{\kappa} \, \hat{z}, \kappa \, z \rangle \in R_*.$$

(g) $\langle \hat{z}, z \rangle \in R \subseteq \hat{V} \times V$ if and only if, for some $\theta \in \{\text{int}, \text{bool}, \text{fun}, \text{tuple}, \text{alt}, \text{cont}\}$ and $\langle \hat{x}, x \rangle \in R_\theta$,

$$\hat{z} = \iota_\theta \hat{x} \text{ and } z = \iota_\theta x.$$

(h) $\langle \hat{x}, x \rangle \in R_* \subseteq \hat{V}_* \times V_*$ if and only if

$$\hat{x} = \iota_{\text{norm}} \hat{z} \text{ and } x = \iota_{\text{norm}} z \text{ for some } \langle \hat{z}, z \rangle \in R,$$

or $\hat{x} = x = \text{tyerr}$ or $\hat{x} = x = \text{err}$ or $\hat{x} = x = \bot$.

(i) $\langle \hat{\eta}, \eta \rangle \in R_E \subseteq \hat{E} \times E$ if and only if, for all $v \in \langle \text{var} \rangle$,

$$\langle \text{get } \hat{\eta} \, v, \eta \, v \rangle \in R.$$

The skeptical reader will notice that this is a mutually recursive definition of relations among domains and predomains that are themselves defined recursively, and will rightly suspect that this kind of definition needs justification. In fact, one can construct relations satisfying the above list of properties, but the mathematics that is needed is beyond the scope of this book.

Once the existence of the relevant relations is assured, one can show

Proposition 12.1 *For any expression e, if $\langle \hat\eta, \eta \rangle \in R_E$ and $\langle \hat\kappa, \kappa \rangle \in R_{\text{cont}}$, then*

$$\langle [\![e]\!]_{\text{fo}} \hat\eta \hat\kappa, [\![e]\!] \eta \kappa \rangle \in R_*.$$

For the most part, the proof is a straightforward induction on the structure of e, but the treatment of recursion depends on the specific construction of the relevant relations.

Bibliographic Notes

A history of the repeated discoveries of continuations (occurring largely in the context of functional languages) is given in Reynolds [1993]; relevant original papers include those by van Wijngaarden [1966], F. L. Morris [1993], Strachey and Wadsworth [1974], J. H. Morris [1972], Fischer [1972; 1993], and Abdali [1976]. The operations **callcc** and **throw** first appeared in Scheme, but are descendents of Landin's [1965b] "J-operator". Both the continuation-passing transformation from direct to continuation semantics and defunctionalization were described, in the setting of programs for interpreting eager-evaluation functional languages, by Reynolds [1972a].

The "SECD machine", an influential operational definition of eager evaluation that is closely related to the first-order semantics of Section 12.5, was defined in the mid-1960's by Landin [1964; 1966b] and used by him to explicate Algol 60 [1965a; 1966a]. The most elaborate flowering of this approach was the formal definition of PL/I by a group of researchers at the IBM Vienna Laboratory [Lucas et al., 1968; Walk et al., 1968].

Beginning with the implementation of Scheme [Sussman and Steele Jr., 1975], continuations and the continuation-passing transformation have played a major role in the design of compilers. More recently, this topic has been explored at book length by Appel [1992].

Exercises

12.1   A simple special case of the syntactic sugar discussed in Section 11.3 of the previous chapter is

$$\textbf{let } v \equiv e \textbf{ in } e' \overset{\text{def}}{=} (\lambda v.\ e')e.$$

(a) From this definition, derive a semantic equation for the direct denotational semantics (discussed in Section 11.6) of **let** $v \equiv e$ **in** e'.

(b) From this definition, derive a semantic equation for the continuation semantics (discussed in Section 12.1) of **let** $v \equiv e$ **in** e'.

(c) Use the continuation semantics obtained in the previous part to prove the following: Let e be an expression such that, for every environment η, there is a value z such that, for all continuations κ,

$$\llbracket e \rrbracket \eta \kappa = \kappa z.$$

Then, for all expressions e' and variables $v' \notin \mathrm{FV}(e) \cup \{v\}$,

$$\llbracket \textbf{let } v \equiv e \textbf{ in } \lambda v'.\ e' \rrbracket = \llbracket \lambda v'.\ \textbf{let } v \equiv e \textbf{ in } e' \rrbracket.$$

(d) Give expressions e and e' and distinct variables v and v' such that **let** $v \equiv e$ **in** $\lambda v'.\ e'$ and $\lambda v'.\ $**let** $v \equiv e$ **in** e' have different meanings.

12.2 Give a semantic equation, to be added to the continuation semantics of Section 12.1, for the **open** construction described in Exercise 11.4.

12.3 The following expressions each contain a β-redex of the form $(\lambda \mathrm{x}. \cdots)(\cdots)$. In each case, give the result of evaluating the expression itself, the expression obtained by contracting the redex within the original expression, and the result of evaluating the reduced expression. (The function fact is the usual recursive function for computing the factorial, as in Section 11.5, so that the expression $\mathsf{fact}(-1)$ does not terminate.)

$$(\lambda \mathrm{x}.\ 3)(\mathsf{fact}(-1))$$

$$(\lambda \mathrm{x}.\ \mathsf{fact}(-1) + \mathrm{x})(3 \div 0)$$

$$\textbf{callcc } \lambda \mathrm{k}.\ (\lambda \mathrm{x}.\ (\textbf{throw } \mathrm{k}\ 3) + \mathrm{x})(\textbf{throw } \mathrm{k}\ 4).$$

12.4 Use **callcc** and **throw** to write a function "test" that accepts a function that in turn accepts two other functions. Specifically, when applied to a function F, test should return

- @ $0\,y$ if an application $F\ f\ g$ returns the value y without calling either of the functional arguments f and g,
- @ $1\,x$ if an application $F\ f\ g$ calls f before any call of g and gives f the argument x on its first call,
- @ $2\,x$ if an application $F\ f\ g$ calls g before any call of f and gives g the argument x on its first call.

(Note that this result does not depend on the functions f or g.) For example, since $e + e'$ is evaluated by evaluating e before e':

$$\text{test} \, (\lambda \text{f}. \, \lambda \text{g}. \, 5) = @ \, 0 \, 5$$

$$\text{test} \, (\lambda \text{f}. \, \lambda \text{g}. \, \text{g}(\text{f} \, 10) + \text{f}(\text{g} \, 20)) = @ \, 1 \, 10$$

$$\text{test} \, (\lambda \text{f}. \, \lambda \text{g}. \, \text{f}(\text{g} \, 20) + \text{g}(\text{f} \, 10)) = @ \, 2 \, 20.$$

12.5   Write two versions of a function that will accept a binary tree (as defined in Section 11.5) whose terminal nodes are labeled with nonnegative integers, and produce the minimum of these labels.

(a) In the first version, use **catch** and **throw** to terminate the computation if a node with a zero label is encountered (which implies that the minimum must be zero).

(b) Use the continuation-passing transformation of Section 12.3 to obtain a second version that terminates when a zero label is encountered without using **catch** and **throw**.

12.6   Extend the transformation to a first-order semantics given in Section 12.4 to permit the construction of tuples of arbitrary length, by transforming the continuation-semantic equation

$$[\![\langle e_0, \ldots, e_{n-1} \rangle]\!] \eta \kappa$$
$$= [\![e_0]\!] \eta \, (\lambda z_0. \, \cdots \, [\![e_{n-1}]\!] \eta \, (\lambda z_{n-1}. \, \kappa(\iota_{\text{tuple}} \langle z_0, \ldots, z_{n-1} \rangle)) \cdots).$$

The problem here is that, just as a binary operation such as addition requires two kinds of records in V_{cont} to accept the values of its two subexpressions, so a tuple constructor should require n kinds of records in V_{cont} to accept the values of its n subexpressions — but now there is no definite limit on n.

One approach to solving this problem is to generalize the semantic function for tuples to a function

$$\text{tuple-eval} \in V^* \to \langle \text{expr} \rangle^* \to E \to V_{\text{cont}} \to V_*$$

that accepts both a sequence of values and a sequence of expressions, and produces a result where the first sequence is appended to the sequence of values of the expressions:

$$\text{tuple-eval} \, \langle z_0, \ldots, z_{m-1} \rangle \langle e_0, \ldots, e_{n-1} \rangle \eta \kappa$$
$$= [\![e_0]\!] \eta \, (\lambda z_m. \, \cdots \, [\![e_{n-1}]\!] \eta \, (\lambda z_{m+n-1}. \, \kappa(\iota_{\text{tuple}} \langle z_0, \ldots, z_{m+n-1} \rangle)) \cdots).$$

One can define $[\![\langle e_0, \ldots, e_{n-1} \rangle]\!]$ in terms of tuple-eval, and then define tuple-eval $\langle z_0, \ldots, z_{m-1} \rangle \langle e_0, \ldots, e_{n-1} \rangle$ by induction on n. The resulting equations are straightforward to defunctionalize.

12.7   Extend the transformation to a first-order semantics given in Section 12.4 to permit multiple recursive definitions.

13

Iswim-like Languages

So far, we have studied two seemingly quite separate kinds of programming languages: imperative languages, where the basic computational notions are assignment and state transitions, and functional or applicative languages, where the basic notions are evaluation and the definition and application of functions. But most practical languages combine these two viewpoints.

In this chapter, we consider languages where assignment and state change are added to a functional language that uses eager evaluation. We call such languages *Iswim-like* in tribute to Peter Landin's Iswim, which, although never implemented, was the first such language to be based on a clear understanding of underlying principles. (These languages should be distinguished from Algol-like languages, to be discussed in Chapter 19, which use normal-order evaluation and incorporate imperative features in a different way.)

13.1 Aliasing, References, and States

Unfortunately, the marriage between imperative and functional programming is never completely blissful. All known ways of combining these approaches (whether Iswim-like or Algol-like) suffer from the phenomenon of *aliasing*. Thus, before developing an Iswim-like language specifically, we begin with an informal and general discussion of aliasing.

Consider for example (in a somewhat different notation than will be defined and used later in this chapter),

> **let** fib $\equiv$ λn. λf.
>
> > **if** n $= 0$ **then** f $:= 0$ **else**
> >
> > > **newvar** k $:= 1$ **in newvar** g $:= 0$ **in** (f $:= 1$;
> > >
> > > > **while** k $\neq$ n **do**
> > > >
> > > > > **newvar** t $:= g$ **in** (g $:= f$; f $:= f + t$; k $:= k + 1$))
> >
> **in** fib a b.

Here we have taken the imperative command for computing Fibonacci numbers from Section 3.6 and embedded it in the definition of a function fib. The resulting entity is not a "function" in the usual mathematical sense, since its application will cause assignments. Such a "function" is often called a *procedure* or if, like fib, its result is trivial, a *proper procedure*. If it assigns to free variables (instead of only arguments or local variables), it is said to have *side effects*. The bound variables, such as n and f, that denote arguments are called *formal parameters*. An application such as fib a b that invokes a procedure is said to *call* the procedure, and the operands of the application, such as a and b, are called *actual parameters*. (This terminology originated with Algol 60, but it has spread to a wide variety of languages.)

If we desugar the function definition as in Section 11.3 and then apply β-contraction, we find that the expression displayed above is equivalent to

$$\textbf{if } a = 0 \textbf{ then } b := 0 \textbf{ else}$$
$$\textbf{newvar } k := 1 \textbf{ in newvar } g := 0 \textbf{ in } (b := 1 ;$$
$$\textbf{while } k \neq a \textbf{ do}$$
$$\textbf{newvar } t := g \textbf{ in } (g := b ; b := b + t ; k := k + 1)),$$

which, as one might hope, will set b to the ath Fibonacci number. But now suppose that the call fib a b is replaced by fib a a. By similar reasoning, the expression will be equivalent to

$$\textbf{if } a = 0 \textbf{ then } a := 0 \textbf{ else}$$
$$\textbf{newvar } k := 1 \textbf{ in newvar } g := 0 \textbf{ in } (a := 1 ;$$
$$\textbf{while } k \neq a \textbf{ do}$$
$$\textbf{newvar } t := g \textbf{ in } (g := a ; a := a + t ; k := k + 1)),$$

which does nothing like setting a to the ath Fibonacci number.

The difficulty is that the substitution of the same actual parameter a for both of the formal parameters n and f is an aliasing substitution in the sense defined in Section 2.5. It creates a situation where, in terms of the original command, an assignment to f changes the values of n as well as f (and vice versa). In this situation, the formal parameters n and f are said to be *aliases*.

Nowadays, methods for detecting, controlling, or eliminating aliasing (and its higher-order generalization, interference) are an active topic of research. But in the mid-1960's, the immediate question was how to describe its semantics rigorously. The answer was that, when one combines an imperative and a functional language, one cannot equate the state used by the first with the environment used by the second. Instead, the denotational semantics of the combined language must employ both of these entities separately: the environment to describe the effect of binding and the state to describe the effect of assignment. When we speak of an assignable variable such as f possessing a value such as 7, we really mean that an environment η maps f into an entity that we will call a *reference*, which in turn is mapped by a state σ into 7.

When two variables f and n are not aliases, they are mapped by η into distinct references r and r'. Even though the state σ may map these references into the same value, an assignment to f will change the state by changing σr but not $\sigma r'$, so that the value $\sigma(\eta n) = \sigma r'$ of n will not change. On the other hand, when f and n are aliases, they are mapped by η into the same reference r. Then an assignment to either variable will change σr and thus the value of both variables.

Before proceeding further, we should clarify terminology. The entities we call states were called "stores" by many early researchers, following Christopher Strachey and his associates, who wished to emphasize the close connection with the physical store of the computer. For similar reasons, some American researchers used the term "memory". For what we call a "reference", Strachey coined the term "L-value", while others have used "name", "pointer", and "address".

Basically, a reference is an abstraction of the hardware concept of an address. Specifically, we assume that there is a countably infinite set $\mathbf{Rf}$ of references, a set $\mathcal{R}$ of finite subsets of $\mathbf{Rf}$ that contains the empty set, and a function "newref" from $\mathcal{R}$ to $\mathbf{Rf}$ such that

$$\forall R \in \mathcal{R}.\ \text{newref } R \notin R \text{ and } R \cup \{\text{newref } R\} \in \mathcal{R}.$$

Then we define the set Σ of states to be

$$\Sigma = \bigcup_{R \in \mathcal{R}} (R \rightarrow V),$$

where V is the set of values.

For example, we might have

$$\mathbf{Rf} = \mathbf{N}$$

$$\mathcal{R} = \{\, 0 \text{ to } n-1 \mid n \in \mathbf{N} \,\} \tag{13.1}$$

$$\text{newref}(0 \text{ to } n-1) = n,$$

so that

$$\Sigma = \bigcup_{n=0}^{\infty} (0 \text{ to } n-1) \rightarrow V = V^*$$

is the set of sequences of values. (The reader may wonder why we do not just take these equations as the definitions of references and states. By allowing these entities to be anything satisfying the axioms in the previous paragraph, we exclude such operations as the addition of a number to a reference. Our intention is not to describe anything, such as arrays, that makes use of such operations, but only simple memory cells with no sense of adjacency or distance from one another.)

One way of adding assignment to a functional language is to change every entity that accepts or produces a value so that it accepts or produces a reference that is mapped by the current state into that value. Thus the evaluation of an expression would produce a reference, environments would map all variables into references, functional values would map references into references, the components of tuples would be references, and alternative values would be references paired with tags. This approach roughly characterizes such languages as Lisp, Iswim, PAL, and Scheme, and to a large extent Fortran, PL/I, and C.

In this book, however, we will pursue a more modern approach that is used in Algol 68, Basel, Gedanken, and Standard ML. Here references are an additional kind of value that can be used by the programmer in those roles for which they are useful, without being forced upon the programmer in contexts where they are irrelevant to his concerns. (This viewpoint is often called the *reference concept*, in contrast to our more general use of the word "reference".)

Syntactically, we extend the language of the previous chapter with

$$\langle\text{exp}\rangle ::= \textbf{mkref }\langle\text{exp}\rangle \mid \textbf{val }\langle\text{exp}\rangle \mid \langle\text{exp}\rangle := \langle\text{exp}\rangle \mid \langle\text{exp}\rangle =_{\text{ref}} \langle\text{exp}\rangle$$

The operation **mkref** e evaluates e, allocates a new reference and initializes it to the value of e (i.e. extends the current state to map the new reference into the value of e), and returns the new reference. The operation **val** e evaluates e, checks that its value is a reference, and returns the value of the reference (in the current state). The operation $e := e'$ evaluates e and e', checks that the value of e is a reference, assigns the value of e' to this reference (i.e. alters the current state to map the reference into the value of e'), and returns the value of e'. (The decision that an assignment returns the value of its right operand is arbitrary, but common to many languages and often convenient for programming.) The expression $e =_{\text{ref}} e'$ tests whether the expressions e and e' denote the same reference (in the sense that assigning to one will change the value of both).

13.2 Evaluation Semantics

To extend the evaluation semantics of Section 11.2 to include assignment and related features, we begin with the realization that the evaluation of an expression may depend on a state and produce a possibly altered state. Specifically, we write the evaluation relation

$$\sigma, e \Rightarrow z, \sigma'$$

to indicate that, beginning in state σ, the expression e will evaluate to z, ending in the state σ'. Moreover, since some expressions will evaluate to references, we expand the range of the metavariable z to include references as well as canonical forms. Similarly, the "values" that are the range of states will be either references or canonical forms. (We use the metavariables r for references and σ for states.)

Now consider an evaluation rule from Section 11.2 such as

EV RULE: Application (β_E-evaluation)

$$\frac{e \Rightarrow \lambda v.\, \hat{e} \qquad e' \Rightarrow z' \qquad (\hat{e}/v \to z') \Rightarrow z}{ee' \Rightarrow z.}$$

To extend such a rule to deal with states, we add state variables to both sides of each evaluation relation, making the state on the left of the first premiss the same as the state on the left of the conclusion, the state on the left of every other premiss the same as the state on the right of the preceding premiss, and the state on the right of the conclusion the same as the state on the right of the last premiss:

EV RULE: Application (β_E-evaluation)

$$\frac{\sigma_0, e \Rightarrow \lambda v.\, \hat{e}, \sigma_1 \qquad \sigma_1, e' \Rightarrow z', \sigma_2 \qquad \sigma_2, (\hat{e}/v \to z') \Rightarrow z, \sigma_3}{\sigma_0, ee' \Rightarrow z, \sigma_3.}$$

It is evident that every rule in Section 11.2 can be extended in this way. (If a rule, such as the rule for canonical forms, has no premisses, then the states on the left and right of its conclusion are the same.) The stereotyped nature of this extension, however, should not obscure its importance: It represents a specific commitment to carry out evaluations in the order of premisses from left to right, which has a vital effect on the behavior of assignment. Although we said nothing about the matter in Section 11.2, we were careful to order the premisses to describe a sensible choice of evaluation order.

What remains are the additional rules for the new syntactic constructs:

EV RULE: Reference Creation

$$\frac{\sigma_0, e \Rightarrow z, \sigma_1}{\sigma_0, \mathbf{mkref}\ e \Rightarrow r, [\,\sigma_1 \mid r\!:\! z\,]} \qquad \text{where } r = \mathrm{newref}(\mathrm{dom}\,\sigma_1),$$

EV RULE: Reference Evaluation

$$\frac{\sigma_0, e \Rightarrow r, \sigma_1}{\sigma_0, \mathbf{val}\ e \Rightarrow \sigma_1 r, \sigma_1,}$$

EV RULE: Assignment

$$\frac{\sigma_0, e \Rightarrow r, \sigma_1 \qquad \sigma_1, e' \Rightarrow z', \sigma_2}{\sigma_0, e := e' \Rightarrow z', [\,\sigma_2 \mid r\!:\! z'\,],}$$

EV RULE: Reference Equality

$$\frac{\sigma_0, e \Rightarrow r, \sigma_1 \qquad \sigma_1, e' \Rightarrow r', \sigma_2}{\sigma_0, e =_{\mathrm{ref}} e' \Rightarrow \lfloor r = r' \rfloor, \sigma_2.}$$

13.3 Continuation Semantics

Iswim-like languages can also be described by an extension of the continuation denotational semantics of Sections 12.1 and 12.2.

The meaning of an expression now accepts the state that is current when evaluation begins, and passes on to a continuation the state that is current when evaluation produces a value. Thus both the semantic function and continuations receive states as extra arguments, so that

$$[\![-]\!] \in \langle \exp \rangle \to (E \to V_{\text{cont}} \to \Sigma \to V_*),$$

where

$$E = \langle \text{var} \rangle \to V$$

$$V_{\text{cont}} = V \to \Sigma \to V_*$$

$$V_* = (V + \{\mathbf{error}, \mathbf{typeerror}\})_\perp.$$

(By omitting any mention of Σ in the equation for the domain V_* of final results, we formalize the behavior of typical implementations of Iswim-like languages, which do not display the final state after evaluating an expression.) It is also useful to define the injections

$$\iota_{\text{norm}} = \lambda z.\ \lambda\sigma.\ \iota_\uparrow(\iota_0 z) \in V \to \Sigma \to V_*$$

$$\text{err} = \lambda\sigma.\ \iota_\uparrow(\iota_1 \mathbf{error}) \in \Sigma \to V_*$$

$$\text{tyerr} = \lambda\sigma.\ \iota_\uparrow(\iota_1 \mathbf{typeerror}) \in \Sigma \to V_*.$$

(Roughly speaking, these are are similar to the ι_{norm}, err, and tyerr used in Chapters 11 and 12, except for the introduction of a state argument that has no effect on the final result.)

As before, the predomain V of values is isomorphic to a disjoint union of values of particular kinds:

$$V \underset{\psi}{\overset{\phi}{\rightleftarrows}} V_{\text{int}} + V_{\text{bool}} + V_{\text{fun}} + V_{\text{tuple}} + V_{\text{alt}} + V_{\text{cont}} + V_{\text{ref}},$$

where now

$$V_{\text{int}} = \mathbf{Z}$$

$$V_{\text{bool}} = \mathbf{B}$$

$$V_{\text{fun}} = V \to V_{\text{cont}} \to \Sigma \to V_*$$

$$V_{\text{tuple}} = V^*$$

$$V_{\text{alt}} = \mathbf{N} \times V$$

$$V_{\text{ref}} = \mathbf{Rf}.$$

Here the domain V_{fun} has been changed so that its members accept the state that is current when function application begins.

The injections from the V_θ to V are still defined in the same way as in Section 11.6:

$$\iota_{\text{int}} = \psi \cdot \iota_0 \in V_{\text{int}} \to V$$

$$\iota_{\text{bool}} = \psi \cdot \iota_1 \in V_{\text{bool}} \to V$$

$$\iota_{\text{fun}} = \psi \cdot \iota_2 \in V_{\text{fun}} \to V$$

$$\iota_{\text{tuple}} = \psi \cdot \iota_3 \in V_{\text{tuple}} \to V$$

$$\iota_{\text{alt}} = \psi \cdot \iota_4 \in V_{\text{alt}} \to V$$

$$\iota_{\text{cont}} = \psi \cdot \iota_5 \in V_{\text{cont}} \to V$$

$$\iota_{\text{ref}} = \psi \cdot \iota_6 \in V_{\text{ref}} \to V.$$

On the other hand, the extension of functions on the V_θ to functions on V must be given a different typing to accommodate the passing of states: If

$$f \in V_\theta \to \Sigma \to V_*,$$

then

$$f_\theta \in V \to \Sigma \to V_*.$$

Nevertheless, the actual equations defining these extensions remain the same as in Section 11.6:

$$f_\theta(\iota_\theta x) = f\, x$$

for $x \in V_\theta$, and

$$f_\theta\, z = \text{tyerr}$$

when z is not in the range of ι_θ.

To extend the semantic equations to describe state changes, we must thread the state through each equation in a way that reflects the order of evaluation. When a constant is evaluated, for example, the state does not change, so that the initial state σ_0 supplied to the meaning of the constant is passed directly to the continuation κ:

CN SEM EQ: Constants

$$[\![\lfloor k \rfloor]\!]\eta\kappa\sigma_0 = \kappa(\iota_{\text{int}}k)\sigma_0.$$

For unary operations, the evaluation of, say, $-e$ causes the same state change as the evaluation of e. Thus the initial state σ_0 is passed to the evaluation of e, and the state σ_1 that is supplied to a continuation by this evaluation is passed to the original continuation κ:

CN SEM EQ: Unary Operations

$$[\![-e]\!]\eta\kappa\sigma_0 = [\![e]\!]\eta\,(\lambda i.\ \lambda\sigma_1.\ \kappa(\iota_{\mathrm{int}}(-i))\sigma_1)_{\mathrm{int}}\sigma_0.$$

For binary operations, the evaluation of, say, $e + e'$ causes the state change due to the evaluation of e followed by the state change due to the evaluation of e'. Thus the initial state σ_0 is passed to the evaluation of e, the intermediate state σ_1 that is supplied to a continuation by this evaluation is passed to the evaluation of e', and the state σ_2 that is supplied to a continuation by this second evaluation is passed to the original continuation κ:

CN SEM EQ: Binary Operations

$$[\![e + e']\!]\eta\kappa\sigma_0 = [\![e]\!]\eta\,(\lambda i.\ \lambda\sigma_1.\ [\![e']\!]\eta\,(\lambda i'.\ \lambda\sigma_2.\ \kappa(\iota_{\mathrm{int}}(i + i'))\sigma_2)_{\mathrm{int}}\sigma_1)_{\mathrm{int}}\sigma_0.$$

In the semantic equation for abstractions (and also the equations for tuples and recursive definitions), something different happens. As with constants, the evaluation of an abstraction never causes a state change, so that the initial state σ_0 is passed to the continuation κ. But now there is a second state σ', which is supplied to the function that is the value of the abstraction when that function is applied to an argument, and which is passed to the evaluation of the body e of the abstraction:

CN SEM EQ: Abstraction

$$[\![\lambda v.\ e]\!]\eta\kappa\sigma_0 = \kappa(\iota_{\mathrm{fun}}(\lambda z.\ \lambda\kappa'.\ \lambda\sigma'.\ [\![e]\!][\,\eta \mid v\!:\!z\,]\kappa'\sigma'))\sigma_0.$$

At this point, we have given enough semantic equations to point out a surprising fact. In each of the semantic equations, by recognizing that two functions on states are equal if the results of applying them to an arbitrary state are equal, we can eliminate all explicit mention of states. (More formally, the occurrences of state variables can be eliminated by η-contraction in the metalanguage.) This reduces the equations given above to

CN SEM EQ: Constants

$$[\![\lfloor k \rfloor]\!]\eta\kappa = \kappa(\iota_{\mathrm{int}}k),$$

CN SEM EQ: Unary Operations

$$[\![-e]\!]\eta\kappa = [\![e]\!]\eta\,(\lambda i.\ \kappa(\iota_{\mathrm{int}}(-i)))_{\mathrm{int}},$$

CN SEM EQ: Binary Operations

$$[\![e + e']\!]\eta\kappa = [\![e]\!]\eta\,(\lambda i.\ [\![e']\!]\eta\,(\lambda i'.\ \kappa(\iota_{\mathrm{int}}(i + i')))_{\mathrm{int}})_{\mathrm{int}},$$

CN SEM EQ: Abstraction

$$[\![\lambda v.\ e]\!]\eta\kappa = \kappa(\iota_{\mathrm{fun}}(\lambda z.\ \lambda\kappa'.\ [\![e]\!][\,\eta \mid v\!:\!z\,]\kappa')).$$

Moreover, as the reader may verify, these equations are identical to those given for the same constructs in Section 12.1.

In fact, all of the semantic equations in Sections 12.1 and 12.2 remain unchanged by the introduction of states. Even the definition of the initial continuation, $\kappa_0 = \iota_{\text{norm}}$, remains the same. All that changes is the typing of the semantic function; the domains V, V_{cont}, V_{fun}, and V_{tuple}; the injections ι_{norm}, err, and tyerr; and the typing of the extension from f to f_θ.

Thus, all we need to do is to give the semantic equations for the newly introduced imperative operations that actually use and change states by allocating, evaluating, and assigning to references.

CN SEM EQ: Reference Creation

$$[\![\mathbf{mkref}\ e]\!]\eta\kappa\sigma_0 = [\![e]\!]\eta\,(\lambda z.\ \lambda\sigma_1.\ \kappa(\iota_{\text{ref}}\,r)[\,\sigma_1\mid r\!:z\,])\sigma_0,$$

where $r = \text{newref}(\text{dom}\,\sigma_1)$,

CN SEM EQ: Reference Evaluation

$$[\![\mathbf{val}\ e]\!]\eta\kappa\sigma_0 = [\![e]\!]\eta\,(\lambda r.\ \lambda\sigma_1.\ \kappa(\sigma_1 r)\sigma_1)_{\text{ref}}\sigma_0,$$

CN SEM EQ: Assignment

$$[\![e := e']\!]\eta\kappa\sigma_0 = [\![e]\!]\eta\,(\lambda r.\ \lambda\sigma_1.\ [\![e']\!]\eta(\lambda z.\ \lambda\sigma_2.\ \kappa z[\,\sigma_2\mid r\!:z\,])\sigma_1)_{\text{ref}}\sigma_0,$$

CN SEM EQ: Reference Equality

$$[\![e =_{\text{ref}} e']\!]\eta\kappa\sigma_0 = [\![e]\!]\eta\,(\lambda r.\ \lambda\sigma_1.\ [\![e']\!]\eta(\lambda r'.\ \lambda\sigma_2.\ \kappa(\iota_{\text{bool}}(r = r'))\sigma_2)_{\text{ref}}\sigma_1)_{\text{ref}}\sigma_0.$$

(Notice that, in the first three of these equations, some of the state variables — specifically σ_1 in the first two equations and σ_2 in the third — cannot be eliminated by η-contraction.) Finally, the initial state that is passed to the meaning of a complete program is the empty function

$$\sigma_0 = [\,].$$

The careful reader may notice a problem with the equation given above for the meaning of **val** e: Since r ranges over the set **Rf** of all references, but the state σ_1 is a function whose domain is a finite set of references, it is conceivable that the application $\sigma_1 r$ could be undefined. In fact it is intuitively evident that this cannot occur, since the domain of the current state is never reduced, and whenever a new reference is introduced by evaluating newref, the domain of the current state is enlarged to include the new reference. But a rigorous proof that undefined state applications cannot occur is difficult and beyond the scope of this book.

It should also be noted that we have made a plausible but not inevitable assumption in taking the references that can be the values of expressions to be the entities that are mapped by states into values. An alternative is to take "reference values" to be *update-evaluate pairs*, which consist of a function describing the state transformation caused by assignment and a function describing the mapping of states into current values. We will use update-evaluate pairs to describe Algol-like languages in Section 19.5.

13.4 Some Syntactic Sugar

Although we have introduced assignment and related operations, our language still lacks the control-flow constructs and variable declarations that are characteristic of imperative languages. In fact, such constructs can be defined as abbreviations in terms of the existing language, so that no further semantic extensions are required.

In particular, we can define

$$\textbf{newvar } v := e \textbf{ in } e' \stackrel{\text{def}}{=} \textbf{let } v \equiv \textbf{mkref } e \textbf{ in } e'$$

$$\textbf{skip} \stackrel{\text{def}}{=} \langle \rangle$$

$$e \,;\, e' \stackrel{\text{def}}{=} \textbf{let } \langle \rangle \equiv e \textbf{ in } e'$$

$$\textbf{while } e \textbf{ do } e' \stackrel{\text{def}}{=} \textbf{letrec } w \equiv \lambda \langle \rangle. \textbf{ if } e \textbf{ then } e' \,;\, w \,\langle \rangle \textbf{ else skip in } w \,\langle \rangle,$$

where the variable w does not occur free in e or e'.

13.5 First-Order Semantics

The continuation semantics of Section 13.3 can be transformed into a first-order semantics in the same way as described in Section 12.4. As before, the sets V_{cont}, V_{fun}, and E of functions become sets of records that are the domains of the interpretive functions cont, apply, and get. But now the first two of these interpretive functions have a more complex functionality:

$$\text{cont} \in V_{\text{cont}} \to V \to \Sigma \to V_*$$

$$\text{apply} \in V_{\text{fun}} \to V \to V_{\text{cont}} \to \Sigma \to V_*$$

$$\text{get} \in E \to \langle \text{var} \rangle \to V.$$

Despite this change in typing, the first-order equations in Section 12.4 remain unchanged, just as the continuation-semantic equations of Section 12.1 remain unchanged. The only difference is that the semantic equations, along with the equations for cont and apply, now describe functions in $\Sigma \to V_*$ rather than results in V_*. Thus, for example, the equations for application:

$$\llbracket ee' \rrbracket \eta \kappa = \llbracket e \rrbracket \eta \langle \mathbf{app}_1, e', \eta, \kappa \rangle$$

$$\text{cont} \, \langle \mathbf{app}_1, e', \eta, \kappa \rangle \, z = (\lambda f. \, \llbracket e' \rrbracket \eta \langle \mathbf{app}_2, f, \kappa \rangle)_{\text{fun}} z$$

$$\text{cont} \, \langle \mathbf{app}_2, f, \kappa \rangle \, z = \text{apply} \, f \, z \, \kappa$$

can be rewritten in a more concrete form by applying both sides of the equations to state variables:

$$\llbracket ee' \rrbracket \eta \kappa \sigma_0 = \llbracket e \rrbracket \eta \langle \mathbf{app}_1, e', \eta, \kappa \rangle \sigma_0$$

$$\text{cont} \, \langle \mathbf{app}_1, e', \eta, \kappa \rangle \, z \, \sigma_1 = (\lambda f. \, \llbracket e' \rrbracket \eta \langle \mathbf{app}_2, f, \kappa \rangle)_{\text{fun}} z \, \sigma_1$$

$$\text{cont} \, \langle \mathbf{app}_2, f, \kappa \rangle \, z \, \sigma_2 = \text{apply} \, f \, z \, \kappa \, \sigma_2.$$

It is also straightforward to transform the new equations for imperative operations:

$$\llbracket \mathbf{mkref} \, e \rrbracket \eta \kappa \sigma_0 = \llbracket e \rrbracket \eta \, \langle \mathbf{createref}, \kappa \rangle \, \sigma_0$$

$$\text{cont} \langle \mathbf{createref}, \kappa \rangle z \sigma_1 = \text{cont} \, \kappa (\iota_{\text{ref}} \, r)[\, \sigma_1 \mid r \colon z \,] \text{ where } r = \text{newref}(\text{dom} \, \sigma_1)$$

$$\llbracket \mathbf{val} \, e \rrbracket \eta \kappa \sigma_0 = \llbracket e \rrbracket \eta \, \langle \mathbf{valref}, \kappa \rangle \, \sigma_0$$

$$\text{cont} \langle \mathbf{valref}, \kappa \rangle z \sigma_1 = (\lambda r. \, \lambda \sigma_1. \, \text{cont} \, \kappa (\sigma_1 r) \sigma_1)_{\text{ref}} z \sigma_1$$

$$\llbracket e := e' \rrbracket \eta \kappa \sigma_0 = \llbracket e \rrbracket \eta \, \langle \mathbf{assign}_1, e', \eta, \kappa \rangle \, \sigma_0$$

$$\text{cont} \langle \mathbf{assign}_1, e', \eta, \kappa \rangle z \sigma_1 = (\lambda r. \, \lambda \sigma_1. \, \llbracket e' \rrbracket \eta \, \langle \mathbf{assign}_2, r, \kappa \rangle \, \sigma_1)_{\text{ref}} z \sigma_1$$

$$\text{cont} \langle \mathbf{assign}_2, r, \kappa \rangle z \sigma_2 = \text{cont} \, \kappa \, z [\, \sigma_2 \mid r \colon z \,]$$

$$\llbracket e =_{\text{ref}} e' \rrbracket \eta \kappa \sigma_0 = \llbracket e \rrbracket \eta \, \langle \mathbf{eqref}_1, e', \eta, \kappa \rangle \, \sigma_0$$

$$\text{cont} \langle \mathbf{eqref}_1, e', \eta, \kappa \rangle z \sigma_1 = (\lambda r. \, \lambda \sigma_1. \, \llbracket e' \rrbracket \eta \, \langle \mathbf{eqref}_2, r, \kappa \rangle \, \sigma_1)_{\text{ref}} z \sigma_1$$

$$\text{cont} \langle \mathbf{eqref}_2, r, \kappa \rangle z \sigma_2 = (\lambda r'. \, \lambda \sigma_2. \, \text{cont} \, \kappa \, (\iota_{\text{bool}} (r = r')) \sigma_2) z \sigma_2.$$

In these equations, we have not defunctionalized states, which are still functions from references to values. If we were to do so, we would obtain a representation by a list of reference-value pairs, similar to the representation of environments (without **recenv**). In an actual interpreter, however, this would be ludicrously inefficient, since the length of such a list would be increased by every execution of an assignment command.

It is better to take advantage of the fact that states are functions on *finite* sets, and to use any of a variety of ways of representing such functions by tabulating their values. Most straightforwardly, one could represent states by tuples, as suggested by Equation (13.1) in Section 13.1, or, for more efficiency, one could use binary search trees.

Even with a sophisticated representation such as binary search trees, however, there is an inherent inefficiency in interpreting a language containing assignment in terms of a purely functional language. The fundamental difficulty is that one cannot express the fact that the state can be updated in place, since the old state will become inactive whenever a new state is constructed. (Recently, however, it has become apparent that this difficulty can be overcome by imposing a novel typing system called "linear typing" on the purely functional language.)

13.6 Examples

As a first example, we give the procedure for computing Fibonacci numbers that was used to illustrate aliasing in Section 13.1. To begin with, we assume that the arguments denoted by the formal parameters n and f are both references:

> let fib ≡ λn. λf.
>
>> if **val** n = 0 **then** f := 0 **else**
>>
>>> **newvar** k := 1 **in newvar** g := 0 **in** (f := 1 ;
>>>
>>>> **while val** k ≠ **val** n **do**
>>>>
>>>>> let t ≡ **val** g **in** (g := **val** f ; f := **val** f + t ; k := **val** k + 1))
>>
> **in** ··· .

Here we have made t into a variable whose value is an integer rather than a reference, since it is an unnecessary complication to use a reference that is never assigned after its initialization. Aside from this change, the only differences from the program in Section 13.1 are the occurrences of the operator **val**.

Even from this simple example, it is clear that the profusion of **val**'s in highly imperative programs can be a nuisance. Some languages, such as Algol 68 and Gedanken, provide an implicit conversion from references to their values in contexts where references would otherwise cause a type error. (This is trickier than it sounds. The conversion must be iterated when the value of a reference is another reference, and can even diverge when a reference is its own value.) On the other hand, Standard ML does not provide such an implicit conversion, though it does replace **val** with the more succinct exclamation point.

As discussed in Section 13.1, aliasing prevents the above procedure from working correctly when it is invoked by a call such as fib a a, where both actual parameters are the same reference. There are two obvious ways to circumvent this problem. One way is to make the input parameter n an integer rather than a reference; then, in place of the aliasing example, we would have let fib ≡ λn. λf.

    if n = 0 **then** f := 0 **else**

        newvar k := 1 **in newvar** g := 0 **in** (f := 1 ;

            while val k ≠ n **do**

                let t ≡ **val** g **in** (g := **val** f ; f := **val** f + t ; k := **val** k + 1))

  in fib (**val** a) a,

which correctly sets a to the Fibonacci number of its initial value.

Changing an input parameter from a reference to its value becomes more complicated if the parameter is assigned to within the body of the procedure. In this case, one must replace the occurrences of the parameter in the body of the procedure by a local reference that is initialized to the input parameter. Thus, for example, the procedure

let power2 ≡ λn. λy.

    (y := 1 ; **while val** n > 0 **do** (n := **val** n − 1 ; y := 2 × **val** y)) ⋯ ,

where n is a reference, becomes

let power2 ≡ λn. λy. **newvar** nn := n **in**

    (y := 1 ; **while val** nn > 0 **do** (nn := **val** nn − 1 ; y := 2 × **val** y)) ⋯ ,

where n is an integer.

In those Iswim-like languages where references are implicitly converted to their values, one must specify explicitly whether a parameter is to be *called by reference* (in which case it will not be converted to a nonreference value) or *called by value* (in which case it will be converted). In Algol 60, where the specification "call by value" was originally introduced, this specification actually invoked a program transformation similar to that shown above.

The other way of avoiding aliasing is to replace an output parameter, such as f in the body of the procedure fib, by a local reference whose final value is assigned to f at the end of the body, after all of the evaluations of other parameters:

let fib ≡ λn. λf. **newvar** ff := 1 **in**

    (**if val** n = 0 **then** ff := 0 **else**

        newvar k := 1 **in newvar** g := 0 **in**

            while val k ≠ **val** n **do**

                let t ≡ **val** g **in** (g := **val** ff ; ff := **val** ff + t ; k := **val** k + 1);

    f := **val** ff)

  in ⋯ .

(Here we have used the initialization of ff to eliminate the first assignment to this reference in the main branch of the conditional expression.) A similar transformation was built into the language Algol W, where it was invoked by specifying that f is *called by result*. (Both call by value and by result will be discussed further in Section 19.3.)

Unfortunately, these examples convey the misleading impression that the vagaries of aliasing are easy to avoid. While this is largely true for parameters that are simple references, the problem is much more serious for parameters that are arrays. For array parameters, the above transformations require the allocation and copying of local arrays, which can waste considerable space and time. In contrast, efficient programming often requires one to use an entirely different "in-place" algorithm when input and output arrays are to be the same rather than different. For example, to transpose an $n \times n$ matrix X in place, one would iterate the exchange of $X(i,j)$ with $X(j,i)$ over $0 \leq i < j < n$. Similarly, one might sort an array using *quicksort* rather than sorting by merging.

Although most popular programming languages fit the Iswim-like mold, they provide a weaker procedure mechanism than what we have described here; many prohibit functions (or procedures) from being the results of functions or the value of references, or sometimes even arguments to functions. In contrast, languages such as Iswim, PAL, Gedanken, Scheme, and ML were built around the rallying cry "functions should be first-class citizens". In comparison with languages like Pascal or C, such "higher-level" languages provided a substantial increase in expressiveness, though originally at considerable cost in efficiency (especially because of the need for garbage collection).

In recent years, the execution speed and memory utilization of higher-level languages have been greatly improved by the development of sophisticated compiling techniques. Nevertheless, it remains true that, for the limited class of programs that can be written straightforwardly in lower-level languages, the lower-level languages make it easier for the programmer to estimate time and storage requirements.

Higher-order procedures that accept procedures as arguments are particularly useful for expressing imperative control structures. For example, the following procedure mimics the **for** command described in Section 2.6:

$$\textbf{let } \mathsf{fordo} \equiv \lambda \mathsf{a}.\ \lambda \mathsf{b}.\ \lambda \mathsf{p}.\ \textbf{newvar } \mathsf{k} := \mathsf{a}\ \textbf{in}$$
$$\textbf{while val } \mathsf{k} \leq \mathsf{b}\ \textbf{do } (\mathsf{p}\,(\textbf{val}\,\mathsf{k})\,;\, \mathsf{k} := \textbf{val}\,\mathsf{k} + 1)\ \cdots.$$

Specifically, this procedure accepts integers a and b and an integer-accepting proper procedure p, and applies p to each integer in a **to** b in increasing order. (Notice that, since a and b are not references, their values cannot be changed by the procedure p. Similarly, p cannot assign to the reference k, since its argument is the value of k rather than k itself.)

A simple example of a recursively defined control procedure is

$$\textbf{letrec map} \equiv \lambda\mathsf{p}. \ \lambda\mathsf{x}. \ \textbf{listcase} \ \mathsf{x} \ \textbf{of} \ (\textbf{skip}, \lambda\mathsf{i}. \ \lambda\mathsf{r}. \ (\mathsf{p\,i}\,; \mathsf{map\,p\,r})) \cdots,$$

which accepts a proper procedure p and a list x, and applies p to each element of x. (Compare this with the definition of mapcar in Section 11.5.)

More interesting things can be done with functions that return functions; for example, one can *memoize* functions. If f is an integer-accepting function, then memo f is a function with the same external behavior that remembers its past history, using a local reference to a list of argument-result pairs, to avoid repeating the same computation:

$$\textbf{let memo} \equiv \lambda\mathsf{f}. \ \textbf{newvar} \ \mathsf{r} := \textbf{nil in} \ \lambda\mathsf{n}.$$
$$\mathsf{search} \ (\textbf{val r}) \ (\lambda\langle\mathsf{i},\mathsf{j}\rangle. \ \mathsf{i} = \mathsf{n}) \ (\lambda\langle\mathsf{i},\mathsf{j}\rangle. \ \mathsf{j})$$
$$(\lambda\langle\rangle. \ \textbf{let} \ \mathsf{y} \equiv \mathsf{f} \ \mathsf{n} \ \textbf{in} \ (\mathsf{r} := \langle\mathsf{n},\mathsf{y}\rangle :: \textbf{val r}\,; \mathsf{y})) \cdots.$$

(The function search used here was defined in Section 11.5.)

13.7 Exceptions

A variety of powerful programming techniques become possible when an eager-evaluation functional language provides both references and continuations as values. One possibility is to use these facilities to provide an exception mechanism. To illustrate exceptions, we will use the syntax

$$\langle\exp\rangle ::= \textbf{raise} \ \langle\exp\rangle \ | \ \textbf{handle} \ \langle\mathrm{var}\rangle \ \textbf{with} \ \langle\exp\rangle \ \textbf{in} \ \langle\exp\rangle$$

Actually, it is straightforward to use continuations by themselves to provide a *static* exception mechanism. In the static approach, **handle** v **with** e **in** e' is a binder of v whose scope is the body e'; when executed, it causes v to denote an *exception* and then evaluates e'. Thereafter, if **raise** e'' is executed and e'' evaluates to the exception denoted by v, we say that the exception is *raised*; this causes e to be evaluated and its value to become the value of the **handle** expression. On the other hand, if the exception is not raised during the evaluation of e', the value of e' becomes the value of the **handle** expression. This behavior can be described by taking exceptions to be procedures that accept a dummy parameter and execute a **throw**, as defined by the desugaring

$$\textbf{handle} \ v \ \textbf{with} \ e \ \textbf{in} \ e' \stackrel{\text{def}}{=} \textbf{callcc} \ \lambda k. \ \textbf{let} \ v \equiv \lambda\langle\rangle. \ \textbf{throw} \ k \ e \ \textbf{in} \ e'$$

$$\textbf{raise} \ e \stackrel{\text{def}}{=} e \ \langle\rangle.$$

Strange things can happen, however, if an exception escapes from the **handle**
expression where it was defined, either by being embedded in the result of this
expression or by being assigned to a reference, and is raised after the **handle** expression has completed evaluation. For example, **raise(handle** v **with** λx. x **in** v)
gives the value $\langle\rangle$, after applying the same continuation twice (much as in the
example at the end of Section 12.2).

A further problem with static exceptions occurs when an exception is raised
in a function that is called from the body of a **handle** expression but is defined
outside of the scope of the **handle** expression:

$$\textbf{let } f \equiv \lambda x. \; \cdots \; \textbf{raise } v \; \cdots \; \textbf{in}$$
$$\textbf{handle } v \textbf{ with } e \textbf{ in } \; \cdots \; f(\cdots) \; \cdots .$$

Here one might expect the raising of v to cause e to become the value of the
handle expression, but in fact, since **raise** v lies outside the scope of **handle** v, an
error will occur (unless v is bound to an exception or function in the surrounding
context).

For these reasons, most languages, such as Standard ML, that provide exceptions use a *dynamic* exception mechanism. In this approach, **handle** v $\cdots$ is not
a binder of v. Instead, exception handling is kept track of in a stack-like manner
by a function-valued reference, which we will call *excphandler* (for "exception
handler"), that is global to the entire program being executed. Whenever an
exception is raised, the current value of the exception handler is applied to the
exception. The initial value of the exception handler is a function that gives an
error stop whenever it is applied:

$$\textbf{let } excphandler \equiv \textbf{mkref } \lambda x. \textbf{ error } \cdots .$$

The effect of **handle** v **with** e **in** e' is to set *excphandler* to a new function for
the duration of the execution of e' and restore its old value upon the completion
of e'. If the new function is applied to an exception that equals v, then the old
value of the handler is restored, e is evaluated, and a **throw** is executed to make
the value of e become the value of the **handle** expression. Thus, **handle** and
raise can be desugared as

handle v **with** e **in** e'

$\qquad \overset{\text{def}}{=} \textbf{let } oldeh \equiv \textbf{val } excphandler \textbf{ in}$

$\qquad\qquad \textbf{callcc } \lambda k. \, (excphandler := \lambda x.$

$\qquad\qquad\qquad \textbf{if } x = v \textbf{ then } excphandler := oldeh \,; \textbf{ throw } k \, e \textbf{ else } oldeh \, x \,;$

$\qquad\qquad\qquad \textbf{let } z \equiv e' \textbf{ in } (excphandler := oldeh \,; z))$

and

$$\textbf{raise } e \overset{\text{def}}{=} (\textbf{val } excphandler) \, e.$$

Here *excphandler*, k, x, and z must be distinct variables such that k, x, and z do not occur free in v, e, or e', and *excphandler* does not occur (except for the specific occurrences in the above definition) in the entire program.

Except for the assumption that exceptions can be tested for equality, the above definition begs the question of what exceptions actually are. The simplest possibility would be to take them to be integers. But this would make it impossible, when writing a part of a program, to use exceptions that are guaranteed not to be used by any other part. Because of this, it is useful to introduce an expression

$$\langle \text{exp} \rangle ::= \textbf{mkexception}$$

such that each evaluation of **mkexception** creates a new exception that is distinct from any other being used in the execution of the program.

One could implement **mkexception** by taking exceptions to be integers and having each execution of **mkexception** produce the "next" integer. But in fact, references already have the properties we need for exceptions. It is simplest to define

$$\textbf{mkexception} \stackrel{\text{def}}{=} \textbf{mkref},$$

and to replace the test $x = v$ in the definition of **handle** by $x =_{\text{ref}} y$. (Notice that this is a use of references where the fact that they possess values is inconsequential.)

Although dynamic exceptions have advantages over the static approach, they are not without their own difficulties. For example, it does not seem possible to devise a form of typing judgement (in the sense to be described in Section 15.1) that can assert that an expression will never raise unhandled exceptions outside of a specified set of exceptions.

In languages such as Standard ML, an argument can be passed to the exception handler when an exception is raised. This generalization is described in Exercise 13.4.

13.8 Backtracking

We have seen that strange behavior can occur when a continuation value escapes from the **callcc** expression that defined it. In this section, we will see how to put this behavior to good use, in computing a list of all possible results of a nondeterministic function.

Consider a function f in our object language that accepts a functional argument amb, which in turn accepts a dummy argument. Imagine that this function is to be evaluated by an ensemble of computers in which, whenever one of the computers evaluates amb$\langle\rangle$, it fissions into two computers, in one of which amb$\langle\rangle$ returns **true** while in the other it returns **false**.

We assume that f always terminates, and does not use references or **callcc** or **throw**. Then the following function, when applied to f, will return a list of all of the results produced by members of the ensemble:

> let backtrack ≡ λf.
>
>> **let** rl ≡ **mkref nil**, cl ≡ **mkref nil in**
>>
>>> (rl := f (λ⟨⟩. **callcc** (λk. (cl := k :: **val** cl ; **true**))) :: **val** rl ;
>>>
>>> **listcase val** cl **of**(**val** rl, λc. λr. (cl := r ; **throw** c **false**)))
>>
>> **in** ⋯ .

This function traces through the tree of executions of f in a depth-first manner. Each time the assignment to rl in the third line is completed, the value of rl will be a list of the results produced so far, and the value of cl will be a list of continuations that, when each is applied to **false**, will compute the remaining results.

When f calls its argument, the result **true** is returned, but beforehand a continuation is added to cl that eventually will be used to return **false** from the same call. Specifically, whenever f completes execution, if cl is not empty, a continuation is removed from this list and is thrown the value **false**.

Thus, for example, the expression

> backtrack(λamb.
>
>> **if** amb⟨⟩ **then if** amb⟨⟩ **then** 0 **else** 1 **else if** amb⟨⟩ **then** 2 **else** 3)

will evaluate to the list 3 :: 2 :: 1 :: 0 :: **nil**.

A more flexible version of backtrack provides f with a second argument, fail, which is also a function accepting a dummy argument. When a computer in the ensemble executes fail⟨⟩, it vanishes from the ensemble. This effect is obtained by having fail⟨⟩ throw to a continuation kf that aborts the evaluation of f without adding anything to the list rl:

> let backtrack ≡ λf.
>
>> **let** rl ≡ **mkref nil**, cl ≡ **mkref nil in**
>>
>>> (**callcc**(λkf. rl :=
>>>
>>>> f (λ⟨⟩. **callcc** (λk. (cl := k :: **val** cl ; **true**)))(λ⟨⟩. **throw** kf ⟨⟩) :: **val** rl) ;
>>>
>>> **listcase val** cl **of**(**val** rl, λc. λr. (cl := r ; **throw** c **false**)))
>>
>> **in** ⋯ .

Thus, for example, the expression

> backtrack(λamb. λfail.
>
>> **if** amb⟨⟩ **then if** amb⟨⟩ **then** 0 **else** fail⟨⟩ **else if** amb⟨⟩ **then** 2 **else** 3)

will evaluate to the list $3 :: 2 :: 0 ::$ **nil**.

As a less trivial example, the following function, when applied to n and s, will produce a list of all those lists of zeros and ones whose lengths are n and whose elements sum to s:

> **let** bitseq $\equiv$ λn. λs. backtrack(λamb. λfail.
>
>   **letrec** bs $\equiv$ λn. λs.
>
>   **if** n $= 0$ **then if** s $= 0$ **then nil else** fail$\langle\rangle$
>
>   **else if** s $= 0$ **then** $0 ::$ bs$(n - 1)$s
>
>   **else if** amb$\langle\rangle$ **then** $0 ::$ bs$(n - 1)$s **else** $1 ::$ bs$(n - 1)(s - 1)$
>
>   **in** bs n s)
>
> **in** $\cdots$.

13.9 Input and Output

It is straightforward to add input and output operations to the language described in this chapter. For output we will use the same notation as in Section 5.2:

$$\langle exp \rangle ::= \;! \langle exp \rangle$$

Now, however, since $! \, e$ is an expression, it must yield a value, which we specify to be the value of e.

We will skirt over the issue of what it means to output a value that is not an integer or boolean. For tuples, alternatives, and references, one can provide output in the same notation as is used in the programming language for constructing such entities. But functions and continuations are more problematical; most implementations of Iswim-like languages merely produce symbols indicating that the value is a function or a continuation, without providing further information.

For input, on the other hand, there is no really satisfactory way of dealing with compound or functional data, so we will consider only integers and booleans. It would be possible to follow the approach of Section 5.6, that is, to provide an expression that assigns input values to references, but the approach most commonly used in Iswim-like languages is to provide expressions that yield input items as their values:

$$\langle exp \rangle ::= \textbf{readint} \mid \textbf{readbool}$$

The evaluation of **readint** (or **readbool**) causes an integer (or boolean) item to be read from the input stream, and yields the value of this item.

Of course, these input expressions are not expressions in the traditional sense of mathematics. For example, **readint** $-$ **readint** may not evaluate to zero. But this kind of behavior becomes possible as soon as expressions can have side effects.

Continuation semantics can be extended to deal with input-output by taking V_* to be a domain of resumptions, similar to Ω in Sections 5.6 and 5.8. Specifically, we redefine V_* to be a solution of the isomorphism

$$V_* \xrightarrow[\psi']{\phi'} (V + \{\mathbf{error}, \mathbf{typeerror}\} + (V \times V_*) + (V_{\mathrm{int}} \to V_*) + (V_{\mathrm{bool}} \to V_*))_\perp,$$

with the injections

$$\iota_{\mathrm{norm}} = \lambda z.\ \lambda\sigma.\ \psi'(\iota_\uparrow(\iota_0\, z)) \in V \to \Sigma \to V_*$$

$$\mathrm{err} = \lambda\sigma.\ \psi'(\iota_\uparrow(\iota_1\, \mathbf{error})) \in \Sigma \to V_*$$

$$\mathrm{tyerr} = \lambda\sigma.\ \psi'(\iota_\uparrow(\iota_1\, \mathbf{typeerror})) \in \Sigma \to V_*$$

$$\iota_{\mathrm{out}} = \psi' \cdot \iota_\uparrow \cdot \iota_2 \in (V \times V_*) \to V_*$$

$$\iota_{\mathrm{intin}} = \psi' \cdot \iota_\uparrow \cdot \iota_3 \in (V_{\mathrm{int}} \to V_*) \to V_*$$

$$\iota_{\mathrm{boolin}} = \psi' \cdot \iota_\uparrow \cdot \iota_4 \in (V_{\mathrm{bool}} \to V_*) \to V_*.$$

Then the semantic equations of Section 13.3 remain unchanged, while the equations for input and output expressions are

CN SEM EQ: Output

$$[\![!\, e]\!]\eta\kappa\sigma_0 = [\![e]\!]\eta(\lambda z.\ \lambda\sigma_1.\ \iota_{\mathrm{out}}\langle z, \kappa\, z\, \sigma_1\rangle)\sigma_0,$$

CN SEM EQ: Input

$$[\![\mathbf{readint}]\!]\eta\kappa\sigma_0 = \iota_{\mathrm{intin}}(\lambda i.\ \kappa(\iota_{\mathrm{int}}i)\sigma_0)$$

$$[\![\mathbf{readbool}]\!]\eta\kappa\sigma_0 = \iota_{\mathrm{boolin}}(\lambda b.\ \kappa(\iota_{\mathrm{bool}}b)\sigma_0).$$

In conclusion, it must be admitted that the input-output facilities described here are hardly adequate for a practical programming language. While a full discussion of the topic is beyond the scope of this book, one point should be emphasized: A serious language must provide a wide spectrum of input-output facilities. At one extreme are constructs that are succinct and easy to use, but that impose specific and inflexible formats on the user; such facilities are appropriate for input-output that is needed only during the development of a program. At the opposite extreme are much lower-level constructs that require extensive programming but provide maximum flexibility; these facilities are needed when the format of input or output must adhere to rigid, externally imposed specifications.

13.10 Some Complications

Despite the addition of imperative features, our language still satisfies the coincidence theorem (10.9) and the soundness of renaming (10.12). One might also expect some analogue of the coincidence theorem for states, for example, that the meaning of a program is unaffected by the value of "inactive" references. However, it is difficult to formulate the notion of "inactive" in denotational semantics, since references can be embedded within data structures and even in closures. For example, the result of the function memo defined in the previous section would be a closure containing a reference to a list of argument-result pairs. (There are also complications due to the fact that the allocation of a reference changes the identity of all later-allocated references.)

The memo example also makes it clear that both references and the closures denoting functional results can remain active long after control has exited from the blocks (e.g. **newvar**, **let**, and **letrec** expressions) in which they are defined. Moreover, references can be used to create cyclic structures. For these reasons, storage cannot be managed with a stack discipline, nor by using reference counts, so that garbage collection is necessary.

A different kind of problem is the unsoundness of β- and η-contraction, as well as various laws of arithmetic. Of course, contraction is unsound even for a purely functional language with eager evaluation, as in Chapter 11, but there the only failure is that a divergent program may contract to a terminating one. In contrast, once assignment is introduced, contraction can change the meaning of terminating programs.

For example,

$$\textbf{newvar } r := 3 \textbf{ in } (r := 4 \,;\, \textbf{val } r) \stackrel{\text{def}}{=} \textbf{let } r \equiv \textbf{mkref } 3 \textbf{ in } (r := 4 \,;\, \textbf{val } r)$$
$$\stackrel{\text{def}}{=} (\lambda r.\ (r := 4 \,;\, \textbf{val } r))(\textbf{mkref } 3)$$

has the value 4, but β-contracts to

$$(\textbf{mkref } 3) := 4 \,;\, \textbf{val } (\textbf{mkref } 3),$$

which has the value 3.

A similar example for η-contraction is

$$\textbf{newvar } r := \lambda x.\ x \textbf{ in let } f \equiv \lambda x.\ (\textbf{val } r)\, x \textbf{ in } (r := \lambda x.\ x + 1 \,;\, f\, 3),$$

which evaluates to 4, but η-contracts to

$$\textbf{newvar } r := \lambda x.\ x \textbf{ in let } f \equiv \textbf{val } r \textbf{ in } (r := \lambda x.\ x + 1 \,;\, f\, 3),$$

which evaluates to 3.

An example of the failure of an arithmetic law is

$$(x := x + 1 \,;\, \textbf{val } x) - (x := x + 1 \,;\, \textbf{val } x),$$

which evaluates to -1 rather than to zero. (A similar example involving input, **readint** − **readint**, was given in Section 13.9.)

Both the need for garbage collection, and the unsoundness of contraction and the laws of arithmetic distinguish Iswim-like languages from the Algol-like languages that will be described in Chapter 19.

Bibliographic Notes

Although many relevant concepts appeared in Lisp [McCarthy, 1960; McCarthy et al., 1962], the first truly Iswim-like language was Iswim itself [Landin, 1966c]. Later untyped languages in this category include PAL [Evans, 1968], Gedanken [Reynolds, 1970], and Scheme [Sussman and Steele Jr., 1975]. Typed Iswim-like languages include Algol 68 [van Wijngaarden et al., 1969; 1975], Basel [Cheatham, Fischer, and Jorrand, 1968], and ML [Gordon et al., 1977; Milner, Tofte, and Harper, 1990]. An excellent text on Iswim-like programming (in Scheme) is Abelson et al. [1985].

The earliest semantics of Iswim-like languages (long before the distinction from Algol-like languages was clear) was given by Landin [1965a; 1966a], using an approach similar to the first-order semantics of Section 12.4. A continuation semantics (of Gedanken) was given by Tennent [1976] and an eager evaluation semantics (of Standard ML) by Milner et al. [1990; 1991].

We have used the term "computational effect" to describe assignment in the context of a functional language, but this term could also describe other deviations from a mathematically pure notion of functions, such as nondeterminacy, **throw**, and even divergence. A general approach to the denotational semantics of such effects, using the category-theoretic concept of a *monad*, has been devised by Moggi [1991]. A less technical explanation of the implications for language design and programming is given by Wadler [1992; 1993].

The idea of memoizing functions is due to Michie [1967; 1968].

Exercises

13.1   The following expression contains a β-redex of the form $(\lambda x.\ \cdots)(\cdots)$. Give the result of evaluating the expression itself, the expression obtained by contracting the redex within the original expression, and the result of evaluating the reduced expression.

$$\textbf{let } r \equiv \textbf{mkref } 0 \textbf{ in } \big(\lambda x.\ (r := 1\,;x)\big)(\textbf{val } r).$$

13.2   The function **memo** defined in Section 13.6 is of little value when applied to recursively defined functions, since it only prevents the recomputation of previously computed results at the top level, rather than at every level of the recursion. Thus, for example, the memoization of

> **letrec** fib ≡ λn. **if** n = 0 **then** 0 **else if** n = 1 **then** 1 **else**
> fib(n − 1) + fib(n − 2) ⋯

would not avoid the exponential time used by the repeated evaluation of recursive calls with the same argument.

Define a function memorec that memoizes a recursively defined function at all levels of its recursion. Specifically, memorec should accept a function F that maps integer-accepting functions into integer-accepting functions, and should produce a memoized version of the function that is the least fixed-point of F, in which repeated evaluation for the same argument is avoided throughout the recursive calculation. (Here we use the term "least fixed-point of F" in the context of the object language to denote the function that would be defined by **letrec** f ≡ λn. F f n **in** f.)

For example,

> **let** fib ≡ memorec(λf. λn. **if** n = 0 **then** 0 **else if** n = 1 **then** 1 **else**
> f(n − 1) + f(n − 2)) ⋯

would define a Fibonacci function such that the call fib 10 would cause a single call of fib applied to each natural number smaller than 10.

13.3   A *reversible reference* has the same behavior as a reference, but also an additional operation undo. The procedure calls listed below on the left have the same effect for reversible references and their values as the expressions listed on the right do for ordinary references and their values:

mkrevref e	**mkref** e
revval r	**val** r
revassign r e	$r := e$
reveq r r'	$r =_{eq} r'$.

In addition, the call

> undo r

causes the reversible reference r to revert to the value it had before the assignment that produced its current value. The restored value is also the result of undo. An attempt to undo an initial value causes an error.

Program the functions mkrevref, revval, revassign, reveq, and undo in the language of this chapter.

Hint Implement a reversible reference by an ordinary reference whose value lists all of the values that have been assigned to the reversible reference but not rescinded by undo.

13.4   In languages such as Standard ML, arguments can be passed to handlers
        when exceptions are raised. To describe such a facility, revise both the
        static and dynamic exception mechanisms of Section 13.7 so that **raise** e''
        is replaced by **raise** e'' **with** e'''. As before, an exception raised by this
        expression will be handled by **handle** v **with** e **in** e', where v matches
        the value of e''. But now e''' will also be evaluated, and then the value of
        e, which must be a function, will be applied to the value of e''', and the
        result of this application will become the value of the **handle** expression.

13.5   When dynamic exceptions are defined in terms of continuations and refer-
        ences, as in Section 13.7, the operations **callcc** and **throw** cease to behave
        correctly, since the value of excphandler may be changed but not restored
        by evaluating **callcc** e if this evaluation is terminated by a **throw**. For
        example, during the execution of

        handle v **with** e_0 **in**

        ⟨**callcc** λk. **handle** v **with** e_1 **in throw** k 0, **raise** v⟩,

        the inner exception handler will still be the value of *excphandler* after the
        evaluation of **callcc** $\cdots$ has been terminated by executing **throw** k 0.
        Thus, **raise** v will cause e_1 to be evaluated.
            Define a function newcallcc that can be used in place of **callcc** to over-
        come this problem.

13.6   Consider a finite directed graph with integers as nodes. It can be repre-
        sented by a list of pairs ⟨x, ℓ⟩, where x is a node and ℓ is a list of those
        nodes y such that there is an edge from x to y. A node appears as the
        first component of such a pair if there is an edge from that node to any
        node.
            A *noncyclic path* from a node x to a node y in such a graph is a
        nonempty list of nodes $x_0, \ldots, x_n$ such that $x = x_0$, $x_n = y$, there is
        an edge from each node in the list to the next, and the nodes in the list
        are all distinct.
            Write a function paths in the language of this chapter such that, when
        x and y are nodes and g is a list representing a finite directed graph,
        paths g x y will produce a list of all noncyclic paths from x to y. This
        function should be defined by applying the function backtrack defined in
        Section 13.8 to a simpler function that traces out a path while calling amb
        whenever it encounters a branch and fail whenever it encounters a dead
        end or an already-visited node.

13.7   The function backtrack defined in Section 13.8 sequences through the tree
        of executions of its argument in a depth-first manner. Write an analogous

function (including the treatment of fail as well as amb) that sequences through the tree of executions in a breadth-first manner.

13.8   The function backtrack in Section 13.8 has the limitation that it can only backtrack functions that do not use references. To overcome this limitation, modify the function so that backtrack f provides f with an additional functional argument called specmkref. Your modification should have the property that f amb fail specmkref will be backtracked correctly, even though it uses references, provided that those references are created by evaluating specmkref e rather than **mkref** e.

Hint Paired with each continuation on the list cl should be a list of reference-value pairs that contains each reference being used by f paired with its current value at the time the continuation was created. When a **throw** occurs to one of these continuations, the references on the associated list should be reset to the values on this list.

To keep track of the references being used by f, one must maintain a list of these references as the value of a reference crefl in backtrack itself. This list should determine the references when reference-value pair lists are created, and it should be reset to the references on the associated pair list when a **throw** occurs to one of the continuations on cl. The value of crefl must also be augmented whenever a new reference is created by specmkref. (This extra side effect is the one difference between specmkref and **mkref**.)

It is possible for a reference to remain on the value of crefl or in one of the reference-value pair lists even though it is no longer being used by f. This can degrade efficiency, but it should not cause an error.

14

A Normal-Order Language

In this chapter, we return to the purely functional world to describe a language using normal-order evaluation. Except for recursive definitions, the syntax of this language is the same as that of the eager-evaluation language in Chapter 11. Semantically, however, the language is quite different: The evaluation of the operands of applications, the components of tuples, and the bodies of alternative constructs is postponed until it is clear that the values are needed to determine the result of the entire program.

As with the lambda calculus, there are expressions that terminate for normal-order evaluation even though they diverge for eager evaluation. In addition, a rich variety of infinite data structures, such as "lazy lists", become possible.

14.1 Evaluation Semantics

Many aspects of the evaluation semantics of our language are unaffected by the change in evaluation order, and remain the same as in Section 11.2. The set of canonical forms is still divided into

$$\langle \text{cfm} \rangle ::= \langle \text{intcfm} \rangle \mid \langle \text{boolcfm} \rangle \mid \langle \text{funcfm} \rangle \mid \langle \text{tuplecfm} \rangle \mid \langle \text{altcfm} \rangle$$

(though the sets $\langle \text{tuplecfm} \rangle$ and $\langle \text{altcfm} \rangle$ will change), and the evaluation relation $\Rightarrow$ still relates closed expressions to canonical forms (and is a partial function since the language is still determinate). In the inference rules, we will still use metavariables with the following ranges:

$$
\begin{array}{llll}
e & \langle \text{exp} \rangle_{\text{closed}} & i & \mathbf{Z} \\
\hat{e} & \langle \text{exp} \rangle & & \\
z & \langle \text{cfm} \rangle & k, n & \mathbf{N} \\
v & \langle \text{var} \rangle & p & \langle \text{pat} \rangle \quad (\text{patterns})
\end{array}
$$

and canonical forms will still evaluate to themselves:

EV RULE: Canonical Forms

$$z \Rightarrow z.$$

The canonical forms for integers and booleans remain the same:

$$\langle intcfm \rangle ::= \cdots \mid -2 \mid -1 \mid 0 \mid 1 \mid 2 \mid \cdots$$

$$\langle boolcfm \rangle ::= \langle boolconst \rangle$$

as do the inference rules for arithmetic, relational, and conditional expressions:

EV RULE: Unary Operations

$$\frac{e \Rightarrow \lfloor i \rfloor}{- e \Rightarrow \lfloor -i \rfloor,}$$

EV RULE: Binary Operations

$$\frac{e \Rightarrow \lfloor i \rfloor \qquad e' \Rightarrow \lfloor i' \rfloor}{e \text{ op } e' \Rightarrow \lfloor i \text{ op } i' \rfloor} \qquad \begin{array}{l} \text{when op} \in \{+, -, \times, =, \neq, <, \leq, >, \geq\} \\ \text{or } i' \neq 0 \text{ and op} \in \{\div, \mathbf{rem}\}, \end{array}$$

EV RULE: Conditional Expressions

$$\frac{e \Rightarrow \mathbf{true} \qquad e' \Rightarrow z}{\mathbf{if}\ e\ \mathbf{then}\ e'\ \mathbf{else}\ e'' \Rightarrow z} \qquad \frac{e \Rightarrow \mathbf{false} \qquad e'' \Rightarrow z}{\mathbf{if}\ e\ \mathbf{then}\ e'\ \mathbf{else}\ e'' \Rightarrow z.}$$

Instead of giving inference rules for boolean operations, however, we will define these operations as syntactic sugar in Section 14.2.

More serious changes appear when we come to the functional aspects of the language. Although the canonical forms for functions

$$\langle funcfm \rangle ::= \lambda \langle var \rangle.\ \langle exp \rangle$$

are the same, the inference rule for application, just as for normal-order evaluation of the lambda calculus, is changed to substitute operands without evaluating them. Thus the evaluation of operands is postponed until when and if the substituted copies are reached in the evaluation of the result of the substitution. In other words, the rule for application becomes the same as the rule for normal-order β-evaluation in the lambda calculus:

EV RULE: Application (β-evaluation)

$$\frac{e \Rightarrow \lambda v.\ \hat{e} \qquad (\hat{e}/v \to e') \Rightarrow z}{e e' \Rightarrow z.}$$

For tuples, the canonical forms are generalized to permit unevaluated subexpressions:

$$\langle tuplecfm \rangle ::= \langle \langle exp \rangle, \dots, \langle exp \rangle \rangle$$

In other words, tuple constructors are always canonical, and thus evaluate to themselves. The evaluation of their subexpressions is postponed until selection occurs, and then only the selected subexpression e_k is evaluated:

EV RULE: Tuples

$$\frac{e \Rightarrow \langle e_0, \ldots, e_{n-1} \rangle \qquad e_k \Rightarrow z}{e.k \Rightarrow z} \qquad \text{when } k < n.$$

The canonical forms of alternatives are also generalized to permit unevaluated subexpressions:

$$\langle \text{altcfm} \rangle ::= @ \langle \text{tag} \rangle \langle \text{exp} \rangle$$

When **sumcase** e **of** $(\cdots)$ is evaluated, the unevaluated subexpression e' of the canonical form of e becomes the operand of an application, which (via the evaluation rule for applications) will be substituted, still unevaluated, into the body of the canonical form of some e_k:

EV RULE: Alternatives

$$\frac{e \Rightarrow @\, k\, e' \qquad e_k\, e' \Rightarrow z}{\textbf{sumcase } e \textbf{ of } (e_0, \ldots, e_{n-1}) \Rightarrow z} \qquad \text{when } k < n.$$

Finally, normal-order evaluation has the particularly pleasant property of permitting the formulation of a general fixed-point operator. We define the abstract syntax

$$\langle \text{exp} \rangle ::= \textbf{rec } \langle \text{exp} \rangle$$

and then introduce the evaluation rule

EV RULE: Fixed Point

$$\frac{e(\textbf{rec } e) \Rightarrow z}{\textbf{rec } e \Rightarrow z.}$$

This rule would be useless under eager evaluation, since there **rec** e could never evaluate to anything. To see this, note that any proof of **rec** $e \Rightarrow z$ would have $e(\textbf{rec } e) \Rightarrow z$ as the premiss of its last step and (since an application in eager order evaluates its operand) **rec** $e \Rightarrow z'$ as a premiss of its penultimate step. Thus, with eager evaluation, there is no shortest proof — and therefore no proof at all — of an evaluation of **rec** e.

With normal-order evaluation, however, the expression **rec** $\lambda v.\, \hat{e}$ evaluates to $\hat{e}/v \rightarrow \textbf{rec } \lambda v.\, \hat{e}$ whenever the latter expression is a canonical form. This will happen when $\hat{e}$ is an abstraction, so that **rec** can be used to define functions recursively, but also when $\hat{e}$ is a tuple or alternative constructor, so that **rec** can be used to define a variety of cyclic data structures recursively.

14.2 Syntactic Sugar

Patterns, **let** definitions, and list-processing operations can be defined as syntactic sugar as in Sections 11.3 and 11.4. Moreover, the fixed-point operator **rec** can be used to define a form of **letrec** definition,

$$\langle \text{exp} \rangle ::= \textbf{letrec } \langle \text{pat} \rangle \equiv \langle \text{exp} \rangle, \ldots, \langle \text{pat} \rangle \equiv \langle \text{exp} \rangle \textbf{ in } \langle \text{exp} \rangle$$

that is more general than that used with eager evaluation (since in each $p_k \equiv e_k$ the pattern p_k need not be a variable and the expression e_k need not be an abstraction).

The free variables of this more general form of recursive definition are given by

$$\text{FV}(\textbf{letrec } p_0 \equiv e_0, \ldots, p_{n-1} \equiv e_{n-1} \textbf{ in } e)$$
$$= (\text{FV}(e_0) \cup \cdots \cup \text{FV}(e_{n-1}) \cup \text{FV}(e)) - \text{FV}_{\text{pat}}(p_0) - \cdots - \text{FV}_{\text{pat}}(p_{n-1}).$$

The simple case where $n = 1$ can be straightforwardly defined by

$$\textbf{letrec } p_0 \equiv e_0 \textbf{ in } e \stackrel{\text{def}}{=} \textbf{let } p_0 \equiv \textbf{rec } \lambda p_0.\ e_0 \textbf{ in } e,$$

but, to handle the general case, one must combine the p_k into a single pattern and the e_k into a single tuple:

$$\textbf{letrec } p_0 \equiv e_0, \ldots, p_{n-1} \equiv e_{n-1} \textbf{ in } e$$
$$\stackrel{\text{def}}{=} \textbf{let } \langle p_0, \ldots, p_{n-1} \rangle \equiv \textbf{rec } \lambda \langle p_0, \ldots, p_{n-1} \rangle.\ \langle e_0, \ldots, e_{n-1} \rangle \textbf{ in } e.$$

Boolean operations can also be defined by desugaring, in terms of conditional expressions:

$$\neg e \stackrel{\text{def}}{=} \textbf{if } e \textbf{ then false else true}$$

$$e \vee e' \stackrel{\text{def}}{=} \textbf{if } e \textbf{ then true else } e'$$

$$e \wedge e' \stackrel{\text{def}}{=} \textbf{if } e \textbf{ then } e' \textbf{ else false}$$

$$e \Rightarrow e' \stackrel{\text{def}}{=} \textbf{if } e \textbf{ then } e' \textbf{ else true}$$

$$e \Leftrightarrow e' \stackrel{\text{def}}{=} \textbf{if } e \textbf{ then if } e' \textbf{ then true else false else if } e' \textbf{ then false else true}.$$

Notice that, in contrast to Section 11.2, the definitions of $\vee$, $\wedge$, and $\Rightarrow$ describe *short-circuit* evaluation: If the result of one of these operations is determined by the first operand, the second operand is never evaluated. (We could have defined these operations to use short-circuit evaluation in Section 11.2, but this kind of evaluation seems more at home in a normal-order evaluation, where functions need not always evaluate all of their arguments.)

14.3 Examples

As we hinted at the end of the previous section, the most obvious advantage of normal-order evaluation is the possibility of functions that do not always evaluate all of their arguments. For instance, one can program functions with the same short-circuiting behavior as the built-in operators $\vee$, $\wedge$, and $\Rightarrow$:

let andfunction $\equiv \lambda$p. λq. **if** p **then** q **else false** $\cdots$

let scmult $\equiv \lambda$m. λn. **if** $m = 0$ **then** 0 **else** m $\times$ n $\cdots$.

Similarly, there is no need for the eager-evaluation technique of using a function of a dummy argument to postpone or avoid unnecessary computation. For example, in place of the function search in Section 11.5, one can define

letrec search $\equiv \lambda$x. λp. λf. λe.

listcase x **of** (e, λi. λr. **if** p i **then** f i **else** search r p f e) $\cdots$,

which only evaluates (and returns) its final argument e if the search fails. Indeed, one can define search in terms of reduce by

let search $\equiv \lambda$x. λp. λf. λe. reduce (λi. λz. **if** p i **then** f i **else** z) e $\cdots$,

since, when p i is true, the functional argument to reduce will not evaluate its second argument z, so that the call of reduce will not recur more deeply.

Another novel programming concept is the infinite list, which is possible because lists are *lazy*, that is, they are built out of tuples and alternatives that do not evaluate their components until necessary. For example,

letrec zerolist $\equiv 0 ::$ zerolist $\cdots$

defines an infinite list whose elements are all zero, and

letrec natlist $\equiv 0 ::$ mapcar (λi. $i + 1$) natlist $\cdots$

defines an infinite list of the natural numbers. (Notice that these are recursive definitions of lists, rather than functions.) More generally,

let arithlist $\equiv \lambda$m. λn. **letrec** a $\equiv$ m :: mapcar (λi. $i + n$) a **in** a $\cdots$

defines a nonrecursive function whose result is a recursively defined list of the arithmetic series that begins with m and increases by n at each step.

Of course, one cannot actually compute all of the elements of an infinite list. But suppose we define

letrec find $\equiv \lambda$k. λx. λe.

listcase x **of** (e, λi. λr. **if** $k = 0$ **then** i **else** find $(k - 1)$ e) $\cdots$,

which finds the kth element of the list x (numbering from zero) or evaluates and returns e if x has fewer than $k + 1$ elements. If x is an infinite list, then, for all $k \geq 0$, find k e will produce a list element rather than evaluate e.

All of the list-processing functions defined in Section 11.5 make sense for infinite as well as finite lists, although a little thought is needed sometimes to understand what this sense is. For example, append x y will give x when x is infinite, eqlist x x' will diverge when x and x' are infinite and equal, search x p f g will diverge if x is infinite and p i is never true, and reduce x $(\lambda m.\ \lambda n.\ m + n)\ 0$ (which sums the elements of x when x is a finite list of integers) will always diverge when x is an infinite list of integers.

The function merge in Section 11.5 can be used to define a function prodlist that accepts two ordered lists of distinct positive integers and returns an ordered list of all products of an element in the first argument with an element in the second argument. The definition of this function, however, reveals some of the subtleties that can arise with infinite lists: The obvious definition

$$\textbf{letrec } \mathsf{prodlist} \equiv \lambda\mathsf{x}.\ \lambda\mathsf{y}.\ \textbf{listcase } \mathsf{x}\ \textbf{of } (\textbf{nil}, \lambda\mathsf{i}.\ \lambda\mathsf{r}.$$

$$\mathsf{merge}\,(\mathsf{mapcar}\,(\lambda\mathsf{k}.\ \mathsf{i} \times \mathsf{k})\,\mathsf{y})\,(\mathsf{prodlist}\ \mathsf{r}\ \mathsf{y}))\ \cdots$$

works for finite lists but not for infinite x, since an attempt to find the first element of the result leads to a recursion that examines all of the elements of x. To define prodlist in a way that works for infinite lists, one must take advantage of the fact that the multiplication is monotone, so that the first element of the result must be the product of the first elements of the arguments, and only the rest of the result needs to be constructed by merging:

$$\textbf{letrec } \mathsf{prodlist} \equiv \lambda\mathsf{x}.\ \lambda\mathsf{y}.\ \textbf{listcase } \mathsf{x}\ \textbf{of } (\textbf{nil}, \lambda\mathsf{i}.\ \lambda\mathsf{r}.$$

$$\textbf{listcase } \mathsf{y}\ \textbf{of } (\textbf{nil}, \lambda\mathsf{j}.\ \lambda\mathsf{s}.$$

$$(\mathsf{i} \times \mathsf{j}) :: \mathsf{merge}\,(\mathsf{mapcar}\,(\lambda\mathsf{k}.\ \mathsf{i} \times \mathsf{k})\,\mathsf{s})\,(\mathsf{prodlist}\ \mathsf{r}\ \mathsf{y})))\ \cdots\ .$$

In addition to finite and infinite lists, there are also partial lists that produce some finite number of elements but diverge if one asks for further elements. For example, if x is an infinite list, but only seven of its elements satisfy the predicate p, then filter x p (where filter is defined in Section 11.5) is a partial list containing seven elements, and find k (filter x p) e will diverge when $k \geq 7$.

Although the infinite case is the dramatic aspect of lazy lists, they are useful in more conventional computations. For example, consider applying eqlist to expressions that perform time-consuming computations, say by applying fringelist (defined at the end of Section 11.5) to large binary trees:

$$\mathsf{eqlist}(\mathsf{fringelist}\ \mathsf{t})(\mathsf{fringelist}\ \mathsf{t}').$$

With eager evaluation, this would be a very inefficient way of comparing the fringes of two binary trees, since the entire fringe lists would be computed even when they differ in their first element. But with lazy lists, the actual computation of the fringes will proceed only as far as the lists are examined by eqlist.

14.4 Direct Denotational Semantics

Much of the domain-theoretic structure of direct denotation semantics is unchanged by the shift from eager to normal-order evaluation. We still have

$$V_* = (V + \{\mathbf{error}, \mathbf{typeerror}\})_\perp,$$

where the predomain V satisfies the isomorphism

$$V \underset{\psi}{\overset{\phi}{\rightleftarrows}} V_{\text{int}} + V_{\text{bool}} + V_{\text{fun}} + V_{\text{tuple}} + V_{\text{alt}},$$

and

$$V_{\text{int}} = \mathbf{Z}$$

$$V_{\text{bool}} = \mathbf{B}.$$

Now, however, an argument to a functional value can be an "uncomputed value" whose computation will diverge or give an error, so that the arguments of such functions belong to V_* rather than V:

$$V_{\text{fun}} = V_* \to V_*.$$

Similarly, since the components of tuples and alternatives can be uncomputed values, these components also range over V_* rather than V:

$$V_{\text{tuple}} = (V_*)^*$$

$$V_{\text{alt}} = \mathbf{N} \times V_*.$$

The one other change to the domains is that variables can stand for uncomputed values, so that the range of environments becomes V_*. Thus,

$$[\![-]\!] \in \langle \text{exp} \rangle \to (E \to V_*) \qquad \text{where} \qquad E = \langle \text{var} \rangle \to V_*.$$

The injections ι_{norm} and ι_θ, the constants err and tyerr, and the function extensions $(-)_*$ and $(-)_\theta$ all are defined as before in Section 11.6.

(As in Section 11.6, V is defined by an isomorphism of predomains rather than domains. But now, in contrast with Exercise 11.12, we can substitute this isomorphism into the equation for V_* to obtain an isomorphism for the domain V_*.)

Within the semantic equations, we will use the following metavariables.

e	$\langle \text{exp} \rangle$	i	$V_{\text{int}} = \mathbf{Z}$
v	$\langle \text{var} \rangle$	b	$V_{\text{bool}} = \mathbf{B}$
η	E	f	$V_{\text{fun}} = V_* \to V_*$
a	V_*	t	$V_{\text{tuple}} = (V_*)^*$.
k, n	$\mathbf{N}$		

The equations for error expressions, constants, arithmetic and relational operations, and conditional expressions remain the same as in Section 11.6. (The equations for boolean operations are no longer needed since these operations have been defined as syntactic sugar.)

For variables, applications, and abstractions, on the other hand, there are several changes that reflect the fact that environments map variables into V_* and functional values accept arguments in V_*:

DR SEM EQ: Variables

$$[\![v]\!]\eta = \eta v,$$

DR SEM EQ: Application

$$[\![ee']\!]\eta = (\lambda f.\ f([\![e']\!]\eta))_{\text{fun}*}([\![e]\!]\eta),$$

DR SEM EQ: Abstraction

$$[\![\lambda v.\ e]\!]\eta = \iota_{\text{norm}}(\iota_{\text{fun}}(\lambda a.\ [\![e]\!][\,\eta \mid v\colon a\,])).$$

In the equation for applications, notice that, if f is a constant function, its result becomes the result of the application, even if the meaning $[\![e']\!]\eta$ is undefined or an error.

For tuples, a divergence or error of one of the components e_k simply determines the corresponding component of the tuple value and has no further effect unless that component is selected:

DR SEM EQ: Tuples

$$[\![\langle e_0,\ \ldots,\ e_{n-1}\rangle]\!]\eta = \iota_{\text{norm}}(\iota_{\text{tuple}}\langle[\![e_0]\!]\eta,\ldots,[\![e_{n-1}]\!]\eta\rangle)$$

$$[\![e.\lfloor k\rfloor]\!]\eta = (\lambda t.\ \textbf{if}\ k \in \text{dom}\,t\ \textbf{then}\ t_k\ \textbf{else}\ \text{tyerr})_{\text{tuple}*}([\![e]\!]\eta).$$

Similarly, when an alternative is constructed, a divergence or error of its body is embedded within the alternative value and, when the value is tested by a **sumcase** expression, is passed on intact to the relevant function:

DR SEM EQ: Alternatives

$$[\![@ \lfloor k\rfloor\ e]\!]\eta = \iota_{\text{norm}}(\iota_{\text{alt}}\langle k, [\![e]\!]\eta\rangle)$$

$$[\![\textbf{sumcase}\ e\ \textbf{of}\ (e_0,\ \ldots,\ e_{n-1})]\!]\eta$$

$$= (\lambda\langle k,a\rangle.\ \textbf{if}\ k<n\ \textbf{then}\ (\lambda f.\ f\,a)_{\text{fun}*}([\![e_k]\!]\eta)\ \textbf{else}\ \text{tyerr})_{\text{alt}*}([\![e]\!]\eta).$$

Finally, the fixed-point operator **rec** is defined by the least fixed-point operator for the domain V_* (which makes sense since V_{fun} is $V_* \to V_*$ rather than $V \to V_*$):

DR SEM EQ: Fixed Point

$$[\![\mathbf{rec}\ e]\!]\eta = (\lambda f.\ \mathbf{Y}_{V_*}\ f)_{\text{fun}*}([\![e]\!]\eta).$$

In fact, **rec** e can be defined as an abbreviation for $Y\ e$, where Y stands for the expression $\lambda \mathsf{f}.\ (\lambda \mathsf{x}.\ \mathsf{f}(\mathsf{x}\mathsf{x}))(\lambda \mathsf{x}.\ \mathsf{f}(\mathsf{x}\mathsf{x}))$ that was found to be a least fixed-point operator for normal evaluation in Section 10.5. When we turn to typed languages in Chapter 15 and later, however, we will find that Y cannot be simply typed, so that an explicit operator such as **rec** must be introduced to treat recursion (see Exercise 15.7).

14.5 Reduction Revisited

An advantage of normal-order over eager evaluation is that β-reduction

TR RULE: β-reduction

$$(\lambda v.\ e)e' \to (e/v \to e')$$

is sound, so that one can replace the left side of an instance of this rule by the right side (or vice versa), in any context, without changing meaning. In addition, there are sound reduction rules, analogous to β-reduction, that describe a variety of language constructs:

TR RULE: Conditional Expressions

$$\textbf{if true then } e \textbf{ else } e' \to e$$

$$\textbf{if false then } e \textbf{ else } e' \to e',$$

TR RULE: Tuples

$$\langle e_0, \ldots, e_{n-1}\rangle.k \to e_k \qquad \text{when } k < n,$$

TR RULE: Alternatives

$$\textbf{sumcase @ } k\ e \textbf{ of } (e_0, \ldots, e_{n-1}) \to e_k e \qquad \text{when } k < n,$$

TR RULE: Fixed Point

$$\mathbf{rec}\ e \to e(\mathbf{rec}\ e).$$

14.6 Lazy Evaluation

Although normal-order evaluation is cleaner and more elegant than eager evaluation, a naïve approach to its implementation can be catastrophically inefficient. Suppose e is an integer expression that takes considerable time to evaluate. Then, although $(\lambda x.\ 3)e$ will evaluate much faster under normal-order than eager evaluation, $(\lambda x.\ x + x)e$ will take about twice as long and

letrec mult $\equiv \lambda$m. λn. **if** n $= 0$ **then** 0 **else** m $+$ mult m $(n - 1)$ **in** mult $e\ k$

will take about k times as long, since the expression e will be repeatedly evaluated k times. Ideally, one would like to have one's cake and eat it too: to postpone evaluating an expression such as e until it is clear that its value is really needed, but also to avoid repeated evaluation. In fact, this can be done by using an approach called *lazy evaluation.*

(Unfortunately, the terminology of this topic has not stabilized. The technique we are going to describe is variously known as "lazy evaluation", "graph reduction", and "call by need". Moreover, the term "lazy evaluation" is also used sometimes as a synonym for normal-order evaluation — where "lazy" merely means stopping at a canonical form rather than at a normal form.)

The basic idea is to use normal-order evaluation, but to represent expressions by graph structures rather than trees. When an operand would be replicated by substitution (during β-contraction), a single copy of the operand is pointed at by all of the positions that contained the variable being substituted for. When the operand is finally evaluated, only the single copy is evaluated — but the replacement of the copy by its value is seen by all of the positions that point to it.

To describe this process formally, we use evaluation semantics but change our viewpoint from the evaluation of a closed expression to the evaluation of a general expression that is paired with a *heap* that maps its free variables into expressions. Such a pair can be thought of as representing the closed expression obtained by substituting the heap repeatedly into the general expression. However, this representation can also be regarded as a graph structure in which the free occurrences of a variable are pointers to the expression obtained by applying the heap to the variable. Moreover, the free variable occurrences in the expression being pointed at can also be interpreted as pointers; indeed, the graph structure can even contain cycles, which can be used to represent recursion explicitly.

As such a pair is evaluated, expressions in the heap are also evaluated, so that the result of the evaluation is a canonical form (or error) paired with an updated heap. Thus heaps behave similarly to states in Chapter 13, except that they map variables into expressions rather than references into values. From this viewpoint, evaluation has the "benign" side effect of changing the heap to map certain variables into canonical forms with the same meanings as their previous values.

Before proceeding further, we make three changes to the syntax of our language. First, we restrict the operands of applications and the subexpressions of alternative constructions to being variables: Instead of $\langle\exp\rangle ::= \langle\exp\rangle\langle\exp\rangle$, we have

$$\langle\exp\rangle ::= \langle\exp\rangle\langle var\rangle$$

and instead of $\langle\exp\rangle ::= @ \langle tag\rangle \langle\exp\rangle$, we have

$$\langle\exp\rangle ::= @ \langle tag\rangle \langle var\rangle$$

The reason for these restrictions is to insure that the substitution performed by β-contraction always substitutes a variable for a variable, and thus cannot expand the size of an expression. (The canonical forms of alternatives are similarly restricted to $\langle altcfm\rangle ::= @ \langle tag\rangle \langle var\rangle$.)

Second, we take the fundamental language construct for recursion to be the recursive definition of a sequence of variables: Instead of $\langle\exp\rangle ::= \textbf{rec} \langle\exp\rangle$, we have

$$\langle\exp\rangle ::= \textbf{letrec} \langle var\rangle \equiv \langle\exp\rangle, \ldots, \langle var\rangle \equiv \langle\exp\rangle \textbf{ in } \langle\exp\rangle$$

Finally, we require that the same variable must never have more than one binding occurrence in an expression. The reason for these last two changes is that, roughly speaking, one can move the **letrec** definitions in an expression outward until they form a single heap specifying all of the recursively defined variables.

It is easy to translate the language used earlier in this chapter into this new form: One simply desugars expressions using the definitions

$$e\, e' \stackrel{\text{def}}{=} \textbf{letrec } v \equiv e' \textbf{ in } e\, v$$

$$@\, k\, e' \stackrel{\text{def}}{=} \textbf{letrec } v \equiv e' \textbf{ in } @\, k\, v$$

$$\textbf{rec } e \stackrel{\text{def}}{=} \textbf{letrec } v \equiv ev \textbf{ in } v,$$

where v does not occur free in e or e'. (The first two definitions should not be applied when e' is already a variable.) Finally, one renames bound variables to eliminate duplicate binders.

We define a *heap* to be a function σ from a finite set of variables to $\langle\exp\rangle \cup \{\textbf{busy}\}$. (Here **busy** is a special symbol whose purpose will be described later.) Then the evaluation relation will relate pairs that each consist of an expression and a heap that are compatible with one another.

More precisely, an expression e and a heap σ are *compatible* when

(a) The free variables of e all belong to dom σ.
(b) For all $v \in$ dom σ, the free variables of the expression σv all belong to dom σ.
(c) The binding occurrences in e and in the expressions σv (for all $v \in$ dom σ) all are distinct from one another and from the variables in dom σ.

Then the evaluation relation $\sigma_0, e \Rightarrow z, \sigma_1$ is defined when e and σ_0 are compatible, z and σ_1 are compatible, and z is a (not necessarily closed) canonical form. (We reverse the order of the expression-heap pair on the left of the evaluation relation to emphasize the similarity with the evaluation relation of Section 13.2.)

The inference rules of Section 14.1 are extended to this relation in exactly the same way that the rules of Section 11.2 were extended to evaluation with states in Section 13.2: We add heap metavariables to both sides of each evaluation relation, making the heap on the left of the first premiss the same as the heap on the left of the conclusion, the heap on the left of every other premiss the same as the heap on the right of the preceding premiss, and the heap on the right of the conclusion the same as the heap on the right of the last premiss. For binary arithmetic operations, for example,

EV RULE: Binary Operations

$$\frac{\sigma_0, e \Rightarrow \lfloor i \rfloor, \sigma_1 \qquad \sigma_1, e' \Rightarrow \lfloor i' \rfloor, \sigma_2}{\sigma_0, e \text{ op } e' \Rightarrow \lfloor i \text{ op } i' \rfloor, \sigma_2} \qquad \begin{array}{l} \text{when op} \in \{+, -, \times, =, \neq, <, \leq, >, \geq\} \\ \text{or } i' \neq 0 \text{ and op} \in \{\div, \mathbf{rem}\}. \end{array}$$

When a rule has no premisses, the heaps on the left and right of its conclusion are the same. For canonical forms, for example,

EV RULE: Canonical Forms

$$\frac{}{\sigma_0, z \Rightarrow z, \sigma_0.}$$

Two rules change because of our restrictions on syntax. For applications, we have

EV RULE: Application (β-evaluation)

$$\frac{\sigma_0, e \Rightarrow \lambda v.\ \hat{e}, \sigma_1 \qquad \sigma_1, (\hat{e}/v \to v') \Rightarrow z, \sigma_2}{\sigma_0, ev' \Rightarrow z, \sigma_2,}$$

which makes it clear that the substitution only maps variables into variables and thus does not expand the size of $\hat{e}$. For alternatives, we have

EV RULE: Alternatives

$$\frac{\sigma_0, e \Rightarrow @\ k\ v', \sigma_1 \qquad \sigma_1, e_k\ v' \Rightarrow z, \sigma_2}{\sigma_0, \mathbf{sumcase}\ e\ \mathbf{of}\ (e_0,\ \ldots\ ,\ e_{n-1}) \Rightarrow z, \sigma_2} \qquad \text{when } k < n,$$

where requiring v' to be a variable in $@\ k\ v'$ insures that the operand in $e_k\ v$ is a variable.

Finally, there are two new inference rules, for variables and recursion. A simple version of the first rule is

EV RULE: Variables (Preliminary Version)

$$\frac{[\,\sigma_0 \mid v\colon e_{\text{renamed}}\,], e \Rightarrow z, \sigma_1}{[\,\sigma_0 \mid v\colon e\,], v \Rightarrow z, [\,\sigma_1 \mid v\colon z_{\text{renamed}}\,].}$$

A variable is evaluated by looking it up in the heap and evaluating the resulting expression. But when the value of the variable is found, the heap is updated to map the variable into its value, thereby avoiding its repeated evaluation. A complication is that one of the duplicated occurrences of e on the left of the premiss must be renamed (to e_{renamed}), and one of the duplicated occurrences of z on the right of the conclusion must be renamed (to z_{renamed}), to avoid duplicate binding occurrences that would violate compatibility. Moreover, to insure compatibility, the bound variables in the renamed expressions should be distinct "fresh" variables that are different from any variables occurring anywhere in the heap and expression being evaluated.

During the evaluation of e invoked by the premiss of this rule, v may be evaluated again. In this situation, the evaluation process is caught in an obvious loop (sometimes called a "black hole") and will diverge. However, it is convenient to signal this fact rather than run on forever. For this purpose, the rule for variables can be improved:

EV RULE: Variables

$$\frac{[\,\sigma_0 \mid v\colon \mathbf{busy}\,], e \Rightarrow z, \sigma_1}{[\,\sigma_0 \mid v\colon e\,], v \Rightarrow z, [\,\sigma_1 \mid v\colon z_{\text{renamed}}\,].}$$

Here, if there is an attempt to evaluate v again before its original evaluation is completed, no rule will be applicable, since the special symbol **busy** is not an expression, and the evaluation will be stuck — a finite form of divergence.

The last inference rule is

EV RULE: Recursion

$$\frac{[\,\sigma_0 \mid v_0\colon e_0 \mid \ldots \mid v_{n-1}\colon e_{n-1}\,], e \Rightarrow z, \sigma_1}{\sigma_0, \mathbf{letrec}\ v_0 \equiv e_0,\ \ldots,\ v_{n-1} \equiv e_{n-1}\ \mathbf{in}\ e \Rightarrow z, \sigma_1.}$$

Here the recursive definitions are simply moved into the heap. Compatibility insures that they will not overwrite any variable-expression pairings that are already present.

As an example, we work out the evaluation of $(\lambda x.\ x + x)(3 + 4)$, beginning with an empty heap, since it is a closed expression. When translated into an appropriate form for lazy evaluation, this expression becomes **letrec** $y \equiv 3 + 4$ **in** $(\lambda x.\ x + x)y$. To show the proof of its evaluation readably, we use the convention (similar to that used at the end of Section 10.3) of displaying a proof whose final step has one or more premisses $p_0, \ldots, p_{n-1}$ and whose conclusion is $l \Rightarrow r$ in the form

$$l$$

$$\text{display of proof of } p_0$$

$$\vdots$$

$$\text{display of proof of } p_{n-1}$$

$$\Rightarrow r.$$

In this format, the proof is

$$[\,], \textbf{letrec } \mathsf{y} \equiv 3 + 4 \textbf{ in } (\lambda \mathsf{x}.\ \mathsf{x} + \mathsf{x})\mathsf{y}$$

$$[\mathsf{y}{:}\,3 + 4], (\lambda \mathsf{x}.\ \mathsf{x} + \mathsf{x})\mathsf{y}$$

$$[\mathsf{y}{:}\,3 + 4], \lambda \mathsf{x}.\ \mathsf{x} + \mathsf{x} \Rightarrow \lambda \mathsf{x}.\ \mathsf{x} + \mathsf{x}, [\mathsf{y}{:}\,3 + 4]$$

$$[\mathsf{y}{:}\,3 + 4], \mathsf{y} + \mathsf{y}$$

$$[\mathsf{y}{:}\,3 + 4], \mathsf{y}$$

$$[\mathsf{y}{:}\,\textbf{busy}], 3 + 4$$

$$[\mathsf{y}{:}\,\textbf{busy}], 3 \Rightarrow 3, [\mathsf{y}{:}\,\textbf{busy}]$$

$$[\mathsf{y}{:}\,\textbf{busy}], 4 \Rightarrow 4, [\mathsf{y}{:}\,\textbf{busy}]$$

$$\Rightarrow 7, [\mathsf{y}{:}\,\textbf{busy}]$$

$$\Rightarrow 7, [\mathsf{y}{:}\,7]$$

$$[\mathsf{y}{:}\,7], \mathsf{y}$$

$$[\mathsf{y}{:}\,\textbf{busy}], 7 \Rightarrow 7, [\mathsf{y}{:}\,\textbf{busy}]$$

$$\Rightarrow 7, [\mathsf{y}{:}\,7]$$

$$\Rightarrow 14, [\mathsf{y}{:}\,7]$$

$$\Rightarrow 14, [\mathsf{y}{:}\,7]$$

$$\Rightarrow 14, [\mathsf{y}{:}\,7].$$

Bibliographic Notes

The functional sublanguages of Algol-like languages [Naur et al., 1960; 1963; Reynolds, 1981b] use normal-order evaluation, but are too restricted to be regarded seriously as functional languages (primarily because their type discipline excludes recursively defined types). Normal-order evaluation is also implicit in Scott's early work on denotational semantics. But normal-order functional languages only became practical after lazy evaluation became widely understood.

Lazy evaluation for the lambda calculus was first described by Wadsworth in his Ph.D. thesis [1971] and was extended to full-blown functional languages by Henderson and Morris [1976] and, independently, by Friedman and Wise [1976]. Our exposition is based on the natural semantics formulated by Launchbury [1993], who gives a proof of correctness relative to a direct denotational semantics.

Concurrent lazy evaluation is treated by Jeffrey [1994]. Modern functional languages using lazy evaluation or related techniques include Ponder [Fairbairn, 1985], Lazy ML [Augustsson, 1984], Miranda[1] [Turner, 1985; Turner, 1990], and Haskell [Hudak and Fasel, 1992; Hudak et al., 1992].

Peyton Jones [1987] has written a text on the implementation of functional languages that discusses lazy evaluation as well as other techniques for the efficient implementation of normal-order evaluation that are based on the use of combinators, which was first suggested by Turner [1979]. Some hardware implications of various techniques are discussed by Koopman, Lee, and Siewiorek [1992].

Exercises

14.1   What goes wrong with the function prodlist, defined in Section 14.3, when one of its arguments contains zero? How can the problem be fixed?

14.2   Consider the function eqlist, when defined using reduce as in Exercise 11.9. Suppose this function is applied to two lists whose first elements are different. How will its execution time depend on the length of these lists when the function is written in a language with normal-order evaluation?

14.3   Define the following infinite lists recursively. In each case, the list itself should be defined by recursion (rather than in terms of a recursive function that maps i into the ith element.) However, you may need to use subsidiary recursive functions on infinite lists, such as functions that apply binary operations elementwise to a pair of lists, or functions along the lines of merge and prodlist.

   (a) The list $1 :: 1 :: 2 :: 6 :: 24 :: \cdots$ of factorials.
   (b) The list $0 :: 1 :: 1 :: 2 :: 3 :: 5 :: \cdots$ of Fibonacci numbers.
   (c) The "Hamming sequence"

$$1 :: 2 :: 3 :: 4 :: 5 :: 6 :: 8 :: 9 :: 10 :: 12 :: 15 :: 16 :: \cdots$$

   consisting of the positive integers (in increasing order) whose prime factors all belong to the set $\{2, 3, 5\}$.
   (d) The prime numbers in increasing order. Do not use the operations of division or remainder.

---

[1] Miranda is a trademark of Research Software Limited.

14.4 Consider Pascal's triangle:

$$1$$
$$1\ 1$$
$$1\ 2\ 1$$
$$1\ 3\ 3\ 1$$
$$1\ 4\ 6\ 4\ 1$$
$$\vdots$$

Each row beyond the first is the componentwise sum of the previous row extended on the left with a zero, and the previous row extended on the right with a zero. For example, 1 4 6 4 1 is the componentwise sum of 0 1 3 3 1 and 1 3 3 1 0.

Define an infinite list **pascallist** of finite lists whose ith sublist is the ith row of Pascal's triangle.

14.5 Define the following functions on lists in such a way that they work for both finite and infinite lists:

(a) A function **alt** such that **alt** x y is the list obtained by alternating the elements of x and y, one at a time, beginning with the first element of x. If one argument is longer than the other, the leftover elements at the end of the longer argument should appear consecutively at the end of the result.

(b) A function **flatten** that, when applied to a possibly infinite list of possibly infinite lists, returns a possibly infinite list containing all elements of every list that is an element of the argument.

14.6 Suppose a single-variable polynomial with integer coefficients

$$a_0 + a_1 \times x + a_2 \times x^2 + \cdots + a_n \times x^n$$

is represented by the list of its coefficients

$$a_0 :: a_1 :: a_2 \cdots :: a_n :: \textbf{nil}.$$

Write list-processing functions to add and multiply polynomials using this representation by lists of coefficients.

By extending the above representation, an infinite power series

$$a_0 + a_1 \times x + a_2 \times x^2 + \cdots$$

is represented by the infinite list of its coefficients

$$a_0 :: a_1 :: a_2 :: \cdots .$$

Your function definitions should also add and multiply infinite power series using this representation by infinite lists.

14.7   Write a program that determines an approximate value of π by counting
        the number of points, selected at random over the unit square, that fall
        within an inscribed quadrant of a circle. Use the language of this chapter,
        extended with real numbers and the common operations and predicates
        on reals that are found in most programming languages (which you may
        write in infix notation). Assume that there is a built-in function rand that
        maps a real number called a seed into a pair $[r, s]$, where r is a random
        real number between zero and one, and s is a seed for generating another
        random number. Thus a sequence of random numbers $r_0, r_1, \ldots$ can be
        generated by

$$[r_0, s_1] = \text{rand } s_0 \qquad [r_1, s_2] = \text{rand } s_1 \qquad [r_2, s_3] = \text{rand } s_2 \qquad \cdots,$$

where s_0 is an initial seed (which can be taken to be 1.0).
        Then write functions to compute:
(a) an infinite list $p_0 :: p_1 :: \cdots$ of random points in the unit square,
(b) an infinite list $h_0 :: h_1 :: \cdots$, where each h_i is 4.0 if the point p_i falls
        within the inscribed circular quadrant and 0.0 otherwise,
(c) an infinite list $z_0 :: z_1 :: \cdots$, where each z_i is the mean of the first i
        members of $h_0, h_1, \ldots$ (this list should converge to π),
(d) z_i for the least i such that $i \geq 10$ and $|z_{i-1} - z_i| \leq 0.01$.

14.8   Show that

$$\textbf{let } v_0 \equiv e_0, \ldots, v_{n-1} \equiv e_{n-1} \textbf{ in } e \to^* e/v_0 \to e_0, \ldots, v_{n-1} \to e_{n-1},$$

and that, for a normal-order language,

$$[\![\textbf{let } v_0 \equiv e_0, \ldots, v_{n-1} \equiv e_{n-1} \textbf{ in } e]\!]\eta$$
$$= [\![e]\!][\eta \mid v_0 \colon [\![e_0]\!]\eta \mid \ldots \mid v_{n-1} \colon [\![e_{n-1}]\!]\eta].$$

Hint Use the desugaring of **let** given in Section 11.3, the result of Exercise
10.10, and the finite substitution theorem (10.11 in Section 10.5).

14.9   Why would it be inadvisable to add references and assignment, as in
        Chapter 13, to a language using lazy evaluation?

15

The Simple Type System

Rudimentary type systems appeared in even the earliest higher-level programming languages, such as Fortran, Cobol, and Algol 60. Soon it was realized that such systems permitted a wide variety of programming mistakes to be detected during compilation, and provided information that could be used effectively to improve data representations. The consequence, beginning in the late 1960's, was a sequence of languages, such as PL/I, Algol 68, Pascal, and Ada, with extensive and complicated type systems.

Unfortunately, the type systems of these languages had serious deficiencies that limited their acceptance: Many of the languages contained "type leaks" that prevented the compile-time detection of certain type errors, many required so much type information that programs became unworkably verbose, and all imposed constraints that made certain useful programming techniques difficult or impossible.

Meanwhile, however, more theoretically-minded researchers began a systematic study of type systems, particularly for functional languages. Over the last two decades, they have shown that the application of sophisticated mathematical and logical techniques could lead to substantial improvements. Polymorphic systems have been devised that permit a procedure to be applied to a variety of types of parameters without sacrificing compile-time type checking. Type-inference algorithms have been developed that reduce or eliminate the need for explicit type information. (These two developments were central to the design of ML in the late 1970's.)

Other researchers, while exploring the connections between types and constructive logic, discovered that (at least in the setting of functional programming) the distinction between the type of a program and a full-blown logical specification of the program's behavior is one of degree rather than kind. This line of research led to the development of such systems as NuPrl and Coq that automatically extract a program from a mechanically verified proof (in intuitionistic logic) that its specification can be met. It also led to the Logical Framework, a metalogic for logical systems, including purely mathematical logics, logics for proving program correctness, and type systems. Most important, perhaps, it led to the realization that specifications of interfaces between program modules are also instances of type systems; this realization led to the module systems of languages such as Standard ML.

At present there is a rich variety of type systems that are the subject of active research. In particular, many questions of how different systems are related, or how they might be unified, are still open research topics. Nevertheless, these systems all share a common starting point that is often called the *simple* type system. (It is essentially the simply typed lambda calculus, with appropriate extensions to deal with the additional features of the functional languages described in previous chapters.) We will begin our treatment of types by describing the simple system in this chapter, and then consider various extensions (largely in isolation from one another) in Section 15.7 and in later chapters.

Our exposition will be limited to purely functional languages. The discussion of syntactic issues (i.e. what are types and when do expressions satisfy typing judgements?) will be largely independent of evaluation order. However, the presentation of semantics (i.e. what do types mean?) will be limited to the direct denotational semantics of normal-order evaluation.

15.1 Types, Contexts, and Judgements

The types of the simple type system themselves constitute a small language, whose abstract syntax is

$$\langle\text{type}\rangle ::= \textbf{int} \mid \textbf{bool} \mid \langle\text{type}\rangle \to \langle\text{type}\rangle$$
$$\mid \textbf{prod}(\langle\text{type}\rangle, \ldots, \langle\text{type}\rangle) \mid \textbf{sum}(\langle\text{type}\rangle, \ldots, \langle\text{type}\rangle)$$
$$\mid \textbf{list}\ \langle\text{type}\rangle \mid \textbf{cont}\ \langle\text{type}\rangle$$

We will also use the following abbreviations:

$$\theta_0 \times \theta_1 \stackrel{\text{def}}{=} \textbf{prod}(\theta_0, \theta_1)$$

$$\textbf{unit} \stackrel{\text{def}}{=} \textbf{prod}()$$

$$\theta_0 + \theta_1 \stackrel{\text{def}}{=} \textbf{sum}(\theta_0, \theta_1).$$

In writing types, we will give operators the following precedences (in decreasing order):

$$(\textbf{list}, \textbf{cont}), \times, +, \to,$$

where $\times$ and $+$ are left-associative but $\to$ is right-associative. For example, $\textbf{int} \to \textbf{list}\ \textbf{int} \times \textbf{bool} \to \textbf{int}$ stands for $\textbf{int} \to (((\textbf{list}\ \textbf{int}) \times \textbf{bool}) \to \textbf{int})$.

We will give precise meanings to types in Sections 15.4 to 15.6, but in the meantime it is useful to give an informal reading:

- The *primitive type* **int** denotes the set of integers.
- The *primitive type* **bool** denotes the set of boolean values.
- The *function type* $\theta_0 \to \theta_1$ denotes the set of functions that return a value of type θ_1 when applied to a value of type θ_0.
- The *product* $\mathbf{prod}(\theta_0, \ldots, \theta_{n-1})$ denotes the set of tuples with n fields of types $\theta_0, \ldots, \theta_{n-1}$.
- The *sum* or *disjoint union* $\mathbf{sum}(\theta_0, \ldots, \theta_{n-1})$ denotes the set of alternative values with tags less than n, where a value tagged with k has type θ_k.
- **list** θ denotes the set of lists whose elements have type θ.
- **cont** θ denotes the set of continuations that accept values of type θ.

The next step is to introduce *contexts*, which are lists that assign types to patterns

$$\langle \text{context} \rangle ::= \; | \; \langle \text{context} \rangle, \langle \text{pat} \rangle : \langle \text{type} \rangle$$

where in $p_0 : \theta_0, \ldots, p_{n-1} : \theta_{n-1}$ the patterns $p_0, \ldots, p_{n-1}$ have no variables in common. (In simple cases, the patterns are merely variables.) Then, if π is a context, e is an expression, and θ is a type,

$$\pi \vdash e : \theta$$

is called a *typing judgement* and is read "e has type θ under π" or "π entails that e has type θ".

(The present use of the word *context* is unrelated to our earlier use, as in Section 2.8, to denote an expression with a hole in it where one can place various subexpressions. Some authors call π a *type assignment* or a *signature*, but these terms can also be confusing: A *type assignment* has nothing to do with the imperative operation of assignment, and the term *signature* usually denotes a specification of the types of constants or primitive operators rather than of variables or patterns.)

The following are examples of valid typing judgements (for the moment, the reader should ignore the underlining):

$$\mathsf{m} : \underline{\mathbf{int}}, \mathsf{n} : \underline{\mathbf{int}} \vdash \mathsf{m} + \mathsf{n} : \underline{\mathbf{int}}$$

$$\mathsf{f} : \mathbf{int} \to \mathbf{int}, \mathsf{x} : \mathbf{int} \vdash \mathsf{f}(\mathsf{f}\,\mathsf{x}) : \mathbf{int}$$

$$\mathsf{f} : \mathbf{int} \to \mathbf{int} \vdash \lambda\mathsf{x}. \, \mathsf{f}(\mathsf{f}\,\mathsf{x}) : \mathbf{int} \to \mathbf{int}$$

$$\vdash \lambda\mathsf{f}. \, \lambda\mathsf{x}. \, \mathsf{f}(\mathsf{f}\,\mathsf{x}) : (\mathbf{int} \to \mathbf{int}) \to \mathbf{int} \to \mathbf{int}$$

$$\mathsf{f} : \mathbf{bool} \to \mathbf{bool}, \mathsf{x} : \mathbf{bool} \vdash \mathsf{f}(\mathsf{f}\,\mathsf{x}) : \mathbf{bool}$$

$$\vdash \lambda\mathsf{f}. \, \lambda\mathsf{x}. \, \mathsf{f}(\mathsf{f}\,\mathsf{x}) : (\mathbf{bool} \to \mathbf{bool}) \to \mathbf{bool} \to \mathbf{bool}$$

$$\langle \mathsf{f}, \mathsf{x} \rangle : (\mathbf{int} \to \mathbf{int}) \times \mathbf{int} \vdash \mathsf{f}(\mathsf{f}\,\mathsf{x}) : \mathbf{int}$$

$$\vdash \lambda\langle \mathsf{f}, \mathsf{x} \rangle. \, \mathsf{f}(\mathsf{f}\,\mathsf{x}) : (\mathbf{int} \to \mathbf{int}) \times \mathbf{int} \to \mathbf{int}.$$

The fourth, sixth, and eighth lines displayed above are typing judgements with empty contexts, which make sense for closed expressions. Such judgements can also be given for the functions defined in Section 11.5:

$\vdash FACT : \underline{\text{int}} \to \underline{\text{int}}$

$\vdash ITERATE : \underline{\text{int}} \to (\text{int} \to \text{int}) \to \text{int} \to \text{int}$

$\vdash ITERATE : \underline{\text{int}} \to (\text{bool} \to \text{bool}) \to \text{bool} \to \text{bool}$

$\vdash APPEND : \text{list int} \to \text{list int} \to \text{list int}$

$\vdash MAPCAR : (\text{int} \to \text{bool}) \to \text{list int} \to \text{list bool}$

$\vdash FILTER : \text{list int} \to (\text{int} \to \underline{\text{bool}}) \to \text{list int}$

$\vdash EQLIST : \text{list } \underline{\text{int}} \to \text{list } \underline{\text{int}} \to \underline{\text{bool}}$

$\vdash MERGE : \text{list } \underline{\text{int}} \to \text{list } \underline{\text{int}} \to \text{list } \underline{\text{int}}$

$\vdash REDUCE : \text{list int} \to (\text{int} \to \text{bool} \to \text{bool}) \to \text{bool} \to \text{bool}$

$\vdash SEARCH : \text{list int} \to (\text{int} \to \underline{\text{bool}}) \to$
$(\text{int} \to \text{bool}) \to (\text{unit} \to \text{bool}) \to \text{bool}.$

(Here each of the uppercase names abbreviates a closed expression for the appropriate function; for example, *FACT* abbreviates **letrec** fact $\equiv \lambda$n. **if** n = 0 **then** 1 **else** n × fact(n − 1) **in** fact.)

Notice that two judgements can give different types to the same expression, even under the same context. In fact, each of the above judgements would remain valid if one replaced all of the nonunderlined occurrences of **int** by some arbitrary type and all of the nonunderlined occurrences of **bool** by some (possibly different) arbitrary type. At the other extreme, there are *ill-typed* expressions, such as **true** + x or x x, that do not satisfy any typing judgement.

15.2 Inference Rules

We use inference rules to specify which typing judgements are valid. Within these *type inference rules* (abbreviated TY RULE), we will use the following metavariables, sometimes with primes or subscripts:

π	⟨context⟩	v	⟨var⟩
θ	⟨type⟩	p	⟨pat⟩
e	⟨exp⟩	k, n	**N**.

The valid typing judgements of the simple type system are those that can be proven using the following rules. (We give rules for the constructs of both the eager-evaluation language of Chapter 11 and the normal-order language of Chapter 14, including constructs defined as syntactic sugar.)

TY RULE: Constants and Primitive Operations

$$\overline{\pi \vdash \mathbf{true} : \mathbf{bool}} \qquad \overline{\pi \vdash 0 : \mathbf{int}} \qquad \text{etc.}$$

$$\frac{\pi \vdash e_0 : \mathbf{int} \qquad \pi \vdash e_1 : \mathbf{int}}{\pi \vdash e_0 + e_1 : \mathbf{int}} \qquad \text{etc.}$$

$$\frac{\pi \vdash e_0 : \mathbf{int} \qquad \pi \vdash e_1 : \mathbf{int}}{\pi \vdash e_0 = e_1 : \mathbf{bool}} \qquad \text{etc.} \qquad (15.1)$$

$$\frac{\pi \vdash e_0 : \mathbf{bool} \qquad \pi \vdash e_1 : \mathbf{bool}}{\pi \vdash e_0 \wedge e_1 : \mathbf{bool}} \qquad \text{etc.,}$$

TY RULE: Conditional Expressions

$$\frac{\pi \vdash e_0 : \mathbf{bool} \qquad \pi \vdash e_1 : \theta \qquad \pi \vdash e_2 : \theta}{\pi \vdash \mathbf{if}\ e_0\ \mathbf{then}\ e_1\ \mathbf{else}\ e_2 : \theta,} \qquad (15.2)$$

TY RULE: Variables

$$\overline{\pi \vdash v : \theta} \qquad \text{when } \pi \text{ contains } v{:}\theta, \qquad (15.3)$$

TY RULE: $\rightarrow$ Introduction

$$\frac{\pi, p{:}\theta \vdash e : \theta'}{\pi \vdash \lambda p.\ e : \theta \rightarrow \theta',} \qquad (15.4)$$

TY RULE: $\rightarrow$ Elimination

$$\frac{\pi \vdash e_0 : \theta \rightarrow \theta' \qquad \pi \vdash e_1 : \theta}{\pi \vdash e_0\ e_1 : \theta',} \qquad (15.5)$$

TY RULE: Product Introduction

$$\frac{\pi \vdash e_0 : \theta_0 \quad \cdots \quad \pi \vdash e_{n-1} : \theta_{n-1}}{\pi \vdash \langle e_0, \dots, e_{n-1} \rangle : \mathbf{prod}(\theta_0, \dots, \theta_{n-1}),} \qquad (15.6)$$

TY RULE: Product Elimination

$$\frac{\pi \vdash e : \mathbf{prod}(\theta_0, \dots, \theta_{n-1})}{\pi \vdash e.k : \theta_k} \qquad \text{when } k < n, \qquad (15.7)$$

TY RULE: Sum Introduction

$$\frac{\pi \vdash e : \theta_k}{\pi \vdash @\, k\, e : \mathbf{sum}(\theta_0, \dots, \theta_{n-1})} \qquad \text{when } k < n, \qquad (15.8)$$

TY RULE: Sum Elimination

$$\begin{array}{c} \pi \vdash e : \mathbf{sum}(\theta_0, \dots, \theta_{n-1}) \\ \pi \vdash e_0 : \theta_0 \to \theta \\ \ddots \\ \pi \vdash e_{n-1} : \theta_{n-1} \to \theta \\ \hline \pi \vdash \mathbf{sumcase}\ e\ \mathbf{of}\ (e_0, \dots, e_{n-1}) : \theta, \end{array} \qquad (15.9)$$

TY RULE: Patterns

$$\frac{\pi, p_0{:}\theta_0, \dots, p_{n-1}{:}\theta_{n-1}, \pi' \vdash e : \theta}{\pi, \langle p_0, \dots, p_{n-1}\rangle{:}\mathbf{prod}(\theta_0, \dots, \theta_{n-1}), \pi' \vdash e : \theta,} \qquad (15.10)$$

TY RULE: **let** Definitions

$$\begin{array}{c} \pi \vdash e_0 : \theta_0 \\ \ddots \\ \pi \vdash e_{n-1} : \theta_{n-1} \\ \pi, p_0{:}\theta_0, \dots, p_{n-1}{:}\theta_{n-1} \vdash e : \theta \\ \hline \pi \vdash \mathbf{let}\ p_0 \equiv e_0,\ \dots, p_{n-1} \equiv e_{n-1}\ \mathbf{in}\ e : \theta, \end{array} \qquad (15.11)$$

TY RULE: **letrec** Definitions

$$\begin{array}{c} \pi, p_0{:}\theta_0, \dots, p_{n-1}{:}\theta_{n-1} \vdash e_0 : \theta_0 \\ \ddots \\ \pi, p_0{:}\theta_0, \dots, p_{n-1}{:}\theta_{n-1} \vdash e_{n-1} : \theta_{n-1} \\ \pi, p_0{:}\theta_0, \dots, p_{n-1}{:}\theta_{n-1} \vdash e : \theta \\ \hline \pi \vdash \mathbf{letrec}\ p_0 \equiv e_0,\ \dots, p_{n-1} \equiv e_{n-1}\ \mathbf{in}\ e : \theta, \end{array} \qquad (15.12)$$

TY RULE: Fixed Point

$$\frac{\pi \vdash e : \theta \to \theta}{\pi \vdash \mathbf{rec}\ e : \theta,} \qquad (15.13)$$

TY RULE: List Introduction

$$\frac{}{\pi \vdash \mathbf{nil} : \mathbf{list}\ \theta} \qquad \frac{\pi \vdash e_0 : \theta \qquad \pi \vdash e_1 : \mathbf{list}\ \theta}{\pi \vdash e_0 :: e_1 : \mathbf{list}\ \theta,} \qquad (15.14)$$

TY RULE: List Elimination

$$\frac{\pi \vdash e_0 : \textbf{list } \theta \qquad \pi \vdash e_1 : \theta' \qquad \pi \vdash e_2 : \theta \rightarrow \textbf{list } \theta \rightarrow \theta'}{\pi \vdash \textbf{listcase } e_0 \textbf{ of } (e_1, e_2) : \theta',} \qquad (15.15)$$

TY RULE: **callcc**

$$\frac{\pi \vdash e : \textbf{cont } \theta \rightarrow \theta}{\pi \vdash \textbf{callcc } e : \theta,} \qquad (15.16)$$

TY RULE: **throw**

$$\frac{\pi \vdash e_0 : \textbf{cont } \theta \qquad \pi \vdash e_1 : \theta}{\pi \vdash \textbf{throw } e_0 \ e_1 : \theta',} \qquad (15.17)$$

TY RULE: **error**

$$\frac{}{\pi \vdash \textbf{error} : \theta.} \qquad (15.18)$$

(The last rule captures the intention that the result of **error** should not be a type error. In contrast, the absence of any rule for **typeerror** captures the intention that the result of **typeerror** should always be a type error.)

The following is a simple example of the use of these rules in proving a typing judgement:

1. $\quad$ $\textsf{f}: \textbf{int} \rightarrow \textbf{int}, \textsf{x}: \textbf{int} \vdash \textsf{f} : \textbf{int} \rightarrow \textbf{int}$ $\qquad\qquad$ (15.3)
2. $\quad$ $\textsf{f}: \textbf{int} \rightarrow \textbf{int}, \textsf{x}: \textbf{int} \vdash \textsf{x} : \textbf{int}$ $\qquad\qquad\qquad$ (15.3)
3. $\quad$ $\textsf{f}: \textbf{int} \rightarrow \textbf{int}, \textsf{x}: \textbf{int} \vdash \textsf{f} \textsf{x} : \textbf{int}$ $\qquad\qquad$ (15.5,1,2)
4. $\quad$ $\textsf{f}: \textbf{int} \rightarrow \textbf{int}, \textsf{x}: \textbf{int} \vdash \textsf{f}(\textsf{f} \textsf{x}) : \textbf{int}$ $\qquad\qquad$ (15.5,1,3)
5. $\quad$ $\textsf{f}: \textbf{int} \rightarrow \textbf{int} \vdash \lambda\textsf{x}. \ \textsf{f}(\textsf{f} \textsf{x}) : \textbf{int} \rightarrow \textbf{int}$ $\qquad$ (15.4,4)
6. $\quad$ $\vdash \lambda\textsf{f}. \ \lambda\textsf{x}. \ \textsf{f}(\textsf{f} \textsf{x}) : (\textbf{int} \rightarrow \textbf{int}) \rightarrow \textbf{int} \rightarrow \textbf{int}$ $\quad$ (15.4,5)

A less trivial example is provided by the recursive definition of the function *append* given in Section 11.5. Let $\pi_1, \ldots, \pi_5$ abbreviate the following contexts:

$$\pi_1 = \textsf{append}: \textbf{list int} \rightarrow \textbf{list int} \rightarrow \textbf{list int}$$

$$\pi_2 = \pi_1, \textsf{x}: \textbf{list int}$$

$$\pi_3 = \pi_2, \textsf{y}: \textbf{list int}$$

$$\pi_4 = \pi_3, \textsf{i}: \textbf{int}$$

$$\pi_5 = \pi_4, \textsf{r}: \textbf{list int}.$$

Then the following is a proof of a typing judgement for an expression for the
append function:

1. $\pi_5 \vdash$ append : list int $\to$ list int $\to$ list int   (15.3)

2. $\pi_5 \vdash$ r : list int   (15.3)

3. $\pi_5 \vdash$ append r : list int $\to$ list int   (15.5,1,2)

4. $\pi_5 \vdash$ y : list int   (15.3)

5. $\pi_5 \vdash$ append r y : list int   (15.5,3,4)

6. $\pi_5 \vdash$ i : int   (15.3)

7. $\pi_5 \vdash$ i :: append r y : list int   (15.14,6,5)

8. $\pi_4 \vdash \lambda$r. i :: append r y : list int $\to$ list int   (15.4,7)

9. $\pi_3 \vdash \lambda$i. λr. i :: append r y : int $\to$ list int $\to$ list int   (15.4,8)

10. $\pi_3 \vdash$ y : list int   (15.3)

11. $\pi_3 \vdash$ x : list int   (15.3)

12. $\pi_3 \vdash$ **listcase** x **of** (y, λi. λr. i :: append r y) : list int   (15.15,11,10,9)

13. $\pi_2 \vdash \lambda$y. **listcase** x **of** (y, λi. λr. i :: append r y) :

    list int $\to$ list int   (15.4,12)

14. $\pi_1 \vdash \lambda$x. λy. **listcase** x **of** (y, λi. λr. i :: append r y) :

    list int $\to$ list int $\to$ list int   (15.4,13)

15. $\pi_1 \vdash$ append : list int $\to$ list int $\to$ list int   (15.3)

16. $\vdash$ **letrec** append $\equiv \lambda$x. λy.

        listcase x **of** (y, λi. λr. i :: append r y) **in** append :

    list int $\to$ list int $\to$ list int   (15.12,14,15)

A third example illustrates the use of products and compound patterns in
typing a function that is similar to append except that it accepts a pair of lists
rather than one list after another. Let $\pi_1, \dots, \pi_5$ abbreviate the contexts:

$$\pi_1 = \text{appendpr: list int} \times \text{list int} \to \text{list int}$$

$$\pi_2 = \pi_1, \langle x, y \rangle \text{: list int} \times \text{list int}$$

$$\pi_3 = \pi_1, x \text{: list int}, y \text{: list int}$$

$$\pi_4 = \pi_3, i \text{: int}$$

$$\pi_5 = \pi_4, r \text{: list int}.$$

Then:

1. $\pi_5 \vdash$ appendpr : **list int** $\times$ **list int** $\to$ **list int** (15.3)

2. $\pi_5 \vdash$ r : **list int** (15.3)

3. $\pi_5 \vdash$ y : **list int** (15.3)

4. $\pi_5 \vdash \langle$r, y$\rangle$: **list int** $\times$ **list int** (15.6,2,3)

5. $\pi_5 \vdash$ appendpr$\langle$r, y$\rangle$: **list int** (15.5,1,4)

6. $\pi_5 \vdash$ i : **int** (15.3)

7. $\pi_5 \vdash$ i :: appendpr$\langle$r, y$\rangle$: **list int** (15.14,6,5)

8. $\pi_4 \vdash \lambda$r. i :: appendpr$\langle$r, y$\rangle$: **list int** $\to$ **list int** (15.4,7)

9. $\pi_3 \vdash \lambda$i. λr. i :: appendpr$\langle$r, y$\rangle$: **int** $\to$ **list int** $\to$ **list int** (15.4,8)

10. $\pi_3 \vdash$ y : **list int** (15.3)

11. $\pi_3 \vdash$ x : **list int** (15.3)

12. $\pi_3 \vdash$ **listcase** x **of** (y, λi. λr. i :: appendpr$\langle$r, y$\rangle$) : **list int** (15.15,11,10,8)

13. $\pi_2 \vdash$ **listcase** x **of** (y, λi. λr. i :: appendpr$\langle$r, y$\rangle$) : **list int** (15.10,12)

14. $\pi_1 \vdash \lambda\langle$x, y$\rangle$. **listcase** x **of** (y, λi. λr. i :: appendpr$\langle$r, y$\rangle$) :

    list int $\times$ **list int** $\to$ **list int** (15.4,13)

15. $\pi_1 \vdash$ appendpr : **list int** $\times$ **list int** $\to$ **list int** (15.3)

16. $\vdash$ **letrec** appendpr $\equiv \lambda\langle$x, y$\rangle$.

    listcase x **of** (y, λi. λr. i :: appendpr$\langle$r, y$\rangle$) **in** appendpr :

    list int $\times$ **list int** $\to$ **list int** (15.12,14,15)

It should be noted that, when using rules 15.4, 15.11, and 15.12, which deal with binding constructs, one must sometimes rename bound variables after applying the rule, to get around the restriction that patterns in contexts must have disjoint variables, For example, there is no instance of 15.4 whose conclusion is x: **bool** $\vdash$ λx. x : **int** $\to$ **int**, since the corresponding premiss, x: **bool**, x: **int** $\vdash$ x : **int**, contains an illegal context. But one can use the rule to prove x: **bool** $\vdash$ λx'. x' : **int** $\to$ **int** and then rename x' in the lambda expression.

Finally, it should be emphasized that the introduction of simple types changes the status of the constructions **letrec** and **rec** for recursive definition and fixed points. As mentioned in Section 14.4, in a untyped language using normal-order evaluation, these constructions can be defined as syntactic sugar by using the expression Y that maps functions into their least fixed-points. (One can also desugar **letrec** in untyped eager-evaluation languages.) Such definitions, however, are ill-typed in most type systems. In fact, it has been shown for the simple type system that, in the absence of any explicit construction for recursion, the

evaluation of an expression that satisfies any typing judgement will always terminate (for either eager or normal-order evaluation). Indeed, this fact remains true
for the extensions of the type system to subtypes and polymorphism that we will
discuss in later chapters (but not for the extension to intersection types to be
discussed in Section 16.3). Thus, we can no longer reduce recursion to syntactic
sugar (although, for normal-order evaluation, we can still define **letrec** in terms
of the fixed-point operator **rec**).

15.3 Explicit Typing

The system of rules given above embodies the assumption that types are properties that can be inferred about expressions but do not actually appear within
the expressions. In this situation the language is said to be *implicitly typed*.

The obvious question about such a language is whether there is any *type inference* algorithm for deciding whether a typing judgement can be inferred for a
given expression (perhaps under a given context, or with a given type). For the
simple type system considered in this section (with minor restrictions), there is
such an algorithm — the Hindley-Milner algorithm — which, although it is theoretically inefficient, has proven itself efficient in practice (for instance, in ML). For
many more elaborate systems, however, such as the intersection types discussed
in Section 16.3 or the polymorphic types discussed in Chapter 17, it is known
that there is no decision procedure for type inference.

Thus many type systems will necessitate the use of an *explicitly* typed language, in which expressions contain enough type information that deciding typing judgements is straightforward. Indeed, even with the simple system, there is
an argument for *explicit* typing: Competent programmers know the types of the
expressions they write; by preventing them from communicating this knowledge
in their programs, an implicitly typed language precludes valuable error checking
and degrades the intelligibility of programs. In practice, type errors are caught,
but they are sometimes poorly localized.

The exact nature of an explicitly typed language will depend on the particular algorithm for inferring typing judgements (which is usually called a *type-
checking* algorithm in the case of explicit typing). The simplest case is *bottom-up*
type checking. Here one defines, by structural induction on expressions, a type-
checking algorithm $\mathcal{B}$ that, given a context π and an expression e, produces a
type θ such that $\pi \vdash e : \theta$, or fails if no such type exists.

Now consider $\mathcal{B}(\pi, \lambda p.\ e)$. In this case, the algorithm can only return a type
if there is a proof of a judgement about $\lambda p.\ e$ under π. But the $\rightarrow$ Introduction
Rule (15.4) is the only type inference rule whose instances have a conclusion
containing an abstraction. Thus the relevant proof must consist of an instance of
this rule, preceded by a proof of the premiss of the instance. It follows from the

form of rule (15.4),

$$\frac{\pi, p: \theta \vdash e : \theta'}{\pi \vdash \lambda p.\ e : \theta \to \theta',}$$

that $\mathcal{B}(\pi, \lambda p.\ e)$ can make the recursive call $\mathcal{B}((\pi, p: \theta), e)$, giving an error stop if the recursive call does so, and otherwise giving

$$\mathcal{B}(\pi, \lambda p.\ e) = \theta \to \theta' \qquad \text{if} \qquad \mathcal{B}((\pi, p: \theta), e) = \theta'.$$

But this is only possible if the type θ of p is given explicitly in the abstraction being type checked. Thus we replace rule (15.4) with a rule that requires the type θ to appear explicitly:

TY RULE: Explicit $\to$ Introduction

$$\frac{\pi, p: \theta \vdash e : \theta'}{\pi \vdash \lambda p_\theta.\ e : \theta \to \theta'.} \tag{15.19}$$

(In the object language, we will write explicit types as subscripts.)

In the specific case of our illustrative language under the simple type system, there are five other places where type information must be provided so that type judgements can be decided by a straightforward bottom-up syntax-directed analysis: alternative constructions for sums, **letrec** definitions, the empty-list symbol **nil**, and the **throw** and **error** operations. (One must also prohibit vacuous expressions of the form **sumcase** e **of** () or require such expressions to be explicitly typed.) These changes are described by the following inference rules:

TY RULE: Explicit Sum Introduction

$$\frac{\pi \vdash e : \theta_k}{\pi \vdash @_{\mathbf{sum}(\theta_0, \ldots, \theta_{n-1})}\ k\ e : \mathbf{sum}(\theta_0, \ldots, \theta_{n-1})} \qquad \text{when } k < n, \tag{15.20}$$

TY RULE: Explicit **letrec** Definitions

$$\pi, p_0: \theta_0, \ldots, p_{n-1}: \theta_{n-1} \vdash e_0 : \theta_0$$

$$\ddots$$

$$\frac{\begin{array}{c}\pi, p_0: \theta_0, \ldots, p_{n-1}: \theta_{n-1} \vdash e_{n-1} : \theta_{n-1} \\ \pi, p_0: \theta_0, \ldots, p_{n-1}: \theta_{n-1} \vdash e : \theta\end{array}}{\pi \vdash \mathbf{letrec}\ p_{0\theta_0} \equiv e_0, \ldots, p_{n-1\theta_{n-1}} \equiv e_{n-1}\ \mathbf{in}\ e : \theta,} \tag{15.21}$$

TY RULE: Explicit Empty List Introduction

$$\overline{\pi \vdash \mathbf{nil}_\theta : \mathbf{list}\ \theta,} \tag{15.22}$$

TY RULE: Explicit **throw**

$$\frac{\pi \vdash e_0 : \mathbf{cont}\ \theta \qquad \pi \vdash e_1 : \theta}{\pi \vdash \mathbf{throw}_{\theta'}\ e_0\ e_1 : \theta',} \tag{15.23}$$

TY RULE: Explicit **error**

$$\overline{\pi \vdash \mathbf{error}_\theta : \theta.} \tag{15.24}$$

Now consider the operation of *erasing* the subscripts that provide explicit type information. It is easy to see that such an operation will convert any instance of an explicitly typed rule into an instance of the corresponding implicitly typed rule. Conversely, one can add appropriate types to any instance of an implicitly typed rule to obtain an instance of the corresponding explicitly typed rule. For the simple type system, by induction on proof length, one can extend this property to proofs: The erasure of types maps explicitly typed proofs into implicitly typed proofs, and every implicitly typed proof is the result of erasing the types of some explicitly typed proof. It follows that type erasure never invalidates a typing judgement for an expression, and that any valid implicit typing judgement can be made explicit by adding appropriate types as subscripts. Thus explicit type information is only a formal commentary that guides and restricts the proofs of typing judgements, but has no effect on the meaning of expressions or judgements.

Although only a few rules change, moving to an explicitly typed language makes expressions significantly longer, as is illustrated by the explicitly typed versions of some of the examples in Section 11.5:

$$\mathbf{letrec}\ \mathsf{fact}_{\mathsf{int}\to\mathsf{int}} \equiv \lambda \mathsf{n}_{\mathsf{int}}.\ \mathbf{if}\ \mathsf{n} = 0\ \mathbf{then}\ 0\ \mathbf{else}\ \mathsf{n} \times \mathsf{fact}(\mathsf{n}-1)\ \cdots$$

$$\mathbf{letrec}\ \mathsf{append}_{\mathsf{list\ int}\to\mathsf{list\ int}\to\mathsf{list\ int}} \equiv \lambda \mathsf{x}_{\mathsf{list\ int}}.\ \lambda \mathsf{y}_{\mathsf{list\ int}}.$$
$$\mathbf{listcase}\ \mathsf{x}\ \mathbf{of}\ (\mathsf{y}, \lambda \mathsf{i}_{\mathsf{int}}.\ \lambda \mathsf{r}_{\mathsf{list\ int}}.\ \mathsf{i} :: \mathsf{append}\ \mathsf{r}\ \mathsf{y})\ \cdots$$

$$\mathbf{letrec}\ \mathsf{mapcar}_{(\mathsf{int}\to\mathsf{bool})\to\mathsf{list\ int}\to\mathsf{list\ bool}} \equiv \lambda \mathsf{f}_{\mathsf{int}\to\mathsf{bool}}.\ \lambda \mathsf{x}_{\mathsf{list\ int}}.$$
$$\mathbf{listcase}\ \mathsf{x}\ \mathbf{of}\ (\mathbf{nil}_{\mathsf{bool}}, \lambda \mathsf{i}_{\mathsf{int}}.\ \lambda \mathsf{r}_{\mathsf{list\ int}}.\ \mathsf{f}\ \mathsf{i} :: \mathsf{mapcar}\ \mathsf{f}\ \mathsf{r})\ \cdots$$

$$\mathbf{letrec}\ \mathsf{reduce}_{\mathsf{list\ int}\to(\mathsf{int}\to\mathsf{bool}\to\mathsf{bool})\to\mathsf{bool}\to\mathsf{bool}} \equiv$$
$$\lambda \mathsf{x}_{\mathsf{list\ int}}.\ \lambda \mathsf{f}_{\mathsf{int}\to\mathsf{bool}\to\mathsf{bool}}.\ \lambda \mathsf{a}_{\mathsf{bool}}.$$
$$\mathbf{listcase}\ \mathsf{x}\ \mathbf{of}\ (\mathsf{a}, \lambda \mathsf{i}_{\mathsf{int}}.\ \lambda \mathsf{r}_{\mathsf{list\ int}}.\ \mathsf{f}\ \mathsf{i}\ (\mathsf{reduce}\ \mathsf{r}\ \mathsf{f}\ \mathsf{a}))\ \cdots.$$

It is obvious that there is a tension between implicit and explicit typing, so that the exact amount of explicit information to be required is a delicate question of language design.

15.4 The Extrinsic Meaning of Types

In this section, we will consider the *extrinsic* view of the direct denotational semantics of types, which is often associated with the logician Haskell Curry (and is sometimes called the "semantical" view). In this view, the meaning of an expression is the same as in an untyped language, while the meaning of a type describes a set of results. When an expression has a type it evaluates to a member of the set described by the type.

(In Sections 15.5 and 15.6, we will explore an alternative *intrinsic* view: that an expression only has a meaning when it satisfies a typing judgement, that the kind of meaning depends on the judgement, and that an expression satisfying several judgements will have several meanings.)

To give a precise description of the extrinsic view, we limit ourselves to normal-order evaluation, so that the type constructor **cont** and the operations **callcc** and **throw** will be disregarded. For simplicity, we also disregard lists, which are special cases of the recursive types that will be discussed in Section 15.7, and other entities that can be defined as syntactic sugar, such as **let**, **letrec**, and patterns other than simple variables. We also give nontype errors, such as division by zero or the effect of the expression **error**, the same meaning $\perp$ as nontermination (rather than the special meaning **error**).

In the direct denotational semantics of Section 14.4 (after eliminating **error** and taking err to be $\perp$), the domain of results is

$$V_* = (V + \{\textbf{typeerror}\})_\perp,$$

where the predomain V satisfies the isomorphism

$$V \xrightarrow[\psi]{\phi} V_{\text{int}} + V_{\text{bool}} + V_{\text{fun}} + V_{\text{tuple}} + V_{\text{alt}},$$

and

$$V_{\text{int}} = \mathbf{Z}$$

$$V_{\text{bool}} = \mathbf{B}$$

$$V_{\text{fun}} = V_* \rightarrow V_*$$

$$V_{\text{tuple}} = (V_*)^*$$

$$V_{\text{alt}} = \mathbf{N} \times V_*.$$

In the earliest extrinsic treatment of types on domains, each type was interpreted as a special kind of subset, called an "ideal", of the domain V_*. For example,

(a) A result $x \in V_*$ belongs to the ideal that is the meaning of **int** if and only if x is $\perp$ or there is an integer i such that $x = \iota_{\text{norm}}(\iota_{\text{int}} i)$.

(b) A result $x \in V_*$ belongs to the ideal that is the meaning of **int** $\to$ **int** if and only if x is $\perp$ or there is a function $f \in V_* \to V_*$ such that $x = \iota_{\text{norm}}(\iota_{\text{fun}} f)$ and, for all a in the meaning of **int**, $f\, a$ belongs to the meaning of **int**.

It soon became evident, however, that in addition to specifying a subset of results, a type also specifies a notion of equality or, more precisely, an equivalence relation, on this subset. To see why this is so, consider the functions

$$\lambda\mathsf{x}.\,\mathsf{x} \qquad \text{and} \qquad \lambda\mathsf{x}.\,\mathsf{x} + 0.$$

Since these function behave differently when applied to, say, **true**, they denote different members of V_*. But when they are applied to any integer, they will give the same result. Thus, when regarded as functions from **int** to **int**, these functions should be regarded as equal. In other words, their denotations in V_* should be related by the equivalence relation specified by the type **int** $\to$ **int**.

A more vivid example occurs if the type **real** is introduced, and the set $V_{\text{int}} = \mathbf{Z}$ of integers is taken to be a subset of the set $V_{\text{real}} = \mathbf{R}$ of real numbers. The function $\lambda\mathsf{x}.\,\sin(\pi \times \mathsf{x})$ (where sin and π have their standard analytical meanings) gives zero whenever its argument is an integer. Thus this function should be related to $\lambda\mathsf{x}.\,0$ by the equivalence relation for **int** $\to$ **int**, or for **int** $\to$ **real**, but not by the equivalence relation for **real** $\to$ **real**.

In brief, in the modern approach to extrinsic semantics, a type denotes both a subset of V_* and an equivalence relation on this subset. However, there is a way of saying the same thing more succinctly. From the properties of relations discussed in Sections A.2, A.4, and A.6 of the Appendix, it is easy to see that ρ is an equivalence relation on a subset $S \subseteq V_*$ if and only if it is a *partial equivalence relation* on V_* — that is, a relation on V_* that is transitive $(\rho\,;\rho \subseteq \rho)$ and symmetric $(\rho^\dagger = \rho)$ — such that

$$S = \operatorname{dom} \rho = \operatorname{ran} \rho = \{\, x \mid \langle x, x \rangle \in \rho \,\}.$$

Thus, instead of saying that a type denotes a subset $S \subseteq V_*$ and an equivalence relation on S, it is simpler to say that a type denotes a partial equivalence relation on V_*, where S is the domain of the partial equivalence relation.

Intuitively, one can think of a type as describing the use of the values of the untyped language to represent some set of entities: A value represents something if it is in the domain of the partial equivalence relation denoted by the type, and two values represent the same thing if they are related by this relation.

We will write $\mathcal{P}(\theta)$ for the partial equivalence relation denoted by the type θ. Even though $\mathcal{P}$ acts on types rather than expressions, it still is defined by syntax-directed equations — but now the syntax is the syntax of types. For primitive types we define

(a) $\langle x, x' \rangle \in \mathcal{P}(\mathbf{int})$ if and only if $x = x' = \bot$ or there is an $i \in V_{\text{int}}$ such that $x = x' = \iota_{\text{norm}}(\iota_{\text{int}} i)$.

(b) $\langle x, x' \rangle \in \mathcal{P}(\mathbf{bool})$ if and only if $x = x' = \bot$ or there is an $b \in V_{\text{bool}}$ such that $x = x' = \iota_{\text{norm}}(\iota_{\text{bool}} b)$.

Then for compound types we define

(c) $\langle x, x' \rangle \in \mathcal{P}(\theta \to \theta')$ if and only if

$$\forall \langle a, a' \rangle \in \mathcal{P}(\theta). \; \langle (\lambda f. \; f \; a)_{\text{fun*}} \, x, (\lambda f. \; f \; a')_{\text{fun*}} \, x' \rangle \in \mathcal{P}(\theta').$$

(d) $\langle x, x' \rangle \in \mathcal{P}(\mathbf{prod}(\theta_0, \ldots, \theta_{n-1}))$ if and only if $x \neq$ tyerr and $x' \neq$ tyerr and

$$\forall k \in 0 \text{ to } n - 1.$$

$$\langle (\lambda t. \; \mathbf{if} \; k \in \operatorname{dom} t \; \mathbf{then} \; t_k \; \mathbf{else} \; \text{tyerr})_{\text{tuple*}} \, x,$$
$$(\lambda t. \; \mathbf{if} \; k \in \operatorname{dom} t \; \mathbf{then} \; t_k \; \mathbf{else} \; \text{tyerr})_{\text{tuple*}} \, x' \rangle \in \mathcal{P}(\theta_k).$$

(e) $\langle x, x' \rangle \in \mathcal{P}(\mathbf{sum}(\theta_0, \ldots, \theta_{n-1}))$ if and only if $x = x' = \bot$ or there are $k \in 0$ to $n - 1$ and $a, a' \in V_*$ such that $x = \iota_{\text{norm}}(\iota_{\text{alt}} \langle k, a \rangle)$, $x' = \iota_{\text{norm}}(\iota_{\text{alt}} \langle k, a' \rangle)$, and

$$\langle a, a' \rangle \in \mathcal{P}(\theta_k).$$

From these definitions, one can show:

Proposition 15.1 *For all types θ:*

(a) $\mathcal{P}(\theta)$ *is a partial equivalence relation.*

(b) $\mathcal{P}(\theta)$ *is a "chain-complete" relation, that is, for all chains $x_0 \sqsubseteq x_1 \sqsubseteq \cdots$ and $x_0' \sqsubseteq x_1' \sqsubseteq \cdots$ of members of V_*:*

$$\text{If } \langle x_i, x_i' \rangle \in \mathcal{P}(\theta) \text{ for all } i \geq 0, \text{ then } \langle \bigsqcup_{i=0}^{\infty} x_i, \bigsqcup_{i=0}^{\infty} x_i' \rangle \in \mathcal{P}(\theta).$$

(c) $\bot \in \operatorname{dom}(\mathcal{P}(\theta))$, *but* tyerr $\notin \operatorname{dom}(\mathcal{P}(\theta))$.

The proof is by structural induction on types. We omit the details, but note that the conditions $x \neq$ tyerr and $x' \neq$ tyerr in part (d) of the definition of $\mathcal{P}$ are needed only to establish tyerr $\notin \operatorname{dom}(\mathcal{P}(\theta))$ in the special case where θ is the empty product **unit**.

Our next task is to show the soundness of our type system, that is, that our type inference rules are in accord with the meanings we have given to types. For this purpose, it is useful to divide the inference rules in Section 15.2 into three categories:

(a) rule (15.3) for variables,

(b) the remaining rules for nonbinding constructs,

(c) rule (15.4) for $\to$ introduction, which (since we are disregarding **let** and **letrec**) is the only rule for a binding construct.

The rules in the second category all have a similar form: The contexts in the premisses are the same as in the conclusion, and no particular structure is placed on these contexts. Thus it is useful to consider the soundness of these rules before dealing with the entire type system:

Proposition 15.2 (Soundness of Nonbinding Type Inference Rules)
Suppose there is a type inference rule of the form

$$\pi \vdash e_0 : \theta_0 \qquad \cdots \qquad \pi \vdash e_{n-1} : \theta_{n-1}$$
$$\overline{\pi \vdash c(e_0, \ldots, e_{n-1}) : \theta,}$$

where c is some constructor of the abstract syntax of expressions, and suppose the untyped semantic equation for this constructor is

$$[\![c(e_0, \ldots, e_{n-1})]\!]\eta = F([\![e_0]\!]\eta, \ldots, [\![e_{n-1}]\!]\eta).$$

If $\langle x_0, x_0' \rangle \in \mathcal{P}(\theta_0)$, $\ldots$, $\langle x_{n-1}, x_{n-1}' \rangle \in \mathcal{P}(\theta_{n-1})$, then

$$\langle F(x_0, \ldots, x_{n-1}), F(x_0', \ldots, x_{n-1}') \rangle \in \mathcal{P}(\theta).$$

PROOF The proof consists of a separate case for each nonbinding type inference rule. We consider only three particularly interesting cases.

For the rule for addition (which is one of the rules (15.1) in Section 15.2),

$$\pi \vdash e_0 : \textbf{int} \qquad \pi \vdash e_1 : \textbf{int}$$
$$\overline{\pi \vdash e_0 + e_1 : \textbf{int},}$$

the semantic equation (the equation for binary operations in Section 11.6, which is the same for normal-order evaluation as for eager evaluation) gives

$$F(x_0, x_1) = \left(\lambda i_0.\ \left(\lambda i_1.\ \iota_{\text{norm}}(\iota_{\text{int}}(i_0 + i_1))\right)_{\text{int}*} x_1\right)_{\text{int}*} x_0.$$

Now suppose $\langle x_0, x_0' \rangle, \langle x_1, x_1' \rangle \in \mathcal{P}(\textbf{int})$. If $x_0 = x_0' = \bot$ or $x_1 = x_1' = \bot$, then the definition of the extension $(-)_*$ insures that $F(x_0, x_1) = F(x_0', x_1') = \bot$, which implies $\langle F(x_0, x_1), F(x_0', x_1') \rangle \in \mathcal{P}(\textbf{int})$. Otherwise, there are integers i_0 and i_1 such that $x_0 = x_0' = \iota_{\text{norm}}(\iota_{\text{int}} i_0)$ and $x_1 = x_1' = \iota_{\text{norm}}(\iota_{\text{int}} i_1)$. Then $F(x_0, x_1) = F(x_0', x_1') = i_0 + i_1$, which again implies $\langle F(x_0, x_1), F(x_0', x_1') \rangle \in \mathcal{P}(\textbf{int})$.

For the rule for $\rightarrow$ elimination ((15.5) in Section 15.2),

$$\pi \vdash e_0 : \theta \rightarrow \theta' \qquad \pi \vdash e_1 : \theta$$
$$\overline{\pi \vdash e_0\, e_1 : \theta',}$$

the semantic equation (the equation for application in Section 14.4) gives

$$F(x_0, x_1) = (\lambda f.\ f\, x_1)_{\text{fun}*} x_0.$$

Thus, if $\langle x_0, x_0' \rangle \in \mathcal{P}(\theta \rightarrow \theta')$ and $\langle x_1, x_1' \rangle \in \mathcal{P}(\theta)$, then the definition (c) of $\mathcal{P}(\theta \rightarrow \theta')$ gives $\langle F(x_0, x_1), F(x_0', x_1') \rangle \in \mathcal{P}(\theta')$.

For the rule for fixed points ((15.13) in Section 15.2),

$$\frac{\pi \vdash e : \theta \to \theta}{\pi \vdash \mathbf{rec}\ e : \theta,}$$

the semantic equation (the equation for fixed points in Section 14.4) gives

$$F(x) = (\lambda f.\ \mathbf{Y}_{V_*}\ f)_{\text{fun}*}x.$$

Suppose $\langle x, x' \rangle \in \mathcal{P}(\theta \to \theta)$. Then the definition (c) of $\mathcal{P}(\theta \to \theta)$ gives

$$\forall \langle a, a' \rangle \in \mathcal{P}(\theta).\ \langle (\lambda f.\ f\ a)_{\text{fun}*}\ x, (\lambda f.\ f\ a')_{\text{fun}*}\ x' \rangle \in \mathcal{P}(\theta),$$

which can be written as

$$\forall \langle a, a' \rangle \in \mathcal{P}(\theta).\ \langle g\ a, g'\ a' \rangle \in \mathcal{P}(\theta),$$

where $g = \lambda a.\ (\lambda f.\ f\ a)_{\text{fun}*}\ x$ and $g' = \lambda a.\ (\lambda f.\ f\ a)_{\text{fun}*}\ x'$. From part (c) of Proposition 15.1, we have $\langle \bot, \bot \rangle \in \mathcal{P}(\theta)$. Then by repeatedly applying the property of g and g' displayed above, we have $\langle g^n \bot, g'^n \bot \rangle \in \mathcal{P}(\theta)$. Thus, by part (b) of Proposition 15.1,

$$\langle \bigsqcup_{i=0}^{\infty} g^n \bot, \bigsqcup_{i=0}^{\infty} g'^n \bot \rangle = \langle \mathbf{Y}_{V_*}\ g, \mathbf{Y}_{V_*}\ g' \rangle \in \mathcal{P}(\theta).$$

To complete the proof, we must do a case analysis on x:

- If $x = \bot$, then $g = \lambda a.\ \bot$, whose only fixed point is $\bot$, while $F(x) = (\lambda f.\ \mathbf{Y}_{V_*}\ f)_{\text{fun}*}x = \bot$.
- If $x = \iota_{\text{norm}}(\iota_{\text{fun}}\ f)$, then $g = \lambda a.\ f\ a = f$, whose least fixed-point is $\mathbf{Y}_{V_*}\ f$, while $F(x) = \mathbf{Y}_{V_*}\ f$.
- If x is any other value, then $g = \lambda a.\ \text{tyerr}$, whose only fixed point is tyerr, while $F(x) = \text{tyerr}$.

In all cases, we have $\mathbf{Y}_{V_*}\ g = F(x)$. By a similar argument, $\mathbf{Y}_{V_*}\ g' = F(x')$. Thus $\langle F(x), F(x') \rangle \in \mathcal{P}(\theta)$.

END OF PROOF

Having dealt with the nonbinding rules, we can now establish the soundness of the entire type system. To state this property succinctly, it is useful to regard contexts as functions from a finite set of variables to types. Specifically, if π is $v_0: \theta_0, \ldots, v_{n-1}: \theta_{n-1}$, then we regard π as the function such that $\text{dom}\ \pi = \{v_0, \ldots, v_{n-1}\}$ and $\pi\ v_i = \theta_i$. (Remember, we are only considering patterns that are variables.) Then:

Proposition 15.3 (Soundness of Typing) *If $\pi \vdash e : \theta$ is a valid typing judgement and η and η' are environments such that*

$$\langle \eta v, \eta' v \rangle \in \mathcal{P}(\pi v) \text{ for all } v \in \text{dom } \pi,$$

then

$$\langle [\![e]\!]\eta, [\![e]\!]\eta' \rangle \in \mathcal{P}(\theta).$$

PROOF The proof is by structural induction on the formal proof of $\pi \vdash e : \theta$, with a case analysis on the rule used in the final step of the proof. Suppose the rule used in the final (and only) step is the rule for variables ((15.3) in Section 15.2),

$$\overline{\pi \vdash v : \theta} \qquad \text{when } \pi \text{ contains } v\!:\!\theta,$$

for which the corresponding semantic equation (the equation for variables in Section 14.4) is

$$[\![v]\!]\eta = \eta v.$$

Then the condition $\langle \eta v, \eta' v \rangle \in \mathcal{P}(\pi v)$ gives $\langle [\![v]\!]\eta, [\![v]\!]\eta' \rangle \in \mathcal{P}(\theta)$ directly.

Next, suppose the rule used in the final step is one of the nonbinding rules described by Proposition 15.2:

$$\frac{\pi \vdash e_0 : \theta_0 \qquad \cdots \qquad \pi \vdash e_{n-1} : \theta_{n-1}}{\pi \vdash c(e_0, \ldots, e_{n-1}) : \theta,}$$

and the corresponding semantic equation is

$$[\![c(e_0, \ldots, e_{n-1})]\!]\eta = F([\![e_0]\!]\eta, \ldots, [\![e_{n-1}]\!]\eta).$$

Assume $\langle \eta v, \eta' v \rangle \in \mathcal{P}(\pi v)$ for all $v \in \text{dom } \pi$. Since we have subproofs of each of the premisses of the rule above, the induction hypothesis gives

$$\langle [\![e_0]\!]\eta, [\![e_0]\!]\eta' \rangle \in \mathcal{P}(\theta_0) \qquad \cdots \qquad \langle [\![e_{n-1}]\!]\eta, [\![e_{n-1}]\!]\eta' \rangle \in \mathcal{P}(\theta_{n-1}).$$

Then Proposition 15.2 gives

$$\langle F([\![e_0]\!]\eta, \ldots, [\![e_{n-1}]\!]\eta), F([\![e_0]\!]\eta', \ldots, [\![e_{n-1}]\!]\eta') \rangle \in \mathcal{P}(\theta)$$

and, by the semantic equation,

$$\langle [\![c(e_0, \ldots, e_{n-1})]\!]\eta, [\![c(e_0, \ldots, e_{n-1})]\!]\eta' \rangle \in \mathcal{P}(\theta).$$

The remaining case is rule (15.4) for $\rightarrow$ introduction,

$$\frac{\pi, v\!:\!\theta \vdash e : \theta'}{\pi \vdash \lambda v.\, e : \theta \rightarrow \theta'}$$

(restricted to patterns that are variables), for which the corresponding semantic equation (the equation for abstraction in Section 14.4) is

$$[\![\lambda v.\, e]\!]\eta = \iota_{\text{norm}}(\iota_{\text{fun}}(\lambda a.\, [\![e]\!][\eta \mid v\!:\!a])).$$

Assume $\langle \eta v, \eta' v \rangle \in \mathcal{P}(\pi v)$ for all $v \in \operatorname{dom} \pi$, and suppose $\langle a, a' \rangle$ is any pair in $\mathcal{P}(\theta)$. Then

$$\langle [\, \eta \mid v\!:\! a \,]w, [\, \eta' \mid v\!:\! a' \,]w \rangle \in \mathcal{P}((\pi, v\!:\!\theta)w)$$

holds for all variables w in the domain of the extended context $\pi, v\!:\!\theta$. Thus the induction hypothesis gives

$$\langle [\![e]\!][\, \eta \mid v\!:\! a \,], [\![e]\!][\, \eta' \mid v\!:\! a' \,] \rangle \in \mathcal{P}(\theta'),$$

which can be rewritten as

$$\langle (\lambda f.\ f\, a)_{\mathrm{fun}*}(\iota_{\mathrm{norm}}(\iota_{\mathrm{fun}}(\lambda a.\ [\![e]\!][\, \eta \mid v\!:\! a \,]))),$$
$$(\lambda f.\ f\, a')_{\mathrm{fun}*}(\iota_{\mathrm{norm}}(\iota_{\mathrm{fun}}(\lambda a.\ [\![e]\!][\, \eta' \mid v\!:\! a \,])))\rangle \in \mathcal{P}(\theta').$$

Finally, since this result holds whenever $\langle a, a' \rangle \in \mathcal{P}(\theta)$, part (c) of the definition of $\mathcal{P}$ gives

$$\langle \iota_{\mathrm{norm}}(\iota_{\mathrm{fun}}(\lambda a.\ [\![e]\!][\, \eta \mid v\!:\! a \,])), \iota_{\mathrm{norm}}(\iota_{\mathrm{fun}}(\lambda a.\ [\![e]\!][\, \eta' \mid v\!:\! a \,]))\rangle \in \mathcal{P}(\theta \to \theta'),$$

and the semantic equation gives

$$\langle [\![\lambda v.\ e]\!]\eta, [\![\lambda v.\ e]\!]\eta' \rangle \in \mathcal{P}(\theta \to \theta').$$

END OF PROOF

Not only is Proposition 15.2 used in the proof of Proposition 15.3, but it can be shown that 15.3 implies 15.2. Thus Proposition 15.2 exactly characterizes the soundness of nonbinding inference rules. From the standpoint of language design this means that, once one has defined the semantics of the untyped language and the partial-equivalence-relation semantics of types, one is free to introduce just those nonbinding inference rules that satisfy Proposition 15.2.

By taking the special case of Proposition 15.3 where $\eta = \eta'$, and using the fact that $\langle x, x \rangle$ belongs to a partial equivalence relation just when x belongs to its domain, we obtain

Proposition 15.4 *If $\pi \vdash e : \theta$ is a valid typing judgement and η is an environment such that $\eta v \in \operatorname{dom}(\mathcal{P}(\pi v))$ for all $v \in \operatorname{dom} \pi$, then*

$$[\![e]\!]\eta \in \operatorname{dom}(\mathcal{P}(\theta)).$$

According to part (c) of Proposition 15.1, $[\![e]\!]\eta \in \operatorname{dom}(\mathcal{P}(\theta))$ implies $[\![e]\!]\eta \neq$ tyerr. This establishes that a well-typed expression, evaluated in a type-correct environment, will not give a run-time type error. This fact is often called the "soundness" of the type system. (When restricted to closed expressions, however, this fact depends only on the meaning of expressions, not the meaning of types — even though we used a particular meaning of types to prove it. Thus it might better be called the "consistency" of the type system.)

15.5 The Intrinsic View

We now turn to the *intrinsic* view of the semantics of types, which is associated with the logician Alonzo Church and is sometimes called the "ontological" view.

In the extrinsic view of the previous section, the meaning of an expression is independent of the type system, while the meaning of a type is a partial equivalence relation whose domain is the set of values of expressions of the type. For example, the meaning of $\lambda x.\, x$ is the identity function on V_*, which belongs to the domains of the meanings of both **int** $\to$ **int** and **bool** $\to$ **bool** (since, roughly speaking, it maps integers into integers and booleans into booleans).

In contrast, in the *intrinsic* view, an expression only has a meaning when it satisfies a typing judgement, the kind of meaning depends on the judgement, and an expression satisfying several judgements will have several meanings. For example, corresponding to the judgement $\vdash \lambda x.\, x : \mathbf{int} \to \mathbf{int}$ the value of $\lambda x.\, x$ is the identity function on the domain that is the meaning of **int**, while corresponding to the judgement $\vdash \lambda x.\, x : \mathbf{bool} \to \mathbf{bool}$ the value of $\lambda x.\, x$ is the identity function on the domain that is the meaning of **bool**. On the other hand, ill-typed expressions such as $\mathbf{true} + x$ or $x\,x$ have no meaning at all.

As in the previous section, to keep things simple we limit our semantic description to normal-order evaluation; we disregard lists, **let**, **letrec**, and compound patterns; and we give nontype errors the same meaning as nontermination.

The first step in developing an intrinsic semantics is to define the meaning of each type θ to be a domain, which we will denote by $\mathcal{D}(\theta)$. The function $\mathcal{D}$ is defined by syntax-directed equations on the syntax of types. For primitive types we have the obvious flat domains

$$\mathcal{D}(\mathbf{int}) = \mathbf{Z}_\perp \qquad\qquad \mathcal{D}(\mathbf{bool}) = \mathbf{B}_\perp,$$

while for compound types we express each type constructor in terms of the analogous constructor for domains:

$$\mathcal{D}(\theta \to \theta') = \mathcal{D}(\theta) \to \mathcal{D}(\theta')$$

$$\mathcal{D}(\mathbf{prod}(\theta_0, \ldots, \theta_{n-1})) = \mathcal{D}(\theta_0) \times \cdots \times \mathcal{D}(\theta_{n-1})$$

$$\mathcal{D}(\mathbf{sum}(\theta_0, \ldots, \theta_{n-1})) = (\mathcal{D}(\theta_0) + \cdots + \mathcal{D}(\theta_{n-1}))_\perp.$$

(Notice the use of lifting in the last equation to convert a predomain into a domain. A lifted disjoint union is often called a "separated sum" of domains.)

The next step is to define the meaning of a context π to be a domain, which we will denote by $\mathcal{D}^*(\pi)$. To do this, we regard the context $\pi = v_0\colon \theta_0, \ldots, v_{n-1}\colon \theta_{n-1}$ as the function on the finite set $\{v_0, \ldots, v_{n-1}\}$ that maps each v_i into the type θ_i. Then the meaning of π is the iterated product, over $\{v_0, \ldots, v_{n-1}\}$, of the domains that are the meanings of the θ_i:

$$\mathcal{D}^*(\pi) = \prod_{v \in \text{dom } \pi} \mathcal{D}(\pi\, v).$$

As with all products of domains, $\mathcal{D}^*(\pi)$ is ordered componentwise. Its members are environments that act on finite sets of variables (rather than the environments used previously in this book, which are defined for all variables). For example, $[\text{x}\colon 7 \mid \text{y}\colon \textbf{true} \mid \text{z}\colon \lambda x\colon \mathbf{Z}_\bot.\ x]$ is an environment in the domain $\mathcal{D}^*(\text{x}\colon \textbf{int}, \text{y}\colon \textbf{bool}, \text{z}\colon \textbf{int} \to \textbf{int})$.

Finally, we consider the intrinsic semantics of expressions, which is fundamentally different from either untyped or extrinsic typed semantics. When we say that an expression has a meaning for every typing judgement that it satisfies, we really mean that meanings are attached to judgements rather than to expressions. For every valid typing judgement $\pi \vdash e : \theta$ there is a meaning

$$[\![\pi \vdash e : \theta]\!] \in \mathcal{D}^*(\pi) \to \mathcal{D}(\theta)$$

that is a continuous function from environments in the meaning of π to values in the meaning of θ. One can think of this as the meaning of e corresponding to $\pi \vdash e : \theta$, but fundamentally it is just the meaning of $\pi \vdash e : \theta$ itself. For example (where $[\,]$ denotes the empty environment),

$$[\![\vdash \lambda\text{x}.\ \text{x} : \textbf{int} \to \textbf{int}]\!][\,] = \lambda z \in \mathbf{Z}_\bot.\ z$$

$$[\![\vdash \lambda\text{x}.\ \text{x} : \textbf{bool} \to \textbf{bool}]\!][\,] = \lambda z \in \mathbf{B}_\bot.\ z.$$

When we attach meaning to judgements rather than expressions, however, it no longer makes sense to define the meaning by syntax-directed semantic equations, which are based on structural induction over expressions. Instead, we define the meaning of judgements by structural induction on the proofs (viewed as trees) of judgements.

For each type inference rule, we give a typed semantic equation that, for every instance of the rule, expresses the meaning of the conclusion of the instance in terms of the meanings of the premisses of the instance. Within these semantic equations, we will use the metavariables:

θ	$\langle$type$\rangle$	z	values in some $\mathcal{D}(\theta)$
π	$\langle$context$\rangle$	η	environments in some $\mathcal{D}^*(\pi)$
e	$\langle$exp$\rangle$	k, n	$\mathbf{N}$
v	$\langle$var$\rangle$	i	$\mathbf{Z}$
		b	$\mathbf{B}.$

In the typed semantic equations themselves (abbreviated TY SEM EQ), we indicate the correspondence with the type inference rules in Section 15.2 by parenthesized references. (Notice that the equation for $\wedge$ defines short-circuit evaluation.)

TY SEM EQ: Constants and Primitive Operations (15.1)

$$[\![\pi \vdash \mathbf{true}\colon \mathbf{bool}]\!]\eta = \iota_\uparrow \mathbf{true}$$

$$[\![\pi \vdash 0\colon \mathbf{int}]\!]\eta = \iota_\uparrow 0$$

$$[\![\pi \vdash e_0 + e_1\colon \mathbf{int}]\!]\eta = (\lambda i.\,(\lambda i'.\,\iota_\uparrow(i + i'))_{\perp\!\perp}([\![\pi \vdash e_1\colon \mathbf{int}]\!]\eta))_{\perp\!\perp}([\![\pi \vdash e_0\colon \mathbf{int}]\!]\eta)$$

$$[\![\pi \vdash e_0 = e_1\colon \mathbf{bool}]\!]\eta = (\lambda i.\,(\lambda i'.\,\iota_\uparrow(i = i'))_{\perp\!\perp}([\![\pi \vdash e_1\colon \mathbf{int}]\!]\eta))_{\perp\!\perp}([\![\pi \vdash e_0\colon \mathbf{int}]\!]\eta)$$

$$[\![\pi \vdash e_0 \wedge e_1\colon \mathbf{bool}]\!]\eta$$
$$= (\lambda b.\,\mathbf{if}\ b\ \mathbf{then}\ [\![\pi \vdash e_1\colon \mathbf{bool}]\!]\eta\ \mathbf{else}\ \iota_\uparrow \mathbf{false})_{\perp\!\perp}([\![\pi \vdash e_0\colon \mathbf{bool}]\!]\eta),$$

TY SEM EQ: Conditional Expressions (15.2)

$$[\![\pi \vdash \mathbf{if}\ e_0\ \mathbf{then}\ e_1\ \mathbf{else}\ e_2 : \theta]\!]\eta$$
$$= (\lambda b.\,\mathbf{if}\ b\ \mathbf{then}\ [\![\pi \vdash e_1 : \theta]\!]\eta\ \mathbf{else}\ [\![\pi \vdash e_2 : \theta]\!]\eta)_{\perp\!\perp}([\![\pi \vdash e_0 : \mathbf{bool}]\!]\eta),$$

TY SEM EQ: Variables (15.3)

$$[\![\pi \vdash v : \theta]\!]\eta = \eta\,v \qquad \text{when } \pi \text{ contains } v\colon\theta,$$

TY SEM EQ: $\to$ Introduction (15.4)

$$[\![\pi \vdash \lambda v.\ e : \theta \to \theta']\!]\eta = \lambda z \in \mathcal{D}(\theta).\,[\![\pi, v\colon\theta \vdash e : \theta']\!][\,\eta \mid v\colon z\,],$$

TY SEM EQ: $\to$ Elimination (15.5)

$$[\![\pi \vdash e_0\,e_1 : \theta']\!]\eta = ([\![\pi \vdash e_0 : \theta \to \theta']\!]\eta)([\![\pi \vdash e_1 : \theta]\!]\eta),$$

TY SEM EQ: Product Introduction (15.6)

$$[\![\pi \vdash \langle e_0, \ldots, e_{n-1}\rangle : \mathbf{prod}(\theta_0, \ldots, \theta_{n-1})]\!]\eta$$
$$= \langle [\![\pi \vdash e_0 : \theta_0]\!]\eta, \ldots, [\![\pi \vdash e_{n-1} : \theta_{n-1}]\!]\eta\rangle,$$

TY SEM EQ: Product Elimination (15.7)

$$[\![\pi \vdash e.k : \theta_k]\!]\eta = ([\![\pi \vdash e : \mathbf{prod}(\theta_0, \ldots, \theta_{n-1})]\!]\eta).k \qquad \text{when } k < n,$$

TY SEM EQ: Sum Introduction (15.8)

$$[\![\pi \vdash @\,k\,e : \mathbf{sum}(\theta_0, \ldots, \theta_{n-1})]\!]\eta = \iota_\uparrow\langle k, [\![\pi \vdash e : \theta_k]\!]\eta\rangle \qquad \text{when } k < n,$$

TY SEM EQ: Sum Elimination (15.9)

$$[\![\pi \vdash \mathbf{sumcase}\ e\ \mathbf{of}\ (e_0, \ldots, e_{n-1}) : \theta]\!]\eta$$
$$= (\lambda\langle k, z\rangle \in \mathcal{D}(\theta_0) + \cdots + \mathcal{D}(\theta_{n-1}).\,[\![\pi \vdash e_k : \theta_k \to \theta]\!]\eta z)_{\perp\!\perp}$$
$$([\![\pi \vdash e : \mathbf{sum}(\theta_0, \ldots, \theta_{n-1})]\!]\eta),$$

TY SEM EQ: Fixed Point (15.13)

$$[\![\pi \vdash \mathbf{rec}\ e : \theta]\!]\eta = \mathbf{Y}_{\mathcal{D}(\theta)}([\![\pi \vdash e : \theta \to \theta]\!]\eta).$$

To see how these rules define the meaning of expressions, consider the first proof of a typing judgement giving in Section 15.2:

1.	$f : \mathbf{int} \to \mathbf{int}, x : \mathbf{int} \vdash f : \mathbf{int} \to \mathbf{int}$	(15.3)
2.	$f : \mathbf{int} \to \mathbf{int}, x : \mathbf{int} \vdash x : \mathbf{int}$	(15.3)
3.	$f : \mathbf{int} \to \mathbf{int}, x : \mathbf{int} \vdash f\,x : \mathbf{int}$	(15.5,1,2)
4.	$f : \mathbf{int} \to \mathbf{int}, x : \mathbf{int} \vdash f(f\,x) : \mathbf{int}$	(15.5,1,3)
5.	$f : \mathbf{int} \to \mathbf{int} \vdash \lambda x.\ f(f\,x) : \mathbf{int} \to \mathbf{int}$	(15.4,4)
6.	$\vdash \lambda f.\ \lambda x.\ f(f\,x) : (\mathbf{int} \to \mathbf{int}) \to \mathbf{int} \to \mathbf{int}$	(15.4,5)

For each step of this proof, corresponding to the type inference rule used to infer the step, there is a semantic equation expressing the meaning of the judgement at that step in terms of the meanings of the earlier judgements that were premisses to the inference. Thus one can obtain the meaning of the judgements in the proof by considering the steps in succession:

1. $[\![f : \mathbf{int} \to \mathbf{int}, x : \mathbf{int} \vdash f : \mathbf{int} \to \mathbf{int}]\!]\eta = \eta\,f$ (15.3)

2. $[\![f : \mathbf{int} \to \mathbf{int}, x : \mathbf{int} \vdash x : \mathbf{int}]\!]\eta = \eta\,x$ (15.3)

3. $[\![f : \mathbf{int} \to \mathbf{int}, x : \mathbf{int} \vdash f\,x : \mathbf{int}]\!]\eta$ (15.5,1,2)

$= ([\![f : \mathbf{int} \to \mathbf{int}, x : \mathbf{int} \vdash f : \mathbf{int} \to \mathbf{int}]\!]\eta)([\![f : \mathbf{int} \to \mathbf{int}, x : \mathbf{int} \vdash x : \mathbf{int}]\!]\eta)$

$= (\eta\,f)(\eta\,x)$

4. $[\![f : \mathbf{int} \to \mathbf{int}, x : \mathbf{int} \vdash f(f\,x) : \mathbf{int}]\!]\eta$ (15.5,1,3)

$= ([\![f : \mathbf{int} \to \mathbf{int}, x : \mathbf{int} \vdash f : \mathbf{int} \to \mathbf{int}]\!]\eta)([\![f : \mathbf{int} \to \mathbf{int}, x : \mathbf{int} \vdash f\,x : \mathbf{int}]\!]\eta)$

$= (\eta\,f)((\eta\,f)(\eta\,x))$

5. $[\![f : \mathbf{int} \to \mathbf{int} \vdash \lambda x.\ f(f\,x) : \mathbf{int} \to \mathbf{int}]\!]\eta$ (15.4,4)

$= \lambda z \in \mathbf{Z}_\perp.\ [\![f : \mathbf{int} \to \mathbf{int}, x : \mathbf{int} \vdash f(f\,x) : \mathbf{int}]\!][\,\eta \mid x\colon z\,]$

$= \lambda z \in \mathbf{Z}_\perp.\ ([\,\eta \mid x\colon z\,]f)(([\,\eta \mid x\colon z\,]f)([\,\eta \mid x\colon z\,]x))$

$= \lambda z \in \mathbf{Z}_\perp.\ (\eta\,f)((\eta\,f)\,z)$

6. $[\![\vdash \lambda f.\ \lambda x.\ f(f\,x) : (\mathbf{int} \to \mathbf{int}) \to \mathbf{int} \to \mathbf{int}]\!]\eta$ (15.4,5)

$= \lambda z' \in \mathbf{Z}_\perp \to \mathbf{Z}_\perp.\ [\![f : \mathbf{int} \to \mathbf{int} \vdash \lambda x.\ f(f\,x) : \mathbf{int} \to \mathbf{int}]\!][\,\eta \mid f\colon z'\,]$

$= \lambda z' \in \mathbf{Z}_\perp \to \mathbf{Z}_\perp.\ \lambda z \in \mathbf{Z}_\perp.\ ([\,\eta \mid f\colon z'\,]f)(([\,\eta \mid f\colon z'\,]f)\,z)$

$= \lambda z' \in \mathbf{Z}_\perp \to \mathbf{Z}_\perp.\ \lambda z \in \mathbf{Z}_\perp.\ z'(z'\,z).$

A subtle question remains: What if there are several proofs of the same judgement (which are distinct as trees, not just sequences)? Clearly, in a sensible intrinsic semantics, all such proofs must lead to the same meaning for the judgement — this property is called *coherence*. For our simply typed language, it is relatively straightforward to establish coherence, since the type inference rules are syntax-directed: For each constructor of the abstract syntax, there is a unique rule that shows how to infer a judgement about a constructed expression from judgements about its subphrases. Thus there is a one-to-one correspondence between proofs (viewed as trees) and abstract syntax trees. In Section 16.6, however, when we consider the intrinsic semantics of subtyping and intersection types, coherence will become a serious constraint.

In Section 10.5, when we discussed the denotational semantics of normal-order evaluation for the untyped lambda calculus, we emphasized the distinction between a closed expression that diverges and one that evaluates to an abstraction whose applications always diverge; in the language of this chapter, an example is provided by $\mathbf{rec}\,(\lambda f.\ f)$ and $\lambda x.\ (\mathbf{rec}\,(\lambda f.\ f))\,x$, both of type $\mathbf{int} \to \mathbf{int}$ (or, more generally, of any type of the form $\theta \to \theta'$). In our untyped denotational semantics, these expressions had the distinct meanings $\bot_{V_*}$ and $\iota_{\mathrm{norm}}(\iota_{\mathrm{fun}}\,\bot_{V_{\mathrm{fun}}})$, respectively. In our intrinsic typed semantics, however, they both have the same meaning, which is the least element of $\mathcal{D}\theta \to \mathcal{D}\theta'$. (Analogously, in our extrinsic semantics, the results $\bot_{V_*}$ and $\iota_{\mathrm{norm}}(\iota_{\mathrm{fun}}\,\bot_{V_{\mathrm{fun}}})$ are identified by the partial equivalence relation $\mathcal{P}(\theta \to \theta')$.)

This raises the fear that the intrinsic semantics might be unsound, in the sense of Section 2.8. But in fact, it is sound if one restricts the observable phrases to closed phrases of *primitive* type (i.e. $\mathbf{int}$ and $\mathbf{bool}$) and only observes whether such a phrase terminates and, if so, its value. It can be shown that, for such phases, this behavior is determined by their intrinsic semantics: When $\vdash e : \mathbf{int}$,

$$e \Rightarrow n \ \text{ if and only if } \ [\![\vdash e : \mathbf{int}]\!] = \iota_\uparrow n$$

$$e \uparrow \ \text{ if and only if } \ [\![\vdash e : \mathbf{int}]\!] = \bot,$$

and similarly for $\mathbf{bool}$. Thus, if O is an observation of termination or of a value, and C is a context that takes on primitive type γ when filled with any phrase e satisfying $\pi \vdash e : \theta$, then

$$[\![\pi \vdash e : \theta]\!] = [\![\pi \vdash e' : \theta]\!]$$

implies

$$[\![\vdash C[e] : \gamma]\!] = [\![\vdash C[e'] : \gamma]\!]$$

(by the compositionality of the intrinsic semantics), which in turn implies

$$O(C[e]) = O(C[e']).$$

On the other hand, the intrinsic semantics is not fully abstract. This surprising result is a consequence of two facts:

- There is a value in $\mathbf{B}_\perp \to \mathbf{B}_\perp \to \mathbf{B}_\perp$,

$$por\ b\ b' = \text{if } b = \mathbf{true} \text{ or } b' = \mathbf{true} \text{ then } \mathbf{true} \text{ else}$$
$$\text{if } b = \perp \text{ or } b' = \perp \text{ then } \perp \text{ else } \mathbf{false}$$

(called the *parallel or*), that is not the meaning of any closed expression of type **bool** → **bool** → **bool**. Roughly speaking, this is because evaluation for our language is purely sequential, so that if a function begins to evaluate an argument of primitive type, it can terminate only if the argument terminates. In contrast, to evaluate an application of *por*, one would need to evaluate the arguments in parallel, terminating if either evaluation terminates with the value **true**. (Despite this need for parallelism, *por* is still a determinate function.)
- There are two closed expressions, both of type (**bool** → **bool** → **bool**) → **bool**,

$$T \stackrel{\text{def}}{=} \lambda\mathsf{p}.\ \textbf{if p true}\,(\textbf{rec}\ \lambda\mathsf{x}.\ \mathsf{x})\ \textbf{then}$$
$$\textbf{if p}\,(\textbf{rec}\ \lambda\mathsf{x}.\ \mathsf{x})\ \textbf{true then}$$
$$\textbf{if p false false then rec}\ \lambda\mathsf{x}.\ \mathsf{x}\ \textbf{else true}$$
$$\textbf{else rec}\ \lambda\mathsf{x}.\ \mathsf{x}$$
$$\textbf{else rec}\ \lambda\mathsf{x}.\ \mathsf{x}$$

$$T' \stackrel{\text{def}}{=} \lambda\mathsf{p}.\ \textbf{rec}\ \lambda\mathsf{x}.\ \mathsf{x},$$

whose meanings are functions that give distinct results when applied to *por*, but give the same result when applied to any other member of the domain $\mathbf{B}_\perp \to \mathbf{B}_\perp \to \mathbf{B}_\perp$.

Clearly, T and T' have distinct denotational semantics. But it can be shown that $C[T]$ and $C[T']$ have the same semantics for all closed contexts C of primitive type; the basic reason is that, when T and T' are applied to any expression, they will yield the same result.

15.6 Set-Theoretic Semantics

At the end of Section 15.2, we remarked that, in the absence of the **letrec** and **rec** constructions, all simply typed expressions of our functional language terminate. This suggests that the sublanguage where recursive definitions and fixed points are eliminated should possess an intrinsic semantics in which partially defined domain elements, and indeed the whole apparatus of an approximation ordering, play no role.

In fact, there is such an intrinsic semantics, in which types denote ordinary sets and $S \to S'$ denotes the set of all functions from S to S'. Indeed, it is this *set-theoretic* semantics that justifies the use of typed lambda expressions (and the other nonrecursive constructions of our simply typed functional language) in ordinary mathematical discourse, as for example in Sections A.3 or 2.5.

It is straightforward to obtain the set-theoretic model by modifying the intrinsic semantics given in the previous section. Equations for the functions $\mathcal{D}$ and $\mathcal{D}^*$, which now map types and contexts into sets, are obtained by dropping the lifting operations:

$$\mathcal{D}(\textbf{int}) = \mathbf{Z}$$

$$\mathcal{D}(\textbf{bool}) = \mathbf{B}$$

$$\mathcal{D}(\theta \to \theta') = \mathcal{D}(\theta) \to \mathcal{D}(\theta')$$

$$\mathcal{D}(\textbf{prod}(\theta_0, \ldots, \theta_{n-1})) = \mathcal{D}(\theta_0) \times \cdots \times \mathcal{D}(\theta_{n-1})$$

$$\mathcal{D}(\textbf{sum}(\theta_0, \ldots, \theta_{n-1})) = \mathcal{D}(\theta_0) + \cdots + \mathcal{D}(\theta_{n-1})$$

$$\mathcal{D}^*(\pi) = \prod_{v \in \mathrm{dom}\, \pi} \mathcal{D}(\pi\, v).$$

Here $\to$, $\times$, $+$, and $\prod$ are given their conventional meanings for sets, as defined in Sections A.3 and A.4.

The semantic equations for judgements are obtained from those in the previous section by eliminating the injections $\iota_\uparrow$ and the function extensions $(-)_{\perp\!\perp}$. (Several equations can then be simplified by β-contraction.)

TY SEM EQ: Constants and Primitive Operations (15.1)

$$[\![\pi \vdash \textbf{true} \colon \textbf{bool}]\!]\eta = \textbf{true}$$

$$[\![\pi \vdash 0 \colon \textbf{int}]\!]\eta = 0$$

$$[\![\pi \vdash e_0 + e_1 \colon \textbf{int}]\!]\eta = ([\![\pi \vdash e_0 \colon \textbf{int}]\!]\eta) + ([\![\pi \vdash e_1 \colon \textbf{int}]\!]\eta)$$

$$[\![\pi \vdash e_0 = e_1 \colon \textbf{bool}]\!]\eta = ([\![\pi \vdash e_0 \colon \textbf{int}]\!]\eta) = ([\![\pi \vdash e_1 \colon \textbf{int}]\!]\eta)$$

$$[\![\pi \vdash e_0 \wedge e_1 \colon \textbf{bool}]\!]\eta = \textbf{if } [\![\pi \vdash e_0 \colon \textbf{bool}]\!]\eta \textbf{ then } [\![\pi \vdash e_1 \colon \textbf{bool}]\!]\eta \textbf{ else false},$$

TY SEM EQ: Conditional Expressions (15.2)

$$[\![\pi \vdash \textbf{if } e_0 \textbf{ then } e_1 \textbf{ else } e_2 : \theta]\!]\eta$$
$$= \textbf{if } [\![\pi \vdash e_0 : \textbf{bool}]\!]\eta \textbf{ then } [\![\pi \vdash e_1 : \theta]\!]\eta \textbf{ else } [\![\pi \vdash e_2 : \theta]\!]\eta,$$

TY SEM EQ: Variables (15.3)

$$[\![\pi \vdash v : \theta]\!]\eta = \eta\, v \qquad \text{when } \pi \text{ contains } v \colon \theta,$$

TY SEM EQ: $\rightarrow$ Introduction (15.4)

$$\llbracket \pi \vdash \lambda v.\ e : \theta \rightarrow \theta' \rrbracket \eta = \lambda z \in \mathcal{D}(\theta).\ \llbracket \pi, v{:}\theta \vdash e : \theta' \rrbracket [\eta \mid v{:}z],$$

TY SEM EQ: $\rightarrow$ Elimination (15.5)

$$\llbracket \pi \vdash e_0\ e_1 : \theta' \rrbracket \eta = (\llbracket \pi \vdash e_0 : \theta \rightarrow \theta' \rrbracket \eta)(\llbracket \pi \vdash e_1 : \theta \rrbracket \eta),$$

TY SEM EQ: Product Introduction (15.6)

$$\llbracket \pi \vdash \langle e_0, \ldots, e_{n-1} \rangle : \mathbf{prod}(\theta_0, \ldots, \theta_{n-1}) \rrbracket \eta$$
$$= \langle \llbracket \pi \vdash e_0 : \theta_0 \rrbracket \eta, \ldots, \llbracket \pi \vdash e_{n-1} : \theta_{n-1} \rrbracket \eta \rangle,$$

TY SEM EQ: Product Elimination (15.7)

$$\llbracket \pi \vdash e.k : \theta_k \rrbracket \eta = (\llbracket \pi \vdash e : \mathbf{prod}(\theta_0, \ldots, \theta_{n-1}) \rrbracket \eta).k \qquad \text{when } k < n,$$

TY SEM EQ: Sum Introduction (15.8)

$$\llbracket \pi \vdash @\ k\ e : \mathbf{sum}(\theta_0, \ldots, \theta_{n-1}) \rrbracket \eta = \langle k, \llbracket \pi \vdash e : \theta_k \rrbracket \eta \rangle \qquad \text{when } k < n,$$

TY SEM EQ: Sum Elimination (15.9)

$$\llbracket \pi \vdash \mathbf{sumcase}\ e\ \mathbf{of}\ (e_0, \ldots, e_{n-1}) : \theta \rrbracket \eta$$
$$= (\lambda \langle k, z \rangle \in \mathcal{D}(\theta_0) + \cdots + \mathcal{D}(\theta_{n-1}).\ \llbracket \pi \vdash e_k : \theta_k \rightarrow \theta \rrbracket \eta z)$$
$$(\llbracket \pi \vdash e : \mathbf{sum}(\theta_0, \ldots, \theta_{n-1}) \rrbracket \eta).$$

The essence of set-theoretic semantics is that no restriction, such as continuity, is imposed on the notion of function. Because of paradoxes such as Russell's, such a semantics is possible only for a sufficiently restrictive typing discipline.

15.7 Recursive Types

In developing types we have tacitly assumed that, like other syntactic phrases, they are finite. In fact, however, our syntactic development extends smoothly to infinite types. For example, as defined in Section 11.4, a list of integers is either $@\,0\,\langle\rangle$ or $@\,1\,\langle i, r \rangle$, where i is an integer and r is a list of integers. Thus the type **list int** is really an abbreviation for the infinite type

$$\mathbf{sum}(\mathbf{unit}, \mathbf{int} \times$$
$$\mathbf{sum}(\mathbf{unit}, \mathbf{int} \times$$
$$\mathbf{sum}(\mathbf{unit}, \mathbf{int} \times$$
$$\cdots))).$$

Similarly, as defined in Section 11.5, a binary tree (with integer-labeled terminal nodes) is either @ 0 n, where n is an integer, or @ 1 $\langle l, r \rangle$, where l and r are binary trees. Thus the type of binary trees is

$$\textbf{sum(int,}$$
$$\textbf{sum(int,}$$
$$\textbf{sum(int,} \cdots)$$
$$\times \textbf{sum(int,} \cdots))$$
$$\times \textbf{sum(int,}$$
$$\textbf{sum(int,} \cdots)$$
$$\times \textbf{sum(int,} \cdots))).$$

At this point, we must warn the reader that our treatment of infinite types will be very intuitive, since a rigorous treatment of languages with infinite phrases is beyond the scope of this book. (In such a treatment, the language itself is regarded as a domain, in which infinite phrases are the limit of interesting chains of partial phrases.)

To make use of infinite types, we must have finite type expressions to denote them; in other words, we must introduce the recursive definition of types (which is quite distinct from the recursive definition of values). For this purpose, we introduce type variables (belonging to the predefined set $\langle \text{tvar} \rangle$) and a binding operator μ:

$$\langle \text{type} \rangle ::= \langle \text{tvar} \rangle \mid \mu \langle \text{tvar} \rangle. \langle \text{type} \rangle$$

(We will use τ as a metavariable ranging over type variables.) Intuitively, $\mu \tau. \theta$ denotes the infinite type obtained by the endless sequence of substitutions

$$\cdots ((\tau/\tau \to \theta)/\tau \to \theta)/\tau \to \theta \cdots .$$

More formally, the "unwinding equation" $\mu \tau. \theta = \theta/\tau \to (\mu \tau. \theta)$ can be used in proofs of typing judgements.

Using this notation, we can define the type constructor **list** as syntactic sugar:

$$\textbf{list } \theta \stackrel{\text{def}}{=} \mu \alpha. \textbf{sum(unit,} \theta \times \alpha). \tag{15.25}$$

Similarly, the type of binary trees is

$$\mu \alpha. \textbf{sum(int,} \alpha \times \alpha).$$

(We will often use the Greek letters α and β, with occasional decorations, as object type variables.)

It should be emphasized that, with the introduction of type variables and μ, the phrases in $\langle$type$\rangle$ have become expressions denoting types rather than types themselves. For such a type expression, the set of free type variables is given by

$$\mathrm{FTV}(\tau) = \{\tau\}$$

$$\mathrm{FTV}(\mu\tau.\ \theta) = \mathrm{FTV}(\theta) - \{\tau\},$$

and for all other forms of type expressions,

$$\mathrm{FTV}(\theta) = \mathrm{FTV}(\theta_0) \cup \cdots \cup \mathrm{FTV}(\theta_{n-1}),$$

where $\theta_0, \ldots, \theta_{n-1}$ are the subphrases of θ. Then the meaning of type expressions is preserved by renaming. For example,

$$\mu\alpha.\ \mathbf{sum}(\mathbf{unit}, \mathbf{int} \times \alpha) \qquad \text{and} \qquad \mu\beta.\ \mathbf{sum}(\mathbf{unit}, \mathbf{int} \times \beta)$$

denote the same type: the type of lists of integers.

Renaming, however, is not the only reason why distinct type expressions may denote the same type. Other expressions denoting the type of lists of integers are

$$\mu\alpha.\ \mathbf{sum}(\mathbf{unit}, \mathbf{int} \times \mathbf{sum}(\mathbf{unit}, \mathbf{int} \times \alpha)),$$

and even

$$\mathbf{sum}(\mathbf{unit}, \mathbf{int} \times \mu\alpha.\ \mathbf{sum}(\mathbf{unit}, \mathbf{int} \times \mathbf{sum}(\mathbf{unit}, \mathbf{int} \times \alpha))),$$

since these type expressions also "unwind" into the same infinite type.

These examples make it clear that the problem of type inference becomes extremely difficult when one is free to replace one recursive type expression by any other denoting the same type. Because of these difficulties, some languages provide a restricted facility for recursive types where one must use explicit transfer functions between a recursively defined type and its expansion. As a simple example, in an explicitly typed language, one might introduce a definition of the form

$$\langle\text{exp}\rangle ::= \mathbf{letrectype}\ \langle\text{tvar}\rangle \equiv \langle\text{type}\rangle\ \mathbf{in}\ \langle\text{exp}\rangle$$

Within the scope of, say,

$$\mathbf{letrectype}\ \mathsf{listint} \equiv \mathbf{sum}(\mathbf{unit}, \mathbf{int} \times \mathsf{listint})\ \mathbf{in}\ \cdots,$$

the types listint and $\mathbf{sum}(\mathbf{unit}, \mathbf{int} \times \mathsf{listint})$ would be distinct, but one could convert from the former to the latter by applying the transfer function **open** listint, and in the opposite direction by applying **close** listint.

Such a facility is described by the following inference rule (for explicit typing):

TY RULE: Explicit-Transfer Recursive Types

$$\frac{\pi, \mathbf{open}\ \tau{:}\,\tau \to \theta, \mathbf{close}\ \tau{:}\,\theta \to \tau \vdash e : \theta'}{\pi \vdash \mathbf{letrectype}\ \tau \equiv \theta\ \mathbf{in}\ e : \theta',} \tag{15.26}$$

where τ does not occur free in θ' or in any type expression in π. (Strictly speaking, we are abusing our formalism here by treating the expressions **open** τ and **close** τ as variables.)

The **datatype** definitions of Standard ML combine this kind of explicit-transfer recursive type definition with a facility for type sums. They also permit the recursive definition of type constructors such as **list**.

The distinction between the unrestricted use of the μ operator and the imposition of explicit transfer functions is closely related to the distinction between transparent and abstract type definitions, which will be discussed in Section 18.1 and Exercise 18.4.

The semantics of recursive types is beyond the scope of this book. An intrinsic semantics using domains can be obtained by using the standard methods for solving domain isomorphisms. An extrinsic semantics can be obtained by placing appropriate restrictions on the partial equivalence relations that are used.

Bibliographic Notes

Early descriptions of the simply typed lambda calculus were given by Church [1940], Curry and Feys [1958, Section 8C], and, in a computer-science context, Morris [1968]. More recent descriptions occur in Barendregt [1984, Appendix A] and the more elementary text by Hindley and Seldin [1986, Chapters 13–15].

Although many early programming languages used types to some extent, it was Algol 68 [van Wijngaarden et al., 1969; 1975] that first embodied the key insight that a fully typed language must employ an infinite number of types, which must be described schematically. Implicit typing, implemented by the Hindley-Milner algorithm [Hindley, 1969; Milner, 1978; Damas and Milner, 1982], appeared a decade later in the Iswim-like language ML [Gordon et al., 1977], which went beyond simple typing to provide a limited form of polymorphism. It was a precursor of the later Standard ML [Milner, Tofte, and Harper, 1990; Milner and Tofte, 1991], which has become the most successful typed Iswim-like language. The main innovation in the latter language is a module system that is based on type theory (in the sense discussed in Sections 18.2 and 18.3). Elementary textbooks on Standard ML include Ullman [1994] and Paulson [1996].

An elaborate type system is provided for object-oriented programming by the popular language Java [Gosling, Joy, and Steele, 1996].

Although the subject is not described in this book, mention should be made of systems for specifying and reasoning about typed functional programs. The first mechanized logic for this purpose was Edinburgh LCF [Gordon, Milner, and Wadsworth, 1979]. More recently, work in this area has focused on the propositions-as-types paradigm, in which types are regarded as propositions and expressions are regarded as proofs of their types. This work stems from an isomorphism between type constructors and logical operators that was discovered by Curry and Howard [Howard, 1980] and has been developed as a theory of proof by Martin-Löf [1984] and Girard et al. [1989]. It has led to a variety of automated systems, including Automath [de Bruijn, 1980], NuPrl [Constable et al., 1986], and Coq [Coquand and Huet, 1988; Paulin-Mohring, 1993; Barras et al., 1998]. Closely related to this work is a framework for defining logics themselves that was developed by Harper, Honsell, and Plotkin [1993a] and implemented in terms of logic programming by Pfenning [1989].

Another topic we have omitted is linear typing, which is based on linear logic [Girard, 1987] and which captures the concept of using a value exactly once. Its application to programming languages has been explored by Lafont [1988], Wadler [1990], Abramsky [1993], and Chirimar, Gunter, and Riecke [1996]. (As mentioned in Section 13.5, linear typing can be used, within a purely functional language, to express the fact that state-like values can be updated in place.)

An early extrinsic model of types, in which types denote certain sets of values called ideals (without any associated equivalence relation) was given by MacQueen and Sethi [1982] and extended to recursive types by MacQueen, Plotkin, and Sethi [1986]. Most work on modeling types by partial equivalence relations, which goes back as far as Kreisel [1959] and includes work by Girard [1972], Troelstra [1973b], and many others, uses relations on natural numbers that model the untyped lambda calculus via Gödel numbering. Much of this work is cast in an elaborate category-theoretic setting, but relatively elementary expositions are given by Longo and Moggi [1991] and by Asperti and Longo [1991, Section 3.4.1]. The use of partial equivalence relations on domains to model types is described by Abadi and Plotkin [1990], who show that recursively defined types can be treated if the relations are appropriately restricted. More recently, Birkedal, Carboni, Rosolini, and Scott [1998] have shown that partial equivalence relations on domains can be used to model a wide variety of mathematical structures and to extend the notion of computability to such structures.

The failure of full abstraction for the domain-theoretic intrinsic semantics of a typed functional language with normal-order evaluation was shown by Plotkin [1977], in the paper where he originally introduced the concept of full abstraction. (Plotkin actually dealt with a language he called PCF, which is obtained from the language of this chapter by removing tuples, alternatives, and recursive types.) The problem of finding a fully abstract denotational semantics of PCF (other than a trivial model in which an expression denotes the class of expressions operationally equivalent to it) remained open for many years, but was finally resolved by using *game-theoretic semantics*, where the meaning of an expression is a strategy for a game, or conversation, between the expression and its environment [Abramsky, Jagadeesan, and Malacaria, 1994, 1998; Hyland and Ong, 1994]. An alternative approach using logical relations has been devised by O'Hearn and Riecke [1995].

Two excellent surveys of type theory are Mitchell [1990] and Barendregt [1992].

Exercises

15.1   For each of the following closed expressions, determine if the expression
        has a valid typing judgement in the simple type system described in Sec-
        tion 15.2 (without recursive types). If so, give a proof of such a judgement;
        if not, briefly explain why.

   (a) $(\lambda\langle x, y\rangle.\ x)\langle 3, \mathbf{true}\rangle$
   (b) $\lambda p.\ \lambda x.$ **if** $p\,x$ **then** x **else** 0
   (c) $(\lambda x.x)(\lambda x.x)$
   (d) $(\lambda f.\ \lambda x.\ f(f\ x))(\lambda z.\ z)$
   (e) **let** $i \equiv \lambda x.\ x$ **in** $i\ i$.

15.2   Replace the question mark in the following typing judgement by a type
        that makes the judgement valid. Then prove the judgement by using the
        inference rules in Section 15.2.

$$\vdash \mathbf{letrec}\ \mathsf{mapcar} \equiv \lambda f.\ \lambda x.$$

$$\mathbf{listcase}\ x\ \mathbf{of}\ (\mathbf{nil}, \lambda i.\ \lambda r.\ f\ i :: \mathsf{mapcar}\ f\ r)\ \mathbf{in}\ \mathsf{mapcar} :$$

$$(\mathbf{int} \to \mathbf{bool}) \to ?.$$

15.3   Give and prove a valid typing judgement for the function **redtree** defined
        in Exercise 11.7.

15.4   In Exercise 11.8, you were asked to define a function **member** nonrecur-
        sively in terms of a given function **lazyreduce**. Let e be your definition.
        Give a formal proof of the typing judgement

$$\vdash \mathbf{letrec}\ \mathsf{lazyreduce} \equiv \lambda x.\ \lambda f.\ \lambda a.\ \lambda\langle\rangle.$$

$$\mathbf{listcase}\ x\ \mathbf{of}\ (a\langle\rangle, \lambda i.\ \lambda r.\ f\ i\ (\mathsf{lazyreduce}\ r\ f\ a))\ \mathbf{in}\ e :$$

$$\mathbf{int} \to \mathbf{list\ int} \to \mathbf{bool}.$$

Hint The appropriate type for the dummy argument $\langle\rangle$ is **unit**, which
        abbreviates **prod**().

15.5   Explain why the **listcase** construction has more desirable typing proper-
        ties than the Lisp primitives null, car, and cdr.

15.6   Derive the type inference rules (15.14) (list introduction) and (15.15) (list
        elimination) in Section 15.2 from the definitions of the list processing op-
        erations as syntactic sugar in Section 11.4 and the recursive type equation

$$\mathbf{list}\ \theta = \mathbf{sum}(\mathbf{unit}, \theta \times \mathbf{list}\ \theta).$$

15.7   Consider the expression

$$\lambda f.\ (\lambda x.\ f(x\,x))(\lambda x.\ f(x\,x)),$$

which was shown in Section 10.5 to behave like a fixed-point operator.

(a) Show that the rules of Section 15.2 cannot be used to prove any typing judgement about this expression.

(b) Show that, if recursive types are permitted as abbreviations for infinite types, then one can use the rules of Section 15.2 to prove

$$\vdash \lambda f.\ (\lambda x.\ f(x\,x))(\lambda x.\ f(x\,x)) : (\mathbf{int} \to \mathbf{int}) \to \mathbf{int}.$$

Hint Give x the type $\mu\alpha.\ \alpha \to \mathbf{int} = (\mu\alpha.\ \alpha \to \mathbf{int}) \to \mathbf{int}$.

(c) Use the **letrectype** construction to give an explicitly typed version of this expression and prove that it satisfies the typing judgement in part (b), by using the rules for explicit typing, including rule (15.26) in Section 15.7.

Since this expression behaves as a fixed-point operator and can be used to invoke Russell's paradox, the fact that it can be typed using recursive types shows that there is no set-theoretic semantics of recursive types.

15.8   Consider the following expression:

> **letrec** taut $\equiv \lambda n.\ \lambda f.$
>
> > **if** n $= 0$ **then** f **else**
> >
> > > **if** taut$(n - 1)(f$ **true**$)$ **then** taut$(n - 1)(f$ **false**$)$ **else false**
> >
> > **in** taut.

(a) Can this expression be given a type by using the simple type system of Section 15.2 (without recursive types)? If so, give a suitable type; if not, explain why.

(b) What is the value (using either eager or normal-order evaluation) of taut $2\,(\lambda x.\ \lambda y.\ x)$?

15.9   Suppose we extend the type system of Section 15.2 (with either the implicit typing rules of that section or the explicit rules of Section 15.3) by introducing type variables:

$$\langle \text{type} \rangle ::= \langle \text{tvar} \rangle$$

Let δ be a substitution map from type variables to types, and let $-/\delta$ denote the result of simultaneously substituting $\delta\tau$ for each type variable τ

in either a type or an expression. Prove that, if

$$p_0 : \theta_0, \ldots, p_{n-1} : \theta_{n-1} \vdash e : \theta,$$

then

$$p_0 : (\theta_0/\delta), \ldots, p_{n-1} : (\theta_{n-1}/\delta) \vdash (e/\delta) : (\theta/\delta).$$

Hint Use structural induction on the formal proof of the judgement $p_0 : \theta_0, \ldots, p_{n-1} : \theta_{n-1} \vdash e : \theta$.

15.10   Prove that Proposition 15.3 in Section 15.4 implies Proposition 15.2.
        Hint To show Proposition 15.2 for an inference rule using the n-ary constructor c, apply Proposition 15.3 to the expression $c(v_0, \ldots, v_{n-1})$, where $v_0, \ldots, v_{n-1}$ are distinct variables.

Subtypes and Intersection Types

Many programming languages provide a variety of implicit conversions (sometimes called "coercions") that serve to make programs more succinct; the most widespread example is the conversion of integers to real (floating-point) numbers. In modern type systems, such conversions are captured by the concept of subtyping.

In this chapter, we extend the simple type system by introducing a subtype relation $\leq$ between types. When $\theta \leq \theta'$, we say that θ is a *subtype* of θ' or, occasionally, that θ' is a *supertype* of θ. Syntactically, this relationship implies that any expression of type θ is also an expression of type θ', and thus can be used in any context that permits an expression of type θ'. In extrinsic semantics, the relationship implies that the set denoted by θ is a subset of that denoted by θ', and that values which are equivalent for the type θ are also equivalent for θ'; more simply, the partial equivalence relation for θ must be a subset of the partial equivalence relation for θ'. In intrinsic semantics, $\theta \leq \theta'$ implies that there is an implicit conversion function from the meaning of θ to the meaning of θ'.

We will also introduce intersection types, which permit the description of values with more than one conventional type. In extrinsic semantics, the intersection of types is modelled by the intersection of partial equivalence relations, and in intrinsic semantics by a constrained product.

We will find that both extrinsic and intrinsic semantics clarify the subtle interactions between subtypes and generic operators.

16.1 Inference Rules for Subtyping

To extend the simple typing system of the previous chapter to encompass subtyping, we introduce a new kind of judgement, called a *subtyping judgement*, of the form $\theta \leq \theta'$. We also introduce a single additional type inference rule to formalize the basic idea that, when θ is a subtype of θ', any expression of type θ is also an expression of type θ':

TY RULE: Subsumption

$$\frac{\pi \vdash e : \theta \qquad \theta \leq \theta'}{\pi \vdash e : \theta'.}$$

(16.1)

If the subsumption rule is to be useful, we must also have rules for inferring the subtyping judgment that is its second premiss. These rules, which we call *subtyping* rules (abbreviated SBTY RULE), have premisses and conclusions that are all subtyping judgments. Thus the main structure of a formal proof of a typing judgment will use type inference rules, but there will be subproofs in which only subtyping rules are used, and each such subproof will be the proof of an instance of the second premiss of the subsumption rule.

The first two subtyping rules are general rules which assert that the subtype relation is a preorder:

SBTY RULE: Reflexivity

$$\overline{\theta \leq \theta,}$$

(16.2)

SBTY RULE: Transitivity

$$\frac{\theta \leq \theta' \qquad \theta' \leq \theta''}{\theta \leq \theta''.}$$

(16.3)

Notice that we do not impose antisymmetry, so that distinct types can satisfy both $\theta \leq \theta'$ and $\theta' \leq \theta$; in this case, we say that θ and θ' are *equivalent* types. (This notion of equivalence of types is quite different from the equivalence of values in extrinsic semantics.)

The remaining subtyping rules deal with specific types or type constructors. For primitive types, there are several possibilities. In the functional language of the previous chapter, for instance, there are two primitive types **int** and **bool**, neither of which can be used in a context calling for the other. But we might decide to regard the meaning of **bool** as a subset of the meaning of **int** by identifying 0 with **false** and 1 with **true**. Then we could take **bool** to be a subtype of **int**. Other possibilities would be to introduce natural numbers as a subtype of the integers and real (floating-point) numbers as a supertype of the integers. These particular possibilities are described by the subtyping rules

SBTY RULE: Primitive Types

$$\overline{\mathbf{bool} \leq \mathbf{nat}} \qquad \overline{\mathbf{nat} \leq \mathbf{int}} \qquad \overline{\mathbf{int} \leq \mathbf{real}.}$$

(16.4)

Except for occasional digressions, we will use these rules for primitive types throughout this chapter. It should be emphasized that this particular choice is intended to provide a variety of useful examples, not as a recommendation for a real programming language.

A subtype relation for arguments or results induces a subtype relation for functions. Suppose f is a function from θ_0 to θ_1. If $\theta_0' \leq \theta_0$, then f can be applied to an argument of type θ_0', while if $\theta_1 \leq \theta_1'$, then the result of such an application will have type θ_1' as well as θ_1. Thus, when both conditions hold, f can also be used as a function from θ_0' to θ_1'. This informal argument is captured by

SBTY RULE: Functions

$$\frac{\theta_0' \leq \theta_0 \qquad \theta_1 \leq \theta_1'}{\theta_0 \to \theta_1 \leq \theta_0' \to \theta_1'.} \tag{16.5}$$

In essence, the type constructor $\to$ is antimonotone in its left argument and monotone in its right argument. For example,

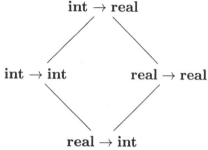

The remaining ways of constructing types have more straightforward subtyping properties. If $\theta \leq \theta'$, then a tuple whose kth component has type θ will also be a tuple whose kth component has type θ', a tagged value whose kth alternative has type θ will also be a tagged value whose kth alternative has type θ', and a list of elements of type θ will also be a list of elements of type θ'. More succinctly, the type constructors for products, sums, and lists are monotone in each of their arguments:

SBTY RULE: Numbered Products

$$\frac{\theta_0 \leq \theta_0' \quad \cdots \quad \theta_{n-1} \leq \theta_{n-1}'}{\mathbf{prod}(\theta_0, \ldots, \theta_{n-1}) \leq \mathbf{prod}(\theta_0', \ldots, \theta_{n-1}'),} \tag{16.6}$$

SBTY RULE: Numbered Sums

$$\frac{\theta_0 \leq \theta_0' \quad \cdots \quad \theta_{n-1} \leq \theta_{n-1}'}{\mathbf{sum}(\theta_0, \ldots, \theta_{n-1}) \leq \mathbf{sum}(\theta_0', \ldots, \theta_{n-1}'),} \tag{16.7}$$

SBTY RULE: Lists

$$\frac{\theta \leq \theta'}{\mathbf{list} \ \theta \leq \mathbf{list} \ \theta'.} \tag{16.8}$$

In the next section, however, we will find that the use of named, rather than numbered, products and sums leads to a more interesting subtyping behavior.

16.2 Named Products and Sums

All that ever happens to a tuple value of type $\mathbf{prod}(\theta_0, \ldots, \theta_{n-1})$ is the selection of fields indexed by the integers 0 to $n-1$. But these selections are also applicable to tuples with additional fields. In fact, in any context requiring an expression of type $\mathbf{prod}(\theta_0, \ldots, \theta_{n-1})$, it makes sense to use an expression whose type is a product with additional fields. Thus we could generalize subtyping rule (16.6) to

$$\frac{\theta_0 \leq \theta_0' \quad \cdots \quad \theta_{n-1} \leq \theta_{n-1}'}{\mathbf{prod}(\theta_0, \ldots, \theta_{m-1}) \leq \mathbf{prod}(\theta_0', \ldots, \theta_{n-1}')} \qquad \text{when } m \geq n.$$

This "field-forgetting conversion" is useful as far as it goes, but there are situations where one needs to forget arbitrary fields, not just the fields at the end of a tuple. This additional flexibility can be obtained by using names rather than numbers as the tags that identify fields. (Named fields also have a mnemonic advantage that can be vital when the variety of tuples and their fields becomes large. They are provided by many programming languages, in tuples that are usually called "records" or "objects".)

For tuples with named fields, we use the syntax

$$\langle \text{exp} \rangle ::= \langle \langle \text{id} \rangle \equiv \langle \text{exp} \rangle, \ldots, \langle \text{id} \rangle \equiv \langle \text{exp} \rangle \rangle \mid \langle \text{exp} \rangle . \langle \text{tag} \rangle$$

$$\langle \text{tag} \rangle ::= \langle \text{id} \rangle$$

$$\langle \text{type} \rangle ::= \mathbf{prod}(\langle \text{id} \rangle : \langle \text{type} \rangle, \ldots, \langle \text{id} \rangle : \langle \text{type} \rangle)$$

where the predefined nonterminal $\langle \text{id} \rangle$ denotes a set of *identifiers*, and the identifiers $\iota_0, \ldots, \iota_{n-1}$ in $\iota_0 \equiv e_0, \ldots, \iota_{n-1} \equiv e_{n-1}$ and $\mathbf{prod}(\iota_0 : \theta_0, \ldots, \iota_{n-1} : \theta_{n-1})$ must be distinct. (The infix type constructor $\times$ no longer makes sense, but it is still useful to write $\mathbf{unit}$ for the empty product.)

In examples, we will use sans serif alphanumeric strings for identifiers, just as for variables. For example, $\langle \mathsf{age} \equiv 61, \mathsf{married} \equiv \mathbf{true} \rangle$ denotes a two-field tuple where the field named age is 61 and the field named $\mathsf{married}$ is $\mathbf{true}$; if x is such a tuple, then x.age and x.married denote its fields.

Corresponding to the type inference rules (15.6) and (15.7) in Section 15.2, we have

TY RULE: Named Product Introduction

$$\frac{\pi \vdash e_0 : \theta_0 \quad \cdots \quad \pi \vdash e_{n-1} : \theta_{n-1}}{\pi \vdash \langle \iota_0 \equiv e_0, \ldots, \iota_{n-1} \equiv e_{n-1} \rangle : \mathbf{prod}(\iota_0 : \theta_0, \ldots, \iota_{n-1} : \theta_{n-1}),} \tag{16.9}$$

TY RULE: Named Product Elimination

$$\frac{\pi \vdash e : \mathbf{prod}(\iota_0 : \theta_0, \ldots, \iota_{n-1} : \theta_{n-1})}{\pi \vdash e.\iota_k : \theta_k} \qquad \text{when } k < n. \tag{16.10}$$

With named fields, one can form a supertype of a product by dropping any component. For example,

$$\mathbf{prod}(\mathsf{age}\colon \mathbf{int}, \mathsf{height}\colon \mathbf{real}, \mathsf{married}\colon \mathbf{bool}) \leq \mathbf{prod}(\mathsf{age}\colon \mathbf{int}, \mathsf{married}\colon \mathbf{bool}).$$

(This kind of relationship is closely related to "inheritance" in object-oriented programming.) The following subtyping rule captures the general idea, as well as monotonicity in the unforgotten fields:

SBTY RULE: Named Products

$$\frac{\theta_{k_0} \leq \theta'_{k_0} \quad \cdots \quad \theta_{k_{m-1}} \leq \theta'_{k_{m-1}}}{\mathbf{prod}(\iota_0\colon \theta_0, \ldots, \iota_{n-1}\colon \theta_{n-1}) \leq \mathbf{prod}(\iota_{k_0}\colon \theta'_{k_0}, \ldots, \iota_{k_{m-1}}\colon \theta'_{k_{m-1}})} \quad (16.11)$$

when $\{\iota_{k_0}, \ldots, \iota_{k_{m-1}}\} \subseteq \{\iota_0, \ldots, \iota_{n-1}\}$.

Notice that, as a consequence of this rule, two product types that differ only in the order of their tag-type pairs are equivalent.

The subtyping behavior of sums is dual to that of products. All that ever happens to a value with a sum type is a **sumcase** branch on its tag, but this operation is also applicable to values with fewer alternatives. In fact, in any context requiring an expression of sum type, it makes sense to use an operation with fewer alternatives.

Just as with products, to obtain more flexible subtyping of sums, we move from numbered to named tags. Specifically, we will use the syntax

$$\langle \mathrm{exp} \rangle ::= @ \langle \mathrm{tag} \rangle \langle \mathrm{exp} \rangle \mid \mathbf{sumcase} \langle \mathrm{exp} \rangle \mathbf{of} (\langle \mathrm{id} \rangle \equiv \langle \mathrm{exp} \rangle, \ldots, \langle \mathrm{id} \rangle \equiv \langle \mathrm{exp} \rangle)$$

$$\langle \mathrm{tag} \rangle ::= \langle \mathrm{id} \rangle$$

$$\langle \mathrm{type} \rangle ::= \mathbf{sum}(\langle \mathrm{id} \rangle\colon \langle \mathrm{type} \rangle, \ldots, \langle \mathrm{id} \rangle\colon \langle \mathrm{type} \rangle)$$

where the identifiers $\iota_0, \ldots, \iota_{n-1}$ in **sumcase** e **of** $(\iota_0 \equiv e_0, \ldots, \iota_{n-1} \equiv e_{n-1})$ and $\mathbf{sum}(\iota_0\colon \theta_0, \ldots, \iota_{n-1}\colon \theta_{n-1})$ must be distinct. (The infix type constructor $+$ no longer makes sense.)

Corresponding to the inference rules (15.8) and (15.9) in Section 15.2, we have

TY RULE: Named Sum Introduction

$$\frac{\pi \vdash e : \theta_k}{\pi \vdash @ \iota_k e : \mathbf{sum}(\iota_0\colon \theta_0, \ldots, \iota_{n-1}\colon \theta_{n-1})} \quad \text{when } k < n, \quad (16.12)$$

TY RULE: Named Sum Elimination

$$\frac{\begin{array}{c} \pi \vdash e : \mathbf{sum}(\iota_0\colon \theta_0, \ldots, \iota_{n-1}\colon \theta_{n-1}) \\ \pi \vdash e_0 : \theta_0 \to \theta \\ \vdots \\ \pi \vdash e_{n-1} : \theta_{n-1} \to \theta \end{array}}{\pi \vdash \mathbf{sumcase} \; e \; \mathbf{of} \; (\iota_0 \equiv e_0, \ldots, \iota_{n-1} \equiv e_{n-1}) : \theta.} \quad (16.13)$$

With named tags, one can form a subtype of a sum by forgetting arbitrary alternatives. For example,

$$\textbf{sum}(\text{exact}: \textbf{int}, \text{absent}: \textbf{unit}) \le \textbf{sum}(\text{exact}: \textbf{int}, \text{approximate}: \textbf{real}, \text{absent}: \textbf{unit}).$$

The following subtyping rule captures this idea, as well as monotonicity in the unforgotten alternatives:

SBTY RULE: Named Sums

$$\frac{\theta_{k_0} \le \theta'_{k_0} \quad \cdots \quad \theta_{k_{m-1}} \le \theta'_{k_{m-1}}}{\textbf{sum}(\iota_{k_0}: \theta_{k_0}, \ldots, \iota_{k_{m-1}}: \theta_{k_{m-1}}) \le \textbf{sum}(\iota_0: \theta'_0, \ldots, \iota_{n-1}: \theta'_{n-1})} \tag{16.14}$$

when $\{\iota_{k_0}, \ldots, \iota_{k_{m-1}}\} \subseteq \{\iota_0, \ldots, \iota_{n-1}\}$.

As with named products, as a consequence of this rule, two sum types that differ only in the order of their tag-type pairs are equivalent.

For the remainder of this chapter, we will use named, rather than numbered, products and sums.

16.3 Intersection Types

We have seen that there are well-typed expressions such as

$$((2+1) \div 2) \times ((2.5+1)/2.5), \tag{16.15}$$

where generic built-in operators such as $+$ are used with more than one type. In the type systems discussed so far, however, one cannot define functions that can be used with similar freedom, as in

$$\textbf{let } \mathsf{f} \equiv \lambda \mathsf{x}. \ \mathsf{x} + 1 \textbf{ in } ((\mathsf{f} \ 2) \div 2) \times ((\mathsf{f} \ 2.5)/2.5). \tag{16.16}$$

This limitation can be overcome by introducing *intersection types* (sometimes called "conjunctive" types). In this approach, we extend the type system of this chapter with a binary type constructor & called *intersection*:

$$\langle \text{type} \rangle ::= \langle \text{type} \rangle \ \& \ \langle \text{type} \rangle$$

along with subtyping rules that characterize $\theta' \ \& \ \theta''$ as a greatest lower bound of θ' and θ'' in the subtyping preorder:

SBTY RULE: Intersection

$$\frac{}{\theta' \ \& \ \theta'' \le \theta'} \qquad \frac{}{\theta' \ \& \ \theta'' \le \theta''}$$

$$\frac{\theta \le \theta' \quad \theta \le \theta''}{\theta \le \theta' \ \& \ \theta''}, \tag{16.17}$$

and a type inference rule saying that an expression has type $\theta' \& \theta''$ if it has both type θ' and type θ'':

TY RULE: Intersection

$$\frac{\pi \vdash e : \theta' \qquad \pi \vdash e : \theta''}{\pi \vdash e : \theta' \& \theta''.} \qquad (16.18)$$

Then, for example, one can prove

1. $x : \mathbf{int} \vdash x : \mathbf{int}$ (15.3)
2. $x : \mathbf{int} \vdash 1 : \mathbf{int}$ (15.1)
3. $x : \mathbf{int} \vdash x + 1 : \mathbf{int}$ (16.27,1,2)
4. $\vdash \lambda x.\, x + 1 : \mathbf{int} \to \mathbf{int}$ (15.4,3)
5. $x : \mathbf{real} \vdash x : \mathbf{real}$ (15.3)
6. $x : \mathbf{real} \vdash 1 : \mathbf{int}$ (15.1)
7. $\mathbf{int} \le \mathbf{real}$ (16.4)
8. $x : \mathbf{real} \vdash 1 : \mathbf{real}$ (16.1,6,7)
9. $x : \mathbf{real} \vdash x + 1 : \mathbf{real}$ (16.27,5,8)
10. $\vdash \lambda x.\, x + 1 : \mathbf{real} \to \mathbf{real}$ (15.4,9)
11. $\vdash \lambda x.\, x + 1 : \mathbf{int} \to \mathbf{int} \,\&\, \mathbf{real} \to \mathbf{real}$ (16.18,4,10)
12. $f : \mathbf{int} \to \mathbf{int} \,\&\, \mathbf{real} \to \mathbf{real} \vdash f : \mathbf{int} \to \mathbf{int} \,\&\, \mathbf{real} \to \mathbf{real}$ (15.3)
13. $\mathbf{int} \to \mathbf{int} \,\&\, \mathbf{real} \to \mathbf{real} \le \mathbf{int} \to \mathbf{int}$ (16.17)
14. $f : \mathbf{int} \to \mathbf{int} \,\&\, \mathbf{real} \to \mathbf{real} \vdash f : \mathbf{int} \to \mathbf{int}$ (16.1,12,13)
15. $f : \mathbf{int} \to \mathbf{int} \,\&\, \mathbf{real} \to \mathbf{real} \vdash 2 : \mathbf{int}$ (15.1)
16. $f : \mathbf{int} \to \mathbf{int} \,\&\, \mathbf{real} \to \mathbf{real} \vdash f\, 2 : \mathbf{int}$ (15.5,14,15)
17. $f : \mathbf{int} \to \mathbf{int} \,\&\, \mathbf{real} \to \mathbf{real} \vdash (f\, 2) \div 2 : \mathbf{int}$ (16.28,16,15)
18. $f : \mathbf{int} \to \mathbf{int} \,\&\, \mathbf{real} \to \mathbf{real} \vdash (f\, 2) \div 2 : \mathbf{real}$ (16.1,17,7)
19. $\mathbf{int} \to \mathbf{int} \,\&\, \mathbf{real} \to \mathbf{real} \le \mathbf{real} \to \mathbf{real}$ (16.17)
20. $f : \mathbf{int} \to \mathbf{int} \,\&\, \mathbf{real} \to \mathbf{real} \vdash f : \mathbf{real} \to \mathbf{real}$ (16.1,12,19)
21. $f : \mathbf{int} \to \mathbf{int} \,\&\, \mathbf{real} \to \mathbf{real} \vdash 2.5 : \mathbf{real}$ (15.1)
22. $f : \mathbf{int} \to \mathbf{int} \,\&\, \mathbf{real} \to \mathbf{real} \vdash f\, 2.5 : \mathbf{real}$ (15.5,20,21)
23. $f : \mathbf{int} \to \mathbf{int} \,\&\, \mathbf{real} \to \mathbf{real} \vdash (f\, 2.5)/2.5 : \mathbf{real}$ (16.28,22,21)
24. $f : \mathbf{int} \to \mathbf{int} \,\&\, \mathbf{real} \to \mathbf{real} \vdash ((f\, 2) \div 2) \times ((f\, 2.5)/2.5) : \mathbf{real}$ (16.27,18,23)
25. $\vdash \mathbf{let}\; f \equiv \lambda x.\, x + 1 \;\mathbf{in}\; ((f\, 2) \div 2) \times ((f\, 2.5)/2.5) : \mathbf{real}$ (15.11,11,24)

Further insight into intersection types is obtained by comparing the types $(\theta \to \theta') \,\&\, (\theta \to \theta'')$ and $\theta \to (\theta' \,\&\, \theta'')$. Intuitively, they both represent the set of functions that, when applied to arguments of type θ, give results with both types θ' and θ''. Thus one would expect these types to be equivalent. Only half of the equivalence, however, is provable from the subtyping rules we have given so far:

1.	$\theta \leq \theta$	(16.2)
2.	$\theta' \,\&\, \theta'' \leq \theta'$	(16.17)
3.	$\theta \to (\theta' \,\&\, \theta'') \leq \theta \to \theta'$	(16.5,1,2)
4.	$\theta' \,\&\, \theta'' \leq \theta''$	(16.17)
5.	$\theta \to (\theta' \,\&\, \theta'') \leq \theta \to \theta''$	(16.5,1,4)
6.	$\theta \to (\theta' \,\&\, \theta'') \leq (\theta \to \theta') \,\&\, (\theta \to \theta'')$	(16.17,3,5)

In fact, we can add the other half of the equivalence as an additional subtyping rule:

SBTY RULE: Distributivity of Intersection and $\to$

$$(\theta \to \theta') \,\&\, (\theta \to \theta'') \leq \theta \to (\theta' \,\&\, \theta''). \tag{16.19}$$

There are also rules that express multiple-field named products as intersections of single-field products, and describe the distribution of intersection with products and sums. In these rules, as in the previous one, the opposite subtyping is provable, so that the subtyping is really an equivalence of types.

SBTY RULE: Named Products as Intersections

$$\mathbf{prod}(\iota_0 : \theta_0) \,\&\, \cdots \,\&\, \mathbf{prod}(\iota_{n-1} : \theta_{n-1}) \leq \mathbf{prod}(\iota_0 : \theta_0, \ldots, \iota_{n-1} : \theta_{n-1}) \tag{16.20}$$

when $n \geq 1$,

SBTY RULE: Distributivity of Intersection and Named Products

$$\mathbf{prod}(\iota : \theta) \,\&\, \mathbf{prod}(\iota : \theta') \leq \mathbf{prod}(\iota : \theta \,\&\, \theta'), \tag{16.21}$$

SBTY RULE: Distributivity of Intersection and Named Sums

$$\begin{aligned}
\mathbf{sum}(\iota_0 : \theta_0, \ldots, \iota_{n-1} : \theta_{n-1}, \iota'_0 : \theta'_0, \ldots, \iota'_{n'-1} : \theta'_{n'-1}) \\
\&\, \mathbf{sum}(\iota_0 : \hat\theta_0, \ldots, \iota_{n-1} : \hat\theta_{n-1}, \iota''_0 : \theta''_0, \ldots, \iota''_{n''-1} : \theta''_{n''-1}) \\
\leq \mathbf{sum}(\iota_0 : \theta_0 \,\&\, \hat\theta_0, \ldots, \iota_{n-1} : \theta_{n-1} \,\&\, \hat\theta_{n-1})
\end{aligned} \tag{16.22}$$

when the ι_k, ι'_k, and ι''_k are all distinct.

(In rule (16.20), the multiple intersections can be parenthesized arbitrarily.) In essence, the equivalence of the two sides of rule (16.20) implies that, in a language with intersection types (such as the Algol-like language Forsythe), one can dispense with multifield products and use intersections of single-field product types in their place.

For some purposes, it is also useful to introduce a type **ns**, called the *nonsense type*, that is possessed by all expressions in all contexts:

TY RULE: Nonsense

$$\overline{\pi \vdash e : \mathbf{ns},} \tag{16.23}$$

and is a supertype of all types:

SBTY RULE: Nonsense

$$\overline{\theta \leq \mathbf{ns}.} \tag{16.24}$$

For example, one can infer typing judgements such as

$$\vdash \lambda x.\ \lambda y.\ x : \mathbf{int} \rightarrow \mathbf{ns} \rightarrow \mathbf{int}$$

$$\vdash \lambda x.\ \lambda y.\ y : \mathbf{ns} \rightarrow \mathbf{int} \rightarrow \mathbf{int},$$

which characterize functions that are constant in some of their arguments. The nonsense type can be thought of as the intersection of zero types; thus it satisfies the "zero-ary" analogues of rules (16.19) and (16.21):

SBTY RULE: Distributivity of Nonsense and $\rightarrow$

$$\overline{\mathbf{ns} \leq \theta \rightarrow \mathbf{ns},} \tag{16.25}$$

SBTY RULE: Distributivity of Nonsense and Named Products

$$\overline{\mathbf{ns} \leq \mathbf{prod}(\iota : \mathbf{ns}).} \tag{16.26}$$

The drawback of introducing the nonsense type is that it restricts the soundness of our type system, since phrases whose type is **ns** or a supertype of **ns** can evaluate to a type error. But such phrases can appear within contexts of other types only when they cannot be executed, so that introducing **ns** gives a kind of dead-code analysis.

Moreover, with the inclusion of **ns**, the intersection type discipline achieves an important property that is not possessed by any other known type system:

Proposition 16.1 (Conservation of Typing Judgements) *If* $e \xrightarrow{\beta}{}^{*} e'$, *then, in the intersection type system with* **ns**, $\pi \vdash e' : \theta$ *is valid if and only if* $\pi \vdash e : \theta$.

Actually, the "if" part of this proposition (often called "subject reduction") holds for any reasonable type system; it is the "only if" part that is peculiar to intersection types.

For example, the expression (16.16), after desugaring, β-contracts in three steps to expression (16.15), which has type **real**. In the simple type system with subtypes but without intersection types, (16.16) is ill-typed. With intersection types, however, we have proven that it has type **real**.

A second example falls within the pure lambda calculus:

$$(\lambda f.\ f\,f)(\lambda x.\ x) \xrightarrow{\beta} (\lambda x.\ x)(\lambda x.\ x).$$

Here the right side has type **int** → **int**, while the left side is ill-typed unless one uses intersection types (or polymorphic types, as described in Chapter 17). With intersection types, however, one can prove

$$\vdash \lambda f.\ f\,f : (((\textbf{int} \rightarrow \textbf{int}) \rightarrow (\textbf{int} \rightarrow \textbf{int})) \,\&\, (\textbf{int} \rightarrow \textbf{int})) \rightarrow (\textbf{int} \rightarrow \textbf{int})$$

$$\vdash \lambda x.\ x : ((\textbf{int} \rightarrow \textbf{int}) \rightarrow (\textbf{int} \rightarrow \textbf{int})) \,\&\, (\textbf{int} \rightarrow \textbf{int}),$$

from which one can infer that the left side has type **int** → **int**.

A third example illustrates the use of **ns**:

$$(\lambda x.\ 3)((\lambda x.\ x\,x)(\lambda x.\ x\,x)) \xrightarrow{\beta} 3.$$

Without **ns**, the left side cannot be typed. With **ns**, however, one can prove

$$\vdash \lambda x.\ 3 : \textbf{ns} \rightarrow \textbf{int}$$

$$\vdash (\lambda x.\ x\,x)(\lambda x.\ x\,x) : \textbf{ns},$$

from which one can infer that the left side has type **int**.

The conservation of typing judgements has important consequences for the use of intersection types in the theory of the pure lambda calculus (without products, sums, or **rec** or **letrec**). Perhaps most important, an expression e has a normal form if and only if $\pi \vdash e : \theta$ is valid for some context π and some type θ, neither of which contains **ns**. Less happily, since deciding whether an expression has a normal form is a form of the halting problem, this result implies that there is no type-inference algorithm for intersection types. In fact, even type checking is known to be inefficient in the worst case, although there are type-checking algorithms that do appear to be reasonable in practice.

16.4 Extrinsic Semantics

In this section, we extend the extrinsic semantics of Section 15.4 to encompass subtypes and intersection types. As a first step, we must make some adjustments to the direct denotational semantics of the underlying untyped language that was given in Section 14.4. First, since we now regard all values of primitive types to be real numbers, we replace V_{int} and V_{bool} by a single discretely ordered set of real numbers (or at least floating-point-representable numbers), so that

$$V \underset{\psi}{\overset{\phi}{\rightleftarrows}} V_{\text{real}} + V_{\text{fun}} + V_{\text{tuple}} + V_{\text{alt}},$$

where $V_{\text{real}} = \mathbf{R}$. We also redefine the operations that use or produce boolean values to replace ι_{bool} **false** by $\iota_{\text{real}}\ 0$ and ι_{bool} **true** by $\iota_{\text{real}}\ 1$.

Second, to shift from numbered to named tuples, we must take a member of V_{tuple} to be a function from a finite set of identifiers to V_*, rather than a sequence of members of V_*:

$$V_{\text{tuple}} = \bigcup \{ (V_*)^F \mid F \overset{\text{fin}}{\subseteq} \langle \text{id} \rangle \}.$$

(Since this is a union of disjoint sets, it is ordered like a disjoint union.) Then the semantic equations for tuples become

DR SEM EQ: Named Tuples

$$[\![\langle \iota_0 \equiv e_0, \ldots, \iota_{n-1} \equiv e_{n-1} \rangle]\!] \eta = \iota_{\text{norm}}(\iota_{\text{tuple}}[\, \iota_0 \colon [\![e_0]\!] \eta \mid \ldots \mid \iota_{n-1} \colon [\![e_{n-1}]\!] \eta \,])$$

$$[\![e.\iota]\!] \eta = (\lambda t. \ \textbf{if} \ \iota \in \text{dom} \, t \ \textbf{then} \ t_\iota \ \textbf{else} \ \text{tyerr})_{\text{tuple}*}([\![e]\!] \eta).$$

The first of these equations makes it clear that the meaning of a tuple constructor is independent of the order of the tag-expression pairs, so that, for example, $\langle \textsf{age} \equiv 61, \textsf{married} \equiv \textbf{true} \rangle$ has the same meaning as $\langle \textsf{married} \equiv \textbf{true}, \textsf{age} \equiv 61 \rangle$.

Third, to shift from numbered to named alternatives, we change the set of tags from numbers to identifiers in the definition of the predomain of alternative values:

$$V_{\text{alt}} = \langle \text{id} \rangle \times V_*,$$

and in the semantic equations:

DR SEM EQ: Named Alternatives

$$[\![@ \, \iota \, e]\!] \eta = \iota_{\text{norm}}(\iota_{\text{alt}} \langle \iota, [\![e]\!] \eta \rangle)$$

$$[\![\textbf{sumcase} \ e \ \textbf{of} \ (\iota_0 \equiv e_0, \ldots, \iota_{n-1} \equiv e_{n-1})]\!] \eta$$
$$= (\lambda \langle \iota, a \rangle. \ \textbf{if} \ \iota \in \{ \iota_0, \ldots, \iota_{n-1} \} \textbf{then}$$
$$(\lambda f. \ f \ a)_{\text{fun}*}([\![e_k]\!] \eta) \ \textbf{else} \ \text{tyerr})_{\text{alt}*}([\![e]\!] \eta)$$

where k is the unique integer such that $\iota = \iota_k$.

(Notice that the meaning of the **sumcase** expression is independent of the order of tag-expression pairs.)

The next step is to adjust the definition given in Section 15.4 of the partial equivalence relations $\mathcal{P}(\theta)$ denoted by each type θ. Here we must modify the definitions for the primitive types to reflect the fact that booleans, natural numbers, and integers all have become special kinds of real numbers. We must also modify the definitions for products and sums to replace numerical tags by named tags, and we must add definitions for intersection types and **ns**. Only the definition for function types remains unchanged:

(a$'_1$) $\langle x, x' \rangle \in \mathcal{P}(\mathbf{real})$ if and only if $x = x' = \bot$ or there is an $r \in V_{\mathrm{real}}$ such that $x = x' = \iota_{\mathrm{norm}}(\iota_{\mathrm{real}}\, r)$.

(a$'_2$) $\langle x, x' \rangle \in \mathcal{P}(\mathbf{int})$ if and only if $x = x' = \bot$ or there is an integer $i \in V_{\mathrm{real}}$ such that $x = x' = \iota_{\mathrm{norm}}(\iota_{\mathrm{real}}\, i)$.

(a$'_3$) $\langle x, x' \rangle \in \mathcal{P}(\mathbf{nat})$ if and only if $x = x' = \bot$ or there is an integer $n \in V_{\mathrm{real}}$ such that $n \geq 0$ and $x = x' = \iota_{\mathrm{norm}}(\iota_{\mathrm{real}}\, n)$.

(b$'$) $\langle x, x' \rangle \in \mathcal{P}(\mathbf{bool})$ if and only if $x = x' = \bot$ or $x = x' = \iota_{\mathrm{norm}}(\iota_{\mathrm{real}}\, 0)$ or $x = x' = \iota_{\mathrm{norm}}(\iota_{\mathrm{real}}\, 1)$.

(c) $\langle x, x' \rangle \in \mathcal{P}(\theta \to \theta')$ if and only if

$$\forall \langle a, a' \rangle \in \mathcal{P}(\theta). \ \langle (\lambda f.\ f\ a)_{\mathrm{fun}*}\, x, (\lambda f.\ f\ a')_{\mathrm{fun}*}\, x' \rangle \in \mathcal{P}(\theta').$$

(d$'$) $\langle x, x' \rangle \in \mathcal{P}(\mathbf{prod}(\iota_0 \colon \theta_0, \ldots, \iota_{n-1} \colon \theta_{n-1}))$ if and only if $x \neq \mathrm{tyerr}$ and $x' \neq \mathrm{tyerr}$ and

$$\forall k \in 0 \ \mathbf{to}\ n - 1.$$
$$\langle (\lambda t.\ \mathbf{if}\ \iota_k \in \mathrm{dom}\, t\ \mathbf{then}\ t_{\iota_k}\ \mathbf{else}\ \mathrm{tyerr})_{\mathrm{tuple}*}\, x,$$
$$(\lambda t.\ \mathbf{if}\ \iota_k \in \mathrm{dom}\, t\ \mathbf{then}\ t_{\iota_k}\ \mathbf{else}\ \mathrm{tyerr})_{\mathrm{tuple}*}\, x' \rangle \in \mathcal{P}(\theta_k).$$

(e$'$) $\langle x, x' \rangle \in \mathcal{P}(\mathbf{sum}(\iota_0 \colon \theta_0, \ldots, \iota_{n-1} \colon \theta_{n-1}))$ if and only if $x = x' = \bot$ or there are $k \in 0 \ \mathbf{to}\ n - 1$ and $a, a' \in V_*$ such that $x = \iota_{\mathrm{norm}}(\iota_{\mathrm{alt}}\langle \iota_k, a \rangle)$, $x' = \iota_{\mathrm{norm}}(\iota_{\mathrm{alt}}\langle \iota_k, a' \rangle)$, and

$$\langle a, a' \rangle \in \mathcal{P}(\theta_k).$$

(f) $\langle x, x' \rangle \in \mathcal{P}(\theta\ \&\ \theta')$ if and only if $\langle x, x' \rangle \in \mathcal{P}(\theta)$ and $\langle x, x' \rangle \in \mathcal{P}(\theta')$.

(g) $\langle x, x' \rangle \in \mathcal{P}(\mathbf{ns})$ is true.

Notice that the relation denoted by $\theta\ \&\ \theta'$ is the intersection of the relations denoted by θ and θ'. Thus a value in the set denoted by the intersection type belongs to the sets denoted by both θ and θ', and two values are equivalent for the intersection type when they are equivalent for both θ and θ'.

Finally, notice that all values belong to the set denoted by $\mathbf{ns}$, and all values are equivalent for this type.

The new definition of $\mathcal{P}(\theta)$ continues to satisfy Proposition 15.1 in Section 15.4, with the exception of part (c), which must be weakened to

(c) $\bot \in \mathrm{dom}\,(\mathcal{P}(\theta))$, *but* $\mathrm{tyerr} \notin \mathrm{dom}\,(\mathcal{P}(\theta))$ *unless* $\mathbf{ns} \leq \theta$,

since even type-incorrect phrases have type $\mathbf{ns}$. (The only interesting change to the proof is the use of the key facts that the intersection of partial equivalence relations is a partial equivalence relation and the intersection of chain-complete relations is a chain-complete relation.)

To show that our extended type system is in accord with this semantics of types, we begin with the subtyping relation:

Proposition 16.2 (Soundness of Subtyping) *If $\theta \leq \theta'$, then $\mathcal{P}(\theta) \subseteq \mathcal{P}(\theta')$.*

PROOF The proof is by structural induction on the formal proof of $\theta \leq \theta'$, with a case analysis on the subtyping rule used in the final step of the proof.

We omit all but the most interesting case, where rule (16.5) for functions in Section 16.1 is used in the final step. In this case, $\theta = \theta_0 \to \theta_1$, $\theta' = \theta'_0 \to \theta'_1$, and there are subproofs of $\theta'_0 \leq \theta_0$ and $\theta_1 \leq \theta'_1$, so that the induction hypothesis gives $\mathcal{P}(\theta'_0) \subseteq \mathcal{P}(\theta_0)$ and $\mathcal{P}(\theta_1) \subseteq \mathcal{P}(\theta'_1)$.

To see that $\mathcal{P}(\theta_0 \to \theta_1) \subseteq \mathcal{P}(\theta'_0 \to \theta'_1)$, suppose $\langle x, x'\rangle \in \mathcal{P}(\theta_0 \to \theta_1)$. Then, by part (c) of the definition of $\mathcal{P}$:

$$\forall \langle a, a'\rangle \in \mathcal{P}(\theta_0).\ \langle (\lambda f.\ f\ a)_{\text{fun}*}\ x, (\lambda f.\ f\ a')_{\text{fun}*}\ x'\rangle \in \mathcal{P}(\theta_1),$$

which implies

$$\forall \langle a, a'\rangle \in \mathcal{P}(\theta'_0).\ \langle (\lambda f.\ f\ a)_{\text{fun}*}\ x, (\lambda f.\ f\ a')_{\text{fun}*}\ x'\rangle \in \mathcal{P}(\theta'_1).$$

It follows from part (c) of the definition of $\mathcal{P}$ that $\langle x, x'\rangle \in \mathcal{P}(\theta'_0 \to \theta'_1)$.

END OF PROOF

Remembering our interpretation of the partial equivalence relations, it is evident that Proposition 16.2 is equivalent to saying that, whenever $\theta \leq \theta'$,

- The set of values denoted by θ is a subset of the set of values denoted by θ'.
- Two values in the set denoted by θ that are equivalent for θ are also equivalent for θ'.

Proposition 16.2 also explains equivalence between types: Two types that are each a subtype of the other must denote the same partial equivalence relation.

We can now show that our extended type system is sound with respect to extrinsic semantics, that is, that Proposition 15.3 in Section 15.4 continues to hold. In the proof of that proposition, which was by structural induction on the formal proof of $\pi \vdash e : \theta$, there are (aside from trivial changes because of our redefinition of the primitive types and the change from numbered to named sums and products) two new cases, which correspond to the two new type inference rules we have added.

ADDITIONAL PROOF (of Proposition 15.3) Suppose the rule used in the final step of the proof is the rule for subsumption ((16.1) in Section 16.1),

$$\frac{\pi \vdash e : \theta \qquad \theta \leq \theta'}{\pi \vdash e : \theta'.}$$

Assume $\langle \eta v, \eta' v\rangle \in \mathcal{P}(\pi v)$ for all $v \in \operatorname{dom} \pi$. By the induction hypothesis applied to the subproof of $\pi \vdash e : \theta$, $\langle [\![e]\!]\eta, [\![e]\!]\eta'\rangle \in \mathcal{P}(\theta)$. By Proposition 16.2 applied to the subproof of $\theta \leq \theta'$, $\mathcal{P}(\theta) \subseteq \mathcal{P}(\theta')$. Thus $\langle [\![e]\!]\eta, [\![e]\!]\eta'\rangle \in \mathcal{P}(\theta')$.

On the other hand, suppose the rule used in the final step of the proof is the rule for intersection ((16.18) in Section 16.3),

$$\frac{\pi \vdash e : \theta' \qquad \pi \vdash e : \theta''}{\pi \vdash e : \theta' \,\&\, \theta''.}$$

Assume $\langle \eta v, \eta' v \rangle \in \mathcal{P}(\pi v)$ for all $v \in \mathrm{dom}\,\pi$. From the induction hypothesis, we find that $\langle [\![e]\!]\eta, [\![e]\!]\eta' \rangle$ belongs to both $\mathcal{P}(\theta)$ and $\mathcal{P}(\theta')$. By part (f) of the definition of $\mathcal{P}$, $\mathcal{P}(\theta \,\&\, \theta')$ is the intersection of the sets $\mathcal{P}(\theta)$ and $\mathcal{P}(\theta')$. Thus $\langle [\![e]\!]\eta, [\![e]\!]\eta' \rangle \in \mathcal{P}(\theta \,\&\, \theta')$.   END OF PROOF

As in Section 15.4, Proposition 15.4 follows from Proposition 15.3. This establishes that a well-typed expression evaluated in a type-correct environment will not give a run-time error unless its only types are supertypes of **ns**.

16.5 Generic Operators

With a rich variety of primitive types, one can have more than one type inference rule for the same arithmetic operator — in the jargon of programming languages, the operator can be *generic*. (For brevity, we will consider only binary operators in this discussion.) For example, one can replace rules (15.1) for addition and multiplication in Section 15.2 by

TY RULE: Addition and Multiplication

$$\frac{\pi \vdash e_0 : \mathbf{nat} \qquad \pi \vdash e_1 : \mathbf{nat}}{\pi \vdash e_0 + e_1 : \mathbf{nat}} \qquad \frac{\pi \vdash e_0 : \mathbf{int} \qquad \pi \vdash e_1 : \mathbf{int}}{\pi \vdash e_0 + e_1 : \mathbf{int}}$$

$$\frac{\pi \vdash e_0 : \mathbf{real} \qquad \pi \vdash e_1 : \mathbf{real}}{\pi \vdash e_0 + e_1 : \mathbf{real}}$$

$$\frac{\pi \vdash e_0 : \mathbf{nat} \qquad \pi \vdash e_1 : \mathbf{nat}}{\pi \vdash e_0 \times e_1 : \mathbf{nat}} \qquad \frac{\pi \vdash e_0 : \mathbf{int} \qquad \pi \vdash e_1 : \mathbf{int}}{\pi \vdash e_0 \times e_1 : \mathbf{int}}$$

$$\frac{\pi \vdash e_0 : \mathbf{real} \qquad \pi \vdash e_1 : \mathbf{real}}{\pi \vdash e_0 \times e_1 : \mathbf{real}.}$$

(16.27)

However, extrinsic semantics places restrictions on such rules for generic operators. In the first place, the operator must denote a single function in the underlying untyped language, so that its result does not depend on its typing. For example, $3+2$ denotes the same number, regardless of whether one is working with natural numbers, integers, or reals. On the other hand, with integer division $3 \div 2$ is 1, while with real division $3/2$ is 1.5, so that $\div$ and $/$ should be distinct operators, even though both are called "division":

TY RULE: Division

$$\frac{\pi \vdash e_0 : \mathbf{nat} \qquad \pi \vdash e_1 : \mathbf{nat}}{\pi \vdash e_0 \div e_1 : \mathbf{nat}} \qquad \frac{\pi \vdash e_0 : \mathbf{int} \qquad \pi \vdash e_1 : \mathbf{int}}{\pi \vdash e_0 \div e_1 : \mathbf{int}}$$

$$\frac{\pi \vdash e_0 : \mathbf{real} \qquad \pi \vdash e_1 : \mathbf{real}}{\pi \vdash e_0/e_1 : \mathbf{real}.}$$

(16.28)

Furthermore, inference rules such as (16.27) must not invalidate Proposition 15.2 in Section 15.4. Consider, for example, the general form of a rule describing a binary operator:

$$\frac{\pi \vdash e_0 : \theta \qquad \pi \vdash e_1 : \theta'}{\pi \vdash e_0 \text{ op } e_1 : \theta'',}$$

and suppose that the semantic equation for this operator is

$$[\![e_0 \text{ op } e_1]\!]\eta = F([\![e_0]\!]\eta, [\![e_1]\!]\eta),$$

where F is some function from $V_* \times V_*$ to V_*. For a rule of this form, Proposition 15.2 asserts that

If $\langle x, x' \rangle \in \mathcal{P}(\theta)$ and $\langle y, y' \rangle \in \mathcal{P}(\theta')$, then $\langle F(x, y), F(x', y') \rangle \in \mathcal{P}(\theta'')$.   (16.29)

This condition implies

If $x \in \operatorname{dom} \mathcal{P}(\theta)$ and $y \in \operatorname{dom} \mathcal{P}(\theta')$, then $F(x, y) \in \operatorname{dom} \mathcal{P}(\theta'')$.   (16.30)

Moreover, when the relations $\mathcal{P}(\theta)$ and $\mathcal{P}(\theta')$ in these conditions are both subsets of the identity relation (so that $\langle x, x' \rangle \in \mathcal{P}(\theta)$ implies $x = x'$, and similarly for $\mathcal{P}(\theta')$), as is the case for the primitive types in the definition of $\mathcal{P}$ in Section 16.4, conditions (16.29) and (16.30) are equivalent.

It is easily seen that condition (16.30) is met by rules (16.27) and (16.28), as well as

TY RULE: Subtraction

$$\frac{\pi \vdash e_0 : \mathbf{int} \qquad \pi \vdash e_1 : \mathbf{int}}{\pi \vdash e_0 - e_1 : \mathbf{int}} \qquad \frac{\pi \vdash e_0 : \mathbf{real} \qquad \pi \vdash e_1 : \mathbf{real}}{\pi \vdash e_0 - e_1 : \mathbf{real},}$$

(16.31)

but not the corresponding rule for subtraction and **nat**, since the difference of two natural numbers can be negative. Moreover, when **false** is identified with zero and **true** is identified with one, condition (16.30) is satisfied by

TY RULE: Boolean Multiplication

$$\frac{\pi \vdash e_0 : \mathbf{bool} \qquad \pi \vdash e_1 : \mathbf{bool}}{\pi \vdash e_0 \times e_1 : \mathbf{bool}.}$$

(16.32)

Indeed, the operation $\times$ can be used instead of $\wedge$ (except that, in our normal-order semantics, we have chosen short-circuit evaluation for $\wedge$ but not $\times$). However, the analogous rule for $+$ violates condition (16.30), since **true** $+$ **true** is $1 + 1 = 2$, which is not a boolean value. Thus $+$ cannot be used instead of $\vee$.

We saw in Section 15.4 that function types are modelled by partial equivalence relations that are not subsets of the identity relation; for example, $\lambda x.\ 0$ and $\lambda x.\ \sin(x \times \pi)$ are distinct functions that are related by $\mathcal{P}(\textbf{int} \to \textbf{int})$. In fact, there are situations where even primitive types might be modelled by partial equivalence relations that are not subsets of the identity relation. Instead of making **bool** a subtype of **nat**, for instance, one might make **nat** a subtype of **bool**, by identifying zero with **false** and all larger natural numbers with **true**. Then any two positive numbers, viewed as boolean values, would be equivalent:

(b″) $\langle x, x' \rangle \in \mathcal{P}(\textbf{bool})$ if and only if $x = x' = \bot$ or $x = x' = \iota_{\text{norm}}(\iota_{\text{real}}\ 0)$ or there are integers $n, n' \in V_{\text{real}}$ such that $n > 0$, $n' > 0$, $x = \iota_{\text{norm}}(\iota_{\text{real}}\ n)$, and $x' = \iota_{\text{norm}}(\iota_{\text{real}}\ n')$.

In this situation, condition (16.29) would permit both of the inference rules

$$\frac{\pi \vdash e_0 : \textbf{bool} \qquad \pi \vdash e_1 : \textbf{bool}}{\pi \vdash e_0 + e_1 : \textbf{bool}} \qquad \frac{\pi \vdash e_0 : \textbf{bool} \qquad \pi \vdash e_1 : \textbf{bool}}{\pi \vdash e_0 \times e_1 : \textbf{bool},}$$

so that $+$ could be used for $\vee$ and $\times$ for $\wedge$ (except for short-circuit evaluation). On the other hand, consider

$$\frac{\pi \vdash e_0 : \textbf{bool} \qquad \pi \vdash e_1 : \textbf{bool}}{\pi \vdash e_0 = e_1 : \textbf{bool}.}$$

Since $\langle 3, 3 \rangle, \langle 3, 4 \rangle \in \mathcal{P}(\text{bool})$ according to (b″), condition (16.29) for this rule would imply that $3 = 4$ has the same value (viewed as a boolean) as $3 = 3$. In essence, once one identifies different numbers with the same boolean value, one cannot use the same equality operator for numbers and booleans. (A possible way around this anomaly would be to use one operator, say $=$, for numbers and another, say $\Leftrightarrow$, for **bool**.)

This example illustrates a general problem that arises when defining an equality operation for a supertype that denotes a partial equivalence relation that is not a subset of the identity relation. Suppose

$$\frac{\pi \vdash e_0 : \theta' \qquad \pi \vdash e_1 : \theta'}{\pi \vdash e_0 = e_1 : \textbf{bool}}$$

and $\theta \leq \theta'$, so that $\mathcal{P}(\theta) \subseteq \mathcal{P}(\theta')$. If $\langle x, x \rangle, \langle x', x' \rangle \in \mathcal{P}(\theta)$ and $\langle x, x' \rangle \in \mathcal{P}(\theta')$, then condition (16.29) implies that $x = x'$ must have the same value (viewed as a boolean) as $x = x$. But if $\langle x, x' \rangle \notin P(\theta)$, this is contrary to the intended notion of equality for the type θ.

It is clear that extrinsic semantics provides a rigid framework that permits a language designer to avoid the anomalous interactions between subtyping and generic operators that have plagued many real programming languages. Once one has given the underlying semantics of the untyped language and defined the partial equivalence relation denoted by each type, the allowable subtyping rules are those that do not violate Proposition 16.2, and the allowable type inference rules (for nonbinding constructions) are those that do not violate Proposition 15.2.

For some purposes, however, this framework is too rigid. If one thinks of a partial equivalence relation as describing the use of the values of the untyped language to represent more abstract objects, then one can think of the "conversion" from a subtype to a supertype as a change in what is being represented; but there is never any conversion of the underlying untyped values.

As we will see in the next section, intrinsic semantics provides a more flexible framework.

16.6 Intrinsic Semantics

In the extrinsic semantics of the previous sections, the values of expressions are unaffected by the type system and so, in particular, are not subject to any kind of conversion from a subtype to a supertype. In an intrinsic semantics, however, the subtype relationship is interpreted by functions that convert values from one type to another.

To extend the intrinsic semantics of Section 15.5 to encompass subtyping and intersection, we must first adjust that semantics to account for our changes to the primitive types, and to products and sums. For the choice of primitive types in Section 16.1, we define

$$\mathcal{D}(\mathbf{bool}) = \mathbf{B} \qquad \mathcal{D}(\mathbf{nat}) = \mathbf{N} \qquad \mathcal{D}(\mathbf{int}) = \mathbf{Z} \qquad \mathcal{D}(\mathbf{real}) = \mathbf{R}.$$

We also replace the product and sum over an interval of integers by products and sums over a finite set of identifiers. In the notation of Section A.3,

$$\mathcal{D}(\mathbf{prod}(\iota_0 : \theta_0, \ldots, \iota_{n-1} : \theta_{n-1})) = \prod [\, \iota_0 : \mathcal{D}(\theta_0) \mid \ldots \mid \iota_{n-1} : \mathcal{D}(\theta_{n-1}) \,]$$

$$\mathcal{D}(\mathbf{sum}(\iota_0 : \theta_0, \ldots, \iota_{n-1} : \theta_{n-1})) = (\sum [\, \iota_0 : \mathcal{D}(\theta_0) \mid \ldots \mid \iota_{n-1} : \mathcal{D}(\theta_{n-1}) \,])_\perp.$$

There are also corresponding changes in the semantic equations for sums and products:

TY SEM EQ: Named Product Introduction (16.9)

$$[\![\pi \vdash \langle \iota_0 \equiv e_0, \ldots, \iota_{n-1} \equiv e_{n-1}\rangle : \mathbf{prod}(\iota_0\!:\!\theta_0, \ldots, \iota_{n-1}\!:\!\theta_{n-1})]\!]\eta$$
$$= [\iota_0\!: [\![\pi \vdash e_0 : \theta_0]\!]\eta \mid \ldots \mid \iota_{n-1}\!: [\![\pi \vdash e_{n-1} : \theta_{n-1}]\!]\eta],$$

TY SEM EQ: Named Product Elimination (16.10)

$$[\![\pi \vdash e.\iota_k : \theta_k]\!]\eta = ([\![\pi \vdash e : \mathbf{prod}(\iota_0\!:\!\theta_0, \ldots, \iota_{n-1}\!:\!\theta_{n-1})]\!]\eta)(\iota_k) \qquad \text{when } k < n,$$

TY SEM EQ: Named Sum Introduction (16.12)

$$[\![\pi \vdash @\,\iota_k\, e : \mathbf{sum}(\iota_0\!:\!\theta_0, \ldots, \iota_{n-1}\!:\!\theta_{n-1})]\!]\eta = \iota_\uparrow\langle \iota_k, [\![\pi \vdash e : \theta_k]\!]\eta\rangle \quad \text{when } k < n,$$

TY SEM EQ: Named Sum Elimination (16.13)

$$[\![\pi \vdash \mathbf{sumcase}\ e\ \mathbf{of}\ (\iota_0 \equiv e_0, \ldots, \iota_{n-1} \equiv e_{n-1}) : \theta]\!]\eta$$
$$= (\lambda\langle k, z\rangle \in \textstyle\sum [\iota_0\!:\!\mathcal{D}(\theta_0) \mid \ldots \mid \iota_{n-1}\!:\!\mathcal{D}(\theta_{n-1})].\ [\![\pi \vdash e_k : \theta_k \to \theta]\!]\eta z)_\perp$$
$$([\![\pi \vdash e : \mathbf{sum}(\iota_0\!:\!\theta_0, \ldots, \iota_{n-1}\!:\!\theta_{n-1})]\!]\eta)$$

where k is the index such that $\iota = \iota_k$.

Next we extend this intrinsic model to deal with subtyping. Whenever $\theta \leq \theta'$, there should be a strict continuous function from $\mathcal{D}(\theta)$ to $\mathcal{D}(\theta')$, which we call the *implicit conversion function* from θ to θ' and denote by $[\![\theta \leq \theta']\!]$.

In Section 15.5, we defined the meaning of a typing judgement by structural induction on the formal proof of the judgement. Here, in a similar manner, we will define the meaning $[\![\theta \leq \theta']\!]$ of a subtyping judgement by structural induction on the formal proof of $\theta \leq \theta'$. For each subtyping rule, we give a *conversion equation* (abbreviated CONV EQ) that, for every instance of the rule, expresses the meaning of the conclusion of the instance in terms of the meanings of the premisses of the instance. (As in Section 15.5, we indicate the correspondence between equations and rules by parenthesized references.)

CONV EQ: Reflexivity (16.2)

$$[\![\theta \leq \theta]\!] = I_{\mathcal{D}(\theta)},$$

CONV EQ: Transitivity (16.3)

$$[\![\theta \leq \theta'']\!] = [\![\theta' \leq \theta'']\!] \cdot [\![\theta \leq \theta']\!],$$

where I_D denotes the identity function on D and $\cdot$ denotes the composition of functions (in functional order).

(The reader who is familiar with the definitions of elementary category theory will recognize what is going on here. If the set of types, preordered by the subtype relation, is viewed as a category, then there is a functor from this category to the category of domains and strict continuous functions that maps each type θ into the domain $\mathcal{D}(\theta)$ and each morphism from θ to θ' into the conversion function $[\![\theta \leq \theta']\!]$. The equations above are simply the standard laws that must be satisfied by such a functor.)

For our choice of primitive types, we have:

CONV EQ: Primitive Types (16.4)

$$[\![\mathbf{bool} \leq \mathbf{nat}]\!] = \lambda b \in \mathcal{D}(\mathbf{bool}). \text{ if } b \text{ then } 1 \text{ else } 0$$

$$[\![\mathbf{nat} \leq \mathbf{int}]\!] = \lambda k \in \mathcal{D}(\mathbf{nat}). \, k$$

$$[\![\mathbf{int} \leq \mathbf{real}]\!] = \lambda i \in \mathcal{D}(\mathbf{int}). \, i.$$

(Notice that the last two conversion functions are identity injections.)

When $\theta'_0 \leq \theta_0$ and $\theta_1 \leq \theta'_1$, a function can be converted from $\theta_0 \to \theta_1$ to $\theta'_0 \to \theta'_1$ by composing it with a conversion of its argument from θ'_0 to θ_0 and a conversion of its result from θ_1 to θ'_1. Diagrammatically,

$$
\begin{array}{ccc}
\mathcal{D}(\theta'_0) & \xrightarrow{\;[\![\theta_0 \to \theta_1 \leq \theta'_1 \to \theta'_2]\!]f\;} & \mathcal{D}(\theta'_1) \\[2pt]
\Big\downarrow{\scriptstyle [\![\theta'_0 \leq \theta_0]\!]} & & \Big\uparrow{\scriptstyle [\![\theta_1 \leq \theta'_1]\!]} \\[2pt]
\mathcal{D}(\theta_0) & \xrightarrow{\;f\;} & \mathcal{D}(\theta_1)
\end{array}
$$

which gives the conversion equation:

CONV EQ: Functions (16.5)

$$[\![\theta_0 \to \theta_1 \leq \theta'_1 \to \theta'_2]\!] = \lambda f \in \mathcal{D}(\theta_0) \to \mathcal{D}(\theta_1).\, [\![\theta_1 \leq \theta'_1]\!] \cdot f \cdot [\![\theta'_0 \leq \theta_0]\!].$$

For named products and named sums, the conversion equations are conceptually straightforward but notationally complicated:

CONV EQ: Named Products (16.11)

$$[\![\mathbf{prod}(\iota_0 : \theta_0, \ldots, \iota_{n-1} : \theta_{n-1}) \leq \mathbf{prod}(\iota_{k_0} : \theta'_{k_0}, \ldots, \iota_{k_{m-1}} : \theta'_{k_{m-1}})]\!]$$
$$= \lambda t \in \prod [\, \iota_0 : \mathcal{D}(\theta_0) \mid \ldots \mid \iota_{n-1} : \mathcal{D}(\theta_{n-1}) \,].$$
$$[\, \iota_{k_0} : [\![\theta_{k_0} \leq \theta'_{k_0}]\!](t(\iota_{k_0})) \mid \ldots \mid \iota_{k_{n-1}} : [\![\theta_{k_{n-1}} \leq \theta'_{k_{n-1}}]\!](t(\iota_{k_{n-1}})) \,],$$

CONV EQ: Named Sums (16.14)

$$[\![\mathbf{sum}(\iota_{k_0} : \theta_{k_0}, \ldots, \iota_{k_{m-1}} : \theta_{k_{m-1}}) \leq \mathbf{sum}(\iota_0 : \theta'_0, \ldots, \iota_{n-1} : \theta'_{n-1})]\!]$$
$$= (\lambda \langle \iota, z \rangle \in \sum [\, \iota_{k_0} : \mathcal{D}(\theta_{k_0}) \mid \ldots \mid \iota_{k_{m-1}} : \mathcal{D}(\theta_{k_{m-1}}) \,].\, \langle \iota, [\![\theta_k \leq \theta'_k]\!]z \rangle)_\perp$$

where k is the index of $\iota = \iota_k$.

(Here $(-)_\perp$ is the lifting operation on functions defined in Section 2.3.)

Finally, we give the one new typed semantic equation needed for subtyping, which corresponds to the type inference rule for subsumption. In essence, to convert the meaning of an expression from a subtype to a supertype, one simply composes the meaning with the appropriate conversion function:

TY SEM EQ: Subsumption (16.1)

$$[\![\pi \vdash e : \theta']\!] = [\![\theta \leq \theta']\!] \cdot [\![\pi \vdash e : \theta]\!].$$

When we discussed the intrinsic semantics of the simple type system in Section 15.5, we pointed out that all of the type inference rules were syntax-directed: Each rule showed how to infer a judgement about a particular kind of expression (i.e. a particular constructor) from judgements about its subphrases. The Subsumption Rule (16.1), however, violates this condition, since it allows one to infer a judgement about a phrase from another judgement about the same phrase. With the introduction of this rule, it is no longer necessary for formal proofs of judgements to have the same shape as abstract syntax trees. As a consequence, it becomes more difficult to establish the property of *coherence*, that all proofs of a judgement must lead to the same meaning for that judgment.

(Actually, the property of coherence is weaker for an explicitly typed language than an implicitly typed one, since the erasure of type information in expressions can convert typing judgements about distinct expressions into judgments about the same expression. In this chapter, we will always use the stronger sense of coherence that is appropriate for implicit typing. Our view is that explicit type information is a kind of annotation that should not affect meaning.)

Although it is beyond the scope of this book to give a proof of coherence, it is illuminating to examine some of its consequences. A first example is based on distinct proofs of the same subtype relation. Suppose θ and θ' are equivalent types, that is, $\theta \leq \theta'$ and $\theta' \leq \theta$. Then we have the proof

1.	$\theta \leq \theta'$	assumption
2.	$\theta' \leq \theta$	assumption
3.	$\theta \leq \theta$	(16.3,1,2)

and, corresponding to this proof,

1.	$[\![\theta \leq \theta']\!] = \cdots$	assumption
2.	$[\![\theta' \leq \theta]\!] = \cdots$	assumption
3.	$[\![\theta \leq \theta]\!] = [\![\theta' \leq \theta]\!] \cdot [\![\theta \leq \theta']\!]$	(16.3,1,2)

(where the right sides of the first two equations would be obtained from the proofs of the assumptions). On the other hand, we also have the trivial proof

1. $$\theta \leq \theta \qquad\qquad (16.2)$$

and corresponding to this proof,

1. $$[\![\theta \leq \theta]\!] = I_{\mathcal{D}(\theta)}. \qquad\qquad (16.2)$$

Thus coherence implies that $[\![\theta' \leq \theta]\!] \cdot [\![\theta \leq \theta']\!] = I_{\mathcal{D}(\theta)}$. Moreover, by a symmetric argument, it also implies $[\![\theta \leq \theta']\!] \cdot [\![\theta' \leq \theta]\!] = I_{\mathcal{D}(\theta')}$. In other words, equivalent types must denote isomorphic domains, and the implicit conversion functions between them must be an isomorphism.

Instances of equivalent but nonidentical types include product and sum types where the $\iota{:}\,\theta$ have been permuted; in this case, the denoted domains are actually identical, and not just isomorphic. There are also a wide variety of equivalent types involving intersection, where we will find that the isomorphic denoted domains are not identical. More interestingly, we could introduce equivalent types denoting distinct representations of the same abstract entities, such as rectangular and polar representations of complex numbers (a situation that would be impossible to describe with extrinsic semantics).

A second example of the consequences of coherence involves the interaction of implicit conversions and generic operators. Suppose that $\theta_0 \leq \theta_1$, $\theta_0' \leq \theta_1'$, and $\theta_0'' \leq \theta_1''$, and that we have two type inference rules for the same operator:

TY RULE: A Rule for a Binary Operator

$$\frac{\pi \vdash e : \theta_0 \qquad \pi \vdash e' : \theta_0'}{\pi \vdash e \text{ op } e' : \theta_0'',} \qquad\qquad (16.33)$$

TY RULE: Another Rule for the Same Operator

$$\frac{\pi \vdash e : \theta_1 \qquad \pi \vdash e' : \theta_1'}{\pi \vdash e \text{ op } e' : \theta_1'',} \qquad\qquad (16.34)$$

along with the corresponding typed semantic equations:

TY SEM EQ: Semantics of (16.33)

$$[\![\pi \vdash e \text{ op } e' : \theta_0'']\!]\eta = f_0([\![\pi \vdash e : \theta_0]\!]\eta, [\![\pi \vdash e' : \theta_0']\!]\eta),$$

TY SEM EQ: Semantics of (16.34)

$$[\![\pi \vdash e \text{ op } e' : \theta_1'']\!]\eta = f_1([\![\pi \vdash e : \theta_1]\!]\eta, [\![\pi \vdash e' : \theta_1']\!]\eta),$$

where $f_0 \in \mathcal{D}(\theta_0) \times \mathcal{D}(\theta_0') \to \mathcal{D}(\theta_0'')$ and $f_1 \in \mathcal{D}(\theta_1) \times \mathcal{D}(\theta_1') \to \mathcal{D}(\theta_1'')$.

Let π be the context $a: \theta_0, b: \theta_0'$. Then we have two proofs of the same typing judgement:

1.	$\pi \vdash a : \theta_0$	(15.3)
2.	$\pi \vdash b : \theta_0'$	(15.3)
3.	$\pi \vdash a \text{ op } b : \theta_0''$	(16.33,1,2)
4.	$\theta_0'' \leq \theta_1''$	assumption
5.	$\pi \vdash a \text{ op } b : \theta_1''$	(16.1,3,4)

and

1.	$\pi \vdash a : \theta_0$	(15.3)
2.	$\theta_0 \leq \theta_1$	assumption
3.	$\pi \vdash a : \theta_1$	(16.1,1,2)
4.	$\pi \vdash b : \theta_0'$	(15.3)
5.	$\theta_0' \leq \theta_1'$	assumption
6.	$\pi \vdash b : \theta_1'$	(16.1,4,5)
7.	$\pi \vdash a \text{ op } b : \theta_1''$	(16.34,3,6)

Suppose $x \in \mathcal{D}(\theta_0)$ and $y \in \mathcal{D}(\theta_0')$, and let η be the environment $[a: x \mid b: y] \in \mathcal{D}^*(\pi)$. Then, corresponding to the first proof,

1.	$[\![\pi \vdash a : \theta_0]\!]\eta = x$	(15.3)
2.	$[\![\pi \vdash b : \theta_0']\!]\eta = y$	(15.3)
3.	$[\![\pi \vdash a \text{ op } b : \theta_0'']\!]\eta = f_0(x, y)$	(16.33,1,2)
4.	$[\![\theta_0'' \leq \theta_1'']\!] = \cdots$	assumption
5.	$[\![\pi \vdash a \text{ op } b : \theta_1'']\!]\eta = [\![\theta_0'' \leq \theta_1'']\!](f_0(x, y))$	(16.1,3,4)

and, corresponding to the second proof,

1.	$[\![\pi \vdash a : \theta_0]\!]\eta = x$	(15.3)
2.	$[\![\theta_0 \leq \theta_1]\!] = \cdots$	assumption
3.	$[\![\pi \vdash a : \theta_1]\!]\eta = [\![\theta_0 \leq \theta_1]\!]\, x$	(16.1,1,2)
4.	$[\![\pi \vdash b : \theta_0']\!]\eta = y$	(15.3)
5.	$[\![\theta_0' \leq \theta_1']\!] = \cdots$	assumption
6.	$[\![\pi \vdash b : \theta_1']\!]\eta = [\![\theta_0' \leq \theta_1']\!]\, y$	(16.1,4,5)
7.	$[\![\pi \vdash a \text{ op } b : \theta_1'']\!]\eta = f_1([\![\theta_0 \leq \theta_1]\!]\, x, [\![\theta_0' \leq \theta_1']\!]\, y).$	(16.34,3,6)

Thus coherence implies that

$$[\![\theta_0'' \leq \theta_1'']\!](f_0(x, y)) = f_1([\![\theta_0 \leq \theta_1]\!]\, x, [\![\theta_0' \leq \theta_1']\!]\, y).$$

More abstractly, since this equation holds for arbitrary $x \in \mathcal{D}(\theta_0)$ and $y \in \mathcal{D}(\theta_0')$, the following diagram of functions must commute:

$$
\begin{array}{ccc}
\mathcal{D}(\theta_0) \times \mathcal{D}(\theta_0') & \xrightarrow{\ \ f_0\ \ } & \mathcal{D}(\theta_0'') \\
{\scriptstyle [\![\theta_0 \leq \theta_1]\!] \times [\![\theta_0' \leq \theta_1']\!]} \downarrow & & \downarrow {\scriptstyle [\![\theta_0'' \leq \theta_1'']\!]} \\
\mathcal{D}(\theta_1) \times \mathcal{D}(\theta_1') & \xrightarrow[\ \ f_1\ \ ]{} & \mathcal{D}(\theta_1'')
\end{array}
$$

where $[\![\theta_0 \leq \theta_1]\!] \times [\![\theta_0' \leq \theta_1']\!]$ is the function such that $([\![\theta_0 \leq \theta_1]\!] \times [\![\theta_0' \leq \theta_1']\!])$
$\langle x, y \rangle = \langle [\![\theta_0 \leq \theta_1]\!]\, x, [\![\theta_0' \leq \theta_1']\!]\, y \rangle$.

For arithmetic operators, the commutativity of this diagram asserts the traditional arithmetic laws that these operators must respect the conversions from **nat** to **int** and from **int** to **real**. With our particular choice of the conversion from **bool** to **nat**, it permits × to be identified with ∧, but not + with ∨.

For an equality operator on primitive types, the diagram reduces to

$$
\begin{array}{ccc}
\mathcal{D}(\theta_0) \times \mathcal{D}(\theta_0) & \xrightarrow{\ \ f_0\ \ } & \mathbf{B}_\perp \\
{\scriptstyle [\![\theta_0 \leq \theta_1]\!] \times [\![\theta_0 \leq \theta_1]\!]} \downarrow & & \downarrow {\scriptstyle I_{\mathbf{B}_\perp}} \\
\mathcal{D}(\theta_1) \times \mathcal{D}(\theta_1) & \xrightarrow[\ \ f_1\ \ ]{} & \mathbf{B}_\perp
\end{array}
$$

where f_0 and f_1 are the equality functions appropriate to the flat domains $\mathcal{D}(\theta_0)$ and $\mathcal{D}(\theta_1)$:

$$f_0(z \in \mathcal{D}(\theta_0), z' \in \mathcal{D}(\theta_0)) = \textbf{if } z = \perp \text{ or } z' = \perp \textbf{ then } \perp \textbf{ else } z = z'$$
$$f_1(z \in \mathcal{D}(\theta_1), z' \in \mathcal{D}(\theta_1)) = \textbf{if } z = \perp \text{ or } z' = \perp \textbf{ then } \perp \textbf{ else } z = z'.$$

The reader may verify that this diagram will commute if and only if the conversion $[\![\theta_0 \leq \theta_1]\!]$ is a strict, injective function.

It is evident that the requirement of coherence plays much the same role in intrinsic semantics that conditions such as (16.29) and (16.30) play in extrinsic semantics. In both cases, the effect is to constrain the interaction of subtyping and generic operators to insure uniform behavior. From the intrinsic viewpoint, the meaning of an expression must be independent of exactly where implicit conversions occur in the structure of an expression.

In early typed languages such as Algol 68 and PL/I, coherence was repeatedly violated, so that the value of an expression depended on the specific points where implicit conversions occurred. In retrospect, it is clear that this was a serious design error that was a major impediment to programming in these languages.

To complete our discussion of intrinsic semantics, we consider nonsense and intersection types. The meaning $\mathcal{D}(\mathbf{ns})$ of the nonsense type must be a singleton set, such as $\{\langle\rangle\}$. (Thus expressions whose only type is $\mathbf{ns}$ are not meaningless, but they all have the same meaning.)

For the meaning $\mathcal{D}(\theta \& \theta')$ of an intersection type, there must be conversions $[\![\theta \& \theta' \leq \theta]\!]$ and $[\![\theta \& \theta' \leq \theta']\!]$ into $\mathcal{D}(\theta)$ and $\mathcal{D}(\theta')$ respectively. This suggests that the members of $\mathcal{D}(\theta \& \theta')$ should be pairs $\langle x, x' \rangle$ such that $x \in \mathcal{D}(\theta)$ and $x' \in \mathcal{D}(\theta')$, and the conversion functions should be the obvious projections,

$$[\![\theta \& \theta' \leq \theta]\!]\langle x, x' \rangle = x \qquad [\![\theta \& \theta' \leq \theta']\!]\langle x, x' \rangle = x'.$$

But whenever θ'' is a common supertype of θ and θ', coherence requires that the diagram of conversions

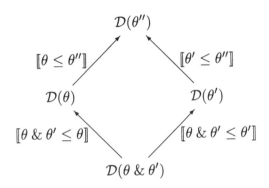

must commute. Thus, we restrict $\mathcal{D}(\theta \& \theta')$ to contain only those pairs for which this diagram always commutes:

$$\mathcal{D}(\theta \& \theta') = \{\, \langle x, x' \rangle \mid x \in \mathcal{D}(\theta) \text{ and } x' \in \mathcal{D}(\theta') \text{ and} \tag{16.35}$$
$$\forall \theta''.\ \theta \leq \theta'' \text{ and } \theta' \leq \theta'' \text{ implies } [\![\theta \leq \theta'']\!]x = [\![\theta' \leq \theta'']\!]x' \,\}.$$

The ordering is componentwise, as with the ordinary product $\mathcal{D}(\theta) \times \mathcal{D}(\theta')$. (The reader should verify that this definition actually gives a domain, with the same least element and limits as the product, which depends on the fact that the conversion functions are strict and continuous.)

(Strictly speaking, Equation (16.35) is a property of $\mathcal{D}(\theta \& \theta')$, but not a true definition. The difficulty is that the meaning of types is defined by structural induction on types, but this equation involves a set of types θ'', some of whom may have more complex structure than $\theta \& \theta'$. In fact, a rigorous definition can be given, but the required construction is beyond the scope of this book.)

An extreme case occurs when the only common supertype of θ and θ' is $\theta'' = \mathbf{ns}$. Then the condition $[\![\theta \leq \theta'']\!]x = [\![\theta' \leq \theta'']\!]x'$ in Equation (16.35) holds for all x and x', since both sides belong to the singleton set $\mathcal{D}(\mathbf{ns})$, and $\mathcal{D}(\theta \& \theta')$ is simply the product $\mathcal{D}(\theta) \times \mathcal{D}(\theta')$.

An example of this case is provided by the intersection of two named products with distinct field names. When $\iota \neq \iota'$, the types $\mathbf{prod}(\iota\!:\!\theta)$ and $\mathbf{prod}(\iota'\!:\!\theta')$ have no common supertype other than $\mathbf{ns}$, so that

$$\mathcal{D}(\mathbf{prod}(\iota\!:\!\theta) \,\&\, \mathbf{prod}(\iota'\!:\!\theta')) = \mathcal{D}(\mathbf{prod}(\iota\!:\!\theta)) \times \mathcal{D}(\mathbf{prod}(\iota'\!:\!\theta')).$$

In fact, since $\mathcal{D}(\mathbf{prod}(\iota\!:\!\theta))$ is isomorphic to $\mathcal{D}(\theta)$, the above product is isomorphic to $\mathcal{D}(\theta) \times \mathcal{D}(\theta')$. Moreover, by the equivalence of the two sides of subtyping rule (16.20) in Section 16.3, it is also isomorphic to $\mathcal{D}(\mathbf{prod}(\iota\!:\!\theta, \iota'\!:\!\theta'))$.

For many intersection types, no expression with the type is provided by our functional language. But the import of intrinsic semantics is that it is consistent to add such a construction to the language whenever the components of the intersection have no common supertype other than $\mathbf{ns}$. A particularly useful case is the intersection of function and product types, such as $(\mathbf{int} \to \mathbf{int}) \,\&\, \mathbf{prod}(\mathsf{length}\!:\!\mathbf{int})$. We can introduce

$$\langle \exp \rangle ::= \mathbf{combine}\ \langle \exp \rangle\ \mathbf{with}\ \langle \exp \rangle$$

with the type inference rule

TY RULE: Combining Functions and Products

$$\frac{\pi \vdash e : \theta \to \theta' \qquad \pi \vdash e' : \mathbf{prod}(\iota_0\!:\!\theta_0, \ldots, \iota_{n-1}\!:\!\theta_{n-1})}{\pi \vdash \mathbf{combine}\ e\ \mathbf{with}\ e' : (\theta \to \theta') \,\&\, \mathbf{prod}(\iota_0\!:\!\theta_0, \ldots, \iota_{n-1}\!:\!\theta_{n-1}),} \qquad (16.36)$$

and the semantics

TY SEM EQ: Combining Functions and Products (16.36)

$$[\![\pi \vdash \mathbf{combine}\ e\ \mathbf{with}\ e' : (\theta \to \theta') \,\&\, \mathbf{prod}(\iota_0\!:\!\theta_0, \ldots, \iota_{n-1}\!:\!\theta_{n-1})]\!]\eta$$
$$= \langle [\![\pi \vdash e : \theta \to \theta']\!]\eta, [\![\pi \vdash e' : \mathbf{prod}(\iota_0\!:\!\theta_0, \ldots, \iota_{n-1}\!:\!\theta_{n-1})]\!]\eta \rangle.$$

In effect, the value of $\mathbf{combine}\ e\ \mathbf{with}\ e'$ behaves like the value of e in contexts that require functions, but like the value of e' in contexts that require tuples. This kind of mechanism is sometimes used to incorporate length or bounds information into arrays.

At the opposite extreme from the cases we have considered so far is the intersection $\theta \,\&\, \theta'$ when θ is a subtype of θ'. In this case, subtyping rules (16.17) imply both $\theta \,\&\, \theta' \leq \theta$ and $\theta \leq \theta \,\&\, \theta'$, so that $\theta \,\&\, \theta'$ is equivalent to θ. Semantically, the condition $[\![\theta \leq \theta'']\!]x = [\![\theta' \leq \theta'']\!]x'$ in Equation (16.35) factors into

$$[\![\theta' \leq \theta'']\!]([\![\theta \leq \theta']\!]x) = [\![\theta' \leq \theta'']\!]x'.$$

This condition holds for all common supertypes θ'' if and only if it holds when $\theta'' = \theta'$. Thus Equation (16.35) reduces to

$$\mathcal{D}(\theta \,\&\, \theta') = \{\, \langle x, x' \rangle \mid x \in \mathcal{D}(\theta) \text{ and } x' \in \mathcal{D}(\theta') \text{ and } [\![\theta \leq \theta']\!]x = x' \,\}$$
$$= \{\, \langle x, [\![\theta \leq \theta']\!]x \rangle \mid x \in \mathcal{D}(\theta) \,\}.$$

Clearly, the pairs $\langle x, [\![\theta \leq \theta']\!]x \rangle$ are in one-to-one correspondence with the $x \in \mathcal{D}(\theta)$. Moreover, it is easy to show that mappings between these domains are continuous (since $[\![\theta \leq \theta']\!]$ is continuous). Thus, as the semantics requires for equivalent types, $\mathcal{D}(\theta \,\&\, \theta')$ is isomorphic to $\mathcal{D}(\theta)$.

Since we have chosen the ordering **bool** $\leq$ **nat** $\leq$ **int** $\leq$ **real** for our primitive types, every conjunction of primitive types is equivalent to a particular primitive type, and all of the conversions among the primitive types and their conjunctions are injections. However, suppose we had not made any primitive type a subtype of any other, but instead had chosen the ordering

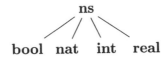

Then the intersections of primitive types would be products, so that a value of type, say **bool** & **real**, would combine a boolean and a real number with no constraints between them. Although this might be useful, it would prohibit having a generic equality operator that was applicable to more than one primitive type, since such an operation would be ambiguous when applied to values with intersection types.

A possible solution would be to introduce a type **primvalue** with the semantics

$$\mathcal{D}(\mathbf{primvalue}) = (\mathbf{B} \cup \mathbf{N} \cup \mathbf{Z} \cup \mathbf{R})_\perp$$

and the subtyping ordering

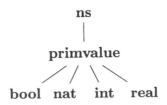

with identity injections as the corresponding conversions. Then, for primitive types θ and θ', Equation (16.35) would reduce to

$$\mathcal{D}(\theta \,\&\, \theta') = \{\, \langle x, x' \rangle \mid x \in \mathcal{D}(\theta) \text{ and } x' \in \mathcal{D}(\theta') \text{ and } x = x' \,\},$$

which is isomorphic to $\mathcal{D}(\theta) \cap \mathcal{D}(\theta')$ — a case where the intersection of types denotes the intersection of sets, as in extrinsic semantics. (Notice that this argument works when $\mathbf{B}$, $\mathbf{N}$, $\mathbf{Z}$, and $\mathbf{R}$ are arbitrary sets with arbitrary intersections; it only depends on the assumption that primitive types denote flat domains.) In this situation, we could introduce an equality operator for **primvalue** that could be used for all primitive values.

Finally, we consider the intersection of two function types. We saw that the condition in Equation (16.35) is vacuous when $\theta'' = $ **ns**. But the only other supertypes of function types are function types. Thus Equation (16.35) becomes

$$\mathcal{D}((\theta_0 \to \theta_1) \,\&\, (\theta'_0 \to \theta'_1))$$
$$= \{\, \langle f, f' \rangle \mid f \in \mathcal{D}(\theta_0) \to \mathcal{D}(\theta_1) \text{ and } f' \in \mathcal{D}(\theta'_0) \to \mathcal{D}(\theta'_1) \text{ and}$$
$$\forall \theta''_0. \, \forall \theta''_1. \, \theta_0 \to \theta_1 \leq \theta''_0 \to \theta''_1 \text{ and } \theta'_0 \to \theta'_1 \leq \theta''_0 \to \theta''_1 \text{ implies}$$
$$[\![\theta_0 \to \theta_1 \leq \theta''_0 \to \theta''_1]\!] f = [\![\theta'_0 \to \theta'_1 \leq \theta''_0 \to \theta''_1]\!] f' \,\}.$$

Using the subtyping rule for functions ((16.5) in Section 16.1) and the corresponding conversion equation, we can rewrite the condition in this equation as

$$\forall \theta''_0. \, \forall \theta''_1. \, \theta''_0 \leq \theta_0 \text{ and } \theta''_0 \leq \theta'_0 \text{ and } \theta_1 \leq \theta''_1 \text{ and } \theta'_1 \leq \theta''_1 \text{ implies}$$
$$[\![\theta_1 \leq \theta''_1]\!] \cdot f \cdot [\![\theta''_0 \leq \theta_0]\!] = [\![\theta'_1 \leq \theta''_1]\!] \cdot f' \cdot [\![\theta''_0 \leq \theta'_0]\!].$$

In other words, for all common subtypes θ''_0 of θ_0 and θ'_0, and all common supertypes θ''_1 of θ_1 and θ'_1, the diagram

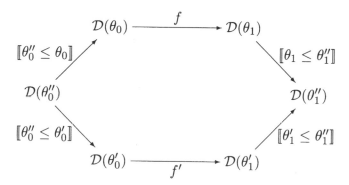

must commute.

For example, consider the special case where θ''_0, θ_0, and θ_1 are all **int** and θ'_0, θ'_1, and θ''_1, are all **real**. Then the hexagon above collapses into a rectangle:

$$
\begin{array}{ccc}
\mathcal{D}(\textbf{int}) & \xrightarrow{\ f\ } & \mathcal{D}(\textbf{int}) \\
{\scriptstyle [\![\textbf{int} \leq \textbf{real}]\!]} \Big\downarrow & & \Big\downarrow {\scriptstyle [\![\textbf{int} \leq \textbf{real}]\!]} \\
\mathcal{D}(\textbf{real}) & \xrightarrow[\ f'\ ]{} & \mathcal{D}(\textbf{real})
\end{array}
$$

Thus a value of an intersection type such as $(\textbf{int} \to \textbf{int}) \,\&\, (\textbf{real} \to \textbf{real})$ (say the value of $\lambda \textsf{x}. \, \textsf{x} + 1$) must consist of components that obey coherence conditions that are similar to those for the primitive operations. This is in sharp contrast to the ad hoc "generic" functions that can be defined in languages such as Ada, which can be given arbitrarily different behaviors for different types.

Bibliographic Notes

The subtype orderings discussed in this chapter were introduced by Reynolds [1980] in a paper that deals with the interaction of implicit conversions and generic operators. Then Cardelli [1984; 1988] discovered the orderings for named products and sums independently and connected the product ordering with the concept of inheritance in object-oriented programming.

Ostensibly, we have said little about object-oriented programming. To a crude approximation, however, it is simply an imposition of exotic terminology on some of the concepts of this chapter: Objects are named tuples, classes are (in a sense) their types, methods are fields with functional values, and inheritance (multiple or otherwise) is subtyping. Nevertheless, there are subtleties, involving the interaction of subtyping, polymorphism, and recursive types, as well as imperative aspects, that are beyond the scope of this book. A compendium on the theoretical aspects of the subject is Gunter and Mitchell [1994]; a unified presentation of a particular viewpoint is Abadi and Cardelli [1996].

Type inference for subtypes has been investigated by Mitchell [1991].

Intersection types were originally introduced in the context of the lambda calculus by Coppo et al. [Coppo and Dezani-Ciancaglini, 1978; Coppo, Dezani-Ciancaglini, and Venneri, 1981; Barendregt, Coppo, and Dezani-Ciancaglini, 1983], who showed the conservation of typing judgements and the undecidability of type inference; these types were discovered independently by Sallé [1978]. An introductory exposition, with an extensive bibliography, is Hindley [1992].

The use of partial equivalence relations to model the subtype relation for named products was first suggested by Bruce and Longo [1990].

Arrays that incorporate bounds information are found in Algol 68 [van Wijngaarden et al., 1969; 1975]. A treatment of arrays that combines them with named tuples giving bounds information (as well as operations for array extension) is found in Dijkstra [1976, Chapter 11].

Intersection types, including a "merge" operation that generalizes the **combine** construction of Section 16.6, are used in the Algol-like programming language Forsythe [Reynolds, 1996]. The worst-case inefficiency of type checking for intersection types is also shown in Reynolds [1996].

The coherence of functional languages with subtyping and intersection has been shown by Reynolds [1991].

Although we have avoided the topic of category theory, it is extremely useful in the investigation of intrinsic semantics. An elementary introduction, with emphasis on computer-science applications, has been given by Pierce [1991].

Exercises

16.1   Using the inference rules in Sections 15.2 and 16.1, including

$$\mathbf{nat} \leq \mathbf{int} \qquad \mathbf{int} \leq \mathbf{real},$$

plus the following rules for exponentiation and subtraction operators:

$$\frac{\pi \vdash e_0 : \mathbf{nat} \qquad \pi \vdash e_1 : \mathbf{nat}}{\pi \vdash e_0 \uparrow e_1 : \mathbf{nat}} \qquad \frac{\pi \vdash e_0 : \mathbf{int} \qquad \pi \vdash e_1 : \mathbf{nat}}{\pi \vdash e_0 \uparrow e_1 : \mathbf{int}}$$

$$\frac{\pi \vdash e_0 : \mathbf{real} \qquad \pi \vdash e_1 : \mathbf{int}}{\pi \vdash e_0 \uparrow e_1 : \mathbf{real}} \qquad \frac{\pi \vdash e_0 : \mathbf{int} \qquad \pi \vdash e_1 : \mathbf{int}}{\pi \vdash e_0 - e_1 : \mathbf{int},}$$

prove the following typing judgement (after replacing the question mark by a type that makes the judgement valid):

$$n : \mathbf{nat} \vdash n \uparrow ((n - (n \uparrow n)) \uparrow n) : ?.$$

16.2   Suppose we extend the language used in this chapter by adding the type **string** (of characters), with the obvious meaning. Consider the following language "features":

(a) **int** is a subtype of **string** with an implicit conversion that converts an integer into a string giving its decimal representation.

(b) **string** is a subtype of **int** with an implicit conversion that converts a string into the integer of which it is a decimal representation. Characters that are not digits (except an initial minus sign) are ignored.

(c) There is a binary operator + that denotes both the addition of integers and the concatenation of strings.

(d) There is a binary operator = that denotes an equality test for both integers and strings.

For each pair of these features, state whether the pair would violate the principles of subtyping. If not, describe how the combination of the two features could be treated, in both the extrinsic semantics of Section 16.4 and the intrinsic semantics of Section 16.6. If so, give an example of a simple program where the two features would cause counterintuitive or ambiguous behavior, and show why the principles of subtyping are violated in terms of both the extrinsic and intrinsic models.

16.3   Show that, when $\mathcal{P}(\mathbf{bool})$ is defined by (b'') in Section 16.5, condition (16.29) permits the inference rules

$$\frac{\pi \vdash e_0 : \mathbf{bool} \qquad \pi \vdash e_1 : \mathbf{bool}}{\pi \vdash e_0 + e_1 : \mathbf{bool}} \qquad \frac{\pi \vdash e_0 : \mathbf{bool} \qquad \pi \vdash e_1 : \mathbf{bool}}{\pi \vdash e_0 \times e_1 : \mathbf{bool}.}$$

16.4   Consider introducing an equality operation for tuples with named numeric
       fields, with the type inference rule

$$\frac{\pi \vdash e : \mathbf{prod}(\iota_0\!:\!\mathbf{real}, \ldots, \iota_{n-1}\!:\!\mathbf{real}) \qquad \pi \vdash e' : \mathbf{prod}(\iota_0\!:\!\mathbf{real}, \ldots, \iota_{n-1}\!:\!\mathbf{real})}{\pi \vdash e =_{\text{tuple}} e' : \mathbf{bool},}$$

and the obvious meaning.

(a) Using extrinsic semantics, show that this construct violates Proposi-
    tion 15.2 in Section 15.4 (assuming part (d′) of the definition of $\mathcal{P}$ in
    Section 16.4).

(b) Using intrinsic semantics, show that the combination of this rule with
    field-forgetting implicit conversions violates coherence.

16.5   Give a type inference rule for the **open** construction of Exercise 11.4.
       Give an example showing why this construction becomes ambiguous when
       combined with rule (16.11) (subtyping named products) in Section 16.2.

16.6   Using intersection types, give a type not containing **ns** for

$$(\lambda x.\ \lambda y.\ y(x(\lambda z.\ z))(x(\lambda z.\ \lambda w.\ z)))(\lambda z.\ z\,z)$$

This expression is notable because it is strongly normalizing but has been
shown not to be typeable in the polymorphic discipline discussed in the
next chapter [Giannini and Ronchi della Rocca, 1988].

16.7   Consider extending Proposition 16.1 in Section 16.3 to some of the other
       kinds of reduction discussed in Section 14.5:

(a) Show that, if $\pi \vdash e_k : \theta$, then $\pi \vdash \langle \iota_0\!:\!e_0, \ldots, \iota_{n-1}\!:\!e_n - 1\rangle.\iota_k : \theta$.

(b) Show that, if $\pi \vdash e\,(\mathbf{rec}\ e) : \theta$, then $\pi \vdash \mathbf{rec}\ e : \theta$.

(c) Give a counterexample to the following statement: If $\pi \vdash e_k\,e : \theta$,
    then $\pi \vdash \mathbf{sumcase}\ @\ \iota_k\ e\ \mathbf{of}\ (\iota_0\!:\!e_0, \ldots, \iota_{n-1}\!:\!e_{n-1}) : \theta$.

(d) Using extrinsic semantics, show that typing remains sound when one
    replaces type inference rule (16.13) for named sum elimination (in
    Section 16.2) by the following stronger rule:

$$\frac{\pi \vdash e : \mathbf{sum}(\iota_0\!:\!\theta_0, \ldots, \iota_{m-1}\!:\!\theta_{m-1}) \qquad \pi \vdash e_0 : \theta_0 \to \theta \qquad \ddots \qquad \pi \vdash e_{m-1} : \theta_{m-1} \to \theta}{\pi \vdash \mathbf{sumcase}\ e\ \mathbf{of}\ (\iota_0 \equiv e_0, \ldots, \iota_{n-1} \equiv e_{n-1}) : \theta}$$

    where $m \leq n$.

(e) Show that the statement in part (c) becomes true if one permits the
    inference rule in part (d).

17

Polymorphism

Perhaps the most serious drawback of early type systems was that they precluded polymorphic functions, which are functions that can be used with arguments and results of an infinite number of types. In this chapter we will explore a type system that overcomes this problem; it is based on the polymorphic lambda calculus, which was discovered in the early 1970's.

An example of a polymorphic function is mapcar, which can have the type $(\theta \to \theta') \to$ **list** $\theta \to$ **list** θ' for any types θ and θ'. Thus, for example, it should be possible to write

$$\textbf{letrec}\ \mathsf{mapcar} \equiv \lambda\mathsf{f}.\ \lambda\mathsf{x}.\ \textbf{listcase}\ \mathsf{x}\ \textbf{of}\ (\mathsf{nil}, \lambda\mathsf{i}.\ \lambda\mathsf{r}.\ \mathsf{f}\ \mathsf{i} :: \mathsf{mapcar}\ \mathsf{f}\ \mathsf{r})\ \textbf{in}$$
$$\lambda\mathsf{x}.\ \mathsf{mapcar}(\lambda\mathsf{n}.\ \mathsf{n} = 0)(\mathsf{mapcar}(\lambda\mathsf{n}.\ \mathsf{n} - 3)\,\mathsf{x}).$$

But this expression cannot be typed according to the simple type discipline, since the two occurrences of mapcar in the last line have different types:

$$(\textbf{int} \to \textbf{bool}) \to \textbf{list int} \to \textbf{list bool} \qquad (\textbf{int} \to \textbf{int}) \to \textbf{list int} \to \textbf{list int}.$$

(Of course, one could type this expression using intersection types as described in Section 16.3, by giving mapcar the intersection of the above types. But polymorphism goes beyond intersection types in giving an infinite family of types to a function such as mapcar, rather than just some finite set of types.)

Two other examples of the need for polymorphism are a function that sums a list of lists of integers:

$$\textbf{letrec}\ \mathsf{reduce} \equiv \lambda\mathsf{x}.\ \lambda\mathsf{f}.\ \lambda\mathsf{a}.\ \textbf{listcase}\ \mathsf{x}\ \textbf{of}\ (\mathsf{a}, \lambda\mathsf{i}.\ \lambda\mathsf{r}.\ \mathsf{f}\ \mathsf{i}\ (\mathsf{reduce}\ \mathsf{r}\ \mathsf{f}\ \mathsf{a}))\ \textbf{in}$$
$$\lambda\mathsf{y}.\ \mathsf{reduce}\ \mathsf{y}\ (\lambda\mathsf{x}.\ \lambda\mathsf{s}.\ (\mathsf{reduce}\ \mathsf{x}\ (\lambda\mathsf{m}.\ \lambda\mathsf{n}.\ \mathsf{m} + \mathsf{n})\,0) + \mathsf{s})\,0,$$

where the two last occurrences of reduce have types

$$\textbf{list list int} \to (\textbf{list int} \to \textbf{int} \to \textbf{int}) \to \textbf{int} \to \textbf{int}$$

and

$$\textbf{list int} \to (\textbf{int} \to \textbf{int} \to \textbf{int}) \to \textbf{int} \to \textbf{int};$$

and a self-application of a function that composes its argument with itself:

$$\textbf{let double} \equiv \lambda\textsf{f}. \ \lambda\textsf{x}. \ \textsf{f}(\textsf{f} \ \textsf{x}) \ \textbf{in double double},$$

where the two last occurrences of **double** might have types

$$((\textbf{int} \rightarrow \textbf{int}) \rightarrow (\textbf{int} \rightarrow \textbf{int})) \rightarrow ((\textbf{int} \rightarrow \textbf{int}) \rightarrow (\textbf{int} \rightarrow \textbf{int}))$$

and

$$(\textbf{int} \rightarrow \textbf{int}) \rightarrow (\textbf{int} \rightarrow \textbf{int}).$$

There are two basic approaches to accommodating polymorphism: a limited but implicitly typed polymorphism, typified by ML, and a broader explicitly typed polymorphism, typified by the polymorphic lambda calculus. Here we will focus on the latter, which requires explicit type information but gives polymorphic functions "first-class citizenship", in particular allowing them to be passed as arguments to other functions.

17.1 Syntax and Inference Rules

We start by extending our explicitly typed functional language with type variables (ranging over the predefined set $\langle\text{tvar}\rangle$), so that types become type expressions:

$$\langle\text{type}\rangle ::= \langle\text{tvar}\rangle$$

(Notice that this includes the type expressions that occur within ordinary expressions in an explicitly typed language.) Then we introduce the ability to define polymorphic functions that accept types as arguments, by abstracting ordinary expressions on type variables (instead of ordinary variables), and the ability to apply such functions to type expressions:

$$\langle\text{exp}\rangle ::= \Lambda\langle\text{tvar}\rangle. \ \langle\text{exp}\rangle \mid \langle\text{exp}\rangle[\langle\text{type}\rangle]$$

In the first form $\Lambda\tau. \ e$, the initial occurrence of the type variable τ binds the occurrences of τ in (the type expressions in) the expression e.

This new kind of function is explained by a new kind of β-reduction that substitutes for type variables instead of ordinary variables:

$$(\Lambda\tau. \ e)[\theta] \rightarrow (e/\tau \rightarrow \theta).$$

Then, for example, one can write

$$\textbf{let double} \equiv \Lambda\alpha. \ \lambda\textsf{f}_{\alpha\rightarrow\alpha}. \ \lambda\textsf{x}_\alpha. \ \textsf{f}(\textsf{f} \ \textsf{x}) \ \textbf{in double}[\textbf{int} \rightarrow \textbf{int}](\textbf{double}[\textbf{int}]),$$

which reduces in a few steps to

$$(\lambda\textsf{f}_{(\textbf{int}\rightarrow\textbf{int})\rightarrow(\textbf{int}\rightarrow\textbf{int})}. \ \lambda\textsf{x}_{\textbf{int}\rightarrow\textbf{int}}. \ \textsf{f}(\textsf{f} \ \textsf{x})) \ (\lambda\textsf{f}_{\textbf{int}\rightarrow\textbf{int}}. \ \lambda\textsf{x}_{\textbf{int}}. \ \textsf{f}(\textsf{f} \ \textsf{x}))$$

(at which stage the polymorphism has disappeared). Similarly, our examples involving mapcar and reduce can be written as follows:

$$\textbf{letrec mapcar} \equiv \Lambda\alpha.\ \Lambda\beta.\ \lambda f_{\alpha\to\beta}.\ \lambda x_{\textbf{list }\alpha}.$$

$$\textbf{listcase } x \textbf{ of } (\textbf{nil}_\beta, \lambda i_\alpha.\ \lambda r_{\textbf{list }\alpha}.\ f\ i :: \textbf{mapcar}[\alpha][\beta]\ f\ r)\ \textbf{in}$$

$$\lambda x_{\textbf{list int}}.\ \textbf{mapcar}[\textbf{int}][\textbf{bool}](\lambda n_{\textbf{int}}.\ n = 0)$$

$$(\textbf{mapcar}[\textbf{int}][\textbf{int}](\lambda n_{\textbf{int}}.\ n - 3)\,x)$$

$$\textbf{letrec reduce} \equiv \Lambda\alpha.\ \Lambda\beta.\ \lambda x_{\textbf{list }\alpha}.\ \lambda f_{\alpha\to\beta\to\beta}.\ \lambda a_\beta.$$

$$\textbf{listcase } x \textbf{ of } (a, \lambda i_\alpha.\ \lambda r_{\textbf{list }\alpha}.\ f\ i\ (\textbf{reduce}[\alpha][\beta]\ r\ f\ a))\ \textbf{in}$$

$$\lambda y_{\textbf{list list int}}.\ \textbf{reduce}[\textbf{list int}][\textbf{int}]\ y\ (\lambda x_{\textbf{list int}}.\ \lambda s_{\textbf{int}}.$$

$$(\textbf{reduce}[\textbf{int}][\textbf{int}]\ x\ (\lambda m_{\textbf{int}}.\ \lambda n_{\textbf{int}}.\ m + n)\ 0) + s)\ 0.$$

The final step is to introduce new types for the polymorphic functions. (Actually, we should have included such types in the **letrec** definitions above.) We introduce the type expression $\forall\tau.\ \theta$, which binds the occurrences of τ in θ and describes the type of polymorphic function that maps a type τ into a value of type θ. For example, double (strictly speaking, the Λ-expression defining double) has the type

$$\forall\alpha.\ (\alpha \to \alpha) \to \alpha \to \alpha,$$

mapcar has the type

$$\forall\alpha.\ \forall\beta.\ (\alpha \to \beta) \to \textbf{list } \alpha \to \textbf{list } \beta,$$

and reduce has the type

$$\forall\alpha.\ \forall\beta.\ \textbf{list } \alpha \to (\alpha \to \beta \to \beta) \to \beta \to \beta.$$

To accomplish this final step, we augment the syntax of type expressions:

$$\langle\text{type}\rangle ::= \forall\langle\text{tvar}\rangle.\ \langle\text{type}\rangle$$

(Concretely, as with other quantifiers, we assume that θ in $\forall\tau.\ \theta$ extends to the first stopping symbol or the end of the enclosing phrase.) We also add two new inference rules (to the rules given in Section 15.2, as modified for explicit typing in Section 15.3):

TY RULE: Explicit $\forall$ Introduction

$$\frac{\pi \vdash e : \theta}{\pi \vdash \Lambda\tau.\ e : \forall\tau.\ \theta} \qquad \begin{array}{l}\text{when } \tau \text{ does not occur free in}\\ \text{any type expression in } \pi,\end{array} \qquad (17.1)$$

TY RULE: Explicit $\forall$ Elimination

$$\frac{\pi \vdash e : \forall\tau.\ \theta}{\pi \vdash e[\theta'] : (\theta/\tau \to \theta').} \qquad (17.2)$$

(The condition in the first of these rules prevents the binding of a type variable that would still have free occurrences in the conclusion of the rule.)

The following is an example of a typing proof using these inference rules. Let π be the context

$$\text{double}: \forall \alpha.\ (\alpha \to \alpha) \to (\alpha \to \alpha).$$

Then:

1. $f: \alpha \to \alpha, x: \alpha \vdash f : \alpha \to \alpha$ (15.3)
2. $f: \alpha \to \alpha, x: \alpha \vdash x : \alpha$ (15.3)
3. $f: \alpha \to \alpha, x: \alpha \vdash f\,x : \alpha$ (15.5)
4. $f: \alpha \to \alpha, x: \alpha \vdash f\,(f\,x) : \alpha$ (15.5)
5. $f: \alpha \to \alpha \vdash \lambda x_\alpha.\ f\,(f\,x) : \alpha \to \alpha$ (15.19)
6. $\vdash \lambda f_{\alpha \to \alpha}.\ \lambda x_\alpha.\ f\,(f\,x) : (\alpha \to \alpha) \to (\alpha \to \alpha)$ (15.19)
7. $\vdash \Lambda\alpha.\ \lambda f_{\alpha \to \alpha}.\ \lambda x_\alpha.\ f\,(f\,x) : \forall\alpha.\ (\alpha \to \alpha) \to (\alpha \to \alpha)$ (17.1)
8. $\pi \vdash \text{double} : \forall\alpha.\ (\alpha \to \alpha) \to (\alpha \to \alpha)$ (15.3)
9. $\pi \vdash \text{double}\,[\text{int}] : (\text{int} \to \text{int}) \to (\text{int} \to \text{int})$ (17.2)
10. $\pi \vdash \text{double}\,[\text{int} \to \text{int}] : ((\text{int} \to \text{int}) \to (\text{int} \to \text{int})) \to$
    $\quad ((\text{int} \to \text{int}) \to (\text{int} \to \text{int}))$ (17.2)
11. $\pi \vdash \text{double}\,[\text{int} \to \text{int}]\,(\text{double}\,[\text{int}]) : (\text{int} \to \text{int}) \to (\text{int} \to \text{int})$ (15.5)
12. $\vdash \text{let double} \equiv \Lambda\alpha.\ \lambda f_{\alpha \to \alpha}.\ \lambda x_\alpha.\ f\,(f\,x)\ \text{in}$
    $\quad \text{double}\,[\text{int} \to \text{int}]\,(\text{double}\,[\text{int}]) : (\text{int} \to \text{int}) \to (\text{int} \to \text{int})$ (15.11)

In conclusion, it should be noted that one can also formulate an implicitly typed polymorphic language where, to eliminate all types from expressions, one erases the type binders $\Lambda\tau$ and the type operands $[\theta]$, as well as the types that appear as subscripts:

TY RULE: Implicit $\forall$ Introduction

$$\frac{\pi \vdash e : \theta}{\pi \vdash e : \forall\tau.\ \theta} \quad \text{when } \tau \text{ does not occur free in any type expression in } \pi, \tag{17.3}$$

TY RULE: Implicit $\forall$ Elimination

$$\frac{\pi \vdash e : \forall\tau.\ \theta}{\pi \vdash e : (\theta/\tau \to \theta').} \tag{17.4}$$

It is known that there is no algorithm that can infer typing judgements for this implicitly typed language. The language ML, however, provides a restricted form of implicit polymorphism for which type inference can be performed by an extension of the Hindley-Milner algorithm. Essentially, ML permits polymorphic functions to be introduced by **let** and **letrec** definitions, as in the examples at the beginning of this chapter. But it does not permit polymorphic functions to be passed as arguments to other functions.

17.2 Polymorphic Programming

Examples such as mapcar and reduce make a strong case for being able to declare polymorphic functions using a **let** or **letrec** definition. But at first sight, the idea of passing polymorphic functions to other functions seems very exotic. Nevertheless, the work of several researchers suggests that using polymorphic functions as data may be the key to a novel programming style. They have studied the pure lambda calculus with polymorphic typing (without explicit recursive definition via **rec** or **letrec**) and have shown that this restricted language has extraordinary properties. On the one hand, all well-typed expressions have normal forms (indeed, they are "strongly" normalizing, which means that they have no infinite reduction sequences), although the proof of this fact requires "second-order arithmetic" and cannot be obtained from Peano's axioms. On the other hand, the variety of functions that can be expressed goes far beyond the class of primitive recursive functions to include any program whose termination can be proved in second-order arithmetic. Beyond this they have shown that certain types of polymorphic functions behave like algebras.

Our purpose here is not to give the details of this theoretical work, but to illustrate the unusual programming style that underlies it. The starting point is a variant of the way that early investigators of the untyped lambda calculus encoded truth values and natural numbers, which we discussed briefly in Section 10.6.

Suppose we regard **bool** as an abbreviation for a polymorphic type, and **true** and **false** as abbreviations for certain functions of this type:

$$\textbf{bool} \stackrel{\text{def}}{=} \forall \alpha.\ \alpha \to \alpha \to \alpha$$

$$\textbf{true} \stackrel{\text{def}}{=} \Lambda\alpha.\ \lambda x_\alpha.\ \lambda y_\alpha.\ x$$

$$\textbf{false} \stackrel{\text{def}}{=} \Lambda\alpha.\ \lambda x_\alpha.\ \lambda y_\alpha.\ y.$$

Then, when e and e' have type θ, we can define the conditional expression by

$$\textbf{if } b \textbf{ then } e \textbf{ else } e' \stackrel{\text{def}}{=} b\,[\theta]\,e\,e',$$

since the reduction rules prescribe the right behavior for the conditional:

$$\textbf{if true then } e \textbf{ else } e' \overset{\text{def}}{=} (\Lambda\alpha.\ \lambda x_\alpha.\ \lambda y_\alpha.\ x)\,[\theta]\,e\,e'$$

$$\rightarrow (\lambda x_\theta.\ \lambda y_\theta.\ x)\,e\,e'$$

$$\rightarrow (\lambda y_\theta.\ e)\,e'$$

$$\rightarrow e$$

and

$$\textbf{if false then } e \textbf{ else } e' \overset{\text{def}}{=} (\Lambda\alpha.\ \lambda x_\alpha.\ \lambda y_\alpha.\ y)\,[\theta]\,e\,e'$$

$$\rightarrow (\lambda x_\theta.\ \lambda y_\theta.\ y)\,e\,e'$$

$$\rightarrow (\lambda y_\theta.\ y)\,e'$$

$$\rightarrow e'.$$

Moreover, we can define

$$\textbf{not} \overset{\text{def}}{=} \lambda b_{\textbf{bool}}.\ \Lambda\alpha.\ \lambda x_\alpha.\ \lambda y_\alpha.\ b\,[\alpha]\,y\,x$$

$$\textbf{and} \overset{\text{def}}{=} \lambda b_{\textbf{bool}}.\ \lambda c_{\textbf{bool}}.\ \Lambda\alpha.\ \lambda x_\alpha.\ \lambda y_\alpha.\ b\,[\alpha](c\,[\alpha]\,x\,y)\,y.$$

Similarly, we can define **nat** and the natural numbers by a typed form of Church numerals:

$$\textbf{nat} \overset{\text{def}}{=} \forall\alpha.\ (\alpha \rightarrow \alpha) \rightarrow \alpha \rightarrow \alpha$$

$$0 \overset{\text{def}}{=} \Lambda\alpha.\ \lambda f_{\alpha\rightarrow\alpha}.\ \lambda x_\alpha.\ x$$

$$1 \overset{\text{def}}{=} \Lambda\alpha.\ \lambda f_{\alpha\rightarrow\alpha}.\ \lambda x_\alpha.\ f\,x$$

$$2 \overset{\text{def}}{=} \Lambda\alpha.\ \lambda f_{\alpha\rightarrow\alpha}.\ \lambda x_\alpha.\ f\,(f\,x)$$

$$\vdots$$

$$n \overset{\text{def}}{=} \Lambda\alpha.\ \lambda f_{\alpha\rightarrow\alpha}.\ \lambda x_\alpha.\ f^n x$$

(where $f^n x$ denotes $f\,(\cdots(f\,x)\cdots)$ with n occurrences of f), so that the number n becomes a polymorphic function accepting a function and giving its n-fold composition. For example, 2 is **double**. (Strictly speaking, we should use some notation such as NUM_n for the nth Church numeral, as in Section 10.6, to indicate that the numeral is an expression denoting a number rather than a number itself. But such formality would make our arguments much harder to follow.)

Using this encoding of the natural numbers, we can define the successor function in either of two ways:

$$\textsf{succ} \overset{\text{def}}{=} \lambda n_{\textbf{nat}}.\ \Lambda\alpha.\ \lambda f_{\alpha\rightarrow\alpha}.\ \lambda x_\alpha.\ f\,(n\,[\alpha]\,f\,x)$$

or

$$\textsf{succ} \overset{\text{def}}{=} \lambda n_{\textbf{nat}}.\ \Lambda\alpha.\ \lambda f_{\alpha\rightarrow\alpha}.\ \lambda x_\alpha.\ n\,[\alpha]\,f\,(f\,x).$$

Now suppose $g : \mathbf{nat} \to \theta$ satisfies

$$g\,0 = c \qquad \text{and} \qquad \forall n \geq 0.\ g(n+1) = h(g\,n), \tag{17.5}$$

where $c : \theta$ and $h : \theta \to \theta$. Then $g\,n = h^n c$, so that we can define $g\,n$ by applying the nth Church numeral:

$$g \overset{\text{def}}{=} \lambda\mathsf{n}_{\mathbf{nat}}.\ \mathsf{n}\,[\theta]\,h\,c.$$

For example, since

$$\mathsf{add}\,m\,0 = m \qquad \text{and} \qquad \mathsf{add}\,m\,(n+1) = \mathsf{succ}\,(\mathsf{add}\,m\,n)$$

fit the mold of Equations (17.5), we can define

$$\mathsf{add}\ m \overset{\text{def}}{=} \lambda\mathsf{n}_{\mathbf{nat}}.\ \mathsf{n}\,[\mathbf{nat}]\,\mathsf{succ}\ m$$

or, more abstractly,

$$\mathsf{add} \overset{\text{def}}{=} \lambda\mathsf{m}_{\mathbf{nat}}.\ \lambda\mathsf{n}_{\mathbf{nat}}.\ \mathsf{n}\,[\mathbf{nat}]\,\mathsf{succ}\ m.$$

Similarly,

$$\mathsf{mult} \overset{\text{def}}{=} \lambda\mathsf{m}_{\mathbf{nat}}.\ \lambda\mathsf{n}_{\mathbf{nat}}.\ \mathsf{n}\,[\mathbf{nat}]\,(\mathsf{add}\ m)\,0$$

$$\mathsf{exp} \overset{\text{def}}{=} \lambda\mathsf{m}_{\mathbf{nat}}.\ \lambda\mathsf{n}_{\mathbf{nat}}.\ \mathsf{n}\,[\mathbf{nat}]\,(\mathsf{mult}\ m)\,1.$$

In fact, this approach can be generalized to define any primitive recursive function on the natural numbers. A function $f : \mathbf{nat} \to \theta$ is said to be *primitive recursive* if it satisfies

$$f\,0 = c \qquad \text{and} \qquad \forall n \geq 0.\ f(n+1) = h\,n\,(f\,n),$$

where $c : \theta$ and $h : \mathbf{nat} \to \theta \to \theta$ are defined nonrecursively in terms of previously defined primitive recursive functions.

Let $g : \mathbf{nat} \to \mathbf{nat} \times \theta$ be such that $g\,n = \langle n, f\,n \rangle$. Then

$$
\begin{aligned}
g\,0 &= \langle 0, f\,0 \rangle \\
&= \langle 0, c \rangle
\end{aligned}
$$

$$
\begin{aligned}
g(n+1) &= \langle n+1, f(n+1) \rangle \\
&= \langle \mathsf{succ}\,n, h\,n\,(f\,n) \rangle \\
&= (\lambda\langle \mathsf{k}, \mathsf{z} \rangle_{\mathbf{nat}\times\theta}.\ \langle \mathsf{succ}\,k, h\,k\,z \rangle)\,\langle n, f\,n \rangle \\
&= (\lambda\langle \mathsf{k}, \mathsf{z} \rangle_{\mathbf{nat}\times\theta}.\ \langle \mathsf{succ}\,k, h\,k\,z \rangle)\,(g\,n).
\end{aligned}
$$

This matches the form of Equations (17.5), so that $g\,n$ can be defined by applying the nth Church numeral:

$$g = \lambda\mathsf{n}_{\mathbf{nat}}.\ \mathsf{n}[\mathbf{nat} \times \theta](\lambda\langle \mathsf{k}, \mathsf{z} \rangle_{\mathbf{nat}\times\theta}.\ \langle \mathsf{succ}\,k, h\,k\,z \rangle)\langle 0, c \rangle,$$

which gives

$$f = \lambda n_{\mathbf{nat}}.\ (n[\mathbf{nat} \times \theta](\lambda \langle k, z \rangle_{\mathbf{nat} \times \theta}.\ \langle \mathsf{succ}\ k, h\ k\ z \rangle) \langle 0, c \rangle).1.$$

For example, since the predecessor function satisfies

$$\mathsf{pred}\ 0 = 0$$

$$\mathsf{pred}(n+1) = n = (\lambda n_{\mathbf{nat}}.\ \lambda m_{\mathbf{nat}}.\ n)\ n\ (\mathsf{pred}\ n),$$

we can define

$$\mathsf{pred} = \lambda n_{\mathbf{nat}}.\ (n[\mathbf{nat} \times \mathbf{nat}]$$
$$(\lambda \langle k, z \rangle_{\mathbf{nat} \times \mathbf{nat}}.\ \langle \mathsf{succ}\ k, (\lambda n_{\mathbf{nat}}.\ \lambda m_{\mathbf{nat}}.\ n)\ k\ z \rangle) \langle 0, 0 \rangle).1$$
$$= \lambda n_{\mathbf{nat}}.\ (n[\mathbf{nat} \times \mathbf{nat}](\lambda \langle k, z \rangle_{\mathbf{nat} \times \mathbf{nat}}.\ \langle \mathsf{succ}\ k, k \rangle) \langle 0, 0 \rangle).1.$$

(Unfortunately, this predecessor function requires time that is proportional to its argument. It is not known how to program a constant-time predecessor function in this formalism.) Similarly, since

$$\mathsf{fact}\ 0 = 1$$

$$\mathsf{fact}(n+1) = (n+1) * \mathsf{fact}\ n = (\lambda n_{\mathbf{nat}}.\ \lambda m_{\mathbf{nat}}.\ (n+1) \times m)\ n\ (\mathsf{fact}\ n),$$

we can define

$$\mathsf{fact} = \lambda n_{\mathbf{nat}}.\ (n[\mathbf{nat} \times \mathbf{nat}]$$
$$(\lambda \langle k, z \rangle_{\mathbf{nat} \times \mathbf{nat}}.\ \langle \mathsf{succ}\ k, (\lambda n_{\mathbf{nat}}.\ \lambda m_{\mathbf{nat}}.\ (n+1) \times m)\ k\ z \rangle) \langle 0, 1 \rangle).1$$
$$= \lambda n_{\mathbf{nat}}.\ (n[\mathbf{nat} \times \mathbf{nat}](\lambda \langle k, z \rangle_{\mathbf{nat} \times \mathbf{nat}}.\ \langle \mathsf{succ}\ k, (k+1) \times z \rangle) \langle 0, 1 \rangle).1.$$

Our ability to define numerical functions, however, is not limited to the scheme of primitive recursion. For example, the exponentiation laws $f^m \cdot f^n = f^{m+n}$ and $(f^m)^n = f^{m \times n}$ lead directly to the definitions

$$\mathsf{add} \overset{\text{def}}{=} \lambda m_{\mathbf{nat}}.\ \lambda n_{\mathbf{nat}}.\ \Lambda \alpha.\ \lambda f_{\alpha \to \alpha}.\ \lambda x_{\alpha}.\ n\ [\alpha]\ f\ (m\ [\alpha]\ f\ x)$$

$$\mathsf{mult} \overset{\text{def}}{=} \lambda m_{\mathbf{nat}}.\ \lambda n_{\mathbf{nat}}.\ \Lambda \alpha.\ \lambda f_{\alpha \to \alpha}.\ n\ [\alpha]\ (m\ [\alpha]\ f),$$

and the law $\lambda f.\ f^{(m^n)} = (\lambda f.\ f^m)^n$ (which can be proved by induction on n) leads to

$$\mathsf{exp} \overset{\text{def}}{=} \lambda m_{\mathbf{nat}}.\ \lambda n_{\mathbf{nat}}.\ \Lambda \alpha.\ n\ [\alpha \to \alpha]\ (m\ [\alpha]).$$

Moreover, if we define

$$\mathsf{aug} \overset{\text{def}}{=} \lambda f_{\mathbf{nat} \to \mathbf{nat}}.\ \lambda n_{\mathbf{nat}}.\ \mathsf{succ}\ n\ [\mathbf{nat}]\ f\ 1,$$

which implies $\mathsf{aug}\ f\ n = f^{n+1} 1$, then we can define

$$\mathsf{ack} \overset{\text{def}}{=} \lambda m_{\mathbf{nat}}.\ m\ [\mathbf{nat} \to \mathbf{nat}]\ \mathsf{aug}\ \mathsf{succ},$$

so that we have

$$\mathsf{ack}\ 0\ \mathsf{n} = \mathsf{n} + 1$$

$$\mathsf{ack}\ (\mathsf{m} + 1)\ 0 = \mathsf{aug}\ (\mathsf{ack}\ \mathsf{m})\ 0$$
$$= \mathsf{ack}\ \mathsf{m}\ 1$$

$$\mathsf{ack}\ (\mathsf{m} + 1)(\mathsf{n} + 1) = \mathsf{aug}\ (\mathsf{ack}\ \mathsf{m})(\mathsf{n} + 1)$$
$$= \mathsf{ack}\ \mathsf{m}\ (\mathsf{aug}\ (\mathsf{ack}\ \mathsf{m})\ \mathsf{n})$$
$$= \mathsf{ack}\ \mathsf{m}\ (\mathsf{ack}\ (\mathsf{m} + 1)\ \mathsf{n}).$$

This establishes that $\lambda \mathsf{n}_{\mathbf{nat}}.\ \mathsf{ack}\ \mathsf{n}\ \mathsf{n}$ is Ackermann's function, which is known to grow so rapidly that it is not primitive recursive. Thus the functions definable in the polymorphic lambda calculus go beyond primitive recursion (which is extraordinary in a language where all expressions terminate).

In addition to primitive types such as **nat** and **bool**, various type constructors can be defined in terms of polymorphic functions. For binary products, we can define

$$\theta_0 \times \theta_1 \overset{\mathrm{def}}{=} \forall \alpha.\ (\theta_0 \rightarrow \theta_1 \rightarrow \alpha) \rightarrow \alpha$$

and, where $e_0 : \theta_0$, $e_1 : \theta_1$, and $p : \theta_0 \times \theta_1$,

$$\langle e_0, e_1 \rangle \overset{\mathrm{def}}{=} \Lambda\alpha.\ \lambda \mathsf{f}_{\theta_0 \rightarrow \theta_1 \rightarrow \alpha}.\ \mathsf{f}\ e_0\ e_1$$

$$p.0 \overset{\mathrm{def}}{=} p\ [\theta_0]\ (\lambda \mathsf{x}_{\theta_0}.\ \lambda \mathsf{y}_{\theta_1}.\ \mathsf{x})$$

$$p.1 \overset{\mathrm{def}}{=} p\ [\theta_1]\ (\lambda \mathsf{x}_{\theta_0}.\ \lambda \mathsf{y}_{\theta_1}.\ \mathsf{y}),$$

since we have the reduction

$$\langle e_0, e_1 \rangle.0 \overset{\mathrm{def}}{=} (\Lambda\alpha.\ \lambda \mathsf{f}_{\theta_0 \rightarrow \theta_1 \rightarrow \alpha}.\ \mathsf{f}\ e_0\ e_1)\ [\theta_0]\ (\lambda \mathsf{x}_{\theta_0}.\ \lambda \mathsf{y}_{\theta_1}.\ \mathsf{x})$$
$$\rightarrow (\lambda \mathsf{f}_{\theta_0 \rightarrow \theta_1 \rightarrow \theta_0}.\ \mathsf{f}\ e_0\ e_1)\ (\lambda \mathsf{x}_{\theta_0}.\ \lambda \mathsf{y}_{\theta_1}.\ \mathsf{x})$$
$$\rightarrow (\lambda \mathsf{x}_{\theta_0}.\ \lambda \mathsf{y}_{\theta_1}.\ \mathsf{x})\ e_0\ e_1$$
$$\rightarrow (\lambda \mathsf{y}_{\theta_1}.\ e_0)\ e_1$$
$$\rightarrow e_0,$$

and similarly

$$\langle e_0, e_1 \rangle.1 \rightarrow^* e_1.$$

For binary disjoint unions, we can define

$$\theta_0 + \theta_1 \overset{\mathrm{def}}{=} \forall \alpha.\ (\theta_0 \rightarrow \alpha) \rightarrow (\theta_1 \rightarrow \alpha) \rightarrow \alpha$$

and, where $e_0 : \theta_0$, $e_1 : \theta_1$, $f_0 : \theta_0 \to \theta$, $f_1 : \theta_1 \to \theta$ and $e : \theta_0 + \theta_1$,

$$@\,0\,e_0 \overset{\text{def}}{=} \Lambda\alpha.\ \lambda g_{\theta_0 \to \alpha}.\ \lambda h_{\theta_1 \to \alpha}.\ g\,e_0$$

$$@\,1\,e_1 \overset{\text{def}}{=} \Lambda\alpha.\ \lambda g_{\theta_0 \to \alpha}.\ \lambda h_{\theta_1 \to \alpha}.\ h\,e_1$$

$$\textbf{sumcase }e\textbf{ of }(f_0, f_1) \overset{\text{def}}{=} e\,[\theta]\,f_0\,f_1,$$

since we have

$$\textbf{sumcase }(@\,0\,e_0)\textbf{ of }(f_0, f_1) \overset{\text{def}}{=} (\Lambda\alpha.\ \lambda g_{\theta_0 \to \alpha}.\ \lambda h_{\theta_1 \to \alpha}.\ g\,e_0)\,[\theta]\,f_0\,f_1$$
$$\to (\lambda g_{\theta_0 \to \theta}.\ \lambda h_{\theta_1 \to \theta}.\ g\,e_0)\,f_0\,f_1$$
$$\to (\lambda h_{\theta_1 \to \theta}.\ f_0\,e_0)\,f_1$$
$$\to f_0\,e_0,$$

and similarly

$$\textbf{sumcase }(@\,1\,e_1)\textbf{ of }(f_0, f_1) \to^* f_1\,e_1.$$

Finally, we consider representing lists by polymorphic functions. If we define the type

$$\textbf{list }\theta \overset{\text{def}}{=} \forall\alpha.\ (\theta \to \alpha \to \alpha) \to \alpha \to \alpha,$$

and the individual lists of this type by

$$x_0 :: x_1 :: \cdots :: x_{n-1} :: \textbf{nil} \overset{\text{def}}{=} \Lambda\alpha.\ \lambda f_{\theta \to \alpha \to \alpha}.\ \lambda a_\alpha.\ f\,x_0\,(f\,x_1\,\cdots\,(f\,x_{n-1}\,a)\,\cdots)$$

(so that a list is its own reduce function), then we can define

$$\textbf{nil} \overset{\text{def}}{=} \Lambda\alpha.\ \lambda f_{\theta \to \alpha \to \alpha}.\ \lambda a_\alpha.\ a$$

$$e :: e' \overset{\text{def}}{=} \Lambda\alpha.\ \lambda f_{\theta \to \alpha \to \alpha}.\ \lambda a_\alpha.\ f\,e(e'\,[\alpha]\,f\,a).$$

Now suppose $g : \textbf{list }\theta \to \theta'$ satisfies

$$g\,\textbf{nil} = c \qquad \text{and} \qquad g\,(i :: r) = h\,i\,(g\,r), \qquad (17.6)$$

where $c : \theta'$ and $h : \theta \to \theta' \to \theta'$. Then $g\,x = \textsf{reduce }x\,h\,c$, so that we can define g by

$$g \overset{\text{def}}{=} \lambda x_{\textbf{list }\theta}.\ x\,[\theta']\,h\,c.$$

For example, if $\textsf{rappend }y\,x = \textsf{append }x\,y$, then

$$\textsf{rappend }y\,\textbf{nil} = y$$

$$\textsf{rappend }y\,(i :: r) = i :: (\textsf{rappend }y\,r),$$

which fits the form of Equations (17.6), so that we can define

$$\textsf{rappend }y \overset{\text{def}}{=} \lambda x_{\textbf{list }\theta}.\ x\,[\textbf{list }\theta]\,(\lambda i_\theta.\ \lambda z_{\textbf{list }\theta}.\ i :: z)\,y$$

or

$$\text{append} \stackrel{\text{def}}{=} \lambda x_{\text{list }\theta}.\ \lambda y_{\text{list }\theta}.\ x\,[\text{list }\theta]\,(\lambda i_\theta.\ \lambda z_{\text{list }\theta}.\ i :: z)\,y.$$

Similarly,

$$\text{length} \stackrel{\text{def}}{=} \lambda x_{\text{list }\theta}.\ x\,[\text{nat}]\,(\lambda i_\theta.\ \lambda z_{\text{nat}}.\ z + 1)\,0$$

$$\text{sumlist} \stackrel{\text{def}}{=} \lambda x_{\text{list nat}}.\ x\,[\text{nat}]\,(\lambda i_{\text{nat}}.\ \lambda z_{\text{nat}}.\ i + z)\,0$$

$$\text{mapcar} \stackrel{\text{def}}{=} \lambda f_{\theta \to \theta'}.\ \lambda x_{\text{list }\theta}.\ x\,[\text{list }\theta']\,(\lambda i_\theta.\ \lambda z_{\text{list }\theta'}.\ (f\,i) :: z)\,\textbf{nil}.$$

These are all functions that recur uniformly down a single list. At first sight, one might expect that it would be more difficult to define a function where the recursion switches back and forth between two lists, such as a function for merging ordered lists of integers. But in fact one can define a curried merging function that uses uniform recursion in its first argument to produce the appropriate function of its second argument.

The first step is to introduce a subsidiary function

$$\text{insertapp} : \textbf{int} \to (\textbf{list int} \to \textbf{list int}) \to \textbf{list int} \to \textbf{list int}$$

such that, when x is an ordered list of integers, $\text{insertapp}\ m\ f\ x$ inserts m into the proper position of x and applies f to the portion of x following this position. (To keep our argument simple, we are using the primitive type **int**, rather than the representation by Church numerals discussed earlier in this section.) Then merge can be expressed in terms of insertapp by

$$\text{merge}\ \textbf{nil}\ y = y$$

$$\text{merge}\ (i :: r)\ y = \text{insertapp}\ i\,(\lambda y_{\text{list int}}.\ \text{merge}\ r\ y)\ y.$$

These equations can be written more abstractly as

$$\text{merge}\ \textbf{nil} = \lambda y_{\text{list int}}.\ y$$

$$\text{merge}\ (i :: r) = \text{insertapp}\ i\,(\text{merge}\ r),$$

which matches the form of Equations (17.6), so that we can define

$$\text{merge} \stackrel{\text{def}}{=} \lambda x_{\text{list int}}.\ x\,[\text{list int} \to \text{list int}]\,\text{insertapp}\,(\lambda y_{\text{list int}}.\ y).$$

The remaining task is to program insertapp, which satisfies

$$\text{insertapp}\ m\ f\ \textbf{nil} = m :: (f\ \textbf{nil})$$

$$\text{insertapp}\ m\ f\ (i :: r) = \textbf{if}\ m \le i\ \textbf{then}\ m :: (f(i :: r))\ \textbf{else}\ i :: (\text{insertapp}\ m\ f\ r).$$

This does not match the form of Equations (17.6), but it can be treated by the same approach that we used for primitive recursive functions on numbers. Let

$$g : \textbf{int} \to (\textbf{list int} \to \textbf{list int}) \to \textbf{list int} \to (\textbf{list int} \times \textbf{list int})$$

be such that $g\ m\ f\ x = \langle x, \text{insertapp}\ m\ f\ x\rangle$. Then

$$g\ m\ f\ \mathbf{nil} = \langle \mathbf{nil}, \text{insertapp}\ m\ f\ \mathbf{nil}\rangle$$
$$= \langle \mathbf{nil}, m :: (f\ \mathbf{nil})\rangle$$

$$g\ m\ f\ (i :: r) = \langle i :: r, \text{insertapp}\ m\ f\ (i :: r)\rangle$$
$$= \langle i :: r, \mathbf{if}\ m \leq i\ \mathbf{then}\ m :: (f(i :: r))\ \mathbf{else}\ i :: \text{insertapp}\ m\ f\ r\rangle$$
$$= (\lambda i_{\mathbf{int}}.\ \lambda\langle y, z\rangle_{\mathbf{list\ int}\times\mathbf{list\ int}}.$$
$$\langle i :: y, \mathbf{if}\ m \leq i\ \mathbf{then}\ m :: (f(i :: y))\ \mathbf{else}\ i :: z\rangle)$$
$$i\ (g\ m\ f\ r).$$

This fits the form of Equations (17.6), so that we can define

$$g \overset{\text{def}}{=} \lambda m_{\mathbf{int}}.\ \lambda f_{\mathbf{list\ int}\to\mathbf{list\ int}}.\ \lambda x_{\mathbf{list\ int}}.\ \mathsf{x}\ [\mathbf{list\ int}\times\mathbf{list\ int}]$$
$$(\lambda i_{\mathbf{int}}.\ \lambda\langle y, z\rangle_{\mathbf{list\ int}\times\mathbf{list\ int}}.\ \langle i :: y, \mathbf{if}\ m \leq i\ \mathbf{then}\ m :: (f(i :: y))\ \mathbf{else}\ i :: z\rangle)$$
$$\langle \mathbf{nil}, m :: (f\ \mathbf{nil})\rangle,$$

and therefore

$$\text{insertapp} \overset{\text{def}}{=} \lambda m_{\mathbf{int}}.\ \lambda f_{\mathbf{list\ int}\to\mathbf{list\ int}}.\ \lambda x_{\mathbf{list\ int}}.\ (\mathsf{x}\ [\mathbf{list\ int}\times\mathbf{list\ int}]$$
$$(\lambda i_{\mathbf{int}}.\ \lambda\langle y, z\rangle_{\mathbf{list\ int}\times\mathbf{list\ int}}.\ \langle i :: y, \mathbf{if}\ m \leq i\ \mathbf{then}\ m :: (f(i :: y))\ \mathbf{else}\ i :: z\rangle)$$
$$\langle \mathbf{nil}, m :: (f\ \mathbf{nil})\rangle).1.$$

17.3 Extrinsic Semantics

The extrinsic semantics of polymorphic types reveals their similarity to intersection types: Just as $\theta_0\ \&\ \theta_1$ denotes the intersection of the partial equivalence relations denoted by θ_0 and θ_1, so the quantified type $\forall \tau.\ \theta$ denotes the intersection of all of the partial equivalence relations that are denoted by θ as one varies the denotation of the type variable τ.

To make this precise, the first step is to accommodate type variables. Let PER stand for the set of chain-complete partial equivalence relations whose domain contains $\bot$ but not tyerr (i.e. which satisfy the conditions of Proposition 15.1 in Section 15.4). In Sections 15.4 and 16.4, we defined a function $\mathcal{P} \in \langle\text{type}\rangle \to$ PER that mapped types into their denotations. But when types can contain type variables, what they denote depends (just as with ordinary expressions) on what the type variables denote. Thus we must introduce the concept of type environments, which map type variables into partial equivalence relations, and redefine $\mathcal{P}$ to satisfy

$$\mathcal{P} \in \langle\text{type}\rangle \to (\text{PER}^{\langle\text{tvar}\rangle} \to \text{PER}).$$

We will use the metavariable ξ for type environments in $\text{PER}^{\langle\text{tvar}\rangle}$.

The various cases defining $\mathcal{P}$ in Sections 15.4 and 16.4 change in a trivial way: The occurrences of $\mathcal{P}(-)$ become occurrences of $\mathcal{P}(-)\xi$. In addition, there are two new cases, which describe type variables and polymorphic types:

(h) $\langle x, x' \rangle \in \mathcal{P}(\tau)\xi$ if and only if $\langle x, x' \rangle \in \xi\tau$.
(i) $\langle x, x' \rangle \in \mathcal{P}(\forall \tau.\ \theta)\xi$ if and only if $\langle x, x' \rangle \in \mathcal{P}(\theta)[\xi \mid \tau{:}\rho]$ for all $\rho \in \mathrm{PER}$.

More succinctly,

(h) $\mathcal{P}(\tau)\xi = \xi\tau$.
(i) $\mathcal{P}(\forall \tau.\ \theta)\xi = \bigcap_{\rho \in \mathrm{PER}} \mathcal{P}(\theta)[\xi \mid \tau{:}\rho]$.

With the introduction of type variables and a binding operator, types exhibit the same behavior as did assertions in Section 1.4 or expressions of the lambda calculus in Section 10.5. The set of free type variables in a type is given by

$$\mathrm{FTV}(\tau) = \{\tau\}$$

$$\mathrm{FTV}(\forall \tau.\ \theta) = \mathrm{FTV}(\theta) - \{\tau\}$$

and, for all other forms, by

$$\mathrm{FTV}(\theta) = \mathrm{FTV}(\theta_0) \cup \cdots \cup \mathrm{FTV}(\theta_{n-1}),$$

where $\theta_0, \ldots, \theta_{n-1}$ are the subphrases of θ. Then one can show

Proposition 17.1 (Coincidence Theorem) *If* $\xi\tau = \xi'\tau$ *for all* $\tau \in \mathrm{FTV}(\theta)$, *then* $\mathcal{P}(\theta)\xi = \mathcal{P}(\theta)\xi'$.

Proposition 17.2 (Substitution Theorem) *If* $[\![\delta\tau]\!]\xi' = \xi\tau$ *for all* $\tau \in \mathrm{FTV}(\theta)$, *then* $\mathcal{P}(\theta/\delta)\xi' = \mathcal{P}(\theta)\xi$.

Proposition 17.3 (Finite Substitution Theorem)

$$\mathcal{P}(\theta/\tau_0 \to \theta_0, \ldots, \tau_{n-1} \to \theta_{n-1})\xi'$$
$$= \mathcal{P}(\theta)[\xi' \mid \tau_0{:}\mathcal{P}(\theta_0)\xi' \mid \ldots \mid \tau_{n-1}{:}\mathcal{P}(\theta_{n-1})\xi'].$$

Proposition 17.4 (Soundness of Renaming) *If*

$$\tau_{\mathrm{new}} \notin \mathrm{FTV}(\theta) - \{\tau\},$$

then

$$\mathcal{P}(\forall \tau_{\mathrm{new}}.\ (\theta/\tau \to \tau_{\mathrm{new}})) = \mathcal{P}(\forall \tau.\ \theta).$$

Moreover, since an intersection of members of PER is a member of PER, Proposition 15.1 in Section 15.4 remains true (with the replacement of $\mathcal{P}(\theta)$ by $\mathcal{P}(\theta)\xi$, where ξ is an arbitrary type environment in $\mathrm{PER}^{\langle \mathrm{tvar} \rangle}$).

The appropriate generalization of Proposition 15.3 is

Proposition 17.5 (Soundness of Polymorphic Typing) *If $\pi \vdash e : \theta$ is a valid typing judgement, ξ is a type environment, and η and η' are environments such that*

$$\langle \eta v, \eta' v \rangle \in \mathcal{P}(\pi v)\xi \text{ for all } v \in \operatorname{dom} \pi,$$

then

$$\langle [\![e]\!]\eta, [\![e]\!]\eta' \rangle \in \mathcal{P}(\theta)\xi.$$

PROOF As before, the proof is by structural induction on the formal proof of $\pi \vdash e : \theta$, with a case analysis on the inference rule used in the final step of the proof. The cases in the proof in Section 15.4 (and its continuation in Section 16.4) remain essentially the same. But now there are two more inference rules to consider. (Since the earlier version of the proposition was stated for implicit typing, we will use the implicitly typed version of the new rules as well.)

Suppose the rule used in the final step is the rule for $\forall$ introduction ((17.3) in Section 17.1),

$$\frac{\pi \vdash e : \theta}{\pi \vdash e : \forall \tau.\, \theta} \qquad \begin{array}{l} \text{when } \tau \text{ does not occur free in} \\ \text{any type expression in } \pi. \end{array}$$

Assume $\langle \eta v, \eta' v \rangle \in \mathcal{P}(\pi v)\xi$ for all $v \in \operatorname{dom} \pi$. Since τ does not occur free in any type expression in π, the coincidence theorem gives $\langle \eta v, \eta' v \rangle \in \mathcal{P}(\pi v)[\xi \mid \tau : \rho]$ for all $v \in \operatorname{dom} \pi$, where ρ is any relation in PER. Then the induction hypothesis gives $\langle [\![e]\!]\eta, [\![e]\!]\eta' \rangle \in \mathcal{P}(\theta)[\xi \mid \tau : \rho]$, and since this holds for any $\rho \in$ PER,

$$\langle [\![e]\!]\eta, [\![e]\!]\eta' \rangle \in \bigcap_{\rho \in \mathrm{PER}} \mathcal{P}(\theta)[\xi \mid \tau : \rho] = \mathcal{P}(\forall \tau.\, \theta)\xi.$$

On the other hand, suppose the rule used in the final step is the rule for $\forall$ elimination ((17.4) in Section 17.1),

$$\frac{\pi \vdash e : \forall \tau.\, \theta}{\pi \vdash e : (\theta/\tau \to \theta').}$$

Assume $\langle \eta v, \eta' v \rangle \in \mathcal{P}(\pi v)\xi$ for all $v \in \operatorname{dom} \pi$. Then the induction hypothesis gives

$$\langle [\![e]\!]\eta, [\![e]\!]\eta' \rangle \in \mathcal{P}(\forall \tau.\, \theta)\xi = \bigcap_{\rho \in \mathrm{PER}} \mathcal{P}(\theta)[\xi \mid \tau : \rho].$$

The intersection here contains $\mathcal{P}(\theta)[\xi \mid \tau : \mathcal{P}(\theta')\xi]$, which equals $\mathcal{P}(\theta/\tau \to \theta')\xi$ by the finite substitution theorem. Thus $\langle [\![e]\!]\eta, [\![e]\!]\eta' \rangle \in \mathcal{P}(\theta/\tau \to \theta')\xi$.

END OF PROOF

Bibliographic Notes

The intuitive concept of polymorphism is due to Strachey [1967]. The polymorphic typed lambda calculus (called the "second-order typed lambda calculus" or "System F" by logicians) was devised by Girard [1971; 1972], who showed that, in the absence of explicit recursion, all expressions reduce to normal form. (In fact, Girard showed "strong normalization" — that there are no infinite reduction sequences, regardless of any evaluation strategy.) The language was rediscovered independently, and connected to Strachey's concept of polymorphism, by Reynolds [1974]. Girard's development also included the existential types that we will discuss in Section 18.2, and an extension called the "ω-order typed lambda calculus" or "System F_ω" that permits quantification over higher "kinds" (such as the kind of type constructors, which can be viewed as functions from types to types).

The representation of lists in Section 17.2 is a special case of the representation of anarchic algebras that was discovered independently by Leivant [1983] and Böhm and Berarducci [1985].

The undecidability of type inference for the full polymorphic typed lambda calculus was shown by Wells [1994; 1998]. In contrast, if one permits the definition of polymorphic functions but prohibits them as arguments to other functions, as in Standard ML [Milner, Tofte, and Harper, 1990; Milner and Tofte, 1991], then type inference can be performed by the Hindley-Milner algorithm [Milner, 1978; Damas and Milner, 1982]. Type inference for more general sublanguages of the polymorphic calculus is discussed by Giannini and Ronchi della Rocca [1994].

Extrinsic models of polymorphism, based on partial equivalence relations, have been developed by Girard [1972], Troelstra [1973a], and, more recently, by Longo and Moggi [1991], Pitts [1987], Freyd and Scedrov [1987], Hyland [1988], Breazu-Tannen and Coquand [1988], and Mitchell [1986]. A variety of domain-based intrinsic models have also been devised; in the earliest, McCracken [1979] interpreted types as closures of a universal domain. She later used finitary retractions in place of closures [McCracken, 1982], while Amadio, Bruce, and Longo [1986] used finitary projections. More recently, Girard [1986] used qualitative domains and stable functions. Other domain-theoretic intrinsic models have been proposed by Coquand, Gunter, and Winskel [1988; 1989].

The general concept of what constitutes a model of the polymorphic calculus has been explicated using category theory by Seely [1987] and Ma and Reynolds [1992]. The impossibility of any model that extends the set-theoretic model of the simply typed lambda calculus has been shown by Reynolds and Plotkin [1993].

When Strachey introduced polymorphism, he distinguished between *ad hoc* polymorphic functions, which can behave in arbitrarily different ways for different types, and *parametric* polymorphic functions, which behave uniformly for all types. Reynolds [1983] formalized parametricity in terms of Plotkin's [1973] concept of logical relations, and Wadler [1989] showed that this formalization can be used to prove a variety of useful properties of parametric polymorphic functions.

Although only parametric functions can be defined in the polymorphic lambda calculus, most of the semantic models of the language include ad hoc functions as well. However, a purely parametric extrinsic semantics, using partial equivalence relations on natural numbers, has been given by Bainbridge, Freyd, Scedrov, and Scott [1990]. On the other hand, although Ma and Reynolds [1992] have managed to define what it would mean for an arbitrary intrinsic semantics to be parametric, no purely parametric domain-theoretic semantics is known.

For a selection of research papers and further references about the polymorphic lambda calculus, see Huet [1990].

In Cardelli and Wegner [1985], polymorphism and subtyping are combined in a language called "bounded fun" (or $F_\leq$) by introducing bounded quantification over all subtypes of a specified type. The coherence of this language was shown by Breazu-Tannen, Coquand, Gunter, and Scedrov [1991] and by Curien and Ghelli [1992]; the latter also gave a semidecision procedure for type checking. However, Ghelli [1991; 1995] gave a complex example showing that this procedure does not always terminate, and Pierce [1992] showed that there is no full decision procedure for type checking. A further extension of $F_\leq$ (called $F_\wedge$) that includes intersection types was also investigated by Pierce [1997].

Although the discussion of polymorphism in this book has been limited to purely functional languages with normal-order evaluation, there has been considerable research on the interaction of polymorphism with features of eager-evaluation and Iswim-like languages, including assignment to references [Tofte, 1990; Harper, 1994] and continuations as values [Harper, Duba, and MacQueen, 1993b]. Interactions with the transformation from direct to continuation semantics have been considered by Harper and Lillibridge [1993b; 1993a].

In the implementation of early typed languages, type information was used to determine the representation of values used by the compiled program. A naïve view of polymorphism seems to prevent this usage: Since a polymorphic function may accept arguments of an infinite variety of types, all values must be represented in a uniform way (say as an address). Indeed, current compilers for languages such as SML discard type information after the type-checking phase and compile the same kind of target code as one would for a untyped language. Recently, however, it has been found that polymorphism does not preclude the type-directed selection of data representations [Harper and Morrisett, 1995; Morrisett, 1995], which can provide a substantial improvement in the efficiency of polymorphic languages.

Primitive recursion is discussed in texts by Mendelson [1979, Section 3.3], Davis and Weyuker [1983, Chapter 3], and Andrews [1986, Section 65]. Mendelson [1979, Section 5.3, Exercise 5.16, Part (11)] and Davis and Weyuker [1983, Section 13.3] give proofs that Ackermann's function is not primitive recursive.

Exercises

17.1 Find an expression e and type expressions θ_0, θ_1, θ_2, θ_3, θ_4, and θ_5 that make the following three typing judgements of the explicitly typed polymorphic lambda calculus true. For each judgement, give a formal proof of the judgement using the rules of Chapter 15 (in their explicitly typed versions) and Section 17.1.

$$\vdash e : \forall \alpha. \; \alpha \to \alpha$$

$$\vdash \lambda x_{\forall \alpha. \; \alpha \to \alpha}. \, x\,[\theta_0]\,(x\,[\theta_1]) : \theta_2$$

$$\vdash \lambda x_{\forall \alpha. \; \alpha \to \alpha}. \, x\,[\theta_3]\,x : \theta_4$$

$$\vdash \lambda m_{\mathbf{nat}}. \, \lambda n_{\mathbf{nat}}. \, \Lambda \alpha. \, n\,[\alpha \to \alpha]\,(m\,[\alpha]) : \theta_5.$$

In the last case, $\mathbf{nat} \overset{\text{def}}{=} \forall \alpha. \, (\alpha \to \alpha) \to \alpha \to \alpha$. (Note that α is a type variable of the object language, while the θ_i are metavariables denoting type expressions.)

17.2 Let e and the θ_i be the expression and types found in Exercise 17.1. Give a reduction sequence to normal form, using the β-reduction for type applications described in Section 17.1 as well as ordinary β-reduction, for each of the following expressions:

$$\left(\lambda x_{\forall \alpha. \; \alpha \to \alpha}. \, x\,[\theta_0]\,(x\,[\theta_1]) \right) e$$

$$\left(\lambda x_{\forall \alpha. \; \alpha \to \alpha}. \, x\,[\theta_3]\,x \right) e.$$

17.3 Give a formal proof of the following typing judgement, using the inference rules of Chapter 15 (in their explicitly typed versions) and Section 17.1.

$$\mathsf{mapcar} : \forall \alpha. \, \forall \beta. \, (\alpha \to \beta) \to \mathbf{list} \, \alpha \to \mathbf{list} \, \beta$$

$$\vdash \lambda f_{\mathbf{int} \to \mathbf{int}}. \, \mathsf{mapcar}[\mathbf{list} \; \mathbf{int}][\mathbf{list} \; \mathbf{int}](\mathsf{mapcar}[\mathbf{int}][\mathbf{int}]\,f)$$

$$: (\mathbf{int} \to \mathbf{int}) \to \mathbf{list}(\mathbf{list} \; \mathbf{int}) \to \mathbf{list}(\mathbf{list} \; \mathbf{int}).$$

17.4 In typing rule (17.1) (and also (17.3)) in Section 17.1, the proviso "When τ does not occur free in any type expression in π" is necessary for type soundness. To demonstrate this:

(a) Use rule (17.1) without this proviso to prove the spurious judgement

$$\vdash \Lambda \alpha. \, \lambda x_\alpha. \, \Lambda \alpha. \, x : \forall \alpha. \, (\alpha \to \forall \alpha. \, \alpha).$$

(b) Construct an expression that reduces to **true** but can be proved, assuming the spurious judgement in part (a), to have type **int**.

17.5   Consider the definition of eqlist in terms of reduce described in Exercise
        11.9.

   (a) Convert the definition of this function into the explicitly typed poly-
       morphic language of this chapter. Here eqlist should not be poly-
       morphic, but reduce should be polymorphic, with the typing given in
       Section 17.1.

   (b) Generalize your definition to that of a polymorphic function called
       geneqlist, which accepts a type α and a function of type $\alpha \rightarrow \alpha \rightarrow$
       bool that compares values of type α for equality, and which returns
       a function of type **list** $\alpha \rightarrow$ **list** $\alpha \rightarrow$ **bool** that compares two lists
       with elements of type α for equality.

   (c) Use the function defined in part (b) to define a typed function that
       compares two lists of lists of integers for equality.

17.6   Using the definition in Exercise 11.8, give and prove a polymorphic typing
        judgement for the function lazyreduce which is general enough that this
        function can be applied to a list with any type of elements and its result
        (after application to x, f, a, and the dummy argument $\langle\rangle$) can have any
        type.

17.7   Using the representation of natural numbers and boolean values in Section
        17.2, define the predicate iszero of type **nat** $\rightarrow$ **bool**.

17.8   Using the representation of natural numbers in Section 17.2, give a non-
        recursive definition of the function that maps a natural number n into
        $n \div 2$.

        Hint Define a subsidiary function that maps the number n into the pair
        $\langle n \div 2, (n + 1) \div 2 \rangle$.

17.9   Suppose we say that $f :$ **list** $\theta \rightarrow \theta'$ is a primitive recursive function on
        lists if it satisfies

$$f \ \mathbf{nil} = c \qquad \text{and} \qquad f \ (i :: r) = h \ i \ r \ (f \ r),$$

        where $c : \theta'$ and $h : \theta \rightarrow$ **list** $\theta \rightarrow \theta' \rightarrow \theta'$ are defined nonrecursively
        in terms of previously defined primitive recursive functions. Using the
        kind of polymorphic programming in Section 17.2, where a list is its own
        reduce function, give a nonrecursive definition of f in terms of c and h.

        Hint The definition of insertapp at the end of Section 17.2 is a special
        example.

17.10   Unlike the version of merge defined in Section 11.5, the version in Section 17.2 does not eliminate duplicates between the lists being merged. Alter the definition of insertapp to remove this discrepancy.

17.11   In the kind of polymorphic programming described in Section 17.2, binary trees can be regarded as their own reduction functions (i.e. redtree in Exercise 11.7), just as with lists. Following this approach, define the polymorphic type **tree** and two functions for constructing trees: term, which maps an integer n into the tree consisting of a terminal node labelled with n, and combine, which maps two trees into the tree whose main node is a nonterminal node with the two arguments as subtrees.

17.12   Generalize Exercise 15.9 to include the inference rules for polymorphism given in Section 17.1. You will need to use a definition of the substitution operation $-/\delta$ where bound type variables are renamed to avoid the capture of free type variables.

17.13   The extrinsic semantics given in Section 17.3 is compatible with that of subtyping and intersection types given in Section 16.4 if one generalizes Proposition 16.2 to encompass type variables:

If $\theta \leq \theta'$, then $\forall \xi \in \mathrm{PER}^{\langle\mathrm{tvar}\rangle}. \; \mathcal{P}(\theta)\xi \subseteq \mathcal{P}(\theta')\xi.$

Show that this generalized proposition remains true if one introduces the subtyping rule

$$\frac{}{\forall \tau. \; \theta \leq \forall \tau_0. \; \cdots \; \forall \tau_{n-1}. \; (\theta/\tau \to \theta'),}$$

where $\tau_0, \ldots, \tau_{n-1} \notin \mathrm{FTV}(\theta) - \{\tau\}$.

Notice that one can derive the implicit rule for $\forall$ elimination ((17.4) in Section 17.1) from the subsumption rule ((16.1) in Section 16.1) and the special case of the above rule where $n = 0$. This kind of combination of polymorphism and subtyping has been investigated by Mitchell [1988] and Giannini [1988].

18

Module Specification

In constructing a large program, it is vital to be able to divide the program into parts, often called *modules*, and to specify these modules with sufficient precision that one can program each module knowing only the specification of the other modules.

One of the main benefits of modern type theory is the realization that the type of a module is in fact a formal specification of the module. Indeed (although we will not discuss them in this book) there are implemented type-based systems such as NuPrl and Coq which can handle specifications of functional programs that are as expressive and flexible as the specifications of imperative programs in Chapter 3. As with the specifications of Chapter 3, however, considerable human assistance is needed to insure that a program meets its specification.

In this chapter, we will examine more limited systems for which the check that a module meets its specification can be performed efficiently and without human intervention. What is surprising is the extent to which these less expressive systems can still detect programming errors.

We begin with a discussion of type definitions, especially abstract type definitions that make it possible to separate the definition of an abstract type, including both its representation and the relevant primitive operations, from the part of the program that uses the abstract type but is independent of its representation and the implementation of the primitives. We then examine a more general approach based on existentially quantified types and polymorphic functions.

18.1 Type Definitions

Many programming languages permit type variables to be defined by type expressions. There are two kinds of such facilities, often called transparent and abstract type definitions. A typical syntax is

$$\langle\text{exp}\rangle ::= \textbf{lettranstype } \langle\text{tvar}\rangle \equiv \langle\text{type}\rangle \textbf{ in } \langle\text{exp}\rangle$$

$$| \textbf{ letabstype } \langle\text{tvar}\rangle \equiv \langle\text{type}\rangle \textbf{ with } \langle\text{var}\rangle \equiv \langle\text{exp}\rangle, \ldots, \langle\text{var}\rangle \equiv \langle\text{exp}\rangle \textbf{ in } \langle\text{exp}\rangle$$

The effect of a *transparent* definition is to introduce a type variable as an abbreviation for a type expression. For example,

$$\textbf{lettranstype } \textsf{realpair} \equiv \textbf{real} \times \textbf{real in } \lambda x_{\textsf{realpair}}. \langle - x.0, - x.1\rangle$$

would have the same meaning and typing behavior as $\lambda x_{\textbf{real} \times \textbf{real}}. \langle - x.0, - x.1\rangle$. More generally, **lettranstype** $\tau \equiv \theta$ **in** e abbreviates the expression obtained from e by substituting θ for τ:

$$\textbf{lettranstype } \tau \equiv \theta \textbf{ in } e \overset{\text{def}}{=} (e/\tau \to \theta).$$

From this definition, it is trivial to derive the type inference rule

TY RULE: Transparent Type Definition

$$\frac{\pi \vdash (e/\tau \to \theta) : \theta'}{\pi \vdash \textbf{lettranstype } \tau \equiv \theta \textbf{ in } e : \theta'.} \tag{18.1}$$

In contrast, the effect of an *abstract* or *opaque* type definition is to provide for a type a representation that is hidden from the scope of the definition. For this to be useful, one must also specify (in the **with** clause) primitive operations for manipulating values of the abstract type. For example, to specify a representation of complex numbers, along with the primitive constant i and primitive functions for converting real to complex numbers, adding, multiplying, and conjugating complex numbers, and computing their magnitude, one might write

letabstype $\textsf{complex} \equiv \textbf{real} \times \textbf{real}$

   with $i_{\textsf{complex}} \equiv \langle 0, 1\rangle$,

     $\textsf{conv}_{\textsf{real} \to \textsf{complex}} \equiv \lambda r_{\textbf{real}}. \langle r, 0\rangle$,

     $\textsf{addc}_{\textsf{complex} \to \textsf{complex} \to \textsf{complex}} \equiv$

        $\lambda x_{\textbf{real} \times \textbf{real}}. \lambda y_{\textbf{real} \times \textbf{real}}. \langle x.0 + y.0, x.1 + y.1\rangle$,

     $\textsf{multc}_{\textsf{complex} \to \textsf{complex} \to \textsf{complex}} \equiv$

        $\lambda x_{\textbf{real} \times \textbf{real}}. \lambda y_{\textbf{real} \times \textbf{real}}. \langle x.0 \times y.0 - x.1 \times y.1, x.0 \times y.1 + x.1 \times y.0\rangle$,

     $\textsf{conj}_{\textsf{complex} \to \textsf{complex}} \equiv \lambda x_{\textbf{real} \times \textbf{real}}. \langle x.0, -x.1\rangle$,

     $\textsf{magn}_{\textsf{complex} \to \textsf{real}} \equiv \lambda x_{\textbf{real} \times \textbf{real}}. \textsf{squareroot}(x.0 \times x.0 + x.1 \times x.1)$

in E.

Within the scope E of this definition, one can manipulate values of type complex by using i, conv, addc, and so forth with the types indicated by the subscripts of these variables. In the definition of these primitives, the type complex is replaced by its representation $\textbf{real} \times \textbf{real}$. In the scope E, however, the abstract type complex and the representation type $\textbf{real} \times \textbf{real}$ are not regarded as equivalent. For instance, an occurrence of i.0 or $(\textsf{conv}(3.5)).1$ in E would be a type error.

In the general case, this behavior is captured by the type inference rule

TY RULE: Abstract Type Definition

$$\pi \vdash e_0 : (\theta_0/\tau \to \theta)$$

$$\ddots$$

$$\pi \vdash e_{n-1} : (\theta_{n-1}/\tau \to \theta) \qquad (18.2)$$

$$\pi, v_0 : \theta_0, \ldots, v_{n-1} : \theta_{n-1} \vdash e : \theta'$$

$$\overline{\pi \vdash \textbf{letabstype } \tau \equiv \theta \textbf{ with } v_{0\theta_0} \equiv e_0, \ldots, v_{n-1\theta_{n-1}} \equiv e_{n-1} \textbf{ in } e : \theta'}$$

when τ does not occur free in θ' or in any type expression in π,

and the reduction rule

$$\textbf{letabstype } \tau \equiv \theta \textbf{ with } v_{0\theta_0} \equiv e_0, \ldots, v_{n-1\theta_{n-1}} \equiv e_{n-1} \textbf{ in } e$$

$$\to ((\lambda v_{0\theta_0}. \cdots \lambda v_{n-1\theta_{n-1}}. e)/\tau \to \theta) e_0 \cdots e_{n-1}. \qquad (18.3)$$

Notice that, although this reduction rule preserves meaning, its two sides do not have the same typing behavior, since the right side may satisfy a typing that (because it violates opacity) is not satisfied by the left side. Also notice that, by combining rule (18.3) with the result of Exercise 10.10, one can obtain the reduction

$$\textbf{letabstype } \tau \equiv \theta \textbf{ with } v_{0\theta_0} \equiv e_0, \ldots, v_{n-1\theta_{n-1}} \equiv e_{n-1} \textbf{ in } e$$

$$\to^* ((e/\tau \to \theta)/v_0 \to e_0, \ldots, v_{n-1} \to e_{n-1}).$$

The abstract type definition is a very simple form of mechanically checkable module specification. In $\textbf{letabstype } \tau \equiv \theta \textbf{ with } v_{0\theta_0} \equiv e_0, \ldots, v_{n-1\theta_{n-1}} \equiv e_{n-1} \textbf{ in } e$, the type variable τ, the ordinary variables $v_0, \ldots, v_{n-1}$, and the types $\theta_0, \ldots, \theta_{n-1}$ provide a specification of the interface between the module where the abstract type is defined, which consists of the representation type θ and the expressions $e_0, \ldots, e_{n-1}$, and the module where the abstract type is used, which consists of the expression e.

Readers who are familiar with **datatype** definitions in Standard ML will recognize that these definitions combine a limited form of abstract type definition with recursive types and sums. Roughly speaking, the SML expression (in our notation)

$$\textbf{letdatatype } \tau \equiv c_0 \textbf{ of } \theta_0 \mid \cdots \mid c_{n-1} \textbf{ of } \theta_{n-1} \textbf{ in } e$$

is equivalent to

$$\textbf{letabstype } \tau \equiv \mu\tau. \textbf{ sum}(\theta_0, \ldots, \theta_{n-1})$$

$$\textbf{with } c_{0\theta_0 \to \tau} \equiv \lambda v_{\theta_0}. @ 0 \, v, \ldots, c_{n-1\theta_{n-1} \to \tau} \equiv \lambda v_{\theta_{n-1}}. @ \lfloor n-1 \rfloor \, v \textbf{ in } e.$$

In SML, however, the identifiers $c_0, \ldots, c_{n-1}$ denote entities called "constructors" that, in addition to being used as functions to construct values of type τ, can also be used within patterns to analyze values of type τ.

18.2 Existential Quantification and Modules

In addition to *universal quantification* over types by the operator $\forall$, the original formulation of the polymorphic lambda calculus (called System F) also permitted *existential quantification* over types by the operator $\exists$. It was later realized that an existentially quantified type is a *signature* that specifies the relationship between an abstract type and its primitive operations, and that values of the existential type are *structures* that implement the abstract type and primitive operations.

To introduce existential quantification we extend our abstract grammar with

$$\langle\text{type}\rangle ::= \exists\langle\text{tvar}\rangle.\ \langle\text{type}\rangle$$

$$\langle\text{exp}\rangle ::= \textbf{pack}\ \langle\text{type}\rangle\ \textbf{with}\ \langle\text{exp}\rangle\ \textbf{as}\ \langle\text{type}\rangle$$
$$|\ \textbf{open}\ \langle\text{exp}\rangle\ \textbf{as}\ \langle\text{tvar}\rangle\ \textbf{with}\ \langle\text{pat}\rangle\ \textbf{in}\ \langle\text{exp}\rangle$$

(Concretely, as with other quantifiers, we assume that θ in $\exists\tau.\ \theta$ extends to the first stopping symbol or the end of the enclosing phrase.)

The effect of **pack** θ **with** e **as** $\exists\tau.\ \theta'$ is to create a value that is a pair consisting of the type θ and the value of the expression e. On the other hand, if the value of e is such a pair, then the effect of **open** e **as** τ **with** p **in** e' is to evaluate e' under a binding in which the type variable τ and the pattern p stand for the components of the pair.

Thus we have the reduction rule:

$$\textbf{open}\ (\textbf{pack}\ \theta\ \textbf{with}\ e\ \textbf{as}\ \exists\tau.\ \theta')\ \textbf{as}\ \tau\ \textbf{with}\ p\ \textbf{in}\ e' \rightarrow ((\lambda p.\ e')/\tau \rightarrow \theta)e. \quad (18.4)$$

Note that, when the pattern p is a variable, the right side reduces further to $(e'/\tau \rightarrow \theta)/p \rightarrow e$.

The occurrence of the type $\exists\tau.\ \theta'$ (which will always be an existential type) at the end of the **pack** expression is an explicit indication of the type of the expression. (According to the usage of previous chapters, we would write this type as a subscript, but it is so central to the usage of the **pack** expression that it is sensible to indicate it more emphatically.) A value of type $\exists\tau.\ \theta'$ consists of a type θ paired with a value of the type obtained from θ' by substituting θ for τ. Thus the inference rule for **pack** is

TY RULE: Explicit $\exists$ Introduction

$$\frac{\pi \vdash e : (\theta'/\tau \rightarrow \theta)}{\pi \vdash \textbf{pack}\ \theta\ \textbf{with}\ e\ \textbf{as}\ \exists\tau.\ \theta' : \exists\tau.\ \theta'.} \quad (18.5)$$

When such a value is opened up, however, the representation type θ is hidden, and the type of the value component is described by θ' as a function of the abstract type τ. Thus:

TY RULE: Explicit $\exists$ Elimination

$$\frac{\pi \vdash e : \exists \tau.\, \theta' \qquad \pi, p : \theta' \vdash e' : \theta''}{\pi \vdash \mathbf{open}\ e\ \mathbf{as}\ \tau\ \mathbf{with}\ p\ \mathbf{in}\ e' : \theta''} \tag{18.6}$$

when τ does not occur free in θ'' or in any type expression in π.

In $\mathbf{open}\ e\ \mathbf{as}\ \tau\ \mathbf{with}\ p\ \mathbf{in}\ e'$, τ is a binding occurrence of a type variable whose scope is the pattern p and the expression e', while the variable occurrences in p are binding occurrences of ordinary variables whose scope is e'. In applying the above rule, it may be necessary to rename the bound type variable in the type of e to match the type variable τ in the $\mathbf{open}$ expression.

Existential types can be used to desugar the abstract type definitions described in the previous section:

$$\mathbf{letabstype}\ \tau \equiv \theta\ \mathbf{with}\ v_{0\theta_0} \equiv e_0,\ \ldots,\ v_{n-1\theta_{n-1}} \equiv e_{n-1}\ \mathbf{in}\ e$$

$$\overset{\mathrm{def}}{=}\ \mathbf{open}\,(\mathbf{pack}\ \theta\ \mathbf{with}\ \langle e_0, \ldots, e_{n-1}\rangle\ \mathbf{as}\ \exists \tau.\ \mathbf{prod}(\theta_0, \ldots, \theta_{n-1})) \tag{18.7}$$

$$\mathbf{as}\ \tau\ \mathbf{with}\ \langle v_0, \ldots, v_{n-1}\rangle\ \mathbf{in}\ e.$$

Using this definition, one can derive reduction rule (18.3) from (18.4), and type inference rule (18.2) from (18.5) and (18.6).

Moreover, existential types are useful in their own right. In particular, a program using an unimplemented abstract type can be realized by a function that accepts an argument, of existential type, that describes an implementation of the abstract type; then the program can be executed with different implementations by applying the function to different arguments.

For example, the existential type

$$\mathbf{lettranstype}\ \mathsf{complexsignature} \equiv \exists\,\mathsf{complex}.$$

$$\mathbf{prod}(\mathsf{complex}, \mathbf{real} \to \mathsf{complex},$$

$$\mathsf{complex} \to \mathsf{complex} \to \mathsf{complex}, \mathsf{complex} \to \mathsf{complex} \to \mathsf{complex}, \tag{18.8}$$

$$\mathsf{complex} \to \mathsf{complex}, \mathsf{complex} \to \mathbf{real})$$

can be used to describe an abstract type of complex numbers with the primitive operations specified in the example given in the previous section. If E is an expression of type θ in which these primitives are used to manipulate complex numbers, then the function

$$\lambda c_{\mathsf{complexsignature}}.\ \mathbf{open}\ c\ \mathbf{as}\ \mathsf{complex}\ \mathbf{with}$$

$$\langle \mathsf{i}, \mathsf{conv}, \mathsf{addc}, \mathsf{multc}, \mathsf{conj}, \mathsf{magn}\rangle\ \mathbf{in}\ E,$$

of type complexsignature $\rightarrow \theta$, expresses E as a function of an implementation of complex numbers and their primitives. To use an implementation of complex numbers via rectangular coordinates (as in the previous section), one could apply this function to

> **pack real $\times$ real with**
>
> $\langle\langle 0, 1\rangle,$
>
> $\lambda r_{\mathbf{real}}.\ \langle r, 0\rangle,$
>
> $\lambda x_{\mathbf{real}\times\mathbf{real}}.\ \lambda y_{\mathbf{real}\times\mathbf{real}}.\ \langle x.0 + y.0, x.1 + y.1\rangle,$
>
> $\lambda x_{\mathbf{real}\times\mathbf{real}}.\ \lambda y_{\mathbf{real}\times\mathbf{real}}.\ \langle x.0 \times y.0 - x.1 \times y.1, x.0 \times y.1 + x.1 \times y.0\rangle,$ (18.9)
>
> $\lambda x_{\mathbf{real}\times\mathbf{real}}.\ \langle x.0, -x.1\rangle,$
>
> $\lambda x_{\mathbf{real}\times\mathbf{real}}.\ \mathsf{squareroot}(x.0 \times x.0 + x.1 \times x.1)\rangle$
>
> **as complexsignature.**

On the other hand, to use a polar-coordinate implementation, one could apply the same function to

> **pack real $\times$ real with**
>
> $\langle\langle 1, \pi/2\rangle,$
>
> $\lambda r_{\mathbf{real}}.\ \langle r, 0\rangle,$
>
> $\lambda x_{\mathbf{real}\times\mathbf{real}}.\ \lambda y_{\mathbf{real}\times\mathbf{real}}.\ \langle \ldots, \ldots\rangle,$
>
> $\lambda x_{\mathbf{real}\times\mathbf{real}}.\ \lambda y_{\mathbf{real}\times\mathbf{real}}.\ \langle x.0 \times y.0, x.1 + y.1\rangle,$ (18.10)
>
> $\lambda x_{\mathbf{real}\times\mathbf{real}}.\ \langle x.0, -x.1\rangle,$
>
> $\lambda x_{\mathbf{real}\times\mathbf{real}}.\ x.0\rangle$
>
> **as complexsignature.**

(It is an accident of the example that the representation type **real $\times$ real** is the same in both implementations. The complicated details of addition in polar coordinates have been cravenly omitted.)

As a second example, we consider finite *multisets* (sometimes called *bags*) of integers. Mathematically, such a multiset is a function from integers to nonnegative integers that gives zero for all but a finite number of arguments. (Informally, this function maps each integer into the number of times it occurs in the multiset.) The existential type

> **lettranstype** multisetsignature $\equiv \exists$multiset.
>
> **prod**(multiset, **int** $\rightarrow$ multiset $\rightarrow$ multiset, (18.11)
>
> **int** $\rightarrow$ multiset $\rightarrow$ multiset, **int** $\rightarrow$ multiset $\rightarrow$ **int**)

describes a constant and three primitive functions:

$$\mathsf{emptymset} = \lambda n \in \mathbf{Z}.\ 0$$

$$\mathsf{insertmset}\ i\ m = [\,m\ |\ i\!:\! m\ i + 1\,]$$

$$\mathsf{deletemset}\ i\ m = [\,m\ |\ i\!:\!\mathbf{if}\ m\ i = 0\ \mathbf{then}\ 0\ \mathbf{else}\ m\ i - 1\,]$$

$$\mathsf{countmset}\ i\ m = m\ i.$$

Computationally, we can represent a multiset by a list of integers, such that the count of an integer in the multiset is the number of its occurrences in the list. This leads to the following representation (where we assume eager evaluation):

> **pack list int with**
>> $\langle \mathbf{nil}_{\mathsf{int}},$
>
> $\lambda i_{\mathsf{int}}.\ \lambda m_{\mathsf{list\ int}}.\ i :: m,$
>
> **letrec** $\mathsf{deletemset}_{\mathsf{int} \to \mathsf{list\ int} \to \mathsf{list\ int}} \equiv \lambda i_{\mathsf{int}}.\ \lambda m_{\mathsf{list\ int}}.$
>> **listcase m of** $(\mathbf{nil}_{\mathsf{int}}, \lambda j_{\mathsf{int}}.\ \lambda n_{\mathsf{list\ int}}.$
>>> **if** $i = j$ **then** n **else** j :: deletemset i n$)$
>
>> **in** deletemset,
>
> **letrec** $\mathsf{countmset}_{\mathsf{int} \to \mathsf{list\ int} \to \mathsf{int}} \equiv \lambda i_{\mathsf{int}}.\ \lambda m_{\mathsf{list\ int}}.$
>> **listcase m of** $(0, \lambda j_{\mathsf{int}}.\ \lambda n_{\mathsf{list\ int}}.$
>>> **if** $i = j$ **then** (countmset i n)$ + 1$ **else** countmset i n$)$
>
>> **in** countmset$\rangle$
>
> **as** multisetsignature.

$$(18.12)$$

Sometimes it is necessary to package several abstract types with primitive functions between them; for this purpose, the existential quantifier can be repeated. As an example, consider a geometry module containing the abstract types **point** and **line**, along with primitive functions such as **through** and **intersect** that map between these types. An appropriate signature would be

> **lettranstype** geometrysignature $\equiv \exists$ point. $\exists$ line.
>> $\mathbf{prod}(\mathsf{point} \to \mathsf{point} \to \mathsf{line}, \mathsf{line} \to \mathsf{line} \to \mathsf{point}, \ldots).$

To create and use values of such a type it is convenient to extend the **pack** and **open** operations to work with more than one type:

> $\langle\mathrm{exp}\rangle ::= \mathbf{pack}\ \langle\mathrm{type}\rangle, \ldots, \langle\mathrm{type}\rangle\ \mathbf{with}\ \langle\mathrm{exp}\rangle\ \mathbf{as}\ \langle\mathrm{type}\rangle$
>
> $\quad\ |\ \mathbf{open}\ \langle\mathrm{exp}\rangle\ \mathbf{as}\ \langle\mathrm{tvar}\rangle, \ldots, \langle\mathrm{tvar}\rangle\ \mathbf{with}\ \langle\mathrm{pat}\rangle\ \mathbf{in}\ \langle\mathrm{exp}\rangle$

The appropriate reduction rule for this generalization is

$$\textbf{open} \, (\textbf{pack} \, \theta_0, \ldots, \theta_{n-1} \, \textbf{with} \, e \, \textbf{as} \, \exists \tau_0. \, \cdots \, \exists \tau_{n-1}. \, \theta')$$

$$\textbf{as} \, \tau_0, \ldots, \tau_{n-1} \, \textbf{with} \, p \, \textbf{in} \, e' \qquad\qquad (18.13)$$

$$\rightarrow ((\lambda p. \, e')/\tau_0 \rightarrow \theta_0, \, \ldots, \, \tau_{n-1} \rightarrow \theta_{n-1})e,$$

while the relevant type inference rules are

TY RULE: Explicit Multiple $\exists$ Introduction

$$\frac{\pi \vdash e : (\theta'/\tau_0 \rightarrow \theta_0, \, \ldots, \, \tau_{n-1} \rightarrow \theta_{n-1})}{\pi \vdash \textbf{pack} \, \theta_0, \ldots, \theta_{n-1} \, \textbf{with} \, e \, \textbf{as} \, \exists \tau_0. \, \cdots \, \exists \tau_{n-1}. \, \theta' : \exists \tau_0. \, \cdots \, \exists \tau_{n-1}. \, \theta',} \quad (18.14)$$

TY RULE: Explicit Multiple $\exists$ Elimination

$$\frac{\pi \vdash e : \exists \tau_0. \, \cdots \, \exists \tau_{n-1}. \, \theta' \qquad \pi, p : \theta' \vdash e' : \theta''}{\pi \vdash \textbf{open} \, e \, \textbf{as} \, \tau_0, \ldots, \tau_{n-1} \, \textbf{with} \, p \, \textbf{in} \, e' : \theta''} \quad (18.15)$$

when $\tau_0, \ldots, \tau_{n-1}$ do not occur free in θ'' or in any type expression in π.

For example, an implementation of the type geometrysignature might be used by a function of the form

$$\lambda g_{\text{geometrysignature}}. \, \textbf{open} \, g \, \textbf{as} \, \text{point}, \text{line} \, \textbf{with} \, \langle \text{through}, \text{intersect}, \ldots \rangle \, \textbf{in} \, E,$$

and might be defined (assuming that points are represented by pairs of reals and lines by triples of reals) by

$$\textbf{pack real} \times \textbf{real}, \textbf{real} \times \textbf{real} \times \textbf{real with}$$

$$\langle \lambda x_{\text{real} \times \text{real}}. \, \lambda y_{\text{real} \times \text{real}}. \, \cdots ,$$

$$\lambda a_{\text{real} \times \text{real} \times \text{real}}. \, \lambda b_{\text{real} \times \text{real} \times \text{real}}. \, \cdots ,$$

$$\cdots \rangle$$

$$\textbf{as geometrysignature}.$$

Readers who are familiar with Standard ML will recognize that

- SML signatures play the same role as existential types.
- SML structures play the same role as values of existential type.
- SML functors play the same role as functions with arguments of existential type.

(The last correspondence raises some complications that will be discussed in the next section.) Actually, signatures in SML are named products in which some components range over types while other components range over values whose types can depend on earlier components. For example, **geometrysignature** might be (in our notation)

$$\textbf{signature}(\text{point: } \textbf{type},$$

$$\text{line: } \textbf{type},$$

$$\text{through: point} \times \text{point} \to \text{line},$$

$$\text{intersect: line} \times \text{line} \to \text{point},$$

$$\cdots),$$

while a value satisfying this signature might be

$$\textbf{structure}(\text{point: } \textbf{real} \times \textbf{real},$$

$$\text{line: } \textbf{real} \times \textbf{real} \times \textbf{real},$$

$$\text{through: } \lambda x_{\textbf{real} \times \textbf{real}}. \ \lambda y_{\textbf{real} \times \textbf{real}}. \ \cdots,$$

$$\text{intersect: } \lambda a_{\textbf{real} \times \textbf{real} \times \textbf{real}}. \ \lambda b_{\textbf{real} \times \textbf{real} \times \textbf{real}}. \ \cdots,$$

$$\cdots).$$

In practice, the approach used in Standard ML provides a more succinct way of associating names with the components of signatures and structures than that developed in this section. To define such a dependent-product approach rigorously, however, would require a sizable digression that would not clarify any basic principles.

18.3 Implementing One Abstraction in Terms of Another

In complex programs, one often needs modules that express the implementation of abstract types and their operations in terms of other abstract types and operations, which are defined by other modules. As a simple example, a module might describe the implementation of finite sets by finite multisets whose count never exceeds one.

The existential type

$$\textbf{lettranstype setsignature} \equiv \exists \text{set}.$$

$$\textbf{prod}(\text{set}, \textbf{int} \to \text{set} \to \text{set},$$

$$\textbf{int} \to \text{set} \to \text{set}, \textbf{int} \to \text{set} \to \textbf{bool})$$

describes a constant and three primitive functions:

$$\text{emptyset} = \{\}$$

$$\text{insertset } i \ s = s \cup \{i\}$$

$$\text{deleteset } i \ s = s - \{i\}$$

$$\text{memberset } i \ s = i \in s.$$

It is straightforward to give a **pack** expression of this type that expresses sets and their primitive operations in terms of multisets and their primitives. One can then use **open** to abstract this expression on the implementation of multisets, which gives the function

> **let** F $\equiv$ λmset$_{\text{multisetsignature}}$.
>
> > **open** mset **as** multiset
> >
> > > **with** $\langle$emptymset, insertmset, deletemset, countmset$\rangle$ **in**
> >
> > **pack** multiset **with**
> >
> > > $\langle$emptymset,
> > >
> > > λi$_{\text{int}}$. λs$_{\text{multiset}}$. **if** countmset i s $= 0$ **then** insertmset i s **else** s,
> > >
> > > deletemset,
> > >
> > > λi$_{\text{int}}$. λs$_{\text{multiset}}$. countmset i s $\neq 0\rangle$
> >
> > **as** setsignature,

of type

$$\text{multisetsignature} \rightarrow \text{setsignature},$$

where multisetsignature is defined by the transparent type definition (18.11) in the previous section. This function can then be applied to any implementation of finite multisets (such as the **pack** expression (18.12) in the previous section) to obtain a representation of finite sets.

Unfortunately, however, things do not always work out so simply. Suppose, for example, that we try to construct a module describing the implementation of complex vectors in terms of complex numbers.

The following expression describes the representation of two-dimensional complex vectors by pairs of complex numbers, and defines two independent basis vectors, a function for adding vectors, a function for multiplying a vector by a complex number, and a function for finding the vector product of two vectors (which is a complex number):

> **pack** complex $\times$ complex **with**
>
> > $\langle\langle$conv 1, conv 0$\rangle$,
> >
> > $\langle$conv 0, conv 1$\rangle$,
> >
> > λv$_{\text{complex}\times\text{complex}}$. λw$_{\text{complex}\times\text{complex}}$. $\langle$addc v.0 w.0, addc v.1 w.1$\rangle$,
> >
> > λv$_{\text{complex}\times\text{complex}}$. λc$_{\text{complex}}$. $\langle$multc v.0 c, multc v.1 c$\rangle$,
> >
> > λv$_{\text{complex}\times\text{complex}}$. λw$_{\text{complex}\times\text{complex}}$.
> >
> > > addc(multc v.0 (conj w.0))(multc v.1 (conj w.1))$\rangle$
> >
> > **as** $\exists$ cvector. θ_{cvector},

where $\theta_{\mathrm{cvector}}$ is the type

$$\textbf{prod}(\mathsf{cvector}, \mathsf{cvector}, \mathsf{cvector} \rightarrow \mathsf{cvector} \rightarrow \mathsf{cvector},$$

$$\mathsf{cvector} \rightarrow \mathsf{complex} \rightarrow \mathsf{cvector}, \mathsf{cvector} \rightarrow \mathsf{cvector} \rightarrow \mathsf{complex}).$$

So far, this is not significantly different from what we have done before. But a problem arises when we try to abstract the above **pack** expression to describe its value as a function of an implementation of complex numbers. Proceeding as in the previous example, we might define the function

> **let** $\mathsf{F} \equiv \lambda\mathsf{c}_{\exists\,\mathsf{complex}.\;\theta_{\mathrm{complex}}}\,.$
>
> > **open** c **as** $\mathsf{complex}$ **with** $\langle\mathsf{i}, \mathsf{conv}, \mathsf{addc}, \mathsf{multc}, \mathsf{conj}, \mathsf{magn}\rangle$ **in**
> >
> > > **pack** $\mathsf{complex} \times \mathsf{complex}$ **with**
> > >
> > > > $\langle\langle\mathsf{conv}\ 1, \mathsf{conv}\ 0\rangle, \dots\rangle$
> > >
> > > **as** $\exists\,\mathsf{cvector}.\;\theta_{\mathrm{cvector}},$

where $\theta_{\mathrm{complex}}$ is the type

$$\textbf{prod}(\mathsf{complex}, \textbf{real} \rightarrow \mathsf{complex},$$

$$\mathsf{complex} \rightarrow \mathsf{complex} \rightarrow \mathsf{complex}, \mathsf{complex} \rightarrow \mathsf{complex} \rightarrow \mathsf{complex},$$

$$\mathsf{complex} \rightarrow \mathsf{complex}, \mathsf{complex} \rightarrow \textbf{real})$$

(so that $\exists\,\mathsf{complex}.\;\theta_{\mathrm{complex}}$ is the type $\mathsf{complexsignature}$ defined by (18.8) in the previous section). One might expect this to give F the type

$$(\exists\,\mathsf{complex}.\;\theta_{\mathrm{complex}}) \rightarrow (\exists\,\mathsf{cvector}.\;\theta_{\mathrm{cvector}}),$$

but this type does not make sense, since there are occurrences of $\mathsf{complex}$ in $\theta_{\mathrm{cvector}}$ that are outside the scope of the binder of $\mathsf{complex}$ — reflecting the fact that $\theta_{\mathrm{cvector}}$ describes a collection of primitive operations that deal with *both* complex vectors and complex numbers.

In fact, the above expression for F is ill-typed, because it violates the proviso "when τ does not occur free in θ'' or ..." (where τ is $\mathsf{complex}$ and θ'' is $\exists\,\mathsf{cvector}.\;\theta_{\mathrm{cvector}}$) in the rule for $\exists$ elimination ((18.6) in the previous section).

To resolve this difficulty, one can pack the type $\mathsf{complex}$ into the result of F:

> **let** $\mathsf{F} \equiv \lambda\mathsf{c}_{\exists\,\mathsf{complex}.\;\theta_{\mathrm{complex}}}\,.$
>
> > **open** c **as** $\mathsf{complex}$ **with** $\langle\mathsf{i}, \mathsf{conv}, \mathsf{addc}, \mathsf{multc}, \mathsf{conj}, \mathsf{magn}\rangle$ **in**
> >
> > > **pack** $\mathsf{complex}, \mathsf{complex} \times \mathsf{complex}$ **with** $\qquad\qquad$ (18.16)
> > >
> > > > $\langle\langle\mathsf{conv}\ 1, \mathsf{conv}\ 0\rangle, \dots\rangle$
> > >
> > > **as** $\exists\,\mathsf{complex}.\;\exists\,\mathsf{cvector}.\;\theta_{\mathrm{cvector}}.$

This expression for F is well-typed, with the type

$$(\exists\,\mathsf{complex}.\;\theta_{\mathrm{complex}}) \rightarrow (\exists\,\mathsf{complex}.\;\exists\,\mathsf{cvector}.\;\theta_{\mathrm{cvector}}). \qquad\qquad (18.17)$$

A problem, however, arises when one tries to use F. After defining F as above, and a complex-number implementation ci of type $\exists$ complex. θ_{complex} (such as the **pack** expression (18.9) in the previous section), one might expect to write

> **open** ci as complex **with** $\langle$i, conv, addc, multc, conj, magn$\rangle$ **in**
>
>   **open** F ci as complex$'$, cvector **with** $\langle$b0, b1, addv, multv, vprod$\rangle$ **in**   (18.18)
>
>   magn(vprod(multv b0 i)(multv b1 (conv 3.5))).

This looks plausible but, as the reader may verify, it does not type check. In the final line, i and (conv 3.5) have type complex but appear in contexts requiring complex$'$, while (vprod $\cdots$) has type complex$'$ but appears in a context requiring complex. (The situation cannot be saved by replacing complex$'$ by complex, since, when rule (18.15) is applied to the inner **open** expression, the proviso in this rule will force a renaming that distinguishes complex$'$ from complex.)

This is more than a failure of renaming. The real problem is that, in the type (18.17), the two bindings of complex can stand for two different types. Thus, for example, (18.16) would continue to have the type (18.17) if **open** c **as** $\cdots$ were replaced by **open** c' **as** $\cdots$, where c' might be any expression (say, (18.10)) of type $\exists$ complex. θ_{complex}. But once c and c' are different, complex and complex$'$ in expression (18.18) can be different, so that the last line of (18.18) does not make sense.

In Standard ML this problem, which might be described as excessive abstraction, is alleviated by the introduction of *sharing* constraints, which are beyond the scope of this book. More general solutions to the problem are a topic of current research in type theory.

Here, we note that a straightforward solution is to make F a polymorphic function accepting the type complex. Suppose we define

> **let** F $\equiv$ Λcomplex. $\lambda\langle$i, conv, addc, multc, conj, magn$\rangle_{\theta_{\text{complex}}}$.
>
>   **pack** complex $\times$ complex **with**
>
> $\langle\langle$conv 1, conv 0$\rangle$, $\dots\rangle$
>
>   **as** $\exists$ cvector. θ_{cvector},

which has the type

$$\forall\, \text{complex}. \ (\theta_{\text{complex}} \to (\exists\, \text{cvector}. \ \theta_{\text{cvector}})).$$

Then F can be used by writing

> **open** ci as complex **with** $\langle$i, conv, addc, multc, conj, magn$\rangle$ **in**
>
>   **open** F[complex]$\langle$i, conv, addc, multc, conj, magn$\rangle$
>
>   **as** cvector **with** $\langle$b0, b1, addv, multv, vprod$\rangle$ **in**
>
>   magn(vprod(multv b0 i)(multv b1 (conv 3.5))).

Bibliographic Notes

The use of existential types to describe abstract types was discovered by Mitchell and Plotkin [1985], who also described the desugaring of **letabstype**. An alternative desugaring in terms of polymorphic types (discussed in Exercise 18.3 below) appeared in Reynolds [1974].

The problem raised in Section 18.3 was discussed by MacQueen [1986], who noted the possibility of using polymorphic functions, but preferred a solution based on "transparent" existential types. A more general approach, based on "translucent" existential types, has been explored by Harper and Lillibridge [1994] and Lillibridge [1997].

The Standard ML module facility has been formalized by Harper, Milner, and Tofte [1987], Harper and Mitchell [1993], and Harper, Mitchell, and Moggi [1990].

Exercises

18.1   Use definition (18.7) of **letabstype** and inference rules (18.5) and (18.6), in Section 18.2, to derive inference rule (18.2) in Section 18.1.

18.2   Show that reduction rule (18.3) in Section 18.1 satisfies subject reduction but not the conservation of typing judgements. Specifically:

   (a) Assume the premisses of inference rule (18.2) in Section 18.1, and prove

$$\pi \vdash ((\lambda v_{0\theta_0}. \ \cdots \ \lambda v_{n-1\theta_{n-1}}. \ e)/\tau \to \theta)\, e_0 \cdots e_{n-1} : \theta'.$$

   Hint You will need to use the results of Exercises 15.9 and 17.12.

   (b) Find a provable instance of the above typing such that the corresponding instance of some premiss of rule (18.2) cannot be proved.

18.3   The abstract type definition can be desugared into a polymorphic expression where one abstracts on the type variable being defined and then applies the resulting polymorphic function to the representation type:

letabstype $\tau \equiv \theta$ **with** $v_{0\theta_0} \equiv e_0, \ldots, v_{n-1\theta_{n-1}} \equiv e_{n-1}$ **in** e

$$\overset{\text{def}}{=} (\Lambda\tau. \ \lambda v_{0\theta_0}. \ \cdots \ \lambda v_{n-1\theta_{n-1}}. \ e)\,[\theta]\, e_0 \cdots e_{n-1}.$$

Use this definition to derive the following typing rule:

$$\pi \vdash e_0 : (\theta_0/\tau \to \theta)$$

$$\vdots$$

$$\pi \vdash e_{n-1} : (\theta_{n-1}/\tau \to \theta)$$
$$\pi, v_0 : \theta_0, \ldots, v_{n-1} : \theta_{n-1} \vdash e : \theta'$$

$$\overline{\pi \vdash \textbf{letabstype } \tau \equiv \theta \textbf{ with } v_{0\theta_0} \equiv e_0, \ldots, v_{n-1\theta_{n-1}} \equiv e_{n-1} \textbf{ in } e : \theta'/\tau \to \theta}$$

when τ does not occur free in any type expression in π. Notice that this rule is more general than (18.2) in Section 18.1, in the sense that this rule will permit the inference of more typing judgments. Discuss whether the extra generality is desirable.

18.4 Show that explicit-transfer recursive types can be defined in terms of implicit-transfer recursive types and abstract types. Specifically, use the definition

$$\textbf{letrectype } \tau \equiv \theta \textbf{ in } e$$
$$\overset{\text{def}}{=} \textbf{letabstype } \tau \equiv \mu\tau.\,\theta$$
$$\textbf{with open } \tau_{\tau\to\theta} \equiv \lambda v.\,v, \textbf{close } \tau_{\theta\to\tau} \equiv \lambda v.\,v \textbf{ in } e$$

to derive type inference rule (15.26) in Section 15.7. (As in the statement of rule (15.26), we are abusing our formalism in treating $\textbf{open }\tau$ and $\textbf{close }\tau$ as identifiers.)

Hint You will need to use the unwinding equation $\mu\tau.\,\theta = \theta/\tau \to (\mu\tau.\,\theta)$.

18.5 Mathematically, a one-dimensional array of length n whose elements have type α is a function from the interval 0 **to** $n-1$ to the set of values of type α. Suitable primitive functions are

$$\textsf{make} \in \textbf{int} \to \alpha \to \textsf{array}$$
$$\textsf{lookup} \in \textsf{array} \to \textbf{int} \to \alpha$$
$$\textsf{update} \in \textsf{array} \to \textbf{int} \to \alpha \to \textsf{array}$$

such that

$$\textsf{make } n\, r = \lambda i \in 0 \textbf{ to } n-1.\, r$$
$$\textsf{lookup } a\, i = \textbf{if } i \in \text{dom } a \textbf{ then } a\, i \textbf{ else error}$$
$$\textsf{update } a\, i\, r = \textbf{if } i \in \text{dom } a \textbf{ then } [\,a \mid i{:}r\,] \textbf{ else error},$$

so that the appropriate type for an implementation of one-dimensional arrays is

$$\textbf{lettranstype } \textsf{onearraysignature} \equiv \forall \alpha.\, \exists \textsf{array}.$$
$$\textbf{prod}(\textbf{int} \to \alpha \to \textsf{array}, \textsf{array} \to \textbf{int} \to \alpha,$$
$$\textsf{array} \to \textbf{int} \to \alpha \to \textsf{array}).$$

(Note that this is an existential type that is universally quantified over the type parameter α describing array elements.) Similarly, a two-dimensional array of width m and length n whose elements have type α is a function from $(0 \textbf{ to } m-1) \times (0 \textbf{ to } n-1)$ to the set of values of type α, with primitives

$$\mathsf{make} \in \mathbf{int} \times \mathbf{int} \to \alpha \to \mathsf{array}$$

$$\mathsf{lookup} \in \mathsf{array} \to \mathbf{int} \times \mathbf{int} \to \alpha$$

$$\mathsf{update} \in \mathsf{array} \to \mathbf{int} \times \mathbf{int} \to \alpha \to \mathsf{array}$$

such that

$$\mathsf{make}\ n\ r = \lambda \langle i \in 0\ \mathbf{to}\ m-1, j \in 0\ \mathbf{to}\ n-1 \rangle.\ r$$

$$\mathsf{lookup}\ a\ \langle i, j \rangle = \mathbf{if}\ \langle i, j \rangle \in \mathrm{dom}\ a\ \mathbf{then}\ a\ \langle i, j \rangle\ \mathbf{else\ error}$$

$$\mathsf{update}\ a\ \langle i, j \rangle\ r = \mathbf{if}\ \langle i, j \rangle \in \mathrm{dom}\ a\ \mathbf{then}\ [\,a \mid \langle i, j \rangle{:}r\,]\ \mathbf{else\ error},$$

so that the appropriate type for an implementation of two-dimensional arrays is

$$\mathbf{lettranstype}\ \mathsf{twoarraysignature} \equiv \forall \alpha.\ \exists \mathsf{array}.$$

$$\mathbf{prod}(\mathbf{int} \times \mathbf{int} \to \alpha \to \mathsf{array}, \mathsf{array} \to \mathbf{int} \times \mathbf{int} \to \alpha,$$

$$\mathsf{array} \to \mathbf{int} \times \mathbf{int} \to \alpha \to \mathsf{array}).$$

(a) Write an expression of type onearraysignature that describes the implementation of one-dimensional arrays of length n by lists of length n, where the array element $a\ i$ is given by the ith list element.

(b) Write an expression of type onearraysignature that describes the implementation of a one-dimensional array by a binary tree, in the sense of Section 11.5, paired with the length of the array. Specifically,

- $\langle @\ 0\ r, n \rangle$ should represent an array of length n, all of whose elements are r.
- $\langle @\ 1\ \langle a_l, a_r \rangle, n \rangle$ should represent the concatenation of the arrays represented by $\langle a_l, n \div 2 \rangle$ and by $\langle a_r, n - n \div 2 \rangle$.

Hint A recursive definition of the type of binary trees is given in Section 15.7.

(c) Write an expression of type onearraysignature $\to$ twoarraysignature that describes the implementation of a two-dimensional array a_2 of width m and length n in terms of the implementation of a one-dimensional array a_1 of width $m \times n$, such that $a_2 \langle i, j \rangle = a_1 (i + j \times m)$.

(d) Write an expression of type onearraysignature $\to$ twoarraysignature that describes the implementation of a two-dimensional array a_2 of width m and length n as a one-dimensional array of length n of one-dimensional arrays of length m.

18.6 The **pack** and **open** operations for repeated existential quantifiers that were introduced in Section 18.2 can be defined in terms of the operations for a single quantifier:

$$\textbf{pack } \theta_0, \ldots, \theta_{n-1} \textbf{ with } e \textbf{ as } \exists \tau_0. \; \cdots \; \exists \tau_{n-1}. \; \theta'$$

$$\overset{\text{def}}{=} \textbf{pack } \theta_0 \textbf{ with}$$

$$\textbf{pack } \theta_1 \textbf{ with}$$

$$\cdot_{\cdot_\cdot}$$

$$\textbf{pack } \theta_{n-1} \textbf{ with}$$

$$e$$

$$\textbf{as } (\exists \tau_{n-1}. \; \theta')/\tau_0 \rightarrow \theta_0, \; \ldots, \; \tau_{n-2} \rightarrow \tau_{n-2}$$

$$\cdot^{\cdot^\cdot}$$

$$\textbf{as } (\exists \tau_1. \; \cdots \; \exists \tau_{n-1}. \; \theta')/\tau_0 \rightarrow \theta_0$$

$$\textbf{as } \exists \tau_0. \; \cdots \; \exists \tau_{n-1}. \; \theta'$$

$$\textbf{open } e \textbf{ as } \tau_0, \ldots, \tau_{n-1} \textbf{ with } p \textbf{ in } e'$$

$$\overset{\text{def}}{=} \textbf{open } e \textbf{ as } \tau_0 \textbf{ with } v_0 \textbf{ in}$$

$$\textbf{open } v_0 \textbf{ as } \tau_1 \textbf{ with } v_1 \textbf{ in}$$

$$\cdot_{\cdot_\cdot}$$

$$\textbf{open } v_{n-2} \textbf{ as } \tau_{n-1} \textbf{ with } p \textbf{ in } e'$$

where $v_0, \ldots, v_{n-2}$ are distinct variables that are not in $\mathrm{FV}(e') - \mathrm{FV}_{\mathrm{pat}}(p)$.

Use these definitions to derive reduction rule (18.13) from (18.4), and type inference rules (18.14) and (18.15) from (18.5) and (18.6) (in Section 18.2).

18.7 If there is a partial order for some type α, one can define an elementwise partial order for type **list** α by saying that $x \leq x'$ if and only if x and x' have the same length and corresponding elements satisfy $x_i \leq x'_i$.

(a) Define the order for lists in terms of the order for the type of their items.

(b) Package this definition as modules of three different types:

$$(\exists \alpha. \; \alpha \rightarrow \alpha \rightarrow \textbf{bool}) \rightarrow (\exists \alpha. \; \alpha \rightarrow \alpha \rightarrow \textbf{bool})$$

$$\forall \alpha. \; ((\alpha \rightarrow \alpha \rightarrow \textbf{bool}) \rightarrow (\exists \alpha. \; \alpha \rightarrow \alpha \rightarrow \textbf{bool}))$$

$$\forall \alpha. \; ((\alpha \rightarrow \alpha \rightarrow \textbf{bool}) \rightarrow (\textbf{list } \alpha \rightarrow \textbf{list } \alpha \rightarrow \textbf{bool})).$$

(c) Discuss the usability of the three packages in part (b).

18.8   Existential quantification and its associated operations can be defined in
        terms of universal quantification. Specifically, one can define

$$\exists \tau.\ \theta' \overset{\text{def}}{=} \forall \alpha.\ (\forall \tau.\ (\theta' \to \alpha)) \to \alpha,$$

where the type variable α is distinct from τ and does not occur free in θ',

$$\textbf{pack } \theta \textbf{ with } e \textbf{ as } \exists \tau.\ \theta' \overset{\text{def}}{=} \Lambda \alpha.\ \lambda v_{\forall \tau.\ (\theta' \to \alpha)}.\ v[\theta]e,$$

where α is distinct from τ and does not occur free in θ, θ', or e, and v
does not occur free in e, and

$$\textbf{open}_{\theta''}\ e \textbf{ as } \tau \textbf{ with } p_{\theta'} \textbf{ in } e' \overset{\text{def}}{=} e[\theta''](\Lambda \tau.\ \lambda p_{\theta'}.\ e').$$

(Note that the left side of the last definition is an explicitly typed variant
of the **open** expression.)

(a) Use the above definitions to derive inference rule (18.5) in Section
    18.2.
    Hint Without loss of generality, you may assume that α does not
    occur free in any type expression in π.

(b) Use the above definitions to derive the explicitly typed version of
    inference rule (18.6):

$$\frac{\pi \vdash e : \exists \tau.\ \theta' \qquad \pi, p : \theta' \vdash e' : \theta''}{\pi \vdash \textbf{open}_{\theta''}\ e \textbf{ as } \tau \textbf{ with } p_{\theta'} \textbf{ in } e' : \theta''}$$

when τ does not occur free in θ'' or in any type expression in π.

(c) Use the above definitions to derive the explicitly typed version of
    reduction rule (18.4):

$$\textbf{open}_{\theta''}\ (\textbf{pack } \theta \textbf{ with } e \textbf{ as } \exists \tau.\ \theta') \textbf{ as } \tau \textbf{ with } p_{\theta'} \textbf{ in } e'$$

$$\to ((\lambda p.\ e')/\tau \to \theta)e.$$

Hint Without loss of generality, you may assume that τ does not
occur free in θ''.

19

Algol-like Languages

In this chapter, we introduce a class of languages that combine imperative and functional features in a very different way than the Iswim-like languages of Chapter 13. Algol-like languages are based on normal-order evaluation, and they distinguish two kinds of types, called data types and phrase types. In contrast to Iswim-like languages, they can be implemented by allocating storage on a stack, without any form of garbage collection; thus they are more efficient but more limited in the variety of programs that can be expressed reasonably. They are theoretically cleaner — in particular, β-reduction preserves meaning. Nevertheless, they still exhibit the complications of aliasing that characterized Iswim-like languages.

The original Algol-like language, Algol 60, was (along with Lisp) the earliest language to combine a powerful procedure mechanism with imperative features. By intentionally concentrating on the desired behavior of the language rather than its implementation, the designers of Algol 60 raised problems of implementation and definition that were a fruitful challenge over the following decade. In particular, the language inspired the definitional ideas of Strachey and Landin that, paradoxically, led to Iswim-like languages.

Since then, a few Algol-like languages, such as Algol W and especially Simula 67, have attracted communities of users. At present, however, the acceptance of Iswim-like languages is far wider. Nevertheless, there has been a spate of theoretical interest in the last decade that suggests the Algol framework may inspire new languages which, if they can overcome the limitations of the stack discipline without compromising linguistic cleanliness, will find significant acceptance. As is usually the case with intellectually significant programming languages, it is the underlying ideas, rather than the language itself, that are likely to prosper.

The distinctive character of Algol-like languages lies in the way procedures are explained, by means of a "copy rule" that is closer to "macro expansion" than to the usual idea of calling a subroutine. In modern terminology, an Algol program is a phrase of a normal-order-evaluation typed lambda calculus with an explicit fixed-point operator. To find the meaning of a procedure application, one simply reduces the program until the application disappears. (We use the term *phrase* rather than "expression" since expressions will be one of several kinds of phrases.)

Roughly speaking, therefore, the first phase of executing a program is to reduce it to normal form. In contrast to the functional languages we have considered in previous chapters, however, this normal form is not a value, but a program, specifically a command of the simple imperative language. Thus the second phase of executing a program is to execute its normal form (as described in Chapter 2):

Reduction of lambda calculus (copy rule)

| normal form

Execution of simple imperative language

The reason this is only roughly speaking is that, in the presence of a recursive procedure, the reduction process may never terminate. In this situation, however, the diagram above continues to make sense if the first phase is executed lazily: One begins the imperative execution as soon as possible, and only does further reduction when it is needed to eliminate a procedure application that is about to be executed.

Even in this interpretation, the diagram indicates that the flow of information between phases is one-way. Nothing that happens in the imperative execution, such as assignment to a variable, ever influences the reduction process. Thus an Algol-like language inherits the basic property of the lambda calculus that meaning does not depend on the order or timing of reductions.

Contrast this with what can happen in an Iswim-like language, where a program might contain a function-valued reference r. Then the result of reducing an application $(\textbf{val } r)(\cdots)$ will depend on the current value of r, and thus on when the reduction occurs, relative to the sequence of assignments that are executed in the imperative phase. In this situation, the procedure mechanism is completely stripped of its functional character.

19.1 Data Types and Phrase Types

The two-phase nature of Algol-like languages leads to two distinct kinds of types. For the simple imperative language, the relevant types, which we will call *data types*, describe sets of the values that are taken on by expressions and variables. In Chapter 2, albeit without being explicit about the matter, we used two data types, **int** and **bool**, but only permitted variables whose values had type **int**. Here (as in Algol 60) we will use three data types,

⟨data type⟩ ::= **int** | **real** | **bool**

and permit variables of all data types. We will also provide an implicit conversion from **int** to **real**, so that the subtype ordering for data types is

For the first phase, the relevant types, which we will call *phrase types*, are those of a simply typed lambda calculus. But the primitive types of this calculus will be quite different than in previous chapters. Since the reduction phase is intended to produce phrases of the imperative language, rather than values, the primitive phrase types will denote the different kinds of such phrases, rather than kinds of values. In fact, except for the addition of real expressions, and real and boolean variables, our primitive phrase types are simply the nonterminal symbols of the simple imperative language of Chapter 2:

$$\langle \text{phrase type} \rangle ::= \textbf{intexp} \mid \textbf{realexp} \mid \textbf{boolexp}$$
$$\mid \textbf{intvar} \mid \textbf{realvar} \mid \textbf{boolvar}$$
$$\mid \textbf{comm}$$

We can emphasize the connection between primitive phrase types and data types if we use the metavariable δ to range over $\langle \text{data type} \rangle$ and replace the above productions by the schema

$$\langle \text{phrase type} \rangle ::= \delta\textbf{exp} \mid \delta\textbf{var} \mid \textbf{comm}$$

Since a variable can always be used as an expression, we make each type of variable a subtype of the corresponding type of expression. Moreover, because of the implicit conversion from **int** to **real**, we can use an integer expression in any context calling for a real expression. Thus we have the subtyping rules

SBTY RULE: Variables to Expressions

$$\frac{}{\delta\textbf{var} \leq \delta\textbf{exp},} \tag{19.1}$$

SBTY RULE: Integer to Real Expressions

$$\frac{}{\textbf{intexp} \leq \textbf{realexp}.} \tag{19.2}$$

On the other hand, there is no subtyping relation between variables of different data types. For example, although an integer variable will always produce a value that can be converted to real, it cannot be assigned an arbitrary real value. Thus the subtype ordering of the primitive phrase types is

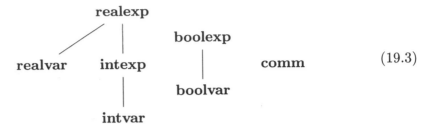

$$\tag{19.3}$$

To construct compound phrase types we need the $\to$ constructor of Chapter 15, which now describes procedures rather than functions:

$$\langle\text{phrase type}\rangle ::= \langle\text{phrase type}\rangle \to \langle\text{phrase type}\rangle$$

The subtyping rule for this constructor is the same as in Section 16.1:

SBTY RULE: Procedures

$$\frac{\theta'_0 \le \theta_0 \qquad \theta_1 \le \theta'_1}{\theta_0 \to \theta_1 \le \theta'_0 \to \theta'_1.} \tag{19.4}$$

We also need the standard rules that are common to all subtyping systems:

SBTY RULE: Reflexivity

$$\overline{\theta \le \theta,} \tag{19.5}$$

SBTY RULE: Transitivity

$$\frac{\theta \le \theta' \qquad \theta' \le \theta''}{\theta \le \theta''.} \tag{19.6}$$

In conclusion, a couple of warnings need to be sounded. We have presented the construction of Algol-like types in a way that emphasizes their naturality: One merely casts the simple imperative language into a typed framework and then adds the types of an equally simple functional language. But the result of this construction is quite different from the languages we have considered previously. For example, in an Iswim-like language, any expression can have side effects, and a command is just an expression that produces a dummy value, so that its only effects are its side effects. But now there is a much sharper distinction: As in the simple imperative language, expressions cannot have side effects, so that a command is in no sense an expression.

We also have two very different kinds of variables. The variables of the imperative language have become a type of phrase, which even includes compound phrases such as the application of a variable-returning procedure to an appropriate argument. On the other hand, the variables of the lambda calculus remain structureless members of a predefined set.

Clearly, this terminological collision must be resolved. It is tempting to call imperative variables "references", but in fact the imperative variables are a type of phrase while the references of Chapter 13 are a type of value. Instead, we will continue to call imperative variables "variables", and will follow the usage of Algol 60 in calling the lambda calculus variables "identifiers". (We have previously used identifiers to name the fields of tuples, but there is no reason not to use the same predefined set for both purposes.)

In what follows, we will have far more to say about phrase types than data types, which are relatively trivial in Algol-like languages. When we speak of a "type" without qualification, we will always mean a phrase type.

19.2 Phrases and Type Inference Rules

Since our Algol-like language combines the simple imperative language with a typed lambda calculus, the first step in describing its syntax and typing rules is to describe the simple imperative language. In addition to providing more data types, this description differs from that of Chapter 2 in using the type system, rather than the abstract syntax, to distinguish different kinds of phrases. Thus the abstract grammar defines only a single nonterminal $\langle$phrase$\rangle$:

$$\langle\text{phrase}\rangle ::= \textbf{true} \mid \textbf{false} \mid 0 \mid 1 \mid 2 \mid \cdots$$

$$\mid\ -\langle\text{phrase}\rangle \mid \langle\text{phrase}\rangle + \langle\text{phrase}\rangle \mid \langle\text{phrase}\rangle - \langle\text{phrase}\rangle \mid \langle\text{phrase}\rangle \times \langle\text{phrase}\rangle$$

$$\mid\ \langle\text{phrase}\rangle \div \langle\text{phrase}\rangle \mid \langle\text{phrase}\rangle\ \textbf{rem}\ \langle\text{phrase}\rangle \mid \langle\text{phrase}\rangle/\langle\text{phrase}\rangle$$

$$\mid\ \langle\text{phrase}\rangle = \langle\text{phrase}\rangle \mid \langle\text{phrase}\rangle \neq \langle\text{phrase}\rangle \mid \langle\text{phrase}\rangle < \langle\text{phrase}\rangle$$

$$\mid\ \langle\text{phrase}\rangle \leq \langle\text{phrase}\rangle \mid \langle\text{phrase}\rangle > \langle\text{phrase}\rangle \mid \langle\text{phrase}\rangle \geq \langle\text{phrase}\rangle$$

$$\mid\ \neg\langle\text{phrase}\rangle \mid \langle\text{phrase}\rangle \wedge \langle\text{phrase}\rangle \mid \langle\text{phrase}\rangle \vee \langle\text{phrase}\rangle$$

$$\mid\ \langle\text{phrase}\rangle \Rightarrow \langle\text{phrase}\rangle \mid \langle\text{phrase}\rangle \Leftrightarrow \langle\text{phrase}\rangle$$

$$\mid\ \langle\text{phrase}\rangle := \langle\text{phrase}\rangle \mid \textbf{skip} \mid \langle\text{phrase}\rangle\ ;\ \langle\text{phrase}\rangle$$

$$\mid\ \textbf{if}\ \langle\text{phrase}\rangle\ \textbf{then}\ \langle\text{phrase}\rangle\ \textbf{else}\ \langle\text{phrase}\rangle$$

$$\mid\ \textbf{while}\ \langle\text{phrase}\rangle\ \textbf{do}\ \langle\text{phrase}\rangle \mid \textbf{new}\ \delta\textbf{var}\ \langle\text{id}\rangle := \langle\text{phrase}\rangle\ \textbf{in}\ \langle\text{phrase}\rangle$$

Here $\langle$id$\rangle$ denotes the predefined set of identifiers. In the type inference rules, we will use the following metavariables:

π	$\langle$context$\rangle$	ι	$\langle$id$\rangle$
δ	$\langle$data type$\rangle$	p	$\langle$phrase$\rangle$
θ	$\langle$phrase type$\rangle$	k, m, n	$\mathbf{N}$,

where contexts are now sequences of identifiers, each paired with a phrase type. The rules for expressions are similar to those in Sections 15.2 and 16.5, adapted to our present choice of data types and operations:

TY RULE: Constants

$$\pi \vdash 0 : \mathbf{intexp} \qquad \pi \vdash \mathbf{true} : \mathbf{boolexp} \qquad (19.7)$$

(and similarly for 1, 2, ..., and **false**),

TY RULE: Arithmetic Operations

$$\frac{\pi \vdash p : \mathbf{intexp}}{\pi \vdash -p : \mathbf{intexp}} \qquad \frac{\pi \vdash p : \mathbf{realexp}}{\pi \vdash -p : \mathbf{realexp}}$$

$$\frac{\pi \vdash p_0 : \mathbf{intexp} \quad \pi \vdash p_1 : \mathbf{intexp}}{\pi \vdash p_0 + p_1 : \mathbf{intexp}} \qquad \frac{\pi \vdash p_0 : \mathbf{realexp} \quad \pi \vdash p_1 : \mathbf{realexp}}{\pi \vdash p_0 + p_1 : \mathbf{realexp}}$$

$$(19.8)$$

(and similarly for $-$ and $\times$),

TY RULE: Division and Remainder

$$\frac{\pi \vdash p_0 : \mathbf{intexp} \quad \pi \vdash p_1 : \mathbf{intexp}}{\pi \vdash p_0 \div p_1 : \mathbf{intexp}} \qquad \frac{\pi \vdash p_0 : \mathbf{intexp} \quad \pi \vdash p_1 : \mathbf{intexp}}{\pi \vdash p_0 \ \mathbf{rem} \ p_1 : \mathbf{intexp}}$$

$$\frac{\pi \vdash p_0 : \mathbf{realexp} \quad \pi \vdash p_1 : \mathbf{realexp}}{\pi \vdash p_0/p_1 : \mathbf{realexp},}$$

$$(19.9)$$

TY RULE: Relational Operations

$$\frac{\pi \vdash p_0 : \mathbf{realexp} \quad \pi \vdash p_1 : \mathbf{realexp}}{\pi \vdash p_0 = p_1 : \mathbf{boolexp}} \qquad (19.10)$$

(and similarly for $\neq, <, \leq, >, \geq$),

TY RULE: Boolean Operations

$$\frac{\pi \vdash p : \mathbf{boolexp}}{\pi \vdash \neg p : \mathbf{boolexp}} \qquad \frac{\pi \vdash p_0 : \mathbf{boolexp} \quad \pi \vdash p_1 : \mathbf{boolexp}}{\pi \vdash p_0 \wedge p_1 : \mathbf{boolexp}} \qquad (19.11)$$

(and similarly for $\vee, \Rightarrow$, and $\Leftrightarrow$),

TY RULE: Conditional Expressions

$$\frac{\pi \vdash p_0 : \mathbf{boolexp} \quad \pi \vdash p_1 : \delta\mathbf{exp} \quad \pi \vdash p_2 : \delta\mathbf{exp}}{\pi \vdash \mathbf{if} \ p_0 \ \mathbf{then} \ p_1 \ \mathbf{else} \ p_2 : \delta\mathbf{exp}.} \qquad (19.12)$$

(Notice that the relational operations apply to integers as well as reals, since **intexp** is a subtype of **realexp**.)

Next we have inference rules for commands:

TY RULE: Assignment

$$\frac{\pi \vdash p_0 : \delta\mathbf{var} \qquad \pi \vdash p_1 : \delta\mathbf{exp}}{\pi \vdash p_0 := p_1 : \mathbf{comm},} \qquad (19.13)$$

TY RULE: **skip**

$$\frac{}{\pi \vdash \mathbf{skip} : \mathbf{comm},} \qquad (19.14)$$

TY RULE: Sequential Composition

$$\frac{\pi \vdash p_0 : \mathbf{comm} \qquad \pi \vdash p_1 : \mathbf{comm}}{\pi \vdash p_0 \,; p_1 : \mathbf{comm},} \qquad (19.15)$$

TY RULE: Conditional Commands

$$\frac{\pi \vdash p_0 : \mathbf{boolexp} \qquad \pi \vdash p_1 : \mathbf{comm} \qquad \pi \vdash p_2 : \mathbf{comm}}{\pi \vdash \mathbf{if}\ p_0\ \mathbf{then}\ p_1\ \mathbf{else}\ p_2 : \mathbf{comm},} \qquad (19.16)$$

TY RULE: **while**

$$\frac{\pi \vdash p_0 : \mathbf{boolexp} \qquad \pi \vdash p_1 : \mathbf{comm}}{\pi \vdash \mathbf{while}\ p_0\ \mathbf{do}\ p_1 : \mathbf{comm},} \qquad (19.17)$$

TY RULE: Variable Declaration

$$\frac{\pi \vdash p_0 : \delta\mathbf{exp} \qquad \pi, \iota{:}\,\delta\mathbf{var} \vdash p_1 : \mathbf{comm}}{\pi \vdash \mathbf{new}\ \delta\mathbf{var}\ \iota := p_0\ \mathbf{in}\ p_1 : \mathbf{comm}.} \qquad (19.18)$$

In the last of these rules, a variable declaration binds an identifier (i.e. a variable of the lambda calculus) that stands for a variable of the simple imperative language.

To complete our language, we add the facilities of the lambda calculus and an explicit fixed-point operator. The syntax is

$$\langle\text{phrase}\rangle ::= \langle\text{id}\rangle \mid \langle\text{phrase}\rangle\langle\text{phrase}\rangle \mid \lambda\langle\text{id}\rangle_\theta.\ \langle\text{phrase}\rangle \mid \mathbf{rec}\ \langle\text{phrase}\rangle$$

and the inference rules are

TY RULE: Identifiers

$$\frac{}{\pi \vdash \iota : \theta} \qquad \text{when } \pi \text{ contains } \iota{:}\,\theta, \qquad (19.19)$$

TY RULE: $\rightarrow$ Introduction

$$\frac{\pi, \iota{:}\,\theta \vdash p : \theta'}{\pi \vdash \lambda\iota_\theta.\ p : \theta \rightarrow \theta',} \qquad (19.20)$$

TY RULE: $\rightarrow$ Elimination

$$\frac{\pi \vdash p_0 : \theta \rightarrow \theta' \qquad \pi \vdash p_1 : \theta}{\pi \vdash p_0\, p_1 : \theta',} \tag{19.21}$$

TY RULE: Fixed Point

$$\frac{\pi \vdash p : \theta \rightarrow \theta}{\pi \vdash \mathbf{rec}\ p : \theta.} \tag{19.22}$$

In keeping with the spirit of Algol (and in deference to the inefficiencies of type inference with subtypes), we have prescribed explicit typing.

Although the above language is theoretically sufficient, in practice it is convenient to add **let** and **letrec** definitions, which can be defined as syntactic sugar, as described in Sections 11.3 and 14.2 (but without the introduction of patterns). The syntax is

$$\langle \text{phrase} \rangle ::= \mathbf{let}\ \langle \text{id} \rangle \equiv \langle \text{phrase} \rangle, \ldots, \langle \text{id} \rangle \equiv \langle \text{phrase} \rangle \ \mathbf{in}\ \langle \text{phrase} \rangle$$

$$\mid \mathbf{letrec}\ \langle \text{id} \rangle_{\theta_0} \equiv \langle \text{phrase} \rangle, \ldots, \langle \text{id} \rangle_{\theta_{n-1}} \equiv \langle \text{phrase} \rangle \ \mathbf{in}\ \langle \text{phrase} \rangle$$

and the inference rules are

TY RULE: **let** Definitions

$$\begin{array}{c} \pi \vdash p_0 : \theta_0 \\ \ddots \\ \pi \vdash p_{n-1} : \theta_{n-1} \\ \pi, \iota_0 : \theta_0, \ldots, \iota_{n-1} : \theta_{n-1} \vdash p : \theta \\ \hline \pi \vdash \mathbf{let}\ \iota_0 \equiv p_0,\ \ldots,\ \iota_{n-1} \equiv p_{n-1}\ \mathbf{in}\ p : \theta, \end{array} \tag{19.23}$$

TY RULE: **letrec** Definitions

$$\begin{array}{c} \pi, \iota_0 : \theta_0, \ldots, \iota_{n-1} : \theta_{n-1} \vdash p_0 : \theta_0 \\ \ddots \\ \pi, \iota_0 : \theta_0, \ldots, \iota_{n-1} : \theta_{n-1} \vdash p_{n-1} : \theta_{n-1} \\ \pi, \iota_0 : \theta_0, \ldots, \iota_{n-1} : \theta_{n-1} \vdash p : \theta \\ \hline \pi \vdash \mathbf{letrec}\ \iota_{0\theta_0} \equiv p_0,\ \ldots,\ \iota_{n-1\theta_{n-1}} \equiv p_{n-1}\ \mathbf{in}\ p : \theta. \end{array} \tag{19.24}$$

Again, in the rule for **letrec**, we have used explicit typing.

Finally, we need the subsumption rule for combining reasoning about subtypes and typing judgements:

TY RULE: Subsumption

$$\frac{\pi \vdash p : \theta \qquad \theta \leq \theta'}{\pi \vdash p : \theta'.} \tag{19.25}$$

19.3 Examples

Simple procedures in our Algol-like language are roughly similar to their analogues in the Iswim-like language of Chapter 13, except that **val** disappears (since variables are now implicitly converted to expressions) and the types are explicit. But there are some subtle differences involving aliasing. For example, the following is a procedure for computing Fibonacci numbers, which was formed by abstracting the program devised in Section 3.6 on its free variables:

> **let** fib $\equiv \lambda n_{\text{intexp}}. \lambda f_{\text{intvar}}.$
>
> **if** $n = 0$ **then** $f := 0$ **else**
>
> **new intvar** $k := 1$ **in new intvar** $g := 0$ **in** $(f := 1 ;$
>
> **while** $k \neq n$ **do**
>
> **new intvar** $t := g$ **in** $(g := f ; f := f + t ; k := k + 1))$
>
> **in** $\cdots$.

This procedure has type **intexp** $\to$ **intvar** $\to$ **comm**. In general, a procedure of type $\cdots \to \theta$ is a procedure whose applications will be phrases of type θ, so that fib is a procedure whose applications will be commands (often called a *proper procedure*). Notice that it doesn't quite make sense to say that an application of fib "returns" a command — in the Algol view, procedure applications denote phrases rather than return values.

When a formal parameter such as n has type **intexp**, it cannot be assigned within the procedure, so that the corresponding actual parameter can be any expression. On the other hand, when a formal parameter such as f has type **intvar**, it may be assigned within the procedure, so that the corresponding actual parameter must be a variable, rather than, say, 3 or $x + 1$. (This distinction was not made in Algol 60 itself, so that some type checks had to be made at run time.)

Notice that the penultimate line of the definition of fib differs from the analogous line in the Iswim-like version of fib in Section 13.6, where t was defined by a **let** definition rather than a variable declaration. If we had written

$$\textbf{let } t \equiv g \textbf{ in } (g := f ; f := f + t ; k := k + 1)$$

in the present language, the effect would be to give t the same meaning as g, not the same value. If one desugars this definition and reduces it, one obtains

$$g := f ; f := f + g ; k := k + 1,$$

which is quite different than introducing a temporary variable. In essence, the **let** definition would make t an alias of g.

Aliasing of procedure parameters can occur in an even greater variety of cases than in the Iswim world. In particular, aliasing can occur between a parameter that is a variable and a parameter that is an expression, as well as between two parameters that are variables. For example, consider using the above definition of fib in

$$\textbf{let fib} \equiv \cdots \textbf{ in fib}\,(a + b)\,a.$$

By desugaring this command and performing three β-contractions, one finds that it is equivalent to

$$\textbf{if } a + b = 0 \textbf{ then } a := 0 \textbf{ else}$$

$$\quad \textbf{new intvar } k := 1 \textbf{ in new intvar } g := 0 \textbf{ in } (a := 1\,;$$

$$\qquad \textbf{while } k \neq a + b \textbf{ do}$$

$$\qquad\quad \textbf{new intvar } t := g \textbf{ in } (g := a\,; a := a + t\,; k := k + 1)),$$

which will not compute the $a + b$-th Fibonacci number correctly since the assignments to a will affect the value of $a + b$. Moreover, even if aliasing does not occur, the procedure fib will be inefficient when its first actual parameter is a compound expression such as $a + b$, since this expression will be repeatedly evaluated by the **while** command.

   Both of these problems can be solved by replacing the input parameter n by a local variable that is initialized to the value of the input parameter (as discussed in Section 13.6):

$$\textbf{let fib} \equiv \lambda n_{\text{intexp}}.\ \lambda f_{\text{intvar}}.\ \textbf{new intvar } n := n \textbf{ in}$$

$$\quad \textbf{if } n = 0 \textbf{ then } f := 0 \textbf{ else}$$

$$\qquad \textbf{new intvar } k := 1 \textbf{ in new intvar } g := 0 \textbf{ in } (f := 1\,;$$

$$\qquad\quad \textbf{while } k \neq n \textbf{ do}$$

$$\qquad\qquad \textbf{new intvar } t := g \textbf{ in } (g := f\,; f := f + t\,; k := k + 1))$$

$$\textbf{in } \cdots.$$

In Algol 60, this kind of transformation could be induced by specifying **value n** in the heading of the procedure definition. A parameter treated in this way was said to be *called by value*; other parameters were said to be *called by name*.

   Nowadays, this terminology has broken loose from the context of Algol. "Call by name" is used generally as a synonym for normal-order evaluation, and more specifically for a parameter that is evaluated, perhaps repeatedly, during the execution of a procedure body. "Call by value" is used generally as a synonym for eager evaluation, and more specifically for a parameter (other than a reference) that is evaluated once, before or at the beginning of procedure execution. A parameter that is evaluated to a reference before procedure execution is said to be "called by reference".

As discussed in Section 13.6, aliasing can also be avoided by replacing an output parameter by a local variable whose final value is assigned to the parameter. For example,

$$\textbf{let fib} \equiv \lambda n_{\text{intexp}}.\ \lambda f_{\text{intvar}}.\ \textbf{new intvar } ff := 1 \textbf{ in}$$
$$\left(\textbf{if } n = 0 \textbf{ then } ff := 0 \textbf{ else}\right.$$
$$\textbf{new intvar } k := 1 \textbf{ in new intvar } g := 0 \textbf{ in}$$
$$\textbf{while } k \neq n \textbf{ do}$$
$$\textbf{new intvar } t := g \textbf{ in } (g := ff\ ;\ ff := ff + t\ ;\ k := k + 1)\ ;$$
$$f := ff)$$
$$\textbf{in } \cdots .$$

In the language Algol W, this kind of transformation was induced by the specification **result** f and was known as "call by result".

Actually, aliasing is a special case of a more general phenomenon known as *interference*, which can occur between between parameters of any type, as long as at least one of the parameters is *active*, meaning that it can be used to cause a change of state. One parameter is said to *interfere* with another if the first can cause a state change that affects the other. For example, consider the analogue of the procedure fordo described in Section 13.6:

$$\textbf{let fordo} \equiv \lambda a_{\text{intexp}}.\ \lambda b_{\text{intexp}}.\ \lambda p_{\text{intexp}\to\text{comm}}.\ \textbf{new intvar } k := a \textbf{ in}$$
$$\textbf{while } k \leq b \textbf{ do } (p\, k\ ;\ k := k + 1)\ \cdots ,$$

of type **intexp** $\to$ **intexp** $\to$ (**intexp** $\to$ **comm**) $\to$ **comm**. Here, since the parameter of p has type **intexp** rather than **intvar**, p cannot assign to this parameter directly. Moreover, since k is a local variable of fordo, one can show that p and k do not interfere. Thus the only assignments to k will be done by the final assignment within the **while** command, so that this variable can be guaranteed to take on successive values starting with the value possessed by a when fordo is called.

However, in a procedure application such as

$$\text{fordo } 0\, x\, (\lambda i_{\text{intexp}}.\ x := x + 1),$$

p can interfere with b so that, in this case, the **while** command may execute forever, chasing an ever-increasing upper limit.

The solution, which also avoids the repeated evaluation of b, is to call b by value:

$$\textbf{let fordo} \equiv \lambda a_{\text{intexp}}.\ \lambda b_{\text{intexp}}.\ \lambda p_{\text{intexp}\to\text{comm}}.\ \textbf{new intvar } k := a \textbf{ in}$$
$$\textbf{new intvar } b := b \textbf{ in while } k \leq b \textbf{ do } (p\, k\ ;\ k := k + 1)\ \cdots .$$

As in a purely functional language, one can use normal-order evaluation to define functions that do not always evaluate all of their arguments. Just as in Section 14.3, one can define short-circuiting functions such as

$$\text{let andfunction} \equiv \lambda p_{\textbf{boolexp}}. \ \lambda q_{\textbf{boolexp}}. \ \textbf{if} \ p \ \textbf{then} \ q \ \textbf{else} \ \textbf{false} \ \cdots$$

$$\text{let scmult} \equiv \lambda m_{\textbf{intexp}}. \ \lambda n_{\textbf{intexp}}. \ \textbf{if} \ m = 0 \ \textbf{then} \ 0 \ \textbf{else} \ m \times n \ \cdots.$$

Moreover, in contrast to the functional case, one can also use repeated evaluation to advantage. For example,

$$\text{let repeat} \equiv \lambda c_{\textbf{comm}}. \ \lambda b_{\textbf{boolexp}}. \ (c \ ; \textbf{while} \ \neg b \ \textbf{do} \ c) \ \cdots$$

defines a proper procedure that mimics the **repeat** command of Exercise 2.2.

19.4 Arrays and Declarators

When we introduced arrays in Chapter 4, we remarked that there are two ways of viewing a (one-dimensional) array:

(a) as an entity that can be applied to an integer to obtain an "array element", which in turn can be either evaluated, to obtain a value, or assigned, to alter the state of the computation,
(b) as a function-valued variable.

In Chapter 4 we pursued the second view; now we will pursue the first. If we recognize that an entity that can be evaluated or assigned is just an ordinary variable, then an array is a procedure that, when applied to an integer expression, denotes a variable. For instance, a real array would be a procedure of type **intexp → realvar**.

Thus we can introduce arrays without introducing new types. If X has type **intexp → realvar**, then the syntax and typing rules we have already given permit an application such as $X(i+1)$ to appear in any context where a variable is permitted, such as within an expression or on the left of an assignment command. (In the jargon of Algol, such an application is called an "array designator".)

The one construction we must introduce is an array declaration. For reasons that will soon become clear, we limit this construction to a simpler form of array than in Chapter 4, by requiring lower bounds to be zero. The new syntax is

$$\langle\text{phrase}\rangle ::= \textbf{new} \ \delta\textbf{array} \ \langle\text{id}\rangle(\langle\text{phrase}\rangle) := \langle\text{phrase}\rangle \ \textbf{in} \ \langle\text{phrase}\rangle$$

and the type inference rule is

TY RULE: Array Declaration

$$\frac{\pi \vdash p_0 : \textbf{intexp} \qquad \pi \vdash p_1 : \delta\textbf{exp} \qquad \pi, \iota : \textbf{intexp} \to \delta\textbf{var} \vdash p_2 : \textbf{comm}}{\pi \vdash \textbf{new} \ \delta\textbf{array} \ \iota(p_0) := p_1 \ \textbf{in} \ p_2 : \textbf{comm}.}$$

$$(19.26)$$

The declaration **new** δ**array** $\iota(p_0) := p_1$ **in** p_2 creates an array whose subscript ranges over the interval 0 **to** $p_0 - 1$, initializes the elements of the array to the value of p_1, and executes p_2 in an environment where ι denotes the array.

In general, the nature of declarations is quite different in Algol-like languages than in Iswim-like languages. In Section 13.4, we defined integer variable declarations in terms of the function **mkref**:

$$\textbf{newvar}\ v := e\ \textbf{in}\ e' \stackrel{\text{def}}{=} \textbf{let}\ v \equiv \textbf{mkref}\ e\ \textbf{in}\ e'.$$

But this does not work in the Algol world. As we pointed out in Section 13.10, **mkref** is not compatible with β-reduction. Moreover, it is a procedure which allocates storage that remains active after the procedure completes execution, which would violate the stack discipline that characterizes storage in Algol.

On the other hand, there is still a way to encapsulate declarations as procedures. Suppose we define

> **let** newintvar $\equiv \lambda$init$_{\text{intexp}}$. λbody$_{\text{intvar}\rightarrow\text{comm}}$.
>
> **new intvar** x := init **in** body x
>
> **in** $\cdots$,

of type **intexp** $\rightarrow$ (**intvar** $\rightarrow$ **comm**) $\rightarrow$ **comm**. Then the procedure application newintvar p_0 ($\lambda\iota_{\text{intvar}}$. p_1) has the same meaning as the variable declaration **new intvar** $\iota := p_0$ **in** p_1. Similarly, if we define

> **let** newrealarray $\equiv \lambda$length$_{\text{intexp}}$. λinit$_{\text{realexp}}$. λbody$_{(\text{intexp}\rightarrow\text{realvar})\rightarrow\text{comm}}$.
>
> **new realarray** X(length) := init **in** body X
>
> **in** $\cdots$,

of type **intexp** $\rightarrow$ **realexp** $\rightarrow$ ((**intexp** $\rightarrow$ **realvar**) $\rightarrow$ **comm**) $\rightarrow$ **comm**, then the procedure application newrealarray p_0 p_1 ($\lambda\iota_{\text{intvar}}$. p_2) has the same meaning as the array declaration **new realarray** $\iota(p_0) := p_1$ **in** p_2.

Clearly, instead of providing variable and array declarations in our language, we could have provided predefined procedures such as newintvar and newrealarray. Procedures, such as these, that mimic declarations are called *declarators*. (This term describes the intended use of the procedures, not their type.)

It is a minor detail of language design whether one provides declarations or built-in declarators. The real point of the matter is that the procedure mechanism is sufficiently powerful that the user can define his own declarators, and use them to declare entities that are not provided directly by the language.

For example, to be able to declare arrays with arbitrary lower and upper bounds, one can define the following declarator, which declares a standard array X of the right length, and then gives the body an "array" that is actually a procedure which accesses X through an appropriate mapping function:

let newtwoboundrealarray $\equiv$ λlow$_{\text{intexp}}$. λup$_{\text{intexp}}$. λinit$_{\text{realexp}}$.

$\quad$ λbody$_{\text{(intexp}\rightarrow\text{realvar)}\rightarrow\text{comm}}$.

$\qquad$ **new intvar** low := low **in new realarray** X(up − low + 1) := init **in**

$\qquad\quad$ body(λi$_{\text{intexp}}$. X(i − low))

in $\cdots$.

(Notice that the parameter low is called by value to avoid repeated evaluation when body uses its array parameter repeatedly.) Then the procedure application newtwoboundrealarray p_0 p_1 p_2 ($\lambda\iota_{\text{intvar}}$. p_3) has the same meaning as the array declaration **new realarray** $\iota(p_0$ **to** $p_1) := p_2$ **in** p_3 — which is why we did not need to build this more general form of declaration into our language.

A slightly less trivial example provides square two-dimensional arrays:

let newsqrealarray $\equiv$ λsize$_{\text{intexp}}$. λinit$_{\text{realexp}}$.

$\quad$ λbody$_{\text{(intexp}\rightarrow\text{intexp}\rightarrow\text{realvar)}\rightarrow\text{comm}}$.

$\qquad$ **new intvar** size := size **in new realarray** X(size $*$ size) := init **in**

$\qquad\quad$ body(λi$_{\text{intexp}}$. λj$_{\text{intexp}}$. X(size $\times$ i + j))

in $\cdots$.

Essentially, once a basic one-dimensional array facility is provided by the language, users have the ability to define any kind of array for which they can program an "indexing" function that maps subscripts of the array into subscripts of an ordinary one-dimensional array. In practice, of course, such expressiveness is only useful if the compiler is able to optimize the resultant program sufficiently. There must be some way of compiling procedures into inline code (perhaps under instructions from the programmer), and the optimization called "strength reduction" (which would eliminate the multiplication in size $\times$ i + j when this expression occured within a loop that increases i by a constant increment) must be applied to arbitrary linear expressions, not just to multiple subscripts.

19.5 A Semantics Embodying the Stack Discipline

In this section, we will discuss the direct denotational semantics of Algol-like languages in an intrinsic framework similar to that of Section 15.5. We will find that a novel approach is needed to capture the stack discipline that is characteristic of these languages.

The separation between the lambda calculus and the simple imperative language induces a separation between environments, which are relevant to the former, and states, which are relevant to the latter. As discussed in Section 13.1, this separation is needed to explain the phenomenon of aliasing.

Thus the meaning of an integer expression, when applied to an appropriate environment, is not an integer, but rather a function from states to integers. Moreover, the meaning of a command applied to an environment is a function from states to states. But in general, in the kind of intrinsic semantics introduced in Section 15.5, the meaning of a phrase of type θ applied to an environment is a member of the domain $\mathcal{D}(\theta)$ that is the meaning of θ. Thus, in such a semantics, we have

$$\mathcal{D}(\delta\mathbf{exp}) = \Sigma \to (S_\delta)_\perp \qquad \mathcal{D}(\mathbf{comm}) = \Sigma \to \Sigma_\perp,$$

where Σ is the set of states and

$$S_{\text{int}} = \mathbf{Z} \qquad S_{\text{real}} = \mathbf{R} \qquad S_{\text{bool}} = \mathbf{B}.$$

The occurrences of the lifting operation $(-)_\perp$ are needed to describe nonterminating expressions and commands.

It is reassuring that the meaning of these types is essentially the same as the meaning of the corresponding set of phrases in our original denotational semantics of the simple imperative language in Section 2.2. The only change is the lifting needed to deal with nonterminating expressions.

Of course, states can no longer be mappings of variables into values, since variables are no longer unstructured names but may be compound phrases such as procedure applications. Instead, we take states to be mappings of *references* into values, as in Section 13.1.

One might expect the meaning of a variable, when applied to an appropriate environment, to be a reference. But this view is too simple to accommodate arrays. An array designator such as $X(i+1)$ is a variable that will denote different references, depending on the value of the subscript $i+1$ in the current state.

There are two ways of dealing with this complication. One, which is similar in spirit to the treatment of Iswim-like languages in Section 13.3, is to take variables to denote functions from states to references, so that $\mathcal{D}(\delta\mathbf{var}) = \Sigma \to \mathbf{Rf}_\perp$. In this section, however, we will pursue a more abstract approach, which is sometimes called *update-evaluate* semantics.

The basic idea is that the meaning of a variable should be a pair of entities corresponding to the two ways that a variable can be used. When a variable is used as an expression, it should have the same kind of meaning as an expression. On the other hand, when a variable is the object of an assignment, the effect is to produce a new state, which will depend on the value being assigned and the old state. Thus the relevant meaning should belong to $S_\delta \to \Sigma \to \Sigma_\perp$. Combining the meanings for the two usages, we have $\mathcal{D}(\delta\mathbf{var}) = (S_\delta \to \Sigma \to \Sigma_\perp) \times (\Sigma \to (S_\delta)_\perp)$.

The choice between these two views of variables has implications for language design. Had we chosen to interpret variables as functions from states to references, it would be straightforward to introduce an equality test $=_{\text{ref}}$ for references, as in Section 13.1. With update-evaluate semantics, however, such an operation does not make sense. On the other hand, as we will find in Section 19.8, update-evaluate semantics permits a generalization of the concept of variable that permits the programmer to define "variables" with unorthodox but useful behaviors.

At this point, we could go on to fill in the details, and obtain a semantics much like that devised by Scott and Strachey in the early 1970's. But such a semantics has a serious limitation: It obscures the *stack discipline* (sometimes called *block structure*) that is one of the basic characteristics of Algol-like languages.

At the outset, it should be emphasized that the stack discipline is more than just a description of a method of implementation. For instance, an informal but implementation-independent characterization would be: After execution of a command, the values of all variables and arrays declared within the command have no further effect on the program.

Such a property does not hold for Iswim-like languages, where references can easily outlive the expressions in which they were created. It does hold for Algol-like languages, and it could be proved from a Scott-Strachey semantics. But such a proof would require a case analysis on every way of constructing phrases. What we want is a semantics whose basic structure implies the stack discipline.

Suppose C is a command such as **new intvar** $t := x + 1$ **in** $x := t \times t$, so that, in a Scott-Strachey semantics,

$$[\![x\colon \mathbf{intvar} \vdash C\colon \mathbf{comm}]\!] \in \mathcal{D}(\mathbf{intvar}) \to \mathcal{D}(\mathbf{comm})$$

$$= (\mathbf{Z} \to \Sigma \to \Sigma_\perp) \times (\Sigma \to \mathbf{Z}_\perp) \to \Sigma \to \Sigma_\perp.$$

(Strictly speaking, we should have $\mathcal{D}^*(x\colon \mathbf{intvar})$ rather than $\mathcal{D}(\mathbf{intvar})$, but the two domains are trivially isomorphic.) In a typical usage, the meaning of C might be applied to an environment that identified the variable x with a reference r_0,

$$\eta = \langle \lambda i.\, \lambda \sigma.\, [\,\sigma \mid r_0\colon i\,], \lambda \sigma.\, \sigma\, r_0 \rangle,$$

and a state containing only the reference r_0.

$$\sigma = [\,r_0\colon 7\,],$$

to give an altered state containing an additional reference, created by declaring the variable t:

$$[\![x\colon \mathbf{intvar} \vdash C\colon \mathbf{comm}]\!]\eta\sigma = [\,r_0\colon 64 \mid r_1\colon 8\,].$$

In fact, the pair $r_1\colon 8$ will remain in the state until the end of the computation, so that any proof that it has no effect on the computation must consider all possible contexts that can contain C.

In contrast, instead of taking Σ to be the set of all possible states that might arise during a computation, suppose we limit Σ to states with the same *shape*, that is (roughly speaking), states whose domain is the same set of references. In the above case, Σ would be the set $\mathbf{Z}^{\{r_0\}}$, and the result of executing C would be

$$[\![x\colon \mathbf{intvar} \vdash C\colon \mathbf{comm}]\!]\eta\sigma = [\,r_0\colon 64\,].$$

Now the fact that $[\![x\colon \mathbf{intvar} \vdash C\colon \mathbf{comm}]\!]\eta\sigma$ belongs to $\mathbf{Z}^{\{r_0\}}$ makes it obvious that the temporary reference r_1 and its value are discarded, independently of the specific nature of either C or the context containing it.

But there is a complication. Although any particular execution of C will leave the shape of the state unchanged, the same command may occur in several places in a program, where it must transform states with a variety of shapes. For example, in

$$\mathbf{new\ intvar}\ x := 0\ \mathbf{in}\ (\ \cdots\ ; C\ ;\ \cdots$$

$$\mathbf{new\ intvar}\ y := 0\ \mathbf{in}\ (\ \cdots\ ; C\ ;\ \cdots\ )),$$

the first occurrence of C will transform states with a single reference, while the second occurrence will transform states with two references. To deal with this complication, instead of taking the meaning of C to be a single function, we must take it to be a family of functions indexed by state shapes.

Before going further, we must make the notion of state shape more precise. In the first place, we can take references themselves to be natural numbers, so that $r_0 = 0$, $r_1 = 1$, and so forth. Second, it will turn out to be sufficient (at least for sequential Algol-like languages) to use states whose domain is an interval beginning with zero, that is, states that are sequences.

This suggests that an adequate notion of state shape would be the length of a state. But this view is too simplistic to deal with more than one data type. In fact, a state shape must specify both the number of components in the state and the set over which each component ranges.

For this reason, we define a *state shape* to be a sequence of countable sets, and we write **Shp** for the collection of such sequences. A state σ has shape $\langle S_0, \ldots, S_{n-1} \rangle$ if it contains n components and each component σ_i belongs to S_i. Thus the set of components of shape $\langle S_0, \ldots, S_{n-1} \rangle$ is $S_0 \times \cdots \times S_{n-1}$. More abstractly, we can use the notation of Section A.3 to define the set of states of shape α to be $\prod \alpha$.

Now, instead of taking C to be a single function,

$$[\![x\colon \mathbf{intvar} \vdash C\colon \mathbf{comm}]\!] \in (\mathbf{Z} \to \Sigma \to \Sigma_\perp) \times (\Sigma \to \mathbf{Z}_\perp) \to \Sigma \to \Sigma_\perp,$$

we take it to be a family of such functions indexed by the state shape α:

$$[\![x\colon \mathbf{intvar} \vdash C\colon \mathbf{comm}]\!]\alpha$$

$$\in (\mathbf{Z} \to (\textstyle\prod\alpha) \to (\textstyle\prod\alpha)_\perp) \times ((\textstyle\prod\alpha) \to \mathbf{Z}_\perp) \to (\textstyle\prod\alpha) \to (\textstyle\prod\alpha)_\perp.$$

Then the meaning of C appropriate to its first occurrence in the example above is $[\![x\colon \mathbf{intvar} \vdash C\colon \mathbf{comm}]\!]\langle \mathbf{Z} \rangle$, while the meaning appropriate to the second occurrence is $[\![x\colon \mathbf{intvar} \vdash C\colon \mathbf{comm}]\!]\langle \mathbf{Z}, \mathbf{Z} \rangle$.

To carry out this generalization systematically, we must alter the basic framework of intrinsic semantics that we established in Section 15.5, so that the meanings of all types, contexts, and implicit conversions, as well as all phrases, become families indexed by state shapes. Thus,

$$\mathcal{D}(\delta\mathbf{exp})\alpha = (\textstyle\prod\alpha) \to (S_\delta)_\perp$$

$$\mathcal{D}(\mathbf{comm})\alpha = (\textstyle\prod\alpha) \to (\textstyle\prod\alpha)_\perp$$

$$\mathcal{D}(\delta\mathbf{var})\alpha = (S_\delta \to (\textstyle\prod\alpha)_\perp \to (\textstyle\prod\alpha)_\perp) \times ((\textstyle\prod\alpha) \to (S_\delta)_\perp)$$
$$= (S_\delta \to \mathcal{D}(\mathbf{comm})\alpha) \times \mathcal{D}(\delta\mathbf{exp})\alpha$$

$$\mathcal{D}^*(\pi)\alpha = \prod_{\iota\in\mathrm{dom}\,\pi} \mathcal{D}(\pi\,\iota)\alpha$$

$$[\![\theta \leq \theta']\!]\alpha \in \mathcal{D}(\theta)\alpha \to \mathcal{D}(\theta')\alpha$$

$$[\![\pi \vdash e : \theta]\!]\alpha \in \mathcal{D}^*(\pi)\alpha \to \mathcal{D}(\theta)\alpha.$$

Once this new framework has been established, the semantics of most of our language is straightforward. In describing it we will use the following metavariables:

π	$\langle$context$\rangle$	i	$\mathbf{Z}$
δ	$\langle$data type$\rangle$	b	$\mathbf{B}$
θ	$\langle$phrase type$\rangle$	x	S_δ
ι	$\langle$id$\rangle$	e	$\mathcal{D}(\delta\mathbf{exp})\alpha$
p	$\langle$phrase$\rangle$	c	$\mathcal{D}(\mathbf{comm})\alpha$
α	$\mathbf{Shp}$	a	$S_\delta \to \mathcal{D}(\mathbf{comm})\alpha$
η	$\mathcal{D}^*(\pi)\alpha$	z	$\mathcal{D}(\theta)\alpha$
σ	$\prod\alpha$	f	$\mathcal{D}(\theta \to \theta')\alpha.$

Several conversion equations and typed semantic equations are the same as for a purely functional language, except for the indexing on state shapes:

CONV EQ: Reflexivity (19.5)

$$[\![\theta \leq \theta]\!]\alpha = I_{\mathcal{D}(\theta)\alpha},$$

CONV EQ: Transitivity (19.6)

$$[\![\theta \leq \theta'']\!]\alpha = [\![\theta' \leq \theta'']\!]\alpha \cdot [\![\theta \leq \theta']\!]\alpha,$$

TY SEM EQ: Subsumption (19.25)

$$[\![\pi \vdash p : \theta']\!]\alpha = [\![\theta \leq \theta']\!]\alpha \cdot [\![\pi \vdash p : \theta]\!]\alpha,$$

TY SEM EQ: Identifiers (19.19)

$$[\![\pi \vdash \iota : \theta]\!]\alpha\eta = \eta\,\iota \qquad \text{when } \pi \text{ contains } \iota\!:\!\theta.$$

Most of the treatment of the simple imperative language is unsurprising. The implicit conversion of expressions is defined by

CONV EQ: Integer to Real Expressions (19.2)

$$[\![\textbf{intexp} \leq \textbf{realexp}]\!]\alpha\, e = J \cdot e$$

where J is the identity injection from $\mathbf{Z}_\perp$ to $\mathbf{R}_\perp$,

and many typed semantic equations are similar to those in Sections 2.2 to 2.4, modified since our present meanings must be applied to state shapes and environments to obtain the more innocent meanings used in Chapter 2. There are also some complications that are needed to deal with nonterminating expressions:

TY SEM EQ: Constants and Primitive Operations (19.7–19.11)

$$[\![\pi \vdash 0 \colon \textbf{intexp}]\!]\alpha\eta\sigma = \iota_\uparrow 0$$

$$[\![\pi \vdash p_0 + p_1 \colon \textbf{intexp}]\!]\alpha\eta\sigma$$
$$= (\lambda i.\, (\lambda i'.\, \iota_\uparrow(i + i'))_{\perp\!\perp}([\![\pi \vdash p_1 \colon \textbf{intexp}]\!]\alpha\eta\sigma))_{\perp\!\perp}([\![\pi \vdash p_0 \colon \textbf{intexp}]\!]\alpha\eta\sigma)$$

(and similarly for the other constants, operations, and data types),

TY SEM EQ: Conditional Expressions (19.12)

$$[\![\pi \vdash \textbf{if}\ p_0\ \textbf{then}\ p_1\ \textbf{else}\ p_2 : \delta\textbf{exp}]\!]\alpha\eta\sigma$$
$$= (\lambda b.\ \textbf{if}\ b\ \textbf{then}\ [\![\pi \vdash p_1 : \delta\textbf{exp}]\!]\alpha\eta\sigma\ \textbf{else}\ [\![\pi \vdash p_2 : \delta\textbf{exp}]\!]\alpha\eta\sigma)_{\perp\!\perp}$$
$$([\![\pi \vdash p_0 : \textbf{boolexp}]\!]\alpha\eta\sigma),$$

TY SEM EQ: **skip** (19.14)

$$[\![\pi \vdash \textbf{skip} : \textbf{comm}]\!]\alpha\eta\sigma = \iota_\uparrow \sigma,$$

TY SEM EQ: Sequential Composition (19.15)

$$[\![\pi \vdash p_0 \, ; p_1 : \textbf{comm}]\!]\alpha\eta\sigma = ([\![\pi \vdash p_1 : \textbf{comm}]\!]\alpha\eta)_{\perp\!\perp}([\![\pi \vdash p_0 : \textbf{comm}]\!]\alpha\eta\sigma),$$

TY SEM EQ: Conditional Commands (19.16)

$$[\![\pi \vdash \textbf{if}\ p_0\ \textbf{then}\ p_1\ \textbf{else}\ p_2 : \textbf{comm}]\!]\alpha\eta\sigma$$
$$= (\lambda b.\ \textbf{if}\ b\ \textbf{then}\ [\![\pi \vdash p_1 : \textbf{comm}]\!]\alpha\eta\sigma\ \textbf{else}\ [\![\pi \vdash p_2 : \textbf{comm}]\!]\alpha\eta\sigma)_{\perp\!\perp}$$
$$([\![\pi \vdash p_0 : \textbf{boolexp}]\!]\alpha\eta\sigma),$$

TY SEM EQ: **while** (19.17)

$$[\![\pi \vdash \textbf{while}\ p_0\ \textbf{do}\ p_1 : \textbf{comm}]\!]\alpha\eta = \mathbf{Y}_{(\Pi\alpha)\to(\Pi\alpha)_\perp}(\lambda c.\ \lambda\sigma.$$
$$(\lambda b.\ \textbf{if}\ b\ \textbf{then}\ c_{\perp\!\perp}([\![\pi \vdash p_1 : \textbf{comm}]\!]\alpha\eta\sigma)\ \textbf{else}\ \iota_\uparrow \sigma)_{\perp\!\perp}$$
$$([\![\pi \vdash p_0 : \textbf{boolexp}]\!]\alpha\eta\sigma)).$$

In fact, the novelty of our semantics appears in only two places, the treatment of variables and of procedures, which are described in the next two sections.

19.6 The Semantics of Variables

In update-evaluate semantics, the conversion from variables to expressions is simply a matter of forgetting the update component:

CONV EQ: Variables to Expressions (19.1)

$$[\![\delta\mathbf{var} \leq \delta\mathbf{exp}]\!]\alpha\,\langle a, e\rangle = e,$$

and the effect of an assignment command is to apply the update component of the left-hand variable to the value of the expression on the right:

TY SEM EQ: Assignment (19.13)

$$[\![\pi \vdash p_0 := p_1 : \mathbf{comm}]\!]\alpha\eta\sigma$$
$$= (\lambda x.\,([\![\pi \vdash p_0 : \delta\mathbf{var}]\!]\alpha\eta)_0 x\sigma)_{\perp\!\perp}([\![\pi \vdash p_1 : \delta\mathbf{exp}]\!]\alpha\eta\sigma).$$

The real machinery of the semantics is concentrated in the equation for variable declarations. Before describing it, however, we must define some notation for sequences. We use the operator $\circ$ to denote the concatenation of sequences, both for states and state shapes. Thus, if σ has shape α and σ' has shape α', then $\sigma \circ \sigma'$ has shape $\alpha \circ \alpha'$.

If σ' has shape $\alpha \circ \alpha'$, then we write $\mathrm{head}_\alpha\sigma'$ and $\mathrm{tail}_{\alpha'}\sigma'$ for the unique states of shape α and α' respectively, such that

$$(\mathrm{head}_\alpha\sigma') \circ (\mathrm{tail}_{\alpha'}\sigma') = \sigma'.$$

In the special case where $\alpha' = \langle S\rangle$ has length one, we write $\mathrm{last}_S\sigma'$ for the unique component of $\mathrm{tail}_{\alpha'}\sigma'$.

Now consider the variable declaration

$$[\![\pi \vdash \mathbf{new}\ \delta\mathbf{var}\ \iota := p_0\ \mathbf{in}\ p_1 : \mathbf{comm}]\!]\alpha\eta\sigma.$$

To execute this command, one first computes the initialization $x = [\![\pi \vdash p_0 : \delta\mathbf{exp}]\!]\alpha\eta\sigma$, and then concatenates the *global* state σ with a *local* state containing the single component x, to obtain the *extended* state $\sigma \circ \langle x\rangle$. Thus the shape of extended states, which will be the shape appropriate for the execution of p_1, is $\alpha \circ \langle S_\delta\rangle$, and the variable being declared is described by the update-evaluate pair $\langle a, e\rangle$, where

$$a = \lambda x.\,\lambda\sigma'.\,\iota_\uparrow((\mathrm{head}_\alpha\sigma') \circ \langle x\rangle)$$
$$e = \lambda\sigma'.\,\iota_\uparrow(\mathrm{last}_{S_\delta}\sigma').$$

The declaration body p_1 is executed for the extended state shape and an environment that extends η to map ι into $\langle a, e \rangle$, beginning with the state $\sigma \circ \langle x \rangle$:

$$\sigma'_{\text{fin}} = [\![\pi, \iota \colon \delta \textbf{var} \vdash p_1 : \textbf{comm}]\!](\alpha \circ \langle S_\delta \rangle)[\, \mathcal{T}^*(\pi)(\alpha, \langle S_\delta \rangle)\eta \mid \iota \colon \langle a, e \rangle\,](\sigma \circ \langle x \rangle).$$

(For the moment, ignore the occurrence of $\mathcal{T}^*(\pi)(\alpha, \langle S_\delta \rangle)$ in this equation.)

After the execution of p_1 produces the state σ'_{fin}, the final value of the local variable is discarded, and the execution of the variable declaration produces the state $\text{head}_\alpha \sigma'_{\text{fin}}$. When we put this all together, and add provisions for the nontermination of p_0 or p_1, we have

TY SEM EQ: Variable Declaration (19.18)

$$[\![\pi \vdash \textbf{new } \delta \textbf{var } \iota := p_0 \textbf{ in } p_1 \colon \textbf{comm}]\!]\alpha\eta\sigma = (\text{head}_\alpha)_{\perp}($$
$$(\lambda x. \, [\![\pi, \iota \colon \delta \textbf{var} \vdash p_1 \colon \textbf{comm}]\!](\alpha \circ \langle S_\delta \rangle)[\, \mathcal{T}^*(\pi)(\alpha, \langle S_\delta \rangle)\eta \mid \iota \colon \langle a, e \rangle\,](\sigma \circ \langle x \rangle)))_{\perp\perp}$$
$$([\![\pi \vdash p_0 : \delta \textbf{exp}]\!]\alpha\eta\sigma)).$$

There is a complication, however, that we have glossed over in the preceding explanation. The environment η belongs to $\mathcal{D}^*(\pi)\alpha$, but the environment needed to execute p_1 belongs to $\mathcal{D}^*(\pi, \iota \colon \delta \textbf{var})(\alpha \circ \langle S_\delta \rangle)$. Thus, before we perform the extension $[\, - \mid \iota \colon \langle a, e \rangle\,]$, we must translate η from the domain $\mathcal{D}^*(\pi)\alpha$ of environments appropriate to global states to the domain $\mathcal{D}^*(\pi)(\alpha \circ \langle S_\delta \rangle)$ appropriate to extended states. This translation is performed by the function $\mathcal{T}^*(\pi)(\alpha, \langle S_\delta \rangle)$.

In general, the effect of a nest of declarations will be to move from a global state shape α to an extended state shape $\alpha \circ \alpha'$, where α' is the sequence of sets introduced by the successive declarations. We must define the translation from a domain appropriate to α to a domain appropriate to $\alpha \circ \alpha'$ for each type,

$$\mathcal{T}(\theta)(\alpha, \alpha') \in \mathcal{D}(\theta)\alpha \to \mathcal{D}(\theta)(\alpha \circ \alpha'),$$

and each context,

$$\mathcal{T}^*(\pi)(\alpha, \alpha') \in \mathcal{D}^*(\pi)\alpha \to \mathcal{D}^*(\pi)(\alpha \circ \alpha').$$

The translation of an environment is performed by translating each of its components according to its type:

$$\mathcal{T}^*(\pi)(\alpha, \alpha')\eta \iota = \mathcal{T}(\pi \iota)(\alpha, \alpha')(\eta \iota).$$

The translation of an expression meaning applies the meaning to the global part of the extended state, which is obtained by head_α:

$$\mathcal{T}(\delta \textbf{exp})(\alpha, \alpha')\, e = \lambda \sigma'. \, e(\text{head}_\alpha \sigma').$$

On the other hand, the translation of a command meaning applies the meaning to the global part of the extended state, while leaving the local part unchanged:

$$\mathcal{T}(\textbf{comm})(\alpha, \alpha')\, c = \lambda \sigma'. \, (\lambda \sigma. \, \sigma \circ (\text{tail}_{\alpha'} \sigma'))_{\perp}(c(\text{head}_\alpha \sigma')).$$

The translation of a variable meaning is obtained by translating the evaluate part as an expression and the update part, after it is applied to a value, as a command:

$$\mathcal{T}(\delta\mathbf{var})(\alpha, \alpha')\langle a, e\rangle = \langle\lambda x.\ \mathcal{T}(\mathbf{comm})(\alpha, \alpha')(a\,x), \mathcal{T}(\delta\mathbf{exp})(\alpha, \alpha')\,e\rangle.$$

We will describe the translation of procedure meanings in the next section.

19.7 The Semantics of Procedures

With parametrization by state shapes, one might expect the set $\mathcal{D}(\theta \to \theta')\alpha$ of meanings of procedures of type $\theta \to \theta'$ to be $\mathcal{D}(\theta)\alpha \to \mathcal{D}(\theta')\alpha$. But procedures in Algol-like languages are more complex than this, since one can define a procedure in an outer block of a program and then apply the procedure within the scope of additional declarations.

For example, consider

$$\begin{aligned}
&\mathbf{new\ intvar}\ \mathsf{x} := 0\ \mathbf{in} \\
&\quad \mathbf{let}\ \mathsf{p} \equiv \lambda \mathsf{a}_{\mathsf{intexp}}.\ \mathsf{x} := \mathsf{x} + \mathsf{a}\ \mathbf{in} \\
&\qquad \mathbf{new\ intvar}\ \mathsf{y} := 0\ \mathbf{in}\ (\ \cdots\ ;\mathsf{p}(\mathsf{y}+1)\ ;\ \cdots\ ; \\
&\qquad\quad \mathbf{new\ intvar}\ \mathsf{z} := 0\ \mathbf{in}\ (\ \cdots\ ;\mathsf{p}(\mathsf{y}+\mathsf{z})\ ;\ \cdots\ )).
\end{aligned} \qquad (19.27)$$

Here the meaning of the procedure p belongs to $\mathcal{D}(\mathbf{intexp} \to \mathbf{comm})\langle\mathbf{Z}\rangle$. But the parameter of the first procedure application belongs to $\mathcal{D}(\mathbf{intexp})\langle\mathbf{Z},\mathbf{Z}\rangle$, while the application belongs to $\mathcal{D}(\mathbf{comm})\langle\mathbf{Z},\mathbf{Z}\rangle$. Similarly, the parameter of the second application belongs to $\mathcal{D}(\mathbf{intexp})\langle\mathbf{Z},\mathbf{Z},\mathbf{Z}\rangle$, while the application belongs to $\mathcal{D}(\mathbf{comm})\langle\mathbf{Z},\mathbf{Z},\mathbf{Z}\rangle$.

In general, a procedure meaning in $\mathcal{D}(\theta \to \theta')\alpha$ must provide a function from $\mathcal{D}(\theta)(\alpha \circ \alpha')$ to $\mathcal{D}(\theta')(\alpha \circ \alpha')$ for all shapes α' of the local state that might be created by declarations intervening between the definition of the procedure and its application. Thus we take the set of such meanings to be a family of functions indexed by α':

$$\mathcal{D}(\theta \to \theta')\alpha = \prod_{\alpha' \in \mathbf{Shp}} \mathcal{D}(\theta)(\alpha \circ \alpha') \to \mathcal{D}(\theta')(\alpha \circ \alpha').$$

In effect, the shape of the intervening local state is a hidden parameter to the procedure application.

As in a purely functional language, the meaning of an abstraction $\lambda\iota_\theta.\ p$, when applied to an environment η, is the function that, when applied to an argument z, gives the meaning of the body p in an extension of η that maps ι into z. But now, if the abstraction meaning is taken for the global shape α and the hidden local shape parameter is α', then the meaning of p is taken for the extended shape $\alpha \circ \alpha'$, and the environment η is translated from α to $\alpha \circ \alpha'$:

TY SEM EQ: $\to$ Introduction (19.20)

$$[\![\pi \vdash \lambda_{\iota\theta}.\, p : \theta \to \theta']\!]\alpha\,\eta\,\alpha'\,z = [\![\pi, \iota\!:\theta \vdash p : \theta']\!](\alpha \circ \alpha')[\,\mathcal{T}^*(\pi)(\alpha, \alpha')\eta \mid \iota\!:z\,].$$

Once a procedure meaning is placed in an environment, it will be translated from a global to an extended state shape each time a declaration is entered. The effect of the translation is to save the local shape, to eventually be concatenated onto the hidden shape parameter when the procedure is applied:

$$\mathcal{T}(\theta \to \theta')(\alpha, \alpha')f\,\alpha'' = f(\alpha' \circ \alpha'').$$

When the procedure is finally applied, its meaning will have been translated to the same shape as the shape for its parameter, so that the hidden shape parameter is the empty shape:

TY SEM EQ: $\to$ Elimination (19.21)

$$[\![\pi \vdash p_0 p_1 : \theta']\!]\alpha\,\eta = [\![\pi \vdash p_0 : \theta \to \theta']\!]\alpha\,\eta\,\langle\rangle([\![\pi \vdash p_1 : \theta]\!]\alpha\,\eta).$$

As an example, consider the program (19.27). The procedure definition in the second line causes the environment to be extended to map p into the meaning f_1, where

$$f_1\alpha'z = [\![\mathsf{x}\!:\mathbf{int\,var} \vdash \lambda\mathsf{a_{intexp}}.\,\mathsf{x} := \mathsf{x} + \mathsf{a} : \mathbf{intexp} \to \mathbf{comm}]\!]\langle\mathbf{Z}\rangle[\mathsf{x}\!:\langle a_1, e_1\rangle\,]\alpha'z$$

$$= [\![\mathsf{x}\!:\mathbf{int\,var}, \mathsf{a}\!:\mathbf{intexp} \vdash \mathsf{x} := \mathsf{x} + \mathsf{a} : \mathbf{comm}]\!](\langle\mathbf{Z}\rangle \circ \alpha')$$

$$[\mathsf{x}\!:\mathcal{T}(\mathbf{int\,var})(\langle\mathbf{Z}\rangle, \alpha')\langle a_1, e_1\rangle \mid \mathsf{a}\!:z\,],$$

where $\langle a_1, e_1\rangle$ is an update-evaluate pair for states containing a single integer:

$$a_1 = \lambda i.\,\lambda\sigma_1.\,\iota_\uparrow\langle i\rangle$$

$$e_1 = \lambda\sigma_1.\,\iota_\uparrow(\mathrm{last}_\mathbf{Z}\sigma_1).$$

(The subscripts on metavariables indicate the length of the relevant state shape.)

Because of the declaration in the third line of (19.27), the meaning f_1 is translated into $f_2 = \mathcal{T}(\mathbf{intexp} \to \mathbf{comm})(\langle\mathbf{Z}\rangle, \langle\mathbf{Z}\rangle)f_1$, so that $f_2\alpha'' = f_1(\langle\mathbf{Z}\rangle \circ \alpha'')$. Similarly, because of the declaration in the fourth line, the meaning f_2 is translated into $f_3 = \mathcal{T}(\mathbf{intexp} \to \mathbf{comm})(\langle\mathbf{Z}, \mathbf{Z}\rangle, \langle\mathbf{Z}\rangle)f_2$, so that $f_3\alpha'' = f_2(\langle\mathbf{Z}\rangle \circ \alpha'') = f_1(\langle\mathbf{Z}, \mathbf{Z}\rangle \circ \alpha'')$. Then f_3 is used as the meaning of p in the procedure application in the last line of the program:

$$[\![\pi \vdash p(y + z) : \mathbf{comm}]\!]\langle \mathbf{Z}, \mathbf{Z}, \mathbf{Z}\rangle\eta$$

$$= [\![\pi \vdash p : \mathbf{intexp} \to \mathbf{comm}]\!]\langle \mathbf{Z}, \mathbf{Z}, \mathbf{Z}\rangle\eta\langle\rangle([\![\pi \vdash y + z : \mathbf{intexp}]\!]\langle \mathbf{Z}, \mathbf{Z}, \mathbf{Z}\rangle\eta)$$

$$= f_3\langle\rangle([\![\pi \vdash y + z : \mathbf{intexp}]\!]\langle \mathbf{Z}, \mathbf{Z}, \mathbf{Z}\rangle\eta)$$

$$= f_1\langle \mathbf{Z}, \mathbf{Z}\rangle([\![\pi \vdash y + z : \mathbf{intexp}]\!]\langle \mathbf{Z}, \mathbf{Z}, \mathbf{Z}\rangle\eta)$$

$$= [\![x : \mathbf{intvar}, a : \mathbf{intexp} \vdash x := x + a : \mathbf{comm}]\!]\langle \mathbf{Z}, \mathbf{Z}, \mathbf{Z}\rangle$$

$$[x : \mathcal{T}(\mathbf{intvar})(\langle \mathbf{Z}\rangle, \langle \mathbf{Z}, \mathbf{Z}\rangle)\langle a_1, e_1\rangle \mid a : [\![\pi \vdash y + z : \mathbf{intexp}]\!]\langle \mathbf{Z}, \mathbf{Z}, \mathbf{Z}\rangle\eta]$$

$$= [\![x : \mathbf{intvar}, a : \mathbf{intexp} \vdash x := x + a : \mathbf{comm}]\!]\langle \mathbf{Z}, \mathbf{Z}, \mathbf{Z}\rangle$$

$$[x : \langle a_3, e_3\rangle \mid a : [\![\pi \vdash y + z : \mathbf{intexp}]\!]\langle \mathbf{Z}, \mathbf{Z}, \mathbf{Z}\rangle\eta],$$

where π and η are the appropriate context and environment, and

$$a_3 = \lambda x.\ \mathcal{T}(\mathbf{comm})(\langle \mathbf{Z}\rangle, \langle \mathbf{Z}, \mathbf{Z}\rangle)(a_1 x)$$

$$= \lambda x.\ \lambda\langle i_1, i_2, i_3\rangle.\ \iota_\uparrow\langle x, i_2, i_3\rangle$$

$$e_3 = \mathcal{T}(\mathbf{intexp})(\langle \mathbf{Z}\rangle, \langle \mathbf{Z}, \mathbf{Z}\rangle)e_1$$

$$= \lambda\langle i_1, i_2, i_3\rangle.\ \iota_\uparrow i_1.$$

In conclusion, we give the remaining equations needed to complete our language definition: the conversion equation for procedures,

CONV EQ: Procedures (19.4)

$$[\![\theta_0 \to \theta_1 \le \theta_0' \to \theta_1']\!]\alpha\, f\, \alpha' = ([\![\theta_1 \le \theta_1']\!](\alpha \circ \alpha')) \cdot (f\, \alpha') \cdot ([\![\theta_0' \le \theta_0]\!](\alpha \circ \alpha')),$$

and the semantic equation for the fixed-point operator,

TY SEM EQ: Fixed Point (19.22)

$$[\![\pi \vdash \mathbf{rec}\ p : \theta]\!]\alpha\, \eta = \mathbf{Y}_{\mathcal{D}(\theta)\alpha}([\![\pi \vdash p : \theta \to \theta]\!]\alpha\, \eta\, \langle\rangle).$$

We leave it to the reader to verify that these are type-correct equations in the metalanguage.

Although we have given a complete definition of a simple Algol-like language (excluding arrays), it is beyond the scope of this book to prove that this definition is coherent and that β- and η-reduction preserve meaning. For those readers who are familiar with category theory, however, we give a brief synopsis: The set $\mathbf{Shp}$ of sequences of countable sets can be partially ordered by defining $\alpha_0 \le \alpha_1$ to hold when α_0 is an initial subsequence of α_1. Then, for every type θ, there is a functor F_θ, from $\mathbf{Shp}$ to the category $\mathbf{Dom}$ of domains and continuous functions, such that $F_\theta\alpha = \mathcal{D}(\theta)\alpha$ and $F_\theta(\alpha \le \alpha \circ \alpha') = \mathcal{T}(\theta)(\alpha, \alpha')$. Similarly, for every context π, there is a functor F_π^* such that $F_\pi^*\alpha = \mathcal{D}^*(\pi)\alpha$ and $F_\pi^*(\alpha \le \alpha \circ \alpha') = \mathcal{T}^*(\pi)(\alpha, \alpha')$. Then the conversion $[\![\theta \le \theta']\!]$ is a natural transformation from F_θ to $F_{\theta'}$, and the meaning $[\![\pi \vdash p : \theta]\!]$ is a natural transformation from F_π^* to F_θ.

These functors and natural transformations are objects and morphisms in the subcategory of the functor category $\mathbf{Dom}^{\mathbf{Shp}}$, whose objects are functors mapping morphisms into strict functions. It can be shown that this subcategory is Cartesian closed.

Of course, one must prove that the laws for functors are satisfied by F_θ and F_π^*, and that the laws for natural transformations are satisfied by conversions and the meanings of phrases. Ultimately, these laws are the properties that are needed to prove coherence and the soundness of reductions.

19.8 Some Extensions and Simplifications

There is an unpleasant asymmetry in the subtyping structure of primitive phrase types, which is displayed in diagram (19.3) in Section 19.1. Although we have implicit conversions from variables to expressions, which can be evaluated but not updated, there is no conversion from variables to some type of entity that can be updated but not evaluated. To introduce such entities, called *acceptors*, we augment our abstract syntax with

$$\langle \text{phrase type} \rangle ::= \textbf{intacc} \mid \textbf{realacc} \mid \textbf{boolacc}$$

and the subtyping rules

SBTY RULE: Variables to Acceptors

$$\overline{\delta \textbf{var} \leq \delta \textbf{acc}}, \tag{19.28}$$

SBTY RULE: Real to Integer Acceptors

$$\overline{\textbf{realacc} \leq \textbf{intacc}}. \tag{19.29}$$

Notice that the ordering in rule (19.29) is the dual of that for expressions in rule (19.2) — since integers can be converted to reals, a real acceptor can be used in any context requiring an integer acceptor. With these additions, the structure of the primitive phrase types becomes

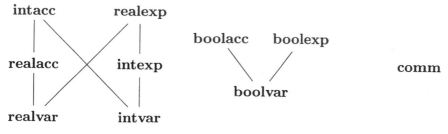

Once acceptors have been introduced, we can revise inference rule (19.13) in Section 19.2 to require acceptors on the left of assignment commands:

TY RULE: Acceptor Assignment

$$\frac{\pi \vdash p_0 : \delta\mathbf{acc} \qquad \pi \vdash p_1 : \delta\mathbf{exp}}{\pi \vdash p_0 := p_1 : \mathbf{comm}.} \qquad (19.30)$$

Clearly, the semantics of acceptors should be that of update components, so that

$$\mathcal{D}(\delta\mathbf{acc})\alpha = S_\delta \to (\textstyle\prod\alpha) \to (\textstyle\prod\alpha)_\bot.$$

The conversion equations corresponding to rules (19.28) and (19.29), and the semantic equation corresponding to rule (19.30), are left to the reader.

Except for identifiers of type $\delta\mathbf{acc}$, there are no phrases in our language that have type $\delta\mathbf{acc}$ but not $\delta\mathbf{var}$. Nevertheless, the new types are useful, particularly for sharpening the specification of parameters to procedures. Instead of

$$\mathbf{let}\ \mathsf{p} \equiv \lambda \mathsf{x}_{\mathbf{intvar}}.\ \mathsf{x} := \mathsf{y} + \mathsf{z} \ \cdots,$$

one can write

$$\mathbf{let}\ \mathsf{p} \equiv \lambda \mathsf{x}_{\mathbf{intacc}}.\ \mathsf{x} := \mathsf{y} + \mathsf{z} \ \cdots$$

to make it clear that the procedure p does not evaluate its parameter, so that its behavior will not depend on the value of the parameter when the procedure application begins execution.

It is clear from the subtype diagram displayed above that the types **intacc** and **realexp** have lower bounds but no greatest lower bound. This is not a problem in the present language, but it becomes one if the conditional construction is generalized to arbitrary phrase types:

TY RULE: General Conditional Phrases

$$\frac{\pi \vdash p_0 : \mathbf{boolexp} \qquad \pi \vdash p_1 : \theta \qquad \pi \vdash p_2 : \theta}{\pi \vdash \mathbf{if}\ p_0\ \mathbf{then}\ p_1\ \mathbf{else}\ p_2 : \theta,} \qquad (19.31)$$

since this generalization permits one to construct a phrase that has both types:

$$\mathsf{b}: \mathbf{boolexp}, \mathsf{n}: \mathbf{intvar}, \mathsf{x}: \mathbf{realvar} \vdash \mathbf{if}\ \mathsf{b}\ \mathbf{then}\ \mathsf{n}\ \mathbf{else}\ \mathsf{x} : \mathbf{intacc}$$

$$\mathsf{b}: \mathbf{boolexp}, \mathsf{n}: \mathbf{intvar}, \mathsf{x}: \mathbf{realvar} \vdash \mathbf{if}\ \mathsf{b}\ \mathbf{then}\ \mathsf{n}\ \mathbf{else}\ \mathsf{x} : \mathbf{realexp}.$$

The difficulty is that, when **if b then n else** x appears as an expression, it must be viewed as a real expression, because it can produce a noninteger value if b is false; but when **if b then n else** x appears as an acceptor, it must be viewed as an integer acceptor, because it cannot accept a noninteger value if b is true. But there is no single type that can be given to this conditional phrase that characterizes both of the ways in which it can be used. If we add such a phrase, which might be called an "integer-accepting, real-producing variable", we would have the ordering

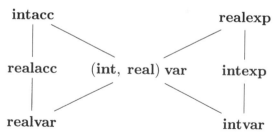

At this stage, our primitive types have become baroque. Fortunately, however, the type system can be substantially simplified if one introduces intersection types, as in Section 16.3. Then one can regard variables as intersection types rather than primitive types:

$$\delta\mathbf{var} \stackrel{\text{def}}{=} \delta\mathbf{acc} \,\&\, \delta\mathbf{exp} \qquad (\mathbf{int}, \mathbf{real}) \; \mathbf{var} \stackrel{\text{def}}{=} \mathbf{intacc} \,\&\, \mathbf{realexp},$$

so that only seven primitive types remain:

The interaction of variables and call by name can cause surprising effects. In Section 4.4, we saw that, in a state where the array X satisfies $X(0) = 0$ and $X(1) = 7$, the assignment $X(X(0)) := 1$ will cause $X(X(0))$ to take the value 7. But now we can pass $X(X(0))$ to a procedure as a parameter of type **intvar**. Thus, for example (where fib is defined as at the beginning of Section 19.3), $\text{fib}(X(X(0)))$ will malfunction when $X(0) = 0$ and $X(1) = 7$, since the first assignment to the formal parameter f will cause f to take on an inappropriate value.

Another example of an oddly behaved phrase of a variable type arises if conditional variables are permitted. For instance, if $x = 0$ and $y = 7$, then the assignment (**if** $x = 0$ **then** x **else** y) := 1 will cause (**if** $x = 0$ **then** x **else** y) to take the value 7. Thus $\text{fib}(\mathbf{if}\ x = 0\ \mathbf{then}\ x\ \mathbf{else}\ y)$ will malfunction.

Such behavior is permissible in update-evaluate semantics, where a variable is simply an entity that produces a state-dependent value when evaluated and causes a value-dependent state change when updated. Indeed, it is possible to extend our language to permit the construction of variables with arbitrary update and evaluate components, so that the programmer can create oddly behaved variables that are more useful than self-subscripting arrays or conditional variables.

For this purpose, we can extend our syntax with

$$\langle\text{phrase}\rangle ::= \mathbf{varcombine}\ \langle\text{phrase}\rangle\ \langle\text{phrase}\rangle$$

and introduce the subtyping rule

SBTY RULE: Procedures to Acceptors

$$\delta\mathbf{exp} \to \mathbf{comm} \le \delta\mathbf{acc},$$
(19.32)

and the type inference rule

TY RULE: Combining Acceptors and Expressions

$$\frac{\pi \vdash p_0 : \delta\mathbf{acc} \qquad \pi \vdash p_1 : \delta\mathbf{exp}}{\pi \vdash \mathbf{varcombine}\ p_0\ p_1 : \delta\mathbf{var}.}$$
(19.33)

The effect of the subtyping is to convert an arbitrary procedure describing a value-dependent state change into an acceptor:

CONV EQ: Procedures to Acceptors (19.32)

$$[\![\delta\mathbf{exp} \to \mathbf{comm} \le \delta\mathbf{acc}]\!]\alpha\, f\, x\, \sigma = f\langle\rangle(\lambda\sigma'.\ \iota_\uparrow x)\sigma.$$

The effect of the **varcombine** operation is to convert an arbitrary acceptor and expression into an update-evaluate pair:

TY SEM EQ: Combining Acceptors and Expressions (19.33)

$$[\![\pi \vdash \mathbf{varcombine}\ p_0\ p_1 : \delta\mathbf{var}]\!]\alpha\eta = \langle[\![\pi \vdash p_0 : \delta\mathbf{acc}]\!]\alpha\eta, [\![\pi \vdash p_1 : \delta\mathbf{exp}]\!]\alpha\eta\rangle.$$

Roughly speaking, when a has type $\delta\mathbf{exp} \to \mathbf{comm}$ and e has type $\delta\mathbf{exp}$, the assignment command $a := e$ has the same meaning as the procedure application $a\, e$. However, the assignment command causes e to be evaluated exactly once, regardless of how many times a evaluates its parameter. In effect, the assignment imposes call by value on the procedure call. (A call-by-name form of assignment has been prescribed for the language Forsythe, but it appears to be seriously inefficient.)

As an example of this kind of generalized variable, consider the declarator

> let newsummingvar $\equiv \lambda\mathrm{init}_{\mathrm{intexp}}.\ \lambda\mathrm{body}_{\mathrm{intvar}\to\mathrm{comm}}.$
>
> **new intvar** x := init **in** body(**varcombine**($\lambda i_{\mathrm{intexp}}.$ x := x + i) x) $\cdots$.

The effect of newsummingvar $p_0\ \lambda\iota_{\mathrm{intvar}}.\ p_1$ is to make ι stand for a new integer variable (initialized to p_0) whose value is increased, rather than reset, by assignment. In other words, $\iota := p$ increases the value of ι by p.

A second example is the declarator

> let newintvarwithmax $\equiv \lambda\mathrm{init}_{\mathrm{intexp}}.\ \lambda\mathrm{body}_{\mathrm{intvar}\to\mathrm{intexp}\to\mathrm{comm}}.$
>
> **new intvar** x := init **in new intvar** m := init **in** body(**varcombine**
>
> $(\lambda i_{\mathrm{intexp}}.\ (\mathrm{x} := i\,;\mathbf{if}\ i > m\ \mathbf{then}\ m := i\ \mathbf{else}\ \mathbf{skip}))\,\mathrm{x})\,\mathrm{m} \cdots$.

The effect of newintvarwithmax p_0 $\lambda \iota_{0\text{intvar}}$. $\lambda \iota_{1\text{intexp}}$. p_1 is to make ι_0 stand for a conventionally behaved new integer variable while making ι_1 stand for an expression whose value is the largest integer yet assigned to ι_0.

Independently of the treatment of acceptors and variables, and the possible introduction of intersection types, it is useful to introduce a product constructor for phrase types. Since implicit conversions that forget fields are often convenient, the named product of Section 16.2 is particularly suitable; the details of its syntax and semantics are the same as in that section. (As mentioned in Section 16.6, if intersection types are used, multifield products can be regarded as intersections of single-field products.)

It should be emphasized that a product of *phrase* types is more like an object, in the sense of object-oriented programming (and in particular, Simula 67), than like a conventional record. For example, suppose we wish to define "counter" objects with three fields: value, which produces the current value of the counter; increment, which increases the current value by one; and increase, which increases the current value by a specified amount. First we define the type variable counter by means of a transparent type definition, as in Section 18.1:

lettranstype counter

$$\equiv \mathbf{prod}(\text{value}: \mathbf{intexp}, \text{increment}: \mathbf{comm}, \text{increase}: \mathbf{intexp} \to \mathbf{comm}) \cdots .$$

Second, we define the declarator

let makecounter $= \lambda \text{body}_{\text{counter}\to\mathbf{comm}}$. $\mathbf{new\ intvar}\ \mathsf{x} := 0\ \mathbf{in}$

  body (value $\equiv$ x, increment $\equiv$ x := x + 1, increase $\equiv \lambda i_{\text{intexp}}$. x := x + i) $\cdots$.

Then the effect of makecounter $\lambda \iota_{\text{counter}}$. p is to create a counter with initial value zero and execute p with ι standing for the counter.

In the jargon of object-oriented programming, the definition of makecounter is a "class definition"; makecounter itself is an "object constructor"; and value, increment, and increase are "methods". However, although one can claim that an Algol-like language with products of phrase types supports the concept of objects, the manipulation of these objects is constrained by the character of the language. In particular, there are no variables whose values are objects, and an object cannot outlive the declarator application that creates it.

Bibliographic Notes

In addition to Algol 60 [Naur et al., 1960; 1963], early Algol-like languages include Simula 67 [Dahl, Myhrhaug, and Nygaard, 1968] and Algol W [Wirth and Hoare, 1966]. (Despite its name, Algol 68 is better classed as an Iswim-like language.)

  The characterization of Algol-like languages presented in this chapter was originally set forth by Reynolds [1981b]. The semantics in Sections 19.5 to 19.7 is a variation on the functor category semantics devised by Oles [1982; 1985; 1997]. The use of such a semantics to structure the translation of an Algol-like language into intermediate code is described by Reynolds [1995]. An operational transition semantics has been devised by Weeks and Felleisen [1993]. The semantics of extensions to concurrency have been investigated by Brookes, for both shared-variable concurrency [1996a] and communicating sequential processes [1997].

The complete design of a modern Algol-like language, Forsythe, is presented in Reynolds [1996].

The specification and verification of Algol-like programs are supported by *specification logic* [Reynolds, 1981a; 1982], which provides two levels of logic corresponding to the lambda-calculus and imperative aspects of the programs. The surprisingly subtle semantics of this logic has been worked out by Tennent [1990] and O'Hearn and Tennent [1993].

In specification logic, the absence of aliasing or interference is a property that must be reasoned about in the same way as other program specifications. An alternative approach, called *syntactic control of interference*, is to restrict the programming language (by means of what is actually a novel type system) so that potentially interfering phrases are syntactically detectable [Reynolds, 1978; 1989; O'Hearn, Power, Takeyama, and Tennent, 1995].

The interaction of variable declarations and procedures makes it difficult to achieve abstraction in the denotational semantics of Algol-like languages. Abstraction and related issues have been investigated by Meyer and Sieber [1988], Sieber [1994], O'Hearn [1996], O'Hearn and Tennent [1995], and Pitts [1996].

Recently, both syntactic control of interference and the search for more abstract semantics have inspired novel approaches to the description of Algol-like languages, using object-based semantics [Reddy, 1996], linear logic and game semantics [Abramsky and McCusker, 1996], and linear typing and polymorphism [O'Hearn and Reynolds, 1998].

Exercises

19.1   Consider the procedure definition

> **let** sum $\equiv \lambda i_{\text{intvar}}.\ \lambda e_{\text{intexp}}.$
>
> $(s := 0\,;\,i := a - 1\,;\,\textbf{while } i < b\textbf{ do }(i := i + 1\,;\,s := s + e)) \cdots.$

At first sight, one would expect that sum i e would merely be an inefficient way of setting s to the product of e times the number of integers between a and b inclusive. But more interesting things can happen if i interferes with e.

Give an example of a useful and interesting application of sum. (This way of using call by name, known as "Jensen's device", was used as an example in the original Algol 60 Report.)

19.2   Define a declarator newintvarres such that newintvarres *init fin* $\lambda\iota_{\text{intvar}} \cdot p$
        behaves similarly to **new intvar** $\iota := init$ **in** p, with the additional effect
        that, after execution of p, the final value of ι is assigned to the integer
        variable *fin*.

        Use this declarator to rewrite the last definition of fib in Section 19.3,
        in a way that encapsulates the use of call by result.

19.3   Write two declarators that are similar to newsqrealarray in Section 19.4,
        except that

        (a) The declared array is symmetric, so that its (i, j)th element is the
            same variable as its (j, i)th element, in the sense that assigning to
            one will assign the same value to both.

        (b) The declared array is antisymmetric, so that assigning a value r to
            the (i, j)th element will assign $-r$ to the (j, i)th element. The di-
            agonal elements indexed by (i, i) should always have zero value, and
            assignment to these elements should have no effect. The initial value
            of the (i, j)th element should be

            if $i > j$ **then** init **else if** $i < j$ **then** $-$ init **else** 0.

            (You will need to use the **varcombine** constructor discussed in Sec-
            tion 19.8.)

19.4   Assume that the language of this chapter has no built-in array declara-
        tions. Give a correct though inefficient recursive definition of the declara-
        tor newrealarray described in Section 19.4.

        Hint At each recursive level, your procedure should declare a local vari-
        able that stores a single array element.

19.5   Define three versions of a declarator newintvarwithsquare. In all cases,
        the effect of newintvarwithsquare p_0 $\lambda\iota_{0\text{intvar}} \cdot \lambda\iota_{1\text{intexp}} \cdot p_1$ should be to
        execute p_1 with ι_0 standing for a conventionally behaved new integer
        variable (initialized to p_0) and ι_1 standing for an expression whose value
        is always the square of the value of ι_0. Operationally, the three versions
        should behave differently, as follows:

        (a) The square should be computed each time ι_1 is evaluated.
        (b) The square should be computed each time ι_0 is assigned to.
        (c) The square should be computed each time ι_1 is evaluated and an
            assignment to ι_0 has occurred after the last evaluation of ι_1.

        In the last two cases, you will need to use the **varcombine** constructor
        discussed in Section 19.8.

19.6   Extend the semantics of Section 19.6 by giving a typed semantic equation
        for array declarations (which are described by inference rule (19.26) in
        Section 19.4).

19.7   In general, we might introduce any of the type constructors $\rightarrow$, **prod**,
        sum, and **list** for either phrase types or data types. What are the con-
        sequences, for the behavior of the language and its implementation, of
        adding **sum** or **list** to act on phrase types? What are the consequences
        of adding each of the four constructors to act on data types?

19.8   Although we have prohibited expression side effects throughout this chap-
        ter, they are not incompatible with the basic structure of Algol-like lan-
        guages. Indeed, they were permitted in Algol 60 and many other Algol-like
        languages.

        A clean way of introducing expressions with side effects (based on the
        "block expressions" of Algol W) is to add type inference rules that permit
        the sequential composition of commands and expressions:

$$\frac{\pi \vdash p_0 : \textbf{comm} \qquad \pi \vdash p_1 : \delta\textbf{exp}}{\pi \vdash p_0 \, ; p_1 : \delta\textbf{exp},}$$

and the use of declarations in commands and expressions:

$$\frac{\pi \vdash p_0 : \delta\textbf{exp} \qquad \pi, \iota\colon \delta\textbf{var} \vdash p_1 : \delta'\textbf{exp}}{\pi \vdash \textbf{new } \delta\textbf{var } \iota := p_0 \textbf{ in } p_1 : \delta'\textbf{exp}}$$

$$\frac{\pi \vdash p_0 : \textbf{intexp} \qquad \pi \vdash p_1 : \delta\textbf{exp} \qquad \pi, \iota\colon \textbf{intexp} \rightarrow \delta\textbf{var} \vdash p_2 : \delta'\textbf{exp}}{\pi \vdash \textbf{new } \delta\textbf{array } \iota(p_0) := p_1 \textbf{ in } p_2 : \delta'\textbf{exp}.}$$

Semantically, the key is to change the semantics of expressions (and the
evaluate component of update-evaluate pairs) to

$$\mathcal{D}(\delta\textbf{exp})\alpha = \left(\textstyle\prod \alpha\right) \rightarrow \left(\left(\textstyle\prod \alpha\right) \times S_\delta\right)_{\perp}.$$

Work out the resulting semantics.

Appendix

Mathematical Background

Here we describe a variety of general mathematical concepts and notations that are used in this book. (Concepts that are more advanced, or are particular to programming-language theory, are explained in the main text when they are first used.) Even though most of these concepts may be familiar, readers are advised to scan this material, especially since some of the notations are novel.

In fact, modern mathematics gives the writer a surprising degree of freedom in defining its fundamental concepts, as long as the definitions are consistent and lead to entities with appropriate properties. In this book, I have made the following choices:

- Pairs are taken to be a primitive notion rather than being defined in terms of sets.

- Relations are defined as sets of pairs, functions as a special kind of relation, sequences as a special kind of function, and pairs as a special kind of sequence. Since a pair, however, cannot be a set containing itself, we break the inconsistent circle by distinguishing between the pairs $\langle x, y \rangle$ that are sequences and the *primitive* pairs $[x, y]$ that are members of relations.

- We define relations (including functions) to be sets of primitive argument-result pairs, rather than calling such a set the "graph" of the relation and defining the relation itself to consist of a domain, a codomain, and a graph. Thus, for example, the function on the integers that increases its argument by one is both a function from integers to integers and a function from integers to reals, and also a partial function from reals to reals. (This view of functions is taken by Gleason [1966, Sections 3-4.1 to 3-4.11]. It is a special case of the view that, in category theory, the morphism sets of a category need not be disjoint.)

- For both finite and infinite sequences, we take zero (rather than one) to be the least index. Thus a sequence of length n, often called an n-tuple, is indexed by the integers $0, \ldots, n - 1$. However, we will sometimes speak of s_0 as the first element of the sequence s, s_1 as the second element, and so on.

A.1 Sets

The most direct way to denote finite sets is to list their members explicitly in braces, for example, $\{1, 4, 9, 16\}$. However, one must remember that sets do not depend on any ordering or repetition of their elements, so that $\{1, 9, 4\}$ and even $\{1, 9, 4, 9\}$ denote the same set as $\{1, 4, 9\}$. (This point can be especially tricky when the notation is used with variables; for example, $\{x, y\}$ denotes a set with one member when $x = y$.) As a special case of this notation, $\{\}$ denotes the empty set.

We will use the following symbols for particular sets:

- **Z** to denote the set of integers,
- **N** or sometimes ω to denote the set of natural numbers (which are the non-negative integers),
- **R** to denote the set of real numbers, or sometimes the countable set of machine-representable (floating-point) real numbers,
- **B** to denote the set $\{\textbf{true}, \textbf{false}\}$ of truth values.

Membership, inclusion, union, intersection, and difference of sets will be indicated by the binary operators $\in$, $\subseteq$, $\cup$, $\cap$, and $-$. The *difference* $S - S'$ is the set of those members of S that do not belong to S'. Two sets are *disjoint* if their intersection is empty. The *powerset* of S, written $\mathcal{P}\, S$, is the set of all subsets of S.

We will occasionally write $x \in! S$ instead of $S = \{x\}$ to assert that x is the unique member of S. We will also write $S \overset{\text{fin}}{\subseteq} S'$ to assert that S is a finite subset of S', and $\mathcal{P}_{\text{fin}}\, S$ to denote the set of all finite subsets of S.

Suppose E is an expression and P is a *predicate*, which is an expression whose values belong to **B**. Then $\{\, E \mid P \,\}$, which is called a *set comprehension*, denotes the set that contains x if and only if there are values for the variables in P and E that make $P = \textbf{true}$ and $E = x$.

For example, we can use set comprehensions to define more specialized notations for consecutive sets of integers:

$$m \textbf{ to } n \overset{\text{def}}{=} \{\, i \mid m \leq i \leq n \,\}$$

$$m \textbf{ to } \infty \overset{\text{def}}{=} \{\, i \mid m \leq i \,\}$$

$$-\infty \textbf{ to } n \overset{\text{def}}{=} \{\, i \mid i \leq n \,\}$$

$$-\infty \textbf{ to } \infty \overset{\text{def}}{=} \{\, i \mid \textbf{true} \,\}$$

$$= \textbf{Z}.$$

Note that ∞ and $-\infty$ are not integers and do not belong to any of these sets. In general, $m \textbf{ to } n$ is called the *interval* from m to n; it is the empty set whenever

$m > n$. (This kind of interval should not be confused with intervals of real numbers.)

When the context makes it clear that a set is intended, we will sometimes write a natural number n to stand for the interval 0 **to** $n - 1$.

The notation $\{ E \mid P \}$ can be abused. One must avoid meaningless expressions such as $\{ x \mid x \notin x \}$. Even more seriously, one must beware of ambiguity. For example, except for the contextual clue "consecutive sets of integers", one might have mistaken the sets defined above for much larger sets of real numbers.

Another source of ambiguity in this notation is the question of which variables are bound. For example,

$$m \text{ to } n \stackrel{\text{def}}{=} \{ i \mid m \leq i \leq n \}$$

only makes sense if one realizes from the context that, on the right side, the variable i is bound but m and n are not bound.

Operations such as union can be generalized in several ways. It is simplest to start with the most general concept and then define more specialized ones. If $\mathcal{S}$ denotes a set whose members are sets, then

$$\bigcup \mathcal{S} \stackrel{\text{def}}{=} \{ x \mid (\exists S \in \mathcal{S})\, x \in S \}.$$

Next, if A denotes a set and, whenever the variable i denotes a member of A, the expression S (usually containing occurrences of i) denotes a set, then

$$\bigcup_{i \in A} S \stackrel{\text{def}}{=} \bigcup \{ S \mid i \in A \}.$$

Then, if a is either an integer or $-\infty$ and b is either an integer or ∞, then

$$\bigcup_{i=a}^{b} S \stackrel{\text{def}}{=} \bigcup_{i \in a \text{ to } b} S.$$

Finally, if $S_0, ..., S_{n-1}$ denote sets, then

$$S_0 \cup \cdots \cup S_{n-1} \stackrel{\text{def}}{=} \bigcup_{i=0}^{n-1} \begin{cases} S_0 & \text{if } i = 0 \\ \quad \vdots \\ S_{n-1} & \text{if } i = n - 1. \end{cases}$$

A similar sequence of specializations can be carried out for intersection (or for any other operation whose most general form is applicable to a set, such as the least upper bound or greatest lower bound of a subset of a partial order). One starts with the definition

$$\bigcap \mathcal{S} \stackrel{\text{def}}{=} \{ x \mid (\forall S \in \mathcal{S})\, x \in S \}.$$

Note, however, that $\bigcap \mathcal{S}$ is meaningless when $\mathcal{S}$ is the empty set (since it would denote the paradoxical "set of everything"). Thus, $\bigcap_{i \in A} S$ is meaningless when A is empty, and $\bigcap_{i=a}^{b} S$ is meaningless when $a > b$.

We write $\#S$ for the size of the set S, which may be either a natural number or infinity.

A.2 Relations

We write $[x, x']$ to denote the *primitive pair* whose first component is x and whose second component is x'. It is possible to define pairs in terms of sets, say, by

$$[x, x'] \stackrel{\text{def}}{=} \{\{x\}, \{x, x'\}\},$$

but such a definition implies properties (such as $\{x\} \in [x, x']$ but $\{x'\} \notin [x, x']$ when $x' \neq x$) that are irrelevant to the concept of "pair". It is better to assume that "pair" is a primitive concept and to regard the above "definition" as merely a way of representing pairs in terms of sets.

A *relation* is a set whose members are primitive pairs. We will sometimes write $\rho: x \mapsto x'$ or $x \, \rho \, x'$ as synonyms for $[x, x'] \in \rho$, and describe this situation by saying that ρ *relates* x to x'.

The empty set is a relation, often called the *empty relation*. When two relations satisfy $\rho \subseteq \rho'$, ρ is said to be a *restriction* of ρ', and ρ' is said to be an *extension* of ρ.

When every pair $[x, x'] \in \rho$ satisfies $x = x'$, ρ is said to be an *identity relation*. For each set S, there is an identity relation

$$I_S \stackrel{\text{def}}{=} \{ [x, x] \mid x \in S \},$$

called the *identity relation on* S. Moreover, every identity relation is I_S for a unique set S.

The set operations $\cup$, $\cap$, and $-$ all carry relations into relations. More generally, if R is a set of relations, $\bigcup R$ is a relation, and if R is a nonempty set of relations, $\bigcap R$ is a relation.

A variety of additional operations on relations are significant. For relations ρ and ρ', we define

- The *domain* of ρ:

$$\operatorname{dom} \rho \stackrel{\text{def}}{=} \{ x \mid (\exists x') \, [x, x'] \in \rho \},$$

- The *range* of ρ:

$$\operatorname{ran} \rho \stackrel{\text{def}}{=} \{ x' \mid (\exists x) \, [x, x'] \in \rho \},$$

- The *composition* of ρ with ρ':

$$\rho' \cdot \rho \stackrel{\text{def}}{=} \rho \, ; \rho' \stackrel{\text{def}}{=} \{ [x, x''] \mid (\exists x') \, [x, x'] \in \rho \text{ and } [x', x''] \in \rho' \},$$

- The *reflection* of ρ:

$$\rho^\dagger \overset{\text{def}}{=} \{\, [x', x] \mid [x, x'] \in \rho \,\}.$$

The two operators $\cdot$ and $;$ describe composition in opposite orders, which are called *functional* order, and *diagrammatic* order respectively.

These operations obey the following laws, where ρ, ρ', ρ'', ρ_1, ρ_2, ρ_1', and ρ_2' denote relations; S and T denote sets; and R and R' denote sets of relations:

- Associativity of composition:

$$(\rho'' \cdot \rho') \cdot \rho = \rho'' \cdot (\rho' \cdot \rho),$$

- Identity laws:

$$\rho \cdot I_S \subseteq \rho$$
$$I_S \cdot \rho \subseteq \rho$$
$$\rho \cdot I_S = \rho \quad \text{when } \operatorname{dom} \rho \subseteq S$$
$$I_S \cdot \rho = \rho \quad \text{when } \operatorname{ran} \rho \subseteq S$$
$$\rho \subseteq I_S \quad \text{if and only if } (\exists T) \; T \subseteq S \text{ and } \rho = I_T$$
$$I_T \cdot I_S = I_{S \cap T}$$
$$\operatorname{dom} I_S - S$$
$$\operatorname{ran} I_S = S,$$

- Reflection laws:

$$(\rho^\dagger)^\dagger = \rho \qquad (\rho' \cdot \rho)^\dagger = \rho^\dagger \cdot \rho'^\dagger \qquad I_S{}^\dagger = I_S,$$

- Laws for the empty relation:

$$\rho \cdot \{\} = \{\} \qquad \{\} \cdot \rho = \{\} \qquad I_{\{\}} = \{\} \qquad \{\}^\dagger = \{\},$$

- Monotonicity laws:

$$(\rho_0 \subseteq \rho_1 \text{ and } \rho_0' \subseteq \rho_1') \text{ implies } \rho_0' \cdot \rho_0 \subseteq \rho_1' \cdot \rho_1$$
$$\rho_0 \subseteq \rho_1 \text{ implies } \rho_0{}^\dagger \subseteq \rho_1{}^\dagger,$$

- Additivity laws:

$$(\bigcup R') \cdot (\bigcup R) = \bigcup \{\, \rho' \cdot \rho \mid \rho \in R \text{ and } \rho' \in R' \,\}$$
$$(\bigcup R)^\dagger = \bigcup \{\, \rho^\dagger \mid \rho \in R \,\}.$$

Since composition is associative, we can write multiple compositions without parentheses, as in $\rho'' \cdot \rho' \cdot \rho$.

For a relation ρ and a set S, we define

$$\rho \rceil S \overset{\text{def}}{=} \rho \cdot I_S,$$

called the *restriction of ρ to S*, and

$$\rho \lceil S \overset{\text{def}}{=} I_S \cdot \rho,$$

called the *corestriction of ρ to S*. Notice the difference between these concepts and the more general one of a restriction of ρ, without the qualification "to S". The restriction or corestriction of ρ to S is a restriction of ρ. However, there are restrictions of ρ that are not restrictions (or corestrictions) of ρ to any set.

A.3 Functions

A function is a relation that does not relate any x to more than one x'. More precisely, a relation ρ is a *function* (or *map*) if and only if, whenever $[x, x'_0] \in \rho$ and $[x, x'_1] \in \rho$, $x'_0 = x'_1$.

One can show that this definition is equivalent to saying that ρ is a function if and only if the composition $\rho \cdot \rho^\dagger$ is an identity relation. It follows that, if f and f' are functions, S is a set, and ρ is a relation, then

$$f' \cdot f \text{ is a function,}$$

$$I_S \text{ is a function,}$$

$$\{\} \text{ is a function,}$$

$$\rho \subseteq f \text{ implies } \rho \text{ is a function.}$$

On the other hand, even when f is a function it may be the case that $f^\dagger$ is not a function; if both f and $f^\dagger$ are functions, f is called an *injection*.

If f is a function and $x \in \text{dom } f$, then f relates x to a unique x' that is called the *result of applying f to x* and is denoted by $f\,x$ (often without parenthesizing x), or occasionally by f_x. We also say that f *maps x into x'* instead of f relates x to x'. Syntactically, we will assume that function application is left associative, so that $f\,x\,y$ stands for $(f\,x)\,y$.

If f and g are functions such that $x \in \text{dom}\,(g \cdot f)$ (which will be a subset of dom f), then $(g \cdot f)\,x = g(f\,x)$ (which shows why $\cdot$ is called composition in functional order).

We will often denote functions by *typed abstractions* (also called *typed lambda expressions*). If S denotes a set and E is an expression that is defined whenever the variable x denotes a member of S, then $\lambda x \in S.\ E$ denotes the function f with domain S such that $f\,x = E$ for all $x \in S$. For example, $\lambda x \in \mathbf{N}.\ x^2$ denotes the function $\{[x, x^2] \mid x \in \mathbf{N}\}$ that squares any nonnegative integer, and $\lambda x \in \mathbf{Z}.\ x+y$ denotes the function $\{[x, x + y] \mid x \in \mathbf{Z}\}$ that adds y to any integer. (Note that this is a different function for each value of y.)

When the body E of a abstraction $\lambda x \in S.\ E$ contains a single occurrence of the bound variable x, we will occasionally abbreviate the abstraction by its body, with the bound variable occurrence replaced by the placeholder "$-$". For example, $\lambda g \in S.\ f(g(x))$ might be abbreviated by $f(-(x))$. (With this notation, the domain S must be inferred from context.)

We will also use a special notation for the variation of a function at a single argument. If f is a function, then $[f \mid x{:}x']$ denotes the function f' such that $\operatorname{dom} f' = \operatorname{dom} f \cup \{x\}$, $f'x = x'$, and, for all $y \in \operatorname{dom} f' - \{x\}$, $f'y = f\,y$. Note that this definition is meaningful regardless of whether x belongs to the domain of f. For example, $[\lambda x \in 0 \text{ to } 1.\ x + 1 \mid 2{:}7]$ and $[\lambda x \in 0 \text{ to } 2.\ x + 1 \mid 2{:}7]$ both denote the function $\{[0, 1], [1, 2], [2, 7]\}$.

We will also use the abbreviations

$$[f \mid x_0{:}x_0' \mid \ldots \mid x_{n-1}{:}x_{n-1}'] \quad \text{for} \quad [\ldots[f \mid x_0{:}x_0']\ldots \mid x_{n-1}{:}x_{n-1}']$$

$$[x_0{:}x_0' \mid \ldots \mid x_{n-1}{:}x_{n-1}'] \quad \text{for} \quad [\{\} \mid x_0{:}x_0' \mid \ldots \mid x_{n-1}{:}x_{n-1}'].$$

In the special case where the x_i are distinct, the latter notation denotes the function with domain $\{x_0, \ldots, x_{n-1}\}$ that maps each x_i into x_i'. In particular, $[]$ denotes the empty function and is therefore a synonym of $\{\}$.

Finally, we write

$$\langle x_0', \ldots, x_{n-1}' \rangle \quad \text{for} \quad [0{:}x_0' \mid \ldots \mid n - 1{:}x_{n-1}'],$$

which denotes the function with domain 0 to $n - 1$ that maps each i into x_i'. A function with domain 0 to $n - 1$ is called an *n-tuple* or a *finite sequence of length* n. Similarly, a function with domain $\omega = 0$ to ∞ is called an *infinite sequence*. Note that the empty sequence $\langle\rangle$ is another synonym for $\{\}$.

We will call the 2-tuple $\langle x, y\rangle$ a *pair*. Strictly speaking, it should be distinguished from the primitive pair $[x, y]$. In practice, however, we will often overlook the distinction and use angle brackets for the members of relations and functions.

When a tuple or sequence f is applied to an argument i, it is more common to write f_i than $f\,i$, and to call the result of the application a *component* or *element* of f. For example, $\langle 3, 4\rangle_0 = 3$ and $\langle 3, 4\rangle_1 = 4$. Unfortunately, this notation can be confused with the use of subscripted variables where, for example, x, x_0, and x_1 may be distinct variables with unrelated values. When the distinction from a subscripted variable is not clear from context (or when f is a compound expression), a tuple application will be written as $(f)_i$.

There are many important notations for sets of functions. Suppose θ is a function, called a *set map*, that maps every member of its domain into a set.

Then the *Cartesian product of* θ is the set of functions

$$\textstyle\prod \theta \overset{\text{def}}{=} \{\, f \mid \operatorname{dom} f = \operatorname{dom} \theta \text{ and } (\forall i \in \operatorname{dom} \theta)\ f i \in \theta i \,\}.$$

If A denotes a set and, whenever the variable i denotes a member of A, the expression S denotes a set, then

$$\prod_{i \in A} S \overset{\text{def}}{=} \textstyle\prod \lambda i \in A.\ S,$$

so that

$$\textstyle\prod \theta = \prod_{i \in \operatorname{dom} \theta} \theta\, i.$$

For example, $\prod_{i \in \mathbf{Z}}\{\, j \mid j > i \,\}$ denotes the set of functions with domain $\mathbf{Z}$ that map each integer into a larger integer. (Products of this form are sometimes called *indexed* products.)

We can now develop more specialized forms of the Cartesian product in much the same way as we did for union. If a is either an integer or $-\infty$ and b is either an integer or ∞, then

$$\prod_{i=a}^{b} S \overset{\text{def}}{=} \prod_{i \in a \text{ to } b} S,$$

and, if $S_0, \ldots, S_{n-1}$ denote sets, then

$$S_0 \times \ldots \times S_{n-1} \overset{\text{def}}{=} \prod_{i=0}^{n-1} \begin{cases} S_0 & \text{if } i = 0 \\ \vdots \\ S_{n-1} & \text{if } i = n-1. \end{cases}$$

Thus, $S_0 \times \ldots \times S_{n-1}$ is the set of n-tuples or finite sequences $\langle x_0, \ldots, x_{n-1} \rangle$ such that each $x_i \in S_i$. In particular, $S_0 \times S_1$, called the *binary Cartesian product* of S_0 with S_1, is the set of pairs $\langle x_0, x_1 \rangle$ such that $x_0 \in S_0$ and $x_1 \in S_1$. (The homage to Descartes honors his discovery that the Euclidean plane is isomorphic to $\mathbf{R} \times \mathbf{R}$.)

The members of the powerset $\mathcal{P}\,(S_0 \times \ldots \times S_{n-1})$ are called *n-ary relations*; as a special case, the members of $\mathcal{P}\,(S_0 \times S_1)$ are called *binary relations*. (Again we have come full circle, since a binary relation is similar to a relation, except that its members are pairs instead of primitive pairs.)

It is also useful to define the *exponentiation* of sets by specializing the Cartesian product to constant set maps. If A and S are expressions denoting sets, and the variable i does not occur in S, then

$$S^A \overset{\text{def}}{=} \prod_{i \in A} S = \{\, f \mid \operatorname{dom} f = A \text{ and } \operatorname{ran} f \subseteq S \,\}.$$

As a special case, using the convention that n stands for the set 0 **to** $n-1$,

$$S^n \overset{\text{def}}{=} S^{0 \text{ to } n-1} = \underbrace{S \times \cdots \times S}_{n \text{ times}}$$

is the set of finite sequences of length n whose components all belong to S. Similarly, S^ω is the set of infinite sequences whose components all belong to S.

Note that $S^0 = S^{\{\}}$ is the singleton (i.e. one-element) set $\{\langle\rangle\}$, and $S_0 \times \ldots \times S_{n-1}$ is the empty set if any S_i is empty. More generally, $\prod_{i \in \{\}} S$ is $\{\langle\rangle\}$, and if S is empty for any $i \in A$, $\prod_{i \in A} S$ is empty.

In addition to exponentiation by a set of natural numbers, the following notation is also commonly used for sets of finite, finite nonempty, and finite or infinite sequences whose components all belong to S:

$$S^* \overset{\text{def}}{=} \bigcup_{n=0}^{\infty} S^n \qquad S^+ \overset{\text{def}}{=} \bigcup_{n=1}^{\infty} S^n \qquad S^\infty \overset{\text{def}}{=} S^* \cup S^\omega.$$

Exponentiation, such as the exponentiation of sets, is the main use of superscripts. Occasionally, however, one needs to use a superscript, in the same way as a subscript, to distinguish otherwise similar variables. In this situation, the superscript will often be parenthesized to avoid mistaking it for an exponent. For example, $S^{(2)}$ and $S^{(3)}$ are distinct variables, while S^2 and S^3 are exponentiations of the same variable S.

For a set map θ, we define the *disjoint union of θ* (also called the *sum* of θ) by

$$\sum \theta \overset{\text{def}}{=} \{\, \langle i, x\rangle \mid i \in \operatorname{dom}\theta \text{ and } x \in \theta i \,\} = \bigcup_{i \in \operatorname{dom}\theta} \{\, \langle i, x\rangle \mid x \in \theta i \,\}.$$

Thus the disjoint union of θ is an ordinary union of sets that are isomorphic to (i.e. in one-to-one correspondence with) the sets θi, but are forced to be disjoint by pairing their members with the "tags" i. As with the Cartesian product, we define indexed and more specialized forms:

$$\sum_{i \in A} S \overset{\text{def}}{=} \sum \lambda i \in A.\, S$$

$$\sum \theta = \sum_{i \in \operatorname{dom}\theta} \theta i$$

$$\sum_{i=a}^{b} S \overset{\text{def}}{=} \sum_{i \in a \text{ to } b} S$$

$$S_0 + \ldots + S_{n-1} \overset{\text{def}}{=} \sum_{i=0}^{n-1} \begin{cases} S_0 & \text{if } i = 0 \\ \vdots \\ S_{n-1} & \text{if } i = n-1, \end{cases}$$

so that

$$S_0 + \ldots + S_{n-1} \stackrel{\text{def}}{=} \{\, \langle 0, x\rangle \mid x \in S_0 \,\} \cup \cdots \cup \{\, \langle n-1, x\rangle \mid x \in S_{n-1} \,\}$$

denotes the union of n disjoint sets that are isomorphic to $S_1, \ldots, S_n$.

When S does not contain i, we have $\sum_{i \in A} S = A \times S$. As a special case,

$$\underbrace{S + \cdots + S}_{n \text{ times}} = n \times S,$$

where n on the right abbreviates the set 0 **to** $n-1$. Also, for any set expression S, $\sum_{i \in \{\}} S = \{\}$.

It is not necessary to introduce functions of several arguments as novel entities. In place of a function accepting n arguments in $S_0, \ldots, S_{n-1}$ and producing results in S, we will usually use a function in $S^{S_0 \times \cdots \times S_{n-1}}$, which is a function accepting a single argument that is an n-tuple. Thus we will write $f\langle x_0, \ldots, x_{n-1}\rangle$ instead of $f(x_0, \ldots, x_{n-1})$.

To facilitate this approach, we extend typed abstractions by defining

$$\lambda\langle\, x_0 \in S_0, \; \ldots, \; x_{n-1} \in S_{n-1} \,\rangle.\ E$$

$$\stackrel{\text{def}}{=} \lambda t \in S_0 \times \cdots \times S_{n-1}.\ (\lambda x_0 \in S_0.\ \ldots\ \lambda x_{n-1} \in S_{n-1}.\ E)(t\,0)\ldots(t(n-1)).$$

For example, the binary addition function in $\mathbf{Z}^{\mathbf{Z} \times \mathbf{Z}}$ could be written as

$$\lambda\langle\, x \in \mathbf{Z},\ y \in \mathbf{Z}\,\rangle.\ x + y.$$

Note that $\lambda\langle\, x \in S \,\rangle.\ E$ is not the same as $\lambda x \in S.\ E$, and that $\lambda\langle\rangle.\ E$ is the function, with the one-member domain $\{\langle\rangle\}$, that maps $\langle\rangle$ into E.

Sometimes we will take an alternative view of multiargument functions called *Currying* (after the logician Haskell Curry). In this approach, an n-argument function accepting arguments in $S_0, \ldots, S_{n-1}$ and producing results in S is regarded as a function with domain S_0 whose results are functions with domain $S_1 \ldots$ whose results are functions with domain S_{n-1} whose results are members of S, so that the set of such functions is $(\ldots (S)^{S_{n-1}} \ldots)^{S_0}$. Such functions can be defined by writing $\lambda x_0 \in S_0.\ \ldots\ \lambda x_{n-1} \in S_{n-1}.\ E$ and applied by writing $(\ldots (f x_0) \ldots x_{n-1})$ or, since function application is left-associative, simply $f x_0 \ldots x_{n-1}$.

Currying and the use of tuples as arguments are equivalent ways of representing multiargument functions, since the sets $(\ldots (S)^{S_{n-1}} \ldots)^{S_0}$ and $S^{S_0 \times \cdots \times S_{n-1}}$ are isomorphic.

A.4 Relations and Functions Between Sets

Instead of considering the collection of all relations or functions in this section we will focus on sets of relations or functions *from* some specified set *to* some specified set.

When dom $\rho \subseteq S$ and ran $\rho \subseteq S'$ or, equivalently, when every $[x, x'] \in \rho$ satisfies $x \in S$ and $x' \in S'$, we say that ρ is a *relation from S to S'*. We write $S \xrightarrow[\text{REL}]{} S'$ for the set of relations from S to S'. A relation from S to S is also called a *relation on S*.

Suppose S, S', and S'' are sets, $\rho \in S \xrightarrow[\text{REL}]{} S'$, and $\rho' \in S' \xrightarrow[\text{REL}]{} S''$. Then

$$\rho' \cdot \rho \in S \xrightarrow[\text{REL}]{} S''$$

$$I_S \in S \xrightarrow[\text{REL}]{} S$$

$$\rho^\dagger \in S' \xrightarrow[\text{REL}]{} S$$

$$\{\} \in S \xrightarrow[\text{REL}]{} S'$$

$$\{\} \in! \{\} \xrightarrow[\text{REL}]{} S'$$

$$\{\} \in! S \xrightarrow[\text{REL}]{} \{\}.$$

In addition, for $\rho \in S \xrightarrow[\text{REL}]{} S'$, we can rewrite the first two identity laws in Section A.2 in the simpler form

$$\rho \cdot I_S = \rho \qquad I_{S'} \cdot \rho = \rho.$$

We now consider certain subsets of $S \xrightarrow[\text{REL}]{} S'$. If $\rho \in S \xrightarrow[\text{REL}]{} S'$ relates every member of S to at least one member of S',

$$(\forall x \in S) \, (\exists x' \in S') \, [x, x'] \in \rho$$

or, equivalently, if dom $\rho = S$, then ρ is said to be a *total relation from S to S'*. We write $S \xrightarrow[\text{TREL}]{} S'$ for the set of total relations from S to S'.

Notice that a total relation from S to S' is not merely a relation from S to S' that is a total relation; the concept of "total relation" is meaningless without the qualification "from S to S'". (Indeed, any relation is a total relation from its domain to any set containing its range.)

If ρ is a relation from S to S', then it is a total relation from S to S' if and only if $\rho^\dagger \cdot \rho \supseteq I_S$. If $\rho \in S \xrightarrow[\text{TREL}]{} S'$ and $\rho' \in S' \xrightarrow[\text{TREL}]{} S''$, then

$$\rho' \cdot \rho \in S \xrightarrow[\text{TREL}]{} S''$$

$$I_S \in S \xrightarrow[\text{TREL}]{} S$$

$$\{\} \in! \{\} \xrightarrow[\text{TREL}]{} S'.$$

A relation from S to S' that is a function is called (rather oddly) a *partial function from S to S'*. We write $S \xrightarrow[\text{PFUN}]{} S'$ for the set of partial functions from S to S'.

If $\rho \in S \xrightarrow[\text{REL}]{} S'$, then $\rho \in S \xrightarrow[\text{PFUN}]{} S'$ if and only if $\rho \cdot \rho^\dagger \subseteq I_{S'}$. If $\rho \in S \xrightarrow[\text{PFUN}]{}$ S' and $\rho' \in S' \xrightarrow[\text{PFUN}]{} S''$, then

$$\rho' \cdot \rho \in S \xrightarrow[\text{PFUN}]{} S''$$

$$I_S \in S \xrightarrow[\text{PFUN}]{} S$$

$$\{\} \in S \xrightarrow[\text{PFUN}]{} S'$$

$$\{\} \in! \{\} \xrightarrow[\text{PFUN}]{} S'$$

$$\{\} \in! S \xrightarrow[\text{PFUN}]{} \{\}.$$

A partial function from S to S' whose domain is S is called a *function from S to S'*; we write $S \to S'$ for the set of functions from S to S'. The terminology here is a little tricky: If a function f satisfies

$$\text{dom } f \subseteq S \text{ and } \text{ran } f \subseteq S',$$

then it is a function that is a relation from S to S', and therefore a function that is a partial function from S to S'. To be a function *from S to S'*, however, it must satisfy the stronger condition

$$\text{dom } f = S \text{ and } \text{ran } f \subseteq S'.$$

It follows that $S \to S'$ is also the Cartesian product of S' over S:

$$S \to S' = (S')^S.$$

From another viewpoint, $S \to S' = (S \xrightarrow[\text{TREL}]{} S') \cap (S \xrightarrow[\text{PFUN}]{} S')$. Thus, if $\rho \in S \xrightarrow[\text{REL}]{} S'$, then $\rho \in S \to S'$ if and only if $\rho^\dagger \cdot \rho \supseteq I_S$ and $\rho \cdot \rho^\dagger \subseteq I_{S'}$. If $\rho \in S \to S'$ and $\rho' \in S' \to S''$, then

$$\rho' \cdot \rho \in S \to S''$$

$$I_S \in S \to S$$

$$\{\} \in! \{\} \to S'.$$

In writing expressions that stand for sets, we will assume that the various arrows are right-associative and have a lower precedence than $\times$. Thus, for example, $S \to T \times U \to V$ stands for $S \to ((T \times U) \to V)$.

A function from S to S' is called

- a *surjection from S to S'* if its range is S' or, equivalently, if its reflection is a total relation from S' to S.
- an *injection from S to S'* if it is an injection or, equivalently, if its reflection is a partial function from S' to S.
- a *bijection from S to S'* if it is both a surjection and an injection from S to S' or, equivalently, if its reflection is a function from S' to S.

(Notice that it makes sense, according to the definition in Section A.3, to say that a function is an injection per se, without adding the qualification "from S to S'". But it does not make sense to say that a function is a surjection or bijection per se.)

An equivalent definition is that a function f from S to S' is said to be a
$$\left\{ \begin{array}{l} \text{surjection} \\ \text{injection} \\ \text{bijection} \end{array} \right\} \text{ from } S \text{ to } S' \text{ when, for all } x' \in S', \text{ there is } \left\{ \begin{array}{l} \text{at least one} \\ \text{at most one} \\ \text{exactly one} \end{array} \right\}$$
$x \in S$ such that $f\,x = x'$.

A function ρ from S to S' is called an *isomorphism* from S to S' when it possesses left and right *inverses*, which are functions $\psi_l, \psi_r \in S' \to S$ such that

$$\psi_r \cdot \rho = I_S \quad \text{and} \quad \rho \cdot \psi_l = I_{S'}.$$

These equations imply $\psi_l = \psi_r \cdot \rho \cdot \psi_l = \psi_r$, so that every right inverse equals every left inverse. Thus an isomorphism ρ from S to S' possesses a unique inverse, which is two-sided and is denoted by ρ^{-1}. Moreover, ρ^{-1} is an isomorphism from S' to S, such that $(\rho^{-1})^{-1} = \rho$. It can be shown that a function is an isomorphism from S to S' if and only if it is a bijection from S to S'.

A.5 More About Products and Disjoint Unions

Associated with products and disjoint unions are special functions and constructions of functions from functions. Although these entities and their properties are defined for products and disjoint unions over arbitrary sets, we limit this exposition to the binary case.

Associated with the product $S \times S'$ are the *projection* functions $\pi \in S \times S' \to S$ and $\pi' \in S \times S' \to S'$ such that, for all $x \in S$ and $x' \in S'$,

$$\pi\langle x, x'\rangle = x \qquad \pi'\langle x, x'\rangle = x'.$$

Also associated with this product is a way of constructing a function from a pair of functions: If $f \in R \to S$ and $f' \in R \to S'$, then $f \otimes f'$ (often called the *target-tupling* of f and f') is the function from R to $S \times S'$ such that, for all $w \in R$,

$$(f \otimes f')\,w = \langle f\,w, f'\,w\rangle.$$

From these definitions, it follows that, for all $w \in R$,

$$\pi((f \otimes f')\,w) = f\,w \qquad \pi'((f \otimes f')\,w) = f'\,w,$$

so that the triangles in the diagram

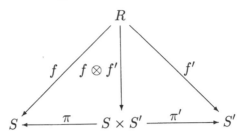

both commute.

Moreover, for all $z \in S \times S'$,

$$z = \langle \pi \, z, \pi' \, z \rangle.$$

Now suppose that g is any function from R to $S \times S'$ that, when taken as the vertical arrow in the above diagram, makes the triangles commute. Then, for all $w \in R$,

$$\pi(g \, w) = f \, w \qquad \pi'(g \, w) = f' \, w,$$

so that

$$g \, w = \langle \pi(g \, w), \pi'(g \, w) \rangle = \langle f \, w, f' \, w \rangle = (f \otimes f') \, w.$$

Thus $f \otimes f'$ is the unique function from R to $S \times S'$ that makes the triangles in the above diagram commute.

There is an additional way of constructing a function from a pair of functions that is associated with the binary product. If $g \in S \to T$ and $g' \in S' \to T'$, then $g \times g'$ (called the *product of functions g and g'*) is the function from $S \times S'$ to $T \times T'$ such that

$$(g \times g')\langle x, x' \rangle = \langle gx, g'x' \rangle.$$

Suppose one has the following functions between sets:

$$Q \xrightarrow{\ e\ } R \xrightarrow[f']{f} \begin{array}{c} S \xrightarrow{\ g\ } T \xrightarrow{\ h\ } U \\ S' \xrightarrow[g']{} T' \xrightarrow[h']{} U' \end{array}$$

Then one can show that

$$(f \otimes f') \cdot e = (f \cdot e) \otimes (f' \cdot e)$$

$$(g \times g') \cdot (f \otimes f') = (g \cdot f) \otimes (g' \cdot f')$$

$$(h \times h') \cdot (g \times g') = (h \cdot g) \times (h' \cdot g')$$

$$I_{S \times S'} = I_S \times I_{S'}.$$

Associated with the disjoint union $S + S'$ are the *injection* functions $\iota \in S \to S + S'$ and $\iota' \in S' \to S + S'$ such that, for all $x \in S$ and $x' \in S'$,

$$\iota x = \langle 1, x \rangle \qquad \iota' x' = \langle 2, x' \rangle.$$

Also, if $g \in S \to T$ and $g' \in S' \to T$, then $g \oplus g'$ (often called the *source-tupling* of g and g') is the function from $S + S'$ to T such that, for all $x \in S$ and $x' \in S'$,

$$(g \oplus g')\langle 1, x \rangle = g\, x \qquad (g \oplus g')\langle 2, x' \rangle = g'\, x'.$$

Thus the triangles in

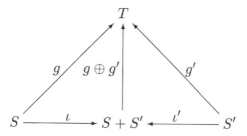

both commute.

Suppose h is any function from $S + S'$ to T that, when taken as the vertical arrow in the above diagram, makes the triangles commute. Then, for all $x \in S$ and $x \in S'$,

$$h\langle 1, x \rangle = g\, x = (g \oplus g')\langle 1, x \rangle \qquad h\langle 2, x' \rangle = g'\, x' = (g \oplus g')\langle 2, x' \rangle.$$

Thus, since these equations equate the results of h and $g \oplus g'$ for every argument in $S + S'$, we find that $g \oplus g'$ is the unique function that makes the triangles in the above diagram commute.

If $f \in R \to S$ and $f' \in R' \to S'$, then $f + f'$ (called the *disjoint union of functions f and f'*) is the function from $R + R'$ to $S + S'$ such that

$$(f + f')\langle 1, x \rangle = \langle 1, fx \rangle \qquad (f + f')\langle 2, x' \rangle = \langle 2, f'x' \rangle.$$

Suppose one has the following functions between sets:

$$Q \xrightarrow{\ e\ } R \xrightarrow{\ f\ } S \xrightarrow{g}$$
$$T \xrightarrow{\ h\ } U$$
$$Q' \xrightarrow[\ e'\ ]{} R' \xrightarrow[\ f'\ ]{} S' \xrightarrow{g'}$$

Then one can show

$$(f + f') \cdot (e + e') = (f \cdot e) + (f' \cdot e')$$

$$(g \oplus g') \cdot (f + f') = (g \cdot f) \oplus (g' \cdot f')$$

$$h \cdot (g \oplus g') = (h \cdot g) \oplus (h \cdot g')$$

$$I_{S+S'} = I_S + I_{S'}.$$

A.6 More About Relations

A relation ρ is said to be *transitive* if and only if $\rho \cdot \rho \subseteq \rho$, *symmetric* if and only if $\rho^\dagger = \rho$, and *antisymmetric* if and only if $\rho \cap \rho^\dagger$ is an identity function. Thus a relation ρ on S is antisymmetric if and only if $\rho \cap \rho^\dagger \subseteq I_S$. Finally, a relation ρ on S is *reflexive on* S if and only if $\rho \supseteq I_S$.

A relation that is reflexive on S and transitive is a *preorder on* S; if it is also antisymmetric, it is a *partial order on* S, while if it is also symmetric, it is an *equivalence relation on* S. A relation that is transitive and symmetric is a *partial equivalence relation*.

The exponentiation of a relation ρ on a set S is defined by

$$\rho^0 \stackrel{\text{def}}{=} I_S \qquad\qquad \rho^{n+1} \stackrel{\text{def}}{=} \rho \cdot \rho^n.$$

Then one can define

$$\rho^+ \stackrel{\text{def}}{=} \bigcup_{i=1}^{\infty} \rho^n \qquad\qquad \rho^* \stackrel{\text{def}}{=} \bigcup_{i=0}^{\infty} \rho^n.$$

(Strictly speaking, since relations are sets, these definitions contradict those of set exponentiation given in Section A.3. However, one can normally tell which definitions are intended by context.)

Conventionally, ρ^+ is called the *transitive closure* of ρ since it is the least transitive relation containing ρ. Similarly, ρ^* is called the *transitive and reflexive closure* of ρ since it is the least transitive and reflexive relation (i.e. the least preorder) containing ρ.

It is easy to see that $\rho \cup \rho^\dagger$ is the least symmetric relation relation containing ρ, and that $-^+$ and $-^*$ preserve symmetry. It then follows that $(\rho \cup \rho^\dagger)^*$ is the least equivalence relation containing ρ.

A set equipped with a preorder is called a *preordered* set. Similarly, a set equipped with a partial order is called a *partially ordered* set or, more briefly, a *poset*.

Any set S can be equipped with the identity relation on S (which is both a partial order and an equivalence relation on S); it is then said to be *discretely ordered*.

Suppose P is a set equipped with a partial order $\sqsubseteq$, $X \subseteq P$, and $y \in P$. If $x \sqsubseteq y$ for all $x \in X$, we say that y is an *upper bound* of X; if any such y exists, we say that X is *upper-bounded* or just *bounded*. If y is an upper bound of X, and $y \sqsubseteq z$ for all $z \in P$ that are upper bounds of X, we say that y is a *least upper bound* of X.

Similarly, if $y \sqsubseteq x$ for all $x \in X$, we say that y is a *lower bound* of X; if any such y exists, we say that X is *lower bounded*. If y is a lower bound of X, and $z \sqsubseteq y$ for all $z \in P$ that are lower bounds of X, we say that y is a *greatest lower bound* of X.

Although the above definitions make sense for preorders, when we make the stronger assumption that P is a partial order, we gain the nice property that every subset of P has at most one least upper bound and at most one greatest lower bound. When they exist, we write

$$\bigsqcup X \text{ for the least upper bound of } X,$$

$$\bigsqcap X \text{ for the greatest lower bound of } X.$$

More specialized forms of this notation can be developed in the same way as with the union operation. For example, when they exist, we write

$$\bigsqcup_{i=0}^{\infty} x_i \text{ for } \bigsqcup \{\, x_i \mid i \in 0 \textbf{ to } \infty \,\}, \qquad x \sqcup y \text{ for } \bigsqcup \{x, y\},$$

$$\bigsqcap_{i=0}^{\infty} x_i \text{ for } \bigsqcap \{\, x_i \mid i \in 0 \textbf{ to } \infty \,\}, \qquad x \sqcap y \text{ for } \bigsqcap \{x, y\}.$$

A particularly useful property concerns the least upper bound of a set of least upper bounds. Suppose $\mathcal{X}$ is a set of subsets of a partially ordered set, such that every member of $\mathcal{X}$ has a least upper bound. If either of the sets

$$\{\, \bigsqcup X \mid X \in \mathcal{X} \,\} \quad \text{or} \quad \bigcup \mathcal{X}$$

has a least upper bound, then both of these sets have the same least upper bound. As a special case, suppose $\bigsqcup_{j=0}^{\infty} x_{ij}$ exists for all $i \geq 0$. If either

$$\bigsqcup_{i=0}^{\infty} \bigsqcup_{j=0}^{\infty} x_{ij} \quad \text{or} \quad \bigsqcup \{\, x_{ij} \mid i \geq 0 \text{ and } j \geq 0 \,\}$$

exists, then both exist and they are equal.

Being the least upper bound of the empty set is equivalent to being the *least* element of P, that is, the unique y such that $y \sqsubseteq z$ for all $z \in P$. Similarly, being the greatest lower bound of the empty set is equivalent to being the *greatest* element of P. When they exist, we write

$$\bot \text{ for the least element,} \qquad \top \text{ for the greatest element.}$$

(The symbols $\bot$ and $\top$ are often called "bottom" and "top".)

Suppose P and P' are partially ordered (or preordered) sets. Then a function $f \in P \to P'$ is said to be a *monotone function from P to P'* if and only if, for all x_0 and x_1 in P, $x_0 \sqsubseteq x_1$ implies $f x_0 \sqsubseteq' f x_1$.

If F is a monotone function from P to P' and f' is a monotone function from P' to P'', then $f' \cdot f$ is a monotone function from P to P''. Moreover, I_P is a monotone function from P to P.

Exercises

A.1   Prove the reflection law

$$(\rho' \cdot \rho)^\dagger = \rho^\dagger \cdot \rho'^\dagger$$

and the identity law

$$\rho \subseteq I_S \text{ if and only if } (\exists T)\ T \subseteq S \text{ and } \rho = I_T.$$

A.2   The use of superscripts, $\times$, and $+$ to represent the exponentiation, Cartesian product, and disjoint union of sets is a notational pun on the meaning of these operators in ordinary arithmetic. Thus, for example, several of the equations between sets given in Section A.3 are identical to laws of arithmetic. In other cases, however, the equations of arithmetic become isomorphisms, rather than equalities between sets.

Each of the following pairs of set expressions would be equal if they were arithmetic expressions. For each pair, give an isomorphism (that is, bijection) from the left expression to the right, and give its inverse (which will also be its reflection):

$$S_0 \times S_1 \qquad\qquad S_1 \times S_0$$
$$(S_0 \times S_1) \times S_2 \qquad\qquad S_0 \times (S_1 \times S_2)$$
$$S_0 + S_1 \qquad\qquad S_1 + S_0$$
$$(S_0 + S_1) + S_2 \qquad\qquad S_0 + (S_1 + S_2).$$

A.3   (a) Prove the additivity law for relations:

$$(\bigcup R') \cdot (\bigcup R) = \bigcup \{\, \rho' \cdot \rho \mid \rho \in R \text{ and } \rho' \in R' \,\}.$$

(b) Give a counterexample showing that the analogous law for intersections of relations,

$$(\bigcap R') \cdot (\bigcap R) = \bigcap \{\, \rho' \cdot \rho \mid \rho \in R \text{ and } \rho' \in R' \,\},$$

is *not* valid.

A.4   Let S be the two-element set $\{\bot, \top\}$, and consider the $2^{2 \times 2} = 16$ relations on S (that is, the relations from S to S). For each such relation ρ, indicate:

(a) Whether ρ is:

1. a total relation from S to S,
2. a partial function from S to S,
3. a function from S to S.

(b) In the cases where ρ is a function from S to S, whether ρ is:

    1. a surjection from S to S,
    2. an injection from S to S,
    3. a bijection from S to S,
    4. monotone with respect to the partial order $\{[\bot, \bot], [\bot, \top], [\top, \top]\}$.

(c) The composition $\rho \cdot \rho$ of ρ with itself.

(d) The reflection $\rho^{\dagger}$ of ρ.

(e) Whether ρ is:

    1. transitive,
    2. symmetric,
    3. antisymmetric,
    4. reflexive on S,
    5. a preorder on S,
    6. a partial order on S,
    7. an equivalence on S,
    8. a partial equivalence on S.

Hint A convenient way of displaying a relation ρ from S to S' (when these sets are finite and small) is by a graph where the members of S are nodes on the left, the members of S' are nodes on the right, and there is an edge from x to x' whenever $[x, x'] \in \rho$. For example, the function

$$\rho = \lambda x \in \{\bot, \top\}. \text{ if } x = \top \text{ then } \bot \text{ else } \top$$
$$= \{[\bot, \top], [\top, \bot]\}$$

is displayed as

while the relation $\rho' = \{[\bot, \bot], [\bot, \top]\}$ is displayed as

Composition is easily worked out by pasting such graphs together. For example, x is related to x'' by the composition $\rho' \cdot \rho$ if and only if there is a path from x to x'' in

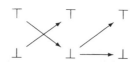

In this case, the composition is

$$
\begin{array}{ccc}
\top & \longrightarrow & \top \\
& \searrow & \\
\bot & & \bot
\end{array}
$$

which displays the relation $\{[\top,\bot],[\top,\top]\}$.

A.5 For each of the following relations ρ on the natural numbers:

$$\{\,[n,2n]\mid n\in\mathbf{N}\,\}$$

$$\{\,[n,2n]\mid n\in\mathbf{N}\,\}\cup\{\,[n,2n+1]\mid n\in\mathbf{N}\,\}$$

$$\{\,[2n,2n]\mid n\in\mathbf{N}\,\}\cup\{\,[2n,2n+1]\mid n\in\mathbf{N}\,\}$$

$$\{\,[2n,2n+1]\mid n\in\mathbf{N}\,\}\cup\{\,[2n+1,2n]\mid n\in\mathbf{N}\,\},$$

(a) Answer the questions in Exercise A.4 for ρ.

(b) Answer questions (a) and (b) in Exercise A.4 for the reflection $\rho^\dagger$.

(c) If ρ or $\rho^\dagger$ is a function, express it as a typed abstraction. Within this typed abstraction, you may use a conditional construction such as **if even n then** $\cdots$ **else** $\cdots$.

In these questions, you should take S to be the set of natural numbers, rather than the two-element set $\{\bot,\top\}$. In part (b4) of Exercise A.4, you should interpret "monotone" as monotone with respect to the usual ordering $0\le 1\le 2\le\cdots$ of the natural numbers.

A.6 Suppose ρ is a relation from S to S'. Prove that

(a) ρ is a total relation from S to S' if and only if $\rho^\dagger\cdot\rho\supseteq I_S$.

(b) ρ is a partial function from S to S' if and only if $\rho\cdot\rho^\dagger\subseteq I_{S'}$.

A.7 Prove the following about least upper bounds in partially ordered sets:

(a) Suppose that, in a partially ordered set, z and z' are both least upper bounds of x and y. Then $z=z'$.

(b) Suppose that Y is the set of upper bounds of a subset X of a partially ordered set. If x is the least upper bound of X, then x is the greatest lower bound of Y.

(c) Suppose $\mathcal{X}$ is a set of subsets of a partially ordered set, such that every member of $\mathcal{X}$ has a least upper bound. If either of the sets

$$\{\,\bigsqcup X\mid X\in\mathcal{X}\,\}\quad\text{or}\quad\bigcup\mathcal{X}$$

has a least upper bound, then both of these sets have the same least upper bound.

Bibliography

Abadi, M. and Cardelli, L. [1996]. *A Theory of Objects*. Springer-Verlag, New York.

Abadi, M. and Plotkin, G. D. [1990]. A Per Model of Polymorphism and Recursive Types. *Proceedings Fifth Annual IEEE Symposium on Logic in Computer Science*. IEEE Computer Society Press, Los Alamitos, California. Pages 355–365.

Abdali, S. K. [1976]. A Lambda-Calculus Model of Programming Languages – I. Simple Constructs, II. Jumps and Procedures. *Journal of Computer Languages*, **1**, 287–301, 303–320.

Abelson, H., Sussman, G. J., and Sussman, J. [1985]. *Structure and Interpretation of Computer Programs*. MIT Press, Cambridge, Massachusetts.

Abramsky, S. [1993]. Computational Interpretations of Linear Logic. *Theoretical Computer Science*, **111**(1–2), 3–57.

Abramsky, S. and McCusker, G. [1995]. Games and Full Abstraction for the Lazy λ-calculus. *Proceedings Tenth Annual IEEE Symposium on Logic in Computer Science*. IEEE Computer Society Press, Los Alamitos, California. Pages 234–243.

Abramsky, S. and McCusker, G. [1996]. Linearity, Sharing and State: A Fully Abstract Game Semantics for Idealized Algol with Active Expressions (Extended Abstract). *Proceedings of Linear Logic 1996. Electronic Notes in Theoretical Computer Science*, http://www.elsevier.{nl,com}/locate/entcs/volume3.html, **3**. Reprinted in O'Hearn and Tennent [1997, vol. 2, pages 297–329].

Abramsky, S. and Ong, C.-H. L. [1993]. Full Abstraction in the Lazy Lambda Calculus. *Information and Computation*, **105**(2), 159–267.

Abramsky, S., Jagadeesan, R., and Malacaria, P. [1994]. Full Abstraction for PCF (Extended Abstract). *Theoretical Aspects of Computer Software: International Symposium TACS '94*. Hagiya, M. and Mitchell, J. C., editors. Lecture Notes in Computer Science 789. Springer-Verlag, Berlin. Pages 1–15.

Abramsky, S., Jagadeesan, R., and Malacaria, P. [1998]. *Full Abstraction for PCF*. To appear in Information and Computation.

Amadio, R., Bruce, K. B., and Longo, G. [1986]. The Finitary Projection Model for Second Order Lambda Calculus and Solutions to Higher Order Domain Equations. *Proceedings Symposium on Logic in Computer Science*. IEEE Computer Society Press, Washington, D.C. Pages 122–130.

Andrews, G. R. [1991]. *Concurrent Programming: Principles and Practice*. Benjamin/Cummings, Redwood City, California.

Andrews, P. B., editor. [1986]. *An Introduction to Mathematical Logic and Type Theory: To Truth through Proof*. Academic Press, Orlando, Florida.

Appel, A. W. [1992]. *Compiling with Continuations*. Cambridge University Press, Cambridge, England.

Apt, K. R. and Olderog, E.-R. [1991]. *Verification of Sequential and Concurrent Programs*. Springer-Verlag, New York.

Apt, K. R. and Plotkin, G. D. [1986]. Countable Nondeterminism and Random Assignment. *Journal of the ACM*, **33**(4), 724–767.

Asperti, A. and Longo, G. [1991]. *Categories, Types, and Structures: An Introduction to Category Theory for the Working Computer Scientist*. MIT Press, Cambridge, Massachusetts.

Augustsson, L. [1984]. A Compiler for Lazy ML. *Proceedings of the 1984 ACM Symposium on Lisp and Functional Programming*. ACM, New York. Pages 218–227.

Bainbridge, E. S., Freyd, P. J., Scedrov, A., and Scott, P. J. [1990]. Functorial Polymorphism. *Theoretical Computer Science*, **70**(1), 35–64. Corrigendum in **71**(3), 431.

Barendregt, H. P. [1984]. *The Lambda Calculus, Its Syntax and Semantics*. Revised edition. Studies in Logic and the Foundations of Mathematics 103. North-Holland, Amsterdam.

Barendregt, H. P. [1992]. Lambda Calculi with Types. *Handbook of Logic in Computer Science: Background: Computational Structures, Vol. 2*. Abramsky, S., Gabbay, D. M., and Maibaum, T. S. E., editors. Oxford University Press, Oxford, England. Pages 117–309.

Barendregt, H. P., Coppo, M., and Dezani-Ciancaglini, M. [1983]. A Filter Lambda Model and the Completeness of Type Assignment. *Journal of Symbolic Logic*, **48**(4), 931–940.

Barras, B. et al. [May 25, 1998]. *The Coq Proof Assistant Reference Manual, Version 6.2*. Tech. rept., INRIA, Rocquencourt, France. http://pauillac.inria.fr/coq /doc-eng.html.

Barringer, H. [1985]. *A Survey of Verification Techniques for Parallel Programs*. Lecture Notes in Computer Science 191. Springer-Verlag, Berlin.

Barringer, H., Cheng, J. H., and Jones, C. B. [1984]. A Logic Covering Undefinedness in Program Proofs. *Acta Informatica*, **21**(3), 251–269.

Bauer, F. L., Brauer, W., and Schwichtenberg, H., editors. [1993]. *Logic and Algebra of Specification*. NATO ASI Series; Series F: Computer and System Sciences 94. Springer-Verlag, Berlin.

Bekić, H., Bjørner, D., Henhapl, W., Jones, C. B., and Lucas, P. [December 20, 1974]. *A Formal Definition of a PL/I Subset: Part I and Part II*. Technical Report TR 25.139, IBM Laboratory Vienna, Vienna, Austria.

Bernays, P. [1936]. Review of "Some Properties of Conversion" by Alonzo Church and J. B. Rosser. *Journal of Symbolic Logic*, **1**, 74–75.

Bird, R. J. and Wadler, P. [1988]. *Introduction to Functional Programming*. Prentice-Hall International, Hemel Hempstead, England.

Birkedal, L., Carboni, A., Rosolini, G., and Scott, D. S. [1998]. Type Theory via Exact Categories: Extended abstract. *Proceedings Thirteenth Annual IEEE Symposium on Logic in Computer Science*. IEEE Computer Society, Los Alamitos, California. Pages 188–198.

Böhm, C. and Berarducci, A. [1985]. Automatic Synthesis of Typed Λ-Programs on Term Algebras. *Theoretical Computer Science*, **39**(2–3), 135–154.

Breazu-Tannen, V. and Coquand, T. [1988]. Extensional Models for Polymorphism. *Theoretical Computer Science*, **59**(1–2), 85–114.

Breazu-Tannen, V., Coquand, T., Gunter, C. A., and Scedrov, A. [1991]. Inheritance as Implicit Coercion. *Information and Computation*, **93**(1), 172–221. Reprinted in Gunter and Mitchell [1994, pages 197–245].

Brookes, S. D. [June 1992]. *An Axiomatic Treatment of Partial Correctness and Deadlock in a Shared Variable Parallel Language*. Report CMU–CS–92–154, School of Computer Science, Carnegie Mellon University, Pittsburgh, Pennsylvania.

Brookes, S. D. [1993]. Full Abstraction for a Shared Variable Parallel Language. *Proceedings Eighth Annual IEEE Symposium on Logic in Computer Science.* IEEE Computer Society Press, Los Alamitos, California. Pages 98–109.

Brookes, S. D. [1994]. Fair Communicating Processes. *A Classical Mind: Essays in Honour of C. A. R. Hoare.* Roscoe, A. W., editor. Prentice-Hall International, London. Pages 59–74.

Brookes, S. D. [1996a]. The Essence of Parallel Algol. *Proceedings Eleventh Annual IEEE Symposium on Logic in Computer Science.* IEEE Computer Society Press, Los Alamitos, California. Pages 164–173. Reprinted in O'Hearn and Tennent [1997, vol. 2, pages 331–348].

Brookes, S. D. [1996b]. Full Abstraction for a Shared-Variable Parallel Language. *Information and Computation,* **127**(2), 145–163.

Brookes, S. D. [1997]. Idealized CSP: Combining Procedures with Communicating Processes. *Mathematical Foundations of Programming Semantics, Thirteenth Annual Conference.* Brookes, S. D. and Mislove, M., editors. *Electronic Notes in Theoretical Computer Science,* http://www.elsevier.{nl,com}/locate/entcs /volume6.html, **6**.

Brookes, S. D. and Older, S. [1995]. Full Abstraction for Strongly Fair Communicating Processes. *Mathematical Foundations of Programming Semantics, Eleventh Annual Conference.* Brookes, S. D., Main, M., Melton, A., and Mislove, M., editors. *Electronic Notes in Theoretical Computer Science,* http://www.elsevier.{nl,com} /locate/entcs/volume1.html, **1**.

Brookes, S. D., Hoare, C. A. R., and Roscoe, A. W. [1984]. A Theory of Communicating Sequential Processes. *Journal of the ACM,* **31**(3), 560–599.

Bruce, K. B. and Longo, G. [1990]. A Modest Model of Records, Inheritance, and Bounded Quantification. *Information and Computation,* **87**(1–2), 196–240. Reprinted in Gunter and Mitchell [1994, pages 151–195].

Burstall, R. M. and Landin, P. J. [1969]. Programs and their Proofs: an Algebraic Approach. *Machine Intelligence 4.* Meltzer, B. and Michie, D., editors. Edinburgh University Press, Edinburgh, Scotland. Pages 17–43.

Burstall, R. M., MacQueen, D. B., and Sannella, D. T. [May 1980]. HOPE: An Experimental Applicative Language. Internal Report CSR-62–80, Department of Computer Science, University of Edinburgh, Edinburgh, Scotland. Updated February 1981.

Cardelli, L. [1984]. A Semantics of Multiple Inheritance. *Semantics of Data Types: International Symposium.* Kahn, G., MacQueen, D. B., and Plotkin, G. D., editors. Lecture Notes in Computer Science 173. Springer-Verlag, Berlin. Pages 51–67.

Cardelli, L. [1988]. A Semantics of Multiple Inheritance. *Information and Computation,* **76**(2–3), 138–164.

Cardelli, L. and Wegner, P. [1985]. On Understanding Types, Data Abstraction, and Polymorphism. *ACM Computing Surveys,* **17**, 471–522.

Cheatham, T. E., Jr., Fischer, A., and Jorrand, P. [1968]. On the Basis for ELF – An Extensible Language Facility. *1968 Fall Joint Computer Conference.* AFIPS Conference Proceedings 33, Part Two. Thompson Book Company, Washington, D.C. Pages 937–948.

Cheng, J. H. and Jones, C. B. [1991]. On the Usability of Logics which Handle Partial Functions. *3rd Refinement Workshop.* Morgan, C. and Woodcock, J. C. P., editors. Workshops in Computing. Springer-Verlag, London. Pages 51–69.

Chirimar, J., Gunter, C. A., and Riecke, J. G. [1996]. Reference Counting as a Computational Interpretation of Linear Logic. *Journal of Functional Programming,* **6**(2), 195–244.

Church, A. [1940]. A Formulation of the Simple Theory of Types. *Journal of Symbolic Logic,* **5**(2), 56–68.

Church, A. [1941]. *The Calculi of Lambda-Conversion.* Annals of Mathematics Studies
  6. Princeton University Press, Princeton, New Jersey.
Church, A. [1956]. *Introduction to ˜Mathematical Logic, Volume 1.* Princeton University
  Press, Princeton, New Jersey.
Church, A. and Rosser, J. B. [1936]. Some Properties of Conversion. *Transactions of
  the American Mathematical Society,* **39**(May), 472–482.
Constable, R. L. et al. [1986]. *Implementing Mathematics with the Nuprl Proof
  Development System.* Prentice-Hall, Englewood Cliffs, New Jersey.
Coppo, M. and Dezani-Ciancaglini, M. [1978]. A New Type Assignment for λ-Terms.
  Archiv für mathematische Logik und Grundlagenforschung, **19**(3–4), 139–156.
Coppo, M., Dezani-Ciancaglini, M., and Venneri, B. [1981]. Functional Characters of
  Solvable Terms. *Zeitschrift für Mathematische Logik und Grundlagen der
  Mathematik,* **27**, 45–58.
Coquand, T. and Huet, G. [1988]. The Calculus of Constructions. *Information and
  Computation,* **76**(2–3), 95–120.
Coquand, T., Gunter, C. A., and Winskel, G. [1988]. DI-Domains as a Model of
  Polymorphism. *Mathematical Foundations of Programming Language Semantics:
  3rd Workshop.* Main, M., Melton, A., Mislove, M., and Schmidt, D. A., editors.
  Lecture Notes in Computer Science 298. Springer-Verlag, Berlin. Pages 344–363.
Coquand, T., Gunter, C. A., and Winskel, G. [1989]. Domain Theoretic Models of
  Polymorphism. *Information and Computation,* **81**(2), 123–167.
Curien, P.-L. and Ghelli, G. [1992]. Coherence of Subsumption, Minimum Typing, and
  Type-Checking in F$_<$. *Mathematical Structures in Computer Science,* **2**(1), 55–91.
Curry, H. B. and Feys, R. [1958]. *Combinatory Logic, Volume 1.* Studies in Logic and
  the Foundations of Mathematics. North-Holland, Amsterdam. Second printing 1968.
Dahl, O.-J., Myhrhaug, B., and Nygaard, K. [May 1968]. *SIMULA 67 Common Base
  Language.* Publication S-2, Norwegian Computing Center, Oslo, Norway.
Damas, L. and Milner, R. [1982]. Principal Type-Schemes for Functional Programs.
  *Conference Record of the Ninth Annual ACM Symposium on Principles of
  Programming Languages.* ACM, New York. Pages 207–212.
Davis, M. D. and Weyuker, E. J. [1983]. *Computability, Complexity, and Languages.*
  Academic Press, New York.
de Bruijn, N. G. [1980]. A Survey of the Project AUTOMATH. *To H. B. Curry:
  Essays on Combinatory Logic, Lambda Calculus and Formalism.* Seldin, J. P. and
  Hindley, J. R., editors. Academic Press, London. Pages 579–606.
Dijkstra, E. W. [1975]. Guarded Commands, Nondeterminacy and Formal Derivation of
  Programs. *Communications of the ACM,* **18**(8), 453–457. Reprinted in Gries [1978,
  pages 166–175].
Dijkstra, E. W. [1976]. *A Discipline of Programming.* Prentice-Hall, Englewood Cliffs,
  New Jersey.
Evans, A., Jr. [1968]. PAL – A Language Designed for Teaching Programming
  Linguistics. *Proceedings of 23rd National ACM Conference.* Brandin Systems Press,
  Princeton, New Jersey. Pages 395–403.
Fairbairn, J. [May 1985]. *Design and Implementation of a Simple Typed Language
  Based on the Lambda-Calculus.* Ph. D. dissertation, Computer Laboratory,
  University of Cambridge, Cambridge, England, Technical Report 75.
Field, A. J. and Harrison, P. G. [1988]. *Functional Programming.* Addison-Wesley,
  Wokingham, England.
Fischer, M. J. [1972]. Lambda Calculus Schemata. *Proceedings of an ACM Conference
  on Proving Assertions about Programs.* ACM, New York. Pages 104–109.
Fischer, M. J. [1993]. Lambda-Calculus Schemata. *Lisp and Symbolic Computation,*
  6(3–4), 259–287.

Floyd, R. W. [1967]. Assigning Meanings to Programs. *Mathematical Aspects of Computer Science.* Schwartz, J. T., editor. Proceedings of Symposia in Applied Mathematics 19. American Mathematical Society, Providence, Rhode Island. Pages 19–32.

Francez, N. [1986]. *Fairness.* Springer-Verlag, New York.

Freyd, P. J. and Scedrov, A. [1987]. Some Semantic Aspects of Polymorphic Lambda Calculus. *Proceedings Symposium on Logic in Computer Science.* IEEE Computer Society Press, Washington, D.C. Pages 315–319.

Friedman, D. P. and Wise, D. S. [1976]. CONS Should not Evaluate its Arguments. *Automata, Languages and Programming: Third International Colloquium.* Michaelson, S. and Milner, R., editors. Edinburgh University Press, Edinburgh, Scotland. Pages 257–284.

Ghelli, G. [1991]. *On the Decidability of Type Checking for Fun.* Unpublished, Dipartimento di Informatica, Università di Pisa, Pisa, Italy.

Ghelli, G. [1995]. Divergence of $F_\leq$ Type Checking. *Theoretical Computer Science,* **139**(1–2), 131–162.

Giannini, P. and Ronchi della Rocca, S. [1988]. Characterization of Typings in Polymorphic Type Discipline. *Proceedings Third Annual Symposium on Logic in Computer Science.* IEEE Computer Society Press, Washington, D.C. Pages 61–70.

Giannini, P. and Ronchi della Rocca, S. [1994]. A Type Inference Algorithm for a Complete Stratification of the Polymorphic Type Discipline. *Information and Computation,* **109**(1–2), 115–173.

Girard, J.-Y. [1971]. Une Extension de l'Interprétation de Gödel à l'Analyse, et son Application à l'Élimination des Coupures dans l'Analyse et la Théorie des Types. *Proceedings of the Second Scandinavian Logic Symposium.* Fenstad, J. E., editor. Studies in Logic and the Foundations of Mathematics 63. North-Holland, Amsterdam. Pages 63–92.

Girard, J.-Y. [June 1972]. *Interprétation Fonctionnelle et Élimination des Coupures de l'Arithmétique d'Ordre Supérieur.* Thèse de doctorat d'état, Université Paris VII, Paris, France.

Girard, J.-Y. [1986]. The System F of Variable Types, Fifteen Years Later. *Theoretical Computer Science,* **45**(2), 159–192.

Girard, J.-Y. [1987]. Linear Logic. *Theoretical Computer Science,* **50**(1), 1–101.

Girard, J.-Y., Lafont, Y., and Taylor, P. [1989]. *Proofs and Types.* Cambridge Tracts in Theoretical Computer Science 7. Cambridge University Press, Cambridge, England.

Gleason, A. M. [1966]. *Fundamentals of Abstract Analysis.* Addison-Wesley, Reading, Massachusetts.

Goguen, J. A., Thatcher, J. W., Wagner, E. G., and Wright, J. B. [1977]. Initial Algebra Semantics and Continuous Algebras. *Journal of the ACM,* **24**(1), 68–95.

Goldstine, H. H. and von Neumann, J. [1947]. *Planning and Coding of Problems for an Electronic Computing Instrument.* Part II, Vol. 1 of a Report prepared for the U. S. Army Ordinance Department.

Gordon, M. J., Milner, R., Morris, F. L., Newey, M., and Wadsworth, C. P. [September 1977]. *A Metalanguage For Interactive Proof in LCF.* Internal Report CSR–16–77, Department of Computer Science, University of Edinburgh, Edinburgh, Scotland.

Gordon, M. J., Milner, R., and Wadsworth, C. P. [1979]. *Edinburgh LCF: A Mechanized Logic of Computation.* Lecture Notes in Computer Science 78. Springer-Verlag, Berlin.

Gosling, J., Joy, B., and Steele Jr., G. L. [1996]. *The Java™ Language Specification: Concepts and Constructs.* Addison-Wesley, Reading, Massachusetts.

Gries, D., editor. [1978]. *Programming Methodology: A Collection of Articles by Members of IFIP WG 2.3.* Springer-Verlag, New York.

Gries, D. [1981]. *The Science of Programming.* Springer-Verlag, New York.

Gries, D. and Levin, G. [1980]. Assignment and Procedure Call Proof Rules. *ACM Transactions on Programming Languages and Systems*, **2**(4), 564–579.

Gries, D. and Schneider, F. B. [1993]. *A Logical Approach to Discrete Math.* Springer-Verlag, New York.

Gunter, C. A. [1992]. *Semantics of Programming Languages: Structures and Techniques.* MIT Press, Cambridge, Massachusetts.

Gunter, C. A. and Mitchell, J. C. [1994]. *Theoretical Aspects of Object-Oriented Programming: Types, Semantics, and Language Design.* MIT Press, Cambridge, Massachusetts.

Gunter, C. A. and Scott, D. S. [1990]. Semantic Domains. *Formal Models and Semantics.* van Leeuwen, J., editor. Handbook of Theoretical Computer Science B. Elsevier, Amsterdam. Pages 633–674.

Harper, R. W. [1994]. A Simplified Account of Polymorphic References. *Information Processing Letters*, **51**(4), 201–206.

Harper, R. W. and Lillibridge, M. [1993a]. Explicit Polymorphism and CPS Conversion. *Conference Record of the Twentieth Annual ACM SIGPLAN-SIGACT Symposium on Principles of Programming Languages.* ACM Press, New York. Pages 206–219.

Harper, R. W. and Lillibridge, M. [1993b]. Polymorphic Type Assignment and CPS Conversion. *Lisp and Symbolic Computation*, **6**(3–4), 361–379.

Harper, R. W. and Lillibridge, M. [1994]. A Type-Theoretic Approach to Higher-Order Modules with Sharing. *Conference Record of POPL '94: 21st ACM SIGPLAN-SIGACT Symposium on Principles of Programming Languages.* ACM Press, New York. Pages 123–137.

Harper, R. W. and Mitchell, J. C. [1993]. On the Type Structure of Standard ML. *ACM Transactions on Programming Languages and Systems*, **15**(2), 211–252.

Harper, R. W. and Morrisett, G. [1995]. Compiling Polymorphism Using Intensional Type Analysis. *Conference Record of POPL '95: 22nd ACM SIGPLAN-SIGACT Symposium on Principles of Programming Languages.* ACM Press, New York. Pages 130–141.

Harper, R. W., Milner, R., and Tofte, M. [1987]. A Type Discipline for Program Modules. *TAPSOFT '87: Proceedings of the International Joint Conference on Theory and Practice of Software Development, Volume 2.* Ehrig, H., Kowalski, R., Levi, G., and Montanari, U., editors. Lecture Notes in Computer Science 250. Springer-Verlag, Berlin. Pages 308–319.

Harper, R. W., Mitchell, J. C., and Moggi, E. [1990]. Higher-Order Modules and the Phase Distinction. *Conference Record of the Seventeenth Annual ACM Symposium on Principles of Programming Languages.* ACM Press, New York. Pages 341–354.

Harper, R. W., Honsell, F., and Plotkin, G. D. [1993a]. A Framework for Defining Logics. *Journal of the ACM*, **40**(1), 143–184.

Harper, R. W., Duba, B. F., and MacQueen, D. B. [1993b]. Typing First-Class Continuations in ML. *Journal of Functional Programming*, **3**(4), 465–484.

Henderson, P. [1980]. *Functional Programming: Application and Implementation.* Prentice-Hall International, London.

Henderson, P. and Morris, J. H., Jr. [1976]. A Lazy Evaluator. *Conference Record of the Third Annual ACM Symposium on Principles of Programming Languages.* ACM, New York. Pages 95–103.

Hennessy, M. C. B. and Plotkin, G. D. [1979]. Full Abstraction for a Simple Parallel Programming Language. *Mathematical Foundations of Computer Science: Proceedings, 8th Symposium.* Bečvář, J., editor. Lecture Notes in Computer Science 74. Springer-Verlag, Berlin. Pages 108–120.

Hindley, J. R. [1969]. The Principal Type-Scheme of an Object in Combinatory Logic. *Transactions of the American Mathematical Society*, **146**(December), 29–60.

Hindley, J. R. [1992]. Types with Intersection: An Introduction. *Formal Aspects of Computing*, **4**(5), 470–486.

Hindley, J. R. and Seldin, J. P. [1986]. *Introduction to Combinators and λ-Calculus*. Cambridge University Press, Cambridge, England.

Hoare, C. A. R. [1969]. An Axiomatic Basis for Computer Programming. *Communications of the ACM*, **12**(10), 576–580 and 583. Reprinted in Gries [1978, pages 89–100].

Hoare, C. A. R. [1971]. Proof of a Program: FIND. *Communications of the ACM*, **14**(1), 39–45. Reprinted in Gries [1978, pages 101–115].

Hoare, C. A. R. [1972]. Towards a Theory of Parallel Programming. *Operating Systems Techniques: Proceedings of a Seminar*. Hoare, C. A. R. and Perrott, R. H., editors. A.P.I.C. Studies in Data Processing 9. Academic Press, London. Pages 61–71. Reprinted in Gries [1978, pages 202–214].

Hoare, C. A. R. [1978]. Communicating Sequential Processes. *Communications of the ACM*, **21**(8), 666–677.

Hoare, C. A. R. [1985]. *Communicating Sequential Processes*. Prentice-Hall International, London.

Hoare, C. A. R. and Lauer, P. E. [1974]. Consistent and Complementary Formal Theories of the Semantics of Programming Languages. *Acta Informatica*, **3**(2), 135–53.

Hoare, C. A. R. and Wirth, N. [1973]. An Axiomatic Definition of the Programming Language PASCAL. *Acta Informatica*, **2**(4), 335–355.

Howard, W. A. [1980]. The Formulae-as-Types Notion of Construction. *To H. B. Curry: Essays on Combinatory Logic, Lambda Calculus and Formalism*. Seldin, J. P. and Hindley, J. R., editors. Academic Press, London. Pages 479–490.

Hudak, P. and Fasel, J. H. [1992]. A Gentle Introduction to Haskell. *SIGPLAN Notices*, **27**(5), T1–T53.

Hudak, P., Peyton Jones, S. L., Wadler, P., et al. [1992]. Report on the Functional Language Haskell: A Non-strict, Purely Functional Language, Version 1.2. *SIGPLAN Notices*, **27**(5), Ri–Rxii, R1–R164.

Huet, G., editor. [1990]. *Logical Foundations of Functional Programming*. Addison-Wesley, Reading, Massachusetts.

Hyland, J. M. E. [1988]. A Small Complete Category. *Annals of Pure and Applied Logic*, **40**(2), 135–165.

Hyland, J. M. E. and Ong, C.-H. L. [1994]. *On Full Abstraction for PCF: I, II, and III*. To appear in Information and Computation. ftp://ftp.comlab.ox.ac.uk/pub /Documents/techpapers/Luke.Ong/.

Jeffrey, A. [1994]. A Fully Abstract Semantics for Concurrent Graph Reduction: Extended Abstract. *Proceedings Ninth Annual IEEE Symposium on Logic in Computer Science*. IEEE Computer Society Press, Los Alamitos, California. Pages 82–91.

Jeuring, J. and Meijer, E., editors. [1995]. *Advanced Functional Programming: First International Spring School on Advanced Functional Programming Techniques, Tutorial Text*. Lecture Notes in Computer Science 925. Springer-Verlag, Berlin.

Jones, C. B. [March 31, 1992]. *The Search for Tractable Ways of Reasoning about Programs*. Technical Report UMCS–92–4–4, Department of Computer Science, University of Manchester, Manchester, England.

Jones, C. B. and Middelburg, C. A. [1994]. A Typed Logic of Partial Functions Reconstructed Classically. *Acta Informatica*, **31**(5), 399–430.

Kahn, G. [1974]. The Semantics of a Simple Language for Parallel Programming. *Information Processing 74: Proceedings of IFIP Congress 74*. Rosenfeld, J. L., editor. North-Holland, Amsterdam. Pages 471–475.

Kahn, G. and MacQueen, D. B. [1977]. Coroutines and Networks of Parallel Processes. *Information Processing 77: Proceedings of IFIP Congress 77*. Gilcrist, B., editor. North-Holland, Amsterdam. Pages 993–998.

Kesner, D., Puel, L., and Tannen, V. [1996]. A Typed Pattern Calculus. *Information and Computation*, **124**(1), 32–61.

Koopman, P. J., Jr., Lee, P., and Siewiorek, D. P. [1992]. Cache Behavior of Combinator Graph Reduction. *ACM Transactions on Programming Languages and Systems*, **14**(2), 265–297.

Kreisel, G. [1959]. Interpretation of Analysis by Means of Constructive Functionals of Finite Types. *Constructivity in Mathematics: Proceedings of the Colloquium*. Heyting, A., editor. North-Holland, Amsterdam. Pages 101–128.

Lafont, Y. [1988]. The Linear Abstract Machine. *Theoretical Computer Science*, **59**(1–2), 157–180. Corrigendum in **62**(3), 327–328.

Landin, P. J. [1964]. The Mechanical Evaluation of Expressions. *The Computer Journal*, **6**(4), 308–320.

Landin, P. J. [1965a]. A Correspondence Between ALGOL 60 and Church's Lambda-Notation. *Communications of the ACM*, **8**(2–3), 89–101, 158–165.

Landin, P. J. [August 29, 1965b]. *A Generalization of Jumps and Labels*. Report, UNIVAC Systems Programming Research.

Landin, P. J. [1966a]. A Formal Description of ALGOL 60. *Formal Language Description Languages for Computer Programming: Proceedings of the IFIP Working Conference on Formal Language Description Languages*. Steel, T. B., Jr., editor. North-Holland, Amsterdam. Pages 266–294.

Landin, P. J. [1966b]. A λ-Calculus Approach. *Advances in Programming and Non-Numerical Computation: Proceedings of A Summer School*. Fox, L., editor. Pergamon Press, for Oxford University Computing Laboratory and Delegacy for Extra-Mural Studies, Oxford, England. Pages 97–141.

Landin, P. J. [1966c]. The Next 700 Programming Languages. *Communications of the ACM*, **9**(3), 157–166.

Larsen, K. G. and Winskel, G. [1991]. Using Information Systems to Solve Recursive Domain Equations. *Information and Computation*, **91**(2), 232–258.

Lauer, P. E. [1971]. *Consistent Formal Theories of the Semantics of Programming Languages*. Ph. D. dissertation, Queen's University of Belfast, Belfast, Northern Ireland. Also Technical Report TR 25.121, IBM Laboratory Vienna, Vienna, Austria, November 14, 1971.

Launchbury, J. [1993]. A Natural Semantics For Lazy Evaluation. *Conference Record of the Twentieth Annual ACM SIGPLAN-SIGACT Symposium on Principles of Programming Languages*. ACM Press, New York. Pages 144–154.

Lee, P. [1991]. *Topics in Advanced Language Implementation*. MIT Press, Cambridge, Massachusetts.

Lehmann, D. J. [1976]. *Categories for Fixpoint Semantics*. Ph. D. dissertation, Department of Computer Science, University of Warwick, Coventry, England, Theory of Computation Report 15.

Leivant, D. [1983]. Reasoning About Functional Programs and Complexity Classes Associated with Type Disciplines. *24th Annual Symposium on Foundations of Computer Science*. IEEE Computer Society Press, Los Angeles, California. Pages 460–469.

Lillibridge, M. [May 1997]. *Translucent Sums: A Foundation for Higher-Order Module Systems*. Ph. D. dissertation, School of Computer Science, Carnegie Mellon University, Pittsburgh, Pennsylvania, Report CMU–CS–97–122.

Loeckx, J., Sieber, K., and Stansifer, R. D. [1987]. *The Foundations of Program Verification*. Second edition. Wiley, Chichester, England.

Longo, G. and Moggi, E. [1991]. Constructive Natural Deduction and its 'ω-set' Interpretation. *Mathematical Structures in Computer Science*, **1**(2), 215–254.

Lucas, P., Alber, K., Bandat, K., Bekić, H., Oliva, P., Walk, K., and Zeisel, G. [June 28, 1968]. *Informal Introduction to the Abstract Syntax and Interpretation of PL/I*. Technical Report TR 25.083, IBM Laboratory Vienna, Vienna, Austria.

Ma, Q. and Reynolds, J. C. [1992]. Types, Abstraction, and Parametric Polymorphism, Part 2. *Mathematical Foundations of Programming Semantics: 7th International Conference, Proceedings*. Brookes, S. D., Main, M., Melton, A., Mislove, M., and Schmidt, D. A., editors. Lecture Notes in Computer Science 598. Springer-Verlag, Berlin. Pages 1–40.

MacQueen, D. B. [1986]. Using Dependent Types to Express Modular Structure. *Conference Record of the Thirteenth Annual ACM Symposium on Principles of Programming Languages*. ACM, New York. Pages 277–286.

MacQueen, D. B. and Sethi, R. [1982]. A Semantic Model of Types for Applicative Languages. *Conference Record of the 1982 ACM Symposium on LISP and Functional Programming*. ACM, New York. Pages 243–252.

MacQueen, D. B., Plotkin, G. D., and Sethi, R. [1986]. An Ideal Model for Recursive Polymorphic Types. *Information and Control*, **71**(1–2), 95–130.

Manna, Z. and Pnueli, A. [1992]. *The Temporal Logic of Reactive and Concurrent Systems: Specification*. Springer-Verlag, New York.

Martin-Löf, P. [1984]. *Intuitionistic Type Theory*. Bibliopolis, Naples, Italy.

McCarthy, J. [1960]. Recursive Functions of Symbolic Expressions and Their Computation by Machine, Part I. *Communications of the ACM*, **3**(4), 184–195.

McCarthy, J. [1963]. Towards a Mathematical Science of Computation. *Information Processing 62: Proceedings of IFIP Congress 1962*. Popplewell, C. M., editor. North-Holland, Amsterdam. Pages 21–28.

McCarthy, J., Abrahams, P. W., Edwards, D. J., Hart, T. P., and Levin, M. I. [1962]. *LISP 1.5 Programmer's Manual*. MIT Press, Cambridge, Massachusetts.

McCracken, N. J. [June 1979]. *An Investigation of a Programming Language with a Polymorphic Type Structure*. Ph. D. dissertation, School of Computer and Information Science, Syracuse University, Syracuse, New York.

McCracken, N. J. [1982]. *A Finitary Retract Model for the Polymorphic Lambda-Calculus*. Unpublished, marked Syracuse University.

McCusker, G. [1998]. *Games and Full Abstraction for a Functional Metalanguage with Recursive Types*. Distinguished Dissertations Series. Springer-Verlag, New York.

Mendelson, E. [1979]. *Introduction to Mathematical Logic*. Second edition. Van Nostrand, New York.

Meyer, A. R. and Sieber, K. [1988]. Towards Fully Abstract Semantics for Local Variables: Preliminary Report. *Conference Record of the Fifteenth Annual ACM Symposium on Principles of Programming Languages*. ACM Press, New York. Pages 191–203. Reprinted in O'Hearn and Tennent [1997, vol. 1, pages 157–169].

Michie, D. [1967]. *Memo Functions: A Language Feature with Rote Learning Properties*. Research Memorandum MIP–R–29, Department of Machine Intelligence and Perception, University of Edinburgh, Edinburgh, Scotland.

Michie, D. [1968]. "Memo" Functions and Machine Learning. *Nature*, **218**(5136), 19–22.

Milne, R. [1974]. *The Formal Semantics of Computer Languages and their Implementations*. Ph. D. dissertation, Programming Research Group, Oxford University, Oxford, England, Report PRG–13 and Technical Microfiche TCF–2.

Milner, R. [1978]. A Theory of Type Polymorphism in Programming. *Journal of Computer and System Sciences*, **17**(3), 348–375.

Milner, R. [1980]. *A Calculus of Communicating Systems*. Lecture Notes in Computer Science 92. Springer-Verlag, Berlin.

Milner, R. [1989]. *Communication and Concurrency*. Prentice-Hall, New York.

Milner, R. [October 1991]. *The Polyadic π-Calculus: A Tutorial*. LFCS Report ECS–LFCS–91-180, Department of Computer Science, University of Edinburgh, Edinburgh, Scotland. Reprinted in Bauer et al. [1993, pages 203–246].

Milner, R. [1993]. Action Calculi, or Syntactic Action Structures. *Mathematical Foundations of Computer Science 1993: 18th International Symposium*. Borzyszkowski, A. M. and Sokołowski, S., editors. Lecture Notes in Computer Science 711. Springer-Verlag, Berlin. Pages 105–121.

Milner, R. [1994]. Higher-order Action Calculi. *Computer Science Logic: 7th Workshop, CSL '93, Selected Papers*. Börger, E., Gurevich, Y., and Meinke, K., editors. Lecture Notes in Computer Science 832. Springer-Verlag, Berlin. Pages 238–260.

Milner, R. [1996]. Calculi for Interaction. *Acta Informatica*, **33**(8), 707–737.

Milner, R. and Tofte, M. [1991]. *Commentary on Standard ML*. MIT Press, Cambridge, Massachusetts.

Milner, R., Tofte, M., and Harper, R. W. [1990]. *The Definition of Standard ML*. MIT Press, Cambridge, Massachusetts.

Milner, R., Parrow, J., and Walker, D. J. [1992]. A Calculus of Mobile Processes, I and II. *Information and Computation*, **100**(1), 1–40, 41–77.

Mitchell, J. C. [1986]. A Type-Inference Approach to Reduction Properties and Semantics of Polymorphic Expressions (Summary). *Proceedings of the 1986 ACM Conference on Lisp and Functional Programming*. ACM, New York. Pages 308–319.

Mitchell, J. C. [1988]. Polymorphic Type Inference and Containment. *Information and Computation*, **76**(2–3), 211–249.

Mitchell, J. C. [1990]. Type Systems for Programming Languages. *Formal Models and Semantics*. van Leeuwen, J., editor. Handbook of Theoretical Computer Science B. Elsevier, Amsterdam. Pages 365–458.

Mitchell, J. C. [1991]. Type Inference with Simple Subtypes. *Journal of Functional Programming*, **1**(3), 245–285.

Mitchell, J. C. and Plotkin, G. D. [1985]. Abstract Types Have Existential Type. *Conference Record of the Twelfth Annual ACM Symposium on Principles of Programming Languages*. ACM, New York. Pages 37–51.

Moggi, E. [1991]. Notions of Computation and Monads. *Information and Computation*, **93**(1), 55–92.

Morgan, C. [1994]. *Programming from Specifications*. Second edition. Prentice-Hall International, London.

Morris, F. L. [1993]. The Next 700 Formal Language Descriptions. *Lisp and Symbolic Computation*, **6**(3–4), 249–257. Original manuscript dated November 1970.

Morris, J. H., Jr. [December 1968]. *Lambda-Calculus Models of Programming Languages*. Ph. D. dissertation, Project MAC, Massachusetts Institute of Technology, Cambridge, Massachusetts, Report MAC–TR–57.

Morris, J. H., Jr. [1972]. A Bonus from van Wijngaarden's Device. *Communications of the ACM*, **15**(8), 773.

Morrisett, G. [December 1995]. *Compiling with Types*. Ph. D. dissertation, School of Computer Science, Carnegie Mellon University, Pittsburgh, Pennsylvania, Report CMU–CS–95–226.

Mosses, P. D. [January 1974]. *The Mathematical Semantics of Algol 60*. Technical Monograph PRG–12, Programming Research Group, Oxford University Computing Laboratory, Oxford, England.

Naur, P. [1966]. Proof of Algorithms by General Snapshots. *BIT*, **6**, 310–316.

Naur, P. et al. [1960]. Report on the Algorithmic Language ALGOL 60. *Communications of the ACM*, **3**(5), 299–314.

Naur, P. et al. [1963]. Revised Report on the Algorithmic Language ALGOL 60. *Communications of the ACM*, **6**(1), 1–17. Also *The Computer Journal*, **5**, 349–367 and *Numerische Mathematik*, **4**, 420–453. Reprinted in O'Hearn and Tennent [1997, vol. 1, pages 19–49].

Necula, G. C. [1997]. Proof-Carrying Code. *Conference Record of POPL '97: The 24th ACM SIGPLAN-SIGACT Symposium on Principles of Programming Languages.* ACM Press, New York. Pages 106–119.

O'Hearn, P. W. [1996]. Note on Algol and Conservatively Extending Functional Programming. *Journal of Functional Programming*, **6**(1), 171–180. Reprinted in O'Hearn and Tennent [1997, vol. 1, pages 89–99].

O'Hearn, P. W. and Reynolds, J. C. [1998]. *From Algol to Polymorphic Linear Lambda-calculus.* To appear in the Journal of the ACM.

O'Hearn, P. W. and Riecke, J. G. [1995]. Kripke Logical Relations and PCF. *Information and Computation*, **120**(1), 107–116.

O'Hearn, P. W. and Tennent, R. D. [1993]. Semantical Analysis of Specification Logic, 2. *Information and Computation*, **107**(1), 25–57. Reprinted in O'Hearn and Tennent [1997, vol. 2, pages 65–93].

O'Hearn, P. W. and Tennent, R. D. [1995]. Parametricity and Local Variables. *Journal of the ACM*, **42**(3), 658–709. Reprinted in O'Hearn and Tennent [1997, vol. 2, pages 109–163].

O'Hearn, P. W. and Tennent, R. D., editors. [1997]. *ALGOL-like Languages.* Birkhäuser, Boston, Massachusetts. Two volumes.

O'Hearn, P. W., Power, A. J., Takeyama, M., and Tennent, R. D. [1995]. Syntactic Control of Interference Revisited. *Mathematical Foundations of Programming Semantics, Eleventh Annual Conference.* Brookes, S. D., Main, M., Melton, A., and Mislove, M., editors. *Electronic Notes in Theoretical Computer Science*, http://www.elsevier.{nl,com}/locate/entcs/volume1.html, **1**. Reprinted in O'Hearn and Tennent [1997, vol. 2, pages 189–225].

O'Keefe, R. A. [1990]. *The Craft of Prolog.* MIT Press, Cambridge, Massachusetts.

Older, S. [December 1996]. *A Denotational Framework for Fair Communicating Processes.* Ph. D. dissertation, School of Computer Science, Carnegie Mellon University, Pittsburgh, Pennsylvania, Report CMU–CS–96–204.

Oles, F. J. [August 1982]. *A Category-Theoretic Approach to the Semantics of Programming Languages.* Ph. D. dissertation, School of Computer and Information Science, Syracuse University, Syracuse, New York.

Oles, F. J. [1985]. Type Algebras, Functor Categories, and Block Structure. *Algebraic Methods in Semantics.* Nivat, M. and Reynolds, J. C., editors. Cambridge University Press, Cambridge, England. Pages 543–573.

Oles, F. J. [1997]. Functor Categories and Store Shapes. *ALGOL-like Languages, Volume 2.* O'Hearn, P. W. and Tennent, R. D., editors. Birkhäuser, Boston, Massachusetts. Pages 3–12.

Owe, O. [1993]. Partial Logics Reconsidered: A Conservative Approach. *Formal Aspects of Computing*, **5**(3), 208–223.

Owicki, S. S. and Gries, D. [1976]. An Axiomatic Proof Technique for Parallel Programs I. *Acta Informatica*, **6**(4), 319–340. Reprinted in Gries [1978, pages 130–152].

Park, D. M. R. [1980]. On the Semantics of Fair Parallelism. *Abstract Software Specifications: 1979 Copenhagen Winter School, Proceedings.* Bjørner, D., editor. Lecture Notes in Computer Science 86. Springer-Verlag, Berlin. Pages 504–526.

Paulin-Mohring, C. [1993]. Inductive Definitions in the system Coq: Rules and Properties. *Typed Lambda Calculi and Applications: International Conference TLCA'93, Proceedings.* Bezem, M. and Groote, J., editors. Lecture Notes in Computer Science 664. Springer-Verlag, Berlin. Pages 328–345.

Paulson, L. C. [1996]. *ML for the Working Programmer.* Second edition. Cambridge University Press, Cambridge, England.

Peyton Jones, S. L. [1987]. *The Implementation of Functional Programming Languages.*
   Prentice-Hall International, London.

Pfenning, F. [1989]. Elf: A Language for Logic Definition and Verified
   Metaprogramming. *Proceedings Fourth Annual Symposium on Logic in Computer
   Science.* IEEE Computer Society Press, Washington, D.C. Pages 313–322.

Pfenning, F. and Elliott, C. [1988]. Higher-Order Abstract Syntax. *Proceedings of the
   SIGPLAN '88 Conference on Programming Language Design and Implementation.
   SIGPLAN Notices,* **23**(7), 199–208.

Pierce, B. C. [1991]. *Basic Category Theory for Computer Scientists.* MIT Press,
   Cambridge, Massachusetts.

Pierce, B. C. [1992]. Bounded Quantification is Undecidable. *Conference Record of the
   Nineteenth Annual ACM SIGPLAN-SIGACT Symposium on Principles of
   Programming Languages.* ACM Press, New York. Pages 305–315. Reprinted in
   Gunter and Mitchell [1994, pages 427–459].

Pierce, B. C. [1997]. Intersection Types and Bounded Polymorphism. *Mathematical
   Structures in Computer Science,* **7**(2), 129–193.

Pitts, A. M. [1987]. Polymorphism is Set Theoretic, Constructively. *Category Theory
   and Computer Science.* Pitt, D. H., Poigné, A., and Rydeheard, D. E., editors.
   Lecture Notes in Computer Science 283. Springer-Verlag, Berlin. Pages 12–39.

Pitts, A. M. [1996]. Reasoning About Local Variables with Operationally-Based Logical
   Relations. *Proceedings Eleventh Annual IEEE Symposium on Logic in Computer
   Science.* IEEE Computer Society Press, Los Alamitos, California. Pages 152–163.
   Reprinted in O'Hearn and Tennent [1997, vol. 2, pages 165–185].

Plotkin, G. D. [October 1973]. *Lambda-Definability and Logical Relations.*
   Memorandum SAI–RM–4, School of Artificial Intelligence, University of Edinburgh,
   Edinburgh, Scotland.

Plotkin, G. D. [1975]. Call-by-Name, Call-by-Value and the λ-Calculus. *Theoretical
   Computer Science,* **1**(2), 125–159.

Plotkin, G. D. [1976]. A Powerdomain Construction. *SIAM Journal on Computing,*
   5(3), 452–487.

Plotkin, G. D. [1977]. LCF Considered as a Programming Language. *Theoretical
   Computer Science,* **5**(3), 223–255.

Plotkin, G. D. [September 1981]. *A Structural Approach to Operational Semantics.*
   Report DAIMI FN–19, Computer Science Department, Aarhus University, Aarhus,
   Denmark.

Plotkin, G. D. [1982]. A Powerdomain for Countable Non-determinism (Extended
   Abstract). *Automata, Languages and Programming: Ninth Colloquium.* Nielsen, M.
   and Schmidt, E. M., editors. Lecture Notes in Computer Science 140.
   Springer-Verlag, Berlin. Pages 418–428.

Plotkin, G. D. [1983]. An Operational Semantics for CSP. *Formal Description of
   Programming Concepts – II: Proceedings of the IFIP Working Conference.* Bjørner,
   D., editor. North-Holland, Amsterdam. Pages 199–225.

Pnueli, A. [1977]. The Temporal Logic of Programs. *18th Annual Symposium on
   Foundations of Computer Science.* IEEE Computer Society, Long Beach, California.
   Pages 46–57.

Pnueli, A. [1981]. The Temporal Semantics of Concurrent Programs. *Theoretical
   Computer Science,* **13**(1), 45–60.

Reade, C. [1989]. *Elements of Functional Programming.* Addison-Wesley, Wokingham,
   England.

Reddy, U. S. [1996]. Global State Considered Unnecessary: An Introduction to
   Object-Based Semantics. *Lisp and Symbolic Computation,* **9**(1), 7–76. Reprinted in
   O'Hearn and Tennent [1997, vol. 2, pages 227–295].

Reynolds, J. C. [1970]. GEDANKEN – A Simple Typeless Language Based on the

Principle of Completeness and the Reference Concept. *Communications of the ACM*, **13**(5), 308–319.

Reynolds, J. C. [1972a]. Definitional Interpreters for Higher-Order Programming Languages. *Proceedings of the ACM Annual Conference.* Pages 717–740.

Reynolds, J. C. [October 1972b]. *Notes on a Lattice-Theoretic Approach to the Theory of Computation.* Report, School of Computer and Information Science, Syracuse University, Syracuse, New York. Revised March 1979.

Reynolds, J. C. [1974]. Towards a Theory of Type Structure. *Programming Symposium: Proceedings, Colloque sur la Programmation.* Robinet, B., editor. Lecture Notes in Computer Science 19. Springer-Verlag, Berlin. Pages 408–425.

Reynolds, J. C. [1977]. Semantics of the Domain of Flow Diagrams. *Journal of the ACM*, **24**(3), 484–503.

Reynolds, J. C. [1978]. Syntactic Control of Interference. *Conference Record of the Fifth Annual ACM Symposium on Principles of Programming Languages.* ACM, New York. Pages 39–46. Reprinted in O'Hearn and Tennent [1997, vol. 1, pages 273–286].

Reynolds, J. C. [1980]. Using Category Theory to Design Implicit Conversions and Generic Operators. *Semantics-Directed Compiler Generation: Proceedings of a Workshop.* Jones, N. D., editor. Lecture Notes in Computer Science 94. Springer-Verlag, Berlin. Pages 211–258. Reprinted in Gunter and Mitchell [1994, pages 25–64].

Reynolds, J. C. [1981a]. *The Craft of Programming.* Prentice-Hall International, London.

Reynolds, J. C. [1981b]. The Essence of Algol. *Algorithmic Languages: Proceedings of the International Symposium on Algorithmic Languages.* de Bakker, J. W. and van Vliet, J. C., editors. North-Holland, Amsterdam. Pages 345–372. Reprinted in O'Hearn and Tennent [1997, vol. 1, pages 67–88].

Reynolds, J. C. [1982]. Idealized Algol and its Specification Logic. *Tools and Notions for Program Construction: An advanced course.* Néel, D., editor. Cambridge University Press, Cambridge, England. Pages 121–161. Reprinted in O'Hearn and Tennent [1997, vol. 1, pages 125–156].

Reynolds, J. C. [1983]. Types, Abstraction and Parametric Polymorphism. *Information Processing 83: Proceedings of the IFIP 9th World Computer Congress.* Mason, R. E. A., editor. Elsevier Science Publishers B. V. (North-Holland), Amsterdam. Pages 513–523.

Reynolds, J. C. [1989]. Syntactic Control of Interference, Part 2. *Automata, Languages and Programming: 16th International Colloquium.* Ausiello, G., Dezani-Ciancaglini, M., and Ronchi della Rocca, S., editors. Lecture Notes in Computer Science 372. Springer-Verlag, Berlin. Pages 704–722.

Reynolds, J. C. [1991]. The Coherence of Languages with Intersection Types. *Theoretical Aspects of Computer Software: International Conference TACS '91, Proceedings.* Ito, T. and Meyer, A. R., editors. Lecture Notes in Computer Science 526. Springer-Verlag, Berlin. Pages 675–700.

Reynolds, J. C. [1993]. The Discoveries of Continuations. *Lisp and Symbolic Computation*, **6**(3–4), 233–247.

Reynolds, J. C. [1995]. Using Functor Categories to Generate Intermediate Code. *Conference Record of POPL '95: 22nd ACM SIGPLAN-SIGACT Symposium on Principles of Programming Languages.* ACM Press, New York. Pages 25–36. Reprinted in O'Hearn and Tennent [1997, vol. 2, pages 13–38].

Reynolds, J. C. [June 28, 1996]. *Design of the Programming Language Forsythe.* Report CMU–CS–96–146, School of Computer Science, Carnegie Mellon University, Pittsburgh, Pennsylvania. Reprinted in O'Hearn and Tennent [1997, vol. 1, pages 173–233].

Reynolds, J. C. and Plotkin, G. D. [1993]. On Functors Expressible in the Polymorphic

Typed Lambda Calculus. *Information and Computation,* **105**(1), 1–29.

Sallé, P. [1978]. Une Extension de la Théorie des Types en λ-Calcul. *Automata, Languages and Programming: Fifth Colloquium.* Ausiello, G. and Böhm, C., editors. Lecture Notes in Computer Science 62. Springer-Verlag, Berlin. Pages 398–410.

Schmidt, D. A. [1986]. *Denotational Semantics: A Methodology for Language Development.* Allyn and Bacon, Boston, Massachusetts.

Scott, D. S. [November 1970]. *Outline of a Mathematical Theory of Computation.* Technical Monograph PRG–2, Programming Research Group, Oxford University Computing Laboratory, Oxford, England. A preliminary version appeared in Proceedings of the Fourth Annual Princeton Conference on Information Sciences and Systems (1970), 169–176.

Scott, D. S. [1971]. The Lattice of Flow Diagrams. *Symposium on Semantics of Algorithmic Languages.* Engeler, E., editor. Lecture Notes in Mathematics 188. Springer-Verlag, Berlin. Pages 311–366.

Scott, D. S. [1972]. Continuous Lattices. *Toposes, Algebraic Geometry and Logic: Proceedings of the 1971 Dalhousie Conference.* Lawvere, F. W., editor. Lecture Notes in Mathematics 274. Springer-Verlag, Berlin. Pages 97–136.

Scott, D. S. [1976]. Data Types as Lattices. *SIAM Journal on Computing,* **5**(3), 522–587.

Scott, D. S. [1982]. Domains for Denotational Semantics. *Automata, Languages and Programming: Ninth Colloquium.* Nielsen, M. and Schmidt, E. M., editors. Lecture Notes in Computer Science 140. Springer-Verlag, Berlin. Pages 577–613.

Scott, D. S. and Strachey, C. [1971]. Towards a Mathematical Semantics for Computer Languages. *Proceedings of the Symposium on Computers and Automata.* Fox, J., editor. Microwave Research Institute Symposia Series 21. Polytechnic Press of the Polytechnic Institute of Brooklyn, New York. Pages 19–46.

Seely, R. A. G. [1987]. Categorical Semantics for Higher Order Polymorphic Lambda Calculus. *Journal of Symbolic Logic,* **52**(4), 969–989.

Sieber, K. [1994]. Full Abstraction for the Second Order Subset of an ALGOL-like Language. *Mathematical Foundations of Computer Science 1994: 19th International Symposium, MFCS'94, Proceedings.* Prívara, I., Rovan, B., and Ružička, P., editors. Lecture Notes in Computer Science 841. Springer-Verlag, Berlin. Pages 608–617. Reprinted in O'Hearn and Tennent [1997, vol. 2, pages 97–107].

Smyth, M. B. [1978]. Power Domains. *Journal of Computer and System Sciences,* **16**(1), 23–36.

Smyth, M. B. and Plotkin, G. D. [1982]. The Category-Theoretic Solution of Recursive Domain Equations. *SIAM Journal on Computing,* **11**(4), 761–783.

Sterling, L. and Shapiro, E. [1986]. *The Art of Prolog: Advanced Programming Techniques.* MIT Press, Cambridge, Massachusetts.

Strachey, C. [1967]. *Fundamental Concepts in Programming Languages.* Unpublished lecture notes for International Summer School in Computer Programming, Copenhagen, August.

Strachey, C. and Wadsworth, C. P. [January 1974]. *Continuations, A Mathematical Semantics for Handling Full Jumps.* Technical Monograph PRG–11, Programming Research Group, Oxford University Computing Laboratory, Oxford, England.

Sussman, G. J. and Steele Jr., G. L. [December 1975]. *SCHEME: An Interpreter for Extended Lambda Calculus.* AI Memo 349, Artificial Intelligence Laboratory, Massachusetts Institute of Technology, Cambridge, Massachusetts.

Tennent, R. D. [1976]. The Denotational Semantics of Programming Languages. *Communications of the ACM,* **19**(8), 437–453.

Tennent, R. D. [1990]. Semantical Analysis of Specification Logic. *Information and Computation,* **85**(2), 135–162. Reprinted in O'Hearn and Tennent [1997, vol. 2, pages 41–64].

Tennent, R. D. [1991]. *Semantics of Programming Languages.* Prentice-Hall, New York.

Tofte, M. [1990]. Type Inference for Polymorphic References. *Information and Computation,* **89**(1), 1–34.

Troelstra, A. S., editor. [1973a]. *Metamathematical Investigation of Intuitionistic Arithmetic and Analysis.* Lecture Notes in Mathematics 344. Springer-Verlag, Berlin.

Troelstra, A. S. [1973b]. Notes on Intuitionistic Second Order Arithmetic. *Cambridge Summer School in Mathematical Logic.* Lecture Notes in Mathematics 337. Springer-Verlag, Berlin. Pages 171–205.

Turing, A. M. [1950]. Checking a Large Routine. *Report of a Conference on High Speed Automatic Calculating Machines.* Marked "Issued by the Laboratory with the cooperation of the ministry of supply". Pages 67–69.

Turner, D. A. [1979]. A New Implementation Technique for Applicative Languages. *Software Practice and Experience,* **9**(1), 31–49.

Turner, D. A. [1985]. Miranda: A Non-Strict Functional Language with Polymorphic Types. *Functional Programming Languages and Computer Architecture.* Lecture Notes in Computer Science 201. Springer-Verlag, Berlin. Pages 1–16.

Turner, D. A. [1990]. An Overview of Miranda. *Research Topics in Functional Programming.* Turner, D. A., editor. Addison-Wesley, Reading, Massachusetts. Pages 1–16.

Ullman, J. D. [1994]. *Elements of ML Programming.* Prentice-Hall, Englewood Cliffs, New Jersey.

van Wijngaarden, A. [1966]. Recursive Definition of Syntax and Semantics. *Formal Language Description Languages for Computer Programming: Proceedings of the IFIP Working Conference on Formal Language Description Languages.* Steel, T. B., Jr., editor. North-Holland, Amsterdam. Pages 13–24.

van Wijngaarden, A., Mailloux, B. J., Peck, J. E. L., and Koster, C. H. A. [1969]. Report on the Algorithmic Language ALGOL 68. *Numerische Mathematik,* **14**(2), 79–218.

van Wijngaarden, A., Mailloux, B. J., Peck, J. E. L., Koster, C. H. A., Sintzoff, M., Lindsey, C. H., Meertens, L. G. L. T., and Fisker, R. G. [1975]. Revised Report on the Algorithmic Language ALGOL 68. *Acta Informatica,* **5**(1–3), 1–236.

Wadler, P. [1989]. Theorems for Free! *Functional Programming Languages and Computer Architecture: FPCA '89 Conference Proceedings Fourth International Conference.* ACM Press, New York. Pages 347–359.

Wadler, P. [1990]. Linear Types Can Change the World! *Programming Concepts and Methods: Proceedings of the IFIP Working Group 2.2/2.3 Working Conference.* Broy, M. and Jones, C. B., editors. North Holland, Amsterdam. Pages 561–581.

Wadler, P. [1992]. Comprehending Monads. *Mathematical Structures in Computer Science,* **2**(4), 461–493.

Wadler, P. [1993]. Monads for Functional Programming. *Program Design Calculi: Proceedings of the NATO Advanced Study Institute.* Broy, M., editor. NATO ASI Series F: Computer and Systems Sciences 118. Springer-Verlag, Berlin. Pages 233–264. Reprinted in Jeuring and Meijer [1995, pages 24–52].

Wadsworth, C. P. [September 1971]. *Semantics and Pragmatics of the Lambda-Calculus.* Ph. D. dissertation, Programming Research Group, Oxford University, Oxford, England.

Wadsworth, C. P. [1976]. The Relation Between Computational and Denotational Properties for Scott's D_∞-Models of the Lambda-Calculus. *SIAM Journal on Computing,* **5**(3), 488–521.

Wadsworth, C. P. [1978]. Approximate Reduction and Lambda Calculus Models. *SIAM Journal on Computing,* **7**(3), 337–356.

Walk, K., Alber, K., Bandat, K., Bekić, H., Chroust, G., Kudielka, V., Oliva, P., and

Zeisel, G. [June 28, 1968]. *Abstract Syntax and Interpretation of PL/I.* Technical Report TR 25.082, IBM Laboratory Vienna, Vienna, Austria.

Wand, M. [1975]. On the Recursive Specification of Data Types. *Category Theory Applied to Computation and Control: Proceedings of the First International Symposium.* Manes, E. G., editor. Lecture Notes in Computer Science 25. Springer-Verlag, Berlin. Pages 214–217.

Wand, M. [1979]. Fixed-Point Constructions in Order-Enriched Categories. *Theoretical Computer Science,* **8**(1), 13–30.

Weeks, S. and Felleisen, M. [1993]. On the Orthogonality of Assignments and Procedures in Algol. *Conference Record of the Twentieth Annual ACM SIGPLAN-SIGACT Symposium on Principles of Programming Languages.* ACM Press, New York. Pages 57–70. Reprinted in O'Hearn and Tennent [1997, vol. 1, pages 101–124].

Wells, J. B. [1994]. Typability and Type Checking in the Second-Order λ-Calculus Are Equivalent and Undecidable. *Proceedings Ninth Annual IEEE Symposium on Logic in Computer Science.* IEEE Computer Society Press, Los Alamitos, California. Pages 176–185.

Wells, J. B. [1998]. *Typability and Type Checking in System F Are Equivalent and Undecidable.* To appear in the Annals of Pure and Applied Logic.

Winskel, G. [1993]. *The Formal Semantics of Programming Languages: An Introduction.* MIT Press, Cambridge, Massachusetts.

Wirth, N. and Hoare, C. A. R. [1966]. A Contribution to the Development of ALGOL. *Communications of the ACM,* **9**(6), 413–432.

Index

Page references to definitions are in boldface, to exercises in italics.